A Sampling of Critical Acclaim

"For a long time I've hoped for a solid, readable, accurate and balanced one-volume history of American Catholicism. Dolan's does the job, and with verve and style. It will be useful both to the general reader and as a fact-filled resource."

> Harvey Cox
> Harvard University Divinity School

"Professor Dolan's balanced, compelling story of Catholicism in America will surely become the standard one-volume work against which all subsequent books will be evaluated."

> Andrew Greeley
> Sociologist and Author

"The perspective and spirit of this innovative history of American Catholicism derive from Vatican Council II and Dolan's concept of social history . . . Elucidating a vast subject with engaging economy, this popular history of the people who comprise the country's single largest religious denomination sets a standard for future researchers."

> *Publishers Weekly*

"[Dolan] has done a masterful job of marshaling a sea of facts while still providing a readable narrative. His own attempt to be fair to the 'church below' is both admirable and in keeping with the spirit of the Catholicism he sees emerging in the post-conciliar period. This is a distinguished piece of historical writing that tells us much about the long struggle in this country to refine and make sense of the two adjectives 'American Catholic.' I recommend it with enthusiasm."

> *National Catholic Reporter*

". . . an exciting and suggestive book . . . a history of real people. For those who dream of an indigenous American Catholicism or a unique American contribution to the universal church, this is where it must start. If Dolan is to be believed it already has."

> *Commonweal*

"Were this book just a history of American Catholicism, it would be well worth the price. But it is much more . . . Dolan has given us a landmark work—must reading for anyone interested in learning how to be both Catholic and American."

> *Catholic Twin Circle*

"Dolan writes in a lively manner and synthesizes vast amounts of material with a flair reminiscent of Martin Marty at his best . . . this is an admirable work that will appeal to general readers and still serve for academic use . . . Highly recommended."

> *Library Journal*

". . . harvests the fruits of a now enormous quantity of sociologically oriented studies of American Catholic history . . . It is a notable achievement."

> *St. Louis Post Dispatch*

"For anyone interested in American Catholic history, Dolan's book is pivotal. The solid research and extensive citations make it a valuable teaching tool, while its solid writing makes its ideas accessible to a literate but broad audience."

St. Anthony Messenger

". . . a major filling of a vast gap in American Catholic historiography."

NC News Service

"[A] synthesis of recent scholarship and reinterpretation of issues from the fresh perspective of a trained scholar living as a committed Catholic layman in the post-Vatican II era . . . *The American Catholic Experience* will deservedly become a central book on the history of the Church, but let us hope it marks a beginning rather than a culmination."

The New York Times Book Review

The American Catholic Experience

A History from Colonial Times to the Present

JAY P. DOLAN

Complete and Unabridged

IMAGE BOOKS
A Division of Doubleday & Company, Inc.
Garden City, New York

Image Book edition published September 1987 by special arrangement with Doubleday & Company, Inc.

Library of Congress Cataloging in Publication Data

Dolan, Jay P., 1936–
  The American Catholic Experience.

  Includes index.
  1. Catholic Church—United States—History.
2. United States—Church history. I. Title.
BX1406.2.D637 1985   282′.73   84-26026
ISBN 0-385-15207-8 (pbk)
Printed in the United States of America

FOR PATRICK AND MARK

Contents

PREFACE   9

THE COLONIAL PERIOD, 1500–1780

I   Conquest and Conversion in the New World   15
The Spanish and French Indian missions in North America

II   Catholicism and Native American Cultures   43
What happened when Catholics came into contact with the world of the Indians

III   Catholics in the English Colonies   69
What it meant to be Catholic in colonial Maryland

A REPUBLICAN INTERLUDE, 1780–1820

IV   A New Beginning   101
The attempt to form an American version of Roman Catholicism

THE IMMIGRANT CHURCH, 1820–1920

V   Immigrant Catholics: A Social Profile   127
The ten major Catholic immigrant groups and their patterns of settlement, work, and economic mobility

VI   The Parish and the People   158
The organization of the local church and the struggle for control

VII   The Neighborhood and Its Gods   195
The relationship between neighborhood, parish, and religion

VIII   The Catholic Ethos   221
*The four marks of devotional Catholicism: authority, sin, ritual, and the
miraculous*

IX   Handing on the Faith   241
The educative role of family, church, school, and the press

X   Schools   262
*The emergence of the parochial school along with the high school and the
college*

XI   Religion and Society   294
*Conflict among immigrant groups and the debate over the role of the church in
the modern world*

XII   Toward a Social Gospel   321
The Catholic response to the Industrial Age

THE END OF AN ERA, 1920–60

XIII   Changes in Church and Nation   349
*The organization of the institutional church, the persistence of immigrant
Catholicism, and the challenges presented by Black and Mexican newcomers*

XIV   Religion, Education, and Reform   384
*The golden age of devotional Catholicism, the expansion of the educational
network, and the move toward social reform*

THE CATHOLIC REFORMATION, 1960–84

XV   A New Catholicism   421
Bringing the church up to date, and the effects of this change

NOTES   455

INDEX   493

Preface

EVERY GENERATION OF HISTORIANS seeks to rediscover the past in a new and enlightening manner. The present generation is no exception. During the past twenty years, historians have reclaimed the history of the family, women, and blacks; in the 1980s they are asking new questions of labor, politics, and economics. Inspiring much of this work is a desire to write a new social history of the United States, a history that goes beyond politicians and power brokers and urges a broader historical vision of American society and its people. Such impulses have also influenced the writing of religious history, most especially European religious history.

As regards the history of Roman Catholicism, another major influence is at work, namely a new understanding of the church. This new understanding of the church, proclaimed at the Second Vatican Council, incorporates the people—lay men and women—into the definition of the church. To outsiders, such a development may seem quite harmless. But for Roman Catholics the effects have been profound. By proclaiming the church to be first and foremost the people of God, the Second Vatican Council sought to revise the more traditional view of the church as a hierarchical institution in which the Pope and his clergy reigned like monarchs. Such a revision stood Roman Catholic theology on its head, and the full implications of this theological development remain to be seen. As Pope John XXIII said more than twenty years ago, a new day is dawning for Roman Catholicism. Today it is still early morning.

One obvious effect of this change is the desire to write a new history of Roman Catholicism. The spirit of Vatican II and the new vision it inspired has had a profound effect on the study of the Bible, theology, ethics, and church law. Less publicized but no less real is its effect on the study of history. A new understanding of the church demands a new history of Roman Catholicism. Reinforcing this development is the current emphasis on the need for a more social history of the past. These two developments, one within the historical academy and the other within Roman Catholicism, have shaped my thinking about the past and persuaded me to write a social history of the American Catholic people from colonial times to the present. Having said this, it is necessary to explain what I mean.

By social history I mean the history of a society that focuses on the ordinary people and their culture; some historians have labeled this "history from the bottom up" or "people's history." Attempting to write a social history that spans more than three hundred years presents problems, a principal one being that for some eras of history the necessary research and sources are not yet available. Thus, some sections of this book follow the traditional narrative style of history; other chapters concern themselves with intellectual history or institutional history. Obviously, bishops are part of the history and so are priests and other church personnel. But my main concern in this book was to focus, as much as it was possible, on the people and not just the prelates, on the experience of religion and not just the development of the institution. I wanted to look at the American Catholic experience from a new angle, from the bottom up if you wish, and write what I believe is a new history of Roman Catholicism in the United States.

In writing this history I have sought to ask new questions of the past and to focus on themes often neglected in American Catholic history. In the colonial period a major issue was what happened when two cultures of religion, Roman Catholicism and native American religions, came into contact with one another. An important question in the English Catholic colonial experience was how these people kept their religion alive in a frontier society in which priests and churches were scarce and Protestants were so numerous. The era of the immigrant church marked a new beginning for Catholicism in the United States. The major questions that concerned me in this period were the social context in which Catholics lived, an economic and social profile of the community, how the people organized their churches, and what leadership roles they assumed in the local church. The focal point in much of this section was the parish community. Another major theme was the nature of religion in the immigrant community. How did Catholics pray, and how did this shape their values? Education and schooling, cultural and theological conflict, and social reform in the immigrant era are other issues examined. These themes continued to dominate the twentieth century as the immigrant church moved into its golden era. Reform movements in the 1940s and 1950s and the increased activity of the laity were other major themes examined. The book concludes with a study of the new Catholicism that has emerged in the past quarter century.

This book is but the first step in the writing of a new social and religious history of American Catholicism. I hope others will take up where I have left off and explore more deeply the vast richness of the American Catholic experience. By doing so they will further enrich a history that deserves to be known in all its fullness.

In writing this book I have acquired many debts, and it is a pleasure to acknowledge them publicly at last. The American Council of Learned Societies provided a fellowship in 1978 that enabled me to begin this project. The University of Notre Dame generously supported my work by allowing me to take some time off from teaching so that I could devote full time to research and writing. The Notre Dame community has also provided an atmosphere and environment of support that have sustained me in my work over the years, and for this I am very grateful.

I am also grateful for the support of many individuals. Martin E. Marty was the first to urge me to pursue the subject, and I am glad he did. Other colleagues, too many to mention, also encouraged me along the way and thus motivated me to complete the task. Daniel McLellan, O.F.M., Steven M. Avella, and James Grummer, S.J., provided valuable research assistance while they were graduate students at Notre Dame. Another student, Jeffrey M. Burns, was especially helpful and did the bulk of the work in the "Parish History Study," cited in the book. Rod Ganey provided us with the necessary sophistication in computer programming to make such a study worthwhile. Henry Warner Bowden, Thomas E. Blantz, C.S.C., Jon Butler, Philip Gleason, David C. Leege, Thomas F. O'Meara, Louis Putz, C.S.C., and Thomas Spalding, C.F.X., read one or more chapters of the manuscript and offered valuable advice. I am especially indebted to James P. Shenton and Joseph M. White, who carefully read all the chapters on the immigrant church. My wife, Pat, was forced to read the entire book and did so cheerfully. Historian that she is, she provided keen insights along the way. She also put up with me throughout the entire project, and for that she deserves a medal. Joseph M. Lauck and the Inter-Library Loan staff of the University of Notre Dame Library were most helpful. Delores Dant Fain, secretary of the Charles and Margaret Hall Cushwa Center for the Study of American Catholicism, did a heroic job in typing the manuscript, and her patience and understanding are sincerely appreciated.

I have dedicated this book to my two sons, who more than once asked me if the book was done yet. When they are old enough to read it, I hope they will be pleased with the result.

JAY P. DOLAN
December 1984

The Colonial Period, 1500–1780

I

Conquest and Conversion in the New World

THE SPANISH MISSIONS

ON A FRIDAY MORNING, the twelfth of October, 1492, Christopher Columbus set foot on a small coral island in the Bahamas. A dream had finally come true. The Italian visionary and explorer had established contact with a new and different world. The Admiral of the Ocean Sea had met the people of America. It was a momentous day in the history of the human race, and Columbus later clothed his discovery with profound religious significance:

> . . . these great and marvelous results are not to be attributed to any merit of mine, but to the Holy Christian faith, and to the piety and religion of our Sovereigns; for that which the unaided intellect of man could not encompass, the spirit of God has granted to human exertions, for God is wont to hear the prayers of His servants who love his precepts even to the performance of apparent impossibilities. Therefore let the King and Queen, our princes and their most happy kingdoms, and all the other provinces of Christendom, render thanks to our Lord and Savior Jesus Christ, who has granted us so great a victory and such prosperity. Let processions be made, and sacred feasts be held, and the temples be adorned with festive boughs—let Christ rejoice on earth, as he rejoices in heaven in the prospect of the salvation of the souls of so many nations hitherto lost.[1]

The "door of the Western sea" was opened at last. Columbus knew that Spain would prosper because of his discovery, and prosper she did when silver and gold from the New World began to pour into the coffers of Spain. But Columbus believed that he was more than a servant of the Crown; he was an instrument of God: a man, he said, "animated by a heavenly fire," whose mission was not only to find a passage to the Indies, but also to inaugurate the last great crusade so that the biblical prophecy of preaching the gospel to all peoples and all races could be fulfilled and the holy city of Jerusalem delivered from the unbeliever.

This visionary side of Columbus, inspired by the book of The Apocalypse and the gospel mandate to "go out all over the world and preach the gospel to all creation," was not unique. Throughout the sixteenth and seventeenth centuries, a similar sense of mission animated other New World explorers, English as well as Spanish, Portuguese as well as French. John Winthrop, the founding father of the Massachusetts Bay Colony, had such a vision when he spoke to his fellow Englishmen about being a chosen people whose task it was to build a Christian society in the New World, where, according to God's will, "we shall be as a city on a hill." Winthrop was not a Columbus, but he was a Puritan, and his vision of the holy commonwealth was as much religious as it was political.

The link between Columbus and Winthrop illustrates an important point. Catholics and Protestants were not terribly different in their motivation to explore and conquer the New World. To acquire wealth was an obvious priority, but to establish a New Israel and extend the boundaries of the kingdom of God on earth was also a major impulse that propelled both the Spanish conquistador and the English Pilgrim across the ocean to America. Seen in this manner, the Spanish conquest of the sixteenth century, which inaugurates the history of Catholicism in the United States, evidences a striking resemblance to the Puritan colonization of the seventeenth century and the beginnings of American Protestantism. American Catholicism, like American Protestantism, was inaugurated with a millennial enthusiasm. It first surfaced on an island in the Bahamas, appropriately renamed San Salvador, and spread across Central and South America, eventually reaching Florida, Texas, Arizona, New Mexico, and California.

There is no denying that the Spanish were greedy; that they robbed, pillaged, and eventually annihilated millions of Indians in South and North America. They were conquistadors, crusaders armed with Toledo steel and mounted on Spanish horses. Theirs was a crusade, made all the more just, precisely because it was conducted on behalf of the Church. Indeed, the Spanish conquest was the last great crusade to abolish "paganism" and establish a city of God in the Promised Land, where the Christianity of the Old World could reach its perfection. Such holy wars are the worst possible kind. But it was the sixteenth century, and conquest and conversion in the name of God and king was the way the Spanish set out to "Christianize and civilize" the people of the New World.

The marriage between conquest and conversion was not unusual in Europe during the fifteenth and sixteenth centuries. Most people were still viewing life through a medieval prism, possessing a worldview that knew no separation between religion and society, church and world. The two realms were interwoven in such a way that it was unthinkable to distinguish the sacred from the secular, to separate religion from the activities of daily life. From birth to death and at every stage in between, the church intervened with ritual and prayer; in the city and the rural countryside, the sacred deeply penetrated the minds of men and women and was never far removed from the surface of human consciousness. Columbus is a good example of this mentality. "His thoughts, deeds, and aspirations were permeated with religious faith," wrote his biographer Samuel Eliot Morison. "He was more particular than many clergymen in saying daily the Divine Office of the Church . . . and seldom missed an opportunity to hear Mass."[2] On his voyage of discovery, Columbus prayed daily and sang the *Salve Regina*, "which all seamen are accustomed to say and sing in their own fashion."[3] He believed he was an instrument of God, whose providence and power had safely brought him to America. Even though Columbus was a sailor, not a saint, religion was the indispensable compass of his life.

Hernán Cortés, the conqueror of Mexico, was a more extreme example of the union between the sacred and the secular in Catholic Spain. The conqueror of Mexico "was greedy, debauched, a politician without scruples, but he had his quixotic moments, for, despite his weaknesses, of which he later humbly repented, he had deep Christian convictions. He always carried on his person an image of the Virgin Mary, to whom he was strongly devoted; he prayed and heard Mass daily; and his standard bore these words: 'Comrades, with true faith follow the sign of the Holy Cross and through it we shall conquer.' "[4] Cortés relentlessly pursued the political and military conquest of Mexico, but he was equally zealous in pursuing a religious crusade as well. All along his journey of conquest to the capital of the Aztec empire he stopped to erect the cross of Christianity and build altars for Mass; at the same time, he pillaged Indian temples, smashed their religious symbols, and killed anyone who tried to stop his march. His was a ruthless faith, which sought to bring a new culture to an old civilization. An essential ingredient of this transfer was religion, and the mission of Cortés would not be complete until he could make the Aztecs Spanish Catholics. Nothing less would satisfy this medieval Catholic who carried a holy card in his pocket and a saber at his side.

It was a thin line that separated Christianity and magic in the sixteenth century. The picture of the Virgin in Cortés's pocket could easily be taken for a good-luck charm as well as a sign of orthodox piety. In the case of Cortés it is hard to say which prevailed; more than likely it was a mixture of both superstition and orthodoxy. Either way, religion was an integral part of Cortés's world; so, too, of that of the common folk. Average Westerners in the sixteenth century were more than likely superficial Christians, possessed of a mentality that knew no sharp distinction between matter and spirit, religion and life. For them, as for Columbus and Cortés, the world was permeated with religion, be it magical, Christian, or a blending of both. But the point is clear. In the sixteenth century and well into the seventeenth, there was no separation between religion and life. Such a mentality helps to explain the crusade launched by Columbus in the name of God and the sovereign. To civilize necessarily meant to Christianize in sixteenth-century Spain.

Another aspect of Spanish culture that shaped the conquest of America was the type of Catholicism prevalent during the sixteenth century. A millennial interpretation of the New World and the intimate bond between religion and life were not uniquely Spanish. They were common to the Western world and explained the founding of Boston as well as the conquest of Mexico. But, for the Spanish, there was a third element at work, a complex of forces which, taken together, made up a special brand of Catholicism that only Spain possessed in the sixteenth century.

A major feature of Spanish Catholicism was the close union between the church and the Crown. Nothing symbolized this better than the *real patronato*, the Crown's right of patronage over the church. Through the *patronato*, granted by the Papacy to the Crown, the sovereign controlled church affairs, generally limited at first to the appointment of bishops. But this authority gradually expanded and soon included appointment to lesser ecclesiastical offices and the right to a portion of the monies collected by the churches. Though it was generally limited in scope, the *real patronato* in Spain enabled the Crown to exercise considerable influence in church affairs. In the New World, however, there was no limit to the Crown's authority. Its control over the church was absolute, and the Spanish king was virtually the Pope of the New World. The papacy conceded such authority to the Crown in a series of papal bulls beginning with the document *Inter Caetera*, of Pope Alexander VI in 1493, which granted to the Catholic kings of Spain exclusive rights in the evangelization of the newly discovered lands in the Indies. Subsequent papal bulls enlarged the privileges of the Crown, so that by the middle of the sixteenth century its control over the church in the New World was complete.

The Crown controlled the appointment of bishops and superiors of religious orders; any cleric going to America had to be approved by the Crown; licenses were issued, and any priest who arrived without one was sent back to Spain. The permission of the civil authority was required for the establishment of every church, monastery, hospital, and other pious institutions; churches and monasteries built without such permission were torn down! The Crown created new dioceses and determined their geographical boundaries; it paid the salaries of the clergy and even furnished the equipment necessary for the missions. Indeed, civil control of the church was so thorough that the very smallest aspect of ecclesiastical life was subject to the scrutiny of civil authorities. Even the transfer of a church sacristan required the king's approval.

Reinforcing this political marriage between the church and the state was an intensely fervent and fanatically vigorous religion. During the fifteenth century, the church in Spain suffered from the abuses common to other European countries. But, for at least two decades before the Protestant Reformation swept across Europe, Spanish Catholicism was already undergoing its own housecleaning. Sponsored by Queen Isabella and eventually entrusted to the scholarly and astute Franciscan Cardinal Ximénez, the new humanism of Erasmus gained a strong following in Spain; a renewed interest in the Bible and a more mystical approach to religion became widespread. Religious orders were reformed and the moral and intellectual life of the clergy improved. Thus, at a time when the church was under attack throughout Europe, Spanish Catholicism was gaining new strength and vigor.

After Ximénez's death in 1517, reform seemed to slow down, but the intellectual and spiritual renaissance he had encouraged flowered again in the 1560s and 1570s. Teresa of Ávila and John of the Cross continued the reform of religious orders. Their mystical writings reinvigorated Spanish mysticism, which was fast becoming "almost a literary mass-movement."[5] Spain gave birth to Ignatius Loyola, and his conversion in 1521 led to the founding of the Jesuits and a new missionary crusade beyond the oceans. Other religious orders were established, and by the middle decades of the century the number of Spanish clergy had increased to more than one hundred thousand. The renewal of religion also unleashed a burst of apostolic activity. Charitable apostolates to the sick and the poor increased, new centers of learning were established, and scores of young men volunteered to travel to the Orient and the Americas to preach the Gospel and spread the faith. A tidal wave of religious enthusiasm had swept across sixteenth-century Spain, and eventually it would spill over into the farthest corners of the empire, in places like Santa Fe, Santa Barbara, and San Francisco.

The religious fervor unleashed by the reform movement also took on an intensity that bordered on the fanatical. It is an understatement, to say the least, that Spanish Catholics were touchy about orthodoxy and horrified by heresy. The seemingly endless crusade against Islam had conditioned the Spanish mind to accept war as persecution and the necessary virtues of a militant faith. The challenge of Protestantism persuaded the Spanish that orthodoxy was the indispensable sign of a faith triumphant. The best symbol of this militant and fanatical orthodoxy was the Spanish Inquisition.

Inaugurated in the thirteenth century, the Inquisition endured right up to the nineteenth century. During the sixteenth century, its principal goal was twofold: racial and religious purity. Its chief victims were Jewish and Moorish converts to Christianity (conversos and moriscos, respectively). Later anyone suspected of Protestant tendencies, humanist inclinations, or mystical aspirations was also hauled before the court of Inquisition. Ignatius Loyola, Teresa of Ávila, and the widening circle of humanists and mystics were all suspects. Sixteenth-century Spain was becoming an increasingly closed society, intolerant of racial or religious diversity. The rise of Protestantism in countries to the north of Spain intensified this intolerance. Philip II, king of Spain during the last half of the century (1556–98), viewed himself as the defender of the faith throughout the world and believed that Spain was the last bastion against the new infidel spawned by Luther and Calvin. Such religious intolerance, which at times reached a level of bloody fanaticism, carried over to the New World, where the Inquisition was finally established in 1569; eventually it became the most feared tribunal in New Spain.

The Spanish conquest of the New World and the beginnings of Catholicism in the United States must be viewed against this cultural and religious backdrop of sixteenth-century Spain. Spanish civilization was indeed permeated with religion; the New World was viewed by many as the Promised Land, the last, best hope of Christianity; and the Catholicism of the conquistador and the friar was a blend of profound spirituality, intense activity, ideological intolerance, and feelings of racial superiority. All of these traits, in one way or another, helped to shape the Spanish phase of colonial Catholic history.

One other feature of Spanish culture must also be set in place, namely, the desire for wealth. Spanish sovereigns sponsored the exploration of the New World to gain wealth and power. Explorers like Columbus searched for fortune and the fame and prestige that money could buy. The historian Bernal Díaz del Castillo, who accompanied Cortés on his conquest of Mexico, put it very bluntly. "We came," he said, "to serve God and the King, and also to get rich."[6] This lust for wealth was a "disease of the heart" which plagued the Spanish; and in the New World, confessed Cortés, "It can only be cured with gold."[7] God, king, and gold, and not necessarily in that order, inspired the conquest of the New World and unleashed such zealous and militant fervor that within fifty years after Columbus' first voyage of discovery, the conquest of Central and South America was complete.

By 1515, the West Indies were completely occupied; by 1521, Cortés had conquered the Aztecs; and fifteen years later Pizarro had overthrown the Incan empire. The great period of Spanish conquest had come to an end, and all of South America (with the exception of Brazil) was under Spanish rule. With the first stage of conquest completed, the Spanish settled down to the more difficult task of consolidating the new kingdom. This would take generations, indeed centuries, and eventually it would mean planting the Spanish flag in areas of the empire that would later become part of the United States.

Scores of Spanish explorers followed Columbus. Ponce de León's search for the fountain of youth led him to Florida in 1513, but he returned home no younger. In the same year, 1513, Balboa came upon the Pacific Ocean. In 1539, De Soto began a three-year journey that would take him through the future states of Florida, Georgia, Tennessee, Alabama, Mississippi, Arkansas, Louisiana, Texas, and Oklahoma. Coronado marched through Texas, New Mexico, Arizona, and the Great Plains looking for the fabled Seven Cities of Cíbola. He met the Pueblo Indians instead; disappointed, he returned to Mexico. God, king, and gold had launched history's most successful and famous group of explorers. Yet, after all their travels, no new settlements were founded on the mainland of the United States.

Florida was the location for Spain's first permanent settlement in the United States. This time the motivation was neither gold dust nor invigorating water, but the presence of French pirates attacking Spanish ships off the coast of Florida. Since Ponce de León had first set foot on Florida, Spain had tried to colonize it, but her efforts were always unsuccessful. Finally, in 1564, French Protestants set up a military post along the Atlantic coast of Florida to use as a jumping-off point to attack Spanish galleons sailing through the Straits of Florida. Since Spain claimed the land, the French presence was a threat to her sovereignty over the peninsula. Under the leadership of Pedro Menéndez de Avilés, a Spanish fleet landed in Florida in 1565, founded the town of St. Augustine, and then proceeded to destroy the French fort. Since Florida never became a vital part of New Spain, the founding of St. Augustine was more important symbolically than politically. To this little Spanish town went the distinction of being the site of the oldest Christian community in the United States.

The next successful colonization effort took place in New Mexico. After the conquest of Mexico, God, king, and gold inspired both conquistadors and friars to find a new Mexico, and several expeditions, most notable that of Coronado in 1540–42, ventured into the land of the Pueblo Indians. Soldiers and priests died trying to find new souls to convert and new riches to exploit. Finally, in January 1598, an expedition led by Juan de Oñate set out to establish the kingdom of New Mexico. Oñate was one of Mexico's richest men, but he dreamed of finding more wealth. Military strategy also played a role in the settlement of New Mexico. Hostile Indians had been attacking the rich mining communities in northern Mexico, and the Crown believed that a Spanish colony farther north would act as a buffer state to bear the brunt of Indian hostility. Thus was launched a colonization program that would have far-reaching effects. After several months of travel, Oñate's entourage of soldiers, friars, and settlers, with their supplies, horses, and cattle, reached the chosen spot of settlement, near the Rio Grande; they named the place San Juan de los Caballeros. In 1610, the administrative center of the new kingdom was established at Santa Fe. The stage was now set for what would eventually become a unique experience in the fusion of Anglo and Hispanic American cultures.

During the seventeenth century, the line of Spanish settlement in Mexico continuously moved north toward the Rio Grande, where small mining communities sprung up. At the same time, the French were moving west from the Mississippi seeking to expand their own empire in America. Rumors of the French presence persistently circulated throughout Mexico City. Then, in 1685, the famous French explorer La Salle landed on the Texas coast, established a fort, and claimed the land for France. As the Spanish put it, "a thorn had been thrust into the heart of America," and it had to be rooted out. La Salle died before the Spanish could find him, and Fort St. Louis was soon abandoned. But the threat of French encroachment remained real for the next half century, and it prompted the Spanish to establish a number of forts and missions in Texas.

The last major Spanish colonization effort took place in Alta (Upper) California in the late-eighteenth century. As in the case of Texas, Spain never really wanted Upper California, but the threat of Russian encroachment into the northernmost frontier of New Spain forced the hand of the Crown. By land and by sea, a Spanish expedition set out from Lower California in 1769; in the summer of that year they rendezvoused at San Diego and founded the first of many Spanish mission towns.

During the two-hundred-year period separating the settlement of St. Augustine and the founding of San Diego, the Spanish Crown reluctantly, but continuously, expanded the perimeter of its empire into what is now the continental United States. Far removed from the heartland of New Spain, these presidios and towns were marginal to the mainstream of colonial Mexican history. They were principally defensive outposts situated on the rim of the empire to protect it from foreign invasion. But the Spanish presence in the United States would eventually have a considerable influence on the future of American history. This is especially true in the Southwest, where the history of the white man begins with the conquistador and the friar, not with the Pilgrim and the parson.

Each time the Spanish ventured into the future territory of the United States, they came into contact with an ancient civilization. Columbus erroneously called these people Indians, and everyone who came after him followed his lead. Yet the people who inhabited North America were more diverse than Columbus could ever have imagined. Recent estimates place the number of Indians living in what is now the contiguous United States in 1492 at about 850,000, and they spoke at least two hundred languages. East of the Mississippi, native Americans lived in settled villages of substantial homes; they subsisted off the land, and their ceremonial life centered around the harvesting of corn. Farther west, the Plains Indians centered their life around the buffalo; they moved from place to place, setting up their tepees wherever they could find the buffalo. In the Southwest, the Indians lived in villages of multistoried houses—*pueblos,* the Spanish called them—raised crops, wove cotton, and excelled in pottery.

Not only did Indian life vary from region to region, but also, within specific regions, there existed great diversity. What we call California was a good example. An estimated 310,000 Indians inhabited the area in 1769; they belonged to more than 105 tribal groups and spoke numerous dialects. Some lived in earthen mound homes, others in wooden plank houses or adobe dwellings. Many were skilled in weaving baskets, while others excelled at rock painting.

Acknowledging such diversity among native Americans, it is still legitimate to speak of certain traits common to most Indian cultures. Three characteristics in particular stand out. Indians had a special love for the land and their natural environment. "The earth is my mother," as one Spokane Indian put it. The Taos Indians, in New Mexico, so respected the land that they walked about in soft shoes during the spring, believing that the earth was pregnant at that time of the year and they should not harm their mother's body. Mountains were sacred shrines, and lakes were the dwelling places of the gods.

This reverence for nature points out another feature common among the Indians: their deep faith in the supernatural. They were a religious people who communed with the world of the spirits through the earth and the sky, through trees and lakes. They had their own priests, who acted as their intermediaries with the supernatural. They also had elaborate rituals and celebrations accompanied with dancing, singing, and the playing of musical instruments. Finally, the Indians whom the Spanish met were a people of culture. They had their own genius for invention and were gifted in various artforms: painting and dancing, in addition to weaving. They were able to tame the earth and, as agriculturalists or hunters, lived off its produce. Even though they were not as technologically advanced as the Aztecs or the Incas, the Indians of North America possessed a sophisticated culture which in many instances would be resilient enough to withstand the onslaught of the white man.

Centuries of cultural contact and decades of research have enabled white Americans to appreciate the culture of the American Indians. But the peoples of conquest—the Spanish, French, and English—did not have such benefits. For centuries prior to the age of exploration, Europeans distinguished between civilized and barbarian peoples. It was a simple way of viewing the human race and one that allowed little room for fine distinctions. When the Spanish, dressed in their shoes, pants, and hats, met barefoot, seminaked Indians, it was fairly evident in which category the conquerors would place the Indians. Years of contact with them during the sixteenth century only reinforced the opinion that these Indians of the New World were indeed barbarians. Some Spaniards, nurtured on ancient myths about the noble savage, were inclined to look upon the Indians in a benign, paternal manner. More often, the natives were simply seen as ignoble savages, useful only for the labor they could provide. All Spaniards agreed on one point, however: the Indians were an inferior race—inhuman, pagan, uncivilized, and lazy—who had to be "taught and trained in the ways of civilization." Father Fermín F. Lasuén, head of the Spanish missions in California, summarized this attitude very succinctly. "The greatest problem of the missionary," he wrote in 1801, "was how to transform a savage race such as these into a society that is human, Christian, civil, and industrious."[8]

By the time the Spanish settled in the United States, they had devised a program to civilize the Indians. The key to their program of cultural conquest was the mission. Shortly after the discovery of America, the Spanish developed a legal institution designed to civilize the Indians and utilize their labor in building a colony. Under this system, called the *encomienda*, a certain number of Indians were given in trust to a colonist who received the right to use their labor in developing his estates, farms, mines, or cattle ranches. The Crown awarded these grants on the condition that the colonist "instruct and teach them [the Indians] in the matters of holy Catholic faith and (to) give them thoroughly good treatment . . ."[9] The system differed from slavery only in that the Indians were legally free people, not property. Though the Crown sought to provide for the spiritual and temporal welfare of the Indians through the *encomienda*, the system broke down. The lust for riches led to brutality and slavery in fact, if not by law. Indians were worked to death, and entire populations began to disappear. Demands for reform soon mounted, and one of the first came in a Sunday sermon in 1511. A Dominican friar, Antonio de Montesinos, mounted a pulpit in Hispaniola and issued an indictment against his fellow colonists that poignantly detailed the harshness of the *encomienda.*

> Tell me, by what right or justice do you keep these Indians in such cruel and horrible servitude? . . . why do you keep them so oppressed and weary, not giving them enough to eat, nor taking care of them in their illnesses? For the excessive work you demand of them, they fall ill and die, or rather you kill them with your desire to extract and acquire gold every day. . . . Are these not men? Have they not rational souls? Are you not bound to love them as you love yourselves? Be certain that in such a state as this, you can no more be saved than the Moors or Turks.[10]

Few people liked what they heard, including Montesinos' superiors. But the struggle for human rights was irrevocably launched in the New World.

Another priest, Bartolomé de Las Casas, followed up the work of Montesinos and urged a crusade for justice on behalf of the Indians. Ordained in 1510, Las Casas was present when Montesinos preached his sermon and was outraged by the friar's indictment. A few years later, in preparing a sermon of his own, he experienced a conversion and became convinced that "everything done to the Indians thus far was wrong and tyrannical."[11] From 1514 until his death in 1566, Las Casas was the protector of the Indians. He argued with popes and kings and debated with scholars; chiefly through his influence, the

Crown issued a series of New Laws in 1542 abolishing the *encomienda* system and restricting the colonists' control over the Indians. But the New Laws were hard to enforce among greedy colonists. Since the *encomienda* system was so firmly entrenched and had so many beneficiaries, it could not easily be abolished. The crusade of Las Casas and other missionaries, however, weakened the system considerably. More important, perhaps, they persuaded both the Crown and the Papacy to acknowledge that Indians had human rights. This crusade for justice, which continued throughout the sixteenth century, was, in the opinion of the historian Lewis Hanke, "one of the greatest attempts the world has seen to make the Christian precepts prevail in the relation between peoples."[12]

Discredited and weakened, the *encomienda* gradually gave way to the mission as the principal agent for cultural conquest. Fundamental to the mission was the Spanish concept of "reduction." Since the Spaniards regarded the Indians as inferior and living in a savage state, it was necessary that they be gathered together in compact settlements so that they could be "reduced to a Christian and civilized way of life insofar as their capacity makes this possible."[13] Years of experience had demonstrated the need for reducing the Indians from a dispersed, sometimes nomadic, existence into a more disciplined, settled way of life. Only in this manner could they successfully be converted and civilized. Once the Indians had been gathered together, either by persuasion or by force, the friars then began the long process of transforming them into a "Christian and civilized" people.

The union between church and state, as well as the interrelationship of religion and culture, meant that the mission was necessarily more than just a religious institution. It was an agent for cultural change, and so the baptism of the Indians was only the first responsibility of the missionary. He also had to train the Indians in the rudiments of a civilized life. As Herbert E. Bolton put it, "The missions were designed to be not only Christian seminaries, but in addition were outposts for the control and training schools for the civilizing of the frontier."[14]

The Spanish mission town was not unique. English Puritans had a similar system—"praying towns," they called them—and Moravian missionaries built a number of similar settlements in Pennsylvania and Ohio. But the Spanish mission was so widespread, so numerous, and lasted so much longer than its Protestant counterpart, that it can legitimately be called the example *par excellence* of the Christian mission town.

It was not until a century after the founding of St. Augustine that the Florida missions reached their high point. The Jesuits had first tried their luck but were so unsuccessful in evangelizing the tribes of Florida that they had abandoned their work in 1572. The Franciscans followed a year later and eventually succeeded in establishing a chain of missions that stretched from St. Augustine to the area around present-day Tallahassee and north into

Georgia. By 1655, seventy friars were working in thirty-eight missions, and they claimed that twenty-six thousand Indians were Christians. This was the "golden age" of the Florida mission. Soon the mission program began to falter. The brutality of Spanish colonists led to Indian revolts, and the zeal of the missionaries seemed to evaporate. Then the English, settled in the Carolinas, challenged the rule of Spain in Florida. In 1702 and again in 1704, English soldiers, along with their Indian allies, destroyed the Florida missions. Reminiscent of the Spanish massacre of French Protestants in 1565, the English invaders left behind a scene of "indescribable horror: scalped and mutilated bodies of men, women, and children lay about the ground, or hung from stakes."[15] More attacks followed, and by 1708 there were no missions left in Florida outside St. Augustine. The death blow came in 1763, when the Spanish handed the territory over to the English.

When the Spanish came to the Southwest, in 1598, they found about forty thousand Pueblo Indians living in four or five dozen villages scattered about the Rio Grande area. Farther west were another six or seven thousand Indians living in isolated pueblos. After quickly subduing the Indian population, the Spanish embarked on their program of reduction. By 1630, the Franciscan superior of the territory, Alonso de Benavides, stated that there were "thirty-three convents and churches in the principal pueblos and more than one hundred and fifty churches throughout the other pueblos."[16] As many as sixty Franciscan missionaries were working at the missions during the early-seventeenth century. The report of Benavides, written to promote the cause of the missions, went on to claim that in the Rio Grande area, "all the Indians are now converted, baptized and very well ministered to"; indeed "they are so well taught," he boasted, "that they now live like perfect Christians."[17] The missionaries were obviously convinced that they had achieved great success with the Indians, but their optimism was unfounded. In 1680 the Pueblo Indians rose up in rebellion, chiefly because of religious oppression, and their first victims were the friars; twenty-one out of thirty-three missionaries were killed. Close to four hundred Spanish settlers also died, while the rest fled south to Mexico. Sixteen years passed before the Spanish were able to reestablish their rule over the Pueblo Indians. After the reconquest, the missions were rebuilt and the Spanish program of reduction began anew.

During the eighteenth century, the New Mexico colony floundered as Spaniards quarreled over the spoils of conquest. Bishops argued with friars about who had the last word of authority in the mission; the clergy constantly accused civil officials of victimizing the Indians, and civil officers blamed the clergy for being too zealous about money and land. Decades of bitter feuding weakened the colony, and time and again it seemed to face extinction. Reports on the conditions in the colony and its missions, in contrast to the glowing accounts of Benavides, painted a deplorable picture of progressive decadence.

In 1776 the Franciscan friar, Francisco Atanasio Domínguez visited the missions in New Mexico and wrote a detailed report on their conditions. At that time there were twenty-four missions in New Mexico, centered in the Rio Grande pueblos; the friar's census counted 18,344 Indian and Spanish Christians. The number of clergy was hardly adequate, with only twenty priests available, and three were so ill that they could not work. Nor were the religious conditions very encouraging. Among the Indians, Christianity was only a veneer, disguising a tenacious adherence to their native religion. The friar's comments about one mission more or less described the general situation:

> "There was great reason to grieve and to sorrow," he confessed; "there is no teaching of the Indians, and consequently no care taken to have them attend catechism and learn it. Their ministers (this does not refer to all of them or to all the missions) aspire only to possess many temporal goods and obtain them at the cost of the poor Indian's sweat and labor."[1]

In subsequent years, the Indian population declined as more and more succumbed to disease or fled to join other tribes; by 1800, only eight thousand Pueblo Indians lived in the territory, a sixth of the sixteenth-century population. The Spanish population, however, had increased substantially, with an estimated twenty thousand living in towns and isolated ranches; a large majority were mestizo, a mixture of Spanish and Indian blood and culture. They formed the nucleus of a population that in later years would be known as Hispanic Americans. Despite the gloomy picture of the colonial period, the Catholic Church has survived in the Southwest to this day. Mission churches still stand at the edges of Indian villages, and many Pueblo Indians consider themselves Catholics. For Hispanic Americans, the Rio Grande area has become a major cultural and political stronghold.

During the seventeenth century, the frontier of the empire inched north and west, finally reaching into present-day Arizona. The one individual most responsible for this expansion was a Jesuit missionary, Eusebio Kino.

Kino was born and raised in a village in the Italian Tyrol. At the age of eighteen he suffered a serious illness and at that time vowed that, if he lived, he would follow in the footsteps of the great Jesuit missionary Francis Xavier. Kino survived the sickness, joined the Jesuits, and eventually headed to New Spain as a missionary, in 1681. After a few years in Lower California, he transferred his energies to Sonora (also in northern Mexico), and his travels eventually took him into the present state of Arizona. He founded a series of missions in the area, most notably at the Indian villages of Guevavi and Bac, the latter renamed by Kino San Francisco Xavier del Bac, after his patron saint. Kino's style was never to stay long in one place. He arrived on the scene laden with gifts for his prospective converts; he preached, baptized, began a church, and instructed the Indians in the material benefits of their new way of life. Then he was off to other parts of the unexplored frontier. He was an "irrepressible expansionist": with the temperament "of a missionary conqueror, not that of a consolidator."[19]

After his death in 1711, other Jesuits settled down to the difficult task of consolidating the mission program begun by Kino. The Pima Indians were hardly as docile and receptive to the new way of life as Kino had portrayed them. But a small contingent of Jesuits, headquartered at Guevavi and periodically traveling to other Indian villages, hung on in the face of incredible hardships and disappointments. In 1767 came the ultimate disappointment. For political reasons, the Crown expelled the Jesuits from the empire, and they left Arizona under military escort. A year later, the Franciscans resumed the missionary enterprise, but they were no more successful than the Jesuits in reducing the Pima Indians of southern Arizona. At the end of the century, Christianity was still confined to two or three small mission settlements. The "glorious harvest of souls" envisioned by Kino had never materialized.

At about the time that Kino was exploring southern Arizona, Franciscan friars marched north through Texas to set up a mission and military fort near the border separating French Louisiana from Spanish Texas. Two years later, in 1692, the mission was abandoned and the Spanish forgot about Texas for more than twenty years. The fear of the French eventually persuaded the government to attempt another colonization of Texas; this time it was to be permanent. An expedition of seventy-five people including Franciscan friars, soldiers, and settlers headed north through Texas in the winter of 1716. By summer they were settled in eastern Texas near the Louisiana border. Shortly afterward, other missions were founded along the gulf coast and in San Antonio, nine in all by 1722. Forty years later, the territory of the present state of Texas numbered twenty-one missions; this forty-year period was the golden age of the Texas missions.

The most famous and significant mission in Texas was San Antonio de Valero; today it is known as the Alamo. Founded in 1718, it was the center of a complex of five missions in and around San Antonio. By 1762, it "had become a prosperous Indian community," with seventy-six Indian families and three Franciscans living at the mission.[20] The number of mission Indians at San Antonio was representative of the size of other missions in the area. Despite forty years and more of progress, the Texas missions were never able to reduce a substantial number of Indians. They were too nomadic for the settled and disciplined life of the mission and did not adapt easily to the Spanish way of life. Two of the most untouchable tribes in Texas were the Apaches and the Comanches. The Apaches were especially fearsome: mounted on mustangs, they were the best light cavalry the Spanish had ever faced. Continually they harassed, attacked, and destroyed the Spanish settlements. As long as they were around, Spanish Texas was constantly on the defensive, and the Crown ended up spending more money in fighting the

Apaches than in developing the colony. Spain's inability to conquer the Apaches was the major reason for its failure to hold Texas.

By 1785, it was evident that the Texas missions were in a state of "decay and dissolution." Only twelve families remained at the San Antonio mission, with young children almost as numerous as adults. The same pattern was true elsewhere. A general decline had set in throughout the colony, and it would not be long before the Spanish Crown completely abandoned the Texas missions. In 1793, the mission of San Antonio had ceased to function and the building was turned over to the military. At that time, the total population of Spanish Texas was less than three thousand, including converted Indians, settlers, and military personnel. Spanish settlers lingered on in Texas, but the evangelization of the Indian had come to an end.

Just when the Texas missions headed into decline, a new field opened up for the Franciscans in California. As was true in Arizona, the stature of one man dominated the missionary enterprise. In California, the name of Junípero Serra is synonymous with the Spanish mission. A seasoned missionary with almost twenty years of work behind him in Mexico before he came to San Diego in 1769, Serra was the exact opposite of Kino. He was not known as an explorer, cartographer, or historian; he is remembered as the founder, organizer, and administrator of the most successful missionary enterprise undertaken by the Spanish in the United States. For fifteen years, he presided over the evangelization of the California Indians and founded nine missions, including such settlements as San Francisco, San Luis Obispo, and San Juan Capistrano. When he died in 1784, approximately 4,646 Indians were living at the missions. In later years, twelve more missions were established in California. The high point of the California missions was reached in the early years of the nineteenth century, when as many as forty-five missionaries ministered to some twenty thousand converted Indians.

The California missions were large complexes; the average size ranged between five hundred and six hundred people, but they often housed as many as a thousand, even occasionally two thousand, Indians. Compared to other Spanish missions in what is now the United States, this was unique. What was also special about California was that, unlike in Texas, Arizona, and New Mexico, the missionary program was an economic bonanza. Taking advantage of the labor of the Indians and a favorable climate, the friars were able to raise cattle, plant orchards, and cultivate vineyards of wine-producing grapes. They eventually built an agricultural corporation that in 1834 was valued at about $78 million.

From the Spanish point of view, the California missions were unusually successful. About fifty-four thousand Indians were converted in a sixty-five-year period, and economically the colony prospered. But, from the Indian point of view, the Spanish colonization was a disaster. In the mission area, centered south of San Francisco Bay, the original population numbered about seventy-two thousand; by 1836, only about fifteen thousand Indians were left. Disease, hard labor, and infant mortality rates as high as 86 percent at the mission had reduced the population substantially. Before long, the old mission population "utterly disappeared."[21] Unlike in New Mexico, where the Indians survived their contacts with the white man, in California the only monuments to the mission era are graveyards and restored mission churches.

The end of the Spanish mission era was inevitably linked to the decline of Spain and its inability to control the political future of New Spain. In the early years of the nineteenth century, a movement for independence was underway in Mexico; it culminated in 1821 with Mexican independence. The California mission towns became part of the new nation, and before long the Mexican Government dissolved them. The friars were ousted, the lands fell into the hands of the government or private individuals, and the mission Indians, now free and independent, were forced to adapt to a new way of life. Many returned to their native villages or joined up with friendly tribes; others drifted to nearby Spanish towns or ranches in search of work and survival.

The end of the California mission era, formalized by the Mexican decree of secularization in 1833, had been coming for a long time. The early-nineteenth century was a time of continued and increasing neglect on the part of both the Spanish and the Mexican governments. The secularization of the California mission system was the final death blow to an institution that was already approaching extinction. In New Mexico, the situation of the mission enterprise was worse. There were not large estates to dissolve, just empty mission churches; in 1832, only five of twenty-two pueblos had missionary priests. People were dying without the sacraments, and corpses were not buried for days; the churches were in shabby condition, and Catholicism itself was in a state of decay. The situation had been worsening since the late-eighteenth century, and by the 1830s the church in New Mexico, virtually abandoned by civil and ecclesiastical authorities in Mexico, had reached its nadir. Unlike in Upper California, the Indians were not victimized by the transfer of power in Mexico City. For them, life went on as usual in the pueblo, and the hold that Catholicism had on them, which was never very deeply ingrained, became even less so.

The dissolution of the mission enterprise and the progressive decay of church life, however, did not mean the end of frontier Catholicism. The church survived, ministering to the needs of Catholic Indians and the increasing Hispanic-American population. Indeed it was in a feeble condition, but the people, with the help of a handful of Mexican clergy, kept the faith alive. Before long, the Americans settled in the Mexican frontier region and eventually gained political control over the area. This ushered in a new era of conquest and cultural conflict. This time its victims were not only the Indians but the Hispanic Americans who had lived and worshiped in some of these areas for more than two hundred years. The shoe was now on the other foot;

those who had once told the Indians to become Spanish European Catholics were now being forced to become American Catholics. The conquerors had become the conquered.

THE FRENCH MISSIONS

The lust for gold and a northwest passage to the Orient led French and English explorers to the North Atlantic seaboard. Instead of gold and a passageway to the East, they found codfish, and lots of it. Throughout the sixteenth century, scores of fishermen set up stations along the coast of Newfoundland to harvest the abundant fish of the North Atlantic. Soon they came upon another valuable commodity, the beaver, and it was not long before the French were involved in a lucrative fur trade with the Indians of North America.

The codfish and the beaver did not quench the French thirst for gold and their desire to match the wealth of Spain. Jacques Cartier, the Columbus of France, made three trips to the Gulf of St. Lawrence looking for a northwest passage and a golden kingdom. On his second voyage, in 1535, he discovered the St. Lawrence River, and the Indians he met told him about the "kingdom and province of the Saguenay" and its rich treasures of gold and silver. The gullible Cartier, like Coronado, believed the Indians' tall tale, claimed the land for France, and reported back home about this golden kingdom and the river that would lead to the Orient. Six years later, Cartier returned to found a colony. This time he realized that he had been had; the St. Lawrence did not lead to the Orient, and the golden kingdom of Saguenay did not exist. Discouraged, he left Canada; France, busy fighting the Spanish and torn apart by its own internal conflicts between Catholics and Protestants, forgot about the idea of a new France. In the meantime, the lucrative fur trade continued and kept alive the hope that wealth and power might lie in the Northwest.

By the opening years of the seventeenth century, France had regained a measure of stability and the Crown once again turned its attention to the New World. This time it was the beaver, not gold, that provided the impetus for colonization. A company of merchants was formed, and the Crown granted them a monopoly in the fur trade; led by a Protestant, Pierre du Gua de Monts, and guided by a Catholic, Samuel de Champlain, a colony was founded at Port Royal, near the Bay of Fundy, in 1605. Within two years, the colony collapsed and its settlers returned to France. The next attempt proved to be more permanent, and this time Champlain became the leading figure in the colonization of New France. In 1608, he founded Québec as the center of the new colony, and from there he went upriver toward the Great Lakes, exploring the territory and expanding the fur trade. He allied himself with the Huron Indians and fought with them against the Iroquois, a decision that would have serious consequences in later years. But Champlain's colony never prospered. The trading companies in France were interested in furs, not in colonization, and as long as the Indians trapped the animals and traded the furs, the merchants at home were content. In 1627, fewer than one hundred French people lived in Canada, and not one could be called a genuine settler. Then along came the English to deal the final, fatal blow to the struggling colony. France and England were frequently waging war against each other; this time the English carried the battle to Canada, where they laid siege to Québec in 1629 and forced Champlain to surrender. New France had apparently come to an end, and the disillusioned Champlain returned home to France. But the intricacies of international politics prevailed, and England returned Canada to French rule in 1632. It was clear, however, that England, with its own colonies beginning to expand south of Canada, would remain a nagging thorn in the side of New France.

A close alliance between the church and the Crown had guaranteed that any efforts of colonization in North America would include a religious as well as an economic motivation. Every commission to establish a colony in New France always singled out the religious purpose of the enterprise as well as its economic aims. Since Cardinal Richelieu was the king's minister in these early years of colonization, it is not surprising to find him urging merchants to introduce the Indians to "the knowledge of the Only God, and cause them to be civilized and instructed in the Catholic, Apostolic, and Roman religion and faith"; nor did he fail to mention that "an advantageous trade" for France would also be useful. Cartier's commission had a similar ring to it, and Champlain envisioned his colony as an opportunity to "establish the Christian faith among an infinite number of souls, who neither hold nor possess any form of religion whatsoever. . . ."[22]

Prior to the English seizure of Québec, some feeble efforts had been made to introduce Christianity to the native populations. Both Protestant ministers and Catholic priests had been part of the original colony at Port Royal. After the colony was restored, two Jesuits returned to Port Royal in 1611 to resume the evangelization of the Indians, but the English raided the small settlement and took the Jesuits off in chains to Jamestown. Champlain's colony along the St. Lawrence received its first missionaries in 1615. They were members of the Recollects, a reformed branch of the Franciscans. For ten years, they traveled up and down the St. Lawrence and its tributaries preaching the gospel to the Indians, vainly seeking converts. Realizing the enormity of the task and their own lack of success, they asked the Jesuits for help. By this time, the Jesuits had become the master missionaries of the church, and the Recollects hoped that perhaps the sons of Ignatius could succeed where they had failed. A group of French Jesuits arrived in 1625 and remained until the English takeover four years later, when they were taken back to England as captives.

During this early period of settlement, the missionaries vainly tried to evangelize the Indians. Even though they met with little success, the possibilities for conversion seemed to be limitless if the opportunity to return to Canada ever presented itself again. Thus, when the French regained control of Canada, the Jesuits were eager to return and resume their work. The Crown granted them undisputed control of the Indian missions, and in 1632 they began a crusade for souls that would take them from Québec to New Orleans and from the St. Lawrence to the upper Great Lakes.

The Jesuits who returned to Canada with Champlain belonged to a religious order whose energy and excellence were unrivaled in Catholic Europe. By the middle of the seventeenth century, the number of Jesuits had increased to fifteen thousand, and they were spread across the globe, preaching the gospel to the Brahmins of India, the natives of Africa, and the Indians of the Americas. "Confessors of European princes and astronomers of the emperors of China, missionaries and remarkable teachers, the Jesuits were the most dynamic element in the Roman Church between 1550 and 1650."[23] They were especially active in France, where they took the lead in the Catholic reform movement.

Unlike Spain, France underwent its religious conversion only after the Protestant Reformation had challenged the legitimacy of Roman Catholicism. Then, for a hundred-year period, roughly 1550 to 1650, France experienced a century of religious renewal, which produced numerous heroes, mystics, and martyrs. This "century of saints" was the high point of Catholic reform in France and throughout Europe.

The popularity of this renaissance in France can be gauged by what people were interested in reading. In Paris, half of the books published in 1643–45 and again in 1699–1701 had to do with the Christian religion. In the countryside, where literacy was not as widespread and Christianity still remained superficial, religious revival was also evident. Rural towns were experiencing parish revivals, religious pilgrimages were very much in vogue, and spiritual confraternities were increasing in number.

During this century of revival, French Catholicism took on a mystical quality similar to that of the Spanish. The writings of Teresa of Ávila and John of the Cross nourished this tendency. In France it acquired a graver and more austere tone through the influence of Pierre de Bérulle, founder of the French Oratory. The Jesuit Louis Lallemant was of a similar bent, and he guided many future missionaries through the sublime and elusive stages of mystical spirituality. The denial of self, or self-dispossession, was a key to this spirituality, and it made for a rigorously disciplined life. This "thirst for mortification" helps to explain the ability, even the desire, of missionaries to suffer incredible hardships, unbelievable tortures, and even death itself in the most forsaken and lonely outposts of North America. Like much of Catholic Europe, French Catholicism also exhibited a very militant quality. The presence of Protestants in France—Huguenots they called them—tempered this militancy somewhat, and even a measure of toleration existed for a while. But this was short-lived, and in the second half of the seventeenth century especially, religious intolerance, enlivened by a strong dose of vigorous orthodoxy in all matters religious, characterized the Catholic Church in France.

Unlike Spain, France did not enjoy the *real patronato,* which granted the Crown papal power in ecclesiastical affairs. In fact, French Catholicism generally was very antipapal, and France became the chief proponent of Gallicanism, a theology of the church which, simply put, meant that the final authority in church affairs was not the Pope, but the general councils of the church. Gallicanism led to a situation in which the church in France tended to become very independent of the papacy, governing itself, rather than being governed by the Vatican. In reality, it evolved into a form of royal Gallicanism (or royal absolutism), with the Crown claiming control over the church. This obviously led to a very close relationship between church and state. Churchmen such as Cardinal Richelieu occupied important positions in the government, wielding extraordinary power. The lower clergy also worked very closely with the monarchy, even though disputes over ecclesiastical prerogatives and privileges were inevitable. In Canada, church and state were even more closely allied, so much so that up until 1663 the "church was the practical master of Canada."[24] At that time, the Crown took over direct control of the colony; this action limited the power of the church, but the bishop of Canada became an influential member of the governing body of the colony, and the church and its clergy remained a force to be reckoned with.

The importance of the church in New France rested on its role as the chief agent responsible for the conversion and acculturation of the Indian population. The Indians of New France, principally the area bounded by the Gulf of St. Lawrence in the east and Lake Superior in the west, were not as numerous as the Indians of the Southwest. An estimated 220,000 Indians lived in all of Canada when the French arrived. Two language groups predominated in the area between Lake Superior and the Gulf of St. Lawrence, the Algonkians in the west and the Iroquois in the east. The Algonkian group included a number of diverse tribes: the Ottawas, Menominees, Chippewas, and Potawatomis, who lived around Lakes Michigan and Superior; to the south, in Indiana and Illinois, were other, less numerous Algonkian-speaking tribes such as the Miamis and the Peorias. In general, the Algonkians were nomadic hunters who moved about in their bark canoes in search of fish and game. Some, like the Miamis and the Potawatomis, were sedentary, basically agriculturalists, who only periodically moved about to hunt or fish. Other tribes, like the Ottawa and the Chippewa, were noted nomads, who traveled long distances to hunt, trade, and make war. Other Algonkian tribes lived along the Atlantic coast from Maine to the Carolinas.

The Iroquois speakers were centered around Lakes Erie and Ontario and along the St. Lawrence River. Included in this language group were the

Hurons, who lived in Ontario on the eastern side of Lake Huron; to the south, in upper New York State, were five tribes—the Mohawks, Oneidas, Onondagas, Cayugas, and Senecas—who together made up the Five Nations, the most powerful group of Iroquoians. The Iroquoian-speaking tribes were primarily farmers and lived in settled villages often housing as many as four thousand people. Fishing was also important to them, and hunting was pursued chiefly to obtain hides for clothing. Similarities of language did not exclude diversity within the Algonkian and the Iroquoian groups. Differences in dialect, religion, and patterns of settlement obviously existed, and often, especially in the case of the Hurons and the Five Nations, tribes of the same language group were engaged in continual warfare.

Like their brothers and sisters in the Southwest, the northeastern Indians had common traits. Chief among these was a reverence for the earth and a way of life that lived in harmony with nature. Closely allied to this was a religious quality that permeated all aspects of native life and a culture which produced successful hunters, fishers, and traders. The Iroquois were especially adept at political organization, and the Five Nations developed a sophisticated and efficient form of government.

These Indians of North America had fascinated the French ever since they first met them. After his explorations in Canada, Cartier returned to France with a few Iroquois Indians. Other explorers did the same, and the Indians were most often displayed at public spectacles, where their presence only served to increase the curiosity of the French about the natives of the New World. The display of the Indians as "curios of the New World"[25] raised a number of questions about the nature of the Indians and their place in human history. The French had the advantage of the Spanish experience and a long written tradition which had examined these questions prior to the founding of Québec. In common with the Spanish and the English, the French viewed the native Americans as barbarians or savages. Two major schools of thought also existed among the French paralleling and influenced by the views of the Spanish. In the tradition of Las Casas and Montesinos, one point of view upheld the innocence and perfection of the Indians, advocated a humanitarian relationship with them, and believed that the peoples of the New World "offered the opportunity to build a new and ideal civilization superior to that of Europe."[26] The other view perceived the Indians as an intrinsically inferior race that could and should be enslaved, forcefully if necessary, by the superior civilization. The French curiosity about the native Americans also encouraged a host of other perceptions during the seventeenth century. A romantic primitivism which inspired the myth of the noble savage was especially enduring; it was employed not only to idealize the American Indians—their innocence, goodness, and rationality—but also to criticize the absence of these virtues in contemporary France.

French perceptions of the Indian were complex and often contradictory, so they cannot be neatly categorized. To do so would do violence to the complexity of the problem. But certain attitudes were dominant and did set the French apart from their Spanish and English contemporaries. The French stressed the good qualities of native life and the Indian potential for virtue and goodness; they advocated a policy of assimilation which, ideally at least, would have given the natives the same rights and privileges as Paris-born colonists; though they judged themselves to be superior to the Indians and racial discrimination did indeed exist, it "never became a dominant attitude in the French colony and it never passed into official legislation."[27] The French also enjoyed more friendly relations with the Indians, since their type of colonization did not involve displacing large numbers of natives. The fur trade depended on a network of traveling French traders and nomadic Indian trappers exchanging goods and hospitality, and not upon the displacement of a native way of life. When colonization meant the displacement or reorganization of a sedentary tribe such as the Iroquois, then relations became less amicable.

All the evidence suggests that the French, of all European nations, knew best how to treat the Indians. One story in particular confirms this tradition in a very direct and simple manner. A German castaway who wandered about sixteenth-century Brazil "recorded that he always talked French or something that sounded like French to the Indians, in order to avoid being eaten. He records one cacique saying in effect, 'Damn it, whenever I select a particularly plump and juicy European for my dinner, he claims to be French and I have to go hungry!' "[28]

The friendly relations between the French and the Indians help to explain the eagerness with which the Jesuits returned to Canada in 1632. In the next five years a total of fifty-four Jesuits had come to New France to evangelize the Indians. Optimistic about the prospects and zealous for the salvation of souls, they fanned out along the St. Lawrence River and began an apostolate whose heroics would be unmatched in North America. For a quarter of a century, they virtually monopolized the Indian apostolate; then other groups began to enter the field. But the Jesuits, because of their superior numbers and their willingness to travel and work in the remotest outposts of the colony, became the most famous missionary group in New France.

One of the first tribes the Jesuits approached was the Hurons. Father Jean de Brébeuf had worked with these Indians prior to the English takeover in 1629. On his return to Canada in 1633, he resumed this apostolate along with four or five other Jesuits. Within a few years, the Huron mission seemed to be prospering. The priests were reaching about twelve thousand Indians and reported more than a thousand baptisms. In the Huron country of Ontario, they built a mission town, Ste. Marie, which was capable of housing as many as one thousand families. It was the center of the mission and the headquarters for the Jesuits. There they gathered for conferences, spiritual retreats, and camaraderie, eighteen missionaries in all by 1648. From there they would fan out across the countryside going to various Huron villages where each maintained his own individual mission, usually no more than a wooden cabin and a bark chapel.

A constant threat to this mission was the age-old hostility between the Huron and the Iroquois. Flying raids and brief skirmishes between the two groups went on for a number of years. Then the Iroquois, desirous of capturing the lucrative fur trade that the Hurons had established with the French, struck the fatal blow. In March of 1649, a band of one thousand Mohawks and Senecas raided the Huron villages, set fire to their homes, and routed the population. Brébeuf and his confrere Gabriel Lalemant were captured by the Iroquois and, after hours of unbelievable tortures, were finally put to death. This marked the end of the Huron mission, as both Jesuits and Hurons made their way back to Québec.

The martyrdom of Brébeuf and Lalemant has become part of the tradition and lore associated with the history of American Catholicism. To sense not just the harshness of the torture but, more important, the tenacity that these missionaries displayed, helps to explain the quality of French piety that many Jesuits possessed. Their thirst for mortification and their willingness to abandon everything for the sake of the Gospel was the key to their heroism, both in life and in death. Here is a report describing the death of Brébeuf and Lalemant:

> Even after they had been stripped naked and beaten with sticks on every part of their bodies, Brebeuf continued to exhort and encourage the Christians who were around him. One of the fathers had his hands cut off, and to both were applied under the armpits and beside the loins hatchets heated in the fire, as well as necklaces of redhot lance blades around their necks. Their tormentors then proceeded to girdle them with belts of bark steeped in pitch and resin, to which they set fire. At the height of these torments Father Lalemant raised his eyes to heaven and with sighs invoked God's aid, whilst Father Brebeuf set his face like a rock as though insensible to pain. Then, like one recovering consciousness, he preached to his persecutors and to the Christian captives until the savages gagged his mouth, cut off his nose, tore off his lips, then, in derision of Holy Baptism, deluged him and his companion martyrs with boiling water. Finally, large pieces of flesh were cut out of the bodies of both the priests and roasted by the Indians, who also tore out their hearts before their death by means of an opening above the breasts, feasting on them and on their blood, which they drank while it was warm.[29]

The fierceness of the Iroquois did not dissuade the Jesuits from attempting to convert them. Father Isaac Jogues had tried first in 1642, when he was a captive of the Iroquois. Then, four years later, after he had escaped and returned to France, he went back again, determined to convert his captors. He did not gain any converts; instead he found the crown of martyrdom at the end of a Mohawk war club.

The destruction of the Huron tribe increased the French fear of the Iroquois. Traffic on the St. Lawrence slowed to a halt and the fur trade suffered; even Montréal and Québec were not safe from attack, and the future of the colony appeared grim. Then, fortunately for the French, the Iroquois began to have their own problems. Their political strength had rested on their alliance with the Dutch in New York, but this broke down; momentarily fearing the power of the French and menaced by opposing Algonkian tribes, they signed a treaty of peace in 1653. This allowed the Jesuits to set up a mission among the Iroquois. Within five years, the peace was broken and the Iroquois again went on the offensive, with the missionaries fleeing for their lives. Finally, in 1666, a French army recruited from the battlefields of Europe attacked the Mohawks and forced them to sign a peace treaty. This blunted the threat of the Iroquois confederation, and almost immediately the Jesuits returned to upper New York State to evangelize the Five Nations of the Iroquois. They established a mission in each tribe and had as many as ten missionaries in the field. Eventually they founded a mission town at Caughnawaga, near Montréal, as a haven for converted Iroquois. For the most part, however, the Iroquois resisted the efforts of the Jesuits. One notable exception was a young Mohawk woman, Kateri Tekakwitha, who not only accepted baptism but, in a brief period of years, attained such a reputation for holiness that the church later recommended her for canonization.

When the English took over New York from the Dutch, they formed an alliance with the Iroquois against the French. They subsequently forced the French out of New York, and by 1687 the Jesuits had abandoned their mission to the Five Nations. In later years, French Jesuit activity in New York consisted of flying visits from their headquarters in Canada.

East of New York was the territory of the present state of Maine, inhabited by several Algonkian-speaking tribes collectively known as the Abnaki. Since Maine was geographically an extension of New England and cut off from New France by the Appalachians, the French were never able to maintain a strong presence in the territory.

Because of the territorial encroachment of the English, King Philip's War (which pitted the English against the Indians), and the attraction of the French settlements along the St. Lawrence, a majority of the Abnaki migrated west into the area around Québec. There the Jesuits established a mission town for the Abnaki, first at Sillery and later at St. François de Sales. The principal thrust of the Jesuit activity in Maine was to get the Abnakis to settle at these mission towns along the St. Lawrence. Within the area of Maine itself, Jesuit and Franciscan priests set up small missions along the coastline in the area north of present-day Portland, where they continued their work intermittently throughout the seventeenth and eighteenth centuries. But the English presence to the south remained a constant menace and curtailed the work of the missionaries. Finally, in 1763, France was forced to hand over the territory to England. With the English takeover, the French missions in Maine came to an end.

After 1670, French colonial policy had taken an expansionist direction. Until then, New France had been centered around the St. Lawrence; fifteen years later, the colony extended into the Mississippi Valley and the western Great Lakes. The expansion was primarily undertaken for economic reasons, the hope being to find a water route to the south, which they eventually did in discovering the Mississippi, and to increase the fur trade, which was being challenged by the English to the south along the lower Great Lakes and to the north in the Hudson Bay region. Explorers like La Salle and Jolliet pushed the boundaries of New France farther west and south until the fleur-de-lis flew over almost the entire heartland of the North American continent. In their tracks came Jesuit missionaries and fur traders, those ubiquitous *coureurs de bois.*

Jacques Marquette was not the first Jesuit to reach the heartland, but he was certainly one of the most famous. His exploration of the Mississippi with Jolliet in 1673 rewarded him with a niche in American history. But Marquette was more than an explorer. Even though he spent less than a decade in New France, he was instrumental in founding three important missions, Sault Ste. Marie and St. Ignace, on the upper Michigan peninsula, and Kaskaskia, in Illinois. He was a zealous missionary, typical of those fearless Jesuits who would chase a potential convert across streams, down rivers, and over mountains until they could catch their prey. But his health failed and he died in 1675, on the eastern shore of Lake Michigan. By the time of Marquette's death, the Jesuits were well established along the western Great Lakes.

The principal center of the western missions was St. Ignace, which had long been a gathering place for the Ottawa Indians. When the French traders and missionaries came west, they established themselves at this center and renamed it in honor of the Jesuit founder. Situated at the northern divide between Lakes Huron and Michigan, it became a jumping-off point for the missionaries who went south by canoe or on foot into the country of the Ottawa. During the winter hunting season of 1679, as many as thirteen hundred Indians gathered at St. Ignace, where they celebrated the feasts of Christmas and Epiphany in incredibly elaborate ceremonies. The mission seemed to hum with religious activity, leading one Jesuit to remark that "nearly everything [was] done here that could have been effected in a well-directed parish."[30]

Farther west was the mission of St. François Xavier, on the southern coast of Green Bay, in Wisconsin. The Jesuit missionary Claude Allouez founded this mission and used it as headquarters for his far-ranging travels throughout the Great Lakes territory. For almost thirty years, Allouez actively pursued the evangelization of numerous Indian tribes in Wisconsin, Illinois, and Michigan. An accomplished linguist who reportedly knew five Indian languages, Jesuit superior of the western missions, and founder of numerous mission stations, he gained the reputation of being the "Apostle to the North-west."

Both Jesuit and Franciscan missionaries worked in the Illinois country, establishing about ten mission stations along the Mississippi and its tributaries. More prominent in this region was the chain of forts and villages that protected the western perimeter of the colony and kept the fur trade in French hands. The French presence also reached into Louisiana and New Orleans, but this area was never very important as far as the evangelization of the Indians was concerned.

The most active period of the missions came to a close in the late 1680s. The religious enthusiasm of the Catholic reform had spent itself, zeal for the missions diminished, and consequently fewer Jesuits followed in the footsteps of Brébeuf and Allouez. Rather than found new missions, the Jesuits began to retrench, consolidating those already established. A report in 1703 listed thirty "very prosperous and well equipped" Jesuit missions in New France. More realistically, only about twenty missions were actively functioning at the time, and the majority of them were situated in the St. Lawrence River area. In 1749, only nineteen Jesuits were active in the Indian missions; a century earlier, the Huron mission alone had had as many black robes.

The decline of the Jesuit missions in the eighteenth century reflected the weakening condition of New France. As so often happened when church and state were intimate partners, the misfortunes of one, most often the state, inevitably affected the other. France certainly had its problems in the eighteenth century. War had become "the sport of princes" and peace a distracting interval between battles. Each war on the Continent had repercussions in the colony, especially when the English were involved. In North America, the English had allied themselves with the Iroquois and were raiding the French colony on all sides of its far-flung but weakly protected perimeters. England needed space for its expanding colonial settlements and continually cast an envious eye at the lucrative fur trade of the St. Lawrence and Great Lakes regions. Since New France was built on the back of the beaver, the loss of this source of trade would inevitably ruin the colony. Moreover, the English out-numbered the French by more than twenty to one; if the French were to be victorious against their North American rivals, they needed reinforcements from home. But when request for aid reached Paris, the reply came back: "When the house is on fire, no one has time to bother about the stables."[31]

Neglected by the Crown and seriously threatened by the English and the Iroquois, New France was doomed. The eighteenth century began peacefully enough, New France seeming to be in control of the situation. Then war broke out between England and France, and after eleven years of battle, they signed a peace treaty, in 1713. For New France it meant the loss of its strategically situated territory in Newfoundland, Acadie, and the Hudson Bay country to the north of Ontario. For the next thirty years, an armed truce characterized French-English relations in North America. They both built forts, strengthened their positions, and waited for events in Europe to sound the battle siren. In 1744, England and France went to war again, but it lasted only three years and had little effect on the realignment of New France. The treaty of 1748 was hardly a truce, and for the next few years the French and the English sparred with each other while the Iroquois were continually harassing the Indian tribes of the Great Lakes, seeking to weaken the hold of France on the fur trade. The final round of war began officially in 1756, the famous French and Indian War, but at least a year earlier the battle was well underway in the Ohio Valley and in Nova Scotia. When the war was over, the French empire in America came to an end. For all practical purposes, the downfall of the colony marked the end of the French missions among the Indians. Canada, described derisively by Voltaire as "a few acres of snow," became part of the British Empire, and Louisiana, west of the Mississippi, was given to the Spanish.

The British takeover of New France coincided with the expulsion of the Jesuits from France; this effectively cut off the supply of new recruits for the Indian missions. The Jesuits remained in British Canada, left to die of old age. In 1773, when the Pope suppressed the Society throughout the world, only eleven Jesuits were in Canada. Other religious orders experienced similar declines in personnel, and the mission enterprise, already weakened substantially by the political upheavals of the eighteenth century, was virtually abandoned. The Catholic church in Canada now turned its attention to consolidating its position in the British-governed colony. As a result of the Quebec Act, passed in 1774, the church received a new lease on life, and French Catholic Canadians were allowed to retain their cultural and religious traditions. This meant that Catholicism would survive along the northwestern frontier, where pockets of French settlers continued to carry on the fur trade. But now the thrust of the French-Canadian church was to minister to its own people, rather than evangelize the Indians. Later, when the United States gained control over this frontier country, Catholicism in the Northwest would enter a new era and evangelization of the Indians would be resumed.

Unlike the Spanish mission program, the French enterprise did not span even one century. It was a brief, though heroic, period of evangelization. The French Jesuits counted their conversions by the hundreds, whereas, along the frontier of New Spain the Franciscans numbered their baptisms by the thousands. Fewer priests were involved in the Canadian enterprise, and their mission towns could never rival the large Franciscan estates of California. But the heroism of the French Jesuits has left a permanent mark in the annals of American Catholic history. However meager their evangelization results were, their heroic exploits and bloody martyrdoms became part of popular Catholic folklore. Growing up Catholic in the early-twentieth century meant reading the lives of these missionaries and hearing tales about their heroism among the Indians. A young Catholic boy or girl did not have to look to Europe for saintly models. They were right there in the forests of New France, and the exploits of Brébeuf, Jogues, and Marquette inspired a number of young people to go and do likewise in China, Latin America, and other missionary regions around the world. What people remembered of the French mission was not the Indian conversions, but the Jesuit heroism. The exploits of the missionaries, not the conversion of the Indians, was the real success story.

II

Catholicism and Native American Cultures

IN A LETTER to his Jesuit superior requesting to be sent to the foreign missions, Jacques Marquette spoke for all Christian missionaries when he wrote that he wanted "to win souls to Christ." This was the primary goal of every missionary who set sail for America: to save the immortal souls of the Indians from eternal damnation. Despite the single-mindedness of Marquette and his confreres, the salvation of souls involved much more than a religious conversion; it entailed a cultural conversion as well. Religion and culture were so interwoven in the minds of both the missionary and the Indian that conversion to Christianity meant a total reorientation of one's life—indeed, "nothing less than a cultural revolution." To Christianize, necessarily meant to civilize, and for the Indian this meant becoming "like Europeans in all aspects of life—in matters of sex, marriage, economy, and government, as well as religion."[1]

The initial contacts between the missionaries and the Indians provide an interesting study in human psychology. The priests were intelligent enough to know that preaching alone would not attract the Indians to their cause. So they invariably brought with them from Europe all types of gifts to dazzle the Indians and win their friendship. A traveling companion of Eusebio Kino described how they spent their time in Spain while waiting for the boat that would take them to America:

> We studied not only astronomy, mathematics, and other interesting fields of knowledge, but we ourselves made all sorts of trinkets and worked at practical things.

Some of us made compasses or sun-dials and others cases for them; this one sewed clothes and furs, that one learned how to make bottles, another how to solder tin; one busied himself with distilling, a second with the lathe, a third with the art of sculpturing; so that with these goods and skills we might gain the good will of the wild heathen and then more easily give them the truths of the Christian faith.[2]

The Franciscan Alonso de Benavides always had "bells, rattles, feathers and beads of different colors" to give to the Indians. Jean Brébeuf told his Jesuit colleagues, "You must provide yourself with a tinder box or with a burning mirror, or with both, to furnish them fire in the daytime to light their pipes, and in the evening when they have to encamp; these little services win their hearts."[3] To "win their hearts" was the first step in the conversion process, and the missionaries generally succeeded for the simple reason that the Indians they met were most often a friendly people. Winning their souls was another problem.

Sometimes this happened rather quickly, or miraculously, as the friar would say. Again, Father de Benavides recounts an incident that illustrated, admittedly in an exaggerated manner, how the missionaries went about converting the Indians to Christianity. During their 1598 journey of conquest to New Mexico, the Spanish had stopped at the Tewa pueblo; they discovered that the Indians were very disturbed because of the lack of rain and the damage this was doing to their crops. Then the priest "told them publicly through interpreters not to be afflicted, to worship the Lord, God, and Creator of all things, as He was the one, and not the idols, who could give them water, and that he could assure them on behalf of God that He would send them rain. The Indians believed him, and the blessed father commissary and his friars, together with all the Christians, offered prayers and invocations to this end. . . . It was remarkable, for, while the sky was clear as a diamond, exactly twenty-four hours after the outcry had gone up, it rained almost throughout the land so abundantly that the crops recovered in good condition. Through this miracle that whole pueblo was converted."[4]

There was nothing like a good miracle to attract the attention of the Indians and demonstrate the power of the Christian God. Most often, however, persuading the Indians to be baptized was a long process. The example of the Jesuits in New France is especially enlightening in this regard. They followed the Indians wherever they went, up and down rivers, over frozen lakes and snow-covered trails, enduring hardships that were unimaginable to these European-bred, university-educated priests. As one Jesuit put it, the life of a missionary was "a long and slow martyrdom . . . an almost continual practice of patience and of mortification." Day and night they followed the Indians, conversing with them about religion; when it came time to go to bed, they slept side by side with their potential converts in cabins so full of smoke that their eyes wept and so loaded with the stench of disease they often got nauseous. In winter they just about froze to death from the cold. "Suffering and hardship," concluded a Jesuit missionary to the Montagnais, "are the appanages of these holy but arduous Missions."⁵ After months, even years, of pursuing the Indians, the missionaries may have persuaded only a few of them to be baptized. But it was well worth the wait. To save one soul from the fires of hell was worth the price of a long and slow martyrdom.

But baptism was only the beginning. Conversion to Christianity involved much more than the sprinkling of a few drops of water on the heads of curious Indians. The lone missionary could travel about baptizing hundreds of Indians in the belief that he was saving their souls from damnation. But to convert them to a new way of life, indeed to a new way of understanding the universe, was a task that took time, lots of time. The principal way the missionaries sought to convert the Indians was through the formation of the mission town. The reasons for the establishment of mission towns were quite obvious and said a great deal about the evangelization of the Indians. Given the lack of missionaries and the nomadic character of many Indian tribes, it made sense to gather together as many Indians as possible at one location, where one or two priests could carry out the evangelization program. In this manner the available personnel could be used efficiently and the necessity of making flying visits to tribes scattered about in any given area would be obviated. The Canadian missionary Paul LeJeune, S.J., summarized this point very clearly. "Not much ought to be hoped for from savages as long as they are wanderers," he wrote. ". . . To try to follow them, as many Religious would be needed as there are cabins. Besides, I do not believe that out of a hundred Religious there would be ten who could endure the hardships to be encountered in following them. . . ."⁶

By gathering the Indians together and segregating them into mission towns, the chances of their apostasizing from the Christian religion were considerably lessened. Experience had proved that leaving the Indians scattered about in their native homes after baptism just did not work. Inevitably they reverted to their old religious customs. Moreover, segregating the Christian Indians from their gentile neighbors would reduce the possibility of friction between the two groups and lessen the social pressure on Christian Indians to abandon their new religion. The mission town also helped to protect the neophytes from the scandalous behavior of the European settlers who lived in the region.

Segregating the Indians was good not only for their souls, but also for their minds. In such a controlled environment the Indians would be better able to assimilate the customs, language, and skills of a European culture. Clearly such a settlement program involved a total social reorganization on the part of the Indian. It meant exchanging a nomadic existence for a sedentary one; life in small clusters or villages for large settlements; an unregulated, individualistic lifestyle for a regimented, bureaucratically regulated community; a native culture for a foreign one. Indeed, joining a mission community involved "nothing less than a cultural revolution."

For those Indians, the Pueblos especially, who already lived in fairly large communities, the settlement program was not necessary. Since the Indians were already settled, all the missionary had to do was build his church on the edge of the village and launch his program of evangelization.

An obvious question is, How were the missionaries able to attract the Indians to these wilderness seminaries? Another way of putting it is, Why did the Indians move to the mission towns? One obvious reason was that this was a new show in town and the Indians were simply curious about life in the village of the black robes. Another reason was equally mundane: food. A Jesuit in Arizona wrote, "Indians do not come to Christian service when they do not see the Maize pot boiling."[7] As hunters and fishers, their lives centered around the search for food, and "Upon the Padre's ability to supply food for his neophytes depended the expansion of his mission."[8]

The personal charisma of the missionary and his seemingly magical powers in curing disease were also very influential in persuading the Indians to accept the spiritual authority of the friar. Through the use of his Christian charms—crucifixes, images, relics, and rosaries—the friar was a potent rival to the Indian shaman. A seemingly miraculous cure was sufficiently impressive to persuade the Indians to accept the authority of this new medicine man. The charisma of the French Jesuit Gabriel Druillettes was not untypical. Like his confreres, he seemed immune to smallpox and the other contagious diseases brought by the white man, and his ability to nurse the sick back to health persuaded some Indians to admit: "He is not a man; . . . he is an extraordinary Genie. . . . It must surely be that the God whom this father announces to us, is powerful, since he so perfectly cures the greatest and the most contagious diseases, which the Manitou or Genie, whom our sorcerers invoke, cannot do."[9]

Obviously the magical powers of the friar could have the opposite effect. When he failed to cure a fatal illness, then he was accused of black magic, and inevitably this destroyed his credibility and the great reputation of the god he invoked.

Thus, through a variety of ways—moral suasion, emphasis on the attraction of mission life with its food, clothing, and shelter, and spiritual arguments on behalf of the Christian god—the missionaries were able to persuade the Indians to live at the mission. But the desire to increase the mission population eventually led some priests to abandon such voluntary means of persuasion in favor of more coercive methods.

During the 1790s the California Franciscans began to seek out prospective converts with the aid of the soldiers. In some instances these were expeditions in search of fugitives from the mission, but many gentiles got caught in the net and were brought back to the mission along with the fugitive Christian

Indians. On other occasions, military expeditions to the interior included both armed subjugation and forced conversions.[10] In Arizona the Jesuits used Christian Indians and soldiers to prod the Pima Indians to become Christian. Most of the population of Guevavi, for example, "was reduced by force."[11]

The populations of some of the French mission towns were increased by gentile Indians captured by Christian Indians who fought alongside the French in their frequent skirmishes with the Iroquois. For some Indians, driven from their native homes by hostile tribes, or in the case of the Abnaki in Maine, by the armed persecution of land-hungry Englishmen, the mission became a refugee camp. Human survival, not religious conviction, persuaded them to join the ranks of the mission Indians.

Ideally, conversion was to be voluntary, but the reluctance of many Indians to commit "cultural suicide" led some missionaries to adopt coercive tactics. As one priest confessed, "The Indians, being children of fear, are more strongly appealed to by the glistening of the sword than by the voice of five missionaries."[12] Conversion was not an easy task, either for the Indians or for the missionaries.

Once the Indians settled at the mission, their daily life became incredibly regimented. It did not matter whether it was a Spanish Franciscan mission in California or a French Jesuit settlement along the St. Lawrence; the daily routine was essentially the same. The schedule at the French mission of Lorette was typical.

> At sunrise, or shortly after, the signal is given for saluting the Mother of God in the words of the angel. They [regard this as a religious duty, and] are careful not to omit it, wherever they may be. Half an hour later, mass is celebrated, at which they all assist. The concourse is the same on working days and holy days. . . . When mass is finished, they leave, if it be a working day, to labor at home or in the fields. In the evening, at sunset, the Signal is given for prayer. All gather in the chapel where prayers are offered up in common for the whole village. Each family also recites prayers privately at home, after which each one with a pious kiss, venerates the most holy wounds of Christ. The order is the same for feast days and working days except for the labor [which the holiness of the day prohibits].[13]

Ora et labora, work and prayer, was the trademark of all mission towns.

A special concern of the missionary were the children. They were generally the first to be baptized and were looked upon as the future hope of the mission. In addition to attendance at mass they had special instructions during the day; some were chosen to sing in the choir, which performed at church services; others were trained to assist the priest at Mass or to act as interpreters at Christian-doctrine classes.

A major purpose of the chapel services was doctrinal instruction. The missionaries most often used Indian interpreters; these individuals, generally men, though the French occasionally used women, occupied a very important position in the mission program. They were the intermediaries between the missionary and the natives; they kept order and decorum in church; sought and punished those who failed to attend chapel; taught their brothers and sisters the mysteries of Christianity; and even acted as interpreters for the sacrament of confession. When the priest was absent from the mission, they took his place preaching the gospel, leading prayer services, and baptizing when necessary. These interpreters, *dogiques* the French called them, were indispensable to the mission program.

Since the missionary seldom baptized adults until they acquired some understanding of Christianity, catechetical instruction was a daily feature of the mission program. Even after their baptism, instruction continued to remain an important part of their Christian formation. The description of a catechism class at a Spanish mission captured the essence of the friar's method of instruction. The Indians

> "were clothed in blankets, and arranged in a row before a blind Indian, who understood their dialect, and was assisted by an alcalde to keep order. Their tutor began by desiring them to kneel, informing them that he was going to teach them the names of the Persons composing the Trinity, and they were to repeat in Spanish what he dictated. The neophytes being thus arranged began: 'Santisima Trinidad, Dios, Jesu Christo, Espirito Santo,' pausing between each name to listen if the simple Indians, who had never spoken a Spanish word before, pronounced it correctly. After they had repeated these names satisfactorily, their blind tutor, after a pause added 'Santos'—and recapitulated the names of a great many saints which finished the morning's tuition."[14]

The technique was very simple—rote memory of the catechism with the hope that the Indians would acquire some understanding of the Christian mysteries. To reinforce the teachings of the catechism, the missionaries, following the old adage of *lex orandi, lex credendi* (the law of prayer establishes the rule of faith), relied on the elaborate ritual of the Catholic liturgy.

Even though these missions were situated in the wilderness frontier of North America, they could rival any European parish in liturgical splendor. Such pageantry was a trademark of Roman Catholic ritual, and it seldom failed to make an impression on the Indians, who were favorably disposed to elaborate ceremonials. As one Spanish Jesuit observed, "There was nothing like a bit of pageantry to awaken interest, deference, and fervor among the Indians."[15] The celebration of feast days was especially elaborate. The Mass of the day was highlighted by music performed by the mission choir and orchestra. The Spanish especially fostered music among the natives as part of their civilizing process; their liturgies included guitars, violins, drums, and bugles, and the humblest church always had a special section for the choir. Outdoor processions were also part of the celebration. The feast of a mission's patron saint was the occasion for a special fiesta; after Mass, a procession took place in honor of the saint; the saint's statue was then put on display in the center of the mission compound, and throughout the day Indian dance groups performed in the plaza and athletic contests took place. The entire day was given over to praying, playing, and partying.

During Holy Week the liturgy was less festive but equally elaborate. In the Southwest, religious plays depicting the passion of Christ, and penitential processions complete with flagellation, became a style of frontier Spanish Catholicism. The Spanish conducted these rituals for their own edification, but occasionally the Indians took part in them. In addition, educational plays depicting various biblical themes were written for and performed by the Indians for their own religious edification.

This emphasis on ceremony and pageantry was common to all mission programs, and it blended in very well with the rich ceremonial practices of the Indians. Every feast-day celebration inevitably involved a substantial mixture of Catholic and Indian ceremonials. This was especially true among the Pueblo Indians, who had developed their own ceremonial tradition. At first the missionaries tried to do away with these native ceremonies, but the Indians resisted, even going to war to preserve their native religious rituals. Eventually the Spanish learned to look the other way and allowed the mixture of Catholic and native ceremonies. The result is that today the Pueblo Indians possess a calendar and a ceremonial life that evidences a considerable mixture of native and Catholic customs. One of the most exhaustive studies of Pueblo religion concluded: "Catholicism has by and large enriched Pueblo religion, contributing God and the saints to the pantheon, fiestas to the calendar, candles and who knows how many other details to ritual."[16]

The liturgy of the mission was an important aspect in the Christian formation of the neophytes. Not only did it reinforce the lessons of the catechism, but the annual cycle of feast days also served to reinterpret the native calendar by integrating Christian holidays with Indian festivals. Even though the missionaries could never destroy the native rituals, their liturgical calendar and ceremonies offered a new interpretation of the universe and a Christian understanding of the seasons of the year.

Another medium used to teach the neophytes was the sacred image. The cross of the crucifixion was a prominent image at the mission, and devotion to the suffering of Jesus was strongly encouraged. The French Jesuits employed a great number of holy images "in order to contribute more effectively toward bringing into sentiments of piety these poor savages."[17] Portraits of the saints and scenes of death, the Last Judgment, hell, and purgatory were used as visual aids to convey the meaning of the Christian way. California mission churches were decorated with "statues and pictures of Christ, the Blessed Virgin, angels and saints, especially of the mission's patron saint. There were also pictures representing heaven, hell, death, judgment, purgatory, etc." The stations of the cross were also "found in every mission."[18] Many of these images were imported from Europe, but in the Southwest the Spanish developed their own art of image-making. Spanish artisans skillfully crafted a variety of holy images *(santos)* such as *retablos* (paintings on wooden panels), *bultos* (figures carved in wood), and paintings on animal skins. These *santos* decorated mission churches and were part of the catechetical network used to instruct both Spanish and Indians in the Christian religion. The *bultos* were often used in processions and were decorated and attired in elegant fashion. Part of the mission church's treasury included a rich wardrobe for these statues: crowns, rings, earrings, necklaces, beads, dresses, mantles, etc. The *santos* clearly had a magical-religious aspect to them and were invoked to repel sickness, natural disasters, and the devil as well as to call forth rain, good crops, and a healthy childbirth. The majority of the *santos* represented male and female saints, "elder brothers and sisters to mankind," who intervened in the realm of the natural, "the world of crops and animals and family serenity and health."[19] Images depicting Jesus and Mary were invoked for more supernatural, salvation-oriented purposes. Indigenous to the Southwest, the *santos* became a conspicuous feature of colonial Spanish Catholicism.

Another feature of the mission's devotional network was the confraternity. These were fraternal and spiritual organizations formed to promote devotion to a particular saint or religious practice. They were part of the Catholic reform tradition, and in transplanting the faith to North America the missionaries never failed to establish these confraternities among the Indians. In the Southwest they were especially popular; among the Spanish they functioned as a surrogate parish, with their own chapels, revenues, and feast-day celebrations. Most of them were in a general state of decline by the late-eighteenth century, but one confraternity appeared at about this time that quickly gained prominence and notoriety. This was the Brothers of Our Father Jesus, commonly known as the Penitentes. Its origin is obscure, but most likely it originated in the Southwest, adapting many of the Franciscan penitential traditions. Its members were men of Spanish descent who committed themselves to practice extreme forms of penitential devotions, especially during Holy Week. These Penitentes were a subgroup, a sect, within the Spanish church in the Southwest, and Indians rarely belonged to this confraternity. They appeared to respect the group, but the Penitentes' harsh style of devotion did not appeal to them. As one Pueblo Indian put it, "The Indian religion is to be happy, but the Spanish religion is to be sad."[20]

In their reports to France, the Jesuits frequently boasted of the well-regulated devotional life at the missions, claiming that they "were ordered like the finest parish of France."[21] Even though this may be an overstatement, it is significant that the model they and their Spanish counterparts had for the mission was the Catholic parish. Indeed the Indian mission was unique in its segregation, its seminary routine, and, in California especially, its regulated work schedule, but when it came to nurturing the piety of the Indians, the mission very much resembled a European parish.

As in the parish, the principal agent of Christian formation was the sermon. Instruction, liturgy, *santos,* and confraternities were essential parts of the network of spiritual formation, but the sermon was the link that bound these activities together. It gave them direction and informed them with religious meaning. Obviously the sermons were geared to the occasion of the day —the feast of a patron saint, the particular devotion of a confraternity, or the celebration of an event in the cycle of salvation. But always the special need of the mission was to convert the Indian to the practice of the Christian religion. Every liturgical event, big or small, sought to nurture the piety of the people and advance them toward Christian perfection. Not unexpectedly, then, the preaching of the missionaries involved a good deal of exhortation, urging the Indians to abandon their native "pagan" practices and fully embrace the Christian way of life. Nor was it surprising that the missionaries adopted a pulpit gospel that was in vogue in Europe at the time. This was the gospel of the parish mission, or what can be called the gospel of Catholic revivalism.

The link with the parish mission in Europe is much more than an impression gleaned from missionary reports. The Jesuits were intensely involved in this work in France; in New France they continued the practice, conducting three- or four-day missions on the occasion of a particular feast or in order to blot out intemperance among their neophytes. The Franciscans were similarly involved in conducting parish missions, and some of those who worked in Texas had been giving such revivals in Mexico. The influence of this style of evangelical preaching also is evident in the accounts given by the missionaries themselves.

It does not take much reading in missionary reports to realize that the priests were preaching an evangelical gospel of terror and fear. The great truths of Christianity such as sin, penance, heaven, hell, and baptism were all there, but the style was fire-and-brimstone. Father Alonso de Benavides described this manner of preaching very clearly.

The word had gone out among the Indians that Benavides was preaching "about the torments of hell which all those who are not baptized must suffer"; curious about this, some Indians questioned Benavides about the truth of the rumor going around. He responded that "it was all true, and I added all that I could about the mysteries of our holy Catholic faith which our Lord inspired me to teach them."[22] In other words, the approach of Benavides and others like him was first to emphasize the terror of eternal damnation and then go on to explain some of the "other mysteries" of Catholicism. Father Kino's technique was somewhat different; he often used a world map to show the Indians where the black robes came from and how they were following in the footsteps of St. James, who long before had converted the Spanish. He pointed out the spiritual and material benefits of becoming Catholic and then gave "other talks of the things of God and of heaven and of hell"; not surprisingly, his talks "on the blazing and eternal fire of hell" were sufficiently vivid to horrify the Indians.[23] The comparison of Kino and Benavides illustrates the point that even though all missionaries did not operate in the same manner, the general thrust of their appeal reflected the fiery tradition of evangelical Catholicism.

The French Jesuits have left the best records in this regard; they clearly indicate that, when it came to persuading the Indians to accept Christianity, no better technique could be used than to instill in them a fear of eternal damnation. They had come to North America "to win souls to Christ." "To do and suffer everything in order to prevent a single mortal sin" was their motivating spirit, and to save the Indians from the consequences of such sin influenced the way they preached. They were men possessed with the thought of death—their own as well as that of the Indians; and the last place they wanted anyone to end up in was hell.

One passage from the *Jesuit Relations* typifies the nature of this stern gospel.

> We have given here, within four or five months, some Instructions on Hell by means of certain Mournful Songs and some spectacular representations, which have had considerable influence upon our savages. I have tried to express in those Mournful Songs, all that is best-fitted, according to The Idea of savages, to torment one damned, and the vices which are the most common among them. This Instruction is repeated from time to time, either in The Church or in some large Cabin. Since we have Begun this form of Instruction, when I wish to give some severe warning to anyone, I ask him at first whether he truly believes all that I have told him about the pains of Hell; then, obliging Him to look with me at a picture of one damned,—which I have placed, for this purpose, in a Room near the hall in which I instruct them,—I allow him to do as he chooses. This Instruction is not given twice to the same person; I have seen few on whom it has not had a very good effect, and whom it has not inclined really to amend their faults.[24]

This was hardly an isolated incident. Similar scenes can be found in every volume of these reports.

Preaching and praying were the *most* important facets of mission life. They served not only a religious purpose in converting and nurturing the native Americans to a new way of belief, but, at the same time, they introduced them to a new culture, a new way of living. New modes of dress, reflective of a European culture, were required for church services; and as Herbert Bolton remarked, the very act of going to church—"with their poor clothes clean, and all washed and combed"—involved a lesson in the amenities of civilization. "There was a virtue then as now in putting on one's Sunday clothes."[25] Musical training which involved making new types of instruments and learning new songs was also an important way of civilizing the Indians. In the case of the Spanish Franciscans especially, learning the gospel of Christianity also meant acquiring a new language, and this, too, was a way to advance the acculturation of the natives. Thus, becoming a mission Indian meant much more than believing in a new God; it also involved accepting a new way of life.

To further the acculturation of the Indians, the mission town fostered other activities. Religious formation was only one half of the *ora et labora* routine; work was the other half. Edward Spicer summarized the significance of this aspect of mission life very well.

> This side of mission operation required at least as much training and supervision as did the church activities. Herds, plows, horses, adobe—and timber building, and in some instances irrigation agriculture were new to the Indians. In addition, the crops introduced by the missionaries, especially wheat and the orchard crops, required new techniques. The missionary, who was aided only by other Christianized Indians sometimes not yet well versed in the new techniques, had to assume the responsibility for getting his neophytes as interested in these as in the novel practices of Christianity. He had to give instruction in handling cattle and in horsemanship, in times and methods of planting, and to select individuals who would take responsibility for instructing others and organizing their work efficiently. The success of a given mission would seem to have depended heavily on the missionary's ability as a farmer and builder, for the size of his congregation was often closely related to the benefits which he offered in the way of food and an impressive church building.[26]

Though Spicer's comments referred to the Spanish mission, the importance of an agricultural way of life at the French mission was similar. The principal difference was that, with the exception of the Hurons, the northern Indian tribes did not take to farming with much enthusiasm. They were more inclined to go off hunting and fishing.

Among the Spanish, the economic aspect of the mission became so important that it led to the development of large plantations distinguished by an elaborate complex of buildings. The layout of the Santa Barbara mission was typical. The church was the most imposing structure in the compound and the first building to be constructed. Adjacent to it was the residence of the friars, which opened out onto the "monks' garden." Behind the church and monastery was the main courtyard, or plaza; on the opposite side of the plaza was the Indian pueblo, which numbered 252 adobe houses enclosed by a wall on three sides. The pueblo opened onto the plaza, where there were a water fountain and a laundry. Situated around the plaza area were the granary, weaving mill, and tannery. Also included in the compound were two reservoirs, a mill, a pottery shed, a horse barn and corral, a cemetery and residences for the soldiers stationed at the mission. Beyond the Indian village were orchards and gardens. Such frontier plantations, strung out along the coastline of California, were the centers of a multimillion-dollar agricultural business.

Because of the intensive economic nature of the Spanish mission, the friars became involved in a host of mundane tasks. They had come to the frontier to save souls, but found that their day was consumed by an endless round of other, less noble activities. A preacher who "lived like a King," the missionary was also the chief mechanic, farmer, rancher, janitor, bookkeeper, and cook. The Indians had to be taught the ways of a new civilization, and the missionary was the one who had to do this by working alongside the Indians in the fields and shops. "I left my paternal hearth," lamented a Spanish Jesuit, "to enter into a spiritual station principally because I saw that business and agriculture were not for me, but in this mission I encountered much more of that sort of anxiety than I would ever have had in my fatherland . . . thus, there remains little time to the father missionary for the performance of his spiritual labors. . . ."[27]

Among the French missionaries, such distractions were not as great, since their mission towns were not terribly large or very elaborate. A typical mission consisted of a small chapel made of wood and animal skin together with a number of bark cabins where the mission Indians lived. Since the economy of New France was built on the back of the beaver, the French mission never became the agricultural enterprise that was commonplace in California; it remained a relatively small village that survived by subsistence farming.

The Spanish mission differed from its French counterpart in one other respect, its political organization. The Spanish had brought with them a system of town government which proved effective in organizing the mission. The system introduced among the Pueblo Indians best represented the ideal of mission town government. Each village had a governor, who represented the Pueblo in dealing with Spanish authorities; a lieutenant governor, who assisted the governor and represented him when he was absent; an *alguacil*, who was the local sheriff; a sacristan, who assisted the priest and maintained the church; the *fiscales*, who were responsible for discipline in spiritual affairs; and the majordomos, who were ditch bosses. The priest appointed his own sacristan and *fiscal;* the other officials, initially appointed by the Spanish, were later elected from the Indian community. Above them in the hierarchy of authority were the Spanish officials who exercised jurisdiction over a specific territory and provided the essential link between the Crown and the frontier communities. Under their jurisdiction were two or three soldiers assigned to the mission town to help preserve law and order among the natives. In California the friars initially resisted such a system of town government, since they were reluctant to yield any authority to the natives; after a good deal of controversy they gave in and accepted the system.

The introduction of a new form of government, like a new religion, was a major force in the acculturation process at the Spanish mission. Though the

Indians had their own form of government, the coming of the Spanish meant that they had to adopt a foreign system of community organization. This involved a tremendous change for the Indians. First they were asked to pledge allegiance to a new authority figure who spoke like a god but was nonetheless a man—the king of Spain. Their land, their rivers, and their hunting ground somehow now belonged to him. They were also asked to work and fight for this man, who lived far away and did nothing for the Indians except "protect them." By introducing this new concept of government, the Spanish "proposed to separate the moral-ritual leadership which was the heart and center of Indian communities from the administrative-executive leadership and to subordinate the former to the latter. This was a thorough turning upside down of the Indian system."[28]

The mission system involved not only a total revolution in Indian culture, but a new way of thinking about the supernatural, a new way of viewing the earth and its fertility, and a new understanding of personal and social relations. The irony is that the Spanish believed that this program of conversion and acculturation would be completed in a short space of time. Theoretically the mission was a temporary institution, designed to last only ten years; then the friars would leave for other frontiers, the land would be distributed among the Indians, and, having been civilized, they would then mix in with the neighboring Spanish community. It never worked that way, however.

To convert and civilize the Indians was a monumental task which ultimately ended up in frustration and failure. The reasons for this are not hard to discover. One of the most obvious was the language barrier. In the early-seventeenth-century Franciscan missions in Florida and New Mexico, it is apparent, the friars did attempt to learn the native language so that they could evangelize the Indians more effectively. In dealing with a nonliterate culture, they realized the necessity of compiling dictionaries and grammars and translating catechetical and devotional works into the native languages. Since this was a policy developed earlier in Mexico, it was not surprising that the missionaries continued it north of the border. But, during the eighteenth century, it was clear that the Spanish Franciscans had become less concerned about learning the native languages. The reasons for this change of attitude are not entirely clear, but it was certainly present by the mid-eighteenth century in New Mexico. When Bishop Tamarón made his visitation of New Mexico in 1760, his severest criticism was aimed at the Franciscans' failure to learn the native languages. One sixty-two-year-old priest had been in New Mexico twenty-eight years, and the bishop "asked him why he had not learned the language of the Keres Indians in so many years . . . ?" The friar, he said, could only offer excuses such as the indifference of the Indians and their unwillingness to go to confession.[29] This was hardly an isolated case. The report of Tamarón as well as the 1776 report of the Franciscan friar Francisco A. Domínguez gave every indication that the missionaries in New

Mexico were sadly deficient in language skills. Although New Mexico offers the most extreme example of the friars' failure to learn the native languages, the situation was not much better elsewhere. The regulations of the order required the Franciscans to learn these languages, but they were not uniformly enforced; the result was that with few exceptions the Franciscan missionaries were unable to speak the language of the people.

A major reason for the friars' failure in this regard was their policy of having the Indians learn the doctrines of Christianity in Spanish. To speak the king's language was not only a mark of civilization, but, in the friars' opinion, it was also the only satisfactory medium for expressing the truths of Christianity. The friars' insistence on Spanish as the language of catechesis forced them to rely on interpreters, for the simple reason that the bulk of the Indian population was indifferent to learning the king's language. They could "recite some of the Christian doctrine in Spanish," observed Bishop Tamarón, but "since they do not understand the language, they might as well not know it."[30] This assessment of Tamarón's could have been made of any Spanish mission; some Indians learned the language sufficiently well to serve as interpreters or civil officials and "in trade and temporal business the Indians and the Spanish understand one another completely." But "this does not extend to the spiritual realm, with regard to which they display great tepidity and indifference."[31] The best that could be said of the Spanish missions was that many Indians "understand a little Spanish but not perfectly."[32]

The Indians of New France were no more enthusiastic about learning French. The Jesuits, however, did show an uncanny ability to learn the native languages. Fundamental to their linguistic talents was their cultural relativism, which persuaded them to adapt their evangelization program to the culture of the people. A French Jesuit eloquently expressed this mentality. "To make a Christian out of a barbarian," he said, "is not the work of a day. . . . A great step is gained when one has learned to know those with whom he has to deal; has penetrated their thoughts; has adapted himself to their language, their customs, and their manner of living; and, when necessary, has been a Barbarian with them, in order to win them over to Jesus Christ."[33] Learning the native language was not "the work of a day," but theoretically no Jesuit could be approved for his final solemn profession unless he was proficient in a native language. Given their cultural relativism, their regulations concerning language proficiency, and their education in the classical languages, it is not surprising that many French Jesuits did become skillful linguists as well as authors of native dictionaries, grammars, and catechetical books. Some obviously were not able to learn the native languages, and even the more proficient were at times anything but fluent. The Hurons "thought it was a joke to ask LeJeune to speak," wrote one Jesuit, "and when he made a stammering attempt at their language, laughter and derision greeted his skilled efforts."[34] Any American tourist in Paris knows how LeJeune must have felt.

Learning the language of the Indians was only the first step. Next came the necessity of translating the gospel message into the language of the natives, and this proved to be a serious problem. Fundamental to this was the difference between the two cultural systems; the Europeans possessed a literate culture and a religious system that thrived on textbook precision; the Indian culture was nonliterate and their language did not possess the equivalents of Catholic theology. One was a language of the New World, while the other expressed the culture of Europe. A Jesuit in New France described this cultural divergence:

> For they have no words which can represent the mysteries of religion, and it would be impossible to translate even the Lord's prayer into their language save by paraphrase. For of themselves they do not know what is sanctification, or the kingdom of Heaven, or supersubstantial bread (which we call daily), or to lead into temptation. The words glory, virtue, reason, beatitude, Trinity, Holy Spirit, angels, archangels, resurrection, paradise, hell, Church, baptism, faith, hope, charity, and an infinity of others are not in use among them.[35]

Reinforcing this cultural and linguistic diversity was a fear that the truths of Catholicism would be misrepresented or, worse, presented in an unorthodox, heretical manner. The Spanish missionaries were touchy about this issue, since some of their confreres in Mexico and elsewhere had been accused of teaching unorthodox theology to the Indians. One Spanish Franciscan advised his fellow missionaries to avoid the problem by expressing "those words, such as God, Trinity, Person, Blessed Sacrament . . . as they sound, and not try to translate them, because not having . . . equivalent terms, if they try to say it all in their language, it is unavoidable either that they will say something different or give rise to errors of which it will not be easy to disabuse the people who hear them, since they usually believe that what the interpreter says is on all occasions the same as what the Father teaches."[36]

Thus in the Spanish mission the inability of the friars to learn the native languages, coupled with the assumed inadequacy of the Indian languages to express the truths of Catholicism, led the friars to resort to the simple memorization of the catechism and the use of interpreters. The use of an interpreter, however, frequently led to "nothing but confusion on the subject of catechism and confession."[37] Confessing one's sins through an interpreter was not terribly comforting, for the simple reason that often "they made their sins public."[38] The linguistic skills of the French Jesuits eliminated many of these problems, but they still had to contend with translating Catholic theology into a New World idiom. It did make for some interesting alterations. The word Brébeuf used for priest could be applied to women as well as to men; the sign of the cross became "in the name of our Father, and of His Son, and of their Holy Ghost."[39] The cannibalism of the Great Lakes Indians, with its evident religious overtones, was a more serious problem. Catholics believed in transubstantiation, "whereby they professed to acquire grace through eating the flesh and drinking the blood of their Saviour. The Jesuits had consciously avoided inculcating the concept of eating the body of Christ and drinking his blood, a notion which might too readily be equated in Amerindian minds with the ritual cannibalism the missionaries were trying to discourage. Brébeuf translated the Eucharist into Huron as *Atonesta,* which signified an act of gratitude and thanksgiving in the sense of a memorial or purely symbolic ceremony."[40] European theologians would hardly have approved of such a substantial alteration in meaning.

Another major obstacle to evangelization was the problem of scandal or the contradiction between the ideals of the gospel and the actions of European settlers. Situated in the vicinity of every Spanish mission was a military presidio and a settlement of Spanish colonists. Their conduct, especially that of the soldiers, was frequently a source of grief to the missionaries because of their crude behavior toward the Indians. "The relation of the soldiers with the Indian women were notorious," noted the scholar Sherburne F. Cook, and such behavior led the Spanish governor to state:

> The officers and men of these presidios are conducting and behaving themselves in the missions with a vicious license which is very prejudicial on account of the scandalous disorders which they commit with the gentile and Christian women.[41]

In New France the fur trader was the principal villain. Many of them led dissolute lives and their relations with Indian women were as notorious as those of the Spanish soldiers. Soldiers stationed at the French forts were no better; these military posts were "virtual bordellos, and the soldiers almost without exception dissolute drunkards."[42] The French introduced the Indians to brandy, and this, too, wrought havoc on the native population and hindered the work of the missionaries.

The behavior of the friars themselves was also puzzling to the neophytes. They preached the gospel of love, but often used the whip and the stocks to punish Indians who refused to attend chapel or work in the fields. Sometimes the friars meted out the punishment themselves; most often, their Indian assistants did the dirty work. Even though such punishment is understandable, given European customs at the time, it served to undermine the attractiveness of the Old World religion. There were many features of the conquest of the Indians that contradicted the tenets of the gospel, and even though historical hindsight makes them understandable, given the culture of the conquerors, they were signs of contradiction to the natives. Even the young children saw this and ridiculed the missionaries, "because they do not see in a French man any of the perfections of a savage and cannot recognize the virtues of a generous Christian."[43]

Another hindrance to evangelization was more subtle but no less wide-spread. This was the rampant disease and high death rate that spread throughout the Indian regions populated by the Europeans. Such malevolent effects were often attributed to the new religion and persuaded many Indians to avoid contact with the missionaries. Their rites, images, and prayers were frequently seen as superstitions "practiced in order to destroy them [the Indians]."[44] A French Jesuit confessed:

> The Algonquins and Hurons . . . have had, and some have still, a hatred and an extreme horror of our doctrine. They say that it causes them to die, and that it contains spells and charms which effect the destruction of their corn, and engender the contagious and general diseases wherewith the Hiroquois now begin to be afflicted.[45]

The mission system itself also suffered from serious internal conflicts which served to weaken the program of Christianization and civilization. The priests were the rulers of the mission towns, possessing ultimate authority over the religious program, but the mission, as an agent of conquest and colonization, was necessarily a political institution. Conflicts between these two spheres, the spiritual and the political, were constant. The heart of the conflict was the opposing views of what the mission should be. Spanish missionaries conceived of the mission as "a transitional institution, the self-sufficient agricultural community, as a necessary vehicle for bringing Indians into Spanish civilization while the civil administrators wanted prompt and direct integration of Indians into Spanish-type communities."[46] On the other hand, the French Jesuits eventually adopted a policy of adapting themselves to Indian life and creating a native American Catholicism; this separation of religion from Frenchification differed from the official policy of assimilating the Indians into one united colony and eventually weakened political support for the Jesuit mission program. Since the missions were politically and financially dependent on the civil government, such conflicts posed serious threats to the viability of the mission program. Other disputes centered on such issues as authority over the assignment of soldiers to the missions, the amount of taxation leveled on the missions, adequate financial support for the missions, the exclusion of brandy trafficking from the colony, and teaching the Indians the language of the conquerors. Such disputes disrupted the mission programs; ultimately this fundamental alliance between church and state destroyed the missions, for when the throne toppled, the altar fell with it.

Ecclesiastical bickering also sapped the strength of the evangelization program. Conflicts between missionaries and bishops over questions of authority and independence of action were frequent and bitter; jealousy and rivalry between religious orders also took their toll. The most fatal blow in this regard was the expulsion of the Jesuits in the Spanish and French colonies.

Given all these conflicts and obstacles, it is amazing that the mission program accomplished as much as it did.

Of all the obstacles to conversion, however, none loomed so large and remained so persistent as the Indians themselves. They had their own ethical and religious beliefs, their own traditions concerning work and community living, and this religious and cultural system proved to be a formidable opponent for the missionary.

Initially the Europeans who came into contact with the Indians believed, as Columbus did, that the Indians "belonged to no religion." Continued contact with Indian civilization began to alter this attitude, and missionaries soon realized that the Indians did possess some form of religion. But to orthodox Catholics any form of primitive religion was pagan idolatry. The testimony of the Franciscan friar Benavides is instructive in this regard. He firmly believed that New Mexico was the devil's empire, and the first thing he did when he arrived at an Indian pueblo "was to conjure and banish the devil from this place through the exorcism of the church."[47] But Benavides realized that, malevolently inspired or not, the Pueblo Indians did possess a very elaborate religious system. "Fire they held in high veneration," he acknowledged; "it would be an endless task to attempt to describe all the different forms of idolatry, for from the house of only one old Indian sorcerer I took out more than a thousand idols of wood [most likely kachina dolls] painted in the fashion of a game of nine pins, and I burned them in the public square."[48] Benavides' destruction of the "idols of wood" was typical of the early Franciscan attitude toward native religion. They eventually became more tolerant of Indian religion and ceremonial practices that were not explicitly contrary to Catholic faith and morals. It is clear, however, that throughout the Spanish mission period the Franciscans believed that the Indian religion was a primitive form of idolatry that had to be rooted out as much as possible. The French Jesuits adopted a more tolerant view of native beliefs, pointing out the similarities between the religion of the Old World and that of the New. But despite such similarities as belief in "God the Father, a Mother, an immortal soul, a son and sun," the Jesuits were as convinced as the Franciscans that native religions were simply primitive forms of paganism. Obviously the Indians did not see it that way. From their point of view, the religion of the Europeans was a bag full of superstitions.

The missionaries' acknowledgment of the religion which the Indians "possessed in their heathen state" was well founded. The Indians were a religious people who had a common belief in the supernatural; their religious beliefs were complex and diverse, varying from region to region, culture to culture, and can scarcely be summed up in the "popular white man's formula of a Great Spirit and a Happy Hunting Ground."[49] A brief glance at a few of the native religions encountered by the Catholic missionaries illustrates the richness and complexity of the religion of the native Americans.

"Easily the most intensive and best written account of the customs and religion of any group of California Indians in the mission days" was *Chinigchinich*, a memoir written by the Franciscan friar Gerónimo Boscana. Focused on the Juaneños (Indians gathered at the mission of San Juan Capistrano), it detailed their "beliefs, usages, and customs, i.e., the religion which these natives possess in their heathen state."[50]

Boscana related two creation stories that existed among the Indians in and around San Juan Capistrano. The first story stated:

Chinigchinich created man, forming him of clay found upon the borders of a lake. Both male and female he created, and the Indians of the present day are the descendants of these. He then said unto them these words: "Him who obeyeth me not, or believeth not in my teachings, I will chastise. To him, I will send bears to bite, serpents to sting, misfortunes, infirmities, and death." He taught them the laws they were to observe for the future as well as their rites and ceremonies.

His first commandment was to build a temple, where they might pay to him adoration, offer up sacrifices, and have religious worship. The plan of this building was regulated by himself. From this time they looked upon Chinigchinich as God. The Indians say he had neither father nor mother and they are entirely ignorant of his origin. The name Chinigchinich signifies "all powerful" or "almighty," and it is believed by the Indians that he was ever present and in all places. He saw everything, although it might be in the darkest night, but no one could see him. He was a friend to the good, but the wicked he chastised.[51]

It is evident from this brief quote that this Indian tribe shared a belief in the origin of human life that was reminiscent of the Judeo-Christian tradition. The similarity between the origin myth of the native Americans and that of the Judeo-Christian tradition was not unique to the Juaneños, and the missionaries were always quick to point out such similarities as hopeful signs for conversion. The Juaneños also had their shaman, "who would know all things and relieve the infirm and the diseased"; they had their own sacred temple, a bush enclosure with altar and sand painting, which they held in great veneration, and "they were extremely careful not to commit the most trivial act of irreverence within."[52] They observed a calendar based on the activity of the sun and the seasons for planting and harvesting; their feast days were celebrated with processions, music, and above all dancing. Ritually they centered their activity around two ceremonies—puberty rites and mourning rituals—both of which were celebrated in an elaborate and prolonged manner.

The religion of the Pueblo Indians was complex and remains so to this day. Though variations existed from pueblo to pueblo, certain common beliefs and rituals existed. The origin myth is a case in point. Human beings came from beneath the earth, emerging through an opening in the roof of the underworld. War gods assisted the people in this emergence from the underworld, after which the people then migrated to their present dwelling place. At death the Indians returned to the world beneath the earth. The original being or creator was often a female whom they called mother. The Pueblo mythology of existence was well ordered, with each natural level of being having its supernatural counterpart; the physical world was organized in a similar fashion, with specific places such as mountains and lakes having sacred significance, and these were interrelated with the human and spiritual levels of existence. In the Pueblo mind the natural and supernatural, the human and spiritual, realms were integrated and no spirit remained "floating homeless in the air," but each had its own dwelling, just as the Indians did.[33]

All Pueblo Indians had very elaborate ceremonies and rituals through which they communicated with the gods of the supernatural world. Some were most sacred, such as the rites of the medicine associations, and these were not seen by the white man, not even by Indians who were not members of these associations. Such native ceremonies included rituals connected with birth, marriage, and death. Other sacred ceremonies were more communal, publicly performed in the pueblo courtyard; in this category were the corn dances. Also included here were the kachina dances of the western pueblos. In these ceremonies, the men of the pueblo impersonated the supernatural spirits through masks, costumes, and dance, petitioning these deities to bring rain and general well-being. Associated with these dance groups were the kivas, ceremonial structures used for private gatherings both sacred and profane. Every pueblo had at least one such structure, generally associated with some ceremonial association. A third category of sacred ceremonies were the rituals of the various ceremonial organizations; there were many such groups in every pueblo, such as the warriors and hunters; they performed their ceremonies both secretly and publicly. These sacred ceremonies made up the Indians' propitiatory rites, "designed to induce the environment to favor all people, not only Indians, with the good things of life."[34] Rich in song, dance, and costuming, they reflected in action the intricate worldview of the Pueblo Indians and were in existence long before the Spanish arrived.

The Huron Indians had their pantheon of supernatural beings, called the Oki. The most powerful Oki was the sky, because it controlled the weather and the seasons of the year; next in the hierarchy of power were the sun and the moon. The sun was a man who created the lakes and rivers and provided good weather and good corn; the moon was the grandmother of the sun and the mother of mankind; she was frequently malevolent, making men die and undoing the work of the sun. All things, such as rocks, rivers, and bushes, also had spirits, while other spirits had power over war, health, and travel.

Dreams had a very important place in the Huron religious system; through dreams they penetrated the spiritual world and discovered the wisdom of the Oki. "[D]reams were their oracles, prophets, physicians, and absolute masters. . . ."[35] A Huron could never act against his or her dreams. The Hurons also believed in life in an afterworld not much different from this world, and their funerals were elaborate and expensive events.

A key person in the Huron religion was the shaman, or in the words of the French, the juggler. They were religious specialists, both male and female, who cured sickness, cast spells, controlled the weather, and predicted the future. Held in great esteem, they proved to be formidable opponents for the missionaries.

From this brief glimpse of selected Indian religions, it is clear that the Indian mind was not a *tabula rasa* as regards religion; it was formed by tribal lore, ritual, and belief; once their religion was challenged by the missionary, they reacted emphatically and critically, evaluating the religion of the white man in relation to their own beliefs and customs. This was especially true as regards the theological concepts of Christianity. James P. Ronda has studied the Indian critique of the Christian ideas of sin, guilt, heaven, hell, and baptism. Using the Hurons as one example, he demonstrated how in these areas of belief the Indians not only challenged the wisdom of the Jesuits, but also perceived how revolutionary these doctrines were. The idea of hell, so prominent in Jesuit preaching, was a case in point. The Hurons believed in an afterlife, but it resembled life on earth, a pleasant existence, not a terrifying experience. The tortures of hell were reminiscent of the punishments inflicted on captured warriors and were very imaginable. But to picture the afterlife as a time of torture was disturbing and contradictory to their belief. If anyone went to such reward, the Huron shamans claimed, it would be those Christian converts who were traitors to the Huron way of life. "Most native Americans," concluded Ronda, "found the concept of hell a meaningless fiction. Even when presented with imagery bound to strike fear in their hearts, they concluded that the ideas of sin, heaven, and hell were just 'so many Fabulous and romantick stories.' "[56]

A similar conflict emerged in the area of moral behavior. Some Indian tribes accorded special esteem to homosexuals and transvestites, and such attitudes disturbed the friars. Much more serious, however, was the issue of marriage. Many Indian tribes did not follow the Christian custom of monogamous marriage. This divergence of behavior led the Guale Indians, of what would later be named Georgia, to revolt and kill the Franciscan friars who preached against their custom of polygamy. Though the Pueblo Indians were traditionally monogamous, Friar de Benavides claimed that some Indians practiced polygamy and that when the friars spoke out against it, they met strong opposition. During the eighteenth century, the Franciscans encountered the practice of concubinage in New Mexico; on one occasion, after a friar spoke out against women living in concubinage (not married in church by a priest), the men went home and "half killed their wives with blows." He never preached this sermon again. From the friars' point of view, any marriage arrangement not blessed by a church ceremony was wrong. The Christian tradition regarding the indissolubility of marriage also posed problems for the friar and the Indian. A French Jesuit summed up the dilemma in the following manner:

> . . . of all the Christian laws which we propound to them, there is not one that seems so hard to them as that which forbids polygamy, and does not allow them to break the bonds of lawful marriage. . . . They no longer look upon Christian marriage as an aid and comfort of human life, but as a servitude full of vexation and bitterness. It is this that prevents most of the infidels from accepting the Faith, and has caused some to lose it who had already embraced it.[57]

Such incongruence between the Indian way of life and the Christian religion led many Indians to conclude that "the missionary was an enigma, his doctrine a mystery, and his ethic a riddle."[58]

From the Indian point of view, other aspects of mission life were also unattractive. The forced settlement in mission towns, in some cases overcrowded living conditions in European-style barracks, the diet, European-type clothes they had to wear, the hard labor they had to perform, and the harsh treatment received from the Europeans were additional stumbling blocks to effecting any type of permanent conversion among the Indians. Due to the incongruities between the Old World and New World religious and cultural systems, many Indians chose to resist the advances of the missionaries. Every region witnessed armed revolts: the Guale revolt in Georgia in 1597, the Pueblo revolt in 1680, and the San Diego uprising in 1775 were some of the more spectacular uprisings. More typical was the Indian pattern of fleeing the mission town and returning to the native village. In California this was especially prevalent, with about one in every ten mission Indians becoming a fugitive from Christianity. Moreover, some tribes, such as the Hopi and the Apache, successfully resisted all conversion attempts of the European missionaries.

Despite the many obstacles to conversion, many Indians did respond positively and sincerely to the call of conversion. The number or percentage is impossible to determine, but the evidence is there to indicate that numerous Indians became ardent Catholics. On the French mission the mystic piety of Kateri Tekakwitha was not an exception; some Indians even became excessive in their fervor and self-mortification; female Indian catechists were often educated in Montréal and returned to the missions as zealous apostles of Christianity. The Abnaki Indians who settled at Sillery were ardent Catholics who appeared to adhere faithfully to the practice of their new religion; the Hurons who settled at the town of Lorette also remained faithful to their new way of life. Father Lasuén believed that out of twenty California mission Indians "there should be one who is so far ahead of the others that he may serve the community profitably and may be of assistance to the missionary."[59] These were the interpreters, the catechists, whose knowledge and piety recommended them for such leadership roles. Undoubtedly, many Indian converts were "rice Christians," who were more interested in food and shelter than the gospel of Christianity; but certainly there were others, whose conversion and fervor testified to the power of the gospel in their lives.

Such ardent and genuine conversions most often involved a break with past religious traditions. It meant adopting new clothes, a new language, a new moral system regarding marriage and sex, and often an apostolic fervor to go forth and persuade others to do likewise. Quite frankly, such radical conversions seemed to have been more the exception than the norm. The bulk of Indian conversions were not so uprooting. They evidenced more a compartmentalization of religious life, with native beliefs and customs coexisting alongside the Christian religious system. The evidence for this is overwhelming.

Despite the intensity of the evangelization program in California, native religious customs persisted. Father Boscana, in his study of the religion of the Juaneños, acknowledged that "superstitions of a ridiculous and most extravagant nature were found associated with these Indians, and even now in almost every town or hamlet the child is first taught to believe in their authenticity. Thus they grow up from infancy familiar with all their fabulous traditions."[60] The shaman, whose presence challenged the authority of the friar, also remained a highly respected figure in the community. One nineteenth-century visitor to the mission of San Luis Rey concluded, ". . . though all are Christians, they still keep many of their old beliefs, which the padres, from policy, pretend not to know."[61]

In New Mexico after almost two hundred years of evangelization the Indians were still firmly rooted in their primitive religious beliefs and customs. "Their condition now," noted Friar Domínguez in his 1776 report, "is almost the same as it was in the beginning, for generally speaking they have preserved some very indecent, and perhaps superstitious, customs."[62] Their Christian name, taken at baptism, was of little importance and was even used in ridicule; they omitted many duties, and those they performed were done "under compulsion"; he went on to say that their knowledge of Christianity was minimal, "and if they sometimes invoke God and his saints or pay for Masses, it is in a confused manner. For example, they pay the father for a Mass and he asked them what the intention is in terms adjusted to their understanding, and they replied: 'You know that saint what more good, more big, him you make mass. I not know, maybe him Virgin, maybe St. Anthony, etc.' " Domínguez also noted, ". . . they are exceedingly fond of pretty reliquaries, medals, crosses, and rosaries, but this does not arise from Christian devoutness (except in a few cases) but from love of ornament."[63] Among the Pueblo Indians the kiva also continued to occupy a prominent place in the community.

This pattern of persistence was true everywhere. Few Indians understood the complex theology of the missionaries, and their primitive religious beliefs remained the principal way they interpreted the meaning of life on Mother Earth. Rather than accepting total conversion, they adapted the religion of the Old World to their own religious values and orientations; some aspects of Christianity they integrated with their own customs, others they observed but kept separate from similar native practices. This was especially true among the Pueblo Indians, and the manner in which they assimilated the Christian religion furnishes a good example of the interaction of two cultures over a prolonged period of time.

Both Spanish Catholics and Pueblo Indians loved elaborate ceremonies. No stage of life, no season of the year, passed without its proper celebration and supernatural invocation. The Indians had their own life-crisis rites, which were performed secretly, and these have persisted to the present day. They also adopted the Christian rituals of baptism, marriage, and death. The two religious systems coexisted, separated from each other but both invoked for the same fundamental purposes. An observer noted this pattern late in the nineteenth century. "These Indians," he wrote, "although professedly Catholic, await only the departure of the priest to return to their sacred ceremonials. The Catholic priest baptizes the infant, but the child has previously received the baptism rite of its ancestors. The Catholic priest marries the betrothed, but they have been previously united according to their ancestral rites. The Romish priest holds mass that the dead may enter heaven, but prayers have already been offered that the soul may be received by Sus-sis-tin-na-ko (their creator) into the lower world whence it came."[64]

Other sacred ceremonies were more public, performed openly in the pueblo, and these native rituals were integrated into Catholic observances and practices such as the Mass and celebration of a saint's feast day. A good example of this integration was the celebration of the village's patron saint and the annual corn dance. After Mass in church, a procession took place with Indians as well as Spanish participating, and the saint's image was carried to the village plaza, where it was properly enshrined. Then the native dancers performed the corn dance, but it was limited to the people of the village, with no outsiders taking part. The dancers paid their respects to the saint and invoked the gods to send rain and the good things of life to the people of the village. At the end of the day, the saint was carried back to the church and the dancers adjourned to the kiva. This type of celebration involved the integration of two religious systems. They were not fused together or amalgamated to create something new, but coexisted alongside one another much like two elements being "combined without losing their separate identities."[65] In other words, the Pueblo Indians compartmentalized their religious life, adhering to their own native beliefs and rituals while accepting the practices of the Spanish Catholic system.

While the Pueblo Indians did selectively accept certain features of the

Catholic ritual system, they clung tenaciously to their own religious values and orientations. They resisted such fundamental Christian ideas as heaven, hell, sin, guilt, and the primacy of Jesus Christ. Their native "life road," or worldview, not the gospel of the missionaries, remained the principal interpretation of the sacred cosmos. As Edward T. Spicer concluded, in accepting Christianity the religion of the Pueblo Indians "acquired more occasions for ceremony and more supernaturals in its pantheon, but lost nothing for nothing was replaced, and its central values and orientation remained the same as before."[66]

Though the evidence is meager, the Pueblo manner of accepting Christianity appeared to be the dominant pattern of conversion among the North American Indians evangelized by the French and Spanish missionaries. Few Indian converts made a complete break with their past religious traditions and beliefs. The majority selectively accepted the Catholic system of belief and ritual and combined this new gospel with their native religion in such a manner that one coexisted alongside the other.

The manner in which the Pueblo Indians accepted the gospel of the missionaries says something about the mission program in general. Insofar as the goal of the priest was to Christianize and civilize the Indians, the evangelization program was only partially successful. The French and the Spanish were bearers of a new culture and did bring elements of civilization to the Indians. They brought not only a new religion, but also new crafts and skills, new concepts of social and political organization, and a new language which made use of writing. But, by the end of the mission era, most Indians still had only a slight familiarity with these elements of civilization, and the majority had either rejected them outright in favor of their own culture or accepted them in a very selective and partial manner.

After more than two centuries of evangelization, the missionaries had remarkably little to show for so much work. Nonetheless, their efforts did testify to the power of the Christian gospel to alter the lives of men and women. But the missionaries also brought disease as well as the gospel, and huge numbers of Indians in California and New France died as a result; others became victims of the social disorganization brought on by the mission program.

As pioneers in a new world, the missionaries helped to prepare the way for other cultures of conquest by taming the wilderness and setting up cultural outposts along the North American frontier. Comparatively speaking, their relations with the Indians were much more humane and considerably less destructive than those of the Anglo-Saxon pioneers who followed after them. Though the Catholic mission clearly had had other power dimensions beyond the proclamation of the gospel, the principle of Christian charity remained an essential force in their dealings with the native Americans. Nor was the tradition of Las Casas and Montesinos forgotten; it gave the mission program a positive, humanitarian orientation that cannot be denied. But as hard as they tried, the missionaries could not convert the Indians. The Indians had to convert themselves, and most of them refused to do so in any meaningful, long-lasting manner.

III

Catholics in the English Colonies

ON THE FIFTH DAY OF MARCH, 1634, two ships, the *Ark* and the *Dove*, sailed up the Potomac River. On board was an unusual group of English adventurers: Catholic noblemen, Jesuit priests, and Protestant servants, they were hardly the types of people you would expect to find joined together by a common dream of founding a colony in the New World. After four months on the high seas, this group of about 140 had at last reached Maryland and was about to begin a new chapter in the English colonization of North America. Unlike that of Virginia or Massachusetts, the founding of Maryland was a joint effort of Catholics and Protestants to establish a colony where "mutuall love and Amity" would prevail among people of differing religious beliefs. Though the dream of Protestants and Catholics working together in "mutuall love and Amity" vanished rather quickly, Maryland did prosper, and it became the New World home for a sizable number of English Catholics. Their presence would eventually alter the contour of the American religious landscape.

The English were quite late in getting involved in the colonization of the New World. During the sixteenth century, while Spain was exploiting the rich natural resources of the American continents, England was still relying on its European trade markets. Gradually these markets began to dry up, and the need for new markets and new routes of trade became evident. At the same time, England was gaining sufficient political strength and confidence to challenge the supremacy of Spain in international affairs. These two basic shifts, one economic and the other political, pushed England into an era of overseas expansion during the closing decades of the sixteenth century. Yet the English colonization enterprise began very slowly, almost reluctantly. Individual entrepreneurs tried their hands in Nova Scotia and later along the coast of North Carolina at Roanoke Island, but both attempts ended in failure. Closer to home, the English were having more success in transplanting a colony to Ireland.

The Irish experience helped to ignite the expansionist impulse of the English, and once the seventeenth century was underway, England plunged into a grandiose colonization program. Included in this were settlements in Virginia, Massachusetts, and Maryland. These English colonies were, first and foremost, profit-making ventures. But closely joined to the hope for economic gain was the more lofty motive of converting the Indian to Christianity. In this regard the English were not very different from the Spanish and the French. The religion of seventeenth-century England, however, was quite different from that of Spain and France.

The Protestant Reformation had revolutionized the religious situation in England. Under Henry VIII, and later and most vigorously under Elizabeth I, England had adopted the reformed gospel and church order of Protestantism. The authority of the Papacy was overthrown, monasteries were ransacked, and Catholics went into exile. The Church of England replaced the Church of Rome, and Queen Elizabeth became the "supreme governor" of English Christianity. But, for many English men and women, the Elizabethan church had still remained too Catholic, too imperfect for their purist tastes. They desired a greater purification of the Church of England from the taint of Romish practices and beliefs. The Puritans, as these reformers came to be known, eventually despaired of the English situation and left their homeland to found new colonies in North America. The major Puritan exodus to a new England began in 1630, and within a decade close to twenty thousand men and women had migrated to settlements in Massachusetts and Connecticut.

The Reformation in England had also made life difficult for Roman Catholics. Henry VIII's break with Rome and his self-proclamation as the "only supreme head" of the Church of England had ushered in a new era. Loyalty to the Pope now became an act of treason. But few people were willing to die for the Papacy. The vast majority of the English went along with Henry, nor was this surprising, ". . . since there was practically no change in religion as they experienced it."[1] A minority did protest Henry's purge of the church and his self-proclaimed spiritual supremacy. For these nonconformists it was either the hangman's noose or exile on the Continent. The tide had briefly turned in favor of Catholics under Queen Mary, but when Elizabeth ascended the throne, every effort was made to wipe out all traces of Roman Catholicism. From 1559 until her death in 1603, Elizabeth and her government passed a series of penal laws against Roman Catholics which effectively reduced the threat of Catholic nonconformity. By the end of her reign, English Catholicism had been substantially changed. The transformation was so complete that some historians believe that the Catholicism of pre-Reformation days disappeared during the Elizabethan period and a new English Catholic community was born, with its headquarters at a seminary in the Flemish town of Douai. However one views the transformation of sixteenth-century English Catholicism, one fact remains clear: during the last years of Elizabeth's reign, Roman Catholics in England were a small, persecuted minority who were "anxious only to live out their lives in peace."[2]

The accession of James I to the throne of England marked the beginning of a prolonged period of moderate toleration for English Catholics. Exiles returned from the Continent, and priests, released from jail, went "openly about the country, the city and private houses saying Mass."[3] The Gunpowder Plot to blow up Parliament, in 1605, served to arouse public fear of Papists, and the government responded with new penal legislation. Once the excitement subsided, the laws were relaxed and Catholics again enjoyed a relatively peaceful existence, tolerated as a minority sect though still publicly feared as potential fifth columnists. The atmosphere of moderate toleration continued under James's successor, Charles I; only occasionally, when the religious zeal of Catholics outraged public opinion, did the government take action against them. This favorable climate of toleration lasted until the 1640s, when the battle between the king and Parliament erupted into civil war. During this period, bracketed by the death of Elizabeth in 1603 and the outbreak of civil war in 1642, the English Catholic community underwent a revival. The number of priests and people doubled, converts were on the increase, and a political *modus vivendi* had been worked out to the advantage of Catholics who had learned how to be loyal to England and faithful to Rome. The community also took on important characteristics in these years; English Catholicism was becoming "an upper-class sect," a community in which the landed gentry dominated. Their manors became the centers of the community, and as lords of the manor they exercised considerable influence over both clergy and lay people in things religious. This predominant position of the upper class and the experience of toleration as a minority sect were two features of English Catholicism that shaped the Catholic experience in colonial America.

The person most responsible for the establishment of a colony in Maryland was George Calvert. Born around the year 1580 in Yorkshire, he was most likely raised a Catholic. When he was twelve years of age, his parents conformed to the Church of England, and George became a member of the Anglican Church at that time. He had a notable career in government service, and King James conferred knighthood on him in 1617. Then, in 1625, after a loss of political power, he was forced to resign his position as secretary of state. At about the same time, he became a Roman Catholic. Honored by the King with the title Baron of Baltimore and awarded a substantial pension, he retired to his estates in Ireland and devoted the rest of his life to investments in overseas colonies.

Calvert's interest in colonization first began while he was a government servant. He had held stock in the Virginia Company and was also a member of the Council of New England. Then, in 1623, the king granted him a charter to found a colony in Newfoundland. But the colony in Newfoundland was not financially successful and the winter weather was so severe that Calvert decided to abandon this enterprise and look for a warmer climate, where the "winters be shorter and less rigorous."[4] His search took him to Virginia. Convinced of the potential of this region, he returned to England and prevailed on the King, Charles I, to grant him a charter to found a colony north of Virginia. But before the papers were drawn up, George Calvert died. A few months later, in June 1632, the charter for the colony of Maryland, named in honor of the king's French Catholic wife, was approved, and the work of colonization passed to Lord Baltimore's twenty-six-year-old son and heir, Cecil Calvert.

The charter granted to Cecil Calvert, similar to the one given to his father for the colony in Newfoundland, was remarkable. By a stroke of the pen, the young second Lord Baltimore received personal ownership of a vast stretch of land bounded on the south by the Potomac River, on the north by Philadelphia, and stretching west into the Appalachian Mountains. Unlike Virginia, to the south, the charter was given to one individual, not to a group of stockholders. Calvert owned the land outright for the nominal fee of "two Indian arrows of those parts" and could do with it what he wished; he possessed extensive governmental powers and could shape the colony's political structure as he chose; his will, not the king's, was the source of legal authority. In reality, the colony of Maryland was a kingdom within a kingdom; theoretically, Lord Baltimore's authority in Maryland was more extensive than the king's in England. Calvert's proprietorship could also be passed on to his heirs.

Cecil Calvert converted to Roman Catholicism most likely when he was in his early or middle twenties, at about the same time that his father became Catholic. The conversion of both father and son to Roman Catholicism is important, because their allegiance to a minority religion would have a significant influence on the early history of Maryland. But it should be emphasized at the outset that the Maryland colony was not founded primarily as an asylum or refuge for Catholics. Maryland was established first and foremost as a commercial enterprise, with profit, not religion, the primary impulse. As one historian put it, "Religion was important, but not too important. In stark contrast to Massachusetts, where a religious outlook dominated, in Maryland religion was not to get in the way of man's other pursuits."[5]

Once Calvert received the charter, he began a year-long campaign to promote his enterprise. It was a low-keyed campaign designed to allay the fears of naturally suspicious Protestants; Calvert also had to contend with the opposition of the "Virginia interest," old Virginia adventurers who wanted to undermine his project. Calvert's influence at court enabled him to overcome his opponents, and his expedition was ready to set sail for Maryland in November of 1633.

A chief inducement offered to prospective settlers was a substantial grant of land. Each "first adventurer" who brought with him or paid the fare of five men between the ages of sixteen and fifty would receive two thousand acres. Another attraction of the Maryland colony was the opportunity for Roman Catholics to live in a land "free from persecution on account of their religion." As Calvert viewed it, it was a unique opportunity for the Catholic aristocracy; they would be able to invest in the first Catholic commercial enterprise in the New World and not have to worry about religious persecution. As it turned out, very few Catholics were willing to invest in Calvert's dream. The explanation for this is simple.

Under Charles I, Catholics were not being severely harassed. The spirit of toleration, dating back to the reign of James I, was especially evident in the king's court. His wife, Henrietta Maria, was a pious Catholic and exercised considerable influence over the appointment of officials to the king's government. As a result, a substantial number of Catholics held patronage positions in the government and even had hopes that Charles himself might become Catholic and grant legal toleration to all English Papists. Convinced that they could not merely survive in England, but survive well, these court Catholics showed little interest in colonization. In the countryside, the landed gentry were also relatively free from harassment, and the idea of investing in an overseas colony was not terribly appealing to them. As for the lower classes, proportionately a small number in the English Catholic community, the majority were dependent on either the nobility or the landed gentry; for this reason, their ability to emigrate was linked with their patrons' decisions regarding colonization. Thus, "By the time Baltimore was looking for immigrants and investors, English Catholics had come to terms with the conditions of their survival . . . and were not predisposed to leap foolishly into colonization."[6]

Moreover, English Catholics were a dispersed community, lacking the advantage of a central network or organization to promote the cause of the "Maryland Design." The Jesuits did campaign on Baltimore's behalf, but their influence was limited, and even those priests who traveled to Maryland had to rely on Protestant, not Catholic, servants. Thus when the *Ark* and the *Dove* set sail for Maryland, the majority of the people on board were Protestants. The passenger list included three Jesuits (the priests Andrew White and John Altham and the brother Thomas Gervase), sixteen "gentlemen-adventurers" most of whom were Catholic, and a host of servants, laborers, and artisans, the majority of whom were Protestants.

Given the small number of Catholics who supported his enterprise, Calvert had to rely on the patronage of Protestants. Yet, English Protestants naturally had reservations about investing in a colony headed by a Catholic proprietor. To allay their fears and safeguard their rights, Calvert made sure that religious toleration was a key element in the Maryland Design. But as the historian John Krugler put it, ". . . religious toleration was not the purpose of founding Maryland. Religious toleration was the *modus operandi* of the 'Maryland Design.' "[7] Calvert's primary concern was profit, not religious freedom. A pragmatic realist, he realized that to achieve success in the New World he had to be open-minded about religion. Considering what things were like at the time in Virginia and New England, or for that matter in New Mexico and Canada, this was indeed an advanced and enlightened policy.

Cecil Calvert's concern for the religious sensibilities of his colonists was clearly articulated in his instructions given to his brother Leonard, governor of the colony, and his two commissioners. The very first paragraph of this lengthy document read as follows:

> His Lo[rp] requires his said Governor and Commissioners th[t] in their voyage to Mary Land they be very carefull to preserve unity and peace amongst all the passengers on Shipp-board, and that they suffer no scandall nor offence to be given to any of the Protestants, . . . and that for that end, they cause all Acts of Romane Catholique Religion to be done as privately as may be, and that they instruct all the Romane Catholiques to be silent upon all occasions of discourse concerning matters of Religion; and that the said Governor and Commissioners treate the Protestants wth as much mildness and favor as Justice will permitt.[8]

These instructions clearly indicated the mind of Cecil Calvert regarding the place of religion in colonial Maryland. Since civil harmony was the primary consideration, religion was to remain a private affair, neither shaping the destiny of the colony nor impeding its progress. Given the history of animosity between English Protestants and English Catholics, it would be difficult, if not impossible, to keep religion out of politics, but Cecil Calvert was determined to try it.

With his instructions in hand, Leonard Calvert and his entourage of adventurers set sail for North America. Cecil wanted to go with the expedition, but prudence dictated that he remain in England to fend off any attempts to undermine his colony. Subsequent events proved this to be a full-time responsibility, and Cecil Calvert never set foot on the Maryland shores.

After stopovers in the Caribbean and Virginia, the *Ark* and the *Dove* finally reached the shores of the Potomac in March of 1634. The first concern of the settlers was to assure the Indians in the area, the Piscataways, that they came with peaceful intentions, "to teach them a divine doctrine, whereby to lead them to heaven, and to enrich them with such ornaments of civil life as our country abounded."[9] The voyagers disembarked on an island which Andrew

White, the Jesuit chronicler of the voyage, named Saint Clement's. "In this place on our blessed Ladies day in Lent [March 25]," wrote White, "we first offered [mass], erected a cross, and with devotion took solemn possession of the country."[10] Two days later, after successful negotiations with the Indians, Leonard Calvert led the group to a site on the mainland, along the banks of a river later named St. Mary's. There they founded St. Mary's City, the first capital of Maryland.

With the founding of St. Mary's City, the Maryland Design finally began to take shape along the shores of the Potomac. All things considered, the settlement of Maryland went rather smoothly. But its future growth and development did not proceed with similar ease and good fortune. A major cause of hardship was political unrest.

Seventeenth-century England was not very peaceful, and when political uprisings occurred at home, the repercussions were felt along the Potomac. Such political revolts not only challenged the rule of Lord Baltimore, but they also threatened the future of the colony. This was especially true during the English civil war which began in 1642 and ended seven years later with the execution of the king. Since Calvert sided with the king against Parliament, his colony was vulnerable to attack by Puritan supporters of Parliament, and attack they did. Led by Richard Ingle, the captain of a tobacco ship trading in the Chesapeake, a contingent of Virginia adventurers and soldiers invaded St. Mary's City in early 1645, took possession of the capital, and plundered the colony. For almost two years Maryland was in a state of chaos; its population dwindled; the government ceased to function; and Jesuit priests and Catholic leaders were led off to England in chains. Ingle's Rebellion nearly destroyed Maryland, but with the restoration of order in late 1646 the colony revived. Then, in 1654, land-hungry Virginia adventurers once again succeeded in overthrowing Calvert's rule. A Puritan regime ruled the colony for four years; then, in 1658, Calvert regained control.

The last major political uprising took place in 1689, and this revolt ushered in a new era in Maryland history. Throughout the late 1670s and 1680s, economic and political discontent was spreading throughout the colony. Closely allied to this was religious discontent among Protestants who disliked the favoritism and partiality that Charles Calvert, the third Lord Baltimore, showed to his relatives and coreligionists. Once again it was events in England, the Glorious Revolution of William and Mary in 1688–89, that ignited the uprising in Maryland. Within two years the rule of the Calverts was overthrown, and Maryland became a royal colony with a governor appointed by the Crown. The revolution of 1689 turned the religious world of colonial Maryland upside down. Religious toleration ended, and the Maryland Assembly established the Church of England as the official state religion in 1692. Though this was not formally approved in England until 1702, it was clear that thenceforth Protestants were in control. Being a Catholic in Maryland was no longer an asset, but a liability. Almost one hundred years passed before another revolution, in 1776, allowed people once again to feel comfortable about being Catholic.[11]

Prior to 1689, the religious world of seventeenth-century Maryland was unique. Unlike in Massachusetts and Virginia, religious toleration was the law of the land. In the first years of settlement, the bases for this policy were Calvert's instructions to the colonists. Then, in 1639, the Maryland Assembly enacted into law the spirit of Calvert's letter by passing legislation that guaranteed that the "Holy Churches within this province shall have all their rights and liberties." Though the Assembly did not specify what church or churches it was referring to, their intention clearly was not to favor the Catholic church but, most likely, to allow religious freedom to the various churches that would be organized in Maryland. Then, ten years later, motivated by the need to attract more settlers after the debacle of Ingle's Rebellion, the Assembly passed the famous "Act Concerning Religion."

The religious wars of the 1640s had underscored the need to keep religion out of politics. Initially Lord Baltimore tried to achieve this by urging people to practice their religion "as privately as may be," but this was not to be. In the seventeenth century, religion was so bound up with politics that it could not remain a purely private affair. Thus, specific legislation had to be enacted that would prevent religion from becoming a socially disruptive force. For Lord Baltimore and the Maryland Assembly, the best way to achieve this was to guarantee the toleration of religion. This would safeguard the rights of the Catholic community, make the colony more attractive to Protestants living in Virginia and elsewhere, and undermine the charges made by Calvert's opponents that Maryland was a seedbed of Papists.

The Assembly defined what it meant by religious toleration principally by prohibiting certain types of behavior. First of all, any one who blasphemed God, "that is, Curse Him or deny Our Savior Jesus Christ to bee the sonne of God, or shall deny the holy Trinity . . . shal be punished with death and confiscation or forfeiture of all his or her lands and goods." Quite clearly, religious toleration did not include people of the Jewish faith. Then, in a very Catholic gesture, it stated that anyone uttering "reproachfull words or Speeches concerning the blessed Virgin Mary, the Mother of Our Savior, or the holy Apostles or Evangelists" shall be fined, and if this did not work, then publicly whipped and imprisoned. In addition, any name-calling, such as labeling a person a "heretick . . . puritan . . . Jesuite, Jesuited papist, Lutheran, . . . Separatist, or any other name or terme in a reproachfull manner relating to matter of Religion" was subject to a fine or, worse, a public whipping and jail. Profaning the Sabbath by swearing, drunkenness, unnecessary work, or any disorderly recreation was also prohibited. Then the law shifted its tone, and in a more positive manner, it stated:

. . . noe person or psons whatsoever within this Province, or the Islands, Ports, Harbors, Creekes, or havens thereunto belonging professing to believe in Jesus Christ, shall from henceforth bee any waies troubled, Molested or discountenanced for or in respect of his or her religion nor in the free exercise thereof within this Province or the Islands thereunto belonging nor any way compelled to the beliefe or exercise of any other Religion against his or her consent. . . .[12]

The only condition stipulated by the Assembly was that in the exercising of religious belief these individuals "be not unfaithfull to the Lord Proprietary, or molest or conspire against the civill Governmen' established or to bee established in this Province under him or his heires." Any violation of this part of the act meant a fine or public whipping and imprisonment.

Anyone who takes the time to read the 1649 "Act Concerning Religion" will not be impressed by its proscriptive tone. It was neither an eloquent statement on behalf of religious freedom nor a radical proposal for the separation of church and state. The historian William Craven assessed it as "sober and sound in its reasoning, the product of good sense rather than of extraordinary intelligence, a call for no surrender of basic convictions, and urged only that men of different faiths live in peace, concede to one another the free right of worship, and eschew in their daily intercourse the use of terms which serve merely to breed ill will."[13] Nevertheless, this piece of legislation was an important step on the road to religious freedom and a noble effort to solve a problem that was peculiarly American: peace and unity among people divided by conflicting religious loyalties.

In addition to religious toleration, another unique feature of seventeenth-century Maryland was the presence of the Jesuits. In other colonies they were considered outlaws, but in Maryland the Jesuits were an integral part of the community. In organizing his colony, Cecil Calvert had worked closely with them. They were major supporters of his enterprise and actively promoted the Maryland colony throughout the English Catholic community. Inspired by the same missionary zeal that sent their French confreres to Québec, English Jesuits traveled to Maryland eager "to devote themselves to procuring the conversion and salvation of the barbarians."[14]

The key figure in the first contingent of Jesuit missionaries was Andrew White. Like his confreres Kino and Brébeuf, he was an educated man who abandoned the comforts of a teaching career for the life of a missionary in the New World. Shortly after his arrival in Maryland, White wrote a description of the voyage and the first days of the colony that has become the classic account of the settlement of Maryland. Once settled at St. Mary's City, White began to evangelize the Indians. Not knowing their language hindered his work at first, but eventually he became fluent enough to write a catechism, a grammar, and a dictionary in the Piscataway language.

A major obstacle in the evangelization of the Indians was the fear of Indian reprisals. An Indian uprising had occurred in Virginia in 1622, and the fear of a similar attack in Maryland was always present. Though the Maryland Indians never responded to the Englishmen's intrusions like the Powhatans of Virginia, they did launch sporadic attacks on outlying farms. This was reason enough to persuade Governor Calvert to force White to give up his Indian apostolate in 1638 and return to the security of St. Mary's City. The following year, White and his confreres, who now numbered four priests and one brother, resumed their apostolate to the Indians. White journeyed north to the principal village of the Piscataway, hoping to convert the chief of the tribe. The Jesuit missionary succeeded, and a year later Chief Chitomachon, his wife, and his son were baptized in an elaborate ceremony attended by the Governor, "together with his secretary and many others." White moved on to the Indian village of Port Tobacco, and ". . . most of the town called Portobacco received the faith with baptism."[15]

Other Jesuits traveled the rivers of southern Maryland evangelizing the Indians and converting a good number of them, perhaps as many as a thousand. But the persistent hostility of some Indian tribes limited the missionaries' ability to travel safely about the countryside. Moreover, most Jesuits were still hindered by their inability to "converse with the Indians without an interpreter." These difficulties notwithstanding, the missionaries continued their work among the Maryland Indians, and it is clear from reading their reports in the first decade of the colony's history that this small band of priests considered this apostolate a major part of their work in Maryland. Ingle's Rebellion brought an end to the Indian mission, and after order was restored, the Jesuits worked exclusively with the English colonists.

A major concern of the Jesuits in those early years was the relationship between church and state. They wanted to establish in Maryland the same type of church-state relationship that prevailed in the Old World, a situation in which religion legally enjoyed a special place in society and the church was invested with a privileged status. A number of prominent Marylanders supported their position, but Calvert and others wanted no such arrangement. Lord Baltimore wanted to fashion a society that would legally remain neutral in matters of religion.

The two opposing factions argued back and forth for more than a decade. In 1638 the Maryland Assembly failed, in the opinion of one Jesuit, "to provide or shew any favor to Ecclesiasticall persons, or to preserve for the church the Immunitye and priveledges which she enjoyeth every where else."[16] The Jesuits countered this by seeking an exemption from taxation for themselves and their servants, the freedom to evangelize the Indians without having to secure government authorization, and the right to acquire land from the Indians without a special license from the proprietor. The Jesuits' demands put Calvert in a delicate position. Publicly he did not want to alienate the Jesuits and thus diminish the attraction of the colony for English Catholics; at the same time, he did not want to weaken his authority as lord and proprietor of Maryland. The dispute between the Jesuits and Calvert continued for some time. Letters passed back and forth between England and Maryland; positions hardened as Calvert refused to grant their demands, and the Jesuits suggested the possibility of his excommunication. Calvert seized the land that the Jesuits had acquired from the Patuxent Indians; he put an embargo on Jesuits going to Maryland; and he sent two secular priests to Maryland to replace the Jesuits and bought back the Jesuit Chapel at St. Mary's for their use. After more than a decade of bitter wrangling, the Jesuits gave in and tacitly accepted the authority of Calvert.

Calvert's victory over the Jesuits not only consolidated his authority, but it also determined the position the clergy would occupy in colonial Maryland. If the Jesuits were going to stay on, they would have to do so without any special privileges from the government. Since the government was not going to support the church, the clergy would have to support themselves. This forced them to become planters and traders as well as Catholic missionaries.

Another distinctive feature of seventeenth-century Maryland was the upper-class nature of the Catholic community. Those Catholics who chose to settle in Maryland came from the gentry class of English society. Though few in number in the early years, they put their stamp on Maryland. Their farms dominated both the landscape and the economy. Much as in manorial society in England, the rest of the settlers lived and worked in a dependent relationship to this gentry class. Politically the Catholic gentry were also very powerful because of their privileged relationship with Lord Baltimore.

Once Maryland recovered from Ingle's Rebellion, immigration to the colony increased at a fairly steady pace, so that, by 1700, Maryland's population had increased to about 34,200. Most of Maryland's seventeenth-century immigrants, nearly three fourths of them, were indentured servants, and they came principally from the Protestant regions of England. Since very few Catholics chose to settle in Maryland, the Catholic community remained quite small in number, only about 2,500 by the year 1700. As was true in the early years of settlement, the seventeenth-century Maryland Catholic community remained predominantly upper class; in other words, Maryland Catholics possessed larger and more valuable estates than their Protestant neighbors. Though there were poor Catholics and wealthy Protestants in seventeenth-century Maryland, to be Catholic meant that a person was most likely prosperous.

Because of their wealth as well as their political power during the Calvert regime, members of the Catholic gentry were numbered among the first families of Maryland. The Darnalls were one such family. Henry Darnall, an associate and relative of the Calverts, had come to Maryland around 1670; he held important political offices in the colony and had put together an estate of forty thousand acres. One of the wealthiest planters in Maryland, Darnall was the principal leader in the Catholic community until his death in 1711. The Brooke family was also well placed politically; Baker Brooke sat on the proprietor's council and was related by marriage to the Calverts. His brother Thomas had three sons who entered the Jesuits; a third brother, Roger, married a daughter of James Neale, and their children married into the Taney family. Like the Darnalls, the Brooke brothers owned considerable land in Maryland. Both the Brooke and the Neale families also had the reputation of being devout Catholics. Another prominent family planted its roots in Maryland in 1688, with the arrival of the young lawyer Charles Carroll. A friend of Charles Calvert, Carroll had migrated from Ireland, where he belonged to the dwindling community of the Irish Catholic gentry. As Calvert's attorney general in the New World, he occupied an important office in the colony and eventually became the chief spokesman for the Catholic community.

Recent research into the world of seventeenth-century Maryland Catholicism has uncovered a tightly knit community. Michael Graham, who did this research, observed:

> Catholics acted as witnesses for the official transactions of other Catholics. When a Catholic died, other Catholics saw to the disposition of the estate and made sure that the orphans were well cared for. Catholic widows and widowers usually remarried a Catholic spouse, while mixed Catholic-Protestant marriages seemed nearly always to have led to the conversion of the Protestant partner and the raising of the children as Catholics. Catholics frequently had godchildren and acted as guardians for Catholic orphans. Catholics entered into business partnerships and engaged in commercial activities with other Catholics. Catholics rose in political life together and together supported the church. They frequently knew their priests outside of Church and socialized with them.[17]

In addition, Catholic families intermarried to such a degree that their family histories became a genealogical nightmare.

Such a Catholic network not only helped to form a community of kindred spirits, but it also enabled people to adjust more successfully to the hardships of life in seventeenth-century Maryland. To be sure, Catholics were involved in the larger social, political, and economic world of Maryland and mingled freely and frequently with Protestants. Yet the intense interaction of Catholics among themselves suggests that they were indeed a tightly knit community.

The cement that bound this Maryland Catholic community together was religion. As regards the institutional development of Catholicism in the seventeenth century, it was indeed meager. There was a small brick chapel in St. Mary's City which Catholics shared with Protestants, who worshipped there without the benefit of clergy. Destroyed during Ingle's Rebellion, it was rebuilt and continued to serve the local Catholic community for much of the remainder of the seventeenth century. The Jesuits established a farm, St.

Inigoes, a few miles from St. Mary's City, and this became "the granary of the mission," the economic base needed to support their apostolic work. By the end of the century, Jesuit farms were also operating at Newtown, in St. Mary's County, and at Port Tobacco, in Charles County; chapels were situated on these Jesuit plantations. In addition, it was reported that there were six or seven wooden chapels scattered about St. Mary's County and Charles County, the area where the majority of Catholics lived.[18]

Even though the Jesuits were among the largest landowners in the colony, life for them was not any more rosy than for the rest of the colonists. Maryland was an immigrant's graveyard during the seventeenth century, and no one was immune to the Chesapeake scourge. Though many Jesuits did sail to Maryland, "they seemed to be coming only to die"; of the twenty-one Jesuits who came to Maryland between 1634 and 1672, seventeen died on the mission at relatively young ages. Such a high rate of mortality kept the number of clergy quite low; in fact, there were never more than four or five Jesuit priests in Maryland at any one time during the seventeenth century. Things got so bad in the 1660s that the Jesuits even considered abandoning the mission, but they stayed on.[19]

As bleak as the situation was, Catholicism was in a favored position prior to the 1689 revolution. Until the 1650s, when Quaker missionaries arrived in Maryland, Catholics had a monopoly on religion. The Jesuits were the only clergy in the colony, and they made good use of this advantage by gaining numerous converts. Even after the establishment of a small Quaker community, the Jesuits still enjoyed success in winning converts. One obvious reason for this was the attraction of the Catholic community itself. To become a Catholic meant that a person joined a tightly knit society that enjoyed notable political and social advantages. The fellowship and status gained by joining the church were not to be disdained in a frontier society, where life could be harsh and lonely. Nonetheless, relatively few people became Catholic or Quaker, with the result that by the end of the seventeenth century the vast majority of the Maryland population remained unchurched.

Though the religion of the people during the seventeenth century remains very much hidden in the past, certain patterns and features stand out which do provide a glimpse into this area of colonial society. The holiday seasons were especially festive and sacred. One of the most important was Christmas. A young English squire, Robert Parker, was traveling in Virginia during December. "The Christmas holidays were drawing near," and Parker, "a Roman Catholic, but not of the kind who are bigoted . . . wished to spend Christmas day in Maryland." His traveling companions, all Protestants, journeyed with him to the banks of the Potomac, crossed the river into Maryland and spent "the night at the home of a Maryland gentleman." The next day was Christmas eve, "& Monsieur Parker wished to perform his religious exercises"; he left his friends and journeyed to a nearby Catholic church.[20] An isolated incident, to be sure, but it was indicative of the determination of some people to fulfill their religious obligations. Parker wanted to be among his coreligionists for Christmas, and like many others in the colony, he was willing to travel great distances to do so. In rural Maryland such travel was not unusual; to attend mass at one of the Jesuit farms or rural chapels on the great feast days such as Christmas involved a good deal of travel as well as overnight lodging with friends along the way. The holiday itself was celebrated by going to church, exchanging gifts, visiting friends, and partying; most often, celebration of such major holidays lasted for two or three days.

By law and by custom, Sunday was the most important day of the week. It was a day of rest from hard labor and a day for going to church. For those who lived in the neighborhood of a Jesuit farm, regular churchgoing was possible; for those who lived in other rural neighborhoods, such a luxury was not possible. They had to do for themselves on most Sundays of the year and hear mass only when the priest visited their area.

A typical rural "neighborhood" in seventeenth-century Maryland included about twelve to twenty families who lived within about two miles of each other. They had frequent contacts with one another and knew each other well.[21] When the Jesuit missionary visited their neighborhood, he would stay at the house of one of the Catholic farmers for a few days while he carried out his pastoral work. He offered mass, heard confessions, conducted classes in Christian doctrine, and spent a good deal of his time with Protestants, hoping to convert them. The missionaries obviously had some success in gaining converts, since their annual reports continually mentioned this point. His work completed, the Jesuit trotted off on his horse to another area to repeat his round of pastoral work. Due to the scarcity of clergy in seventeenth-century Maryland, such pastoral visits did not occur very frequently in any one neighborhood.

The gentry were well-bred, educated people who valued books and education. As one contemporary gentleman put it, "Better be never born than ill-bred."[22] The Jesuits had a lending library of religious and devotional literature, and the books circulated among the community. Families also had their own small collections of books, and many of these, as was typical of the time, had to do with religion. Formal schooling was almost nonexistent in colonial Maryland. The Jesuits had begun a small school at Newtown in the middle of the seventeenth century, but it operated only intermittently and closed after the 1689 revolution. Among the gentry, the more usual pattern was to send their children off to Europe for an education. This was a common custom in Chesapeake society, and the Catholic gentry followed it by sending their children to Catholic schools in Europe.

The wills left by Maryland Catholics provide a special glimpse into their religious world. Composing their last wills with an eye toward the future, they most commonly began their testaments with the phrase "In token that I dye a true Roman Catholique." After this self-congratulatory statement that left no doubt as to what religion they professed in life, they would then proceed to bequeath their worldly possessions. A very high percentage of Catholics, perhaps as many as 60 percent, left bequests for the support of the church; Jesuit clergymen were frequently singled out for bequests, and this clearly suggests that most people held the Jesuits in high esteem. Such bequests to the church and clergy were common not only among prosperous Catholics, but among the less prosperous as well. Another striking feature was that large numbers of single people left bequests to the church; they were consistently the group that contributed most. What this suggests is that because of its cohesiveness and the sense of community it offered, the Catholic Church had a special meaning for these individuals, who did not enjoy the community of family life. Catholics requested a Catholic burial and appointed fellow Catholics to oversee their estates. One other notable pattern was that Catholics often stipulated in their wills that their heirs, especially their children, be disinherited if they abandon the Roman Catholic religion.[23]

A study of Catholic wills also suggests that women enjoyed a special status in the community. John Bossy's study of English Catholicism underscored this point by noting that the survival of Catholicism depended upon the women, who maintained the rhythms of Catholic life in the home by observing the ritual of fast days and feast days; they were also the ones who made sure that the children were raised Roman Catholic even when their husbands conformed to the Church of England. Since there was no Church of England to conform to in seventeenth-century Maryland, this did not pose a problem for Catholic families. Nevertheless, women most likely exercised the same critical religious role in Maryland that they did in England. In Maryland, Catholic widows clearly were the object of special solicitude and regularly were left a larger portion of their husband's estate than the law prescribed. Such sizable bequests not only ensured the widow's survival, but also gave her greater bargaining power in contracting future marriages and would not force her to abandon her religion for the sake of economic security. This special treatment for widows suggests a special status for women in the community.[24]

Religion was obviously important to this pioneer generation of American Catholics. They practiced it in an unostentatious manner, with little of the public pageantry so commonplace in the Spanish Southwest. For Maryland Catholics, religion remained a private affair, centered around the home and the family, principally because of the precedent for this in England, but also because clergy were few and churches were scarce. Reflecting this domestic character of seventeenth-century religion, the Catholic rites of passage took place within the home. Children were baptized at home, and the priests frequently recorded the number in their annual reports. If the priest was not available, most often the parents or the midwife baptized the newborn infants. Marriage was a very informal ritual, with vows often exchanged at home without the benefit of clergy. Since many seventeenth-century Marylanders did not become "seasoned" to the new disease environment of the Chesapeake, the colony experienced a very high mortality rate. As a result, a good deal of the missionaries' time was spent burying the dead. The one constant throughout the century was the faith itself. The people kept it alive, and Catholicism survived into the eighteenth century politically defeated but spiritually undaunted.

With the political and religious changes ushered in by the 1689 revolution, Catholicism became in law as well as in fact a minority sect. Moreover, the virulent anti-Catholicism so prevalent in English society during the Elizabethan period reappeared in England and Maryland. Thenceforth, the Maryland Government sought to curb "the growth of popery" and prevent Catholics from regaining political power. This was accomplished by the passage of a series of laws that proscribed the rights and privileges of Catholics. Known as the penal laws, the bulk of them were enacted during the first two decades of the eighteenth century, and they effectively isolated Catholics from the sources of political power. Thenceforth, Catholicism became a distrusted and persecuted religious sect. Though the Quakers were in a similar situation, Catholics were more feared and treated more harshly.

One of the harshest pieces of anti-Catholic legislation was enacted in 1704. Entitled "An Act to prevent the Growth of Popery within this Province," it was aimed at curbing the work of the Jesuits. It was clear that the convert work of the Jesuits, so prominent a part of their apostolate throughout the seventeenth century, had aroused the ire of Maryland Protestants. To prevent such proselytizing, the Assembly forbade any "Popish Bishop Priest or Jesuite" from persuading anyone "to embrace and be reconciled to the Church of Rome." They also prohibited any priest from baptizing children "other than such who have Popish Parents." In addition, to "say Mass or exercise the ffunction of a Popish Bishop or Priest" was outlawed. In effect they wanted to drive the Jesuits out of the colony. Violations of these laws meant a fine and six months in jail. More severe penalties were reserved for second offenders who continued "to say Mass or exercise any part of the Office or ffunction of a Popish Bishop or Priest"; the penalty for these felons was exile to England and further punishment. Within two months the Assembly modified this legislation by allowing priests to exercise their "ffunction in a private family of the Roman communion" for a period of eighteen months or until the Queen ruled otherwise. As the grace period for private worship was coming to a close, members of the Catholic gentry, notably Henry Darnall, Charles Carroll, Richard Bennett and James Carroll, petitioned the Assembly in the name of their coreligionists to further extend the period in which private worship could legally take place. Their intervention was successful, and the Maryland Assembly allowed Catholics the right to private worship. This law, passed in 1707, set the pattern for private religious services in eighteenth-century Maryland and reinforced the domestic character of religion in the Catholic community.

Other penal laws passed by the Assembly prohibited Catholics from practicing law, banished from the colony any Catholic involved in the education of children, and sought to protect "Protestant Children of Popish Parents" from being forced to become Roman Catholics; if parents did attempt to do this by denying their children "a fitting Maintenance," then the government could intervene and take the children away from them. To curb the growth of Catholicism, the Assembly levied taxes on "Irish Papist" servants in order to slow their immigration to Maryland. Finally, in 1718 the Maryland Assembly disenfranchised Catholics by requiring all voters, Quakers excepted, to take oaths that were explicitly offensive to Catholic belief.[25]

Not all of these penal laws were rigorously enforced, but they certainly restricted the political and religious activities of the Catholic community. Catholics were able to survive, but they felt the oppression levied on them by their neighbors. As one group of petitioners noted, ". . . by these Laws we are almost reduced to a Levell with our Negros not having even the privilege of Voting . . . in short they deprive us of all the Advantages promised our Ancestors on their Coming into this Province. . . ."[26]

After 1720 the climate changed and Catholics admitted that "tho' deprived of our Rights & Privileges" they "enjoyd peace & Quiet." Then, in the 1750s, during the French and Indian War, the fear of Catholics intensified once again. Factionalism divided the Maryland Assembly; the lower house approved harsh legislation aimed at penalizing both people and clergy, but the upper house, composed of the gentry class who had often collaborated with the Catholic gentry to mitigate the severity of the popularly supported penal legislation, would not approve such severe laws. Nonetheless, the Assembly did approve a special tax on Catholics in 1756 aimed at raising money for the militia. This double tax rankled the Catholic gentry. Charles Carroll of Annapolis, one of the wealthiest persons in Maryland, was so disturbed that he made plans to leave the colony and found a refuge for Catholics in the Louisiana Territory. Nothing came of his plan, but his anger and frustration indicated how bad things could get even for the wealthiest of Catholics. After the 1750s a climate of toleration prevailed and Catholics once again enjoyed a prolonged period of freedom from harassment.[27]

In addition to the political revolution that transformed Maryland in the late-seventeenth and early-eighteenth centuries, the colony was also undergoing major economic and social change. In the mid-seventeenth century, Maryland was "a good poor man's country," where families of modest means could prosper. But this had changed by the turn of the century. Opportunity declined, wealth was more unevenly distributed, and slavery had become an essential part of the economy. As a result, eighteenth-century Maryland was "a slave-based, gentry-dominated society" in which a landed elite of native families emerged as the ruling class; as one historian put it, Maryland had become "a society that kept most of its laborers in perpetual bondage and offered others a choice between permanent poverty and exile."[28]

As the poor became more numerous, the size of the wealthy gentry class declined, so that by the middle of the eighteenth century only one in twenty families possessed "sufficient wealth to put it in the class of the great planters."[29] Included in this group would be such Catholic families as the Carrolls, Brents, Diggeses, and Brookes. But the Catholic gentry was also shrinking in size. Though these families were still recognized as the leaders of the Catholic community, most Catholics were small planters, subsistence and commercial farmers who lived off the land; others were tenant farmers, people who rented land from the great planters. At the bottom of the social structure were the slaves. Many Catholics owned slaves. The Jesuits were among the largest slaveholders, with 192 of them working on their farms. Charles Carroll, one of the wealthiest men in the colonies, employed 300 slaves at his plantation at Doughoreagan. How many of these slaves were Catholic is difficult to determine. A 1785 report put their number at 3,000; undoubtedly the figure had been much smaller at mid-century.

Though singled out for political discrimination and abuse, the Catholic community remained steadfast. A study of their wills suggests that the sense of community so evident in the seventeenth century still existed in the eighteenth century, though to a less intense degree. Though intermarriage among Catholics remained a dominant pattern, it seemed clear that more and more religiously mixed marriages were taking place. Fewer Catholics left bequests to the church or threatened to disinherit their children if they abandoned the Roman Catholic religion. Nevertheless, in proportion to the rest of the population, Catholics were still more generous in their bequests to the church and more zealous in controlling their children's religious life.[30]

One striking development in the eighteenth century that suggests an impressive measure of vitality and commitment in the community was the large number of vocations to the religious life. During the seventeenth century, only three or four Marylanders entered the Society of Jesus; one of these, Robert Brooke, became the first native of the English colonies to become a Roman Catholic priest. In the eighteenth century the situation changed dramatically. Thirty-six native Marylanders entered the Jesuit order prior to its suppression in 1773, and four other young men entered seminaries affiliated with other religious orders. Young women also began to enter religious life in impressive numbers. Mary Digges, the first native female from Maryland to enter religious life, joined the Sepulchrine Convent in Liège in 1724. Afterward an increasing number of young Maryland women entered convents in Europe; prior to the revolution, a total of at least thirty-six women entered such orders as the Benedictines, the Poor Clares, the Carmelites, the Dominicans, and the Augustinians. Only the sons and daughters of the upper class could aspire to such a life. The cost of the journey to Europe was prohibitive for most families, and in the case of women the dowries required to enter the convent were so large, ranging from one hundred to four hundred pounds, that only the well-to-do could afford the high cost of religious life.[31]

Another indicator of Catholicism's sustained vigor was the increase in the number of lay people and clergy as well as the expansion of the Catholic presence throughout Maryland and even north into Pennsylvania. By 1765 the number of Catholics in Maryland was approximately 20,000; this was almost a tenfold increase since 1700 and a higher rate of increase than that of the population at large. A major reason for this increase was the large number of Irish immigrants to Maryland. Though the bulk of Catholics still lived in St. Mary's and Charles counties, large estates of the gentry could also be found in the more northern counties, where a sizable number of Catholics of more modest means also lived. Catholics also began to settle in Pennsylvania, where the liberal Quaker policy of religious toleration proved to be most appealing. It was reported that by 1741 Philadelphia had a "growing congregation," and the number of "country Catholiks" was also multiplying. A census taken in 1756 recorded 1,365 adult Catholics in Pennsylvania; about three out of five were German, and the bulk of them lived along the rural frontier. Philadelphia, which accounted for about one quarter of the Catholic population, had both an Irish and a German congregation. Immigration continued to expand the population, and by 1765 Pennsylvania Catholics numbered around 6,000. Even though no one knew exactly how many Catholics lived in Maryland or Pennsylvania, these population figures, based on estimates given at the time, reflect the substantial growth of the community in the decades preceding the American Revolution.[32]

As in the seventeenth century, the key Catholic institution in Maryland was the Jesuit farm. By the 1770s the Jesuits owned and operated seven farms. Two of these farms, one at Deer Creek, north of Baltimore, and the other at Tuckahoe, on the eastern shore, were relatively small farms of 200 acres or less. The other five were major plantations ranging in size from 1,100 acres to 4,400 acres; these plantations were situated at St. Inigoes and Newtown, in St. Mary's County; at Port Tobacco, in Charles County; at Bohemia, in Cecil County near the Delaware border; and at White Marsh, in Prince Georges County. The total acreage of these farms in 1765 was 12,777; owning such a vast amount of land placed the Jesuits in the select ranks of the great planters. Given the average size of a Maryland farm at this time, about 200 acres, the magnitude of the Jesuit plantations is even more striking.

Managing such extensive plantations proved to be quite burdensome for clergymen interested in more spiritual endeavors. Joseph Mosley, the priest in charge of the small farm at Tuckahoe, bemoaned the extent of his more mundane chores:

. . . My time also was greatly taken up in looking out for provisions for myself, workmen, and negroes, which at one time could hardly be got for love or money. . . . I have now my cows, my sheep, hogs, turkeys, geese, and other dunghill fowl: I've my own grain, and make my own bread. In fine, I had a thousand other difficulties to go through, which at present I can't call to mind and which then took up all my time and thoughts exclusive of all the hardships and fatigues of a very laborious mission. . . ."

On larger plantations the chores were clearly more numerous and more time-consuming. As the number of Catholics increased and the extent of the mission circuit expanded, priests like Mosley became more and more "taken up with Evangelical Ministries" and had less time to "apply their minds to temporalities." As a result the Jesuit farms deteriorated and were never as economically profitable as they might have been; "either the fields are badly tilled," as one Jesuit put it, "or their produce is in great part wasted."[34]

Although its main purpose was to provide for the economic well-being of the clergy, the Jesuit farm was also a principal center of religious activity. Every plantation had its small chapel, generally attached to the clergy's residence, but as the eighteenth century progressed, separate church buildings began to be built on the plantations. Sunday services were held in these churches at least twice a month for the people who lived in the surrounding area; on weekdays and Sundays, the priests were out on the mission circuit traveling as much as fifty to sixty miles a day on horseback, visiting remote settlements of Catholics. Sunday at the farm included more than just church services; the Jesuits had adopted the southern custom of hospitality and provided food as well as opportunities for socializing for those who had journeyed to church. This was necessary, since many people had been fasting from food and drink for several hours in preparation to receive Communion at Mass. Though the clergy complained of the "heavy burthen" of such expenses, the custom remained in vogue throughout the period.

As time passed, a major development took place at these farms. They became the center of stable congregations, which began to exhibit the features of a parish church. This development seems to have taken shape in the middle of the eighteenth century; prior to this time the farm served principally as the central headquarters of an extensive missionary network and not primarily as a center of a parish community. But in the 1760s these plantations began to function as parish churches. New churches were built on many of the farms; parish registers for baptism, marriage, and death appeared, detailing the performance of these rites of passage, most of which now took place at the parish church; lists of parishioners were compiled and maintained, and parish devotional societies, composed of women, were also organized. Thus, at a time when Catholics were still legally discriminated against, denied the ballot, and allowed to have only private worship services, the church was going public by building "publick meeting places of divine worship" and organizing communities. As a result, religion was becoming less domestic or private and more congregational or public. This can be seen in the congregational setting of the rites of passage, the organization of parish devotional societies, and the maintenance of parish membership rosters. This was a significant step toward the strengthening of the institutional church and a decisive move away from the more private practice of religion so commonplace in the seventeenth and early-eighteenth centuries.

In Pennsylvania the parish had served as the vehicle for building community from the very beginning, most especially in the urban villages of Philadelphia and Lancaster. But, in Maryland, more than a century had elapsed before a recognizable parish structure emerged. The irony is that it took place at a time when the public exercise of religion was forbidden to Catholics. Obviously this suggests that the penal laws were not very zealously enforced in the period immediately preceding the American Revolution.

This same trend can be observed in the more remote areas the missionaries visited on their circuits. Maryland was a predominantly rural colony, with 95 percent of the people in 1770 living on farms dispersed at lengthy distances from one another along the rivers and streams that fed into the Potomac and the Chesapeake Bay. Scattered about this rural countryside was an increasing number of Catholic families, whose farms served as magnets for the Jesuit and his horse. Father Mosley left extensive reports of his travels in Talbot County along Maryland's eastern shore; they provide a fascinating view of missionary life in eighteenth-century Maryland.

Mosley worked his farm along with his slaves, about eight in number, stripping tobacco, cutting wood, slaughtering cattle, smoking meat, and raising crops. When he was not busy at the farm, he was off visiting one of eight "congregations" situated on his missionary circuit. Six of these were within twenty-five miles of the farm, and he visited each of them once every two months; the other two were more remote, and these he visited only twice a year. Eventually he regularized his missionary circuit so that he could visit each congregation once every two months, apparently abandoning the two more remote regions for areas closer to his residence. He spent a good deal of time on horseback or, as he put it, "daily on horseback, visiting the sick, comforting the infirmed, strengthening the pusillanimous, etc." Riding all day "in excessive heats, the use of bad water, salt meats, bad accommodations, violent colds, poor open lodging, often out whole nights in the woods," took their toll and Mosley eventually complained of attacks "of the gravel and stone."[35] It was not an easy life and Mosley confessed that he did "grumble much" about it, but he continued at his work for twenty-nine years, until he died, in 1787, at the age of fifty-six.

The itinerant Mosley, like other Jesuit circuit riders, would spend a few days, even as much as a week, in one region, celebrating Mass, preaching, catechizing, visiting the sick, and administering the sacraments. In many respects his missionary agenda resembled the format of a parish mission which the Jesuits had conducted in Europe. The same rationale seemed to be present, "to remain a week together in a congregation. To instruct after the Jesuit missioners from Europe."[36] Unlike his European counterpart, however, the American missionary traveled alone, and the center of his work was not a parish community, but the residence of a Catholic family, most often a member of the gentry whose farm or plantation included a private chapel. Those weeks when the missionary was not around, the people performed their religious exercises in private, reciting the prayers of the Mass and other devotions from prayer books obtained from England.

During the 1760s, the mission circuit underwent a transformation similar to the one that took place on the Jesuit farm. This did not happen all at once or in every region, but a noticeable pattern of parish organization did appear. In St. Mary's County, for example, five chapels were built between 1760 and 1775 at what were formerly mission stations centered at a private residence. On Mosley's mission, no such chapels were constructed, though he did begin building a combination residence and chapel at his Tuckahoe farm shortly after the American Revolution began. The church-building activity of the 1760s and 1770s on these missions reinforced the pattern of development taking place at the major Jesuit farms. In the wake of this church-building activity came a more public, less domestic, practice of religion.

The key to this development was the Jesuit farm. As an economic institution, it provided the funds needed to keep a band of itinerant missionaries and well-traveled horses on the road; it furnished the means to buy land, build churches, and foster the institutional development of Maryland Catholicism. In addition, the farm was both a center from which emerged an identifiable parish community and the catalyst that hastened the development of other parishes scattered about the Maryland countryside.

Catholicism did not just survive in eighteenth-century Maryland, it prospered. For Maryland Quakers, the Protestant revolution of 1688–89 and the subsequent legal establishment of the Church of England proved to be a fatal blow to their future as a vibrant religious community. Catholics, however, adjusted more successfully to the religious and political revolts that turned Maryland into an Anglican citadel. Part of the reason for this successful adaptation was the English Catholic tradition of survival as a distrusted and persecuted religious sect. This tradition became part of the Maryland Catholic identity and enabled them to adjust successfully to the anti-Catholic atmosphere that prevailed in the eighteenth century. Though some Catholics did renounce their religion for social or political gain, the majority kept the faith. An increase in the number of lay people, clergy, and churches was a good indication of the vitality of this minority community; the large number of vocations to the religious life was another positive sign of the group's vitality.

Thus, on the eve of the American Revolution, all signs pointed to a Catholic community that was growing both in numbers and in strength.

During the eighteenth century, the religion of the people strongly resembled that of the seventeenth century. In each era, the symbol of Catholic religion was a book, the ever-present manual of prayers. In the seventeenth century, the favorite book of English Catholics was a *Manual of Godly Prayers* . . . ; it was a book of prayers "distributed according to the dayes of the weeke" and compiled with monastic thoroughness. A compendium of morning and evening devotions for each day of the week, it also included various litanies and psalms as well as devotions for Mass, confession, and Communion. Popular throughout the seventeenth and early-eighteenth centuries, this manual of prayers underscored the importance of the English Catholic tradition of morning and evening prayers.

In the eighteenth century, the favorite spiritual guide in terms of popularity and formative influence was John Gother. A convert from Protestantism and later a priest, he wrote sixteen volumes of instructions, meditations, and prayers before he died, in 1704. The special feature of Gother's writings was that they were not just manuals of prayer, but manuals of instruction as well.

The prayers of Gother were "simple and straight forward resembling an overheard conversation between close friends rather than the rhetorical flourish of many prayers of that period which were more like an ambassador's presentation of his credentials to a prince, or in the case of continental ones, too embarrassingly sentimental to English ears."[37] Gother fostered devotion to Jesus and the events of his life, a "Christian devotion" that gave "almost no place" to devotion to saints and relics. Neither militant nor triumphal, his spirit of devotion was, as one writer put it, "subtly undenominational," the type that fostered "peace with other Christians." His instructions on Christian living were "practical and ethical rather than theoretical," commonsense advice for various states of life: master and servant, parent and shopkeeper as well as for the fearful, the lukewarm, and the intemperate. In this manner, people would learn how to live "a life conformed to the principles of the Gospel."[38]

The type of piety that emanates from the manuals of John Gother can best be described as personal and interior. Rooted in the personal relationship between the Christian and God, it did not demand incessant exercise of external rituals or an exaggerated reliance on the sacraments, but only faith, to enter into personal communion with God. The sermons of the Jesuit Peter Atwood reflected this type of personal and interior religion. The best example of this was Atwood's sermon for Ash Wednesday, which sought to instruct people on the need for prayer and self-denial during Lent. In his sermon, Atwood made no mention of the need for special devotions or the sacraments; for him the way to overcome sin was through prayer; in his Christmas sermon he also stressed a familiar theme of Gother, namely the individual's personal relationship with Christ.[39]

The piety encouraged by Gother and Jesuits like Atwood was especially appropriate for Maryland. With few priests and a scarcity of pulpits, people could readily turn to their manuals of prayer and have at their fingertips a devotional guide that encouraged a type of prayer not grounded in the mediative function of priest or ritual. The irenic, or noncombative, spirit of Gother's manuals also blended in with the tradition of toleration prevalent among the Catholic gentry who prided themselves on being "inoffensive" in regard to the practice of religion. The sermons of the Jesuits reflected a similar "inoffensive" tone.

Gother's central position in the spiritual life of the people was eventually taken over by Richard Challoner. Born in 1691, he came under the spiritual guidance and instruction of Gother at an early age, and this relationship, compared to that of a master and his disciple, had an important influence on Challoner's later life. After ordination to the priesthood and pastoral work in England, Challoner was selected to be a bishop and later the vicar apostolic of London. As head of the church in England he exercised jurisdiction over the church in the colonies, but distance and the independent spirit of the Jesuits did not allow Challoner to have much say about affairs in the colonies. His influence in the colonies derived more from his spiritual writings than from his ecclesiastical position. Like Gother, Challoner wrote a variety of spiritual works prior to his death in 1781. These included a manual of prayer, meditations, and a catechism. Undoubtedly his most important spiritual work was *The Garden of the Soul,* first published in 1740. It was a manual of prayer and instruction "for Christians, who living in the World aspire to devotion." Like the popular *Manual of Godly Prayers, The Garden of the Soul* included morning and evening prayers, prayers for Mass, for feast days and Sundays, and numerous other prayers and litanies; like Gother, Challoner also included appropriate instructions along with all these prayers. Prayers of devotion and instruction in a Christian life were the heart of this little book, and before long it became the *vade mecum* of English Catholics. It was so successful that the expression "Garden of the Soul Catholic" eventually was used to describe the spirituality of the late-eighteenth-century English Catholic community.

Garden of the Soul Catholicism was "deep and strong but very sober in character"; Challoner did not emphasize external rituals or devotions, but stressed an interior, personal piety reminiscent of his spiritual tutor. The Garden of the Soul Catholic was also urged to be engaged in the world, actively involved in his or her particular vocation in a manner consistent with the Christian gospel and the Commandments. The type of piety outlined by Challoner clearly mirrored the spirituality of his tutor, John Gother.[40]

One theme common to both Gother and Challoner was devotion at Mass. For Catholics this was the principal act of prayer and worship, to be performed on Sundays and feast days. If attendance at Mass was not possible, then Catholics would turn to their devotional guides and for a half hour alone or with family "hear Mass in Spirit" by reading the prayers in their pocket-size manuals. In the seventeenth century, devotion at Mass consisted of private prayers such as saying the beads, that is, the rosary. Since such devotion had no relation at all to the prayer of the Mass, Gother tried to encourage congregational participation by urging his readers "to join with the Priest in offering it [i.e., the Mass] to Almighty God."[41] This practice, similar to the spirit of worship that emerged from the Second Vatican Council, did not seem to take hold. Challoner certainly was not as insistent as Gother in this respect and did not even include the main prayer of the Mass in his manual. Though Challoner underlined the congregational aspect of the Mass, he put more emphasis on private devotion, enabling the worshiper to follow the action of the Mass with appropriate prayers and instructions. This style of private devotion at Mass definitely became the norm for Catholic worshipers by the time of Challoner's death and would remain so for quite some time.

An important part of worship at Mass was reception of Holy Communion. The minimum requirement was to receive Communion once a year during the Easter time; priests even compiled lists of Easter communicants and used these as a gauge of piety in their parish. The Jesuit preachers urged the people to receive Communion frequently; their continual emphasis on this throughout the eighteenth century suggests that Maryland Catholics did not receive Communion very frequently, most likely only at Easter and a few other times throughout the year, on such major feasts as Christmas or Pentecost.

Preparation for Communion centered around the sacrament of penance; this was to be practiced well in advance of the feast day, and in the interval the prospective communicant was to prepare devoutly for the reception of Communion. Only out of necessity, which was often the case in Maryland, did the penitent go to confession on the day of the Communion Mass. Preparation for Communion also included fasting from food and drink from midnight.

The tradition of fasting underscored the austere tone of Catholic piety. Not only was fasting necessary for the reception of Communion, but it was required throughout Lent and Advent, on all Fridays of the year, and on the vigils of the great feasts as well as several other days of the year; in fact, about one third of the year were days of fast for Catholics. Such fasting meant eating only one full meal a day. There was agitation both in England and the colonies to reduce the number of fast days, and eventually, in 1781, the number was reduced. Undoubtedly the practice caused hardship for a farming community, and the clergy regularly dispensed people from the rigors of fasting.

Instruction in the Christian life was another essential ingredient in Catholic piety. It was a constant theme in the literature and a serious obligation for both priest and people. Reflecting this was the widespread availability of catechisms in colonial Maryland. For the clergy, instruction was a primary responsibility; they always mentioned it as part of their pastoral work, along with Mass and the administration of the sacraments. The nature of the Maryland mission and the domestic character of religion also made it an important responsibility for the laity; they underscored this point in their wills by appointing someone to care for the education of their children. Only one Catholic school existed in eighteenth-century Maryland. Though it did educate some members of the more famous Catholic families in the colony such as Charles Carroll of Carrollton and the future American bishop John Carroll, this school, at Bohemia Manor, was definitely limited to the gentry class and was very short-lived. The home was the main school for religious instruction, and by the eighteenth century the mother of the family was the accepted teacher.

As in the seventeenth century, women occupied a special place in the Catholic community. Not only was the mother of the family the principal instructor in religion, but she was also the chief cook, who saw to it that fast days were observed; the parish devotional societies that developed in the eighteenth century were primarily female in membership. This central place of women may also be seen in penal legislation passed by the Maryland Assembly; the lawmakers recognized the important place of the mother in the religious training of children and were intent upon reducing this influence when Protestant children were left with a Catholic mother.

In summary, three qualities distinguished the religion of the Catholic community: personalism, discipline, and sobriety. The prayer life of the people was essentially personal, demanding no intermediary between God and believer; the ethical code of the community, outlined in the manuals of instruction, stressed the importance of the individual and a personal, responsible Christian way of life. Religion was also very disciplined; the tradition of beginning and ending each day with prayer was long-standing; the desired regularity of Sunday worship and observance of numerous holy days of obligation, as many as twenty-five prior to the 1770s, imposed a regular rhythm on the liturgical year; fasting underscored another dimension of this discipline, namely self-discipline; the emphasis on annual examination of conscience and confession reinforced this trait. It was also a sober piety; it was not extravagant or ostentatious; it lacked the enthusiasm of Evangelical Protestantism, which was emerging in the eighteenth century, as well as the visible intensity of Spanish Catholicism.

The shift that took place in the middle of the eighteenth century as more parish churches were built and Catholics became increasingly more regularized and institutionalized had a noticeable influence on the religion of the people. In shifting the center of religion from the home to the parish church, it not only altered the domestic character of religion, it also introduced a more public, more congregational dimension to religion. More so than before, people were encouraged to worship as a group, as a parish community, and not primarily as individuals or families. Such rituals as adoration of the Blessed Sacrament and devotion to the Sacred Heart came into vogue, and with this development came an increased emphasis on external ritual. In other words, additional mediums of prayer were set in place; they not only emphasized a more public and congregational form of worship, but began to mediate the prayer of the Christian through church rituals. Thus, the external practice of religion through devotional ritual began to appear together with the more interior, personal style of prayer. These two types of piety had long been present in Roman Catholic spirituality, but in eighteenth-century Maryland the interior, Garden of the Soul, type of piety remained the dominant strain. Once the Catholic community lost its English character, however, it would lose this style of piety as well. In its place would come a more public, devotional Catholicism.*

Two events in the 1770s altered the course of history for colonial Catholics. The first was the papal suppression of the Jesuits in 1773. For the priests in Maryland and Pennsylvania, this was a personally devastating blow. These missionaries were more than just priests, they were Jesuits, members of a unique and famous religious order. Now the Pope, Clement XIV, had suppressed their order, and like their confreres in Canada, the Maryland Jesuits became disillusioned and discouraged. For John Carroll it was a "fatal stroke," a "shock" from which he doubted he ever would recover; he told his mother that now "the greatest blessing which in my estimation I could receive from God, would be immediate death. . . ."[42] These were harsh words, but it was obvious that something especially dear to Carroll and his confreres had died. By the stroke of a pen, a central part of their identity and a major reason for their living had been destroyed. Joseph Mosley expressed his sense of loss as well as anyone:

> To my great sorrow, the Society is abolished; with it must die all that zeal that was founded and raised on it. Labour for our neighbour is a Jesuit's pleasure; destroy the Jesuit, and labour is painful and disagreeable. . . . with joy I impaired my health and broke my constitution in the care of my flock. It was the Jesuit's call, it was his whole aim and business. The Jesuit is no more; . . . in me, the Jesuit and the Missioner was always combined together; if one falls, the other must of consequence fall with it.[43]

Despite such disillusionment and sadness, Mosley and the rest of his Jesuit confreres remained in Maryland and Pennsylvania and continued their priestly ministry. For these Jesuits, twenty-one in number at the time of the

---

* See Chapter VII, especially page 211, for a definition of the phrase "devotional Catholicism."

suppression, a new challenge awaited. They would have to regroup, devise some plan of organization for the future, and eventually select someone to guide them through this period of reorganization. The choices they made and the man they selected (John Carroll) were decisions that would significantly shape the future of the Catholic community in the new nation.

In December of 1773 another event took place which signaled the beginning of another, more significant change in the history of colonial America. This was the Boston Tea Party, the symbolic beginning of the American Revolution. As was true in other colonies, Maryland had been caught up in a revolutionary fervor for several years. The patriot cause in Maryland, however, had a special twist to it. For decades, the lower and upper houses of the Assembly had been at odds over the authority of the proprietary government of the Calverts, which had been restored in 1715. This factionalism led to the emergence of two loosely organized groups: the proprietary or court party, which supported the proprietor's cause, and the country party, which attacked the privileges and powers of the proprietary government. By the 1770s the country party was becoming increasingly identified with the patriot cause, while the proprietary faction became known as supporters of the royal government. Into this debate stepped Charles Carroll of Carrollton; his first public political encounter marked the beginning of a major shift in the political life of Maryland's Catholics. Charles was the grandson of Charles Carroll the seventeenth-century Catholic spokesman, and the only son of Charles Carroll of Annapolis. Belonging to a wealthy gentry family, he received the best European education available. He studied the classics with the Jesuits at St. Omer, poetry at Rheims, philosophy in Paris, and law in Bourges and London. When he finally returned to the Chesapeake in 1764, he was an educated aristocrat who had not only imbibed the intellectual spirit of the Enlightenment, but also believed that one day "America . . . will and must be independent."[44]

Carroll's political debut was sparked by a letter of Daniel Dulany published in the *Maryland Gazette* in January 1773. Dulany wrote his letter in support of the governor's right to impose fees related to the official inspection of tobacco. The country party viewed this position as a usurpation of authority, "taxation by executive action." Carroll aligned himself with the popular cause of the country party and took Dulany on in a newspaper debate. More than just politics motivated Carroll, however. In recent years the Dulany and Carroll families had been feuding with each other, and in 1773 the bad blood between them was worsening. Carroll saw an opportunity to attack and seized it. Writing under the pseudonym of "First Citizen," Carroll attacked Dulany's political stance as well as his personal character; Dulany, signing his responses "Antilon," slashed back in a similar fashion. "Dulany spoke the language of a constitutional lawyer," noted his biographer, "Carroll that of natural rights. But the telling hits were personal and cheers went up in proportion to the intemperance of the blows."[45]

From his very first letter, First Citizen was acclaimed a hero, a celebrated spokesman for the country party and the cause of natural rights. Charles Carroll soon achieved widespread popularity and was acknowledged as "a most flaming patriot." Thrust into the political arena, he emerged as a major figure in the struggle for independence. He was present at the First Continental Congress, in Philadelphia, in 1774; later that year, he was elected to the Maryland Convention, the first Catholic to hold political office in Maryland since the seventeenth century. Two years later, Carroll was a delegate to the Continental Congress and fixed his signature to the Declaration of Independence. Returning to Maryland, he helped to draft the new state constitution, which ended the era of anti-Catholic penal legislation by proclaiming that "all persons, professing the Christian religion, are equally entitled to protection of their religious liberty."

Carroll's support of the patriot cause was a decisive step for the Catholic community. Thenceforth, Catholics would be united with Protestants in the common struggle for independence. The contagion of liberty had broken down the barriers of religious bigotry, and an increasing number of Catholics stepped into the political arena during the revolutionary period. In Maryland, Catholics were elected to the state convention; they also served on the local committees of observation organized in each county. As a new state government evolved, Catholics took their places alongside their Protestant peers in the state assembly. They also took up arms on behalf of the revolutionary cause in Maryland and Pennsylvania. Though Pennsylvania could claim some Catholic loyalists, the vast majority of colonial Catholics, in the words of George Washington, took a "patriotic part" in achieving the Revolution of 1776.

The revolution hardly destroyed the spirit of anti-Catholicism, but it dealt bigotry a severe blow. The patriotism of Carroll and others who followed him into the political arena demonstrated the loyalty of colonial Catholics. The support of Catholic France in the revolution also helped to improve the public image of Roman Catholics. The irenic spirit of the Enlightenment reinforced this shift away from religious bigotry. But most important of all was the contagion of liberty that swept across the landscape during the revolutionary period. Though it could not root out bigotry, it did usher in freedom. For Catholics, a dream deferred had finally been realized. They stood on the threshold of a new age, ready to build a new church which would attempt to graft the spirit of the new nation onto their colonial tradition and create something new in the history of Roman Catholicism, an American Catholic Church.

A Republican Interlude, 1780-1820

IV

A New Beginning

MORE THAN AN ARMED REBELLION, the American Revolution was an ideological revolution the effects of which were felt long after the last shot was fired at Yorktown. John Adams put it well. The real American Revolution, he said, took place "in the minds and hearts of the American people," and it gave birth to an ideology of republicanism that turned American society on its head. Political life was reordered as the people entered into electioneering and constitution making; a new emphasis on equality repudiated a colonial society rooted in privilege and patronage; and a spirit of independence, of rugged individualism, became idealized as genuinely American. From this emphasis on individuality and equality emerged a new spirit of toleration in things religious and a radical democratization of American church life.

This revolution of the mind affected all Americans, but for one group in particular, the small colony of Catholics, the change was especially dramatic. Because of their religious beliefs, they had lived as second-class citizens, discriminated against politically, professionally, and socially. The revolution changed all this. New laws and new constitutions gave them religious freedom, and in those states—Maryland and Pennsylvania—where the bulk of Catholics lived, this meant political freedom as well. Not only could they now vote, but they even could run for political office, and it was startling how quickly Catholics jumped into the political arena. In Maryland the political achievements of Charles Carroll became legendary, but other, less famous men also became politically involved, at the county and state levels of government. Such a turn of events led the priest John Carroll to observe in 1779 that Roman Catholics "are members of Congress, assemblies, and hold civil and

78320

military posts as well as others."[1] When the time came to write a new federal constitution, two Catholic laymen, Daniel Carroll of Maryland and Thomas Fitzsimmons of Philadelphia, were elected to the Constitutional Convention. Both of these men had been politically active in their own states and would now achieve a niche in history as framers of the federal constitution. When Catholics migrated west to Kentucky, they continued the same pattern of political involvement, serving as elected officials at both the county and the state levels. Such political involvement was a new experience for Catholics, but they took to it like ducks to water.

Another significant change took place "in the minds and hearts" of America's Catholics during the 1780s and 1790s. Because of the atmosphere of the prerevolutionary period, Catholics had been very conscious of their minority status. Such an attitude surfaced time and again in their petitions to the Maryland legislature during the penal days of the eighteenth century. But with the Revolution the atmosphere changed. Protestants became more tolerant of Catholics, and relationships between the two groups improved considerably. To be sure, religious bigotry existed on both sides, but what was most noticeable in the republican era was the absence among Catholics of a conscious minority mentality. Indeed, they were a minority group in terms of their numbers and religious beliefs, just as the Quakers and the Jews, but Catholics no longer evidenced a sense of being oppressed outsiders, as they had in the 1750s. The Revolution had given Catholics a sense of belonging to and being an integral part of the new nation. One concrete result of this sense of belonging was their political involvement; another, equally visible result of this new mentality was a prolonged period of cordial relations between Catholics and Protestants.

One incident, which took place in Lebanon, Pennsylvania, in 1810, summed up this new ecumenical spirit. The occasion was the dedication of a Catholic church. A Jesuit priest, John William Beschter, presided, and he preached both in German and English "to a mixed congregation of Catholics and Protestants. Three Lutheran, three Reformed, and one Moravian minister listened attentively as Beschter spoke on Protestant misrepresentations of Catholicism and the solidity with which Christ had built his church. After the services, all of the clergy dined at the home of the local Lutheran minister."[2]

This was not an unusual occurrence. Lebanon was America writ small in the republican era. Throughout the nation, Catholics and Protestants were learning how to live together; mutual respect had improved; they attended services in each other's churches, sometimes out of necessity, more often out of a genuine interest and curiosity; Protestants gave money and land for the construction of Catholic churches and sent their children to Catholic schools; Catholics and Protestants were partners in politics, and mixed marriages were commonplace.[3]

Such amicable relations were more than just manifestations of good feelings. They were signs of a fundamental shift in the mentality of the people. The republican spirit of the Enlightenment, endorsed and legitimated by the Revolution, had as a fundamental ideal freedom of conscience and its corollary, religious toleration. In such an atmosphere, Catholics not only experienced considerably less hostility, but they no longer envisioned themselves as an embattled minority group. In addition to altering the way Catholics thought about themselves, the republican ideas of the Enlightenment also influenced the way Catholics thought about their church.

To understand how the republican revolution affected the way Catholics thought about their church, it is first necessary to look at the life and thought of John Carroll. As the first Roman Catholic bishop in the United States, he became the principal spokesman for the Catholic community, and his voluminous writings are the best available record of the history of Catholicism in this early period. They not only unveil the thinking of this clerical leader, but they also are an indispensable resource for understanding the development of the Catholic community in the republican era.

John Carroll was born into the gentry society of Maryland in 1736. His family was part of the Catholic aristocracy, and among his relatives were the Darnalls, the Brents, and the Carrolls of Annapolis—the first families of Catholic Maryland. As was the custom among the Chesapeake gentry, John Carroll was sent to Europe to obtain the best education possible. At the age of thirteen he enrolled with the English Jesuits at their college, St. Omer, in Flanders; five years later, Carroll decided to join the Jesuits. After sixteen years of spiritual and intellectual formation, John Carroll was ordained a priest. He stayed on in Europe teaching for a while and then spent two years touring the Continent as tutor and travel guide for an English nobleman's son. With the suppression of the Jesuits in 1773, John Carroll decided it was time to return to Maryland, where he could live far removed from the "scandal and defamation" which had followed in the wake of the Society's dissolution.

When John Carroll returned home to Maryland, in 1774, he was thirty-eight years old; half of his life was already behind him, but the most significant part awaited him. For his first few years in Maryland, Carroll lived at his mother's manor at Rock Creek; from there he carried out the work of a missionary priest, traveling about Montgomery County ministering to a "very large congregation"; once a month he visited "another congregation in Virginia."[4]

In 1776, John Carroll had an unusual experience as a revolutionary diplomat. In that year of independence the Continental Congress attempted to gain the support of Canada in their struggle against the British. To this end, Congress appointed a committee to travel to Canada; the members of the committee were Benjamin Franklin, Charles Carroll of Carrollton, Samuel

Chase, and Father John Carroll. The appointment of a Catholic priest was extraordinary, but it was thought that Carroll's presence might have some influence with the French Catholic Canadians. John Carroll was chosen because he was "a man of liberal sentiments, enlarged mind and a manifest friend to civil liberty."[5] Though the mission to Canada was unsuccessful, it had a decided benefit for John Carroll. During the course of his travels to and from Canada, he became friendly with Benjamin Franklin, and this friendship would help Carroll later on, at a critical point in his career.

Shortly after the war had ended, John Carroll began to ponder the future of the Catholic community in the colonies. It was clear to him that the old guard of ex-Jesuits were not only getting on in age, but they also were lacking in leadership and initiative. They had a superior, Father John Lewis, but he had given little direction to the small band of aging missionaries, and the outlook for the future appeared uncertain. Since the suppression of their religious order in 1773, the ex-Jesuits had taken no concrete steps to provide for the future of the church in the colonies. There was an obvious need for organization if the American church was to have a future; in addition, there was the issue of ownership of the farms, the large estates acquired by the Jesuits in the colonial period.

John Carroll sought to resolve these issues by drawing up a plan of organization for the clergy. The purpose behind this plan, as he explained to an English colleague, was "to establish some regulations tending to perpetuate a succession of labourers in this vineyard, and to preserve their morals, to prevent idleness, and secure an equitable and frugal administration of our temporals."[6] Representatives of the clergy met at the Jesuit farm at Whitemarsh in 1783 and discussed Carroll's idea of a constitution. Using his draft as a basis, they drew up a constitution that would "establish a form of government for the clergy and lay down rules for the administration and preservation of their property."[7]

The Whitemarsh meeting was also the occasion for a petition to the Pope asking him to confirm Father Lewis as superior of the American mission and to grant him the spiritual privileges and authority needed to govern the church. The reason behind the petition was clearly stated in the letter to Pius VI. "Because of the present arrangement in government in America," explained Carroll and his fellow petitioners, "we are no longer able as formally to have recourse for our spiritual jurisdiction to bishops or vicars apostolic who live under a different and foreign government. Again and again this fact has been urged on us in unmistakable terms by the officials of the Republic; neither could we acknowledge any such person as ecclesiastical superior without offense to the civil government."[8] The significance of this petition and the accompanying cover letter by Carroll, which more forcefully opposed any foreigner's being appointed head of the American church, was that the clergy obviously had their own ideas of what the Catholic church in the United States should look like.

First and foremost, they wanted to avoid "any dependence on foreign jurisdiction." When Carroll heard that the Vatican, independent of the American clergy, was in the process of appointing a superior for the American church, he was more than a little upset. "This you may be assured of," he wrote to his English colleague Charles Plowden, "that no authority derived from the Propaganda will ever be admitted here; that the Catholick Clergy and Laity here know that the only connexion they ought to have with Rome is to acknowledge the pope as the Spiritual head of the Church; that no Congregations existing in his states shall be allowed to exercise any share of his spiritual authority here; that no Bishop Vicar Apostolical shall be admitted; and if we are to have a Bishop, he shall not be *in partibus* (a refined political Roman contrivance), but an ordinary national Bishop, in whose appointment Rome shall have no share."[9] Fortunately, the Vatican made the right decision, and after much diplomatic consultation with American and French diplomats, appointed an American to head the church in the United States. But, much to the surprise of the clergy, the choice was not John Lewis, but John Carroll. This was where Benjamin Franklin entered into the picture.

During the course of the Vatican's diplomatic endeavors to determine whom to appoint, the name of Carroll had emerged as a possible candidate. He was younger than the sixty-four-year-old Lewis and had a reputation for "piety and zeal." Once his name surfaced, Franklin, at the time on diplomatic duty in Paris, "exerted all his influence to press his good friend's appointment," and "there is little doubt that Franklin's influence was considerable."[10]

Carroll's appointment, in June of 1784, as "Superior of the Mission in the thirteen United States" and the clergy's acceptance in the fall of that year of the constitution drawn up earlier at Whitemarsh were two events that marked the beginning of an organized Catholic "religious society."

Once he received notice of his appointment as "Superior of the Mission," John Carroll began to plan for the future. He knew that the American political revolution was extraordinary, but he believed that religion had "undergone a revolution, if possible, more extraordinary, than our political one." The revolution had created a new religious situation, and for Catholics it was "a blessing and advantage."[11] In a very real sense all things were beginning anew; a new political and social order was being born; a new religious environment was taking shape as well. Onto this stage stepped John Carroll, and together with his colleagues among the clergy and laity he began to articulate an understanding of Roman Catholicism that was unique in Western Christendom.

This new understanding of Roman Catholicism first surfaced during the 1780s. Central to this understanding was the desire of American Catholics to be free and independent from all foreign influence or jurisdiction. Both the clergy and the people envisioned themselves as members of a "national" church. They were citizens of a new nation that had overthrown the yoke of foreign oppression, and as Catholics they did not want to be subject to a foreign authority, be it English or Roman.

This issue of an "independent national church" emerged most clearly and forcefully in the discussion about the appointment of a superior for the American Catholic Church. Neither John Carroll nor the other priests were satisfied with his appointment as superior of a mission church, because this meant that the church in America would be dependent on the Propaganda, the Vatican congregation in charge of the missions. Such an arrangement meant that the Vatican would govern the American church—something no one wanted, least of all the ex-Jesuits who had already experienced its capricious will when their order was suppressed. Carroll summed this feeling up in a letter to his fellow priests:

> I consider powers issued from the Propaganda not only as improper, but dangerous here. The jealousy in our Governments of the interference of any foreign jurisdiction is known to be such that we cannot expect, and in my opinion ought not to wish, that they would tolerate any other, than that which being purely spiritual, is essential to our Religion, to wit, an acknowledgement of the Pope's spiritual Supremacy, and of the see of S. Peter being the center of Ecclesiastical unity. The appointment therefore by the Propaganda of a Superior for this Country appears to be a dangerous step, and, by exciting the jealousy of the governments here may lend much to the prejudice of Religion, and perhaps expose it to the reproach of encouraging a dependance on a foreign power, and giving them an undue internal influence by leaving with them a prerogative to nominate to places of trust and real importance, and that *ad suum beneplacitum* [at their own pleasure]."[12]

He went on to say that, by virtue of the revolution, Catholicism "had acquired equal rights and privileges with that of other Christians" and we priests form "a permanent body of national Clergy, with sufficient powers to form our own system of internal government, and I think, to choose our own Superior."[13]

This desire for independence from "all foreign jurisdiction" in the government of the American church was also evident among the lay people. In fact a group of "outstanding Catholics were of a mind to point this out" in a letter to the Pope, but Carroll persuaded them to allow him to be the spokesman on this issue.[14] Carroll summed it up when he stated that Rome should grant the Church in the United States "that Ecclesiastical liberty, which the temper of the age and of our people requires."[15]

This desire for independence eventually persuaded Carroll and the rest of the clergy that what American Catholicism needed was a bishop who by virtue of his office would be dependent on the Pope alone and only in matters spiritual. Moreover, they wanted this bishop to be elected by the American clergy "instead of being appointed by a foreign tribunal which would shock the political prejudices of this Country."[16] They conveyed their sentiments to the Pope and he went along with their request. The first election of a bishop in the United States took place in May 1789, and not surprisingly the popular choice of the clergy was John Carroll.

The election of a native American as the first bishop in the United States was not only a major step forward in the ongoing organization of the church, but it also symbolized the spirit of independence prevalent among American Catholics. They were Roman Catholic to be sure, but their loyalty to the Papacy was neither exaggerated nor uncritical. It was rooted in an ancient religious tradition which acknowledged the "pope as Spiritual head of the Church," and in the words of John Carroll, "the Catholick Clergy and Laity here know" that this is "the only connexion they ought to have with Rome."[17]

Closely joined with this independent attitude was a consciousness of being a national church. Like most Americans, Catholics were caught up in the enthusiasm of the birth of a nation. They were Americans, and they wanted their church to reflect the spirit of the new nation, rather than mirror the ethos of a foreign country. This desire for a specifically American quality came through very clearly in the issue concerning the need for priests in the United States.

A constant lamentation during the 1780s and indeed well into the nineteenth century was the shortage of priests. Catholic communities up and down the Atlantic seaboard begged Carroll to send them a priest; the same plea came from beyond the Alleghenies, where Maryland Catholics were beginning to migrate in the 1780s. "Words scarcely reveal the extent of our lack of laborers," bemoaned Carroll in a report to Rome.[18] "To combat this bad situation" he proposed that a school be founded where American youth could be educated and, he hoped, candidates for the priesthood recruited. These young recruits would then enter a national seminary to pursue a "theological education." As early as 1783, Carroll had this idea of founding a school which would serve as a "nursery for the seminary"; he was so convinced of its need that "on this academy," he wrote, "is built all my hope of permanency and success to our Holy Religion in the United States."[19] He persuaded the other priests to go along with his idea and finally saw his wish fulfilled in 1791, when Georgetown Academy, now known as Georgetown University, opened its doors to students. In that same year, a few miles away, in Baltimore, St. Mary's Seminary also began a distinguished history of education, in a reconstructed tavern. In less than a decade, Carroll's hope for a national college and a national seminary was realized.

Behind this desire to found a college and a seminary was Carroll's conviction that the United States needed a native clergy, "men," he said, "accustomed to our climate, and acquainted with the tempers, manners, and government of the people, to whom they are to dispense the ministry of salvation."[20] It would be a long time, however, before Carroll's dream of having a steady and continuous supply of native American priests was realized. He knew this and so was forced to accept just about any priest who turned up in the United States. He revealed the extent of his desperation when he urged an English colleague to "encourage all you can meet with, Europeans or Americans, to come amongst us."[21] But in accepting Europeans to alleviate the severe shortage of clergy, Carroll insisted that they not only learn English, but also become sensitized to American culture. He rebuked a French priest for being insensitive to "the people of Boston" and for not becoming "better acquainted with the temper and habits of thinking in America." He urged a young European nobleman preparing to be a priest in the United States "to study our constitution, our laws, our customs" and observe as well as possible "the American way of life."[22] This insistence on foreign priests becoming Americanized underscored the conviction of Carroll and his contemporaries that Catholicism in the United States was to be both American and independent. To accomplish this, a clergy in tune with "the American way of life" was indispensable.

In addition to being independent and American, a third dimension of the republican blueprint of Catholicism was an insistence on the separation of church and state. In the seventeenth century, Lord Baltimore had implemented this practice when he refused to allow the Jesuits any special privileges; at the time, it was a pragmatic decision rooted in the necessity for religious toleration in a Catholic colony populated by Protestants. With the Protestant takeover in Maryland, religious toleration became an orphan. Only with the Revolution did this republican idea become actualized once more. This time it emerged not as a pragmatic concession to a religiously plural environment, but as a fundamental human right endorsed by the Revolution. Catholics accepted this rights-of-man philosophy and enthusiastically supported the concept of a free church in a free society. Such thinking placed American Catholics squarely in the mainstream of Catholic Enlightenment thought.

The Catholic Enlightenment was a movement in Europe and England which "attempted to bridge the ever-widening gap between the Roman Catholic Church and the social and intellectual forces of the Enlightenment."[23] It surfaced in the United States principally through the influence of the writings of a handful of English Catholic thinkers who were seeking to reconcile Catholicism with the new questions raised by the Age of Reason. John Carroll certainly shared this Enlightenment mentality, and numerous other Catholics were of a similar frame of mind. How widespread the pattern was is hard to determine, but there is no question that "to a greater degree than has been realized, American Catholics participated in the mentality of the Enlightenment."[24]

American Catholics did not appropriate the complete platform of Catholic Enlightenment thinkers; rather, they supported certain intellectual positions and attitudes about religious practice that were most applicable to the American political, social, and religious environment. The acceptance of the separation of church and state was the most important issue that found support among American Catholics. Such a mentality persuaded them to look upon religious pluralism in a positive manner, and it would be hard to find a stronger endorsement of this position than that penned by John Carroll. "If we have the wisdom and temper to preserve [civil and religious liberty], America may come to exhibit a proof to the world, that general and equal toleration, by giving a free circulation to fair argument, is the most effectual method to bring all denominations of christians to an unity of faith."[25]

A concrete example of how normative this attitude was in the Catholic community can be found in the Maryland state assembly during the mid 1780s. In 1784, the assembly considered passing a bill which would tax the people for the support of all religious denominations. Most of the Catholic delegates opposed such a union between the state and religion; one reason for their opposition was a fear that such legislation would only be the first step toward the reestablishment of the Protestant Episcopal Church in Maryland. As John Carroll put it, ". . . we have all smarted heretofore under the lash of an established church and shall therefore be on our guard against every approach towards it."[26] When the issue was resolved, in 1785, the assembly voted against the proposed legislation, and "there can be little doubt that Catholic opinion weighed heavily in the final outcome of the tax bill."[27]

Such positive support for the separation of church and state went against the traditional medieval Catholic position, which envisioned a society in which church and state were united and religious pluralism was not tolerated. This was the majority viewpoint among European Catholics and remained so throughout the nineteenth century. In the United States, however, where religious pluralism was as American as Uncle Sam, Catholics thought differently about the relationship between church and state. The uniqueness of the American experience and the influence of Enlightenment thought led them in this direction and enabled them to become a voice for religious toleration within Roman Catholicism. Eventually this American tradition of religious freedom did gain acceptance in the Roman Catholic Church, but it took almost two hundred years before the Church, at the Second Vatican Council, would endorse the position of the Catholic Enlightenment.

Another aspect of the Catholic Enlightenment platform endorsed by Carroll and his contemporaries was an apologetic based on reason and intelligibility. As a minority religion in a Protestant nation, they were well aware of the potential for conversions to Roman Catholicism, but in an Enlightenment age, prospective converts had to be persuaded of the reasonableness of religion, rather than coerced. Thus, a concern for intelligibility in religion became prominent among Catholics in this republican period. The most visible manifestation of this was the desire to have Catholic worship services celebrated in English, rather than Latin.

John Carroll vigorously supported the use of English in the liturgy and claimed that most of the clergy "feel the Necessity of such a Change in this Country equally with myself." The reason behind this support for an English liturgy was quite evident. "Latin is an unknown Tongue, and in this Country, still more than yours," explained Carroll to an English colleague, "either for want of Books or desirability to read, the greatest part of our Congregation must be entirely ignorant of the meaning and Sense of the publick Offices of the church."[28] Though no official change was ever adopted in favor of a vernacular liturgy, the use of English in church services was quite common. Along with a vernacular liturgy, the translation of the Bible into the vernacular was another aspect of the Catholic Enlightenment which Carroll and his contemporaries supported. This project was realized when the Philadelphia publisher Mathew Carey published an English Catholic version of the Bible in 1790; one of his most energetic salesmen was Bishop John Carroll.

Another important component in the Catholic Enlightenment movement in Europe was the active participation of the laity in the life of the church. In the United States this took its most concrete form in the move toward the democratization of local church government through the adoption of the trustee system. What this system meant was that lay trustees, elected annually by those people in the parish who rented pews, presided over the government of the parish in the area of temporal affairs. Such an arrangement went against the traditional form of parish government, which invested all authority in the clergy. Though there were precedents in Europe for the trustee system long before the outbreak of the American Revolution, it is clear that its emergence in almost every major city and parish in the United States was due in large part to a widespread attempt of the Catholic community "to adapt the European Catholic Church to American culture by identifying that Church with American republicanism."[29] This move toward a democratization of church life signaled a new understanding of the church. As one Charleston trustee put it, American Catholics should "rear a National American Church, with liberties consonant to the spirit of the Government, under which they live; yet, in due obedience in essentials to the Pontifical Hierarchy, and which will add a new and dignified column to the Vatican."[30]

The movement toward a trustee system of parish government began in the 1780s in such urban centers as New York and Philadelphia. A similar pattern emerged along the Kentucky and Indiana frontier, where pioneer Catholic communities without the benefit of clergy would join together to form a "religious society," elect their leaders, purchase land for a church, and assume responsibilities for the future of Catholicism in the local community. Many conditions accounted for the emergence of the trustee system, such as the shortage of priests, national consciousness among various immigrant groups, and European precedents. But, without a doubt, the contagion of republicanism unleashed by the revolution was a major reason for its widespread acceptance among Catholics in the United States.

Thus, by 1790 a unique vision of the church was beginning to surface in the United States. This republican blueprint envisioned a national, American church which would be independent of all foreign jurisdiction and would endorse pluralism and toleration in religion; a church in which religion was grounded in intelligibility and where a vernacular liturgy was normative; and finally a church in which the spirit of democracy permeated the government of local communities.

It should be emphasized that this republican blueprint was not a packaged program of reform endorsed and championed by the Catholic community. Without a doubt, these positions, inspired by the spirit of republicanism and the ideals of the Enlightenment, were taking hold in the Catholic community during the 1780s. Still it was not an organized national program for reform; rather, it was a decisive turn toward a new understanding of Catholicism which sought to adapt the church to American culture. This new view of Catholicism was still in its formative stages in 1790, and it had some way to go before it could become the final blueprint to guide the future of the church in the United States. The significant point was that Catholics in the United States were embarking on a new experiment seeking to fashion a church in tune with the republican age.

Though this vision of Catholicism was unique among Roman Catholics, precedents for it can certainly be found in the American colonial experience. Colonial Catholics necessarily emphasized the importance of the laity in religion and their active participation in church affairs; likewise, a tradition of religious toleration was something sacred to Maryland Catholics, and they were also accustomed to being independent of any type of foreign jurisdiction or interference when it came to religion. Thus, as unique as it was in the Roman Catholic world of the 1780s, the thrust of this new republican blueprint was not totally alien to the American Catholic experience.

During the summer of 1790, John Carroll traveled to England, where on August 15 he was ordained as the first bishop of Baltimore. At that time, the Catholic church in the United States was a small missionary outpost, numbering only about thirty-five thousand people, the equivalent of a large urban parish in France or Spain. The bulk of the population still lived in Maryland and Pennsylvania, but recognizable communities were beginning to emerge in New York and Boston. Some Maryland Catholics had joined the migration West and settled in Kentucky; other Catholic settlements were situated at old French trading posts and forts such as Vincennes and Detroit; once a part of New France, they were now American frontier towns.

Despite its small size, its scattered population, and its meager resources, this missionary church was beginning to articulate a new understanding of the relationship between the Roman Catholic church and the modern world. Given the religious and political environment of the United States, there was reason to hope that such a vision would be actualized. But it never happened. The republican blueprint, fashioned in the 1780s, began to come apart during the 1790s; as striking as its emergence was in the 1780s, the more startling was its disintegration in the 1790s. The evidence for this is overwhelming.

The first indication of a turning away from a new, American version of Roman Catholicism was the church synod held in Baltimore in 1791. Realizing that church affairs were "badly regulated," John Carroll wanted to hold a synod, or meeting of the clergy, at which issues of importance could be discussed and "an uniform discipline may be established in all parts of this great continent."[31] For several days in early November, Carroll and the clergy, a total of twenty-two priests, met to discuss the future of the church. What resulted was a body of legislation pertaining to the administration of the sacraments, the celebration of Mass, and the financial support of the clergy. These new statutes lacked any hint of innovation or imagination reminiscent of the thinking of the 1780s. In fact, the legislation turned out to be nothing more than the adoption of laws issued in earlier European synods. As Carroll admitted, there were "no innovations in the decrees—everything was copied from former synods" and in his opinion they were even "too unimportant" to be published.[32] Thus, at a decisive moment in the early history of the church, both the bishop and the clergy failed to step boldly into the future and fashion a church in tune with the republican spirit of the new nation. Rather, they looked to the past, to the European tradition of Roman Catholicism, for their model of the church.

This tendency to shape American Catholicism according to a traditional European model, rather than one inspired by the spirit of republicanism and the Catholic Enlightenment, became more pronounced as time went on.

The most telling example of this change in thinking was the attitude concerning the election of new bishops for the United States. A year after his consecration as bishop, Carroll was already looking for help. At the 1791 synod, he and the other clergy discussed the issue and agreed that the new bishop, like Carroll himself, should be elected by the priests. "Otherwise," observed Carroll, "we never shall be viewed kindly by our government here, and discontents, even amongst our own Clergy, will break out."[33] Carroll carried out his plans by consulting "the older and more worthy" clergy, and the person they selected was Laurence Graessel.[34] Unfortunately he died of yellow fever in 1793. The second choice, Leonard Neale, was selected in the same manner; Carroll considered this process of selection by consultation tantamount to election, since he wanted to be sure that the new bishop was the "choice" of the "most experienced Brethren" and not, as he said, a result of "my arbitrary will."[35] In December of 1800 Carroll ordained Neale as the coadjutor bishop of Baltimore.

When the time came to organize new dioceses in the United States, additional bishops were chosen, but this time there was no general election among the clergy. Carroll himself selected the men and recommended their names to Rome, in 1807. The Vatican approved Carroll's choices for the new dioceses of Boston, Philadelphia, and Bardstown, Kentucky. Contrary to his wishes, however, Rome created the diocese of New York and appointed as bishop an Irish priest who had never set foot in the United States. A major reason for the appointment of Richard Luke Concanen as the first bishop of New York was the recommendation Rome had received from the hierarchy of Ireland. Concanen died before he could ever get to New York, and his successor was another Irishman, also recommended by the Irish bishops and a total stranger to both Carroll and the United States. Carroll feared the consequences of such a "dangerous precedent," but there was little he could do. What he promised never to permit, he reluctantly accepted: papal control over episcopal nominations. The concern now was not maintaining a spirit of "ecclesiastical democracy" in the American church, but maintaining control over the appointment of future bishops, as well as preventing any meddling in this area by the Irish or French hierarchy. The clearest expression of this change in mentality came in 1813, when Carroll, in a letter to the Pope, Pius VII, asked him "to instruct us as to how we are to provide in the future for vacant sees [dioceses] . . . and how should the bishops be chosen?" Such a subservient attitude was a far cry from his thinking in 1788, when he feared such dependence on Rome "would shock the political prejudices of the Country."[36]

With the spirit of independence, so manifest in the 1780s, gone, Carroll became increasingly dependent on the Papacy. All throughout his career as a leader in the American Catholic community, he sought to maintain a balance between being a loyal American and a faithful Roman Catholic. It was a delicate balancing act; in his younger years, as a priest, he leaned toward the American spirit of independence; in his later years, as bishop, he moved closer to the stance of a Roman Catholic for whom the Papacy was the vital center of the church. Though he still held firm to his belief that the authority of the Papacy was limited to "things purely spiritual," he no longer supported the idea of an independent American Catholic church.[37]

Another indication of the conservative shift in the church was the use of English in the liturgy. In the 1780s Carroll and most of the clergy supported this practice; the 1791 synod encouraged the use of the vernacular at Mass and at other liturgical services but said nothing about its replacing Latin as the principal language of the liturgy. During the 1790s and early in the nineteenth century English was widely used both in the celebration of Mass and in the administration of the sacraments. By the time of the bishops' meeting in 1810, however, it was clear that official support for this practice was waning. To achieve uniformity of practice, the bishops ordered the clergy to celebrate "the whole Mass in the Latin language" and to use Latin in the essential prayers of the sacraments; English could be used only for the nonessential prayers connected with the administration of the sacraments. Though the 1810 legislation was not totally against the use of the vernacular at religious services, it was clear that John Carroll and his episcopal colleagues were opposed to promoting the cause of an English liturgy. What he had once considered "as essential to the Services of God and Benefit of Mankind" was now a dead issue for Bishop Carroll.[38]

One area in which the republican thrust remained consistent was that of local church government. The lay-trustee system was the most successful example of how Catholics adapted their church to the American republican ethos. Throughout these formative years, it became the normative type of parish government, and it fostered the growth of a particular type of parish, the congregational parish.

Two major tendencies set the congregational parish apart from the traditional European parish: an emphasis on a democratic model of authority, rather than a hierarchical model, and an emphasis on local autonomy, in which the relationship to authority beyond the local level was poorly defined and only minimally actualized. Clearly, such a model of parish was characteristic of American Protestant denominations, and those Catholics opposed to the lay-trustee system did not fail to point this out. But theirs was a minority voice during the republican period of American Catholicism.

The diaspora condition of early American Catholicism favored the growth of the congregational parish. The absence of clergy in such diverse places as Vincennes and St. Louis, Charleston and New York, forced the laity to become the organizing force in these communities. This particular pattern of organization led them to assume not only such mundane tasks as buying land and building a church, but also other, more spiritual responsibilities such as leading the community in prayer and teaching catechism to the children. John Carroll clearly approved of this, but he really had little choice, due to the lack of clergy; some bishops even officially commissioned such lay leaders to preside over the community's religious services and catechetical instructions. In addition to the scarcity of clergy, the scattered nature of the Catholic population favored the development of local lay autonomy. The fact that there was but one bishop for the entire United States was hardly a situation that fostered episcopal control over distant communities; Carroll knew this and pleaded with Rome to create more dioceses in the United States so that the work of administration could be divided up among several bishops. In 1808, four new dioceses were organized: Boston, New York, Philadelphia, and Bardstown, Kentucky; but the bishops for these dioceses were not consecrated until 1810, and New York didn't get its first episcopal leader until 1815. Appointing one bishop for the Trans-Allegheny region, however, or one bishop for all of New England, did not drastically increase episcopal control in these areas. Such an underdeveloped state of ecclesiastical organization naturally fostered lay initiative at the local level.

The democratic dimension of the congregational parish was rooted in the custom of holding annual elections to choose the board of lay trustees. People clearly saw this from a republican point of view and believed that such a democratic procedure should be adopted by the Catholic church. In addition, they wanted "to participate in a selection of their pastors, and to dismiss them if they abused their authority, were scandalous to the general public, or were incompetent in their ministry."[39] By exercising control over the temporal affairs of the parish and by sharing with the clergy the responsibility for the spiritual welfare of the community, lay trustees believed that they were establishing a more democratic church, and they articulated this belief time and again in their correspondence and pamphlets.

The democratization of church government was the one feature of the republican blueprint which gained the most popular and widespread support. Unlike other issues, the trustee system was never discussed at the 1791 synod or the 1810 meeting of bishops. Such silence, in contrast to the fears expressed at other councils later in the nineteenth century, suggests satisfaction with the congregational parish. In contrast, the election of bishops had become a dead issue by 1810, and the same was true as regards an English liturgy. Support for the separation of church and state was still strong, and most Catholics desired a church whose clergy was sensitive to "the American way of life." But supporting these positions did not demand any profound change in the daily lives of American Catholics or in the way the church functioned. To support the concept of the congregational parish, however, did mean effecting a substantial shift in the understanding of the Roman Catholic church and the way it traditionally operated. Instead of a clerical monopoly it meant popular democracy. Rather than emphasizing the hierarchical nature of the church, this view stressed its communal character. This was a unique vision in the Roman Catholic world and represented a decisive advance toward a new definition of the Church.

The widespread acceptance of the congregational parish was not without its problems, however. The most troublesome issue centered about the right to appoint and dismiss the parish priest. Some trustees and clergy asserted that this right rested with the lay people; Bishop Carroll adamantly opposed this point of view, stating that the bishop alone possessed the final authority in such decisions. These disputes became quite bitter at times and lasted for years, not months. The New York Catholic community was involved in such a dispute with Carroll even before he was named bishop of Baltimore; the Germans in Philadelphia and in Baltimore carried on a bitter battle against Carroll for more than a decade; and in Charleston the Irish locked horns with him over this issue of authority. There was no doubt where John Carroll stood on this question, and his firmness meant that he "would sooner see a whole Congregation leave the communion of the Church than yield" on this point.[40] As adamant as he was about this aspect of ecclesiastical authority, Carroll was equally consistent in supporting the concept of the trustee system. For him it was not a question of tolerating a bad idea, but of actively supporting a republican concept of the church. In so doing he recognized the congregational parish as a viable and legitimate accommodation of the Church to the American situation. His episcopal colleagues, Benedict Flaget of Bardstown and Jean Cheverus of Boston, together with the pioneer priest of Boston, Francis Matignon, concurred in this position and supported the people in their efforts to establish congregational-type parishes. There were others, however, who thought otherwise; the most well known opponents of the trustee system were Carroll's auxiliary bishop, Leonard Neale, and the pioneer priest of Kentucky, Stephen Badin. These men, along with other clergy and laity, viewed the church in a hierarchical manner, as a church which, in Neale's words, "places the clergyman over the vestrymen whom he appoints and dismisses at will."[41] Despite such a hard-line attitude among some clerics, the concept of the congregational parish was not to be denied, and it remained the most popular form of local church government during the first quarter of the nineteenth century.

Other features of the republican blueprint also remained intact during this period of increasing conservatism. Support for the separation of church and state continued, with its most articulate advocates being the lay trustees; closely related to this was a positive stance toward religious pluralism and religious toleration. In addition, cordial relations with Protestants remained normative through the 1820s, and Catholic laymen continued to be politically active in the new nation.

Thus the picture of Catholicism that emerged by 1820 was more than a little complex. From one angle of vision, American Catholics had obviously assimilated the spirit of republicanism and supported ideas which, as far as Roman Catholicism was concerned, were indeed innovative: the congregational parish, separation of church and state, and religious pluralism. Yet at the same time there was a clear shift toward a more traditional posture: reliance on a European model of Catholicism, an increasing dependency on Rome for guidance in church affairs, and suppression of an English liturgy.

The explanation for the republican posture of early American Catholicism can be traced to the ideological revolution unleashed by the war for independence, the influence of Enlightenment thought, and the colonial tradition of American Catholicism. All these forces combined to sustain a spirit of republicanism in the area of parish government and in the relationships between Catholics and American society. But why, in other areas, was there a shift to a more conservative, European stance by the turn of the century? In other words, why did the republican blueprint of the 1780s and the vision of a "National American Church" begin to come apart in the 1790s?

An obvious reason for the conservative swing of the 1790s was that the times were changing; the heady republican atmosphere of the 1780s, set on fire by a victorious revolutionary struggle, was on the wane, and a more conservative, federalist attitude rose up to challenge the "excesses of democracy." This swing toward conservatism had an obvious impact on the American Catholic community.

Charles Carroll of Carrollton was a classic example of a revolutionary gentleman who turned into a federalist aristocrat. Since he had always been a wealthy aristocrat, such a shift was hardly a radical conversion for Squire Carroll, and it was a political swing that appeared to be common among many of the Maryland Catholic gentry. It was certainly the case with John Carroll. In the 1780s he was clearly a champion of republican ideas, but after his consecration as bishop, he became more and more hesitant in his endorsement of the proposed marriage between Catholicism and republicanism. The "anarchy and insurrection" of the French Revolution scared Carroll, as it did most Americans; its destructive impact on the Church was especially chilling, and this cautioned the Federalist bishop against "the prevailing spirit of ecclesiastical no less than civil democracy."[42] Once appointed head of the church in the United States, he became preoccupied with the issue of authority and feared that the American spirit of independence would persuade both clergy and lay people to act independently of any legitimate ecclesiastical authority. This fear, coupled with his concern that the church in America would lose all identity with Rome, led him to do all he could to prevent any "disunion with the Holy See."[43] This meant an emphasis on obedience to episcopal authority and on uniformity in church discipline. Closely allied to this was the Roman Catholic tradition concerning the authority of the bishop; simply put, he was supreme monarch in his own diocese. Carroll acted out of this belief, and so did the vast majority of Catholics. This meant that the republican movement in the church could go only so far before it clashed head-on with a fundamental teaching of Roman Catholicism. It also meant that the bishop had tremendous power and could exercise this as he wished. Thus, if Carroll no longer saw the wisdom of a vernacular liturgy, he could pass a law to that effect, which is essentially what he did in 1810 along with his episcopal colleagues. If he no longer saw the wisdom of electing new bishops, he could cease conducting his consultations, which is what he did in 1807. By acting this way, he believed that he was cementing the bond between Rome and America and providing for the selection of the right type of individuals to govern the church.

Thus, the conservative swing of the 1790s and the ensuing split this caused in American society between supporters of a Federalist ideology and those of a Republican one; the anarchy of the French Revolution, coupled with Carroll's federalist inclination and the responsibility of the episcopal office; and the Roman Catholic tradition on authority in the Church, pushed American

Catholicism into a more traditional, conservative posture. Not surprisingly, the areas in which this swing to traditionalism was most evident were those areas over which the bishop had control: worship, the election of bishops, and official relations with Rome. In those areas over which his control was limited —local church government and the thinking of the people regarding the role of the Church in a democratic society—the republican spirit remained intact.

The swing to a traditional version of Catholicism, however, cannot be totally ascribed to the power of one person or to American influences alone. A major reason for this shift and for the permanent status it quickly acquired was the influx of European clergy and the importation of a European, continental understanding of Roman Catholicism.

Given the shortage of clergy, John Carroll was forced to turn to Europe for immediate help. He realized the cultural problems involved and urged foreign clergymen to adapt as much as possible to the American way of life. But, as a missionary bishop in dire need of help, he could be neither too particular nor too demanding. Though foreign-born clergy never inundated the country, their presence within the Catholic community was overwhelming. In 1791, at the first church synod held at Baltimore, 80 percent of the clergy present were foreign-born. To overcome such dependence on foreign clergy, Carroll had established a seminary in Baltimore, but even this step could not stem the tide of foreign influence. In its first decade of operation, 1791–1801, more than 60 percent of the students at St. Mary's Seminary were foreign-born, and 60 percent of all the priests ordained from this seminary during the period 1791–1829 were foreign-born; in fact, the first ordination in the United States of an American-born priest did not take place until 1800, when John Carroll ordained William Matthews of Maryland. When it came time to select bishops for the new dioceses of Boston, New York, Philadelphia, and Bardstown, none of the men selected were native-born Americans.

Though the foreign-born clergymen came from various European countries, France was by far the nation with the most influence. Not only did it supply the most priests, but it also furnished a large number of future bishops. Moreover, the Society of St. Sulpice, a French society of priests, was in charge of St. Mary's Seminary and thus responsible for the training of clergy for the American church. It was obvious that their model of priestly formation was grounded in the French Sulpician tradition; as one Sulpician boasted, ". . . our rule is now established in all points like in France. . . ."[44] Though this French influence was present in virtually all regions of the American Catholic community, it was most striking in Kentucky.

The Kentucky Catholic community was founded in the 1780s by transplanted Marylanders who had abandoned the Chesapeake for the more fertile and more promising territory west of the Alleghenies. The community continued to expand as more and more people joined the westward movement, with the result that by 1815 Catholics in Kentucky numbered about ten thousand. They were concentrated in the central part of the state, where the village of Bardstown was the center of the Catholic settlement. Though the majority of these people were native-born Americans, there was only one American-born priest in Kentucky in 1815; the rest were Europeans, with Frenchmen being the most numerous.

The pioneer priest of Kentucky was Stephen Badin. Born in Orléans, France, he came to the United States as a seminarian and completed his studies for the priesthood at St. Mary's Seminary, in Baltimore. Ordained a priest by Bishop Carroll in 1793 (the first such ceremony in the United States), he was assigned to the Kentucky mission. Badin worked in Kentucky for twenty-six years, and for the first twelve years of his ministry he was virtually the only priest in the state; those few who came to assist him quickly succumbed to death or discouragement. He was so singularly identified with Catholicism in the Bluegrass State that he is rightly remembered as the "Apostle of Kentucky."

After Badin's arrival in 1793, the flow of French clergymen remained slow but steady; for the most part, these priests were refugees from the French Revolution and came to the United States seeking asylum. Among them was Charles Nerinckx, a Belgian priest who arrived in Kentucky in 1805. Like Badin, Nerinckx would have a decisive influence on the development of Kentucky Catholicism. Not surprisingly, the first bishop of Kentucky was another refugee from the French Revolution, Benedict Flaget. After his appointment as bishop of Bardstown in 1808, Flaget initiated a practice many of his episcopal colleagues later imitated: he traveled to France to recruit priests and seminarians for his vast diocese, which included not just Kentucky but everything west of the Alleghenies and east of the Mississippi. In later years, coadjutor bishops were appointed to assist Flaget in his work, and these two men, John B. David and Guy I. Chabrat, were also French. In fact, of the twenty-three bishops appointed to work in the West during the first half of the nineteenth century, eleven were French; the others were Irish (three), Belgian (two), German (two), Italian (two), and American (three).[45]

Such a dominant presence of French clergy had a decisive influence on the development of Catholicism in Kentucky. Badin's influence was especially visible in the stern code of morality he encouraged along the frontier and in his opposition to "the extravagant pretentions of Republicanism" in local church government.[46] Nerinckx held stern views about dancing, dress, and theatergoing, but his continental tastes were most manifest in his promotion of an elaborate devotionalism—a style of piety identified with eighteenth-century-baroque Catholicism. It was clear that Badin and Nerinckx, as well as other French clergy, were acting out of a European model of Roman Catholicism. This was the type of religion that shaped them, and as far as they were concerned, there was no other alternative. For them, an American Catholicism, inspired and guided by the spirit of republicanism, was unthinkable. Inevitably, conflict was bound to erupt between the French clerical mentality and the aspirations of American-born priests and people. In fact, such conflict surfaced frequently: congregations wrote republican constitutions despite Badin's opposition, and people spent their Saturday evenings dancing, much to his displeasure. Resistance finally reached a crisis point in the 1830s, when there erupted "an emotional tempest that nearly tore the Church in Kentucky apart."[47] The episode centered around Flaget's decision to appoint Guy Chabrat as his coadjutor. The Frenchman Chabrat was not a happy choice for many reasons, one of which was his nationality. Once word of Flaget's plan got out, both the clergy and the laity mounted a vocal and prolonged attack. The ladies of Louisville spoke for many Catholics when, in a letter to Flaget remonstrating with him for his choice, they said, "Must we have another Frenchman as bishop?"[48] For the women of Louisville, two French bishops, Flaget and his ailing assistant, John B. David, were enough. Flaget eventually won out when Rome appointed Chabrat as a coadjutor bishop of Bardstown.

There was more to this episode than nationality differences. Beneath it all was a basic cultural difference regarding religion. Time and again the French clergy referred to the spirit of independence ("republicanism," they called it) as the principal trait of American Catholics. For these political refugees, who could still vividly recall the upheavals of the French Revolution, such wide-eyed republicanism was not a healthful sign, and they continually sought to tame it. Their model of Catholicism was clearly alien to the American republican movement and evidenced no influence at all from the Catholic Enlightenment; it was a traditional European model of Roman Catholicism grounded in a monarchical view of authority, moral rigorism, elaborate devotionalism, and an exaggerated loyalty to the Papacy. Though the contrast was most striking in Kentucky because of the predominantly American-born laity and the heavily French clergy, it was hardly confined to that one region.

Georgetown College was plagued by a similar division during the presidency of Father William Dubourg, who was too French for the former Jesuits attached to the college; they quickly developed "strong prejudices against everything which was derived in any shape, from France."[49] Such nativism also wreaked havoc in the newly restored Jesuit community. The Pope had partially restored the Society in 1801, when he recognized the legitimacy of the Russian Province of the Jesuits and allowed it to accept members from outside Russia. For the former Jesuits in Maryland, this was a happy event, and they soon affiliated with the Society in Russia. Then, in 1814, the Society was restored throughout the world and the Jesuits began a new chapter in their American mission. Most of the American branch of the Society, however, were European priests who had brought with them a strong foreign prejudice "toward American institutions and ideas." Like the French émigrés, they were suspicious of the republican spirit that characterized native-born Catholics. This prejudice clashed with the aspirations of the American Jesuits, with the result that a "Jesuit Nativism grew up which impeded the revival of the Society here for years."[30] This tension between Europeans and Americans also affected the development of communities of women religious.

During this republican period, 1780 to 1820, five communities of women religious were founded in the United States: the Carmelites, at Port Tobacco, Maryland, in 1790; the Visitation Nuns, founded at Georgetown in 1799; the Sisters of Charity, founded at Emmitsburg, Maryland, in 1809; and the Sisters of Loretto and the Sisters of Charity of Nazareth, both founded in Kentucky in 1812. Though these communities were made up predominantly of American-born women, the model of religious life most often forced upon them by male ecclesiastical superiors was a European one. This obviously caused serious problems. The best-known episode took place among the Sisters of Charity at Emmitsburg, Maryland. The founder of this community, the holy woman Elizabeth Seton, waged an intense struggle against her clerical superior, the Frenchman John B. David, and his plan to structure the community according to a French model of religious life. Seton won this struggle, and for successfully putting up with the harassment of David and other French male superiors she deserved canonization![51] The Sisters of Loretto in Kentucky, who were 90 percent American-born had a similar problem with their founder, Father Charles Nerinckx. He wrote the rule for the community, and his austerity bristled on every page of the regulations. Rather than adapting the rule of life to the frontier, he composed a very austere rule; the sisters, for example, had to go barefoot much of the year and remain silent throughout the day. It was so demanding and out of harmony with the environment that the community experienced a large number of deaths; for example, in one twelve-month period, September 1823 to September 1824, fifteen Loretto sisters under the age of thirty died. Nerinckx, however, was so convinced of the correctness of the European model that he even wanted to import women religious "from Europe to teach the young women the rudiments of religious life, but they protested that he could do it better himself."[52] The unrealism of Nerinckx's rule finally persuaded Bishop Flaget to intervene and have it modified.

The heart of this cultural conflict between a European and an American model of religious life was succinctly captured in a letter from the French bishop of New Orleans, William Dubourg, to a Vatican official:

> It is scarcely possible to realize how contagious even to the clergy and to men otherwise well disposed, are the principles of freedom and independence imbibed by all the pores in these United States. Hence I have always been convinced that practically all the good to be hoped for must come from the Congregations or religious Orders among which flourish strict discipline. . . .[53]

Such independence on the part of Americans even led some Europeans to believe that few vocations to religious life would come from the United States. The most significant result of this shift toward a traditional European model of Roman Catholicism was the emergence of a new type of piety. In the colonial Catholic community, the dominant strain of piety was grounded in the English tradition of John Gother and Richard Challoner, a school of spirituality that fostered a personal and interior piety. This tradition remained strong in the 1780s and 1790s and indeed would persist as a viable option well into the nineteenth century, but another school of spirituality was beginning to emerge. Like the Gother-Challoner tradition, it was imported into the United States, but it came from the Continent, from France in particular, and it evidenced the rigorism and excessive devotionalism of baroque Catholicism. According to Joseph Chinnici, who has studied this shift in piety, the personal, interior approach to the Christian life characterized the Enlightenment view of the person. "This tradition," observed Chinnici, "did not dwell excessively on fallen nature but encouraged individual participation in the mystery of salvation. As a result, the necessity of structures, the mediation of the hierarchical Church and the saints and external religious behavior (e.g., baroque devotionalism) did not play a preponderant role. The tendency of the works was to create *interior* communion with Christ. The person was evaluated as good, a possessor of the Spirit, one having direct access to the supernatural."[54]

What can rightly be called the baroque tradition fostered a very pessimistic view of the human person; personal moral weakness was a dominant theme, with self-discipline and control of the passions the chosen remedies. As a result, confessional practices became very elaborate as people were urged to conduct an excessively detailed examination of conscience; emphasis on the external practice of religion encouraged an elaborate devotionalism, which in turn was nourished by an increased commitment to spiritual confraternities.

Nerinckx was an especially enthusiastic booster of confraternities and went so far as to enroll young babies, even unborn infants, in his societies. John B. David was another representative of this tradition; he compiled a prayer book, *True Piety,* which became the most popular and representative manual of the baroque tradition of piety. As an itinerant missionary in Kentucky, he also conducted numerous missions, or what can be called revivals, and these, too, reinforced the continental tradition. This tradition of piety, promoted through prayer books, sermons, and confessional practices, reinforced the conservative shift taking place in other areas of Catholic church life. As Chinnici rightly noted, "Internal sentiments and external realities combined to form a definite religious sensibility, one which placed a primary value on order, control, subordination, and disciplinary uniformity."[55] By 1820, such a religious sensibility was becoming more widespread in Catholic America. The plain style of religion, associated with Garden of the Soul Catholicism, remained popular, but, like the other characteristics of republican Catholicism, its days were numbered.

By the time of John Carroll's death in 1815, it was clear that Catholicism in the United States was undergoing a major transition. Trademarks of colonial Catholicism—the predominance of the landed gentry and Garden of the Soul Catholicism—were slowly losing their significance. The vital center of the community was shifting from the rural counties of southern Maryland to Baltimore, Philadelphia, and Bardstown. Perhaps the best symbol of this change was the deterioration of the Jesuit farms and the decline of the Jesuits themselves. Once the spiritual centers of Catholicism, these farms had become run-down reminders of a vanished past; as their farms deteriorated, the Jesuits became more covetous about the monetary value of these estates; pastoral lethargy settled in as the Jesuits bickered over ownership and control of the farms. While they worried about their farms, time passed them by, and the Sulpicians took over the leadership role among the American clergy.

Despite the deterioration in southern Maryland, Catholicism still remained a southern church. The southern flavor of pre-1820 Catholicism is often overlooked, yet it is a significant point which provides a dramatic contrast with subsequent developments. Colonial Catholicism was clearly a southern institution in which the gentry were the most influential group and slaveholding was commonplace. Yet, even after the Revolution, Catholics remained heavily concentrated in the upper South; Maryland and Kentucky were key centers, and both states were attached to the slave-based economy of the South. In both regions, Catholics supported the slave market; priests owned slaves, women religious owned slaves, and the laity owned slaves; even John Carroll had his black servants, one free and one slave. Slaveholding being commonplace in the South, it should not be surprising to find Catholics supporting the system in the early-nineteenth century. What was surprising, however, was how quickly European priests accepted this practice, which by 1820 had died out in most parts of the Western world. The southern character of Catholicism goes a long way toward explaining why in later years Catholics were so reluctant to join the antislavery crusade.

The attempt to fashion an American national church, so visible in the 1780s, had failed as each subsequent decade witnessed an increasing Europeanization of the church. John Carroll certainly played a decisive role in this shift from the republican blueprint of the 1780s to a more traditional model of Roman Catholicism. Traditionally he is looked upon as a leading force in the Americanization of Roman Catholicism, and in recent years, the liberal wing of Vatican II Catholicism has viewed his episcopacy most favorably because of his liberal tendencies. Yet this is an erroneous assessment. John Carroll the priest was indeed a champion of an independent American church imbued with the spirit of republicanism and the Catholic Enlightenment; John Carroll the bishop was not so enthusiastically inclined, and the older he got—he was seventy-nine when he died—the more committed he became to a traditional understanding of Roman Catholicism. Though Carroll the bishop never repudiated the American system of separation of church and state, the concept of the congregational parish, or the need for foreign-born clergy to adjust to the American way of life, he still came off considerably more traditional than many of his contemporaries who were eager to fashion a uniquely American Roman Catholic church.

This fascination with shaping an American Catholicism still remained a popular option during the early years of the nineteenth century despite the increasing Europeanization of the church. Priests continued to use English in the celebration of Mass and the sacraments, despite the 1810 regulations to the contrary. The American spirit of independence certainly fostered such deviant liturgical practices, and European clerics were quick to point this out. The same spirit also prevailed in communities of women religious when they were forced to challenge the cultural excesses of their European clerical superiors. The continued popularity of the congregational parish was another indicator of an American influence in the church. But it should be mentioned that a major reason for its success was undoubtedly the ability of French and German clergy to adapt to this type of local church government. Such a style of government, which involved the active participation of lay people, was not unknown in France and Germany, and for this reason, many priests from these countries supported the concept of the congregational parish.

Thus, by 1815, two schools of thought were manifest in the American Catholic community. One desired to fashion an indigenous church, an American Catholicism; the other wanted to transplant to the new nation a continental European version of Roman Catholicism. These two positions constituted the opposing forces of an ongoing dialectic that would challenge Catholicism in the United States for decades to come. It was clear, at the time of John Carroll's death, in what direction the church was heading; if there was any doubt about this, the massive immigration of European Catholics would decisively settle the issue.

The Immigrant Church, 1820-1920

V

Immigrant Catholics: A Social Profile

DURING THE NINETEENTH CENTURY, the United States exerted a powerful influence on the peoples of Europe. As historian Philip Taylor put it, it acted like "a distant magnet," and in the course of a hundred years, 1820–1920, the United States attracted 33.6 million immigrants to its shores.[1] Other nations, such as Canada, Australia, and Brazil, possessed a similar attraction, but no nation could match the United States in the diversity of its immigration. Walking through city neighborhoods, nineteenth-century visitors marveled at the number of languages spoken and "in some mining and mill towns one might find a dozen ethnic groups inter-mixed in more or less the same neighborhood."[2] Such diversity of peoples was unparalleled, and it has contributed to the well-founded legend that America is indeed a "nation of immigrants." A stunning example of such diversity of people was the American Catholic Church.

As a world religion, Roman Catholicism had set its roots into many nations and cultures. Catholics could be found in the many countries of Europe and throughout the Middle East. But, within each nation, Catholicism was culturally quite homogeneous, with the native culture clearly the dominant force in the church. In the United States it would be quite different. Immigration brought millions of people from diverse cultures and backgrounds to these shores, and this posed a mighty challenge to both nation and church. People of different nationalities were mixed together, and somehow they had to adjust to the American way of life while preserving their own unique heritages. Unity had to be achieved in the midst of diversity. For the Catholic Church, this would prove to be a delicate balancing act, but its continued existence in the United States meant accomplishing this feat. Despite the unusual variety of people who called themselves Catholic, certain groups, by their numbers and influence, stood apart from the rest. During the first half century of immigration, the Irish and the Germans were the two groups that had the most visible impact on American Catholicism.

The Irish had been migrating to the United States since the founding of the colonies. Servants, artisans, merchants, and political exiles journeyed to the New World in hopes of a better life. By the time of the American Revolution, Philadelphia and New York had sizable Irish communities, and numbers of Irish lived in the Catholic counties of southern Maryland. When the time came to take the first federal census, in 1790, people of Irish birth or descent numbered about four hundred thousand. Though Ulster Protestants made up the bulk of this colonial population, Irish Catholics were well represented. During the nineteenth century the Irish presence in the United States increased dramatically, and in contrast to the colonial period the bulk of these immigrants were Catholic.

Though the Irish famine of the latter half of the 1840s is rightly regarded as a watershed in Irish history and a major reason for emigration to the United States, it did not inaugurate the nineteenth-century Irish migration. Long before the potato blight, people had been leaving Ireland in rather impressive numbers; in fact, between 1820 and 1840, more than 260,000 Irish emigrated to America. Once the famine struck, however, the exodus escalated dramatically, and in a brief, six-year, period, 1846–51, over 1 million people left Ireland. The passing of the famine hardly halted the flow of migration, with the result that, between 1851 and 1920, 3.3 million Irish immigrants settled in the United States, bringing the total Irish migration to the United States during this hundred-year period, 1820–1920, to 4.3 million people.[3]

Such massive emigration from a small country was the result of a complex of social and economic changes which took place in nineteenth-century Ireland. Substantial population increase in the early decades of the century was one major cause of the Irish exodus. An outmoded agricultural economy could not keep pace with such massive population growth. Moreover, the heavy reliance on the potato compounded the problem, so that the slightest crop failure could spell disaster. This happened several times in the prefamine years, but the potato blight of the late 1840s and the great famine which followed stretched the limits of human comprehension as one million people starved to death. Such a cosmic catastrophe dramatically accelerated the Irish exodus. Increasing literacy among the peasant population was also a contributing force, as it opened up a world beyond Ireland to a new generation of youth, and the attraction of this world proved irresistible to many young Irish men and women.

The strong kinship network among the Irish and the role this played in financing emigration from Ireland also contributed to the exodus. At home, families and relatives pooled their resources to send the younger men and women to the United States. After their arrival in the United States, these individuals then sent money back to the old country to pay the passage of those left behind. The experience of John O'Connor of County Galway was typical. Leaving his family at home, he set sail for the United States. Soon after his arrival in Baltimore in 1848 he wrote to his wife and children:

> I send home this 10 pound; I hope that it will not be long until I send for ye all. I would make arrangements to send for some of ye, but I expect to bring ye all from Liverpool. I would rather ye would all together than to separate ye from each other. You will be careful as you can about this money, for perhaps I might get a chance before a month . . . [to send for all].[4]

Such remittances amounted to enormous sums of money, over $8 million in some years, and they enabled many poor peasants to make the journey across the ocean.

No single reason can fully explain Irish emigration to the United States. Population growth, an outmoded economy, and famine were major reasons; an increase in literacy and also the Irish kinship tradition contributed to the exodus. During the nineteenth century, all these forces came together, with the result that large numbers of people left Ireland. It was clear, however, that such "significant movement was far from random process, for those who departed shared distinct age, marital status, occupational, and religious characteristics."[5]

The emigrants came from a variety of regions in Ireland. Even though pronounced differences existed between certain areas, such as the western province of Connaught, with its Gaelic-speaking peasant farmers, and the comparatively more prosperous farming area situated in the English-speaking counties of eastern Ireland, Irish emigrants had similar characteristics. Before the 1830s the typical emigrant was a Protestant farm laborer who traveled to the United States as part of a family group. In the 1830s a change took place as more unmarried Catholics from the lowest levels of society began to leave Ireland; by the time of the famine, Catholics made up a clear majority of the emigrants. When the famine struck, it hit the "small farmers and laborers with unprecedented fury," and these individuals, living at the lowest level of Irish society, left Ireland in record numbers.[6] Continuing the trend noticeable since the 1830s, the vast majority of these emigrants were literate single Catholic men and women under thirty-five years of age. The postfamine migration reinforced this pattern, with the typical Irish emigrant being a young man or woman, unmarried, and poor.

The Germans were the other major Catholic immigrant group that settled in the United States during the antebellum period, and like the Irish, they continued to emigrate to America right up until World War I. The first sizable presence of German Catholics developed in colonial Pennsylvania, where the first German parish, Holy Trinity, was organized in Philadelphia in 1787. Once the nineteenth-century wave of emigration got under way, Germans began to emigrate to the United States in record numbers: between 1820 and 1920, close to 5.5 million Germans settled in the United States. Prior to the Civil War, about 1.5 million Germans came to the United States (1,491,985); in the next forty years, 1860–1900, 3.5 million Germans came (3,499,756). The high point of this migration took place in the 1880s, when close to 1.5 million Germans arrived in a single decade. Though it is difficult to determine how many of these immigrants were Catholic, a reasonable estimate would place their number at about 30 percent of the total; in other words, an estimated 1,648,407 German Catholics emigrated to the United States between 1820 and 1920.[7]

The historian Kathleen Neils Conzen has divided German migration into three phases. The first phase, or what she calls the preindustrial phase, lasted until about 1865. During this period, Germany was beginning to experience the problems of overpopulation: too little agricultural land for too many people; in addition, the Industrial Revolution was slowly transforming the economy, as new factories began to take over the traditional work of the artisans. Confronted with forces beyond their control, many farmers and craftsmen decided to emigrate to the United States. Unlike the Irish, these emigrants did not come from the lowest levels of society. John Martin Henni, a German priest in Cincinnati, noticed this and correctly observed:

> It is only the middle classes and especially from the Rhine area who emigrate and venture across the ocean. Mostly they are fathers with large families and single people. Hence, because of the great expense incident to it, it is not the poorest classes who emigrate.[8]

As Henni noted, during this phase of emigration Germans traveled as families, with as many as two thirds to three quarters of all immigrants arriving in family groups. The second phase of migration lasted until about 1895. During these years, Conzen noted, "The number of independent farmers and artisans declined," while the number of farm laborers, displaced by an expanding industrial economy, increased. Consistent with earlier years, most German immigrants, about two thirds of them, arrived as parts of family groups.[9] Of significance to Catholics at this time was the *Kulturkampf,* a period of religious persecution against the Catholic Church. Reaching a high point in the 1870s, this campaign forced many priests and nuns to leave Germany, and a large number of them settled in the United States. The third phase of migration took place during the twentieth century at a time when Germany was becoming more and more industrialized. Emigration to foreign countries slowed down considerably, and the people who did come to the United States in those years tended to be unmarried industrial workers in search of better jobs.

The next sizable group of nineteenth-century Catholic immigrants were the Italians. They did not start emigrating to the United States in any significant numbers until the 1880s; at that time, their numbers began to increase slowly but steadily, with the result that close to one million Italians (959,202) settled in the United States during the last two decades of the century. By 1900, the slow but steady stream of migration had become a tidal wave, and in the next twenty years over three million Italians (3,155,401) emigrated to the United States, and just about all of these people were Catholic.

As was true throughout much of eastern and southern Europe at the time, Italy was experiencing a pronounced increase in population in the late-nineteenth century; between 1880 and 1910, the population increased by more than 6 million people. This significant increase produced a predictable problem: too many people seeking a livelihood on too little decent agricultural land. Coupled with this was a decline in nonagricultural employment opportunities. Unlike Germany, Italy was not entering a period of mature industrialization at the turn of the century; on the contrary, Italian industry was experiencing a depression. Thus, unable to find a piece of land to farm and with the chances of finding work in the village or a nearby city not very promising, millions of Italians turned to emigration as the answer to their dilemma. Since this transformation was most pronounced in the provinces of southern Italy, the vast majority of Italian immigrants came from this region. Emigration, however, was not a fatalistic solution to substantial demographic and economic changes. As historian Josef Barton has shown, those Italians who left their homeland did so "not merely to escape the misery of the village but to survive threats to an old way of life."[10] For these people, emigration was an opportunity for self-improvement and economic advancement; for the vast majority, the United States was "the pot of gold" they were seeking.

The Italians who emigrated to the United States came from a variety of occupations. A study analyzing the occupational backgrounds of a 1909 group of immigrants revealed that about one third were agriculturalists—farmers, shepherds, gardeners, etc.; another third were unskilled workmen and day laborers employed in the construction industry; the remaining individuals were skilled workers such as masons, carpenters, and tailors. Hardly a homogeneous group, these immigrants were also men on the make; as one observer described them, they were "the more frugal, thrifty, and energetic" type.[11]

Unlike the Irish, Italian emigration was a decidedly male phenomenon, with men outnumbering women three to one. These individuals, ranging in age from fourteen to forty-four, included both single and married men. Once they were settled and working in the United States, they began to send for the other members of their families. The saga of Marion Callendrucci of Buffalo was quite typical. "I was thirty when I came here," she said; "My husband was in America and called me. He was here over six years. . . . He took so long because he couldn't get [citizenship] papers. . . . There are many women [in Italy] in the same position."[12] According to a study of the Buffalo Italian community, "The average family waited three and a half to four years to reunite."[13] Of course such chain migration—that is, one person following in the footsteps of an earlier, related emigrant—was quite common among most groups. What was unique about the Italians was the large number who returned to their homeland. Between 1899 and 1924, 3.8 million Italians came to the United States, but 2.1 million returned to Italy; in fact, in some years the numbers of Italians leaving the United States was larger than those arriving. The reason behind this return migration was that many Italian emigrants came to the United States as migrant laborers; "birds of passage," they were called. Once they found work and acquired what they considered sufficient capital, they returned to their families and homeland. With their savings they paid off old debts and, most likely, bought some land. These *Americani,* as the repatriated immigrants were known in Italy, became a sizable presence in many Italian villages.

The other major group of Catholic immigrants who settled in the United States in the post-1880 period were the Polish. Like the Italians, very few Polish had migrated to the United States before 1880; in 1870, for example, only fifty thousand Poles lived in the United States. In the next fifty years, however, more than 2 million Polish immigrants came to America, and the vast majority of them were Catholic.

These immigrants came from Germany, Austria, and Russia, the three countries that had dismembered the ancient kingdom of Poland in the late-eighteenth century. The first wave of emigrants came from German Poland in the 1870s and 1880s; the reason behind their emigration was predictable: too little agricultural land available for too many people. By the 1870s, German Poland had become a region distinguished by large landholdings controlled by local aristocrats; this left a mass of landless or nearly landless peasants, and it was this group of people that decided to emigrate in the 1870s and 1880s. Their motivation was primarily economic and ultimately, as one contemporary observer put it, "a desire to purchase land on more favorable terms than he can do at home and thus become an owner of property."[14] Another contributing cause was the anti-Catholic, anti-Polish *Kulturkampf* of the 1870s. By the 1890s, the situation in German Poland changed as Germany became more and more industrialized; new industries began to develop, and increasingly they absorbed the surplus of farm workers. So great was the demand for industrial labor that after 1890 very few Poles emigrated from Germany.

The next group of Polish emigrants came from Austrian Poland, from the area known as Galicia. The situation in this region was much worse than in German Poland; in fact, "Galicia was the most backward of all Polish regions and one of the most poverty-stricken pockets in Europe."[15] Because of population growth, land was continually subdivided, to the point that a peasant's plot was so small "that, as the saying ran, when a dog lay on a peasant's ground, the dog's tail would protrude on the neighbor's holdings."[16]

In need of work to support his family and desirous of buying a plot of land, the peasant farmer left Galicia to market his labor. During the 1890s, emigration from Galicia picked up, but after 1900 it increased substantially, with the result that close to half a million people emigrated to the industrial areas of Austria, Germany, and other European countries; eventually many of these people came to the United States. Like the Italians, these Polish emigrants were basically migrant workers in search of a well-paying job, and they planned to return to their homeland; in fact, two thirds of all Galician emigrants to the United States between 1905 and 1914 did go back. This phenomenon of return migration was also very evident in Russian Poland.

A principal reason for emigration from Russian Poland was the common problem of Eastern Europe: a sizable increase in the peasant population with no increase in the growth of peasant landholdings. "The result," as historian Caroline Golab put it, "was an upsurge in the number of landless or nearly landless peasants."[17] Industrial expansion alleviated the problem by enabling many landless peasants to find work within Russia. But after 1900 the economic situation changed as the Russian industrial economy went into a tailspin. Countless factory workers joined the landless peasantry, and before long the Poles of Russia turned to emigration as the solution for economic survival. As in Galicia, many of these emigrants planned to return to their homeland once they had acquired sufficient capital to help themselves and their families. "The peasant left," wrote Golab, "only so he could return a better man."[18] The outbreak of World War I, however, took away this possibility, and many Polish immigrants became permanent members of the Polish-American community.

Though there was no typical emigrant, the Polish newcomers had certain traits in common. Almost all of them came from the lower levels of society— peasants or agricultural laborers. As in the Italian migration, men were in the majority, an estimated two of every three immigrants; in addition, the majority of these men, ranging in age from fifteen to forty-four, were single; in 1912, for example, 60 percent of the Polish arrivals were unmarried.[19]

A major immigrant group often overlooked in the history of American immigration is the French Canadians. A proudly Catholic people, they began their migration to the United States during the second half of the nineteenth century, reaching a peak in the 1880–1900 period. By 1910 the United States census counted close to 1 million people (932,238, to be exact) of French-Canadian background, and six years later a religious census reported that over 1 million Catholics (1,026,966) worshiped in parishes where the French language was used; comparative figures for the Polish (1,425,193) and the Italians (1,515,818) indicate the relatively large presence of French Canadians in the American Catholic community in 1916.[20]

The causes behind the emigration of French Canadians were similar to those prevalent in eastern Europe. The Canadian economy was on the decline in the late-nineteenth century, with the milling and lumber industries being especially depressed; the French-Canadian population was on the increase, and this created a shortage of decent agricultural land. Given these conditions, many French Canadians naturally thought of emigration as a strategy for survival, and the closeness of the United States was especially attractive. Moreover, in nearby New England the textile industry was expanding and there was a need for cheap labor. To help direct the flow of emigration, the textile mills sent labor recruiters throughout the Quebec countryside to recruit families for work in the mills. Thus it was not surprising that two of every three French-Canadian immigrants settled in the mill towns of New England.

The southwestern United States experienced a similar immigration because of the closeness of the United States to another country, Mexico. During the colonial period, the Southwest was part of the Spanish empire; in the nineteenth century it became part of the new nation of Mexico. Then, with the Mexican-American war (1846–48), the United States conquered and annexed a vast northern portion of the Mexican nation. At that time, about eighty thousand people of Mexican heritage were incorporated into the United States, three fourths of these people living in one area, namely what was to become the state of New Mexico. In the next fifty years, migration from Mexico across the Mexican-American frontier took place at a rather slow pace, with many people coming only for seasonal work as migrant laborers. The twentieth century, however, witnessed a substantial increase in immigration. Though most of this took place after 1920, an estimated 216,500 Mexicans migrated to the United States during the previous twenty-year period, 1900–1920. Census figures, though underestimated in this instance, do offer some indication of the size of the Mexican community in relation to other Catholic immigrant groups in the United States. The 1910 census numbered 382,002 people of Mexican heritage, while the 1916 religious census stated that 552,244 people belonged to Spanish-speaking parishes; the vast majority of these people were Mexican, and they lived in the border region of the Southwest, an area that has had a Spanish presence since the early-seventeenth century.

These six groups—the Irish, Germans, Italians, Polish, French Canadians, and Mexicans—were the largest Catholic communities in the United States. Using the 1916 religious census as an indicator, they accounted for at least 75 percent of the American Catholic population of 15,721,815.[21] Of the rest of the "foreign" Catholic community (i.e., first- and second-generation), the vast majority was made up of a variety of Eastern European peoples. Among these, several groups stood out in terms of their size.

The Slovaks emigrated from the nineteenth-century Hungarian kingdom that is known today as Czechoslovakia. How many emigrated to the United States is difficult to determine, but historian Mark Stolarik estimated that 500,000 "emigrated to the United States in the late nineteenth and early twentieth centuries"; the vast majority, about 80 percent, were Roman Catholic.[22] Neighbors to the Slovaks were the Czechs, or Bohemians as they were called in the nineteenth century. Prior to World War I, about 350,000 came to the United States, and like the Slovaks, the vast majority of them were Catholics, but they were notoriously indifferent to religion. Unlike other eastern European groups, the Czech emigrants were generally skilled workers, and rather than emigrate individually, they came in family groups.[23] In this respect they resembled the Germans, rather than the Slovaks.

Another major group from eastern Europe were the Lithuanians, 300,000 of whom emigrated to the United States in the fifty years prior to World War I. Peasant Catholics, they left the western frontier of Russia for the land of promise and economic survival. Like their Polish neighbors, a good number of these emigrants were male migrant laborers who planned to return to their homeland, and about 20 percent of them did just that prior to the outbreak of World War I. Another sizable and noteworthy emigrant group were the Ruthenians, referred to today as Ukrainians. Most of these emigrants, about 85 percent, came from the Ukrainian areas of Austria and Hungary; the others emigrated from Russia. Primarily peasant farmers, they left for the same reason as the Poles, the Lithuanians, and the Slovaks: too many people trying to survive on too little available agricultural land. The best estimate of the size of this wave of migration placed the number at 250,000 between 1880 and 1914; on the eve of World War I it was estimated that 500,000 Ruthenian Catholics lived in the United States.[24] In addition, these people were Eastern-Rite Catholics; that is, they worshiped in and observed the customs of an ancient Byzantine liturgical tradition, rather than the Latin liturgical rite of Rome, followed by the overwhelming majority of Catholics in the United States.

These ten groups of immigrants made up the bulk of Catholics living in the United States in the early-twentieth century. Not only did they transform the ethnic profile of the Catholic Church, but they created an incredibly diverse religious denomination. In 1820 the Catholic church included no more than three foreign-language groups; a century later it was a cosmopolitan church speaking twenty-eight languages. In addition to the groups already mentioned, there were sizable numbers of Hungarians, Slovenians, Croats, and Portuguese, as well as numerous smaller groups such as the Syrians, Arabs, and Dutch. Moreover, each one of these groups possessed a measure of cultural diversity within its own boundaries. This was evident among the Italians, for example, a group that included Sicilians, Calabrians, and Romans—three types of people as diverse as Germans, French, and Irish. All groups shared such regional diversity as well as the more particular contrasts associated with differing village origins and language dialects. A study of the Lithuanians in Lawrence, Massachusetts, succinctly captured the extreme diversity inherent in a particular immigrant community; the 1,324 Lithuanians living in Lawrence in 1906 came from all three provinces of czarist Lithuania, and they represented seventy-eight Old World parishes or villages as well as all the major peasant folk cultures and dialects.[25]

When the European emigrants set sail for the United States, it might have been their first trip across the Atlantic, but it was hardly the first time that they had set out in search of work. For these folk, the transatlantic journey was the culmination of a long series of migrations in search of work throughout Europe. What Caroline Golab wrote about the Poles could be said of all immigrant groups: "It was rare to find a Polish immigrant who had not migrated to some other part of Europe or within his own country before coming to America."[26] Once people decided to make the long journey across the Atlantic, their travels were facilitated greatly by a transportation and communication revolution which had developed during the late-nineteenth century.

For the Irish and Germans who emigrated before the Civil War, a transatlantic crossing could be a harrowing experience. Day after day for four to five weeks, the emigrants huddled together in cramped, dingy living quarters on wooden sailing ships; babies were born en route and people died; young folks sang and danced, while others wept and mourned. With the advent of the steamship, in the late 1860s, emigrant travel changed. It became a big business complete with advertising, travel agents, prepaid tickets, and regularly scheduled departures on ships designed to carry people, not lumber, as had been the case in the early days of emigrant travel. The time it took was shortened considerably—seldom more than twelve days from a northern European port such as Hamburg or about three weeks from an Italian port. For the poor in steerage class the journey was hardly an "ocean cruise"; it was a voyage to be endured in cramped living quarters with overtaxed toilet facilities. One redeeming feature, according to the reports available, was the food: it was not bad; in fact some claimed that people ate better on board ship than "they ever did before."[27] Once the voyage ended in an American port, most often New York, the next phase of the emigrant journey began: locating a settlement in the United States.

Finding a home in America was not a random process. Most often, the immigrants followed in the footsteps of relatives and friends who had arrived earlier. In fact, the one spark that often ignited the enthusiasm of people for the United States was the immigrant letter; it passed among family and friends in the Old World village, most often extolling the advantages of America, where as one Pole noted in a letter to his brother, "I live better than a lord in our country. I wish you also to come."[28] Such positive letters were the best advertisement the United States had, and they persuaded many people to join their families and friends in America. But people did not emigrate to the United States merely to enjoy a family reunion; they came in search of work, and the immigrant pattern of settlement clearly indicates this.

Irish immigrants were very inclined to settle in a city along the northern Atlantic seaboard. The reasons for this are not hard to discover. During the nineteenth century the United States was undergoing a period of rapid urbanization; cities were expanding in size and number, and the growing urban economy offered numerous job opportunities to ambitious immigrants. To travel farther inland required additional funds, which the Irish did not have, and to embark on a rural farming career required far too much capital. As a result, the bulk of the Irish gathered along the East Coast in port cities—Boston and New York—where in 1850 they made up one quarter of each city's population. Since the northeastern region—the New England and Middle Atlantic states—remained the economic core of the nation up until the 1870s, this was the region that offered the Irish the best job opportunities and this was where they chose to settle. As such cities as Chicago and San Francisco began to develop, after mid-century, they, too, attracted a relatively large number of Irish, but the pattern that took shape in the 1830s and 1840s remained consistent well into the twentieth century; in fact, in 1970 two thirds of the first- and second-generation Irish-born still chose to live in New England and the Middle Atlantic states.

The Germans adopted a different pattern of settlement. Better off financially than the Irish and more inclined toward farming, they set out for the interior United States, where the westward movement of people was pushing the frontier settlement beyond the Mississippi. By 1850, half of the German immigrants lived in the North Central region of the country—an area stretching from Cincinnati to St. Louis to Milwaukee—"the German triangle," as it was known; the vast majority of the remaining Germans settled in the Middle Atlantic states, New York and Pennsylvania especially. Though the majority of German immigrants came in search of farmland, the city still acted as a magnet for many of them. Milwaukee was a good example of this. The urban center of Wisconsin attracted German "immigrants hoping to earn funds to buy their own farms, those who tried farming and failed, those who saw opportunity for themselves in providing urban services for their farming compatriots, those who realized, instinctively perhaps, that a booming urban frontier provided opportunity in conjunction with the expansion of the agricultural frontier."[29] During the late-nineteenth century, the third phase of German emigration, more German immigrants settled in the cities, so that, by 1920, 67 percent of the German-born were living in the city (places twenty-five hundred or larger in population). This pattern continued so that, by 1950, close to 80 percent of the German population lived in cities in the Middle Atlantic and North Central regions of the country.

The Italian pattern of settlement was more diversified. Large numbers of them chose Middle Atlantic states—Pennsylvania, New York, New Jersey—along with southern New England towns such as New Haven and Providence. These commercial centers, along with New York and Philadelphia, offered a variety of employment opportunities. Relatively large Italian communities also developed in New Orleans and San Francisco, reflecting the sizable presence of Italians in the South and in the Pacific coastal region.

After 1870, the economic industrial core of the nation moved westward, so that by 1910 it stretched from Boston to Milwaukee and from Philadelphia to St. Louis, encompassing the Great Lakes region and the Ohio Valley. By 1910, 85 percent of the foreign-born immigrants lived in this core area. Situated in the western half of this economic core, the Great Lakes area in particular, were such new industrial cities as Cleveland and Chicago. Unlike the older cities of the East, these midwestern industrial cities had many more openings for unskilled workers in the late-nineteenth and early-twentieth centuries and, like magnets, they attracted sizable numbers of Eastern European immigrants; an interlocking transportation system of canals and railroad lines facilitated this move into the Midwest. The other favorite residence of Eastern European groups was the Middle Atlantic region, especially the mining towns of Pennsylvania.

The settlement pattern of the Lithuanians reflected this pattern of regional concentration very well. Large Lithuanian communities were found in Cleveland and Chicago as well as Boston and New York; they also settled in the mining towns of central Pennsylvania and the factory towns of Connecticut and Massachusetts. In other words, the Lithuanians settled throughout the economic industrial core of the Northeast, where jobs for unskilled laborers were most readily available. As was true of most immigrants, the Catholics from Eastern Europe were a very urban people. The one exception were the Czechs, who, like the Germans, were oriented toward farming; over one half of the foreign-born Czechs in 1900 were engaged in agriculture in such farm states as Texas, Nebraska, Wisconsin, Iowa, and Minnesota. The 1920 census confirmed this pattern, noting that 66 percent of the foreign-born Czechs lived in cities, a relatively low figure in comparison with other immigrant groups. Of the 150 Czech Catholic parishes at this time, 120 were in rural areas.[30]

The pattern of settlement of Catholic immigrants clearly exhibited certain features. First of all, the overwhelming majority of Catholic immigrants—the

Mexicans being the one notable exception—settled in the economic core of the nation, an industrial region stretching from Boston to Milwaukee and from Philadelphia to St. Louis. This was the heartland of Catholic America, where, in 1916, seven of every ten Catholics lived (72 percent). Within this area certain groups evidenced a measure of regional preference: the Irish liked New England, as did the French Canadians; the Germans favored the Midwest, as did the Czechs, while half of the Slovaks lived in Pennsylvania. Yet, most shared one trait: they had city addresses.

The immigrants settled in the city principally because they came to the United States in search of work, and the cities of the nation's economic core were the most likely places to find jobs. But not all immigrants gravitated toward the same type of work. A group's cultural and economic background steered them to certain types of work; in the case of rural German immigrants, for example, this meant farming, whereas their urban counterparts were attracted to such trades as carpentry and tailoring. In addition, within each group a definite social hierarchy existed based on the type of work people did. This became more apparent within each group as time passed and more people experienced upward economic mobility.

The work experience of the Irish is the most extensively studied of all immigrant groups; it illustrates very well the tendency of a particular group to concentrate in one area of the economy, as well as the development of a distinct social and economic structure within an immigrant community.

In the early and middle decades of the nineteenth century, roughly the period from 1820 to 1880, the Irish were concentrated at the bottom of the occupational hierarchy. Arriving with no marketable skills except a strong back and a desire for work, large numbers of Irish-born men found employment as unskilled laborers. In Boston in 1850, for example, 62 percent of Irish-born workers were unskilled laborers; in Sacramento it was 53 percent and in Detroit 50 percent. Thirty years later, a similar pattern existed in Boston, where 67 percent of Irish-born workers were unskilled laborers; in Detroit it was 42 percent and in Sacramento, California, 46 percent.[11] As unskilled workers, the Irish performed a variety of tasks: unloading coal and cotton at a New England textile plant, hauling iron at a Pittsburgh foundry, and driving railroad spikes in Chicago. Their wages were frightfully low—no more than a $1.50 a day at mid-century and often less; since they worked only about two thirds of the year, a typical laborer might have earned about $360 a year; a family could not live on such an income except in dismal poverty.

A level above the Irish laborer was the skilled worker such as the machinist, mason, cooper, and blacksmith; about 30 percent of Irish workers were employed in these occupations; the rest, seldom no more than 20 percent in any city, and most often lower, were listed as white collar workers, i.e., people engaged in the professions or as clerks, salesmen, or self-employed artisans.

The concentration of Irish immigrants at the bottom of the social structure necessarily meant that such working-class families needed more than one breadwinner. This meant that wives and children went to work to support the family. In recent years historians have begun to uncover the work patterns of immigrant women, and though the literature on this topic is not very large, some general observations can be made.

The first observation is that a sizable percentage of women did work for wages; in Poughkeepsie, New York, for example, in 1860, 38 percent of all Irish women over fifteen years of age were employed; the study of an Irish neighborhood in New York found that 44 percent of the Irish women between ages fifteen and forty-nine worked.[32] Among those women who were employed, the wife who worked outside the home was the exception. Generally she worked at home by taking in boarders. Using this category of "boarding house keeper" as a type of employment, a study of Poughkeepsie found that, in 1880, 14 percent of Irish wives worked.[33] If the wife did not take in lodgers, then most likely she was employed in industrial homework; i.e., earning money in a particular industry working at home. Such jobs ranged through making hats, umbrellas, baseballs, shoes, and numerous other items in a piecework arrangement.

The unmarried daughter, not the wife, was the typical working woman in the Irish family, and most often she was employed as a domestic servant. In Jersey City, New Jersey, 76 percent of the Irish female work force were employed as domestic servants in 1860; in Poughkeepsie the percentage was 55 percent.[34] Wherever you went, from Poughkeepsie to San Francisco, the pattern was the same, Irish-born women were heavily concentrated in domestic service. Although the job of servant was supposedly an unskilled occupation, it required a diversity of talents. A New York resident's recollections of the life of a domestic suggested as much: ". . . generally an Irish girl. She washed on Monday, ironed on Tuesday, swept on Wednesday, went courting on Thursday, cleaned on Friday, and baked on Saturday. She was cook, waitress, chamber maid, and butler."[35] What was not mentioned were the long hours—sometimes fifteen hours a day and often seven days a week; the pay was not much either, about six dollars a month in addition to room and board. Not surprisingly, the bulk of Irish domestic servants came from lower-working-class families, since it was their extra salary that helped these families survive during the early years of settlement in the United States.

Despite the heavy concentration of Irish men and women at the bottom levels of the occupational hierarchy, a surprisingly large percentage of Irish families owned property, most often no more than a small house and lot. In his study of the Newburyport Irish, Stephan Thernstrom discovered "that Irish working class families were especially successful in accumulating property."[36] Nor was this "land hunger" limited to Newburyport. In Poughkeepsie at mid-century, half of the unskilled Irish laborers owned property; studies of the Irish in San Francisco, Detroit, and Albany also found a relatively high level of property ownership, roughly between 25 and 35 percent, within the Irish community.[37] Though this level of property ownership may appear small by contemporary standards, it compared very favorably with other nineteenth-century immigrant groups. Moreover, the longer the Irish lived in the United States the more they outperformed other groups in terms of property ownership. Though the amount of property owned was not excessive, seldom more than a thousand dollars in value at mid-century, such small successes were a significant achievement for these immigrant families, and they could congratulate themselves that, "thank God, 'tis are own, anyhow, and nobody can take it from us."[38]

The one institution that fed this Irish hunger for land was the building and loan association. A people's bank, it encouraged immigrants to save money and provided them with the mortgage necessary to buy a home. Philadelphia had six hundred such building and loan associations by 1875; they were a common sight across urban America. One of the more successful Irish building and loan associations was the Hibernia Savings and Loan Society, founded in San Francisco in 1859; within ten years it had 14,544 depositors and assets of over ten million dollars.[39]

Property ownership, like occupation, was a good index of the social structure within the Irish community. The unskilled laborer, if he owned property, most likely possessed a modest amount such as a house valued at about six hundred dollars, while the more wealthy members of the community lived in houses valued at five thousand dollars and more. A study of the Irish in Milwaukee pointed out such social differentiation very clearly. One third of Milwaukee's Irish owned property in 1860, with 2 percent owning more than ten thousand dollars' worth of property, 17 percent owning between one thousand and ten thousand dollars' worth, and the remaining 15 percent having less than one thousand dollars' worth. Studies of Philadelphia, Detroit, and San Francisco have come up with similar patterns of property ownership and point to the presence of a sizable Irish middle class during the middle decades of the nineteenth century.[40]

Such eastern cities as New York and Philadelphia had been favorite residences of the Irish since the late-eighteenth century, and by the 1850s they had a large middle class. In New York the "lace curtain" Irish, the snobbish, upwardly mobile part of the community, allegedly first emerged as early as 1831 at the Erin Ball, where "the high price and strict limitation of tickets assured a select attendance, warning away the unwanted 'paddies.' "[41] Counted among the upper ranks of Irish society were such men as the lawyer Charles O'Conor and the merchant Cornelius Heeney. In Philadelphia, such men as Dennis Kelly, a textile manufacturer, and Thomas Cahill, a coal shipper, represented the upper crust of Irish society. In the midwestern city of Detroit the same pattern was present. About 20 percent of the Detroit Irish in

1850 were white-collar workers—such as proprietors of small businesses, real estate salesmen, bankers, builders, lawyers, and physicians. Numbered among them were such success stories as the businessman Richard R. Elliott and the industrialist Jeremiah Dwyer. In San Francisco the Irish were making their mark on Nob Hill in the 1850s. The Irish-born John Sullivan, one of the founders of the Hibernia Savings and Loan Society, had made a fortune out of real estate; Daniel Murphy owned one of the largest dry-goods stores west of Chicago, and the Donahue brothers were wealthy bankers and industrialists.[42]

Though the Irish laborer made up about half of the Irish work force in each of these cities, the presence of men like Richard Elliott of Detroit and John Sullivan of San Francisco pointed out the social stratification present among the Irish at mid-century. Though they had a common heritage and a common faith, the urban Irish were divided along economic and social class lines.

The reason for this diverse social structure is not hard to discover. The Irish had been emigrating to the United States in sizable numbers since the 1820s, and by 1860 or so a good number of Irish were beginning to experience upward economic mobility. The large influx of the poverty-stricken famine immigrants, at least 80 percent of whom were peasants, clearly overshadowed this development within the antebellum Irish community. After 1880 the trend became more noticeable as large numbers of Irish began to experience economic mobility; this was especially true of the second generation, American-born Irish.

Most studies of the Irish work force do not go beyond 1880, due to the unavailability of necessary census data. Those few studies examining this topic have arrived at one major consensus about the Irish laboring community in the 1880–1920 period. The second-generation Irish, the American-born sons and daughters of immigrant parents, experienced significant economic mobility in the post-1880 period, and this in turn led to the development of a large Irish middle class by the early-twentieth century.

Stephan Thernstrom has done the most extensive historical study of economic mobility for the post-1880 period, and as regards the Boston Irish he found, "The American-born children of Irish immigrants fared notably better than their fathers."[43] Though they did not do as well as their Yankee rivals, the Irish increased the size of "their middle class element from 10 percent to 38 percent, and reduced the fraction of low manual workers from 65 to 36 percent."[44] A study of Albany, New York, confirmed this pattern graphically, pointing out the disadvantage of being a foreign-born Irish person at the turn of the century. In 1905, 31 percent of the city's American-born Irish were working in white-collar jobs, whereas only 7 percent of Albany's foreign-born Irish were so employed. The same pattern was true at the other end of the occupational scale, with 43 percent of the foreign-born employed in low manual jobs, while only 25 percent of the American-born Irish were so employed. Other studies have confirmed this pattern of the development of a sizable middle class among the American-born Irish community.[45] The writer James Farrell captured this development in his novels and re-created for his readers the urban neighborhood of Washington Park, home of Chicago's "steam heat" Irish, the middle class who had arrived by the early-twentieth century and could afford the luxury of steam heat.[46]

Another trend evident in the post-1880 period was a dispersal of the Irish work force throughout various sectors of the economy. Unlike the situation at mid-century, when both men and women were heavily concentrated in the unskilled labor market, the situation in the early-twentieth century found the Irish employed in a broader range of occupations, reflecting the development of diversity taking place in industrial America. The work experience of the women illustrates this point very well.

Those few studies done of the Irish female work force in the post-1880 period form a consensus. Like their male counterparts, American-born Irish women moved out of the unskilled labor category and into more middle-class occupations. By 1905, single Irish women in Albany had moved into low white-collar jobs in impressive numbers; shunning the role of domestic servant, they moved into a variety of jobs, with 42 percent of them working as clerks, stenographers, telephone employees, and teachers. An interesting point of comparison is that 90 percent of the foreign-born Irish women in Albany in 1905 still remained locked into the work of domestic servant.[47] As was true elsewhere, social origin had a lot to do with where a person ended up in the occupational hierarchy. Another pattern present in Albany and elsewhere was the development of career women among the American-born Irish. Unlike the situation at mid-century, many single women went to work in 1900 with the hopes of pursuing a career, and among the Irish the most popular career choice was teaching. In fact, the Irish schoolteacher became a common sight in urban America; in some public school systems, Chicago's and Albany's, for example, they accounted for more than half of the faculty.[48]

If teaching was a favorite profession of the Irish woman, politics and the church attracted an unusually large number of Irish men. Politics had become an Irish preserve in urban America, and by the late-nineteenth century, many Americans were bemoaning the fact that the Irish ran the cities of the nation. Though the fear was exaggerated, the Irish were politically in control of many major cities. In addition, they had moved into national political prominence, with numerous Irishmen serving in the House of Representatives and the Senate. In the church, their presence was even more prominent. Though the Irish did not account for more than 50 percent of the Catholic population in 1900, the percentage of Irish priests and bishops was much higher. Among the hierarchy, for example, 62 percent of the bishops in the United States were Irish, and more than half of them had been born in

Ireland. A similar though lesser dominance could be found among the parish clergy. One of the few historical studies done on the Roman Catholic clergy found that 45 percent of all the clergy affiliated with the diocese of St. Paul, Minnesota, from 1850–1930 were of Irish heritage. This Irish hegemony has remained consistent throughout the twentieth century, so that, by 1972, 37 percent of the American clergy and 48 percent of the hierarchy still identified themselves as Irish.[49]

In addition to the presence of a growing Irish middle class, by the early-twentieth century an Irish aristocracy had also emerged. The saga of Thomas E. Murray, the son of an Albany carpenter, rivaled anything Horatio Alger could imagine. Born in 1860 and at work by the age of ten, he eventually made his mark as an engineer and inventor. A genius, he would hold eleven hundred patents, second in number only to Thomas Edison. This Irish Catholic patriarch lived at a fashionable address in Brooklyn with his wife, Catherine, and their eight children, and like an earlier Irish patriarch, Charles Carroll, he had a chapel in his home. Along with the McDonald and Cuddihy clans, Tom and Catherine Murray made Southampton, Long Island, the Newport of the New York Irish aristocracy. When he died in 1929, Thomas Murray's estate was worth about nine million dollars. Rich as he was, Murray's wealth could scarcely rival that of Thomas Fortune Ryan, undoubtedly the wealthiest Irishman in the United States. He was worth about a hundred million dollars in 1910, and it is reported that during his life he gave twenty million dollars to the church. Out West, in California, the Irish aristocracy made it in mining, and the Irish "silver kings" were a prominent fixture in San Francisco society.[50]

Though the Irish aristocracy made up a small percentage of the community, they were a very visible and prominent segment of that society. Furthermore, their presence pointed to the very diverse nature of the American Irish people. Such diversity, present in the middle decades of the nineteenth century, became more pronounced as time passed. Though the foreign-born Irish still worked with their hands in 1900 and experienced very little occupational mobility, their American-born counterparts had done quite well. Many of them hung lace curtains from their windows, while others bragged about their steam heat.

The next-largest group in the Catholic community were the Germans, who made up about 20 to 25 percent of the American Catholic community in 1900. In discussing the work pattern of German immigrants, it would be helpful to be able to differentiate between Christian and Jew, Protestant and Catholic. Most studies of the German immigrant community have been able to distinguish the work patterns of Christians and Jews, with the latter being clearly more urban and more oriented toward retail business and nonmanual work in general. Unfortunately, very few studies have been able to distinguish the work patterns and economic careers of Protestant and Catholic Germans.

Those that have, still remain more speculation than fact regarding what influence religion exercised, if any, in the work careers of these immigrants.[51] Given this limitation, sufficient data do exist to make some sound observations about the work patterns of German Catholic immigrants.

Unlike the Irish, a large number of Germans were attracted to rural America. In 1870, 27 percent of the German work force were in agricultural work, and by 1900 Germans owned 11 percent of the farms in rural America. This tendency to settle in rural areas was especially evident prior to 1900; during the third phase of German immigration, in the early-twentieth century, most newcomers shunned the rural areas in favor of manufacturing jobs available in the cities. German Catholics, many of them coming from the rural areas of the Rhineland provinces, were a very visible part of the rural German community. In southern Indiana, such farming communities as Jasper, Oldenburg, and Ferdinand were German Catholic enclaves. In Stearns County, in rural Minnesota, 36 percent of the population were still German in 1910, and in such villages as St. Martin, St. Cloud, and St. Joseph, German Catholics were just about the only type of people who walked down the street. In St. Martin, for example, 102 of the 118 families living there in 1905 were German, and most if not all were Catholic.[52] Among the urban German community, estimated at 67 percent in 1920, certain distinct patterns of work emerged.

The most thorough study of an urban German community in the pre-1880 period is Kathleen Neils Conzen's work *Immigrant Milwaukee*. Conzen found that among the Milwaukee Germans in 1850, 51 percent of the work force were employed in skilled jobs, whereas 51 percent of the Irish were working as unskilled laborers.[53] This comparative snapshot very accurately portrayed the differing work patterns of the Germans and the Irish. Unlike the Irish, most Germans arrived in the United States with marketable skills and were able to acquire decently paying jobs as carpenters, bakers, shoemakers, tailors, brewers, etc. The situation in Milwaukee was hardly unique. In whatever city they settled, German immigrants were concentrated in skilled occupations. This heavy concentration of Germans in the middle ranges of the occupational hierarchy, however, did not preclude the presence of a sizable number of Germans in the unskilled labor market. In Milwaukee at midcentury, 22 percent of the Germans were so employed; in Detroit, the level was 35 percent; and among New York German Catholics, 25 percent.[54] Though this level of concentration at the bottom of the occupational hierarchy was less than that of the Irish, it certainly was greater than that of native-born Americans. Predictably the worst available jobs went to Irish and German immigrants. As regards white-collar occupations, Germans evidenced a slightly better record than the Irish. In Milwaukee, for example, 17 percent of the Germans, as opposed to 11 percent of the Irish, in 1850 were employed in white-collar occupations such as professionals, managers, petty proprietors, clerks, etc. In some cities, such as Detroit, the opposite was true, with the Irish outperforming the Germans in gaining the more choice jobs. This was the exception, however.[55]

A comparison of urban Irish and German work patterns indicates that about half of the Irish work force were concentrated at the bottom levels of the occupational hierarchy, while the same percentage of the German work force were concentrated in the middle ranges; just about an equally small number of Germans and Irish were engaged in white-collar work (less than 20 percent), while about one quarter to one third of the Irish were engaged in skilled occupations, with a similar number of Germans in unskilled labor. Like the Irish, the Germans were a diverse group occupationally, but their cultural and economic background shaped this diversity in a particular way. Coming from a country that was experiencing the beginnings of an industrial revolution, German immigrants brought skills with them that were marketable in a developing industrial nation. Thus it is not surprising to find the majority of German immigrants employed in skilled trades, whereas the Irish, coming from an underdeveloped, rural country, carried very little in the way of industrial skills or experiences.[56]

The work patterns of German female city dwellers strongly resembled those of the Irish. Unlike the situation of their male counterparts, the cultural and economic experience of the old country appeared to have little influence in shaping the work experience of Irish and German women. A major reason for this was that, given the limited job opportunities for women prior to 1880, immigrant women had a very narrow range of occupations from which to choose; in 1870, for example, half of all women wage earners in the United States worked as domestic servants. Like the Irish, the majority of employed German women worked as domestic servants, while a small percentage were employed in skilled work such as sewing or baking.[57] Like the Irish, the typical German working woman was unmarried; married women remained at home, and their contribution to the economic needs of the family generally consisted of either taking in boarders or doing industrial homework. Though the similarities between the Irish and the German female work experiences were quite striking, the differences, though minor, should be noted. A higher percentage of Irish women worked outside the home, and the Irish had a larger number of unskilled jobs, while more German women were employed in skilled occupations. A study of female workers in Poughkeepsie illustrated these differences. In 1860, 38 percent of Irish women over fifteen years of age worked for wages, as opposed to 13 percent of the Germans; 84 percent of these Irish women were employed in unskilled work, as opposed to 58 percent for the Germans; finally, 13 percent of the Irish worked in skilled jobs, while the corresponding figure for German women was 23 percent. These differences remained consistent up to 1880.[58]

The data on German working women after 1880 are quite limited, but the patterns resembled those of the Irish. In other words, more American-born German women worked for wages than their foreign-born sisters; rather than domestic service jobs, they chose more skilled occupations such as secretary and clerk.

Like the Irish, German immigrants evidenced a hunger for property ownership. This was not surprising, given their concentration in skilled middle-class occupations. Predictably, those studies examining German property ownership have discovered that in comparison with the Irish a slightly larger percentage of the German work force owned property and their holdings tended to be more substantial than those of the Irish.[59] This pattern of property ownership among the Germans pointed to the large middle class that existed in the Catholic community throughout the nineteenth century. Present in the middle decades, it began to expand as time passed, and the second generation acquired a more secure place in the social and economic structure of American society. Among the Germans, however, the path toward upward economic mobility did not appear to rise very high.

In their study of Poughkeepsie, New York, Clyde and Sally Griffen discovered that the immigrant generation of skilled German workers experienced remarkable upward mobility. Half of Poughkeepsie's German-born artisans moved from a wage-earning status to self-employment as the owner of a shop. This success, however, did not extend to their sons, who experienced less occupational mobility than expected. The reason for this was that, given their high status to begin with, the children of self-employed artisans did not have much area for upward mobility. Moreover, as the Griffens noted, these "native-born sons concentrated disproportionately in a narrowing range of crafts which can be interpreted as cul-de-sacs."[60] Still there seems to be no question that at the turn of the century American-born German workers fared much better in gaining white-collar jobs than their foreign-born countrymen.[61] It was these second-generation Germans who made up a large part of the Catholic middle class in 1900, a middle class that had achieved near parity with the American-born white community.

Most historical images of the American Catholic people have focused on the stereotype of a poor, lower-class, immigrant community. By 1900 this was hardly the case. At the beginning of the twentieth century, the American Catholic community had a large middle class made up of American-born sons and daughters of Irish and German immigrants. Though it is difficult to determine how large this group was, one recent study estimated that 20 percent of the Irish and an equal percentage of the Germans were engaged in middle-class occupations, with the bulk of these people working in low white-collar jobs.[62] Beneath this group were blue-collar working-class Catholics, people employed in skilled occupations, many of whom owned their own homes. These two groups, the white-collar middle class and the skilled blue-collar working class, made up a large part of the Catholic community at the turn of the century. These were the people who were sending their sons and daughters to college in increasing numbers in the late-nineteenth and early-twentieth centuries; these were the ethnic and religious leaders in the community. In 1850 their ancestors constituted the Catholic working-class poor, but by 1900 Irish and German Catholics had achieved a modest though significant measure of social mobility. As recent studies have indicated, the pattern of this upward mobility was sufficiently consistent across the country for it to be called characteristically Roman Catholic; in other words, Catholics "moved largely into the skilled and propertied working class and into low white-collar occupations."[63] Situated below these people were the new Catholic immigrants: the Italians, Poles, Slovaks, and other eastern European people. In 1900 these newcomers, along with the Mexican-Americans, made up the bulk of the Catholic lower-class poor.

The Italian newcomers came from rural areas, but in America they settled in the city in such overwhelming numbers that 84 percent of the Italian foreign-born in 1920 were listed as city dwellers. Eight out of ten of these immigrants were unskilled workers who had been employed in the old country as farmers, construction workers, or day laborers. Since few Italian professionals emigrated, the rest of the emigrants were skilled workers such as barbers, tailors, shoemakers, and masons.[64]

Lacking job skills marketable in an urban economy, the bulk of Italian immigrants found employment as unskilled laborers—digging ditches, hauling cement, or loading ships. Their concentration in unskilled jobs recalled earlier Irish patterns, and as the Irish had moved up the occupational ladder, the new immigrants, in this case the Italians, took their place. Stephan Thernstrom pointed this out in his study of Boston, where the occupational profile of the Italians in 1910 strongly resembled that of the Irish twenty years earlier, with 65 percent of the Italians employed in low manual jobs.[65] The work pattern of the New York Italians was similar. In 1880, 60 percent were employed in low manual jobs; twenty-five years later, after the bulk of Italian immigrants had arrived in the United States, 58 percent of the immigrant work force were employed as longshoremen and construction workers. In Buffalo, Chicago, and San Francisco the same pattern prevailed.[66]

For Italians looking for work, a key person was the *padrone*. A labor broker, he was one person who could find what they wanted most: work. As a middleman, the *padrone* negotiated with contractors, government officials, and employment agencies, offering them a pool of workers at a low price. As a godfather to the workers, he took care of such basic needs as housing, food, and transportation. Since many *padroni* financially exploited both workers and employers, the institution had obvious drawbacks, yet it helps to explain why Italian immigrants concentrated in certain types of labor.

The most popular type of job for unskilled Italian immigrants was construction work. In the old country, many Italians were employed as farm laborers, and in urban America the work that came closest to this was excavation work.[67] Moreover, Italians liked to work in groups, avoiding jobs that forced them to be alone, isolated from their countrymen, for long periods of time. Construction work was ideally suited for such group work, and before long the Italian labor gang became an integral part of the construction industry. Italian laborers were especially vital in large work projects, building such urban monuments as New York's Grand Central Station, Washington's Union Station, and Philadelphia's City Hall. Such projects required large numbers of workers, and the *padrone* system could solve that problem; in addition, such group-type labor, involving hundreds of workers, appealed to the Italians. Another industry that attracted Italian laborers was the railroad. This type of work, requiring large numbers of laborers working together, attracted the Italians; before long they became so essential to the railroad industry that it was thought to "be a difficult thing . . . to build a railroad of any considerable length without Italian labor."[68]

Neither the *padrone* system nor the Italian fondness for group work originated in the United States. They were features of the Old World culture and economy that helped to shape the work patterns of Italians in the United States. Other aspects of the Old World culture and economy also influenced the Italian immigrant work experience. Chief among these was the family. A study of San Francisco's Italians revealed how such influence was exercised.

For the Italian newcomer seeking a job, the influence of the father was decisive. The father's occupation had a lot to do with the type of work his son was attracted to in the United States. In the case of the San Francisco Italians, ". . . the sons of fishermen were the most likely of all immigrants to stay in the same line of work in San Francisco. About 50 percent of the immigrant sons of fishermen remained in that business. . . ." In other areas of work—trade and manufacturing—the link with the father's occupation was also very noticeable. Another source of parental influence was land ownership; the correlation between land tenure in Italy and occupations in San Francisco indicates, "On the average, the immigrants whose fathers were either landowners or share-farmers had better jobs than immigrants whose fathers were renters or day laborers." A final source of parental influence was literacy; immigrants who had literate fathers had a decided advantage over those with illiterate fathers and thus gained better jobs in San Francisco.[69]

The economic situation in the Old World also influenced the work patterns of Italian newcomers. Those who came from a more diversified and more modern economic area fared better than those immigrants who came from a town or region whose economy was not so diversified and modern.[70]

The influence of the Old World culture was also evident among Italian women. First of all, few Italian mothers worked outside the home. Even though married women working outside the home was uncommon among women in general, among Italian women it was especially rare. In Buffalo, for example, less than 2 percent of Italian families reported wives working outside the home; in New York City in 1905 it was less than 6 percent.[71] As Virginia Yans-McLaughlin has convincingly demonstrated, this reluctance of married women to work outside the home was particularly pronounced among Italians because of their strong devotion to the family and "the Italian ideal . . . to keep women at home."[72] If they did work outside the home, it was often in work that was family oriented, such as migrant farm work, in which mother and children worked together. In Buffalo, for instance, Italian married women worked in the cannery, principally because they were able to work there side by side with their children. Few Italian women, whether married or single, sought employment as domestic servants. The reason for this was also rooted in cultural traits, in this case the reluctance of Italian men to "permit their wives to work under another man's roof" and the preference of women to avoid work that would separate them from their families.[73] But not all Italian women shunned work outside the family context. Young unmarried women did work in factories in such cities as New York, Chicago, and Philadelphia, but characteristically they preferred to work in garment or textile factories, "where women would be the only workers and where sisters, mothers, daughters and other female relatives could serve as chaperones."[74] Single Italian women were also represented in the teaching profession, but their numbers were few in comparison with the Irish.[75]

Like most other immigrant groups, the Italians were eager to own property. The way to achieve this goal was by saving money, and according to one Sicilian, "The immigrants knew how to save money." One way they saved, he said, was by eating "Pasta and beans every day."[76] What money they saved they put into savings banks founded by the Italian community; San Francisco had four such savings banks in 1910, with the deposits totaling 14 million dollars.[77] As regards property ownership, a study of Cleveland found that more than half of the Italians owned property (57 percent), which compared favorably with other immigrant groups. A similar level of Italian property ownership seemed to prevail in Chicago and Buffalo as well.[78]

Property ownership was certainly a symbol of success, and like other immigrants, Italians shared in the American success story. Thomas Kessner has done the most thorough study of this question; in his study of New York he found, "If an Italian immigrant remained in the city one decade his chance of proceeding from a blue collar job to a white collar position was 32 percent—not bleak by any standard." Studies of San Francisco, Chicago, and Cleveland arrived at similar conclusions of modest social mobility among Italian immigrants.[79]

An important aspect of Italian mobility and one not really pertinent to the Irish and German experience was the issue of returning or not returning to the old country. Many Italian immigrants came to the United States in search of a job, not a career, and planned to return to Italy, where their savings would enable them to become small landowners. Undoubtedly this attitude had a negative influence on the rate of Italian economic mobility, but at the same time, those Italians who remained in the United States—and as the twentieth century progressed, their numbers grew larger—were intent on making it in America. Though they may not have initially fared as well as their countrymen who returned to Italy, their persistence found its rewards in the second generation. Among these children of the immigrants the usual pattern emerged: they outperformed their fathers and mothers in terms of social mobility. Compared with the children of Irish and German immigrants, however, they lagged behind in occupational achievement; when compared with the children of the Italian returnees, they did much better.[80]

Like the Italians, Polish Catholic immigrants came to the United States as unskilled migrant laborers in search of jobs. Eager to work, they headed for the factories and steel mills of the Midwest. In Chicago, Polish workers were concentrated in the meat-packing industry and the steel mills of the South Side. On the city's North Side they worked in garment factories. The nearby steel mills of Gary, Indiana, also attracted large numbers of Polish workers, as did the factories of South Bend. In Detroit they concentrated in the automobile industry, whereas in Cleveland large numbers worked in the steel mills. The coal-mining region of Pennsylvania was the other area that attracted large numbers of Polish immigrant workers. The state's first Polish settlements were in the heart of coal country: Shamokin (1870), Shenandoah (1873), Nanticoke (1875), and Blossburg (1875). As immigration increased, large numbers of Poles continued to settle in the mining towns of Pennsylvania, where the demand for unskilled labor grew as Pennsylvania's industries expanded.[81]

Though the vast majority of Polish immigrants were employed as unskilled laborers, a minority were able to acquire skilled jobs. A study of the small Polish community in Philadelphia found that in 1915 about 24 percent of the city's Polish workers were employed in such semiskilled and skilled occupations as carpentry, cabinet-making, and blacksmithing, and as machinists. A study of Catholic Polish heads of families in Minneapolis found 41 percent of the sample group so employed, while in Cleveland a similar sample of Polish workers had about 30 percent working in semiskilled and skilled jobs.[82] These studies underscore the point that a minority of Poles did acquire skilled jobs in urban America.

Given the preponderance of unskilled workers in the Polish community and their meager wages (the average daily wage in Pennsylvania's mines and steel mills in 1915 was $2.22), most families needed additional income to survive, and this invariably meant that women went to work in factories, but as Caroline Golab noted, ". . . unmarried Polish girls in America did not remain unmarried very long."[83] Once married, Polish women shunned factory work and took up one or more of the usual occupations of immigrant women: domestic service, taking in boarders, and industrial homework. Domestic service was especially popular with Polish women, and they gravitated toward the higher-paying jobs of cleaning offices, hotels, businesses, schools, and churches. Not surprisingly the stereotype of the "Polish cleaning lady" became very common.

The ability of Polish women, along with their children, to add additional income to the family meant that many Polish households not only survived, but were able to build up a modest savings account. As was true with other immigrant groups, such savings formed the basis for a famous neighborhood institution, the Polish Building and Loan Society. These societies were founded for one basic purpose: to help immigrants purchase their own homes. Like the Irish before them, the Polish had a strong desire to own land. A Polish proverb put it very succinctly: "A man without land is like a man without legs: he crawls about but cannot get anywhere."[84] Unable to realize their wish in the old country, Polish immigrants sought to attain it in the New World, where owning land most often meant a small lot with a home and garden, rather than a farm. The newcomers realized "from past experience," noted a Polish observer, "that the man without his own land and home has always been a serf, a slave."[85] Home ownership thus had a special meaning for Poles, and the proliferation of building and loan associations was eloquent testimony to this; in the small town of South Bend, Indiana, two building and loan associations existed by the 1890s; one of them, the Kosciuszko Building and Loan Association, had assets of $2 million early in the twentieth century; it was the largest building and loan association in the state outside of Indianapolis. At least 60 such societies were established in Chicago by 1925; nationwide the number reached 550, with a membership of 400,000 people and assets of $330 million.[86]

Home ownership among the Polish, as was true with other immigrant groups, should not be misunderstood as a sign of upward economic mobility. Indeed it was a clear sign of thrift, but not of economic advancement. To the steelworker and the coal miner, home ownership was clearly something to be proud of, an obvious improvement from the Old World. To measure economic advancement, however, it is necessary to look beyond home ownership for other evidence of economic mobility; in the case of the Polish, the data are scarce indeed.

A study of three cities, Minneapolis, Cleveland, and Utica, New York, found that prior to 1900, Polish workers remained concentrated in unskilled work. Between 1900 and 1920, Polish heads of families were better represented in skilled occupations and low white-collar jobs, but as regards individual economic mobility in this period, the evidence, though scanty, suggests very little advancement. One sign of advancement was the number of small proprietors who set up their stores in the ethnic neighborhood. Small entrepreneurs, they ran groceries, saloons, bakeries, and other stores that met the needs of the immigrants. But these business men and women made up a small minority in the community. The majority of workers remained locked into unskilled or semiskilled jobs. Nor did this pattern, evident before 1920, change very much in the pre-World War II era.[87]

An immigrant group that experienced even less social mobility than the Polish were the French Canadians. Attracted to the United States by the expansion of the New England textile industry, the vast majority of French Canadians were employed as factory workers in the small and medium-size mill towns of New England. This pattern was evident from the very beginning of immigration, and by 1890 over 70 percent of the French Canadians working in New England "were in manufacturing and mechanical industries; and, of this number, quite the largest proportion were to be found in factories and mills."[88] In Holyoke, Massachusetts, for instance, 40 percent of the men working in the local cotton mills in 1885 were French Canadians; in the Amoskeag Mills, in Manchester, New Hampshire, 40 percent of the work force in 1900 were French Canadians. In other mill towns in New Hampshire and Maine, French Canadians made up as much as 60 percent of the work force in the textile industry.[89]

A unique feature of the French-Canadian work experience was its family orientation. Unlike the steel mills and the mines, where strength and physical endurance were essential requirements, work in textile mills was well suited to women, and many French-Canadian mothers and daughters did work in the mills; a 1910 study, for example, found that 70 percent of French-Canadian working women were employed in factories; only 10 percent were employed as domestic servants.[90] This preference for factory work set French-Canadian women apart from Polish and Italian working women. In addition to large numbers of women working in textile factories, many children worked there as well, contributing as much as one third of the total family income. Though the percentage of French-Canadian child breadwinners was most likely not higher than that of other groups, their concentration in the mills, where they worked alongside brothers and sisters, mothers and fathers, was peculiarly French Canadian. The textile industry encouraged such family work patterns and even sought to recruit entire French-Canadian families, with larger families receiving more preference. Such emphasis on the family had an obvious influence on the French-Canadian work experience. According to historian Tamara Hareven, "the family and the kin group served as the labor recruiter, the organizer of migration roots, and the housing agent. Within the mill itself, the family exercised job controls in the workrooms, directed the work choices of its members within certain limits, and influenced their placement in the mill. Finally, the family also became a major socializer of its members for industrial life."[91]

The heavy concentration of French Canadians, both young and old, in a single industry remained persistent throughout the early decades of the twentieth century, and as a result French Canadians experienced very little social mobility. What social mobility there was took place after 1910 as American-born French Canadians became more numerous; for those working in the mills, mobility most often meant acquiring a skilled job in the factory. As was true in other immigrant communities, a small middle class had developed composed mainly of small businessmen and storekeepers who served the particular needs of the closely knit French-Canadian community; after 1910 a number of professionals such as doctors and lawyers also emerged. The dominant pattern in the pre-1920 period, however, was the blue-collar, working-class nature of the French-Canadian community, and in this regard they more closely resembled the Polish and the Italians, rather than the Irish and the Germans. This blue-collar dominance, coupled with very meager social mobility, persisted throughout the first half of the twentieth century.

Even though large numbers of French Canadians lived in factory-owned tenements, ". . . one of the strongest desires among them," observed a contemporary, "is to own their own homes"; to accomplish this, they established their own building and loan associations.[92] Though it is difficult to determine the extent of home ownership among French-Canadian workers, it is clear that it did increase after 1910 as lower-middle-class and middle-class residential areas emerged on the periphery of crowded tenement districts in towns like Nashua, New Hampshire, and Woonsocket, Rhode Island.

The work experience of the Mexican Americans was very different from all other Catholic ethnic groups. In the Southwest, land was the basis of the economy, and many Mexican Americans owned their own ranches and farms; others farmed and raised cattle on the communal lands of the *pueblos*. But after the American conquest of 1848 the Mexican people began to lose control over their land. This loss of land took place throughout the entire Southwest, and its effect on the Mexican-American people was disastrous. "The loss of land," Carlos Cortes noted, "eroded their economic base, undermined their political power, and displaced ranch workers, small farmers, and residents of towns with lost or truncated communal land grants."[93] Dispossessed of their land and displaced from their traditional pastoral economy, most Mexican Americans were forced into the unskilled labor market of the new, expanding American economy. In Texas they picked cotton, and in the California fields they harvested fruit; in New Mexico they worked as sheep herders and miners, and throughout the entire Southwest, Mexican Americans helped to build the railroad. These four industries—farming, ranching, mining, and railroad construction—employed the vast majority of Mexican Americans, and predictably they were concentrated in unskilled occupations. Nor was it any better for those who lived in the cities. In 1880 in San Diego, 80 percent of the Mexican work force were unskilled laborers; in Santa Barbara, it was 80 percent, and in Los Angeles, 65 percent.[94] This pattern of downward mobility from landowner to unskilled laborer did not change during the nineteenth century, nor did the situation improve in the early-twentieth century. The best that can be said of the pre-World War I experience of the Mexican Americans is that their situation did not deteriorate any further. They experienced little downward or upward mobility during the early-twentieth century. Of all Catholic ethnic groups, they were clearly the most disadvantaged. While other groups experienced various degrees of upward mobility, the Mexican Americans remained stuck at the bottom of the socioeconomic ladder.

Because of the economic decline of the Mexican Americans, many women were forced into the labor market. This pattern began to develop during the 1880s and 1890s, and with each passing decade the number of working women increased. One type of work widespread among Mexican Americans was farm labor; employed at piecework rates, entire families worked in the fields harvesting the crops. For many Mexican-American women, such part-time, seasonal employment was their principal type of work outside the home. Other women worked in the more traditional areas of female labor, such as domestic service or in jobs at garment factories and food-processing plants. As was true with other immigrant groups, after 1910 or so, Mexican-American women living in urban areas began to move into service jobs such as sales clerk; the vast majority, however, still worked in unskilled positions.[95]

The work experience of the Slovaks, Lithuanians, and Ukrainians closely resembled that of other immigrants from eastern Europe. Employed in mines, steel mills, and factories, they worked with their hands at tasks requiring physical strength and endurance but few skills. This concentration in manual labor persisted throughout the immigration generation; for the fortunate few who experienced economic mobility, it generally meant acquiring a semiskilled or skilled job in the mill or factory. Given this situation, women entered the labor market either as domestic servants or as boardinghouse keepers; children in these communities also went to work at an early age, taking up menial jobs for very meager wages. The one eastern European immigrant group that deviated from the norm were the Czechs. Resembling the Germans, large numbers of Czechs were employed in skilled-labor jobs in the garment industry and in manufacturing; in 1900, only 14 percent of the foreign-born Czech men were employed as unskilled laborers, an incredibly low number. More than half of the immigrant Czechs, about 55 percent, were engaged in agriculture, and the vast majority (80 percent) owned their own farms. In urban communities, Czech women worked as tailors, cigar makers, and domestics.[96]

The Czech experience illustrates a major point about the Catholic immigrant community: no easy generalizations can adequately describe the community, because it was so diverse. Ethnic diversity was its most obvious feature, with six major groups—Irish, Germans, Italians, Polish, French

Canadians, and Mexican Americans—accounting for at least 75 percent of the population by 1920; the remainder was made up of twenty-two groups, with four—the Slovaks, Lithuanians, Ukrainians, and Czechs—being the largest of these. No single reason can explain why these people emigrated to the United States. Famine drove many of the Irish to the shores of America in the 1840s, the availability of work attracted the Italians, religious persecution persuaded the Germans to leave the old country, and the likelihood of military conscription motivated young Polish men to emigrate. Upon arrival, immigrant Catholics, like most newcomers, chose to settle in cities in the economic core of the nation, a region which by 1900 stretched from Milwaukee to Boston. The one exception to this, of course, was the rural-based Mexican Americans of the Southwest. Within the cities immigrant communities took shape, and clearly defined boundary lines of language and culture set them apart from one another; even within particular communities regional differences and loyalties transplanted from the old country created internal divisions. Ethnic and regional differences, however, were not the only sources of diversity. Equally important was the influence of social class.

The immigrant Catholic community was a multilayered society differentiated by occupational status or what is more commonly referred to as class. In the middle of the nineteenth century, the bottom level of Catholic society was made up of recently arrived Irish and German immigrants, with the Irish clearly outnumbering the Germans by as much as two to one in some cities. Unskilled workers with their families, they accounted for the majority of Catholics in the 1850s. German immigrants and native-born Americans made up the bulk of the middle class; these were the skilled workers and lower-level white-collar workers such as clerks, managers, and small businessmen. The upper level of the Catholic community was much smaller, made up principally of American-born individuals of Irish and German heritage who were either professionals or well-to-do businessmen. At mid-century the Catholic community, in terms of economic class, resembled a pyramid with very few professionals or families of wealth at the top and large numbers of immigrants situated at the bottom level of society; in between was a small middle class of immigrants and native-born Catholics.

By the early-twentieth century, economic class continued to draw very bold lines of division throughout the community, but within the various levels of society, changes had occurred. The more recent immigrants were clustered at the bottom. Polish, Italians, French Canadians, and Mexican Americans were the most numerous groups situated at this level, which was composed of the unskilled working class. Some Irish and Germans were at this level of society, especially the more recent arrivals, but they were clearly outnumbered by immigrants from eastern and southern Europe. Though the size of the Catholic upper class did not appear to increase in any dramatic way, more people of Irish descent were represented at this level of society than a half century earlier. A more striking change was the size of the middle class. This had increased since the mid-nineteenth century as second- and third-generation Irish and Germans experienced a measure of social mobility; also visible at this level were the small entrepreneurs of the Polish, Italian, and French-Canadian communities. Though the basic pyramid shape had not changed, its midsection was clearly larger than before. What was significant, however, was not so much the shape or the size of each level of society, but the lines of division these levels created within the community. Like ethnicity, economic class divided the community, and in so doing it reinforced the pattern of a multilayered Catholic community.

VI

The Parish and the People

FOR IMMIGRANTS, the shock of change upon arrival in the United States was enormous. Nothing could fully prepare them for the strange, new world they entered as they stepped off the boat. A language barrier immediately put most of them at a decided disadvantage and clearly underscored their newcomer, foreigner status. A new way of counting money, different housing arrangements, and strange styles of dress were just some of the adjustments immigrants had to make. For Catholic immigrants, there also was the reality that the United States was a Protestant nation, not a Catholic country. They knew this before they came, but experiencing it at first hand was still a shock. Those arriving in the early-nineteenth century could walk up and down Main Street and never see a Catholic church. If they were fortunate enough to be in a large city like New York or Philadelphia, they could eventually find a church, but invariably it was a modest structure on a side street. In smaller cities and towns, immigrants would be lucky if they found a Catholic church at all. This was quite a change from the old country, where the church occupied a prominent place in the rural village, and cathedrals decorated city squares. Like the immigrants, the Catholic Church was in a very real sense a newcomer to the United States. Columbus may have prayed to Mary, Jesuit missionaries may have worked with the Indians, and Catholics could claim to be the founders of one of the original thirteen colonies. But after the passage of three hundred years, Catholics were still a quaint oddity in the United States. In Baltimore, Philadelphia, and Bardstown, Kentucky, they were quite visible. That was clearly the exception, however; in most towns and cities, Catholics were an invisible minority.

Since there were few churches and barely the semblance of any institutional structure or organization in the early years of the nineteenth century, "everything," as one priest put it, was "beginning from scratch."[1] Catholics had to organize themselves and build churches where, before, there were no churches. The key institution in this organizational process was the parish.

In a local community or neighborhood, the parish is a particular representation of the Church universal; this is where the local Catholic community manifests its beliefs. Given the complexity of late-twentieth-century society, this was more true in the nineteenth century than it is today. In fact the nineteenth century was a time when the parish was undergoing a revival, and by the second half of the century it had become the vital center of Catholic life. Thus, for the historian interested in understanding the development of Catholicism during the century of immigration, the parish is an excellent focal point. It is a window in the wall, through which Catholic life can be observed.

As a religious institution, the parish was the focal point for the manifestation of Catholic beliefs. To discover the religion of the people, historians must necessarily turn to the local church. But the parish was also a social institution, and it can and should be studied from this perspective as well. Specifically this means looking at the parish as a community organization that brought people together. How did Catholic immigrants organize themselves in the strange, new world of Protestant America? Were there particular patterns or styles of organization noticeable across the country? Did these ways of organization change over the course of time? What was the role of lay people and clergy in this area of parish life? Were there differences among immigrant groups as regards involvement in parish affairs? To understand the parish more fully, answers to these questions must be found. Such information will uncover the social function of the parish, and when combined with a study of the parish as a religious institution, the theme of the next chapter, a more comprehensive understanding of immigrant Catholic life will be available. Too often, church historians have limited their horizons to the study of the parish as a religious institution, and seldom have they sought to examine its social functions. At the same time, social historians most often have limited themselves to a study of the parish as a social institution and have left the area of religion untouched. A study of the parish as both a social and a religious institution is necessary so that the perspectives and insights of religious history and social history can be joined together to enrich our understanding of not just the parish, but of immigrant Catholic life as well.

No more than two hundred Catholics lived in New York City in the 1780s. From time to time, an itinerant priest celebrated Mass for them, but they had no resident pastor. The absence of a priest, however, did not cool the people's desire to organize themselves and establish a Catholic presence in New York. This occurred in 1785, when a group of twenty-two Catholic laymen petitioned the city's common council for "a suitable site on which we can construct a church, being in this encouraged by the happy tolerance accorded by the new constitution of this State and the privilege of professing publicly our religion here."[2] Though the petition was unsuccessful, they pressed on, and in June of that year the leaders of the community incorporated themselves as "The Trustees of the Roman Catholic Church in the City of New York." With money collected from both Catholics and Protestants, they bought five farm lots from Trinity Episcopal Church, and on October 5, 1785, the cornerstone of St. Peter's church was put in place.

In Boston, the organization of the first parish community, in 1788, began somewhat differently. Boston's Catholics had the benefit of a resident French priest, Abbé Claude de la Poterie, and lay people and priest worked together to draw up regulations for the local Catholic community. They decided to hold regular monthly meetings on the first Sunday of each month; they set the time for services on Sunday with Mass in the morning and vespers and benediction in the afternoon, and they elected two church wardens or trustees to take care of the church. A few weeks later, the people took on the responsibility of providing a residence for the *abbé* and paying him a salary.[3]

In Kentucky, a general pattern prevailed as regards the organization of the local community. The procedure in Bardstown was typical. About seventy families made up the local Catholic community in the late 1790s. After meeting for religious services in private residences for some time, they finally decided to build their own church. Land was donated by a Catholic, and the "congregation" began to build a church. But because of "the difficulty of raising money in the country" it took almost four years for the small log chapel to be completed.[4]

Other examples from the late-eighteenth and early-nineteenth centuries could be given, but the pattern is clear. Lay people were very involved in the organization of local Catholic communities. In some instances, they acted on their own as in New York City; at other times, priest and people worked together to form the local congregation. During the republican period of American Catholicism, the central role of the laity in the formation of local congregations eventually became institutionalized in the lay-trustee system of parish government. This tradition carried over into the era of the immigrant church, principally because the parish continued to serve as the primary form of association for local Catholic communities.

Immigration clearly transformed the church. In 1820, American Catholicism was still a missionary outpost equal in significance to a small diocese in Europe and surpassed in importance by the church in Canada and Cuba. Compared with other religious denominations in the United States, Roman Catholicism was in a subordinate position. In 1820 it had fewer churches, 124, than any other denomination, and its estimated population of 195,000 people placed it behind the Methodists and the Baptists. But the situation changed dramatically in the next few decades as thousands of Irish and Germans immigrated to the United States. The impact upon the church was astounding. Population increased by leaps and bounds, so that in 1850 Catholics numbered 1,606,000, and not only had they become the single largest denomination in the country, but they outnumbered the Methodists by more than a quarter of a million people. In the next decade the number of Catholics just about doubled, reaching a total of 3,103,000 by 1860. The number of churches had increased to 2,385 by 1860, and the 150 clergymen of 1820 had multiplied almost fifteen times, reaching a total of 2,235.[5]

Since John Carroll had become bishop of Baltimore, American Catholicism had steadily been moving in the direction of becoming a church of immigrants. Although the Anglo-American ethos left over from colonial days in Maryland was still very much alive in the early years of the nineteenth century, it had vanished for all practical purposes by 1860. Catholicism had become a church of immigrants. New York City illustrates this change as dramatically as any other community. In 1810, one Catholic parish served a community of ten thousand people in New York; fifty years later, Catholics numbered about four hundred thousand and the city had thirty-two Catholic churches. Of these churches, 70 percent could be described as Irish, and the clergy was said to be "almost entirely Irish." The next-largest group were the Germans, who occupied one out of every four churches in the city, with a total of about fifty thousand Germans belonging to these parishes in 1865.[6]

The other noticeable trend was the increased urbanization of the Catholic community. Since the Revolution, Catholicism was steadily becoming an urban church. Baltimore had replaced St. Mary's County as the center of Maryland Catholicism; sizable communities were beginning to develop in Philadelphia, New York, and Boston. This trend intensified as immigrants flooded the urban centers of the nation. In fact, by 1890 the Catholic urban population was so large that it outnumbered the urban populations of all other religious denominations combined. There were obviously many rural Catholic communities scattered across the country, but the city had become the favorite home for immigrant Catholics. This can be clearly seen in Kentucky. The small village of Bardstown was for years the center of Kentucky Catholicism. But the movement of population shifted away from Bardstown in the early decades of the nineteenth century; realizing this, Bishop Flaget moved the administrative center of the diocese to Louisville in 1841. By that time, Louisville had become not only the metropolitan center of Kentucky, but also the home of one quarter of the state's Catholic population.[7]

Whether talking about the rural frontier or the urban metropolis, historians have increasingly come to acknowledge the importance of religion in shaping the identity of the immigrants. "Ethnic association," observed historian Timothy Smith, "was determined largely by the immigrant's identification with a particular religious tradition. The appeal of common language, national feeling, and belief in a common descent was sufficient in only a few minor cases to outweigh the attraction of religious affiliation as an organizing impulse."[8] The most common way this took place was through the organization of a local church community. In the antebellum period, the clearest example of a people organizing themselves around a local church was the Germans.

German Catholics organized the first national parish in Philadelphia in 1787 in order "to keep up their respective nation and language." Two years later, Holy Trinity Church was open for services. In New York, German Catholics wanted to organize their own parish in 1808, where they could worship in their "Mother Tongue," but their plans did not materialize until twenty-five years later, when St. Nicholas Church was finally organized. In both instances the people strongly desired to preserve their culture and religion, and the way they wanted to achieve this was by practicing their religion in their native language. This was the key. The Germans, like other foreign-speaking groups, strongly believed that "language saves faith." As one German priest put it, ". . . religion and nationality go hand in hand," and the most concrete expression of this union between religion and nationality was the national parish.[9]

In the republican period, the ideal was to establish "not Irish, or English, or French Congregations and Churches, but Catholic-American Congregations and Churches."[10] Philadelphia's Holy Trinity Church was clearly the exception to this view of John Carroll. But as immigration increased and more Germans arrived in the United States, the national parish soon became the norm.

Traditionally, American Catholic parishes had been organized territorially; this meant that all the people living in a designated geographical area belonged to the same parish. Such territorial parishes disregarded any distinction of people based on nationality. But the arrival of large numbers of immigrants posed a problem. Even though they might have lived in the same area of the city, German and Irish Catholics were not willing to worship in the same church. Each group wanted to worship and pray in its own language and according to the tradition and custom of the Old World; as more diverse groups of Catholic immigrants arrived in the United States, the problem became even more acute. The national parish was a pragmatic response to this problem, and it became the principal institution the immigrants established in their attempt to preserve the religious life of the old country. The distinguishing element in the national parish was language, rather than nationality, even though the two are often thought to be identical. This was especially true during the nineteenth century, when the sense of nationality was not yet very well developed among European immigrants.

By organizing their own national parishes, immigrant Catholics hoped to hear sermons in their mother tongue, practice the devotions and customs of the old country, and raise their children in the faith of their fathers and mothers. In the words of one missionary, such parishes enabled the immigrants to "preserve incorrupt the sacred treasures of religion and to transmit it to their children."[11] For the immigrants, then, religion became a center around which they organized, and at the local level this meant the founding of a national parish. Though religion was not the only focal point for organization, it was clearly one of the principal ways by which immigrants identified themselves. Moreover, it was one area that involved the participation of the entire family, both adults and children, and this gave it added importance as a primary source of association and identification.

Immigrant settlement patterns reinforced this tendency to establish national parishes. The newcomers not only settled in cities, but they also chose to live in distinct neighborhoods. As each wave of newcomers followed in the footsteps of their predecessors, certain neighborhoods eventually took on a decidedly ethnic character and acquired such names as Corktown in Detroit and Little Germany on New York's Lower East Side. Such clustering heightened the sense of group consciousness, and in seeking a badge of identification in a cosmopolitan city, religion became an obvious choice. In fact, it was often the first step in the mobilization of a community's sense of group consciousness. Invariably this meant the founding of a national parish. Of course, this was as true of German Protestants as it was of German Catholics. A historical tour of any urban German neighborhood would clearly point this out and underscore the observation of Timothy Smith that religious affiliation was a major organizing impulse for the immigrants.

In the German community, lay people had a central role in the organization of parishes. In New York, Philadelphia, and other cities a familiar pattern emerged. Lay leaders in the community would emerge and organize their countrymen around the goal of founding a parish; they would purchase some land, canvass the city for funds, and then proceed to build a church. Then they would ask the bishop to send them a priest who, as one group put it, "is capable of undertaking the Spiritual Care of our souls in the German language, which is our Mother Tongue."[12] The founding of the German parish of St. John the Baptist in Cincinnati illustrated the extent to which lay people became involved in the organization of a parish.

The new church was to be situated in the Over the Rhine area, Cincinnati's little Germany. The first organizational meeting took place during the last week of October 1844 in a German church in Over the Rhine. A building committee of ten laymen were chosen, and they then proceeded to draft a constitution outlining the procedures for building the church. At another public meeting, German Catholics ratified the constitution, and the establishment of St. John the Baptist parish was underway. The people purchased land for the church in the name of the bishop, John Purcell, and voted to name the church after his patron saint. Between October and March they held eight public meetings and voted upon such issues as the maximum price to be paid for the property, the number of doors in the church, the thickness of its walls, and the size of its windows. As was true elsewhere, a collection committee, organized at a public meeting, solicited funds throughout the city for the church's construction.

On March 25, 1845, the laying of the cornerstone took place highlighted by an elaborate procession through Over the Rhine. The people had planned the ceremony, procession, and accompanying festivities. Then, in November of 1845, the dedication of the church took place. While all this was going on, the people also decided to build a school, and like the planning of the church, this "was agreed to and carried out with the accustomed meetings."[13]

Lay involvement in the parish did not end with the opening of the new church. In Cincinnati and in other places as well, German congregations established the lay-trustee system of parish government. In Cincinnati as in Chicago, the lay-trustee system had a unique twist to it: even though the bishop in each place owned all church property, the Germans still maintained a tradition of lay government in the parish. Every German parish in Cincinnati had lay trustees, and their sphere of activity was outlined in regulations issued by the bishop in 1851. This system of parish government persisted throughout the nineteenth century, and all the evidence suggests that in Cincinnati both prelates and people were satisfied with it.[14]

Even though language was a key reason for the close relationship among religion, nationality, and parish in the German community, a similar relationship prevailed among the English-speaking Irish. The Irish publicist Thomas D'Arcy McGee observed that among the Irish, religion was "the most important of all topics."[15] Two centuries of attack and discrimination had strengthened the importance of religion among Irish Catholics, and as Oscar Handlin put it so well, "Beliefs maintained at great personal sacrifice are not lightly held."[16] Nor was an ocean journey sufficient to erase deeply rooted beliefs. Among the immigrants, religion remained an important identifying mark. Like nationality, it defined the person, helping to explain who he or she was. A world of difference separated Catholic and Protestant Irish, and the discriminating quality was not the land of one's birth, but the faith of one's family. Much exaggerated romanticism has crept into Irish-American history extolling the faith of the people and their devotion to the Catholic Church. Even after discounting for such exaggeration, it still remains obvious to the unbiased observer that religion occupied a central place in the lives of the Irish. In an urban neighborhood or a rural town, the most visible expression of this was the parish church.

The parish church was a standard landmark in the Irish neighborhood. In Detroit the church was so central to the community that when the Irish population began to concentrate in one specific neighborhood the parishioners "jacked up the building and rolled it 15 blocks northwest to the corner of Porter and Sixth Streets in the eighth ward." This church, Holy Trinity, then acted as a magnet, drawing hundreds more Irish to Detroit's West Side so that by 1853 Irish Catholics made up 45 percent of the ward's population. In

New Haven, Connecticut, the Irish had built a small church in the 1830s; in 1848 it was destroyed by fire. Within six months the community of Irish laborers had raised thirteen thousand dollars to buy and furnish a former Congregational church.[17] Such commitment to the church was not uncommon. In the poorest of Irish neighborhoods, the people invariably found the means to build the parish church and support it through both good and bad times.

The organization of Irish parishes differed from that of the Germans. Among the Irish, lay initiative was most evident in the people's request for priests. Such petitions to church authorities were commonplace in the formative stages of every Irish Catholic community. As bishop of Boston, Benedict Fenwick was responsible for the church throughout New England, and in 1830 he acknowledged, "The cry from every quarter is: send us a Priest—and they are mad because I have none to send them."[18] Left without the benefit of clergy, groups of Catholics would gather at homes, barns, and store fronts to pray together. The instructions of the bishop of Boston, Jean Cheverus, to Catholics in Hartford, Connecticut, in 1823 depicted a common scenario. "You will do well," he wrote, "to procure a room and meet every Sunday to perform together your devotions. Let one who reads well and has a clear voice, read the prayers of the Mass, a sermon, or some instructions out of a Catholic book. . . ."[19] This was the style of religion for Catholics in much of the Northeast during the 1820s and 1830s, and it was commonplace in the western territories half a century later. Once a resident priest arrived, a parish community was formally organized and the church was open for services. In other words, most Irish parishes were formally organized by clergy and lay people working together. Rare was the case, so common among the Germans, of an Irish community organizing, buying land, and building a church on their own initiative without the input of the clergy. One obvious reason for the difference was the greater availability of priests for the English-speaking Irish, and this became more true as the nineteenth century progressed. Another reason was the Irish inclination to be more dependent on the clergy in religious affairs. Furthermore, the English-speaking Irish could conveniently attend religious services in a Protestant church; such a practice, customary in such southern regions as the Carolinas, was undoubtedly more widespread than is realized. How widespread it actually was, however, is unknown.

The central role of the priest in the establishment of Irish parishes hardly meant that the Irish were passive parishioners. Like the Germans, they became actively involved in the government of the local church through their participation in the trustee system. In almost every urban community during the antebellum period, the Irish supported this congregational style of church government. In the diocese of Albany, for example, it was quite commonplace; Irish parishes in New York and Philadelphia favored it also; in the southern regions of Virginia and the Carolinas it was not only the accepted pattern, but it had become the official church policy during the episcopacy of John England.

When the Irish-born England became bishop of Charleston, South Carolina, in 1820, he promoted the lay-trustee concept and made it an integral part of local church government. Viewing such a republican form of government as a harmonious blend of American and Roman Catholic traditions, England sought to achieve a situation in which, he said, "the laity are empowered to cooperate but not to dominate."[20] The system was spelled out in detail in the church constitution drawn up by England and adopted by Catholics in the Carolinas and Georgia. Similar to that found in other communities, it provided for the annual election of a board of trustees by the adult males of the parish; this board met regularly throughout the year, with the local pastor acting as president at these meetings. In some areas of parish life the decision of the lay trustees was not subject to a clerical veto, and if necessary, they could even petition the bishop for the pastor's removal. But they had to abide by the bishop's decision unless it was overturned by a "superior ecclesiastical tribunal," which would have been highly unlikely.[21] All the evidence suggests that throughout England's episcopacy, 1820–42, the system worked well, and by sharing authority between priest and people it fostered cooperation and harmony, rather than domination and discord.

In emphasizing this tradition of lay initiative and involvement in the local church, it is important to avoid romantic illusions about the past. First of all, women were excluded from this sphere of activity; as liberal as John England's constitution was, a woman could not "be considered a member of the Roman Catholic church of the diocese of Charleston, nor of any Roman Catholic church within the same"; thus, women were excluded from participation in the vestry and in all regional and state church conventions.[22] Moreover, a reading of the minutes of parish trustee meetings clearly indicates that these men were business managers of the parish. Their principal concern was financial: collection of pew rents, salaries of clergy, purchasing a new organ, managing the cemetery, and paying off church debts. They also supervised the work of such church personnel as organist, choir director, and maintenance men. Not only was this pattern of management evident in both Irish and German parishes, but it was also similar to the type of concerns evident among Protestant lay trustees. The major difference was that the Catholic pastor enjoyed more independence from the trustees than his Protestant counterpart.[23]

This issue of authority and clerical independence in the local parish was a source of many problems and controversies. As was true in John Carroll's day, laymen and clergy battled over the control of power and authority. The lay people who most often had bought the land and built the church with their own funds wanted a voice in how their parish would be managed. Many clergy understood this concern and worked in a harmonious relationship with the trustees and the people of the parish. Some failed to achieve such harmony, and invariably the people would vote to dismiss their pastor. Then a battle ensued between people, priest, and bishop over authority in the parish. In the diocese of Albany, New York, for example, as many as twenty-six parish communities experienced such conflict during the middle decades of the nineteenth century.[24] Many times, the bishop resolved the issue by removing the pastor and sending a more congenial, cooperative priest to the parish. In quite a few places, such as Philadelphia, Norfolk, New Orleans, and Buffalo, Catholics were especially recalcitrant, and bishops proceeded to place parishes under interdict and excommunicated the parishioners.

The Philadelphia story was the most notorious. In this city of brotherly love, the Irish parishioners of St. Mary's, the city's principal Catholic parish, went to battle over the issue of authority. The trustees claimed the right to appoint and dismiss their priests, and the bishop denied such claims. Conflict erupted periodically during a twenty-year period, reaching a high point in the 1820s, when opposing factions of people and priests battled one another for control of the parish. Bitter pamphlet wars ensued, tumultuous parish meetings took place, and even a trustee election riot occurred, in 1822, in which Irish Catholics, armed with clubs and bricks, fought with one another in the front of the church; numerous people, "perhaps two hundred," were injured. As one Philadelphia lawyer put it, Catholics had turned "the temple of religion into a place of tumult, riot and bloodshed."[25]

Such struggles over power and authority were typically American and Catholic. In the United States, nineteenth-century Catholics, unlike their Protestant neighbors, did not go to battle over theological issues; they fought over power: the issue of authority in the local church; this was the one issue that provoked schism in the church during the nineteenth century. It was also typically Catholic in that it was another chapter in the ongoing debate over authority in the church, a debate that had divided Catholics since the Middle Ages, when the issue of a more representative form of church government, commonly referred to as conciliarism, first surfaced. In the United States, clergy and laity were lined up on both sides of the debate; one side supported the traditional, monarchical form of church government, in which the lay people were left to pay, pray, and obey. The other side, best exemplified in John England's diocese, supported a more representative, republican form of church government in which cooperation, rather than domination, was the goal.

Until recently, historians have painted a negative picture of the trustee system, interpreting it "as an heretical and rebellious attempt by lay and clerical trustees to control the temporal and sometimes spiritual welfare of the local congregation."[26] This was an inadequate, biased view tainted by a twentieth-century monarchical interpretation of authority in the church. As a result, the tradition of lay involvement in the organization of parish life was overlooked and ignored until very recently. In the wake of the Second Vatican Council and with an increased interest in social history, historians have reexamined the nineteenth century and discovered a strong tradition of lay involvement in both the organization and the government of parish life. Though that tradition obviously had created some problems, what is especially significant was not the conflict it precipitated, but the extent to which the tradition prevailed and how popular and successful it was during the antebellum period.

Though both Irish and Germans were active in the organization and government of local parish communities, some differences between them were noticeable. First of all, it was obvious that both lay initiative in the organization of parish communities and lay involvement in local church government were more customary and more extensive among the Germans than among the Irish. In the republican period, roughly from 1780 to 1820, the differences were not very striking, given the small number of Germans. In the antebellum era, however, the differences emerged more clearly as time progressed. A study of three hundred Irish and German parishes clearly pointed this out. Among the Germans, about three out of five (62 percent) of the parishes had lay trustees, whereas among the Irish the ratio was approximately two out of five (42 percent).[27] As regards lay initiative in the organization of parish life, the same pattern was evident, with Germans clearly exhibiting more independence and initiative in this phase of church life. One reason for the difference can be traced back to the cultural and religious experience of the old country. Among German Catholics there was a strong tradition of lay involvement in parish affairs, and this was maintained in the United States. Moreover, the ideal of the German hometown, a distinctive autonomous form of local government that developed in the seventeenth and eighteenth centuries, was a strong tradition that formed the political and social experience of many immigrants. Independence, self-government, and a community closely bound together by consensus were trademarks of the German hometown, and it would not be surprising to find such ideals surfacing in the United States. Though it was impossible to re-create the integrated life of the hometown in the New World, people did form associations—surrogate hometowns—in which they could "find communal intimacy . . . exercise the satisfactions of community participation, and . . . perpetuate German values."[28] The church was certainly one such surrogate hometown.

Moreover, German Catholics needed the church more than the Irish did. Catholicism was clearly not the dominant religion in the German community; only 25 to 30 percent of German immigrants were Catholic. This meant that the church had to compete with rival beliefs and allegiances; Germans were also more prone to indifference in religion and could boast of such God killers as Feuerbach, Marx, and Nietzsche. In such a religiously fragmented and pluralist community, the church took on a special importance. There were not just Protestant Americans to contend with, but, more important, there were German-speaking Protestants, freethinkers, and radicals who competed with the Catholic Church for the allegiance of the immigrants. One priest summarized the situation quite succinctly: ". . . the German Catholic, unlike the Irish, is surrounded by countrymen, who, as Protestants, infidels, secret-society-men, do everything in their power to lure him away from his church."[29] To ward off such threats, Catholic Germans gathered around the parish and closely identified with it. As a result, the parish became much more than a religious center; it was also a social center. This is clearly evident from the very rich organizational life, known in German as *Vereinswesen*, which surfaced in their parishes. In addition to the usual devotional societies, they had life insurance organizations, music societies, military groups, and other cultural and socially oriented organizations. Compared with the Irish, the German parish clearly had a more elaborate organizational network.[30]

A final reason why the church was so important was the need to preserve language among the Germans and the close relationship between faith and language. In an English-speaking country, this took on a special meaning. It was all right to learn English, counseled one priest, because ". . . in English you must count your dollars, but in German you speak with your children, your confessor, and your God."[31] For Catholics, the major institution that encouraged the preservation of the mother tongue was the church.

The importance of the church for the Germans does not mean that the parish was not important or vital for the Irish or that the latter were passive participants in parish life. Hardly! But when compared with the Germans it is clear that the relationship of the Irish to their parish church was different. Irish immigrants came from a culture in which clerical authoritarianism in church affairs and deference on behalf of the laity were more normative. Clerical leadership, rather than lay initiative, was a distinctive mark of the Irish experience in the prefamine period. Moreover, in the United States the Irish developed a very rich associational life beyond the parish; a glance at the line of march of any St. Patrick's Day parade clearly suggests this.[32] In addition to parish organizations, the Irish affiliated with political groups, labor associations, burial societies, benevolent and fraternal organizations, and temperance societies. Though the parish was important as a center for religion and ethnic identification, it was not so vital to the total Irish experience as it was for the Germans. Moreover, unlike the Germans, religious competition hardly existed among the Irish immigrants, since the bulk of them, 90 percent or more, were Catholic, and to join an Irish association not affiliated with the parish would not necessarily pose a threat to one's religious beliefs.

With the passage of time, the involvement of the laity in the parish began to change. As the church became more developed institutionally and thus better able to cope with the influx of Irish and German immigrants, lay involvement in the parish began to wane. In the early, formative years of a community, people often acted on their own, due to the absence of clergy; for the Irish and the Germans, this was no longer the case in most parts of the United States by the latter part of the century. In some places, such as Nebraska and Colorado in the 1870s and 1880s, the church was still in its formative stages, and lay initiative, especially among the Germans, was still in evidence. But, in the heartland of Catholic America, the northeastern states, where 70 percent or more of the people lived, the mission church of the 1820s had been transformed into a large, bureaucratic organization that was able to recruit the manpower needed for an expanding constituency. Throughout the nineteenth century, the vast majority of these recruits were foreign-born; the few studies of the clergy that have been done illustrate this very clearly. In Minnesota, for example, nine out of ten priests, between 1844 and 1880, were foreigners; in the next thirty years the ratio dropped off to two out of three, but this was still a very high percentage of foreign-born clergy working in an American diocese. In St. Louis a similar pattern prevailed at the turn of the century, with well over half of the clergy being immigrants. Reflecting the nationality of the people, the vast majority of these priests, at least 70 percent in Minnesota, were Irish and Germans.[33]

As their numbers increased, the clergy became more involved in the organization of the local parish. Of course, priests had always organized parishes on their own initiative, but in the formative years of the community this was but one of several possible ways of founding a parish. As time passed, however, the model of the priest-founder became more normative. The organization of Epiphany parish in New York City in 1868 is instructive in this regard. Richard L. Burtsell, the first pastor of the parish, was a young priest with liberal ideas. Concerned about the need for more parishes in the city, he asked his bishop, John McCloskey, to permit him to organize a parish in a poor neighborhood on the East Side of Manhattan. Though reluctant at first, the bishop finally gave in to Burtsell's persistence, in December of 1867. Burtsell then set about to raise the necessary money and, through an agent, purchased the land for the church; this done, he began to organize the parish community. The key role of the laity in all this was to help Burtsell raise money for the church by canvassing the community for donations; in addition, they were to run the Sunday-school program, which in Burtsell's mind was the most important work the laity could do in the parish. The trustee system did not exist in the parish, nor would it have been allowed, given the history of conflict in New York City between people and clergy over this issue.[34]

Burtsell was hardly unique, and the more priests became involved in organizing parish communities and building churches, the more common became the "brick and mortar" pastor, whose claim to fame was how much he built. Virtually invisible in the early years of the century, the priest-builder image became a dominant one by the mid-nineteenth century. A papal visitor noticed this and remarked quite accurately that "The most outstanding priest is the one that built the most churches and begun the most institutions."[35] This image remained a favorite theme of eulogists throughout the nineteenth and twentieth centuries when they preached at priests' funerals. It now was the priest, not the lay people, who organized the parish and built the church, school, rectory, convent, and any other parish buildings. This was how he was remembered, and it was quite accurate.[36]

Another development that enhanced the authority of the priest was the increased length of a pastor's tenure. This was a trend that developed over the course of the nineteenth century and was especially notable in English-speaking communities. A study of 290 nineteenth-century Catholic pastors revealed that two out of three of them (67 percent) served less than six years in the same parish; by the twentieth century, however, the average tenure had increased significantly, so that among a group of 428 pastors examined, nearly two out of three (63 percent) served more than six years; indicative of this trend was a large number, about one out of three, of these twentieth-century pastors who served for more than eleven years in the same parish.[37] Such long tenures served to strengthen the authority of the pastor and enabled some priests to become virtual lords of the manor. One such colorful figure was Maurice J. Dorney of Chicago.

Dorney was an American-born Irishman, and in 1880 he founded the parish of St. Gabriel, near the Union Stockyards on the South Side of the city. He remained pastor of the parish until his death in 1914. Known as "King of the yards," he was a legend in the neighborhood and in the stock yards. A brick-and-mortar priest, he built the church, designed by the famous Chicago architects Daniel H. Burnham and John Wellborn Root, as well as a grammar school, high school, rectory, and convent. His authority was such that he was called on to arbitrate labor strikes; he acted as an employment agent and single-handedly kept the saloons off residential streets in the neighborhood. No one in St. Gabriel's parish doubted for a moment who held the authority in the church, and if one did, Dorney would mount the pulpit to remind his parishioners that he was indeed king of the yards and pastor of the parish.[38]

There was more involved in the demise of the trustee system than an increase in the availability of clergy and the increased tenure of pastors. These certainly influenced the move toward clerical supremacy in the parish, but a major reason for the demise of the trustee system was the persistent opposition to it on behalf of both bishops and clergy. Ever since the days of John Carroll, opposition to lay trusteeism had existed. Individual bishops opposed it, and church councils legislated against it; as one historian wrote, in a typically biased manner, "The serpentine trail of trusteeism, winds its way along the high road of canonical legislation from 1791 to 1884."[39]

The key issue in the entire discussion was authority. Through ownership of church property, lay trustees exercised control of the local parish; due to the conflict such an arrangement occasionally caused, the hierarchy sought to overturn this custom and in so doing restore their own authority. At the first council of Baltimore, in 1829, the bishops made their first concerted attack against lay ownership of church property, and every major council thereafter not only discussed this issue, but progressively strengthened the hierarchy's position, so that by the Third Plenary Baltimore Council, in 1884, the bishops' authority in this area was absolute. But in asserting their authority over the Church by insisting on ownership of all church property, the hierarchy did not totally eliminate lay participation in the government of the local church. In fact, they encouraged this by allowing for the election of parish church committees or trustees. The legislation of the major church councils, such as the plenary Baltimore councils of 1866 and 1884, provided for such popularly elected committees and spelled out in detail the qualifications needed by prospective councilmen: i.e., men over twenty-one years of age who had made their Easter duty (confession and Communion during the Easter time), who supported the church financially, did not belong to secret societies, and finally, according to the 1884 directive, men who would not neglect to send their children to the parochial school.

Episcopal support for such popularly elected committees was a compromise that had developed in the middle decades of the nineteenth century. Having obtained control of the ownership of parish property and control over the appointment and dismissal of the parish clergy, they continued to allow lay people a voice in the operation of parish affairs through their elected trustees. But it is clear from a reading of conciliar legislation on this issue that as time passed, the activities of such committees were becoming progressively more limited, while the authority of the bishop was continually expanding. Thus, by 1884 such church committees could exist, but only at the discretion of the local bishop.[40] This helps to explain why some dioceses continued the tradition of lay involvement in local church government and others did not.

Though opposition to the trustee system centered around the specific issues of ownership of church property and the authority of the bishop over the appointment and dismissal of parish clergy, the implications were much wider. Two concepts of local church government were at odds: a congregational model in which there was an emphasis on a democratic exercise of authority, and a hierarchical model, which meant clerical supremacy in church affairs. In English-speaking communities, clerical supremacy clearly became the norm. In other words, at the turn of the century a little more than half of the Catholic community were organized in parishes in which the priest's authority was supreme. The Irish tradition of an authoritarian clergy and a deferential laity had become the normative model in the United States.[41] Other immigrant communities, however, refused to adopt the Irish model and stuck to their own tradition of lay initiative and independence as long as they could. The Germans were a good example.

The German tradition of lay involvement in local church government was not limited to the formative years of the community. It persisted into the twentieth century. This can be clearly seen in Cincinnati, where there is comparatively rich documentation for the German Catholic community. Both Bishop Purcell and his successor, William Henry Elder, supported the tradition among the Germans and issued regulations "for the administration of temporal affairs of German Roman Catholic churches of Cincinnati."[42] The history of St. Paul's parish in Cincinnati illustrates quite clearly how involved the laity were in the decision-making process. As in the founding years, public meetings were held in the 1890s to plan the golden jubilee of the parish, and a few years later they met to plan the rebuilding of the church after it was damaged by fire. Throughout its nineteenth-century history, the parish had lay trustees; this was the German tradition in a city in which Irish parishes from the very beginning were governed by the clergy alone. Nor was Cincinnati unique; an examination of 287 German parishes revealed that support for the lay trustee system persisted throughout the nineteenth century, and though it declined somewhat in the early-twentieth century, it still remained popular.[43] The Germans were not the only people who refused to adopt the Irish model of parish government. The new immigrants who arrived in the late-nineteenth and early-twentieth centuries had their own traditions regarding lay involvement in parish life, and they, too, were quite different from the Irish model.

Religion was a major force in the lives of the immigrants from southern Italy. But the religion of the people was not the same as the official religion of the church. Italian popular religion was a complex system of magical practices inherited from a pre-Christian past and sustained throughout centuries of coexistence with Christianity. Alongside this system was the religion of Roman Catholicism. In some areas the two religious systems overlapped and intermingled, much like the commingling of Indian and Christian beliefs and practices. In other areas, popular religious beliefs were opposed to official practices of the church. This duality of religion, one popular and the other official, helps to explain the religious behavior of Italian immigrants. Frequently they were described as a people for whom religion was all-pervasive, but at the same time their lukewarm attitude toward attendance at Mass and their anticlericalism shocked their coreligionists. Given the dual religious system prevalent among the people, such apparently contradictory behavior was not uncommon among Italians, and it clearly affected their relationships with the larger Catholic community.[44]

In some communities such as Chicago and San Francisco, Italian anticlericalism was quite powerful. Immigrants in these cities came from towns in Italy that had an anticlerical tradition, and they brought this with them to the

United States. In other cities such as Rochester and Utica, anticlericalism was not a major force. But it was obvious that in any city, involvement in the local parish community was scarcely a priority for the anticlerical faction; indeed, it was to be ridiculed and attacked. Despite such anticlericalism and indifference toward official church religion, a tradition of involvement in the organization of parish life did exist among the people.

When Italians arrived in the United States in the late-nineteenth century, the church was totally unprepared for them. They were expected to worship in the local parish, which was most likely Irish, and little initiative was taken by prelates or priests to deal satisfactorily with the religious needs of the new immigrants. A common strategy was to turn over the basement of a parish church to the Italians so they could come together for Sunday Mass. Such discrimination was not only humiliating, but it was also not a very successful pastoral strategy. Many Italians did not associate with such parishes, in which they were clearly second-class members. Faced with such discrimination, immigrants would gather together and petition the local American bishop, or even clergy in the old country, to send them an Italian-speaking priest so that they could establish their own parishes, where they could "unite to pray and worship the Lord and preserve intact the rites as transmitted to them by their ancestors."[45] Very often, the catalyst for such petitions was an already existing mutual benefit society.

Mutual benefit societies were popular in the old country and quickly became commonplace in the United States. Each one had a specific purpose, and some of them were religiously based; very often it was from these religiously based societies that the impetus came for the establishment of an Italian parish. In Corona, New York, for example, the people were "gathered in religious congregation under the title of *Maria SS Assunta in Cielo,*" and having met together they asked the bishop of Brooklyn for "a church in which they may be instructed in the faith according to the traditional, glorious millenary decoro of which Italy is the noble example to the world."[46] Most often, the bishop would acknowledge their request, and after having obtained the services of an Italian-speaking priest, he would then establish the parish. Some of these mutual benefit societies predated the formation of their parishes by several years, and during this time they served as the vital center of religion for the people. A good example of this could be found in Berwick, Pennsylvania, where the Maria Assunta Society, a mutual aid society, predated the founding of the parish by eleven years. During this period, from 1910 to 1921, the society celebrated its own religious festival on August 15 in honor of the Assumption of Mary.[47] Societies such as Maria Assunta, so commonplace in the Italian community, clearly promoted lay initiative and independence in the area of religion, and such traits often carried over into the organization of the parish community. A good example of this was the organization of the first Italian parish in St. Paul, Minnesota.

The archbishop of St. Paul, John Ireland, had invited Father Nicola Carlo Odone from Genoa to take charge of the Italian mission in St. Paul. Odone arrived in 1899, and for several years the people worshiped in the dark and humid basement of the cathedral. It was a humiliating experience for "we children of Catholic Italy," bemoaned Odone, to have "to meet under the feet of a different people [the Irish] which looks at us from above with contempt."[48] Both priest and people wanted their own church, and like the Germans in Cincinnati, they gathered together in 1905 to discuss the building of a church. They held organizational meetings, appointed a committee to collect funds for the new church, and elected their own parish trustees and councilors. The independence of the people was such that they even wanted to keep control over the money collected and purchase the property for the church in their own name, rather than that of the bishop. Neither Father Odone nor Archbishop Ireland would accept such an arrangement; this opposition dampened the enthusiasm of the people. In addition, the people argued over the location of the new church, and this division of opinion delayed the founding of the parish. Finally, in 1910, after five years of struggling with a divided congregation, Odone resigned. Though the significance of this episode can be evaluated from a variety of perspectives, it was clear that the St. Paul Italian community manifested a strong sense of lay initiative and independence in the area of religion.

Episodes similar to the St. Paul experience took place in Boston and Marlborough, Massachusetts, and other cities where Italians settled. Such examples of an immigrant people's actively seeking to organize their own parish church suggest that the Italians were hardly indifferent and passive toward the formation of local church communities. They had a strong tradition of establishing all types of voluntary associations, and they brought this with them to the United States. Included in this tradition were religiously based mutual aid societies, which frequently served as the catalyst for the organization of Italian parishes.[49] Though it is unknown how extensive this pattern of lay initiative was in the establishment of Italian parishes, it is clear that it was not the most common way in which their parishes were organized. Most often, they were established by prelates and priests, not the lay people. Chicago offers a good example of this pattern. Both Archbishop Patrick A. Feehan (1880–1902) and his successor, James E. Quigley (1903–15), were the prime movers in the formation of Italian parishes. As in other cities, they brought in Italian religious-order priests, in this case the Servites and the Scalabrini, to establish parishes and minister to the needs of the people. The same pattern of episcopal leadership was evident in San Francisco, and in both places little evidence exists for lay involvement in the formation of parish communities.[50]

Unlike in the German parishes, the lay-trustee form of parish government was not very widespread in Italian parishes in the United States. In the old country, laymen were involved as trustees in the administration of church finances, but these men were appointed by the pastor, and they were seldom representatives of the people, but, rather, personal friends of the priest. Thus, "From the organizational point of view the peasant had almost no voice in the conduct of his parish church."[51] A few communities in the United States did support a trustee system of parish government for a while, but it seems not to have endured very long. Predictably, in those communities—Boston and St. Paul would be two examples—conflict erupted between bishop and people over ownership of church property. In the Italian community the focal point for lay involvement in religion was not in the government of the local church, but in the mutual aid societies they brought with them from the old country.

The Mexican tradition was somewhat similar to the Italian in that they, too, placed a good deal of emphasis on the importance of voluntary associations such as the mutual benefit society and the religious confraternity. The reasons for this are rooted in the decades of neglect by the Mexican church toward the people living in the northern rim of Mexico. Throughout this area, the American Southwest, the mission churches were in a state of near collapse and the number of priests in the area was frightfully inadequate. When the first bishop of Santa Fe, New Mexico, Jean B. Lamy, arrived, in 1851, he found only twelve clergymen—and not very good ones at that—to serve an estimated sixty-eight thousand Catholics scattered across an area as large as France.[52] For the majority of people in the Southwest, Catholicism was a church without clergy, and this "condition of neglect, more than any other, gave it its special character."[53] Without clergy, the Mexican people were forced to improvise their own religious expressions. Mixing Catholic practices and folk traditions, they became accustomed to baptizing their children, burying their kinfolk, and celebrating marriage without the benefit of clergy. Since a priest came so infrequently to their village, Mass was a rare occasion, but they regularly celebrated their religious festivals with elaborate processions honoring their beloved *santo*.

In spite of the collapse of the institutional church, religion remained a very central part of the lives of the people. For them the most important religious organization was not the parish, but the religious confraternity, the *cofradía*. Rooted in medieval Spain, *cofradías* were quickly established in the New World. The vital center of religion, they could be found in every *pueblo* in New Mexico and throughout the Southwest. Together with the celebration of religious festivals, they nurtured the religion of the people and helped them to maintain their identity as a people once they became part of the United States.

Another feature of the religion of the Southwest was the proliferation of private chapels. In 1851, Lamy found forty such chapels in his diocese, almost double the number of churches. Replicas of the large mission churches, these small adobe structures were built by individual families or *cofradías*. Like the religious brotherhoods, they often eluded the control and approval of church authorities in Mexico, and quite naturally they also fostered independence in religion.[54] Thus it was clear that when the Southwest became part of the Church in the United States, the people had become accustomed to a great deal of independence in religion. Neither parish-centered nor clergy-centered, theirs was a religion rooted in devotion to the *santo* and promoted by the religious confraternity.

Once the Southwest became part of the United States, bishops were assigned to the various regions. Joseph S. Alemany went to California, Jean B. Lamy to New Mexico, and John M. Odin to Texas. These men sought to establish discipline and control in their respective dioceses. Ownership of church property was an important issue, since previously the Mexican Government had controlled all church property. Eventually the bishops did acquire the ownership of church property, parish churches included, and this helped to consolidate their authority in the Catholic community. In need of clergy, these bishops turned to Europe—France in particular—for priests. They were relatively successful, and eventually the French began to dominate the clergy; in Texas, for example, twenty-eight out of thirty diocesan priests were Frenchmen in 1866.[55] A similar pattern prevailed in New Mexico, where both French and Italian clergy ministered to Mexican-American Catholics. These men, along with their European-born bishops, brought a new understanding of church and religion to the Southwest, and it was clearly different from the Mexican tradition. The contrast could be seen most dramatically in New Mexico, where the Frenchman Jean B. Lamy and his clerical countrymen sought to establish French Gothic Catholicism among Mexican people.

The most visible manifestation of this was in the churches and chapels they built. In Santa Fe, Lamy built a Romanesque-styled cathedral around the old parish church. In the *pueblo* of San Juan, the French priest Camille Seux of Lyons "had a life size Our Lady of Lourdes shipped from France and erected in the center of the plaza on a lofty stone pedestal." Then he built a Gothic chapel of stone across the road from the church. Next he remodeled the old *pueblo* church itself "until, with pitched roof, rose window, and pretty French steeple, it stood wholly unrecognizable."[56]

More than architectural styles were at stake, however. For these French clergymen, lay independence in religion and lay involvement in the government of the local church were not acceptable. Clerical control in parish affairs was the norm. Thus, when new parish communities were formed, the clergy, both bishops and parish priests, were most often responsible for their organization. But the persistent shortage of priests throughout the nineteenth and early-twentieth centuries limited the extent to which they could effectively exercise this control.

Because of the shortage of clergy, much of the rural Southwest remained no-priest country. Once or twice a year a padre on horseback would visit a settlement. "In the morning, Mass at about seven," noted one such itinerant priest traveling through the Mexican communities of Nueces County, in southern Texas, in 1876. "Then on horseback to the next ranch, in the evening after supper Catechism, Rosary, a little instruction to the people, next day the same as before."[57] Such a situation naturally encouraged lay initiative in the organization of local Catholic communities. Left on their own, people formed their own religious confraternities, built their own chapels, petitioned the bishop for priests, and then waited for the day when a resident priest would come to their village. But if upon his arrival the priest sought to exercise too much control over their religious life, their confraternities in particular, he met with strong resistance.[58] Thus it is evident that the shortage of clergy in the Southwest, a condition most acute in rural areas, fostered lay initiative and independence in religion. When parish churches were finally and officially established by the bishop and his clergy, the people maintained this tradition through their confraternities, which became the heart of Mexican parish life.

The French-Canadian experience was quite different from both the Italian and the Mexican situations. One reason for this was the close connection between religion and nationality among French Canadians. The roots of this connection go back to the eighteenth century, when Protestant Great Britain defeated Catholic French Canada in war and for thirty years thereafter ruled over the country as "a conquered province of Great Britain without representative government."[59] The English conquest of 1760 thus became "the single most important event in French Canadian history."[60] Since then, French Canadians have fought for survival (survivance, they called it) as a people seeking to maintain their own foi, langue, et moeurs (faith, language, and customs). Religion, la foi, was an integral part of this struggle for survivance in both Canada and New England, and the key to the survival of religion was the Catholic parish.

In French Canada, "The parish was the basic social unit." In rural areas, where most of the immigrants came from, it served as both a religious and a civil unit, a church and village whose boundaries and constituents were one and the same.[61] It was the single most important institution in maintaining la foi, la langue, et les moeurs among French Canadians. In New England and other parts of the United States the parish continued to serve, in the words of one romanticist, as "the most beautiful poem of faith, of hope, and of devotion to survivance catholique et française in the United States."[62] More than a place of worship, it was a vital force in maintaining French-Canadian culture and nationality. In Canada the people took an active part in the government of the parish through the trustee, or fabrique, system of parish government. Elected by the people, lay trustees, known as marguilliers, controlled and administered the financial affairs of the parish. Moreover, there was a strong tradition of independence and local control among Canadian parish communities; this endured until the late-nineteenth century. In the United States such lay involvement was notable in the organization of French-Canadian parishes.[63]

When French Canadians settled in the United States they invariably organized a mutual aid society such as the Union of St. Jean Baptiste, in Duluth, Minnesota, or the Association Canadienne-Française, in Concord, New Hampshire. These societies became the social and cultural centers for the immigrant community. As regards religion, the French Canadians would attend the local parish, most often Irish, and their experience was not much different from that of the Italians. French-speaking newcomers were not very welcome in Irish parishes, and such discrimination precipitated bitter relations between the two groups. In some cities competition for jobs between French and Irish hardened the lines of division. Thus it was not long before French Canadians would petition the local bishop for their own national parish, where they could sustain *la foi, la langue, et les moeurs* as in Canada; most often, a mutual benefit society acted as a catalyst in this decision. This pattern of lay initiative resembled that found in other immigrant communities, and as was true elsewhere, the bishop generally granted the request of the people and established a French-Canadian parish with a priest recruited from Canada. Yet it is clear from the evidence available that this pattern of parish organization was not the most common way in which French-Canadian parishes were formed.

In New England—in most of the Northeast, for that matter—the church was fairly well developed institutionally by the late-nineteenth century, when the French Canadians were arriving on the scene. Numerous dioceses had been established in which a modest form of ecclesiastical bureaucracy was in place, rules and regulations governing church life existed, and sufficient numbers of clergy were available to staff parish churches. Bishops generally recognized the need for parishes with French-speaking clergy and tried to establish them; the closeness of Canada and the availability of priests there facilitated the work of the bishops. Though there clearly were some instances of lay initiative, especially in the pre-1890 period, this pattern of episcopal initiative in the organization of parish communities eventually became the most common pattern.[64] The dominant role of the bishop and his clergy was also the pattern as regards the government of the local church.

Even though they came from a culture in which lay involvement in parish government and independence of the local church were accepted customs, French Canadians were not able to transplant this tradition to the United States. In New England they met a church controlled by Irish priests and bishops, and by the late-nineteenth century the tradition of lay trustees had become a curious antique. In Rhode Island, for example, an 1866 law made the bishop president of the local parish corporation; in Maine an 1887 law made him the sole owner of all parish property; such centralized control did not allow for much independence at the parish level.[65] Yet, several parish communities did resist such episcopal control. French Canadians in Fall River, Massachusetts, in 1886 and in North Brookfield in 1900 rebelled when the bishop did not appoint a French-Canadian priest; they refused to contribute money to the church and even stopped attending Mass. In North Brookfield, the people went so far as to establish a new parish with their own pastor, and this led the bishop to excommunicate those involved. Danielson, Connecticut, was the scene of a controversy during the 1890s between a group of French Canadians and their bishop over the appointment of a French-Canadian pastor to their parish. They unsuccessfully appealed to Rome for support of their cause and eventually established their own parish. In Maine, French Canadians challenged the Irish rule of the church and waged a lengthy controversy (1906–14) over the issue of episcopal control of the local church. In no instance did the people win, and in the end there was usually ". . . a grudging and halfhearted acquiescence to the authority of the Church hierarchy."[66]

These incidents of a local French-Canadian community's resisting what they felt was discrimination and persecution by the hierarchy reflected the problem of adjustment these immigrants experienced in trying to transplant their religion to Irish Catholic New England. It was clear that, once they crossed the border, they had to leave behind their tradition of a democratically governed parish community. Many resisted abandoning this tradition for the good of *la survivance,* but they fought a losing battle.

The French-Canadian experience offers a clear example of how one immigrant group was forced to abandon part of its own religious tradition because of the powerful opposition of the dominant group, in this case the Irish. The single largest group of Catholics in the United States, the Irish dominated the ranks of both clergy and hierarchy; this dominance was so extensive that by 1900 two out of every three Catholic bishops in the United States were of Irish descent; in New England the ratio was three out of four. Such control of the positions of authority meant that the Irish tradition regarding the role of lay people in parish affairs would become the dominant tradition. Moreover, during the late-nineteenth century, Roman Catholicism was moving toward a more monarchical, less democratic, style of church government. The Vatican Council of 1870 decisively pushed the church in this direction when it proclaimed the infallibility of the Pope and encouraged the centralization of the church in Rome. Such centralization of authority filtered down throughout the church, enhancing the authority of both bishop and pastor. The Third Plenary Council of Baltimore (1884) mirrored this development by making the will of the bishop supreme in all local church affairs. Such a way of thinking was clearly articulated in a directive issued in 1907: "The Church is not a republic or democracy, but a monarchy; . . . all her authority is from above and rests in her Hierarchy; ,   while the faithful of the laity have divinely given rights to receive all the blessed ministrations of the Church, they have absolutely no right whatever to rule and govern."[67] Such thinking, coupled with the Irish tradition of the priest's dominant role in parish life, obviously posed a serious obstacle to any attempt of lay people to gain a decision-making role in parish affairs. But the Irish were not the Church, and directives from Rome or from the local bishop were not always accepted by the people. The clearest example of such resistance could be found among eastern European Catholic immigrants.

In the old country the parish was the center of village life for Polish Catholics. "The most important events of individual, familial, and communal life" took place there, and it bound people together, giving them a sense of identity as both Polish and Catholic. When they emigrated to the New World, the parish became the primary form of association among Polish Catholics. It was "simply the old primary community, reorganized and concentrated" in the United States.[68] A Polish priest underscored the importance of the parish for the immigrants in the following manner. "The Polish Catholic," he wrote, "who doesn't belong to any parish is homeless—without any support, religious or national, he is a social bankrupt, a bandit on the open highway, and sooner or later he must perish because without support and help he will not be able to meet the test."[69] As both a social and a religious institution, the parish provided "the support and help" that the immigrants needed in the New World. It became so central to the life of the community that Polish neighborhoods were even named after the local Catholic parish. Thus, in Chicago, Polish immigrants did not live in the North Side of the city, they lived in what they affectionately called *Stanislaswowo*, that is, the village of St. Stanislaus, the name of the local parish church.

The organization of the parish in the Polish community followed a pattern similar to that of other immigrant groups. When people first arrived, they generally attended services in a local Catholic church. For many Poles, this often meant a German church, since those from Prussia and Austria could understand German. But this was not a satisfactory arrangement. Like all immigrants, they wanted to pray in their native language and sing Polish hymns, not German ones. One Ukrainian immigrant spoke for all immigrants when he wrote, "We are not entirely the same as we were in our country because we are missing something. What we miss is God Whom we could understand, Whom we could adore in our own way."[70] To remedy this, Polish immigrants organized themselves into the mutual benefit society, whose express purpose was to found a Polish parish church.

The mutual benefit society was a commonplace organization in immigrant communities. Most often transplanted from the Old World, such societies provided insurance benefits for their members in times of sickness and death and gave the newcomers a sense of identity and belonging in the New World.

More than an insurance institution, the mutual benefit society became a source of initiative in the broader community, and among the Polish "the great work of the society . . . is the formation of a parish."[1]

In any city where Polish Catholics were, a mutual benefit society was quickly organized, and it became the catalyst in the organization of a parish church. The pattern was a familiar one. Feeling a deep need for their own, national parish, where they could hear sermons in Polish and practice their own religious customs, the society would collect money to purchase land for a church; then they would petition the local bishop to send them a Polish-speaking priest. Once a resident priest arrived, the church was built and the parish began to take shape.

The organization of Holy Cross parish in Minneapolis illustrates the way one Polish community operated, and shows the great pride they took in their accomplishments. With the "guidance and assistance" of a Polish priest from St. Paul, Dominic Majer, they organized their "first parish society and voted for officers" in 1885. "Then," they went on to write, "we made a collection among ourselves which brought quite a sum into our treasury. On the advice of Fr. Majer, our officers sought and found three lots in a fine location at a reasonable price, and much to our joy, purchased them. Through the planning and leadership of our committee, the building of the new Polish church was begun."[2] The bishop, John Ireland, approved their work and was able to acquire the services of a young Polish priest for the people of Holy Cross parish.

Even though every parish community was not organized in the same way, a definite pattern of lay initiative existed in each instance. Sometimes people acted on their own, sometimes they acted with the aid of a priest, as in Minneapolis, but with few exceptions the source of the initiative for the organization of the parish was the people's mutual benefit society.

A key issue in the establishment of Polish parishes was the ownership of property. Most often, the parish was incorporated in the name of the mutual benefit society, and its officers became the trustees of the parish. This arrangement obviously conflicted with the prevailing custom, in the late-nineteenth century, of bishop and clergy owning all church property. Thus the stage was set for conflict, and conflict there was. In virtually every city where they settled, Polish Catholics went to battle over the issue of the ownership of church property. From their point of view, the tradition of the old country allowed for lay involvement in parish affairs and they sought to continue this in the United States. One Polish editor expressed this point of view quite persuasively:

In the old country the founders and benefactors [of a parish] had a voice not only in the running of church affairs, but in the selection of the pastor. Here in America, the founders and benefactors of the Polish churches, that is the Polish people, should certainly have the same rights and privileges."[3]

The editor had made an important point. In the Old World, Polish nobles enjoyed the right of patronage *(jus patronatus)* and could not only appoint parish priests, but also exercise control over parish affairs. In the New World, the people wanted to transform "the old world individual patron into a more democratic form of collective patronage."[74] But the bishops and clergy, many Polish priests included, would not go along. For them, the clergy, not the people, should run parish affairs and hold title to all church property. Unlike the French Canadians, however, the Polish did not give in on this issue. They resisted strongly and even accepted excommunication, rather than go along with the Irish-Roman tradition of clerical control in parish affairs. The controversy surrounding St. Stanislaus Kostka parish in Chicago illustrates the type of conflict this issue could precipitate.

St. Stanislaus Kostka was founded in 1867 by a mutual benefit society of the same name. From the very beginning, conflict divided the community; one group of people could be labeled nationalists, and for them politics and nationalism were more important than religion; for the others, the clerical party, religion was more important than politics. With this ideological split as a backdrop, the issue of parish ownership became the spark that ignited the flames of conflict. Within five years the nationalists founded a new church, Holy Trinity, three blocks from St. Stanislaus. The priests at St. Stanislaus tried to take over Holy Trinity parish, but the people would not allow it. For the next twenty years the two groups fought. One priest walked the neighborhood armed with a pistol; people rioted in the streets and demonstrated in church, throwing hymnals, yelling, and stamping their feet; several times, the parish was closed by the bishop, and finally the people appealed their case to Rome. In a surprise move, Vatican authorities supported the dissidents in Holy Trinity parish, and in 1893 the parish was turned over to the Holy Cross priests from the University of Notre Dame. Peace was restored and Father Casimir Sztuczko, a twenty-six-year-old Holy Cross priest, became the new pastor of Holy Trinity parish; he remained in this position for the next fifty-five years!"[75]

The controversy in Chicago had all the ingredients of a classic parish war. Independent-minded lay people who wanted a voice in parish affairs; a strong-willed priest who told the people to "obey the pastor"; street riots, church demonstrations, and appeals to Rome; all ended when a new priest arrived on the scene to calm the waters and restore harmony to the divided community. Though nationalism was certainly a factor in the Chicago episode, lay ownership of parish property and, more important, lay involvement in the government of the parish were the issues that led people to take to the streets and demonstrate in church. As extreme as this episode may seem, such conflict was a fact of life in Polish parishes across the country. Moreover, all parish wars did not end as harmoniously as the one in Chicago. In fact, conflict over the issue of ownership of church property and lay involvement in the government of the local church was the cause for the first major schism in American Catholic history.

Schism in the American Catholic Church had occurred throughout the nineteenth century. Generally it involved dissident parish congregations who chose to separate from the Roman Catholic Church because of a difference of opinion with their bishop over the issue of ownership of parish property. Most often, time healed the wounds and the people rejoined the church. Things did not go so smoothly among the Polish, however. During the 1890s, schismatic independent churches began to emerge in Chicago, Buffalo, Scranton, and other cities in the Northeast. Then, in 1904, Rev. Francis Hodur, leader of the Scranton independents, called a meeting of several independent parishes; this gathering was the formal beginning of the Polish National Catholic Church. A major part of the dissidents' platform focused on the issue of democracy in the government of the local church, a concern with which all Polish immigrants could readily identify. Hodur became the bishop-elect of the new denomination and headed it until his death in 1953. By World War I, twenty-five parishes belonged to the Polish National Catholic Church. Though it never reached more than 5 percent of the entire Polish population, the existence of the Polish National Catholic Church served as a continual reminder of the conflict that permeated the Polish Catholic community.[76]

Schism from the Roman Catholic Church, however, was not the normal pattern. Most Polish congregations went along with the local bishop and if necessary turned over ownership of the church to him and his clergy. But such transferral of ownership rights hardly meant that the Poles abandoned their tradition of lay involvement in parish affairs. Many parishes supported popularly elected "parish committees"; approved by the Baltimore church councils, these committees functioned much like the more official and clerically controlled boards of trustees. Thus, in effect Polish parishes frequently had two committees, one appointed by the clergy and approved by the bishop, and the other elected annually by the people. In this manner, Polish parishes evaded the hierarchy's opposition to lay trustees, and lay people continued to have influence in local church government even though they were not the owners of the church property.

Thus, among the Poles it was clear that lay people wanted to have a voice in the government of the local church. They went to battle for this; some accepted schism, rather than give in on this point, while most found other ways to exercise a time-honored tradition. Despite the widespread custom of Irish and American parishes, in which clerical supremacy was the standard, the Poles, like the Germans, maintained a strong voice in the government of the local church. They may not have owned the property, but they did have a say in how it was managed. As long as Polish priests and people were willing to cooperate, democracy continued to remain a trait of Polish parishes. When one faction tried to dominate the other, then conflict, even schism, erupted.

Immigrant Catholics from other parts of Eastern Europe followed a pattern similar to the Polish. Upon arrival in the United States, Slovaks went to the local Polish parish for religious services, but this was not very satisfying. Language as well as strong national feelings posed a problem, and inevitably the Slovaks would form their own parish. The catalyst for this would be the mutual benefit society. This same pattern was repeated among the Lithuanians as well—attendance at a Polish parish, formation of a mutual benefit society, and finally the founding of a Lithuanian parish. With both groups, lay initiative was prominent in the organization of the parish.

As regards ownership of parish property and authority in the government of the local church, both Slovaks and Lithuanians sought this type of involvement. As with the Polish, it was not the custom of the common folk in the old country to have a voice in local church government; this was the prerogative of the local noble or, in some regions, the privilege of the state. In the United States the people democratized this tradition and sought to exercise control over parish affairs. This would mean ownership of church property, an elected board of trustees, and even removal of uncooperative pastors. In their mind the rationale for this was quite simple and clear-cut: "The people have built the churches," wrote a Lithuanian immigrant, "therefore the people are the owners of the churches; and not the will of the bishop or of the Pope, but that of the people must be the rule in the parishes."[77] When such populist-minded individuals confronted an authoritarian bishop or priest, conflict inevitably erupted. Nor was it any less violent among others than it was among the Poles. In Bridgeport, Connecticut, for example, one hundred Slovak women in SS. Cyril and Methodius parish "marched on the rectory, broke down the door, and chased" the newly appointed pastor "into the attic where he barricaded himself." The problem, as the ladies saw it, was that the priest, Gaspar Panik, was appointed by the bishop against their wishes. Only the intervention of the police stopped the women from destroying the rectory.[78] As with the Polish, some Slovak and Lithuanian parishes went into schism and formed independent churches, rather than give in on this question of ownership of church property. Among the Lithuanians, for example, a dozen such independent churches came into being.[79] But they were never organized in the manner that the Polish National Catholic Church was, and their numbers diminished over time, as many of these independent parishes eventually sought reconciliation with the local Roman Catholic bishop.

Though the Czechs were not as committed as the Polish to religion and the church, those who were followed the Eastern European style in the organization of their parishes, and the same types of issues and conflicts became an accepted part of Czech parish life.[80]

It should be noted that the clergy were also very active in the organization of parish communities among Eastern European Catholics. In most instances, they worked with the people in organizing the local congregation, and frequently a single priest stood out as a catalyst and driving force behind the organization of several parish communities. One such person was the Lithuanian immigrant Joseph Zebris. Based in Waterbury, Connecticut, and later in nearby New Britain, this priest was "instrumental in the founding of at least fifteen parishes" in Lithuanian settlements throughout Connecticut, Massachusetts, New York, and New Jersey. As his biographer put it, "His practical instruction and persuasive rhetoric goaded newly-formed colonies to keep alive and implement their desire for a separate parish."[81] A Polish counterpart to the itinerant Zebris could be found in northern Indiana. Father Valentine Czyzewski, C.S.C., was pastor of St. Hedwig's Polish parish in South Bend, Indiana; from 1877, when he first became pastor at St. Hedwig's, until his death in 1913, ". . . he acted as the undoubted leader of the Poles in Northern Indiana." From his base at St. Hedwig's he traveled throughout the region, helping to found Polish parishes in such places as Terre Coupee, Rolling Prairie, and South Bend, as well as in Chicago.[82] There were many like Zebris and Czyzewski across Catholic America—priests who took on the stature and reputation of patriarchs in specific regions. The achievements of such men as Zebris and Czyzewski illustrate that even in eastern European communities, where lay authority in the organization and government of the parish was so zealously advocated, the clergy could still exercise a very formative role in the organization of parish life.

The other major eastern European group were the Ukrainians, and as Eastern-rite Catholics, their experience was different from that of the Latin-rite immigrants. In fact it was so different that American Catholic bishops were unable to adjust to the Ukrainian Catholic way of life.

In the old country, Ukrainian culture was permeated with religion; as one scholar noted, "The Church accompanied the life of the Ukrainian peasant from the cradle to the grave. His familial, social, and cultural life was unthinkable without the presence of church and priest."[83] As Eastern-rite Catholics (often referred to as Uniates), Ukrainians worshiped in a manner that was quite different from the Latin rite; not only was the language of worship different, but they also had different religious customs and traditions. Upon their arrival in the United States, Ukrainian immigrants at first would attend a Polish or Slovak church, but nostalgia for their own church, where they could practice the familiar rituals of the old country, motivated the people to found their own parishes. But there was one obstacle; their clergy married. Though this was the custom in the Eastern-rite church in Europe, it was not accepted by American bishops, who belonged to the Latin rite, in which clerical celibacy was the norm. The persistent refusal of the American hierarchy to yield on this point precipitated the second major schism to divide the Catholic church in the United States. Rather than become Latin-rite Catholics, as American bishops would have preferred, large numbers of Ukrainian people and priests left the Roman Catholic Church and joined the Russian Orthodox Church, in which a married clergy was accepted and Ukrainians could worship in their traditional manner.

This schism began in Minneapolis in 1891, when hostility developed between the bishop, John Ireland, and Father Alexis Toth, who had been asked by the people to become pastor of the newly established Ukrainian Catholic church.

Shortly after his arrival in Minneapolis in 1889, Toth went to introduce himself to Archbishop John Ireland. It proved to be a fateful meeting. Their conversation illustrated the cultural chasm that separated the American bishop from the Ruthenian priest, and it deserves to be reprinted since it clearly points out the problem that Eastern-rite Catholics faced in the United States. According to Toth the meeting went as follows:

I appeared before Bishop Ireland December 19, 1889, kissed his hand according to custom and presented my credentials, failing, however to kneel before him, which, as I learned later, was my chief mistake. I remember that no sooner did he read that I was a "Greek Catholic," his hands began to shake. It took him fifteen minutes to read to the end after which he asked abruptly—we conversed in Latin:

"Have you a wife?"

"No."

"But you had one?"

"Yes, I am a widower."

At this he threw the paper on the table and loudly exclaimed:

"I have already written to Rome protesting against this kind of priests being sent to me!" "What kind of priests do you mean?"

"Your kind."

"I am a Catholic priest of the Greek Rite. I am a Uniate and was ordained by a regular Catholic Bishop."

"I do not consider that either you or this bishop of yours are Catholic; besides, I do not need any Greek Catholic priests here; a Polish priest in Minneapolis is quite sufficient; the Greeks can also have him for their priest."

"But he belongs to the Latin Rite; besides our people do not understand him and so they will hardly go to him; that was the reason they instituted a church of their own."

"They had no permission from me and I shall grant you no jurisdiction to work here."

Deeply hurt by the fanaticism of this representative of Papal Rome, I replied sharply: "In that case, I know the rights of my church, I know the basis on which the Union was established and shall act accordingly."

The Archbishop lost his temper. I lost mine just as much. One word brought another, the thing had gone so far that our conversation is not worth putting on record.[84]

This was not an isolated event; many Eastern-rite priests experienced such humiliation from American Catholic bishops. Dressed in a long soutane, with a long beard, often with a wife and family gathered around them, these priests were more than American bishops could handle. They wanted no part of them and refused them permission to work in their dioceses, telling the priests to go back to Europe, where they belonged.[85] Toth, like many others, defied the bishop. Rather than leave Minneapolis, he remained as pastor of St. Mary's Church; then, in March of 1891, he and his congregation of 365 Ukrainian immigrants joined the Russian Orthodox Church. This marked the beginning of a major exodus of Ukrainian Catholics from the Roman Catholic Church in the United States. By 1907, sixty-five congregations had followed the lead of the St. Mary's congregation and joined the Orthodox Church, nor did the exodus slow down. By 1916, about 163 Eastern-rite Catholic parishes, with over two hundred thousand members, had joined the Orthodox Church. Conversion to Orthodoxy continued throughout the twentieth century, and today "as high as 65 percent of the faithful of the Orthodox Church of America are former Uniates who are ethnically Ukrainian-Ruthenians."[86]

Clerical celibacy, however, was only one reason for the conflict. Another was the Ukrainian insistence on ownership of parish property. Like other immigrant Catholics, Ukrainian lay people founded their own churches and incorporated church property in the name of the parish committee. Given the shortage of Eastern-rite clergy, such a development was not surprising. Yet it was something new for the Ukrainians, who did not enjoy such control of church affairs in the old country. Like other Eastern European Catholics in the United States, they democratized an Old World custom and gained control of the local church.[87] Like the Polish, Ukrainian Catholics were not about to yield on this issue, and they strongly resisted the attempts of American Latin-rite bishops to gain control over Ukrainian parishes. Though some parishes did turn over ownership of church property to the local bishop, this was clearly the exception. A major reason for such widespread resistance was the fear that ownership of their parish church by the American bishop would be but the first step in the Latinization or Romanization of their religion. In the opinion of one historian, lay ownership of parish churches "was the only thing that saved the fledgling Greek Catholic churches from being absorbed by the Latin Rite."[88] Throughout the 1920s, this issue remained a major point of discussion, and along with the celibacy issue it was one of the main reasons why Eastern-rite Catholic priests and lay people left the Roman Church during the pre-World War II period.

The loss of hundreds of thousands of Eastern-rite Catholics along with thousands of Poles, Lithuanians, and Slovaks illustrates how critical the issue of lay involvement in parish government was. Insistence of Catholic immigrants on preserving their authoritative role in managing local church affairs was such that they would accept excommunication, rather than give in on this point. At the same time, the Catholic hierarchy, along with the majority of the clergy, were so adamant that they were willing to allow an exodus of lay people, rather than give in to their demands on this issue. An irresistible force had met an immovable object, and the encounter produced bitter and prolonged conflict. Nationality differences certainly intensified the conflict, but more than just cultural differences were involved. Fundamentally it was a conflict between two radically differing views of the church. One view advocated a congregational model of the church, which emphasized a democratic functioning of authority with an emphasis on local autonomy. According to this model, lay people and clergy would work together and share responsibility for the organization and government of the parish. The other view supported a hierarchical model of the church; championed by the hierarchy, this emphasized the authority of the clergy over the lay people, with the bishop exercising supreme authority over everyone, priests and lay people alike.

By the early years of the twentieth century, certainly by the 1920s, most Catholic communities in the United States had accepted the prevailing hierarchical concept of the church. Eastern-rite Catholics remained the most notable exception, and the vestiges of congregationalism could also be found in some Slovak and Polish parishes, in which elected parish committees were still very popular.

The shift from a congregational model of the parish to a clerical model, in which the priest was the one supreme authority, took place gradually. It was first noticeable in the Irish communities during the 1820s and 1830s; by the 1850s, most Irish parishes had accepted the hierarchical concept of the church. Other immigrant groups resisted the trend, with some being more successful than others. Though there was never unanimous agreement among all ethnic groups on this point, resistance was widespread enough to cause conflict and even schism. By the 1920s, however, the clergy controlled the parish, and the tradition of lay people participating in the organization and government of the local church had come to an end.

No one reason can satisfactorily explain why this shift took place. A variety of influences must be considered which, taken together, will help to explain the transition.

In the early years of the nineteenth century, the spirit of republicanism unleashed by the American Revolution was still exerting its influence. This could be clearly seen in the area of religion, where ". . . by the early nineteenth century the religious liberalization begun by the Revolution had created a democratic religious world that few in 1776 had expected."[89] The democratization of religion was most striking in Protestant churches, but to limit its impact entirely to Protestants does not make sense. Catholic America was also caught up in the republican spirit, and the widespread popularity of the trustee system was a good example of the democratization of Catholicism during the republican period. Reinforcing this was the Catholic Enlightenment school of thought, which was still enjoying substantial support in Europe and England as well as in the United States. After 1820 or so, the Catholic Enlightenment began to falter; the democratization of religion also started to wane, so that by mid-century, religion in America was becoming once again more hierarchical in nature, with the clergy, both Catholic and Protestant, enjoying a regained status and control in the area of religion.

Another very important reason for the demise of the congregational concept of the church was the restoration of the papacy in the nineteenth century and the strengthening of papal authority throughout the Catholic world. This was achieved most decisively during the pontificate of Pius IX (1846–78) and reached its symbolic apex with the declaration of papal infallibility in 1870 at the First Vatican Council. The traditional hierarchical view of authority in the church was now reasserted with an absolutism that at times bordered on the extreme. This concept of the church became the standard view, and every priest and bishop learned this during his seminary education. The strengthening of papal authority and the hierarchical concept of the church meant that episcopal authority was likewise magnified. Each bishop became Pope in his own diocese. Such extreme emphasis on episcopal authority can be clearly seen in the legislation of the 1884 Baltimore Council, which gives the distinct impression that the bishop is the church. At the parish level the pastor's authority was also magnified. He benefited from the strengthening of the hierarchical church, so that in the parish he enjoyed a supremacy over the laity not unlike that of the Pope over the entire church. Such a development continued to gain strength during the early decades of the twentieth century.

The Irish attitude of deference to clerical authority, which grew stronger during the nineteenth century, reinforced this trend. Because of their numerical dominance among clergy and laity, the Irish tradition of deference became a standard which others were expected to follow.

The shortage of clergy and the unorganized state of the church's administrative bureaucracy encouraged the prevalence of congregationalism in the early decades of the nineteenth century. These conditions changed in much of the northern and eastern regions of the country by mid-century, but in the western regions such a state of affairs continued well beyond the 1860s, and not surprisingly, lay involvement was quite widespread in the West. But as the supply of clergy increased and ecclesiastical administration developed, clerical control became more realizable. Among new immigrants, however, church life in the United States was just beginning in the late-nineteenth century; churches had to be organized from scratch; there was a shortage of clergy who could speak their parishioners' mother tongues, and the experience of the Old World and its traditions were still very vivid. Given these conditions, congregationalism did become quite widespread. Even though the church was fairly well organized by this time and episcopal control was the standard, congregationalism did persist among many immigrant communities into the twentieth century. But as the supply of foreign-language-speaking clergy increased, as the local bishop gained more familiarity and experience in dealing with the new immigrants, and as the tradition of the Old World customs faded into the background, especially among the second generation, clerical control increasingly became the standard in these communities as well.

A final reason for the triumph of the clerical church was the social forces that were reshaping the Catholic community during the century of immigration. During the course of the nineteenth century, Catholicism changed from a small, relatively homogeneous community in terms of nationality and class to a large, radically diverse population made up of people from at least twenty-eight nationalities situated at various levels of the social and economic hierarchy. As Catholicism was becoming increasingly more divided along ethnic and class lines, so too was the rest of American society. Cities had become more segregated along racial, ethnic, and class lines by the late-nineteenth century; the emergence of a permanent wage-earning class of workers had hardened the lines dividing one class of people from another. Streetcar suburbs had emerged to accommodate the new middle class, and more exclusive residential areas sprung up to attract the upper classes. To counter this trend, city governments sought to acquire greater control over their people and neighborhoods. This desire for control was also evident in industry, which was experiencing rapid growth and expansion of services. The railroad industry provides a classic example of this move toward a more centralized control of operations in the late-nineteenth century.

Like their secular counterparts, church leaders also sought a more centralized control of their people and institutions. In a community divided along class and ethnic lines, such control made sense if the bishop was going to protect and strengthen his position as the supreme authority in a local church. A hierarchical concept of church could not operate very effectively if in each local community the lay people enjoyed a significant amount of authority and independence in the governance of the church. Unity in the church had been a keenly sought-after objective since the middle of the nineteenth century, and the increasing fragmentation of the church only intensified this rage for unity and order. This meant not only unity of belief, but also a uniform standard of religious practice; included in this of course were the organization and the government of the local church. To achieve this standard, control was necessary; the hierarchical concept of the church clearly fostered a more centralized control over church affairs.

These reasons help to explain the shift from a congregational concept of the church to the clerical church of the twentieth century, which has so prominent a place in the memory of Catholics raised in the pre-Vatican II church. The early years of the nineteenth century were a time when Catholic congregationalism was widespread; for most Catholic laity, the parish was a place where they could become involved in the management and administration of church affairs. But as the bishops proceeded to win the battle against lay trusteeism, Catholic congregationalism began to disintegrate. Unlike the one-hoss shay of Oliver Wendell Holmes, it did not collapse all at once, but came apart a piece at a time. First the Irish succumbed, and in their wake followed the French Canadians, the Italians, and the Mexicans; among the Eastern European peoples, resistance was stronger and longer. A remnant of congregationalism remained in the popularly elected lay committees, sanctioned by church councils, but by the 1920s these committees were a faded memory in most Catholic communities. Clericalism had become the standard, and the pastor, now enjoying a relatively long tenure in office, ruled as lord and master of his parish, where the lay people were left to pay, pray, and obey. This was a major shift in the history of Catholicism in the United States and one that has been overlooked for too long. The post-Vatican II era has rightly been labeled the age of the emerging laity, but history reminds us quite clearly that, even in the brief past of Catholic America, lay people at one time had a major responsibility for the growth and development of the local church.

Before concluding this study of the people and the parish, it would be wise to answer two questions that naturally come to mind. The first is, To what extent did the lay trustees represent the parish community? The second question seeks to know the social and economic background of these elected representatives.

Unfortunately, not very much research has been done on these issues, but from the studies available, certain patterns do emerge. Trustees, elected by the male pewholders of a given parish, clearly represented that particular constituency. Many people, however, did not rent pews; this was especially true of poorer Catholics, whose budget could not afford the added burden of a monthly pew-rental fee. Thus the question arises, What portion of the local Catholic community rented pews? Though it is difficult to give an exact answer, the best estimate, at least in the early-nineteenth century, was that less than 25 percent of the eligible families rented pews.[90]

Discrimination against the poor was a major complaint voiced against the pew-rental system, and for that reason many parishes did not adopt it. The most extensive example of this was in Bishop John England's diocese, in Charleston, South Carolina. Since England did not allow the pew-rental system precisely because it discriminated against the poor, parish trustees were elected by all male members of the parish over twenty-one years of age. Nineteenth-century church councils clearly favored this type of a more general, more representative election of trustees or church committeemen, and many Catholic parishes did begin to adopt this style of election, rather than limiting it to pewholders. This was especially notable in Polish and Slovak parishes, where church committees were elected by the male members of the parish at large.[91] Thus a definite pattern did emerge; in the early years of the nineteenth century, when the lay-trustee system was still very strong, elections were most often limited to those who rented pews; in subsequent decades, when the lay trustee-system was beginning to decline, elections became more representative of the entire parish population. The point to be made of course is that such elections, regardless of the extent of their representativeness, did mean that a certain measure of democracy existed in the government of local Catholic parishes. The two best examples of this would be the diocese of Charleston, South Carolina, during the episcopacy of John England (1820–42) and Eastern European (Polish and Slovak especially) parishes in the late-nineteenth and early-twentieth centuries.

What type of men were these trustees? This is the other question that must be answered, and again the evidence is sketchy. Patrick Carey writes that during the first half of the nineteenth century, "lay trustees were not from the poor and uneducated classes. Some of them were wealthy, but most were middle class professionals, e.g. physicians, lawyers, publishers, business executives, and skilled laborers."[92] My own research in a New York Irish parish supports this statement; the trustees of Transfiguration parish in the 1830s and 1840s represented the upper levels of the occupational hierarchy: professional men, proprietors of small neighborhood businesses (grocers especially), and skilled artisans. The same pattern appears to have prevailed among the Germans. A study of the German parish of St. Louis in Buffalo, New York, during the 1850s, concluded that the majority of the trustees were of high socioeconomic status, with 61 percent owning their own businesses.[93] From these few studies it seems clear that among native-American, Irish, and German parishes the trustees were men of social and economic standing in the community who had lived in the area for some time and had achieved a measure of economic status not common among the majority of their coreligionists. Predictably they represented the Catholic middle class, which was growing larger in the native-American, Irish, and German communities during the nineteenth century.

In Eastern European communities, however, the majority of church trustees came from the lower classes. The most thorough documentation for this comes from a study of Slovak parishes in Pittsburgh in the early-twentieth century. This study, by Sylvia Granatir Alexander, indicates that about two thirds of the trustees elected in the four Slovak parishes of Pittsburgh in the 1906–15 period were laborers; the others were small businessmen and professionals. Alexander also noted, ". . . in general it was laborers, not businessmen or professionals, who initiated efforts to establish churches." Moreover, a strong bond existed between the local Slovak fraternal societies and the parish, with the result that the leaders in these lodges were often the chosen leaders in the church as well.[94] This pattern of Pittsburgh's Slovaks appears to have been the pattern in other Eastern European communities. This is not surprising, given the recent arrival of these peoples and the small sizes of their middle classes. It would also reinforce the pattern of diversity observable in early-twentieth-century Catholicism: a sizable middle-class constituency made up of Irish and Germans, alongside a large lower-class community made up principally of Eastern European immigrants. The result was that lay leadership in the Irish and German communities came from the middle class, while among Eastern Europeans it emerged from the lower, laboring class.

By the 1920s, however, lay leadership in the Catholic church was a contradiction. A remnant of it may have remained in some Eastern European parishes, but, for all practical purposes, the clergy led and the laity followed. They were like the biblical sheep; as Pope Pius X put it, ". . . the one duty" of the laity "is to allow themselves to be led, and like a docile flock, to follow the Pastors."[95] Pushed out of the decision-making sphere of parish life, lay people were encouraged to take up other types of activity. The new spheres of lay involvement became the social and devotional areas of the parish.

VII

The Neighborhood
and Its Gods

WHEN IMMIGRANT CATHOLICS came to the United States, the vast majority of them headed for the neighborhoods of urban America. The city was where they had their best chance of finding a job; it was also where they could find their relatives and friends, those enthusiastic letter writers who had urged them to come in the first place. Arriving in such places as New York, Philadelphia, Chicago, and San Francisco, the newcomers went to the local ethnic village, the immigrant neighborhood where they would find their own kind of people. Every city had such areas. Walking through these neighborhoods, a nineteenth-century visitor could not help but notice their foreign quality. The immigrants "create for themselves," observed one such visitor, "distinct communities, almost as impervious to American sentiments and influences as are the inhabitants of Dublin or Hamburg. . . . They have their own theaters, recreations, amusements, military and national organizations; to a great extent their own schools, churches, and trade unions; their own newspapers and periodical literature."[1]

For New York's Germans, Little Germany on the Lower East Side was their home, not Manhattan; Chicago's Irish lived on the South Side in such neighborhoods as Bridgeport and Canaryville; San Francisco's Italians lived in North Beach, near the fishing wharfs; Chicago's Polish lived in such neighborhoods as Stanislawowo, named after the local parish church; New England's French Canadians lived in neighborhoods such as Enfant Jésus and St. François-Xavier, areas also named after Catholic parishes. Distinctive landmarks of urban America, they possessed an innate magnetism that attracted the immigrants, and once the newcomers settled in, these neighborhoods became their reference point within the larger, more impersonal city, their home in a strange new world.

The immigrant neighborhood had developed over the course of the nineteenth century. In the late-eighteenth and early-nineteenth centuries, American cities were small enough that a leisurely afternoon walk could take you from one end of the city to the other. Even though these "walking cities" had certain areas for business and trade as well as distinctive residential quarters, they had not yet developed recognizable immigrant neighborhoods. The walking cities of this era had a measure of urbanity about them in the sense that home and shop, rich and poor, foreign-born and native were mingled together throughout the city. Church steeples dominated the skylines of these early cities and underscored the importance of this urban institution. But most of the churches were not neighborhood churches; they served a citywide clientele made up of various classes and nationalities. St. Peter's Church in New York was a classic example of such a cosmopolitan institution. Masses were offered in three languages: English, French, and German. Rich and poor, Irish and German, black and white attended the same church. A similar situation prevailed in other urban Catholic communities in the early-nineteenth century, and even the few distinctively ethnic parishes such as Holy Trinity German parish in Philadelphia served a citywide population, rather than a particular neighborhood community.

Once the war of 1812 came to an end, immigration began in earnest; hundreds, then thousands, and finally millions of people emigrated to the United States. An urban explosion took place along the Atlantic coast, and the old colonial cities burst their boundaries. Beyond the Alleghenies, old towns such as St. Louis and Cincinnati became the centers of an urban frontier, while such new towns as Chicago and Milwaukee were founded. With the arrival of the immigrants and the expansion of the city, recognizable immigrant neighborhoods began to take shape. New York's Lower East Side took on a decidedly German flavor, Cincinnati experienced the same development in the German quarter of Over the Rhine. The Irish in Detroit congregated in Corktown, while in San Francisco the Irish were concentrated in the Seventh Ward, along the waterfront. Then, at mid-century, the streetcar appeared; at first powered by horses and later by electricity, this technological development pushed city boundaries even farther out from the center of the city. As the city expanded, residential streetcar suburbs emerged, and the city gradually became more segregated according to class, race, and ethnicity. By the late 1800s the old walking city had become the residential center for new immigrants from southern and Eastern Europe, along with Irish and German lower classes; along streetcar lines, middle-class neighborhoods sprung up, and they attracted second- and third-generation-American Catholics.[2]

Every neighborhood had its distinguishing marks—institutions that served the needs of its people and cemented city blocks together into a cohesive, identifiable area. The major institutions were political club, church, school, and saloon; other centers, such as police station, firehouse, and athletic club, were also important. Chicago's Bridgeport, an Irish Catholic neighborhood settled in the mid-nineteenth century, offers a fine example of how certain institutions geographically defined a particular neighborhood. Famous today because it was the lifelong residence of Chicago's mayor Richard J. Daley, the major institutions of Bridgeport—Nativity Catholic Church, the Eleventh Ward regular Democratic organization headquarters, and Schaller's Pump— were situated within a few blocks of one another. Bible, ballot, and bottle, these were the symbols that defined the space of Bridgeport. Each of these institutions served a specific purpose and was important in its own right, but during the century of immigration the church remained the most enduring cultural institution in the neighborhood and the matrix within which immigrant Catholicism was nurtured and sustained.[3]

As the city took on a new shape during the century of immigration, the Catholic parish also changed, with the result that class and ethnicity became the identifying marks of a particular parish; race was only infrequently a determinative feature, given the small number of black Catholics in any one city. The polyglot, cosmopolitan parish of the early-nineteenth century had disappeared, and parishes were now set apart by geographical boundaries that most often corresponded to the natural boundaries of city neighborhoods. Given the ethnic and class distinctions of these neighborhoods, however, this meant that the church, like the city, was really divided not by geography but by class and nationality.

Shaped by the forces of urbanization and immigration, the local Catholic church took on the features of nineteenth-century neighborhoods. Like the city, urban Catholicism became a multiethnic, multiclass community. Given the predominantly lower-class nature of Catholicism, however, the immigrant neighborhood was the dominant type of urban Catholic communities. Three selected examples will illustrate what these neighborhoods were like.

New York has always been a major center of the Irish-American community and with good reason. The roots of the New York Irish go back deep into history, and by the 1830s the city already had a vibrant Irish community, the center of which was the Sixth Ward. The Sixth Ward had both its dark and its bright sides. A potpourri of poverty and wealth, it included the fashionable avenue of Broadway, with its stores and fancy shoppers, as well as the Five Points slum just a few blocks away. Most people lived in wooden tenements or shanty cottages, with some of the worst tenements in the city being in the Irish Sixth Ward. Mortality rates were high and life was harsh. During the 1840s and 1850s, a large percentage of the men and women in the neighborhood were unskilled workers; a smaller number were engaged in neighborhood trades such as groceries, liquor, and oysters. But the vast majority of Irish were employed in some type of skilled or semiskilled trade such as carpentry, tailoring, or shoemaking. The Sixth Ward Irish worshiped at Transfiguration Church, which, together with the school, were the religious and educational centers of their lives.[4]

A half century later and a thousand miles west, in the city of Chicago, was another immigrant neighborhood which outsiders did not hesitate to call a slum. It was the Polish community of Stanislawowo, on the city's northwest side. The massive structure of St. Stanislaus Church dominated the skyline of the neighborhood, but within its shadows were some of the most densely populated areas in the United States. On one block alone, 2,327 people were jammed into 96 lots; such overcrowding hastened the deterioration of the neighborhood housing stock, with the result that the tenements of Stanislawowo were some of the city's worst. The vast majority of people worked in neighborhood sweatshops, earning meager wages as unskilled workers. Men and women, adults and children, had to work to support their large families. Reflecting the precarious nature of life in the neighborhood, the infant-mortality rate was one of the highest in Chicago—in 1900 each Polish mother, on the average, buried two of her infant children. It was with good reason that some reformers labeled "the Polish slums of Stanislawowo as among the worst in Chicago and in the nation."[5]

Like the Polish in Chicago, Mexican Catholics in El Paso, Texas, were also struggling to survive. The largest Mexican *barrio*, or neighborhood, in the city was situated along the Rio Grande adjacent to the stockyards and the railroad. Like New York's Sixth Ward and Chicago's Stanislawowo, the *barrio* on the South Side of El Paso had all the characteristics of a lower-class immigrant neighborhood. In Chihuahuita, as the Mexicans called it, people lived in small adobe huts with dirt floors and little or no plumbing and heating. Situated along the banks of the river, they were easy prey to spring and summer flooding. Overcrowding was a common sight in the adobe homes, and this encouraged an unusually high incidence of sickness and disease; the infant mortality rate in the *barrio* was also very high. The Catholic Church was well represented in South El Paso, with the parish of St. Ignatius and its multiple religious confraternities, social-service agencies, and school doing a great deal to aid the immigrants in their adjustment to American society.[6]

Chihuahuita, Stanislawowo, and the Sixth Ward were not unique. They were representative of lower-class immigrant neighborhoods scattered across urban America. Slovaks in Pittsburgh, Irish in Milwaukee, Germans in New York, French Canadians in Nashua, New Hampshire, and Italians in San Francisco lived in similar environments. Nineteenth- and twentieth-century outsiders often called these places slums, but the people who lived there called them home. Life was certainly harsh and survival was the goal of most. Yet despite these realities people clung to their homes with unusual tenacity. As one observer noted of the Germans on New York's Lower East Side, they "were satisfied, happy and contented." The immigrant neighborhood enabled them to live among their own people, with whom they could speak their native language and observe their ethnic customs. Moreover, the standard of living was such that, unlike in the old country, they could live in New York like a prince "for $10.00 to $14.00 a month."[7] Life in the immigrant neighborhood clearly was an experience both bitter and sweet, and your vantage point determined how you interpreted it. One woman who grew up in the French-Canadian mill town of Manchester, New Hampshire, put it very well. "We found out later," she said, "as we were growing up and we started realizing we never had this or we never had that, that we must have been poor. But as we were growing, I never felt poor. We never felt that we were any less than other people. . . ."[8]

Even though the lower-working-class neighborhood was clearly the dominant type of Catholic community in the United States, other types of neighborhoods and parishes existed. The most significant of these was the middle-class neighborhood. Reflecting the multilayered nature of the Catholic community, such neighborhoods existed throughout the century of immigration. Before the Civil War, for example, New York's Greenwich Village had a fashionable residential area, and situated in the heart of this neighborhood was St. Ann's Church. A small parish, its parishioners lived in the fine residences of the Washington Square district, and many had country homes as well, complete with servant help.[9] St. Ann's parish, however, was unusual for its time. Later on, as the streetcar pushed city boundaries outward and second- and third-generation immigrants began to make it economically, more middle-class neighborhoods emerged.

The Dorchester section of Boston experienced this development in the 1870s and 1880s; it became a favorite home for many of Boston's growing Irish middle class. By the 1880s, St. Peter's in Dorchester was one of the most prosperous parishes in the city. Similar developments took place in Philadelphia as Catholics followed the expansion of the city into new residential areas east of the Schuylkill River. In this region emerged such middle-class parishes as St. James, St. Agatha, and St. Francis de Sales. A famous example of a Catholic middle-class neighborhood was Chicago's Washington Park. Famous because it was the setting for James Farrell's novels, most especially the Studs Lonigan trilogy, the neighborhood of Washington Park was typically middle-class Catholic America in the early-twentieth century. It was where the "steam heat" Irish lived, "a description compounded of jealousy mingled with derision." For Chicago's South Side Irish, owning a home in Washington Park was the epitome of the good life. Raised in poor working-class neighborhoods, these descendants of immigrants were the lucky ones who had made it. As in the old neighborhood, the parish church remained an important center of the world encompassed within Washington Park.[10]

Washington Park represented the quintessence of the Catholic middle-class neighborhood in the early-twentieth century. Yet, Catholics were not the only people who lived there. Protestants also called Washington Park home, and this points out a very important point: Catholic immigrant neighborhoods were by no means exclusively Catholic. Chicago's Bridgeport was the home of German Lutherans as well as Irish Catholics; New York's Little Germany was also the home of large numbers of German Protestant immigrants; the same was true of Cincinnati's Over the Rhine neighborhood.

Moreover, Catholic immigrant neighborhoods housed several ethnic groups. Immigrant "ghettos" with an unusually high concentration of one foreign-language group were simply not the norm in most cities. The following exceptions prove the point. In Manchester, New Hampshire, French Canadians made up 80 percent of the city's Fourth Ward population in 1882; before World War I, a ten-block section of Chicago's Stanislawowo neighborhood was 95 percent Polish; unusually high concentrations of Germans could be found in Milwaukee and Cincinnati. But these were clearly exceptions. "Only rarely," noted historian Howard Chudacoff, "did one immigrant group constitute a majority of residents in an area one half to one square mile in size."[11] Most often, several immigrant groups lived in the same neighborhood, though within these areas informal but real boundary lines existed. Chicago's Bridgeport provided a good example of such an ethnic hodgepodge with its own internal boundary lines. The area was about one square mile in size; five Catholic immigrant groups—Irish, Polish, Czechs, Germans, and Lithuanians—made up about 70 percent of the area's population. At the turn of the century the Polish and the Lithuanians were concentrated in one section of Bridgeport and zealously avoided living near the Irish. Irish homes were quite evenly distributed throughout the area, and the Czechs and the Germans were also residentially dispersed, though sizable concentrations of them lived near their respective parish churches.[12] Even within each area it was not unusual to find regional loyalties and distinctions. German neighborhoods evidenced this, as did Italian districts, where people from Sicily or the Abruzzi would congregate together on a certain street or block.

Little Italies and Little Germanies, those famous ethnic colonies where a particular nationality group made up a plurality, though not a majority, of the population, certainly did exist. These were areas where certain streets and blocks took on distinctive characters. Reminiscing about Manchester, New Hampshire, a Greek woman talked about such "little cities within a city":

> Manchester was divided into an amazing network of ethnic communities. Cedar Street was the Middle East in all its splendor, mostly, Syrians. Little Greece was on Spruce Street one thoroughfare away. The French in west Manchester were so ethnic that you needed an interpreter to enter. The Chinese, with their impeccable laundries, had scattered throughout the city.[13]

The major importance of such ethnic colonies was cultural, rather than residential. As Chudacoff put it, these neighborhoods "centralized institutions rather than group residence."[14] They nurtured and sustained a variety of institutions within the community and established a web of social relationships that bound each group together. Little cities within a city, they created a new world for people, a world of the mind wherein they could function, as well as a spatial world where they could meet people of their own kind, reminisce about the old country, hear the Word of God spoken in a familiar tongue, and watch their children grow up speaking and praying as they did. Living in such neighborhoods was as much living in a special state of mind as it was living in a special residential area. Even though they all lived within a stone's throw of each other, Irish seldom mingled with Italians, Catholics hardly ever met Protestants or Jews. These immigrant neighborhoods were cultural ghettos, not residential ghettos.

A long-time resident of a Chicago South Side neighborhood articulated how simple it was to live in such a cultural ghetto cut off from the surrounding world. She spoke of her neighborhood in the 1920s and 1930s as "an Irish neighborhood"; "everybody was Irish," she said. She went to St. Columbanus Church and "everybody," as she remembered it, was "Catholic." But these reminiscences conflict with the reality. Her neighborhood housed between twenty-six and thirty-three ethnic groups, with the Irish making up only 13 percent of the area, which was predominantly Protestant, not Catholic. This woman remembered her old neighborhood as Irish Catholic because this was the world she experienced, a world peopled with Irish Catholics.[15]

A major influence in shaping such cultural isolation was ethnic and religious prejudice. Prejudice among Catholic immigrant groups was widespread and led to overt discrimination and even open conflict in the parish. Irish-Italian and Polish-German disputes were perhaps the most notorious; later, the Mexicans felt the brunt of discrimination from their coreligionists. Such conflict created parish schisms and helped to underline the necessity of the national parish. As real and persistent as such discrimination was, it could not match the virulence of the anti-Catholic, anti-foreign prejudice experienced by Catholic immigrants.

Anti-Catholicism was a leftover from the Protestant Reformation. It was an integral part of American colonial culture, and after a period of religious harmony during the republican era, it surfaced again in the early-nineteenth century. The main reason was the large influx of Catholic foreigners, whose presence threatened the homogeneity of the Anglo-Saxon Protestant culture of the United States. By the 1830s, the threat was real enough to persuade many Protestants to act. Convents were a special target of curiosity, and convent raids and even burnings took place; churches were also attacked, and in New England ". . . mob attacks . . . became so frequent that many congregations posted regular armed guards to patrol and protect their property."[16] Pornographic anti-Catholic literature also was published. The *Awful Disclosures of the Hotel Dieu Nunnery of Montreal,* a scurrilous and false account of life in a Catholic convent published in 1836 and frequently reprinted, permanently etched the name of Maria Monk, its author, into the annals of American history. Such animosity toward Catholics also helped to ignite city riots. Philadelphia was the site of the most famous. For several days in May 1844 and again in July, Protestants and Irish Catholics clashed in violent street battles; homes in Irish neighborhoods were burned, as were two Catholic churches, and thirteen people were killed, with many others injured. Though cultural as well as economic factors may help to explain the 1844 riots, religion was clearly a major issue.

The antiforeign sentiment became so popular that a new national political party was organized around this issue. Voting an anti-Catholic and antiforeign platform, the Know-Nothings gained wide popular support in the 1850s. Before their collapse in the midst of the dispute over slavery, the Know-Nothings had gained control of several city and state governments. Such stirring victories at the polls reminded Catholic newcomers of their precarious place in the New World. Nor was this anti-Catholic paranoia a regional phenomenon. Despite the absence of large numbers of Catholics, the South witnessed anti-Catholic outbursts; the new towns of the Midwest also experienced it, nor was it absent from California. Transplanted New Englanders and other Protestants led the crusade to clean up San Francisco in the 1850s; in other words, to get rid of the poor Irish immigrants. Their campaign reached a high point in 1856, when the Committee of Vigilance took over control of the city government and proceeded to execute four people and sought to banish from the city close to one hundred more; the anti-Irish tenor of the Vigilance campaign was evident. Two out of the four people hanged and 75 percent of those ordered out of the city were Irish.[17]

Some semblance of mutual accord among Catholics and Protestants, native-born and foreign-born, was restored during the 1860s. But the calm in the storm only raised the fears of some people that trouble would soon resurface. In the presidential election campaign of 1876, the anti-Catholic issue emerged once again, as it did once more in 1884, when a Protestant minister's warning against "rum, Romanism, and rebellion" angered many Catholics. Then, in 1887, in the small town of Clinton, Iowa, the American Protective Association was founded. An anti-Catholic organization, it reached its high point of popularity in the 1890s; the popularity of the APA, coupled with the resurgence of antiforeign feelings against the new immigrants—Italians, Polish, Lithuanians, and other Eastern European peoples—would not allow Catholic immigrants to forget their second-class status in the United States. Although support for the anti-Catholic crusade had diminished considerably since the 1850s, it remained a threat well into the twentieth century. The emergence of the Ku Klux Klan, with its anti Catholic platform and its popularity during the 1920s, was indicative of this.[18]

Catholics, of course, were not the only people in the United States who experienced the ugliness of discrimination. Jews and Mormons endured persecution because of their religious beliefs; among Protestants, a great deal of religious discrimination was evident, with Methodists and Baptists, Presbyterians and Congregationalists waging wars of words against each other. Religious prejudice cut wide chasms in the fabric of American society, and anti-Catholicism was only one aspect of this larger cultural phenomenon. Racial and ethnic discrimination reinforced such division and widened the gulfs separating Americans from one another.

The point to be made is that religious and ethnic conflict tended to harden the lines of the Catholic cultural ghetto, thus expanding the gap between Catholics and Protestants as well as between differing Catholic ethnic groups. Over time the gap between Catholic ethnics narrowed. The increasing number of ethnically mixed marriages after 1880 was a sure indicator of this; such mixed marriages were a rare occurrence in the first generation, but they became increasingly more notable in the second and third generations.[19]

Despite this tendency to marry outside one's own ethnic group, the cultural ghetto remained a powerful reality in the early-twentieth century. Even though some individuals may have breached the gap that separated them from other Catholic nationality groups, the ethnic parish remained the last bastion of cultural exclusivism through the 1920s. Although the gap dividing Catholic ethnics narrowed, there is little evidence to suggest that a similar development took place between Catholics and Protestants. Well into the twentieth century, religion remained a major point of division, as well as contention, in American society. Thus, throughout the century of immigration, the immigrant neighborhood remained a powerful force in shaping the culture of Catholics. Ethnicity and religion were the major elements in this culture, and they shaped Catholicism into a very ethnocentric and religiously exclusive community.

As central as the immigrant neighborhood was in the lives of the newcomers, most people did not live there for long periods of time. The image of the stable ethnic neighborhood from which nobody moved is, like the ethnically homogeneous neighborhood, a myth. It never existed. Americans have always been on the move, and the nineteenth century was not very different in this regard from the twentieth century. During the nineteenth century only between 40 and 60 percent of the population in a given city at one time was likely to be living there a decade later; in other words, within a ten-year span, about one half of the city's population would have moved.[20] Moreover, the other half of the population, who stayed behind, were also on the move within the city, moving from neighborhood to neighborhood. In Omaha, Nebraska, for example, ". . . less than 25 percent of the city's young and middle-aged family heads lived in one place for as long as five years; only 3 percent failed to move in twenty years." Among the New York Irish, ". . . four out of five families moved at least once while they lived in New York; of these families two out of five moved more than once."[21] Such mobility belies the image of the stable neighborhood and parish. Even though neighborhood populations were continually changing, such change was neither traumatic nor threatening, because the newcomers generally resembled the transients in both ethnic and religious background. Polish replaced Polish in Little Poland, and Italians replaced Italians in Little Italy. This gave the appearance of a stable neighborhood population, when in fact it was quite mobile.

One institution that remained in the neighborhood and helped to give it a special identity was the immigrant parish. Most often founded by the people, the church was the most enduring and important cultural institution in the neighborhood. As a social organization that brought people together through a network of societies and clubs, it helped to establish a sense of community. As an educational organization, it taught both young and old the meaning of America, its language as well as its culture; as a religious organization, it brought the presence of God to the neighborhood, nurturing and sustaining the presence of the holy through worship, devotional services, and neighborhood processions.

Important as this religious dimension was, the immigrant parish was more than just a religious institution in which people could satisfy their spiritual needs and desires. This was the manifest purpose of the parish, but it also was a key social institution. Indeed in most Catholic neighborhoods it was the cement that bound the people together, enabling them to establish some semblance of a community life. Families were indeed the building blocks of every immigrant community, but the church was the mortar that sought to bind them together.

In the early years of the nineteenth century, the Catholic parish was primarily a religious institution. Its identity was associated with the church structure, where worship and devotional services took place on a regular, though infrequent basis. The church was a Mass house and not much more. The absence of any significant network of organizations confirms this, with only one or two devotional confraternities being the norm in a Catholic parish at this time. As the city expanded and immigrant neighborhoods developed, the parish was transformed into a community institution.

As historian Sam Bass Warner noted about Philadelphia, "The mid-nineteenth century was par excellence, the era of the urban parish church, the lodge, the benefit association, the social and athletic club, the fire company, and the gang." In a changing city, people were searching for "a sense of social place and community," and many immigrants found this in the parish.[22] This trend continued throughout the rest of the nineteenth century as Americans became joiners in a multitude of organizations. The transformation of the parish mirrored this trend. Prior to 1880, most parishes had a few societies, and the vast majority of these, such as the Rosary Society, were manifestly devotional, though they certainly could have had a social dimension to them. But the parish with the large organizational network was clearly the exception prior to the 1880s. The parish history study referred to previously is very suggestive in this regard. All societies in each of the more than nine hundred parishes studied were tabulated by date of origin, and even though more than half of the parishes were founded prior to 1880, only about one out of five parish societies (19 percent) had been organized by that date. Moreover, these were decidedly devotional or spiritual, with two out of every three societies founded between 1800 and 1880 being of this type. The purpose of these societies was explicitly spiritual; dedicated to a particular saint or to a specific devotion associated with Jesus or a saint, each had its own constitution and regulations, which spelled out the spiritual obligations of the members. These included the regular recitation of certain prayers, attendance at Mass, and reception of Communion. Some of the more popular societies were the Sodality of Mary, Confraternity of the Holy Childhood, and Confraternity of the Sacred Heart.

After 1880 the picture changed dramatically when not only were many more parish societies founded, but they also represented a greater diversity of purpose. Now societies with explicit social, recreational, charitable, and educational goals were beginning to appear. With the multiplication of a vast and diverse array of societies, the immigrant parish was transformed into a major social and cultural institution in the neighborhood. This change went hand in glove with the segregation of the city and the development of strong ethnic neighborhoods. This is not to say that strong ethnic neighborhoods or organizationally complex parishes did not exist prior to 1880; not at all. The point is that such neighborhoods and parishes were in the process of development during this period, with the result that by the 1880s the configuration of city and parish differed visibly from previous decades. The pattern, noticeable by the 1880s, intensified in the next twenty years.[23]

Just about any parish could be cited as an example of the type that emerged after 1880, the parish that, as one observer put it, ". . . aimed to meet every need of the parishioner, and to deal with every condition."[24] A famous old Chicago parish, Holy Family, was a good example of this type of institution. Situated on the near West Side of Chicago, Holy Family was an Irish working-class parish, undoubtedly one of the largest in the country in the 1880s and 1890s. About seventy-five thousand people lived within its boundaries in 1895, and twenty-five thousand of them belonged to the parish. In 1896 the parish bulletin listed twenty-five societies; they were spiritual, recreational, educational, and charitable in nature; though the total membership was never listed, based on other evidence it had to number well over ten thousand people, with some of them most likely belonging to more than one society.

Holy Family had a society for every age group; the societies sponsored a dizzying array of events and activities: bands, baseball clubs, dramatic groups, picnics, bazaars, and parades as well as the usual weekly or monthly group meetings. Each society had its list of officers, and their history was proudly chronicled in the parish history.[25] A more modest-size German parish, St. John the Baptist in Cincinnati, had a similar organizational network. In 1895 it had sixteen parish societies; as in Holy Family, the majority had a manifestly spiritual purpose, and the rest included mutual benefit societies, a charitable society, a literary society that sponsored debates and plays, and fraternal insurance societies affiliated with national organizations. As the parish history noted, the people found "strength in unity," and this sense of community was an important value fostered in the parish.[26]

Holy Family and St. John the Baptist were not unique. Urban Catholic communities spawned a multitude of societies in the late-nineteenth century. In Pittsburgh, for example, when an attempt was made in 1899 to unite Catholic societies throughout the city, representatives from ninety societies showed up at the meeting; the majority of these were centered in local parish communities.[27]

The trend, first noted in the 1880s, continued into the twentieth century. According to the parish history study, the period 1900–20 matched the previous twenty-year period in the number of societies founded; diversity of purpose continued, with the most notable shift being the establishment of more societies for young people. By the 1920s the immigrant church had reached a level of strength and confidence not previously known. This decade, bracketed on one side by war and on the other by economic depression, was the golden age of the Catholic parish. This was the time when it reached the height of its activity. Some parishes had as many as eleven or more social events a year; dances, plays, minstrel shows, card parties, parish bazaars, and picnics were commonplace. In New York, parish social life was so hectic that the local Catholic newspaper even published a weekly column, "What's Going On in City Parishes," to keep people abreast of the activity; it filled a full page and a half of notices. Clerical magazines carried many articles which instructed priests about the value of parish theater groups and other types of parochial activities. In these years the priest was "cult leader, confessor, teacher, counselor, social director, administrator, recreation director for young and old, and a social worker."[28] A New York Catholic, a member of Sacred Heart parish on Manhattan's West Side, recalled this time in her life. "My recollection," she said, "of Sacred Heart is a very happy one, of my own family, my friends and neighbors. Our lives were centered around Sacred Heart church and one another." Her family went to Mass daily; her father belonged to the Holy Name Society—a very popular men's organization in the twentieth century—and her mother belonged to the Altar and the Rosary societies; she belonged to the Dramatic Club, which was quite popular in the

1920s. She went on parish excursions to Rockaway Beach and took part in May processions that filled West Fifty-first Street with hundreds of people.[29]

The obvious commitment of this woman's family to the church raises the question of how typical she was. Clearly she and her family were not typical parishioners in terms of their daily attendance at Mass, but their social involvement in parish societies and events was quite standard. For this family and many others, life did center around the parish church. Such people formed the core of the parish. But the question remains as to what percentage of immigrant Catholics were included in the parish as members, and an even more difficult question is, What part of these made up the core, those for whom the parish represented "the center of their lives," a phrase found continually throughout the history of immigrant Catholicism? Since little research has been done in this area, no substantive conclusion can be drawn, but some light can be shed on the question.

One study of New York in the early-twentieth century revealed that, in Irish neighborhoods, at least 70 percent of the people belonged to the parish church, whereas, in German neighborhoods, the number of Catholics belonging to the parish was less, about 46 percent. The level of membership appeared to increase as the social class of people improved, though the Irish were still more frequently affiliated with the parish than the Germans. My own study of the same area in the late-nineteenth century found that only between 40 and 50 percent of the Catholics in the neighborhood were members of the local parish. In Lawrence, Massachusetts, 68 percent of the city's Lithuanian Catholics made their Easter duty in 1910, and this would have been the minimal criterion for parish membership at that time.[30] This does suggest that religious commitment could and did indeed vary among differing ethnic groups. But another issue, regular church attendance, must be considered, and here the evidence is more consistent. In most Catholic parishes, no more than 50 percent attended church regularly, and in some communities where regular church attendance was not invested with high religious value, among the Italians and Mexicans for example, the level was much lower. The final question remains—what percent of the people made up the core? My estimate, based on membership figures for parish societies, the percentage of people belonging to the parish, and figures for regular churchgoers, would put this group most likely in the 25–30 percent range, possibly lower, certainly not higher. As small as the core may appear, most families in the parish likely had at least one member who was actively involved in some parish society.

Regardless of their level of involvement, however, all Catholics could identify with the local parish. An important neighborhood institution, it meant different things to different people. For some it was a reference point, a place that helped them to remember who they were in their adopted homeland; for others it was more, a place where a sense of community could be found; for still others it gave life meaning, and it helped them to cope with life in the emerging metropolis or the small town. Because it was more than just a religious institution, the immigrant parish touched both the indifferent and the devout in differing ways and for varying reasons. The central place of the parish in the neighborhood was dramatically underscored on the occasion of neighborhood processions.

Associated with religious events, such processions traveled through the streets of the neighborhood, and large numbers of people marched in line while hundreds of others stood and watched. During such festivals, the neighborhood took on new life: stores were decorated with flags and banners, people hung decorations in their windows, and streets were swept clean. As the procession filed through the streets, Catholics were marking off their neighborhood, laying claim to it, and telling people that this was their piece of the earth. People from other religions or ethnic groups might have lived in the area and even watched the parade march by, but on these days Catholic Irish, Polish, Italians or Mexicans were laying claim to the neighborhood and saying in a very clear and symbolic way that this was their Little Poland or Little Italy, etc. As was true of other parish involvement, some people walked at the head of the procession and others at the end; some did not march at all but merely stood and watched. Yet, despite their differing levels of involvement, all Catholics could easily identify with the procession of their countrymen and countrywomen. Such processions helped to forge a sense of solidarity among Catholics and reminded them all that this was their neighborhood, and these were their people parading along the street with the symbols, the icons, of their God.[31]

Such religious processions clearly served several purposes, but their explicit, manifest purpose was religious. The same was true of the parish. Though it was more than just a religious institution, the parish's primary purpose was spiritual. This is where people publicly manifested their faith, and for most Catholics it was the center of their religious world. To understand the religion of the people, it is necessary to penetrate the religious world of the parish. Though it may not have encompassed the totality of an individual's religious experience, a study of religion at the parish level can uncover a great deal by pointing out the major contours of the religious landscape in the immigrant Catholic community.

It is important to understand that the religious world of Catholics in the early-nineteenth century was quite different from its counterpart in the closing decades of the century. Unlike churches in Europe, Catholic churches in the United States were very plain, not terribly large, and decorated in a Spartan style. One European Jesuit, John Grassi, described them as "unpretending structures, without ornament." He went on to note that they had "galleries all around the inside in order to have more room and the organ, if they possess one, over the main entrance, and they have only one altar. Behind or alongside the altar, there is a small sacristy, in which confessions are heard, and it is provided with a fireplace."[32] Notably absent were the statues and pictures commonly found in Roman Catholic churches. For European missionaries, this was something of a culture shock; Ambrose Marechal, the French-born archbishop of Baltimore, "grieved" very much that the Baltimore cathedral was "almost completely lacking in decoration." He wanted "to buy two statues, namely one of Our Lord and Saviour and one of the Blessed Virgin" for the cathedral, but "none whatsoever could be found in these regions."[33] In Kentucky, Father Stephen Badin wrote a report in 1821 describing the state of the church; he noted that people needed prayer books, catechisms, and rosaries; in addition, ". . . chalices, ciboriums, crucifixes, vestments and church ornaments, altar pictures—in fact, everything relating to divine service" was also needed, and he urged future missionaries to America to bring such things with them.[34]

European missionaries such as Grassi, Marechal, and Badin clearly noticed the plain style of Catholicism in the United States. To them it was most visible in the simplicity of church architecture and decoration. For these foreigners, such simplicity was a deficiency of the missionary church that could be remedied only by importing the necessary statues, pictures, and ornaments. But the plain style of American Catholicism was not a weakness or deficiency attributable solely to its missionary status. Rather, such simplicity, most visible in church architecture and decoration, was reflective of a style of religion that was popular throughout the republican period. To the newly arrived European missionary, such plainness was a fault that needed correction; to the American-born lay people, it was a familiar quality.

John Carroll's pastoral letters clearly reflected this plain style of religion; lacking any emphasis on the practice of external devotional rituals, he encouraged a personalist religion rooted in the imitation of Christ. For John Carroll, prayer, meditation, spiritual reading, and works of charity were the core of Catholic piety.[35] A reading of parish trustee minutes during this period also suggests that the practice of religion was not very complicated; notably absent was the elaborate network of societies and devotional practices so commonplace by the 1890s. The practice of religion centered around Sunday, with the celebration of morning Mass, afternoon vespers, and benediction constituting the core of Catholic devotions. This emphasis on Sunday as the focal point for Catholic piety was encouraged at the first church synod held in Baltimore in 1791; prayer books published in the United States during this early period were organized around the Sunday focus. Beyond the Sunday rituals of Mass, vespers, and benediction were a few devotional practices such as praying the rosary, which were done privately and individually.[36]

The plainness of Catholic religion at this time was very noticeable in the pastoral work of itinerant priests who evangelized scattered Catholic settlements. The Jesuit John Grassi left a description of a typical visit:

On Saturday, the missionary leaves his residence, and goes to take up his lodging with some Catholic living near the church. Having arrived at the house, he puts the Blessed Sacrament in some decent place, and also the Holy Oils, without which he never sets out on a journey. On the following morning he rides to the church, and ties his horse to a bush. The whole morning is spent in hearing confessions: meantime, the people from distances of four, six, ten miles, and even more, are coming in on horseback, so that often the church is entirely surrounded with horses. Mass begins towards noon; during the celebration, those who can read make use of prayer books, and pious hymns, for the most part in English, are sung by a choir of men and women. The sermon comes after the Gospel, and it is preceded by the Gospel read in the vernacular. The preacher either reads or delivers his sermon, according to his inclination, and sometimes it is deferred until after Mass, to enable the priest to take some refreshment, which the faithful never fail to supply. There is no necessity to recommend attention, because they display the greatest eagerness to listen to the word of God. Vespers are not said, as the people live so far off and are so scattered; and so, when Mass is over, the children recite the catechism, infants are baptized, or the ceremonies are supplied in the case of those already baptized in danger, prayers for the dead are recited or the funeral services are performed over those who have been buried in the churchyard during the absence of the priest. Finally, one must attend to those who ask for instruction in order to join the Church, or who wish to be united in the bonds of Holy Matrimony.[37]

The picture painted by Grassi was commonplace. Confessions, celebration of Mass, a sermon, and catechism were the standard routine for the missionary. During those months when the people were on their own, their instructions were quite simple: "meet every Sunday to perform together your devotions. Let one who reads well and has a clear voice, read the prayers of the Mass, a sermon, or some instructions out of a Catholic book. . . ."[38] In rural settlements as well as in urban communities the pattern was the same; simplicity and plainness were the distinctive marks of religion.

A principal characteristic of Catholic piety at this time was its emphasis on Jesus as a model of virtue; people were encouraged to follow his example and in so doing achieve a personal union with Jesus. Jesus as a lawgiver or the suffering servant was not emphasized; rather, the humanist portrait of Jesus as ". . . model and exemplar for everyone, a person with whom each individual in the Christian community could identify," was stressed, so that in imitating Christ people fulfilled their own humanity. Such a vision of the Christian life quite naturally had an impact on the practice of religion. Devotional works emphasized an interior, personal piety, and in encouraging devotional practices the emphasis was placed on a personal relationship to Jesus as well as the interior disposition of the individual; the actual performance of pious acts meant nothing without the proper interior disposition.[39] This type of spirituality, which deemphasized the mediating role of priests and sacraments, blended in well with the social situation of the Catholic community, in which there was a scarcity of both clergy and churches.

The plain style of Catholic piety was an obvious holdover from the republican age. As was noted earlier, however, another style of religion was beginning to take hold among American Catholics. Imported from Europe by missionary priests like Badin and Marechal, this style can be labeled devotional Catholicism. The heart of devotional Catholicism was the exercise of piety, or what was called a devotion. Since the Mass and the sacraments were never sufficient to meet the spiritual needs of the people, popular devotions distinct from the Mass and sacraments have arisen throughout the history of Roman Catholicism. Each devotion has a very specific focus—e.g., the passion of Jesus—and for this reason the spiritual life of an individual became centered around a particular person—e.g., Jesus, Mary, or one of the saints—and the devotion connected with that person. Though they could be performed privately, devotions were often celebrated in church at a public ceremony presided over by the priest. Since devotions required the recitation of many prayers, they were readily adaptable to such communal ritual; before long, these public celebrations of devotions surpassed the Sunday Mass in terms of popular response.[40]

Because devotions could easily become the end, rather than the means, in the spiritual life, they were often subject to criticism. They could often lead to the glorification of self, rather than the service of God; hypocrisy was another charge leveled against false devotionalism. In the nineteenth century, however, devotions enjoyed a renaissance in the Catholic community. Most of these devotions had originated centuries earlier, and after a period of neglect in the late-eighteenth century they were revived with a new vigor during the papacy of Pius IX. They soon became the hallmark of a new type of religion, devotional Catholicism.

Some of the more popular devotions were devotion to the Sacred Heart of Jesus, devotion to Jesus in the Eucharist through public exposition of the Blessed Sacrament, devotion to the passion of Jesus, devotion to the Immaculate Conception of Mary, the recitation of the rosary, which included repetition of the Marian prayer Hail Mary, meditation on the life of Jesus, and, of course, devotion to particular saints such as St. Joseph, St. Patrick, and St. Anthony; novenas, or nine days of prayers in connection with the celebration of a saint's feast day, were especially popular.

By the late-nineteenth century this style of religion clearly dominated Catholic life, and the more interior, humanist tradition associated with Garden of the Soul Catholicism was scarcely visible. A key question is, When did one style of religion give way to the other?

It is clear that these two traditions coexisted side by side in the early decades of the nineteenth century. Devotional Catholicism was making some headway, but the plain style of religion was a dominant trait of American Catholicism throughout the 1820s and even into the 1830s. The key shift took place during the 1840s. The shift occurred slowly but perceptibly during this decade, so that by the 1850s, devotional Catholicism was clearly gaining the ascendency. By the 1860s, it had become the dominant trait of American Catholicism.

One convincing piece of evidence for this shift was the multiplication of prayer books; that is, books of collected prayers, hymns, instructions, and meditations for Catholics. From 1800 to 1880, eighty prayer books were published in English in the United States; 73 percent of these were published after 1840, with 32 percent of them appearing in the 1850s. The multiplication of devotional guides—that is, books devoted to a few specific devotions such as devotion to the Sacred Heart, the Way of the Cross, and the rosary—followed the same trend. One hundred and thirty such guides were published between 1830 and 1880, with 98 percent being published after 1840; once again, the decade of the 1850s surpassed other decades in terms of the largest number of publications, with fifty-one, or 39 percent, of the total number of devotional guides published in that decade.[41]

The proliferation of prayer books and devotional guides was an essential element in the shift to a new style of religion. Aiding this were the technological and social changes which fostered a mass market for books. Changes in the printing process during the 1830s paved the way for the mass production of books; the crusade for public education and literacy encouraged book sales; and publishers sought to meet the rising demand by selling books at prices common people could afford. The result was a publishing boom during the 1840s and 1850s, a boom in which Catholics shared. The sale of prayer books increased significantly, and for Catholic publishers, according to one observer, their "best customers are devout people of the poorer classes who have generally too little education to take an interest in literature, and for whom books of piety have to be manufactured in the cheapest possible way."[42]

Not only were many more prayer books now available to people, but the style of religion promoted by these books was decidedly different from the plain style of religion associated with early-nineteenth-century Catholicism.

Historian Ann Taves, in her analysis of these prayer books, has convincingly documented this shift. Prior to 1840, prayer books included only a few devotions—the rosary and benediction of the Blessed Sacrament being the most popular; after 1840, the number of devotions increased dramatically, featuring such rituals as devotion to the Sacred Heart of Jesus, the passion of Jesus, the Way of the Cross, and devotions in honor of St. Joseph, as well as numerous others. Devotional guides reflected the same trend, noted Taves, with devotions to Mary, the Blessed Sacrament, the Sacred Heart of Jesus, and the passion and death of Jesus being the most popular.[43]

The significance of the 1840s and 1850s was again underscored in the development of the Catholic revival, or, as it was more commonly known, the parish mission. Catholic revival meetings increased significantly during the 1840s, with three times the number of missions being held in this decade as in the previous one; the trend continued in the 1850s with a large increase, and the curve continued to climb throughout the following decades. Through its sermons and rituals, the parish mission fostered devotional Catholicism. Moreover, the mission also was a primary occasion for the sale of large numbers of prayer books and devotional guides as well as rosaries, pictures, and other religious articles. It was ". . . the super bowl of Catholic piety; the main attraction, the revival itself, was the occasion for all types of ancillary devotional promotions. Everything a pious Catholic needed to keep him or her spiritually busy was sold at the revival. Holy cards and schedule programs could be preserved as mementos of the great event; rosaries, medals, scapulars, and crucifixes could be purchased and worn as badges of an individual's religious allegiance, depicting his or her favorite holy hero. . . . Just about every item in the church's devotional treasury was on public display."[44]

The importance of this shift to devotional Catholicism can also be noted in the legislation of the 1866 Plenary Council of Baltimore. Considerable attention was given to the forty hours devotion to the Eucharist and benediction of the Blessed Sacrament and the need for processions associated with these devotions; legislation was enacted which encouraged the organization of confraternities associated with various popular devotions such as those of the Eucharist, the Sacred Heart of Jesus, Mary, St. Joseph, the Holy Angels, and others. Such extensive consideration of the Catholic devotional network was absent from previous and subsequent church councils and suggests that by the 1860s the importance as well as the newness of devotional Catholicism in the United States was very much in the forefront of episcopal consciousness.

The importance of the devotional confraternity or sodality in fostering devotional Catholicism cannot be underestimated. Clarence Walworth, pastor of St. Mary's Church in Albany, spoke for many pastors when he said, "Sodalities are invaluable for forming virtuous habits. The sodalities are the life of my parish."[45] Encouraged by church councils, promoted and often initially organized at the parish mission, they were a trademark of the immigrant parish. Parish confraternities enrolled large numbers of people and contributed greatly to building up a sense of community among Catholics. Through their emphasis on devotions and ritual, they explicitly encouraged the development of devotional Catholicism. For Italians and Mexicans, the devotional confraternity was the primary focus of religious activity.

Throughout the nineteenth century, the devotional confraternity was clearly the most important parish society. In fact, prior to 1860 it was just about the only parish society, with seven out of ten societies being of this type. In subsequent decades its hegemony declined somewhat as other types of societies were organized, but the devotional confraternities still represented about 60 percent of all societies founded during the 1860–1900 period. The founding of these societies also reflected the chronological development noted with the publication of prayer books and the inauguration of parish missions.

Prior to 1840, only 2 percent of all devotional societies organized in the nineteenth century were founded; between 1840 and 1860, an increase took place, with 14 percent of the total number being founded. But the dramatic rise took place after 1860, when 84 percent of all nineteenth-century parish devotional societies were founded. These figures suggest that the organization of parish confraternities lagged behind the publication of prayer books and the inauguration of the parish mission movement.[46] Most likely, the promotion of the parish confraternity at the 1866 Baltimore Council had something to do with their subsequent popularity. But it also was true that in the closing decades of the nineteenth century the parish confraternity became increasingly important for Catholics, as a social organization that bound them together and gave them a sense of identity in an increasingly segregated urban environment. This social function blended in well with its explicit religious purpose and helped to nourish the culture of piety which was setting Catholics apart from other Americans.

Once the devotional revolution was underway, it continued to intensify and expand. Technological developments in the newspaper industry during the second half of the century helped it along. By the 1880s, newspapers could be produced more quickly and more cheaply than before; the advent of the telegraph, transmitting news reports from faraway cities and towns, speeded up the circulation of news. The number of magazines also increased, and popular journals for the masses were changing the reading habits of Americans. The large increase in population fueled these developments, and newspaper and magazine publishing quickly became big business. Such developments provided the opportunity for the Catholic publishing industry to expand, with the result that each successive decade saw an increase in magazines and newspapers. The number of new serials published in the 1860s doubled the number of those established during the 1850s; the 1870s figures were twice those of the decade of the 1860s; during a single decade, the 1890s, 546 new Catholic magazines and newspapers were created; though much of these new magazines and newspapers were short-lived, the proliferation of these information media was important for the popularization of devotional Catholicism.[47]

The Catholic press lived off religious news. This was more true in the late-nineteenth century than previously, when Catholic newspapers carried a good deal of secular news. By the 1880s and 1890s, however, the primary focus of the Catholic press was religious, and it featured numerous articles related to and promoting devotional Catholicism. They could be edifying stories of the deeds of the saints, accounts of miraculous healings, reports of religious festivals or parish missions, or news about the latest papal encyclical promoting a particular devotion. Such newspapers as the *Pilot* in Boston and the *Catholic News* in New York enjoyed large circulations, with the *Pilot* claiming a circulation of 75,000 by 1906 and the *Catholic News* reaching the figure of 150,000 by the 1890s. During this period, devotional magazines such as *Ave Maria*, founded in 1865, and the *Messenger of the Sacred Heart*, founded in 1866, began to appear; nurturing devotional Catholicism was a primary focus of these magazines, and they, too, enjoyed a respectable circulation among Catholics, reaching figures of 20,000 and more.[48]

Accompanying the growth in newspapers and magazines was an increase in books and pamphlets. The numbers of Catholic publications rose dramatically in the 1880s and 1890s, with 1890 the apparent "high water mark, at least in terms of the number of titles published. It was also the year during which the largest number of specifically Catholic publishers were doing business; and eleven of them issued at least ten titles." In 1891 Benziger Brothers in New York, ". . . the largest publisher of Catholic novels, advertised a list of one hundred and sixteen novels." This literature was "self-consciously didactic" and concerned primarily with religious subjects; like Catholic newspapers and magazines, it fostered devotional Catholicism.[49]

Church architecture reflected the shift taking place in the religious world of Catholics. Gone were the plain structures of the early years as large, expensive churches became commonplace across Catholic America; most often Gothic or Romanesque in style, their interiors were elaborately decorated in a manner that visually instructed the people in the basics of devotional Catholicism. A large marble altar, often decorated with figures of saints and angels carved into the stone, was the focal point of each church; the crucified Christ was most often portrayed above the altar either in stained glass or a painting. Smaller altars were placed at either side of the main altar in the front of the church and, traditionally, on one was placed a statue of Mary, and on the other a statue of Joseph occupied a place of honor. Stained-glass windows became commonplace during this period; they usually depicted scenes from the life of Christ as well as scenes from the lives of various saints. Reflecting the trend toward the multiplication of devotions, numerous statues and pictures associated with particular devotions were placed about the church; statues of the Sacred Heart of Jesus, of St. Ann, and of St. Anthony were quite popular; in addition, each ethnic group often had small shrines in their churches honoring their own special patrons, such as Our Lady of Guadalupe among the Mexicans and Our Lady of Mount Carmel among the Italians.

When boys and girls entered Catholic school, religious instruction became an important part of their education. In addition to learning the religion of the catechism, they were introduced into the celestial community of the saints and the elaborate network of devotions that brought these heavenly relatives into their lives. The atmosphere in a convent school run by the women religious of the Society of the Sacred Heart exemplified the minute attention given to cultivating Catholic devotional piety. "Statues and paintings of the Sacred Heart, the Blessed Virgin Mary, various saints and biblical scenes decorated every room and corridor in the school," noted one historian. "The prize for academic excellence, good behavior, or victory in school games was a statue, holy picture, a medal or a book of a religious nature. Holy days in school celebrations were saints days or feast days of one of the Religious."[50] A former student described the effect of this atmosphere on a young girl:

> She really did begin to live all day long in the presence of the Court of Heaven. God the Father and God the Holy Ghost remained awe-inspiring conceptions, Presences who could only be addressed in set words and with one's mind, as it were, properly gloved and veiled. But to Our Lady and the Holy Child and the saints she spoke as naturally as to her friends. She learnt to smooth a place on her pillow for her guardian angel to sit during the night, to promise St. Anthony a creed or some pennies for the poor in return for finding her lost property, to jump out of bed at the first beat of the bell to help the Holy Souls in purgatory. She learnt, too, to recognize all around her the signs of heaven on earth.[51]

May devotions to Mary were especially important in Catholic schools. At St. Francis Xavier men's college in New York, ". . . elaborate processions of the entire student body arranged according to rank—first classes, then sodalities, and finally clergy—marched from the school to the church bearing a statue of Mary for the opening and closing of the month. Special altars decked with flowers in honor of the Virgin were erected in classrooms or study halls." At other schools, young men would gather around an outdoor Marian shrine and recite the rosary. Students were also introduced to the "literature of eternity" as well as more secular reading appropriately called "literature of time." What was striking about the literature of eternity encouraged at one Jesuit college was the extensive attention given to the saints; these were the spiritual heroes presented to young men as male models of virtue and piety.[52]

The liturgical calendar also reflected the shift taking place. By the 1880s, Sunday still remained the day for worship, but vespers was no longer very popular, having gradually been replaced by the recitation of the rosary. Moreover, the centrality of Sunday was being overshadowed by certain practices encouraged by devotional Catholicism. First-Friday-of-the-month devotions in honor of the Sacred Heart became increasingly popular, and people were encouraged to attend Mass on these days; certain months of the year became identified with specific devotions, and people were encouraged to practice them at these special times. May was the month of Mary, and children became especially involved in the month's activities of processions, praying the rosary, and dramatic performances. June was set aside for devotion to the Sacred Heart; March honored St. Joseph; October became the special time for praying the rosary; and November was dedicated to prayers for the dead. All these devotions were enhanced by special indulgences granted by the Pope to those people who performed the prescribed prayer and rituals. Such indulgences or spiritual rewards were not new for Catholics, but during the era of

Pope Pius IX they were zealously promoted, with the result that the number of indulgences substantially increased.

New immigrants from southern and Eastern Europe brought with them a strong attachment to devotional Catholicism. Unlike the early Irish immigrants, these people had been raised in the elaborate tradition of baroque piety; their styles of religion were neither plain nor simple. The churches they built reflected their traditions very strongly, as did their attachment to devotional confraternities. The most striking example of this attachment to devotional Catholicism would be the celebration of religious festivals in these communities. The Italians were especially noted for this. Italians in Newark, New Jersey, spent three days every September honoring their heavenly hero St. Gerardo with processions, carnivals, and feasting. Every July, East Harlem, in New York, came alive with a week-long celebration in honor of Our Lady of Mount Carmel. Chicago, St. Louis, San Francisco, and other cities with Italian communities celebrated similar religious festivals in honor of the saints of the old country.[33] Among the Polish and the Lithuanians, the celebration of the forty hours devotion to the Eucharist became very elaborate when, after three days of prayers, sermons, and Masses, the celebration ended with a solemn and lengthy procession.

Mexican Catholics were also raised in this school of piety, and their settlements annually came alive with the celebration of the Feast of Our Lady of Guadalupe, in December. A contemporary described one such procession in Conejos, Colorado, in 1873:

> The procession left at 1 in the afternoon. It was preceded by some 160 men on horseback guided by Don Pablo Ortega and Antonio Maria Vigil. In front of the horsemen rode Don Victor Garcia, carrying a beautiful waving flag. They were followed by boys and girls each carrying a flag, then the men and women. Finally came Fathers Fede and Maffei, preceded by the statue of Our Lady of Guadalupe, which was borne by eight young ladies under a canopy carried by Don Rafael Cabeza, Don Manuel Sabino Salazar, Don Celedonio Valdes, and Don José Gabriel Martinez. The procession made one turn around the Church and then entered it the next time around. All the girls stationed themselves in the sanctuary around the altar. High Mass and sermon by Father Fede. The attendance was extremely good and everyone was happy with how splendid the fiesta turned out to be. A beautiful day also contributed to this joy. Glory to Mary Most Holy who chose to favor us in such a manner.[34]

In those villages where there were no priests, the Mexicans developed their own network of devotional practices, "which ranged from the Santos themselves through Corpus Christi processions with a bulto of Christ and velorios for the dead, Christmas and Passion Plays, an enactment of the passion of Christ using a statue of Jesús Nazareno, all the way to the Penitente Crucifixion by tying one of the members of the brotherhood to a cross. In other words, what the Sacraments and the Mass were to a village with a priest, the communal Penitente initiations, penances, wakes and enactments of the death of Jesus were to a village without one."[55]

Prayer books, devotional confraternities, newspapers, magazines, church architecture, schools, the church calendar, and the celebration of religious festivals shaped the sacred cosmos of Catholics, educating them into a specific style of religion: devotional Catholicism. In a very real sense, Catholics were surrounded by symbols of their religion; neighborhood churches and schools were important reminders of who they were; neighborhood processions underscored the point; the seasons of the year also had their special religious importance, with Christmas and Easter holding special places; certain months of the year and even days of the week also possessed religious significance.

Domesticity was an important virtue in Victorian America, and by the end of the nineteenth century, Catholics were vigorously promoting a domestic ideology. A key part of this was religion and the need to establish a proper spiritual environment in the home. Catholics accomplished this by decorating the home with the religious symbols of devotional Catholicism. These symbols—crucifixes, statues, holy pictures, and candles—were advertised in the Catholic press and readily available at the local religious-goods store. A social worker's description of the apartment of an Irish Catholic family revealed how elaborate and extensive such decoration could be:

> In the living and bedroom stands a large wooden wardrobe, which contains all the family clothes, treasures, cast-off clothing, etc. Next to this is the bureau. . . . On the bureau is the family shrine, a brown wooden box with a slanting roof. In this there is an image of the Virgin, over whom is hung a rosary. The family Bible and a picture of St. Anthony are also placed on the bureau. On the mantel piece there are a brown wooden clock, several brightly colored vases filled with artificial flowers, two glass crucifixes, a china image of the Virgin, a plaster image of Mary with the Infant Jesus and some gaudy calendars. . . . On the walls hang colored pictures of St. Benedict and Christ healing the sick, a newspaper print of Pope Leo XIII and of Pope Pius; a photograph of a family tombstone in Ireland; a color print of a praying child and several insurance, grocer, and brewery calendars. Over the mantle hangs a chromo of the father in a bright gilt frame decorated by palm leaves. On either side hang bright prints of saints, also a picture of a young woman and child under a shower of apple blossoms. . . . a door opens on the west side of this room to the smaller bedroom. . . . the walls are decorated with bright pictures of angels and saints.[56]

The Irish were not unique in this regard. Houses of other Catholics prominently displayed such religious symbols. Among Mexican Catholics it was even commonplace to have a small altar and shrine in the home, where the family regularly prayed.

The growth and consolidation of devotional Catholicism was the most significant reform that took place in American Catholicism during the era of the immigrant church. It ranks in significance with another period of reform, that of the post-Vatican II era of the 1960s and 1970s. Begun in the 1840s and fairly well consolidated by the 1860s, devotional Catholicism brought about an interior, religious transformation among the people. The plain, undemonstrative style of religion, with its emphasis on a personal union with Christ through the mediation of the Bible and other books, gave way to a demonstrative, emotion-packed religion distinguished by its emphasis on the practice of external rituals of devotion, communion with a heavenly host of saintly relatives, and devotion to a suffering savior, all of which was mediated through a sacramental system controlled by the clergy.

By the early-twentieth century it was clear that the mass of Catholics were more assiduous than formerly in practicing their religion. In the early-nineteenth century, priest confessors frequently remarked about the length of time people had been away from the sacraments of confession and Communion; by the late-nineteenth and early-twentieth centuries, such comments were rare. Catholics were more inclined now to make their Easter duty; that is, receive Communion once a year during the Easter season. In the early decades of the nineteenth century, churchgoers received Communion infrequently, but by the end of the century, monthly Communion had become the norm for these people; by the early-twentieth century, even more frequent reception of Communion became popular. Revivals were frequent events in Catholic parishes, and attendance at them was quite good. Prayer books, devotional pamphlets, novels, magazines, and newspapers became commonplace in Catholic families. Catholic grammar schools and academies grew at a fast pace, and they became culture factories for devotional Catholicism. Whether or not Catholics in 1900 were any more religious than Catholics in 1820 is hard to say. Most likely they were not. But they were practicing their religion much more —attending Mass more regularly, receiving Communion more frequently, and performing a greater variety of devotional rituals. A new culture of piety, devotional Catholicism, had developed, and it not only reinforced American Catholicism, it also changed the way people thought.

It is important to understand that what was happening throughout Catholic America at this time was also taking place in Europe. The American reform was but one phase of a larger, worldwide reform of Roman Catholicism. The nineteenth century was a unique period of spiritual revival in the history of Roman Catholicism. What emerged from this was " . . . a piety more accessible to the masses and giving greater scope, because of its stress on a multiplicity of exterior devotions and on frequent attendance on the sacraments, to emotional participation."[7] Exported throughout the world, it effected an interior transformation of Catholics everywhere. France experienced such a revival; Ireland had its own devotional revolution, as did Australia. The papacy promoted the revival by awarding new indulgences to those who practiced the devotions, by issuing encyclical letters promoting specific devotions, and by organizing worldwide Eucharistic congresses to promote devotion to Christ. The American hierarchy, as evidenced by their actions at the 1866 council, supported the Papacy in this. Many of the American bishops were educated in Rome and were obviously influenced by the style of piety promoted by the Papacy. Loyalty to the Pope was a key ingredient of a Roman seminary education, and it meant support for a certain style of religion as well as a specific brand of theology.

A sizable growth in the number of men's religious orders at this time provided the necessary personnel for the spread of the revival. In the United States, the number of male religious orders increased throughout the second half of the century, growing from nineteen in 1850 to forty-five by 1900. The number of diocesan clergy also increased. This increase in the number of priests was critical, since devotional Catholicism relied so heavily on their mediating function in the celebration of Mass, the sacraments, and devotional rituals.

Devotional Catholicism influenced the way Catholics thought about themselves and the world in which they lived. Made up of many ethnic groups as well as a number of classes, Catholics in the United States were a very diverse group of people. Such diversity caused tension, often serious conflict and even schism. But a Catholic ethos or worldview did exist which cut across class and ethnic boundaries, and even though it did not bind Catholics together into a unified community, it did shape the way they thought. It was the bedrock of the cultural ghetto, which was so striking a trademark of the immigrant church. Theological principles presented to the people in the catechism were indeed critical in shaping this ethos. Devotional Catholicism, however, was theology in practice; it was a popular affirmation and manifestation of belief. Though expressed in a manner different from the dry, intellectual style of the catechism or the manual, devotional Catholicism arose out of a specific theology; in attempting to understand the Catholic mind of the past century, it is necessary to examine some of the main traits of the Catholic ethos fashioned by devotional Catholicism.

VIII

The Catholic Ethos

IN DESCRIBING THE WAY Catholics thought about themselves and the world
in which they lived, the focus will be on the central features of this mental
landscape, those major landmarks or traits which, in towering above all else,
had a major influence in shaping the Catholic worldview. There were four
such central traits: authority, sin, ritual, and the miraculous. Such concepts
are found in other religious traditions as well, since they are so fundamental
to the Christian system of belief. Yet, within the Roman Catholic tradition,
they took on a special meaning and set Catholics apart from other people in
the United States.

A major influence on the Catholic mind was the concept of *authority*. The
late-eighteenth and the nineteenth centuries was a time when the authority of
the Roman Catholic Church was being seriously challenged. Napoleon had
made the Pope his prisoner; Garibaldi's cannons shelled the Vatican; Bismarck outlawed the clergy; and before long the Pope was a prisoner in his
own house. The influence of modernity, with its new sciences and technology,
redefined the universe, making it less mysterious and less dependent on religion to solve its riddles. New philosophies and new theologies transformed
the meaning of God and ultimately the meaning of religion. A modern
schism, as historian Martin Marty put it, was taking place during the nineteenth century, and religion was being relocated to the periphery of society.[1]
Though the schism ushered in by these forces of modernity affected all religions, Roman Catholicism was especially threatened, and its reaction at times
became extreme. The church's authority, now that it was being challenged,
was reasserted with excessive vigor. The high point was the declaration of

papal infallibility in 1870 at the first Vatican Council. Yet the crusade to establish the supreme authority of Pope and church within the Catholic community did not end in 1870. This view of the church, in which papal authority reigned supreme, soon became standard Catholic theology. The centralization of the church around Rome and the Papacy increased the power of church bureaucrats in the Vatican so that, before long, *"Roma locuta est; causa finita est"* (Rome has spoken; the case is closed) became an accurate description of internal church affairs.

Though Catholicism in the United States did not have a Napoleon or a Bismarck, church officials were still concerned with the issue of authority. The United States prided itself on freedom and democracy, and new immigrants as well as longtime citizens cherished these qualities. Time and again, European priests bemoaned this "spirit of independence" prevalent among Americans, since such a spirit weakened the respect for authority deemed so necessary in the church. American culture encouraged such freedom and independence, especially in things religious; church authorities recognized this not only as a weakness of the culture, but as a threat to Catholicism as well.[2] Of course, the forces of modernity, be they embodied in Darwin or Hegel, the machine or the factory, were also undermining respect for traditional authorities and encouraging a spirit of individualism. This cultural backdrop, part European and part American, helps to explain why authority occupied so central a place in the Catholic mind during the age of the immigrant church.

The relationship between clergy and lay people defined the meaning of the Catholic lay person. "The Church," wrote Pope Pius X, "is essentially an unequal society . . . comprising two categories of persons, the Pastors and the flock." The pastors alone had the authority, and ". . . the one duty of the multitude is to allow themselves to be led, and, like a docile flock, to follow the Pastors."[3] What this meant theologically was that the bishops ruled the church, and as bishop of Rome, the Pope was the supreme ruler, the monarch of the church. The supremacy of papal authority was a basic tenet of nineteenth-century Catholic theology, and it was proclaimed throughout the community. Sermons frequently instructed people about the reality of papal authority. Papal flags and papal portraits in church and school constantly reinforced the preacher's words. The fiftieth anniversary of Pope Pius IX's ordination to the priesthood was celebrated with solemnity in many parishes, as was the twenty-fifth anniversary of his coronation as Pope. Such activities and attention clearly strengthened the position of the Pope in the church. Pius IX's popularity with the masses also gave him the confidence needed to pursue his own theological and political course of action regardless of what critics might say.[4]

Local bishops shared in the church's renewed emphasis on authority. The Third Baltimore Council, in 1884, was a ringing affirmation of their authoritative position in the church, and subsequent decades did little to change this. Basking in the power of Pope and bishop, the local pastor became a dominant figure in the parish community. Pius IX was in Rome, the bishop was downtown or in a different city, but the pastor was only a few blocks away; visible in the neighborhood and church, he was the chief authority figure for Catholics. Parish missions reminded people of this when preachers dutifully told the people to heed his counsel and be docile parishioners; mission prayer books included an exhortation on the "duties of parishioners towards their pastor."[5] One immigrant pastor, Vincent Barzynski, in a very succinct explanation of the basis for a pastor's authority, captured the essence of the hierarchical model of government operative in the Catholic church:

> If you desire to work in the name of God, pay heed to the words of Christ, because God the Father gave us only one Christ; if you wish to labor for Christ, then listen to Peter, for Christ gave us only one Peter; if you want to work in Peter's name, obey the Pope, because he is the only true successor to the first Pope; if you wish to work in the Pope's name, obey the bishop, because only the bishop rules the diocese; if you wish to obey the bishop, then you must obey your pastor, for the bishop gave you only one pastor.[6]

This focus on authority permeated Catholic culture so thoroughly that religious authority became "the preeminent doctrinal concern of Catholic fiction." As apologists for American Catholicism, novelists stressed the authoritative position of Roman Catholicism, endorsing its claims to absolute and infallible authority in matters of faith and morals and "for the hierarchical structure through which that authority flowed."[7]

Another way in which authority shaped the Catholic mind was through church laws, those rules and regulations that seemed to pop up everywhere. First there were the church commandments, such as attending Mass on Sundays and holy days and going to confession and Communion at least once a year. Invested with the church's authority, they assumed the gravity and importance of the biblical Commandments. In addition, there was the body of legislation that American bishops enacted during the course of the nineteenth century. The hierarchy was anxious to establish discipline in the Catholic community, and it passed a wide variety of laws to do this. These ranged from outlawing membership in such secret societies as the Oddfellows to prescribing the proper form of clerical dress. Finally, in 1917, a new Code of Canon Law was promulgated for Catholics throughout the world. A major overhaul of church laws, its publication spawned a cottage industry of canon lawyers, with their commentaries, books, and journals.

Parishes also had their own regulations regarding membership, and pastors enforced them. This often meant the faithful payment of pew rents and at least annual reception of Communion, during the Easter time. Some Polish parishes had an especially elaborate system of monitoring parish membership.

They kept family account books which recorded each family's financial contribution to the parish, and those who did not contribute did not receive their Easter confession cards. These cards were to be turned over to the priest when the person went to confession during the Easter time; the priest then turned all the cards over to the parish secretary, who marked them to signify fulfillment of the Easter obligation. The name of the penitent, indicated by a registration number on the card, was then placed in the parish records. If someone did not make his or her Easter confession, then he or she was no longer a member of the parish and could not be married in church or receive a Christian burial. If you did not "get your card punched," as the people would say, then you were in deep trouble. But a family received its set of confession cards at Easter only if its minimum donation for the previous year was paid.[8]

Laws of fast and abstinence regulated the behavior of people throughout the year, especially during the season of Lent. When Catholics joined a religious confraternity, they also were subject to certain rules of behavior. The practice of religion itself was, basically, fulfilling a series of obligations, and every prayer book spelled out such laws and obligations as it sought to help people prepare for a general confession.[9]

Catholicism was clearly a religion of authority, and people learned not only to pray, but also to obey. Being Catholic meant to submit to the authority of God as mediated through the church—its Pope, bishops, and pastors. In such a culture, the rights of the individual conscience were deemphasized, as each person was conditioned to submit to the external authority of the church. A nineteenth-century prayer expressed this ethos:

> Most gracious and merciful God . . . who hast made me . . . a member of the one only and true Catholic Church, wherein I am secured from error, and guided in the road that leads to eternal bliss. Grant, oh my God, that I may never prove so ungrateful as to waver in this faith, or to contradict it by my conduct; but that, until the end of my life, firmly believing what it teaches, and earnestly endeavoring to comply with the duties it lays down, I may merit the eternal reward thou hast promised to those who persevere to the end in the profession of Thy faith in the observance of Thy commandments.[10]

The importance of the Mass and the sacraments, so central to Catholic spirituality, also enhanced the authority of the clergy and the institutional church in the lives of people. The Mass and the sacraments, as opposed to private devotions, were the official public worship of the church and the principal way that people gained access to the supernatural. But the church, through its clergy, controlled this important realm of the spiritual life. This is seen most vividly in the Eucharist, the sacrament in which Jesus becomes present in the midst of the people under the signs of bread and wine. The Eucharist could take place only through the action of the priest at Mass; the priest could be present only by the authority of the bishop, who acted on behalf of the church. Such a close identification between priesthood, institutional church, and access to the divine magnified the importance of both priest and church.

Moreover, by virtue of his ordination, the priest, according to Catholic theology, had a unique relationship with Jesus. Sharing in his divine priesthood, the priest became completely identified with Jesus, and thus " . . . he becomes the mediator with Christ for all. The priest is he who sets into operation on earth the whole divine economy of religion and salvation."[11] Such a theology of priesthood elevated the priest to a realm above and beyond that of the laity. Possessor of the keys of the kingdom, another Christ, salvation was unthinkable without his mediation. Such a lofty view of the priest not only enhanced his position in the community, but it also served to reinforce the move toward clerical control in the immigrant church.

Raised in such a culture of authority, Catholics were taught to be docile and submissive. The most persuasive image used to cultivate such docility was that of Jesus, the suffering Savior. Evoked to persuade others to follow his example, the image portrayed was one of docile obedience; indeed, Jesus was obedient even unto death. Absent from this portrait were any signs of independence or rebellion. Obedience and docility, not dissent and independence, were the ideals cherished in the Catholic community. Clearly this did not mean that all were submissive servants. Trustee conflicts, parish wars, and church schisms were a fact of life in immigrant Catholicism. Yet, as the authoritarian culture of devotional Catholicism strengthened its grip on people, obedience, rather than rebellion, became the standard. The emergence of clerical control by the early-twentieth century was a good indicator of how strong this mentality had become. People could and did rebel, but such dissent became more isolated and more private. More common was the attitude expressed by a French-Canadian immigrant. Speaking about the practice of birth control among Catholics, she observed that "most of the French people were not rebellious in any way. . . . They were people with a deep, simple, religious faith."[12] In a culture of authority, simple meant docile.

A second dominant trait of devotional Catholicism was its emphasis on *sin*. All theistic religions acknowledge the reality of sins, those transgressions against God and others which affect the spiritual well-being of the sinner. Nevertheless, some religions put more emphasis on sin than others. New England Puritans, for example, were very aware of the reality of sin, and it weighed heavily on their consciences. Occupying a central position in Puritan spirituality, sin shaped people's thought and behavior. For some, the reality of sin turned their lives into a torturous spiritual pilgrimage. Nineteenth-century Catholics resembled Puritans in their emphasis on sin. The major reason for this was that the tradition of Augustine was an important influence in shaping the religious world of both Catholics and Puritans.

The Augustinian tradition espoused a very pessimistic concept of the human being. Original sin had undermined the strength of men and women and made them victims of sin. Gifted with freedom but bewitched by sin, men and women had to struggle to attain holiness on earth and salvation afterward. In some religious traditions, the Calvinist being the most notable, salvation was reserved for a chosen few, the elect of God. For others, Catholics among them, holiness and salvation was open to all, but you had to earn it; the way you did this was through a victorious struggle over sin. Since humanity was so inclined to evil, however, people needed a great deal of assistance in their battle against sin.

Because sin was so pervasive and powerful, the evil inclinations of people had to be curbed. The way this was done was through a multitude of laws and regulations that helped to discipline and strengthen Catholics in their struggle against sin. The church, with its culture of authority as well as its sacramental system, became a necessary companion in this struggle. In other words, a culture of sin demanded a culture of authority.

The evidence for this culture of sin is quite convincing. First of all was the importance of confession. Throughout much of the nineteenth century, confessing one's sin to the priest in the sacrament of penance was an infrequent experience, once a year for many, once a month for the devout. But, with increased emphasis on the Eucharist and more frequent Communion, confession also became a more frequent experience. Crowds of people would line up in church on Saturday afternoons and evenings in order to go to confession; in the 1860s, priests complained about the long hours spent in the confessional. It was no better in the 1920s, when, on the eve of Christmas, a priest could spend as many as seven hours hearing confessions.[13]

Prayer books focused a good deal of attention on sin and confession. *The Ursuline Manual,* for example, had sixty pages devoted to this topic; eighteen pages alone were given over to an examination of conscience, which consisted of question after question about all the possible sins one might have committed. *The Mission Book,* a most popular work, set aside forty-two pages for the discussion of sin and confession. The theme of sin frequently reappeared at other places in these manuals. Given the culture of Catholicism, such emphasis was to be expected.[14]

Devotional guides also reinforced the culture of sin. The Sacred Heart devotion stressed the sinfulness of mankind and the need of reparation for past sins. Mary was honored because she was immaculate, free from sin; other, less immaculate saints were also prized because of their victory over sin. Catholic fiction continuously focused on the struggle between good and evil; in these moral dramas, a sinful villain was always a major actor.

Yet, nothing stressed the horror of sin more forcefully than the parish mission. At these revival meetings, Catholics were continually reminded of it.

Indeed, the one purpose of the revival was to convert people from sin to virtue. Sin, the people were reminded, has

> given the deathblow to your immortal soul; you have drawn down upon yourself the anger and punishment of the living God, a God who in his just vengeance is awful and terrible; that he it is who cast forever into hell the holy angels when they first rebelled against Him; that, alas! many of the damned who are now groaning in the eternal pains of hell, have not committed so great and so many sins as you.[15]

Sermons on hell, portraying the torment of condemned sinners, sought to move people to convert from their sinful ways. Hearing such strong denunciations of sin, people flocked to the confessionals; revival preachers prided themselves on such large numbers of confessions and kept a running count of them so they could proudly note this in their mission reports.[16]

This emphasis on sin and the corresponding need for conversion pointed out the evangelical nature of devotional Catholicism. The revival clearly illustrated this. An immediate, heartfelt conversion, the essence of evangelicalism, was the goal of every parish mission. Emotionalism was also a part of this evangelical thrust, and it fed on the sentimental, "full of unction" sermons given during the course of the mission.

Clearly some sins seemed to be more important than others. Using the revival as an indicator, it is clear that an evangelical code of morality was fostered in the Catholic community. At the heart of this code was opposition to the sins of drunkenness and impurity; in the opinion of the clergy, these were the two major vices that confronted Catholics. Special mission sermons hammered against intemperance, and people were frequently urged to take the pledge. The revivalist concern for temperance was but a part of a larger cultural phenomenon in the United States. Like other Americans, Catholics had launched a crusade against intemperance, or what one preacher described as ". . . the seven headed monster of the Apocalypse, a vice that encircles the globe and stops short of nothing" in subduing its victims.[17]

The sin of impurity was clearly a sensitive topic for the clergy, and in public they discussed it with careful discretion. Even prayer books were circumspect in their discussion of this theme, lest too vivid a presentation be an occasion of sin for an innocent reader. For young men and women, the archetypes of moral perfection tended to be virginal—frequently virgin martyrs—". . . indicating that symbolically at the very least sexuality posed the foremost threat to Baptismal innocence." Sodality sermons and popular literature, especially the lives of the saints, sought to persuade young Catholics of the importance of purity and the evils of lust, because, as one prayer book warned, ". . . nothing can injure or dishonor you more than the sin of impurity."[18]

To acquire the strength (i.e., spiritual graces) needed to combat sin, people turned to prayer and devotions. Since these rituals of devotional Catholicism promised the spiritual muscle needed in the fight against sin, people turned to them in every need. Catholics prayed to Jesus, Mary, and the saints to ask for help so that they could resist the allurements of sin. This was the way a Catholic waged war against sin, and with such heavenly soldiers on their side, Catholics were inclined to feel confident about victory. In a culture of sin, the system of devotional Catholicism made sense, and the more help—i.e., devotions—was available, the better was the chance for victory. This helps to explain the popularity of devotional Catholicism.

Coloring the Catholic view of sin was an attitude toward the world or secular society that was quite negative. Church leaders frequently spoke as if Armageddon was just around the corner. The power of darkness seemed to be in control, and religious error, like "a wolf in sheep's clothing," prowls about the earth seeking whom it may devour. Though European Catholics were more extreme in this regard, Americans also evidenced a hostile attitude toward the world.[19] The anti-Catholic crusade of the 1840s and 1850s seemed to justify such suspicion, and the Catholic press took great pains to defend the church against its critics in American society. The city was seen as an especially wicked place; the rapid growth of cities, with all the problems this created, appeared to justify this evaluation.

Negative evaluation of the world and antiurban bias were not uniquely Catholic; they were common among many American Protestants as well. What was special about Catholic hostility toward secular society was its strong anti-Protestant tone. Protestants grew up learning to fear Catholics; Catholics grew up believing Protestants were a "perishing and debauched multitude of heretics and infidels."[20] Catholics were continually urged to avoid contact with them, and many Catholics grew up never knowing any Protestants. Liberal Catholics attempted to break down such prejudice, but the popular culture of Catholicism was clearly not irenic. The most revealing indication of this was the attitude toward marriages between Catholics and Protestants. Though such marriages were not totally forbidden, they were only allowed for "just and grave causes."[21] Since the church taught that marrying a Protestant was clearly a threat to one's salvation and to the salvation of the children as well, it was strongly and continuously discouraged. Catholic fiction stressed the peril, especially to children, of such mixed marriages; spiritual guidebooks somberly discussed this "grave question," and only in exceptional cases could such a marriage be allowed. Though the numbers did increase during the twentieth century, religiously mixed marriages were not common during the nineteenth century.[22]

The dominance of sin in the Catholic culture meant that guilt was a very important influence in shaping the minds of people. "In those years," as one man put it, people were more conscious of being "miserable sinners."[23] Sins "like a mountain lie heavy upon" people, and confession was necessary not only because it absolved one of sin, but also because it relieved that "anxiety of mind" brought on by sin.[24] The special stress on intemperance and impurity intensified the degree of guilt attached to them; intemperance was especially evil because of its effect on the family; impurity was so "dreadful" because it was ". . . a dishonor to God, our Sovereign Lord, an injury to Jesus Christ who redeemed us, and a profanation of the Holy Ghost who sanctifies us."[25] Guilt was also a major theme in Catholic literature, and such concentrated focus suggests that it most likely influenced the way people thought and behaved. Moreover, a sense of guilt was necessary for confession, a sacrament that was an integral part of devotional Catholicism; to promote confessions, the preacher had to nurture guilt, and the Catholic culture of sin made this an easy task.

A specifically Catholic trait in the economy of sin was the element of mercy and forgiveness guaranteed at confession. Sin may have been deadly and guilt may have been intense, but the "waters of grace" washed it all away and restored the sinner to virtue and life. This indeed was an important part of the Catholic theological system, and it clearly tempered the harshness of the culture of sin.

Not all Catholics accepted the culture of sin and authority. Some rebelled against priest and bishop; many never went to church on a regular basis; mixed marriages did occur; and men continued to frequent the saloon. That is not the point, however. The standard was there to follow, and the culture was present to form you, and growing up Catholic in the era of the immigrant church meant that a person had to cope with a culture built on sin and sustained by authority. You could resist and rebel, as many did, but even in your resistance the culture pursued you like Francis Thompson's "Hound of Heaven," never letting you forget what you were fleeing.

A third dominant feature of devotional Catholicism was its emphasis on *ritual.* For Catholics, the way to the sacred was through ritual, and the central ritual was the Mass. Celebrated in an atmosphere of solemn silence amid the sights, smells, and sounds of burning candles and tinkling bells, fragrant incense and colorful flowers, the Mass was the epitome of liturgical theater. The main actor, the priest, walked about the altar dressed in special, often imported, robes, while he prayed in Latin, the unknown language of the holy. On special feast days, the Mass was celebrated with extraordinary grandeur: more candles, flowers, incense, music, and actors gave it a special solemnity. The central importance of this ritual was underscored by the church commandment that Catholics were obliged to "hear Mass every Sunday and holy day."[26]

Next in importance were the rituals of the sacraments; baptism, marriage, confession, and Communion were the most important rites for the people. Like all rituals, they helped to define the meaning of being Catholic, i.e., one who was baptized in the church and went to confession and received Communion at least once a year. That was a minimal definition to be sure, yet it illustrates how essential the rituals of these sacraments were to the culture of Catholicism. Without them, one was simply not Roman Catholic. The ritual quality of Catholicism, however, went beyond the celebration of Mass and the sacraments.

A major ritual dimension of Catholicism was associated with devotion to the saints, who occupied a central place in the lives of Catholics. Children were to be given a saint's name at birth; churches and schools were named after saints; so, too, were baseball teams and sodalities. They were the popular spiritual heroes and were offered to young men and women as models of virtue. Unlike God, saints were human; they walked the earth, and lived and died like other mortals. Consequently they were more approachable than the unseen God of the heavens. People treated the saints like distant relatives, heavenly aunts and uncles whose pictures hung on the wall. Children learned about them at school, and popular biographies spread their fame. Among various ethnic groups, certain saints were singled out. The Irish honored St. Patrick; the Mexicans, St. James; the Germans, St. Boniface; and the Polish, St. Stanislaus. Some saints gained their popularity because of special powers attributed to them. St. Anthony, for example, could help you find what you had lost; St. Ann would help you find a husband; and Mary would intercede on your behalf with her son, Jesus. No more complex than the family tree, the network of heavenly relatives was there to call on in time of need.

Associated with devotion to the saints was a wide array of rituals. Some were publicly performed in church, such as the novena, a devotion of nine days to honor a particular saint or to obtain a particular request. The celebration of Mass on a saint's feast day was obviously an important ritual. More common was the private, individual ritual. In his study of Catholic fiction, Paul Messbarger noted:

Private devotions played perhaps a larger part in the religious life of the nineteenth century Catholic than the Mass and the sacraments, according to fictional accounts. To begin with it is the rare hero or heroine who does not practice a special devotion to a saint or to one of the anatomical mysteries of Christ; and this devotion is frequently the badge of special sanctity. Moral identification is not the only function of devotions, however; they also serve as talismans. The Catholic who says the rosary daily, who makes the nine First Fridays, or who prays to St. Anthony, can expect anything, from protection against physical harm to reconciliation with an estranged husband or material success. Thus, in one short story an army sergeant who has fallen away from the church, wears from habit a badge of the Sacred Heart and is by that gesture led back to the Faith. In another story, a boy who is about to succumb to the temptations of drink is, because he has made the nine First Fridays, given the grace to resist. A prayer to St. Anthony leads to the discovery of a lost waif. A medal of the Blessed Virgin protects a Civil War soldier from the effects of a bullet.["]

Few of these rituals were new to the nineteenth century. They were traditional Catholic practices which had been revived with great vigor during the devotional revolution of the nineteenth century. New papal indulgences attached to these devotions made them especially appealing, and their popularity kept an entire industry of religious publishers and merchants in business.

All religions emphasize the importance of ritual, but for some it is clearly more central to their identity. This was certainly true of devotional Catholicism. Religion was associated with the performance of certain external acts. The divine was accessible only through the ritual—that was clearly the message conveyed. It may not have been completely orthodox, but the centrality of ritual in devotional Catholicism clearly suggested that it was the popular, working theology of both priests and people. The importance of the priest and the church in this culture was clear. Without the priest, the critical public rituals could not be performed; as regards the extensive world of private ritual, to be effective they had to be performed as the church instructed, and indulgences could be obtained only after a prescribed ritual within the ritual had been completed. For these reasons, the ritual culture enhanced the culture of authority and made the church and its hierarchical system all the more essential to devotional Catholicism.

The culture of ritual was important in and of itself, but it also fostered two qualities that were very characteristic of devotional Catholicism. The first was individualism. The salvation of souls is the supreme law, was the motto of Tridentine Catholicism, a style of religion promoted by the sixteenth-century Council of Trent. In other words, personal salvation was the highest goal for Catholics. This law was still dominant during the era of the immigrant church. Though salvation was to be achieved through the mediation of the church, it was a personal responsibility. As one preacher said, "Save your soul, . . . it is your affair."[28] Nineteenth-century Catholicism preached an individual gospel, not a social gospel. The multiplicity of private, personal rituals reinforced this. Through their private devotion, people established personal relationships with saintly heroes; other rituals, such as devotions to the Sacred Heart or the rosary, let them build up their personal attachment to Jesus and Mary. Indeed, the public performance of rituals and the community celebration of festivals built up a sense of group consciousness, of belonging to a particular community. But salvation, like sin, was always thought of as personal, and the ritual culture did nothing to change this.

A second major characteristic of the culture of ritual was its emphasis on certain key values which in the nineteenth century were identified with the feminine personality. There was no question that Catholic devotions were riddled with emotionalism and sentimentalism, qualities identified as feminine. The paraphernalia of this devotional milieu—pictures, statues, prayer cards, religious imagery in general—was, as one historian put it, notoriously "lacrimose, sentimental and effeminate."[29] The plastic Jesus, popularized in song in the twentieth century, had its counterpart in the smooth, clean, manicured imagery of devotional Catholicism. An Anglican clergyman who espoused a more muscular Christianity characterized the feminine quality of Roman Catholicism in a letter to a cleric who was about to convert to the Roman church.

> If by holiness you mean "saintliness," I quite agree that Rome is the place to get *that*—and a poor pitiful thing it is when it is got—not God's ideal of man, but an effeminate shaveling's ideal—look at St. Francis de Sales' or St. Vincent de Paul's face—and then say, does not your English spirit loathe to be such a prayer-mongering eunuch as *that?* God made man in His image, not in an imaginary Virgin Mary's image.[30]

Docility was another virtue that was clearly identified with the feminine personality. In such an authoritarian culture as Roman Catholicism, obedience and docility were important virtues. A major inspiration for these virtues was the death of Jesus, who was obedient, even unto death; the saints, too, were blessed because they learned to be docile servants.

Toward the end of the nineteenth century, both Catholic and Protestant clergy began to challenge the feminization of religion by promoting a more muscular Christianity. Catholic literature reflected this development very clearly, especially the popular novels of Francis Finn, the Jesuit author. Set in a Catholic boarding-school culture, Finn's heroes were athletic, all-American boys. But because religion was so identified with feminine character traits, Finn had to create secondary heroes who were the ". . . epitome of passivity and acquiescence, in whose manner and characteristic expression we recognize the equivalent of the feminine in adult fiction."[31] The all-American boy, imperfect because of his aggressive masculinity, becomes more perfect, more Catholic in this case, by following the example of these secondary figures and practicing virtues ". . . usually associated with women in nineteenth century English speaking societies and with the saints of the church—a certain artistic, emotional and devotional sensibility, greater modesty about their accomplishments, and submission of their willfulness to higher authority."[32]

A further indication of the feminine character of devotional Catholicism was the active role that women had in the church. There was no doubt that, for Catholic women, and for Protestant women also, the church was a major sphere of activity. Recalling the early years of his life in an Irish immigrant community, a priest observed that "life for all the women centered about the parish churches." One Italian woman observed that "religion is a woman's job," and there was no doubt that church attendance was left largely to women in the Italian community.[33] In Providence, Rhode Island, for example, it was estimated that 80 percent of the Italians who received the sacraments in a given year in the early-twentieth century were women. Women also played a very prominent role in the celebration of religious festivals and in Italian parish life in general.[34] The pattern did not vary among other ethnic groups either. A study of church attendance in the borough of Manhattan, New York, in 1902 concluded that 73 percent of all Catholic churchgoers were women; though that was a very high figure, it does underscore the point that devotional Catholicism was especially attractive to women.[35] Attendance at Catholic revivals tended to moderate this somewhat. Though women generally outnumbered men, the difference was insignificant. Also, a study of converts from Protestantism indicates that men were as likely to convert as women.[36] A study of parish histories in the nineteenth century, however, leaves no doubt about the central place of women in the devotional life of the church.

In general, the number of parish societies with either an exclusively male or female membership was fairly equal. The differences show up in the types of societies each group populated. Mutual-aid and charitable societies were clearly the domain of men, while devotional societies were overwhelmingly the sphere of women. This changed in the 1900–20 period with the widespread organization of the Holy Name Society. This society was for men only, and its purpose (to defend and uphold the holy name of Jesus) reflected the more militant, muscular version of Catholicism that was beginning to surface at this time. Yet, throughout the nineteenth century, parish devotional societies were clearly identified with women. An analysis of the marital status of the members of these societies shows that, among the Irish, single women predominated. The reason for this seemed to be that unmarried Catholic career women, most likely schoolteachers, had few organizational activities in which they could participate. As a result, single women gravitated to the church and its devotional societies, where they could establish their own separate social world.[37]

The delineation of male and female spheres within the parish was also illustrated in the operation of local church government. Men were the only people who could vote in parish elections, and they alone could act as trustees. Such secular activities as managing money and buying property were seen as a man's job, while religion was, as the Italian lady put it, "a woman's job."

The fourth and final trait of devotional Catholicism was its openness to the *miraculous*. A sense of mystery, a sense of the holy, was part of the mystical tradition of Roman Catholicism. Identified closely with the monastic way of life and certain saints, it also found a niche among the common people. The celebration of Mass certainly evoked this atmosphere of the holy, as did the numerous religious processions in and about the church and the neighborhood. But even more telling was the popular belief in miraculous cures. Part of the cultural baggage that Catholics brought with them was an attachment to a non-Christian religious culture. Distinct from the official religion of the church, it was the realm of folk tales and magic, banshees and charms, a supernatural world of good and evil forces. Catholicism, with its elaborate network of saints, its use of sacred objects such as relics, rosaries, candles, scapulars, and holy water, and its emphasis on the need for ritual to bridge the chasm between human and divine, blended in nicely with this folk religion. Rather than try to abolish such deep-seated cultural beliefs, the church sought to channel them into its official network of prayer and worship. The result was a curious blend of official and folk beliefs and practices.

A study done of the Irish living on Manhattan's West Side at the turn of the century uncovered widespread belief in the supernatural powers of scapulars, charms, and relics, as well as certain folk practices associated with birth and marriage. The Irish tradition of the festive wake was another example of the persistence of folk religious beliefs, despite prolonged opposition on the part of church authorities.[38] Marriage among Hispanic Catholics mixed together Hispanic and Anglo, folk and institutional religious customs. Belief in a supernatural world of the spirit beyond the realm of the official church was commonplace among Italians. One such aspect of this was belief in the healing power of certain women in the community, individuals who could ward off the effects of the evil eye.[39] Also quite common was belief in the supernatural power of such objects as scapulars and relics. Mission preachers, in their stories about the miraculous power of these objects, nurtured this belief; such religious periodicals as Ave Maria regularly reported cures and other miraculous events attributed to the use of such objects.[40] Catholic literature also encouraged such popular beliefs by frequently singling out in a positive way the miraculous power of such objects.

This belief in miraculous healings was quite common throughout Roman Catholicism during the nineteenth century. Shrines such as Our Lady of Lourdes, in France, and Ste. Anne de Beaupré, in Canada, attracted large numbers of pilgrims. Though the United States did not have such nationally renowned shrines, there were many local shrines associated with the healing powers of certain statues, relics, or pictures. Most of these shrines were founded during the 1920s, a time when devotional Catholicism was reaching its zenith of popularity. Nevertheless, at least eighteen local shrines were established during the nineteenth-century phase of the devotional Catholic awakening (i.e., after 1860). At St. Jean-Baptiste Church in New York, a relic of Ste. Anne was enshrined in 1892, and it quickly became the center of popular devotion because of the numerous cures attributed to the relic. Equally famous was the shrine at Our Lady of Mount Carmel Church in Italian Harlem. Beginning in the 1880s and continuing up until the 1950s, thousands of Italian Catholics came to 115th Street every July 16 to celebrate the festival of Our Lady of Mount Carmel. The festival was popular for many reasons, but chief among them was the tradition of numerous favors and healings received through the intercession of the Madonna. One hundred miles west of St. Louis was the German settlement of Starkenburg, Missouri, site of the Shrine of Our Lady of Sorrows. Established in the 1880s, it soon became a favorite destination for pilgrims from Kansas and Missouri.[41]

The fascination with the miraculous was a distinctive trait of devotional Catholicism. The Catholic God was a personal figure who listened to the prayers of people and acted on their behalf. God was not some distant, disinterested force, but one who would reach down and touch the lives of the people. The saints were frequently called on to persuade God to act, and such successful intervention understandably made them very popular among the people. The linking of such temporal favors as health, personal safety, and individual success with the rituals of devotional Catholicism was another major reason for the popularity of these devotions among the people. This was especially true when dramatic cures or healings took place in association with the performance of certain devotions such as prayers at a Marian shrine or the shrine of some saint. The reporting of such miracles was commonplace, and such news served to enhance the popularity of these shrines and devotions.[42]

The God of devotional Catholicism was a God of many faces. He was a lawmaker who exercised his authority through a myriad of rules established by the church which Jesus founded. Clearly an authoritarian figure, He punished sinners severely through the everlasting pains of hell. Yet, another side of Him was more benign. In His mercy He would forgive repentant sinners, cure the sick and heal the lame. Other cultures in other times represented God in different ways, but, for devotional Catholics, He was both stern judge and kind father. This is what made Him at once so fearsome and attractive, dreaded and loved. A culture of authority and sin emphasized the dark side of the divine, while the practice of ritual and belief in the miraculous underscored the bright side.

Though there can be no question about the popularity of devotional Catholicism in the immigrant community, some Catholics did attempt to articulate a different concept of God and religion. This divergent attitude was closely associated with Isaac Hecker, a few of his Paulist colleagues, and other liberal Catholics who sought to fashion a more American style of Catholicism in the New World.

Born in New York, Hecker converted to Roman Catholicism in 1844. Shortly afterward, he entered the Redemptorist order of priests; after his ordination to the priesthood, in 1849, he became very involved in preaching parish missions. Then, in 1858, he founded a new order of priests, the Congregation of Missionary Priests of St. Paul the Apostle, commonly known as the Paulists. Raised in the New England school of transcendental thought and influenced by Catholic mystical writers, Hecker thought quite differently from most Catholics about religion and society. His views on spirituality clearly demonstrated this.

Hecker articulated his vision in an 1875 essay in which he called for a new spirituality ". . . in view of the needs of the age."[43] The key to his vision was the Holy Spirit and its action within the souls of men and women who, thus energized, would renew the earth by advancing God's providential work. Hecker believed in the importance of authority and viewed the declaration of papal infallibility as the final necessary step toward the restoration of authority in the church and society. Yet he balanced this with the interior action of the Holy Spirit. As he put it, ". . . the exclusive view of the external authority of the Church, without a proper understanding of the nature and work of the Holy Spirit in the soul, would render the practice of religion formal, obedience servile, and the Church sterile."[44] Docility and passivity were qualities that did not fit into this energetic vision. More active, aggressive qualities were needed to renew religion and society. Hecker clearly had a more positive view of human nature than that of devotional Catholicism and continually stressed the possibility and indeed the need for union with the Holy Spirit on the part of individuals. His vision was certainly open to the miraculous, the realm of the supernatural, but absent from it was a dwelling on the cult of miracles; his view was more contemplative and mystical. For him, ". . . the sum of the spiritual life consists in observing and yielding to the movements of the Spirit of God in our soul, imploring for this purpose all the exercises of prayer, spiritual reading, sacraments, the practice of virtues, and good works." "The immediate guide of the Christian soul is the Holy Spirit," he wrote; contrary to this was "a mechanical piety," which, he said, "fixes the attention of the soul almost, if not altogether, on outward observances, and inculcates nothing beyond a complete submission to her external authority and discipline."[45] Though Hecker did not believe that Catholicism fostered such "mechanical piety," others did.

Other Paulists reacted against excessive attention given to "little devotions and religious sentimentality." The Paulist George Deshon wrote a popular guidebook for young working women, and though he encouraged special devotions, he did so in a moderate way, cautioning his readers to avoid being "loaded down with a great number of special devotions." Other guidebooks for women made the same point, advising mothers, for example, not "to cumber their daughters with too many of these practices."[46]

Catholic intellectuals associated with the Americanist movement in the late-nineteenth century articulated a view of religion and the spiritual life quite similar to Hecker's. Though their number was small, they clearly had a concept of the church, the human being, and devotional practices quite different from that of devotional Catholicism. Like Hecker, the Americanist movement followed in the tradition of the humanist school of religion visible during the republican period.[47]

A major complaint of this school of piety centered on the excessive reliance on the ritual of devotionalism; associated with this complaint was criticism of sentimental emotionalism, which devotional Catholicism also fostered. Reflecting a middle-class background, such critics sought a more subdued and refined type of piety. The same point was made about Catholic revival preaching. Enthusiasm was all right, but "noisy or demonstrative" excitement was not very Catholic; rather, it should be "all within, quiet, subdued."[48] Such complaints indicate that despite the popularity of devotional Catholicism, it did have its critics. Even more vociferous were those mainline Catholics who complained that the devotional practices of some immigrant groups bordered on pagan superstition.

The Italians offered the classic example of one group's practice of religion being misunderstood and consequently labeled by others as pagan superstition. Italian Catholicism was rooted in the confraternity and festive celebrations in honor of popular saints, rather than regular attendance at Mass and frequent reception of the sacraments. This shocked many American clergy— the Irish especially—and led to a litany of complaints, criticisms, and even conflict. One group of New York Italians, in fact, stormed the rectory of their Irish priest and "destroyed" it after he refused to support their demand to have a procession through the streets on the feast of St. Rosalia.[49]

Hispanic Catholics faced similar discrimination. The loudest complaints were voiced against the folk practices associated with the cult of the passion and death of Jesus. Holy Week was a special time for such manifestations, and the live performance of a passion play was quite common in Hispanic communities. Rooted in the colonial period, such plays were part of Spanish folk religion and were a very demonstrative and dramatic display of popular belief in the passion and death of Jesus. The Penitentes, a popular religious confraternity in the Southwest, encouraged this tradition by staging their own passion plays and other religious theater in a penitential manner that at times became excessive. French and Italian clergy working in the Southwest spoke out against such folk religious practices; too demonstrative and perhaps excessive for their taste, they were also not part of the official ritual of Catholicism.[50]

Devotional Catholicism fostered the practice of ritual and a demonstrative piety, but orthodoxy had its limits. This meant church-sanctioned rituals, rather than popular folk practices; moderate displays of piety and emotion, rather than excessive demonstrations. Nevertheless the Italian *festa* and the Spanish passion play survived despite the persistent opposition of church authorities. The popularity of the *festa* and the passion play illustrated the cultural diversity of Catholicism in the United States. In their efforts to standardize devotional Catholicism, church authorities could not overcome such deep-rooted practices and grudgingly allowed them to survive. Only later, as the people themselves became more acculturated to the American way of life, did such folk practices disappear.

Devotional Catholicism was the expression of a people's faith, and this fact alone can help to explain why it was so popular. But, as the noted medieval philosopher and theologian Thomas Aquinas said, grace builds on nature. Thus, in trying to explain why immigrant Catholics were so attached to religion, devotional Catholicism in particular, the historian necessarily must examine other, more natural explanations. The church, from the Pope down to the lowest parish priest, promoted this type of religion; developments in printing facilitated its dissemination; the use of the vernacular in most of the private and public devotional rituals was especially appealing. In addition, other social as well as personal reasons fostered the spread of devotional Catholicism.

In trying to understand why devotional Catholicism was so popular, certain social and psychological reasons should be noted. Catholics were clearly outsiders in the United States. White, Anglo-Saxon Protestants shaped the cultural, economic, and political life of the nation. Like other outsiders, Catholics experienced a good deal of ethnic and religious discrimination. Yet, religious discrimination worked both ways, with the anti-Protestant tone of devotional Catholicism only serving to widen the chasm that divided Catholics and Protestants. The political situation in the United States also encouraged such division. Religious freedom meant that as many religions as the people wanted would be able to compete in the marketplace. Such competition not only nurtured division, but it also meant that each group had to define itself clearly so that its identity would be recognizable in the midst of the religious marketplace. The segregation of urban America along racial, ethnic, and class lines meant that Catholics lived in neighborhood cultural ghettos separated from the rest of society. Even in small rural towns, where many Catholics lived, such social and residential segregation was common; towns were either preponderantly Catholic in population or, if not, were often so geographically divided that Catholics lived segregated from Protestants. In such a social situation, Catholic outsiders needed to acquire an identity. They were newcomers, and the history and lore of the American past was foreign to them; unlike their experience in the Old World, they did not have a tradition or an *ancien régime* to identify with. Devotional Catholicism thus became a means of social identity; it gave people a specifically Catholic identity in a Protestant society. Certainly ethnicity, or one's nationality, was a vital trademark with which both the first and the second generations identified. But religion was such an essential part of ethnic identity that, in the United States, religious affiliation became the "organizing impulse" among immigrants.[51] Moreover, in a society that still strongly believed in religion as a major element in the American way of life, religious identity was especially meaningful and valuable.

Personal reasons also account for the popularity of devotional Catholicism. Living in a Protestant society, it would be extremely difficult for Catholic immigrants to appropriate an American—i.e., Protestant—worldview. Throughout the era of the immigrant church, the United States was still perceived by most Catholics as too Protestant and thus too threatening. For some, a truly secular view of life and reality became a viable option, but, for the vast majority of Catholics, the Catholic devotional culture remained the major influence in shaping their mental world. It gave them a system of meaning in a society which at the time was able to offer few viable alternatives.

For the lower-class people who made up the majority of the Catholic population, religion became important in the personal struggle to survive. Life was harsh in the nineteenth century: mortality rates were high, living conditions were poor, and wages were low. Because of this, people suffered a great deal. In a special way, devotional Catholicism told them that such suffering had meaning and would receive its reward. One woman, not an avid churchgoer herself, put it this way. "I've only been an occasional church-goer," she said. "Only when the load got too heavy to bear did I share it with God." Another person wrote that the parish "has been and always will be a place of refuge for me. I draw whatever strength I need from it—it isn't just a place of worship, it's Sacred Heart—full of wonder, hope, faith, mystery, and yes, miracles."[52] Though isolated comments, they point to the very real personal value people found in their religion.

For immigrant Catholics, devotional Catholicism was especially appropriate. The culture of authority nurtured a sense of certainty, since they alone possessed the truth. Both church and Pope were infallible, and such claims to certitude gave Catholic outsiders a confidence that, despite their marginal position in American society, made them believe that they were the ones on whom the future of America rested. Such Catholic boosterism was a constant theme throughout the era of the immigrant church, and the confidence nurtured by a culture of authority gave it meaning and vitality. For people confronting the harshness of nineteenth-century city living, a culture of sin was not unreal; it surrounded them. The suffering of Jesus could be readily understood and the salvific mercy of his death appreciated. The struggle against such sins as intemperance and impurity was real in a Victorian culture bathed in alcohol, but those heavenly heroes, the saints, who had triumphed over sin, offered encouragement and example. The festive pageantry of a ritual culture enlivened drab city neighborhoods and quiet rural towns. The emphasis on private devotional practices through the use of pocket-size prayer books and devotional guides, together with portable sacred objects, was well suited to a very mobile population. Through a culture of the miraculous, the finger of God reached down and touched people, and such divine attention strengthened them in their belief that God indeed was on their side. They always knew they were correct in their beliefs, but such miraculous interventions confirmed this belief. The emotional and psychological relief that miraculous cures brought to individuals was unquestionable; religious solace was equally evident.

The old rituals and traditional beliefs of Roman Catholicism were restructured and acquired a special meaning in the United States during the era of the immigrant church. Separated from this social context, they may well appear meaningless and strange; set against the backdrop of urban, industrial, immigrant America, they become more understandable. For people living in the closing decades of the twentieth century, the sacred cosmos of this period may seem as remote as the Middle Ages. For several generations of Catholics, however, it was the only ethos that made sense.

IX

Handing on the Faith

CATHOLICS IN THE UNITED STATES possessed a distinctive ethos, a value system, that set them apart from their Protestant and Jewish neighbors. As immigrants, they also brought with them specific ethnic heritages, and parents zealously sought to transmit such cultures and traditions to the children of the New World. This desire to pass values and tradition on to future generations is a central concern of every culture. New England Puritans had the same aspiration, and so did Jewish immigrants in New York and Cincinnati. The way a people pass their culture on from generation to generation is through education.

For a long time, historians defined education narrowly, limiting it to formal pedagogy, or what took place in the schoolhouse. In recent years, however, scholars have defined education more broadly. It includes not only formal schooling but "the entire process by which a culture transmits itself across the generations."[1] This is clearly a seemingly limitless definition, but it does point out that education cannot be identified only with schools. It must include other agencies and institutions which serve to transmit a culture from one generation to the next. In this chapter, education will be understood in this broad manner, but in order to give the study a clear focus, only certain major institutions and agencies will be considered. For Catholics, the primary educative institutions during the century of immigration were family, church, school, college, and publications (i.e., newspapers and books). Other agencies and institutions that had a less significant educative influence will also be considered. All these institutions and agencies had one thing in common: they made a deliberate attempt to educate people in the spirit and meaning of the Catholic religion.[2]

Because of its central importance in American culture in general, and in the Catholic community in particular, the school demands special attention. For Catholics and also for German Lutherans, the parish school taught the four R's: reading, writing, arithmetic, and religion. Teaching secular subjects was essential, but religion was the bedrock of the school. "The teaching of the religion of Jesus Christ," wrote one Catholic school official in 1908, "is the reason for the existence of our separate system of schools."[3] Ignatius F. Horstmann, bishop of Cleveland at the turn of the century, was an ardent advocate of the parochial school; in a letter to a Cleveland priest, he expressed a similar point of view:

> . . . my dear father you can tell your faithful people that a parish without a parochial school is not a Catholic parish. The parochial school is a rock foundation, the soul of the future. Their divine faith understood fully is the most precious inheritance parents can leave their children. With it practically lived up to they will gain heaven. Without it all else is valueless—a priest's work without a parochial school can only be half done and is very discouraging.[4]

Though Horstmann's views may seem exaggerated, they represented a point of view in the Catholic community in which the school, not the church, was the hope of the future. Such a dedication to the parochial school gave Catholicism in the United States a special imprint that set it apart from that in other nations. By 1920, Catholics across the country were supporting over five thousand parish schools, and in some cities the Catholic school population was larger than the public school population. Such a situation was unique not only in the world of Roman Catholicism, but also in the United States.

In studying the Catholic school, it is very important not to view the past through the present. Such anachronism can distort the past and confuse the present. Catholic schools of recent times are products of the twentieth century, not the nineteenth century. The parochial school developed over the course of time; trying to compare the schools of the past twenty-five years with their predecessors in the nineteenth century is like comparing jet planes with tricycles. The same can be said of the public school. There is a substantial difference between twentieth-century schools and their nineteenth-century predecessors.

In looking at the educational experience of Catholics during the century of immigration, it would be helpful to examine briefly the period of the early republic, roughly from 1790 to 1830. With this background in place, the developments that took place in subsequent decades will stand out with greater clarity.

Surprisingly little is known about *family* life in the early republic. The daily activities of such personages as Thomas Jefferson, Charles Carroll, and Abigail Adams can be gleaned from their correspondence, but the family lives of more common folk remain hidden in the past. Such people did not leave behind diaries and voluminous correspondence, and if they did, it was most likely lost. Nevertheless enough material does exist for historians to talk intelligently about the family, the white middle-class family in particular, and its role in education and religion.

An economic transformation took place during this period that greatly affected the future of the family. For decades, work had been centered around the home, which was both hearth and workplace, but in the early-nineteenth century a separation took place as first the shop and then the factory replaced the home as the central place of work. Once a cradle of the economy, the home now became a nursery of domesticity. With this shift, the private sphere of the home became the domain of women. As historian Carl Degler noted, "Women's activities were increasingly confined to the care of children, the nurturing of husband, and the physical maintenance of the home. Moreover it was not unusual to refer to women as the 'angel of the house,' for they were said to be the moral guardians of the family. They were responsible for the ethical and spiritual character as well as the comfort and tranquillity of the home."[5] Portrayed as morally superior to men, women were responsible for the rearing of children and instructing them in discipline, skills, and religion. In other words, the educational responsibility of the woman in the home was central, whereas the man's responsibility rested in the public sphere of business, politics, and work. This model of family, with the woman as moral guardian and principal educator, was a pervasive theme in the literature of the early-nineteenth century, and it changed little during the rest of the century.[6] Though clearly identified with a white middle-class culture, it defines the boundaries of our knowledge about the family and its educative role in the early republic. In seeking to understand the educative role of the Catholic family at this time, even less hard information is available. Nevertheless, some insights can be gleaned from a variety of sources that reinforce, rather than contradict, the prevailing image of the family as educator.

Since Catholicism during this period was so centered in the book, catechisms and prayer books were standard items in Catholic homes. People imported such books from England, borrowed them from priests, or bought them from the Philadelphia publisher Mathew Carey.[7] Many Catholics lived in towns or villages devoid of clergy and church, and thus religion necessarily became a very domestic and private affair, with the book as the focal point. Bristol, Maine, was such a place; a letter of Father Jean Cheverus to the Hanley family in 1797 was most informative:

> Every day, say your prayers on your knees, morning and evening with attention and devotion. Every Lord's day and Holy day meet together morning and afternoon. In the morning, begin by the morning prayer on your knees. Read in the

Manual, What every Christian must believe. P.3 . . . Then the prayers at Mass with the Epistle and the Gospel of the Day. One chapter at least in the poor man's Cathechism. Acts of Faith, Hope, Charity and Contrition, kneeling. P.108.

In the afternoon, a Litany for Sunday, P.306, kneeling, or else the Universal prayer, or some other. One chapter at least in the poor man's Cathechism. Paraphrase on the Lord's Prayer, or some other prayers. Let the children recite by heart, every Sunday, something out of the Christian Doctrine. Keep days of fasting and abstinence as they are set down in the prayer book. Be careful to be well prepared for Confession and Communion against the next time that you will have a priest with you. . . .[8]

One of John Carroll's first pastoral letters strongly emphasized the educative role of the family. Carroll was vitally concerned about "the Christian instruction of youth" and saw this as a "special duty" that "rests on parents and heads of families." The church, he wrote, through the clergy, could lighten this "burthen" and schools would complement it, but, for Carroll, "Fathers and Mothers" had a primary responsibility to raise their "children in the discipline and correction of the Lord."[9] The 1829 pastoral of the American bishops, written by John England, was another eloquent statement on the importance of the family in educating the children.

Such few inferences about family and religion do not provide much raw material to fashion what might be called a Catholic understanding of family as educator in the early years of the republic. Given the underdeveloped nature of the church in the young nation, the severe scarcity of clergy, and the reliance on the book for religious guidance and inspiration, the family clearly had a key educational responsibility in religious affairs as well as secular concerns. The prevailing concept of woman as the moral guardian of the family and chief domestic educator was most likely as true among middle-class Catholics as it was in the rest of middle-class America. No evidence exists to contradict this presumption. In fact, the evidence that does exist for a later period would suggest that, in the early republic, middle-class Catholics were as Victorian in this regard as their Protestant neighbors.

During these early years, the Catholic Church in America was very underdeveloped. Comparatively speaking, the size of the community was quite small in relation to other denominations, and in 1815 Catholics claimed fewer churches than any other religious denomination. With the beginning of mass immigration, the number of bishops and dioceses slowly increased, so that by 1833 the Catholic hierarchy consisted of eleven bishops, who presided over as many dioceses. Nevertheless, the bishop remained very much a glorified pastor; he was not saddled with much administrative work, since the institutional structure of the church was not very developed. As a result, most bishops spent a good deal of time administering the sacraments and acting as ordinary pastors. This was quite a difference from Europe, where history and tradition had made bishops into princes. In the United States they had to be pastors. This impressed Europeans, and as late as 1847 one woman religious remarked that the bishop of Pittsburgh, Michael O'Connor, lived "the life of a simple priest," earning his livelihood "like any other priest" and "taking care of things like any ordinary priest."[10] These visitors also noticed something else. The church in this country was in its infancy, "like a newborn infant . . . comparable with the first years of Christianity."[11] One only had to glance at the U.S. Catholic Almanac published in 1833 to realize this. The state of Connecticut had but one church, seven were scattered across Massachusetts, and the Michigan territory claimed one church and a few mission chapels. The situation was much better in the cities than in the rural areas. New York State was quite typical. New York City numbered about thirty-five thousand Catholics, with four churches and only a few clergymen to care for their needs. North of the city, the situation was much more bleak. In upper New York State "endless numbers of neglected souls" were scattered far and wide. In a tour of the diocese, Bishop John Dubois discovered that wherever he visited he found "ten times as many Catholics as I expected; seven hundred are found where I understood there were but fifty or sixty; eleven hundred, where I was told to look for two hundred."[12] Along the northern boundary of the state, two thousand Irish and French Catholics lived scattered across an area of one thousand square miles, and rarely, if ever, did they see a priest. Given this underdeveloped state of the church, in rural areas especially, it is not surprising that a major responsibility for education rested with the family. Nevertheless, the *church* did engage in some educative activities.

Preaching was a key agency in this regard and was highly valued by the people. "Preaching is an indispensible duty," wrote one priest, "and the minister who pleases the people in that respect possesses unlimited influence over his flock."[13] Despite this assessment, priests preached only one major sermon on Sunday, at the principal Mass; the other Masses generally featured either brief, five-to-ten-minute, talks or most likely no sermon at all; Sunday evening devotions also included a brief sermon.

Parish missions, or revivals, were also aimed at instructing the faithful and converting sinners. John B. David preached such revivals along the Kentucky frontier during the 1790s, and others followed in his footsteps. Elsewhere they seemed to be scattered and infrequent happenings until the 1820s. In 1825, Pope Leo XII proclaimed a Holy Year in the hopes of launching a crusade for spiritual renewal. During that year and afterward, revivals were held in many cities and towns across Catholic America. Between 1826 and 1828, more than twenty took place in Kentucky alone. By 1829 it was clear that the revival had become an accepted feature of Catholic evangelization. Revivals sought conversion and the renewal of religion in "congregations cold and neglectful of their Christian duties." Instruction in Catholic doctrine was also a key focus of the revival. Like the sermon, the revival sought to educate people in the Catholic ethos.[14]

Another traditional form of education was Sunday school, or what was then simply called catechism. Every Sunday, catechism classes were held in Catholic churches as part of the usual Sunday schedule; for those areas without churches and clergy, the catechism class was always a regular feature of the itinerant missionary's visit.

During these early years, not much else existed in terms of the educative thrust of the church. Sermon, revival, and catechism made up the core. Some city parishes may have had one or two devotional societies which also sought to strengthen religion among the people, but beyond the city such organizations were quite exceptional. The goal of all these agencies was to convert the sinner, revive the faithful, and instruct the curious so that the Catholic ethos might take root in the soil of Protestant America. It was a big order for a denomination with too few clergy and not enough churches.

The *newspaper* was another important educator of the people. In the early years of the republic, no Catholic newspaper existed, but after 1810 or so a few did appear (a total of six by 1819). These first papers shared one trait: they did not last very long, most often less than a year. Obviously, this said something about their popularity and influence. During the 1820s, fifteen more Catholic newspapers were established, and of these, two had a relatively prolonged and important influence in the community. The *United States Catholic Miscellany* first appeared in print on June 5, 1822, in Charleston, South Carolina, and remained in circulation until 1861. The *Miscellany* was the brainchild of Bishop John England of Charleston. He served as its editor but received help from his sister, Joanna Monica England, until her death in 1827; afterward, he got assistance from various priests. A weekly paper, it was the first Catholic diocesan newspaper published in the United States. As the title suggests, the *Miscellany* was meant to serve the entire United States, and in its prime as many as seventy agents were selling the newspaper throughout the East and the Midwest. It carried news from Europe—Ireland in particular—kept people informed about the activities of the church in the Carolinas and elsewhere, and, most important, furnished a forum through which John England could educate the scattered Catholic population of his diocese. As England's reputation as a leading progressive churchman spread and the paper began to circulate beyond the Carolinas, it became England's pulpit to Catholic America. A contemporary assessment of the paper underscored its educational value. "The *United States Catholic Miscellany* is a leading Catholic weekly in the country," noted an observer, "not only telling about the Catholic faith but uniting scattered Catholics in the States . . . educating and encouraging them in the midst of the dangers to the faith."[15]

The other important paper of this period was the *Truth Teller*. A weekly paper, it was founded in New York City in April 1825. It was an Irish paper aimed at the immigrant community in New York and beyond; in addition to the usual news about the old country, it included a good deal of information about the church in New York. "Good priest writers" contributed to the *Truth Teller,* and this helped to strengthen its educative quality.[16]

In addition to the few newspapers circulating through the community, other media existed for passing on the culture of Catholicism; chief among these were *books, catechisms,* and *pamphlets.* Catholic books, that is, books written by Catholics with a religious or doctrinal focus, such as works in apologetics, doctrine, and history, circulated quite widely. Many of these were imported from England, France, and Germany, often brought over by the immigrants themselves. Priests themselves frequently acted as circulating libraries, lending books to people whom they met in the course of their ministry.[17] By far the most widely circulated book was the catechism. *The Catholic Christian Instructed,* by Bishop John Challoner of London, was the most popular, but many other catechisms compiled by European clergymen were published in the United States at this time. Individual dioceses also published their own; one adopted in many places was a catechism approved by John Carroll, *A Short Abridgement of Christian Doctrine.* At this time, catechisms were strikingly similar in content; those aimed at the clergy and educated laity were substantial compendiums of Catholic theology written in an apologetical style. Smaller, more popular editions were arranged in a question-and-answer format, and these also contained the essence of Catholic doctrine. Prayer books such as *The Garden of the Soul* were also circulating among Catholics; about a dozen such books were published prior to 1830. Devotional literature was also being published in the United States; the most popular books of this type were *The Imitation of Christ,* by Thomas à Kempis, and *The Introduction to the Devout Life,* by St. Francis de Sales.[18]

In addition to importing books from Europe, attempts were made to print books in the United States. The Jesuit priest Robert Molyneux started this practice in Philadelphia in 1786, printing Challoner's catechism and one or two other books. Out West, in the Michigan Territory, Father Gabriel Richard set up a press in 1809. Richard was a remarkable individual; a French Sulpician, he came to the United States in 1792 and spent the greater part of the next forty years as a missionary in the Michigan Territory. Bishop Joseph-Octave Plessis, an admirer of Richard, left a valuable glimpse of Richard and the mundane and varied nature of missionary life in the early-nineteenth century, a way of life reminiscent of eighteenth-century Maryland.

> This ecclesiastic is, moreover, thoroughly estimable on account of his regularity, of the variety of his knowledge, and especially of an activity of which it is difficult to form an idea. He has the talent of doing, almost simultaneously, ten entirely different things. Provided with newspapers, well informed on all political matters, ever ready to argue on religion when the occasion presents itself, and thoroughly learned in theology, he reaps his hay, gathers the fruits of his garden, manages a

fishery fronting his lot, teaches mathematics to one young man, reading to another, devotes time to mental prayer, establishes a printing press, confesses all his people, imports carding and spinning-wheels and looms to teach the women of his parish how to work, leaves not a single act of his parochial register unwritten, mounts an electrical machine, goes on sick calls at a very great distance, writes letters and receives others from all parts, preaches every Sunday and holyday both lengthily and learnedly, enriches his library, spends whole nights without sleep, walks for whole days, loves to converse, receives company, teaches catechism to his young parishioners, supports a girls' school under the management of a few female teachers of his own choosing whom he directs like a religious community, while he gives lessons in plain-song to young boys assembled in a school he has founded, leads a most frugal life, and is in good health, as fresh and able at the age of fifty as one usually is at thirty.[19]

Richard had a keen interest in education, and this led him to become a moving force behind the establishment of what is now known as the University of Michigan, serving as its first vice president for four years and later as a member of its board of trustees. His interest in the general welfare of the region persuaded him to run for political office, and in 1823 he was elected to Congress and served for two years. During one of his trips East, Richard had purchased a printing press, most likely in Utica, New York, and had had it shipped back to Detroit, where he had set up shop and begun printing books. During the seven years of its existence, 1809–16, Richard's press published a total of fifty-two books. Most of these were of European, mostly French, origin. The majority were religious in nature—catechisms, prayer books, devotional literature—and reflected the pastoral, educative purpose of Richard's press.[20]

The other notable publisher of Catholic books was Mathew Carey. Born in Ireland in 1760, he came to the United States in 1784 after a brief but stormy political career. Shortly after he arrived in Philadelphia, he set up shop as a printer and bookseller; in 1787 he began publication of what became a noted literary magazine, *The American Museum;* soon after, he began to print Catholic books. In 1790 Carey printed the first English Catholic Bible in the United States, and he also published English editions of European works, mostly prayer books and catechisms. For the next twenty years he remained a major Catholic publisher in the United States. He published other types of books as well, so that by 1817 his firm had become the "greatest publishing and distributing firm" in the nation.[21] Like Richard, Carey published books families could use to educate themselves and their children in the Catholic religious tradition. Since formal schooling was a sometime experience, the responsibility for education rested heavily on the shoulders of parents, the mother especially; Carey and Richard made their job a little easier.

Formal education was the work of the *schools,* and the Catholic community, like other denominations, established such institutions. During this early period, three types of Catholic schools came into existence. The first was the church school established for the young boys and girls of the parish; the second was the female academy, and the third was the men's college.

The most important school during this period, in the opinion of the bishops, was the men's college. There is no more convincing evidence for this than the founding of Georgetown University. Bishop John Carroll was personally responsible for the establishment of this academy. He frequently said that the founding of Georgetown was the object nearest his heart. "On this academy," he once wrote, "is built all my hope of permanency and success to our holy religion in the United States."[22] Later bishops shared Carroll's enthusiasm for a men's college. In Kentucky, Benedict Flaget founded a seminary in 1811; eight years later its companion institution, St. Joseph's College, opened its doors, with another college to follow two years later. In Ohio, Bishop Edward Fenwick had a college and seminary in operation by 1831. William Du Bourg was bishop of the vast New Orleans diocese; one of his first projects was to found a seminary and college in a place in Missouri called "the Barrens," now known as Perryville; in 1819, he also established a college in St. Louis, which today is known as St. Louis University. In Alabama, hardly a Catholic stronghold, Michael Portier, bishop of Mobile, established Spring Hill College, in 1830. In fact, by 1830 a total of fourteen Catholic men's colleges had been founded; four of these are still in operation today—namely, Spring Hill College, St. Louis University, Georgetown University, and Mount St. Mary's College in Emmitsburg, Maryland.[23]

The reason for the bishop's concern for a men's college was the dire need for priests. Throughout this period, decent and reliable clergy were in short supply, and bishops viewed the college as a way of recruiting and training young men for the priesthood. As Carroll said of Georgetown, ". . . it will become a nursery for the seminary."[24] Later bishops also assigned top priority to the founding of colleges.

In these early days, college and seminary most often developed together as one institution. The college not only acted as a feeder of students for the seminary, but it also provided financial support for the seminary. On the other hand, the seminary provided unsalaried teachers for the college in the persons of the seminarians, who guided the educational and moral development of younger students. As historian Philip Gleason observed, ". . . the college/seminary relationship was a symbiotic affair," with each supporting the other.[25]

These early Catholic colleges were mixed institutions that engaged in educational activities that today would be carried out by "three or four distinct types of schools." The combination of college and seminary work under one roof was one indication of this lack of differentiation and specialization. Even more telling was the makeup of the student body. Students ranged anywhere from eight to twenty-two years of age. William Gaston, for example, was a twelve-year-old lad from North Carolina when he entered Georgetown as its first student, in 1791. Such a mixture of young and old students meant that the college had to offer "instruction ranging from elementary courses like spelling, penmanship, and basic English grammar to college-level work in Latin, Greek and Philosophy." Another point worth noting is that Protestants regularly attended Catholic colleges at this time; for example, out of seventy-eight new students entering St. Joseph's College in Bardstown, Kentucky, in 1848–49, one third (36 percent) were Protestants.[26]

Though these institutions hardly resembled today's college, they were considered colleges at that time. Their model, however, was European and not American. The reason for this was that the founders of the schools were European-educated priests, and the institutions they established were designed to resemble the colleges they had attended. In addition, such European religious orders as the Jesuits, Dominicans, Sulpicians, and Vincentians constituted the faculty of these institutions, and their educational roots were European as well.[27]

The women's academy was the second-most-important school at this time. In the early years of the republic, the education of women was promoted as an integral part of the development of a new American culture. As historian Frederick Rudolph put it, ". . . the American female was recognized as capable of being educated—up to a point," and college was the point of resistance; for this reason, female education at this time focused on the academy.[28] Following this development, Catholic female academies began to appear with consistent regularity in the early-nineteenth century. Like their Protestant counterparts, they were founded for religious and moral reasons. Mother Elizabeth Seton, the saintly founder of the Sisters of Charity, emphasized this point in a talk to students at St. Joseph's Academy, which she had founded, in Emmitsburg, Maryland. "I would wish to fit you for that world in which you are destined to live," she said, "to teach you how to be good mistresses and mothers of families." In other words, "the moral and religious training of their pupils as future American mothers" was the chief goal of all Catholic academies.[29] Once educated in moral and domestic virtues, their graduates could become the moral guardians of the home.

Of course, the female academy was not an American invention. It was a transplanted European institution. The founding of the first Catholic female academy, in New Orleans in 1727, points this out most clearly. Ursuline nuns came from France to organize the academy, the first of its kind in the French Louisiana Territory. As educators, they were eager to transplant the academy concept to New Orleans; in fact, more nuns than necessary volunteered for the Louisiana mission. As in France, they accepted both boarders and day students and also established a free school in conjunction with the tuition academy. It was not until 1790 that the next academy, Visitation, was founded, in Georgetown. After the turn of the century, additional academies began to appear with regularity; ten were in operation by 1820 and one hundred by 1852.[30]

The female academy resembled the men's college in the sense that it, too, was a catchall institution. It had both boarding and day students ranging from seven to fifteen years of age; it attracted Protestants as well as Catholics; and it tailored its curriculum and schedule as needed. Beginning at a primary level and advancing to a secondary level, it offered spelling, reading, writing, and arithmetic, as well as courses in French, drawing, music, needlework, and other subjects thought to be proper for a young female's "domestic" education.[31]

The key to the establishment of female academies was the availability of women religious. Catholic sisters ran the academies, and most often a new religious order was founded specifically to operate such an educational institution. Of the first eight women religious congregations founded in the United States, for example, seven were organized specifically for educational reasons.[32] Such a concern for education on the part of these women illustrates how central female education was considered to be in the life of the Catholic community. Behind this, of course, was the ideal of the woman as mother and moral guardian of the home; to fulfill this role as well as possible, a sound moral and religious education was desirable. Viewed from this perspective, the female academy served the family and sought to strengthen it in its educative function. This underscores the point that the family, not the academy, was the primary educational institution in this era.

The most common school of the period was the parish school, established for young boys and girls. It is also the school about which least is known. These schools most often originated from the desires of the local community. People wanted their children to know the principles of their faith, and so they pushed for a school in the parish. Reflecting this tradition of localism, parish schools varied considerably from place to place. Diversity, rather than uniformity, best describes this early period of elementary schools. Since the line between public and private schools was not well defined, Catholic schools were also more integrated into the local community than would be true later. As a result, some Catholic schools received financial support from the local government; such was the case in New York City until 1825. In some rural towns the Catholic school was the only school; in effect, it served as the "public" school. In some towns, classes were taught in a foreign language and no one seemed to mind.

Another major feature of the schools in this period was their transiency. Like a morning fog, they were quite visible for a brief period and then they vanished without notice. They were very modest enterprises: a small log cabin in a rural town or a basement operation in a city church; some charged a small tuition, others were free. Most often, they were run by male teachers called schoolmasters, who, since pay was low, worked at other jobs and tended to be quite mobile. As a result, turnover was high, and one-room schools opened and closed depending on the availability of a schoolmaster. Nor were students accustomed to regular attendance; they moved in and out of schools according to the seasons of the year and the need for work on the farm or in the shop. In addition to these church schools, women religious often opened a free school for those children who could not afford their tuition academy. In all these schools the curriculum was quite basic and very similar: "reading, writing, arithmetick, and Catechism."[33] This was the basic core of elementary education, with moral and religious training being the central purpose of the school.

With the 1830s, the educational enterprise in the United States began to change substantially. The most significant development was the emergence of the common-school system. In addition to the elementary school, high schools and colleges developed, so that by 1920 a public educational system was emerging in the United States which sought to educate children from early childhood to young adulthood. Schooling clearly had become a central concern of the American people, and this would greatly influence the shape of education in the Catholic community. With the growth of the nation, the emergence of an industrial economy, and the popularization of culture, major changes took place which affected the educational thrust of family, church, and press. The emergence of a school system hardly negated the educational role of these institutions; rather, they would supplement the work of the school, thus helping to shape an identifiable American culture.

Throughout this period, from 1830 to 1920, the model of *family and home* prevalent in the early years of the republic remained dominant. The importance of domesticity was continually stressed throughout the culture, and woman was placed upon a pedestal, enshrined as the moral guardian of the family. The nineteenth century became the century of the child, and proper child rearing was the primary role of the mother. This was the dominant model of family and motherhood in white middle-class America, and it became the norm against which all else was measured. In this model, the family clearly was viewed as an educational institution, with the mother being the primary teacher. This ideal clearly was the norm among middle-class English-speaking Catholics. Guidebooks and etiquette books for women clearly supported this model, and sermons on family life implied as much. Such books as the *Mirror of True Womanhood* enshrined the home as "the true woman's kingdom" and urged women to be the Catholic superwoman.[34] Parish missions generally included a sermon on the duties of parents, and the telling point was that the mother was portrayed as the active person, the teacher at whose knee the children would sit to learn the catechism or recite their prayers. In the words of one preacher, the children's "best school teacher is at home and she has been appointed by the Holy Spirit."[35] Though preachers emphasized the responsibilities of both parents, the mother was

clearly the active educator, while the father instructed by example. Guidebooks for young men made this point as well.

The principal way mothers taught their children the ethos of Catholicism
was by the recitation of prayers, instruction in the catechism, and the practice
of devotions. The family rosary was clearly one practice held up as an ideal.
Mission preachers promoted it and often stated that it was a prevalent practice among the people they met. Though the family rosary appeared to be the
main domestic ritual among both Irish- and American-born families, other
devotions "such as the Sign of the Cross, the use of Holy Water, of Blessed
candles" were also encouraged, and mothers were urged to be "zealous" in
communicating such devotions "to their sons and daughters."[36] In addition,
homes were often decorated with holy pictures and statues, and these helped
to reinforce the educative environment of the home.

This ideal, portrayed in books and sermons, reflected a middle-class culture
within a particular segment of the community, namely the Irish and American-born Catholics. How widespread this ideal was in practice is difficult to
know, but it clearly was the normative model and was the moral standard
against which the lives of parents, mothers especially, were measured. Catholics, however, were a very diverse people; and family behavior patterns varied
among different immigrant groups.

If comparatively little is known about the history of the middle-class family
in the United States, even less is known about working-class immigrant families. Nevertheless, from what studies have been done, a general portrait of
immigrant family life can be drawn. It is important to realize, however, that
important differences separated rural families from urban families, and middle-class families from working-class families; moreover, within the immigrant community, each group had its own traditions, with the result that the
role of family in the Italian community, for example, differed substantially
from that of the Irish and the Slovak traditions. Given these caveats, some
generalizations can still be made that will provide a context in which the
educational role of the immigrant family can be understood.

Most immigrants arrived as individuals, either as single unmarried persons
or as one piece in the chain migration of a family. These people had to
establish new families in the United States through marriage or reconstitute
their Old World families, which were separated by emigration. Some immigrants, like the Germans, generally emigrated as families. The majority of
these families were nuclear families; that is, they were made up of mother,
father, and children. The mothers of these families seldom worked outside the
home, though they frequently did take in boarders or do some type of work at
home such as sewing or industrial homework to supplement the family income. The children of immigrant families often went to work at an early age,
around ten or so, but the age of entry into the work force rose as schooling
lengthened and compulsory-attendance laws became more effective. Immi-

grant families tended to be larger than American-born families, and rural families were larger than urban ones. Though desertion and death did claim victims, the two-parent household was the norm in the immigrant community. Among the Irish, however, desertion—or what is generally referred to as divorce, Irish style—did account for more female-headed households than among other groups. As was true elsewhere, the mother was the "heart of the home; it was she who managed the home and reared the children."[37] As primary educator, she was responsible for raising the children in the family's culture and religion. But she was also cook and banker, cleaning lady and decision maker. The home was her castle, and men clearly understood this.

In the immigrant family, passing on the religious heritage took place in a variety of ways. Learning the language was an essential step; once this was achieved, children learned to pray in the language of their parents; in other words, at home, religion was transmitted through the immigrant's language, and this gave it a strong ethnic identification. Like their American or Irish counterparts, foreign-language-speaking mothers taught children their prayers and their catechism; if religion was passed on at all, this was how it was done. Pictures and statues depicting popular ethnic saints were common sights in these working-class homes; among Mexican and Italian families, it was common to find small household shrines to favorite saints. Domestic rituals were also more numerous among the non-Irish foreign-born.

Most religious rituals in the immigrant household were associated with major feast days. Easter was especially important for Eastern European immigrants. Families baked bread, gathered together foodstuffs, and had the priest bless them at home or at church; then they celebrated the feast with a family meal which gathered together uncles and aunts, grandparents and cousins. Mexican and Italian families also baked special breads for Easter, thus underlining the distinctive influence of religion on family life. On Palm Sunday, people brought palms home from church and used them to decorate shrines, pictures, or statues; some even placed them under their beds to ward off sickness. Christmastime found manger scenes decorating immigrant homes. The celebration of baptism, first Communion, and confirmation were prolonged by family parties and banquets; first-Communion family portraits were also quite commonplace. In this manner, religious events became the occasion for family celebrations.

The Italians provide a good example of the close bond between family, home, and religion. The family was the core of Italian culture, and religion was "narrowed within the walls of their home"; or, as one recent study put it, ". . . the Italian home and family *is* the religion of Italian Americans."[38] Though official church religion was marginal to the religion of family and home, the Italians did celebrate church festivals with religious enthusiasm; such *feste* became family-oriented events celebrated to bind families together or heal the wounds that divided them. Within the home itself, ". . . the immigrants also clung tenaciously to their 'sacred, ancestral traditions.' Religious images adorned the walls; votive lamps burned before shrines to the saints and madonnas. Saints days were observed with special foods and prayers, and few homes lacked a *presepio* (manger scene) at Christmas."[39] Since religion among the Italians was the woman's domain, the role of mother as moral guardian was commonly accepted; it was the mother who taught the children the mysteries of religion. Among the Italians and among other immigrant groups as well, the family was clearly an important institution for educating children in the ethos of Catholicism, and though there were differences of degree and of style, each group passed on its religion through the family. But the family was not alone. The church also sought to transmit the culture of Catholicism across the generations, and in doing so it supplemented the work of the family in a variety of ways.

From 1830 to 1920, the institutional *church* underwent a period of tremendous expansion. The numbers of Catholics increased from an estimated 318,000 in 1830 to close to 18 million by 1920 (17,735,553); the number of priests rose from 232 to 21,019, and the number of churches from about 230 to 16,181. With this growth came more systematic organization and control as the number of dioceses, a geographical region established for administrative and juridical purposes, increased from 10 to 112. Accompanying the growth was an expansion in the educational work of the church on both parish and regional levels.

In the parish, preaching remained an important way for the clergy to reach the people. Not as central to Catholic worship as it was to Protestant liturgy, the sermon was limited to Sunday Masses, and even then it was still a sometime happening, always at the principal Mass, but only occasionally at other Masses. It was the mission preacher, the itinerant professional, who became the major pulpit educator during these years. After a slow beginning in the pre-1830 period, the parish mission soon emerged as the most popular and effective means of evangelization of the masses. For a period of one, two, or even four weeks, night and day, through both sermons and catechetical instructions, a team of Catholic revival priests would lay out before the people the Catholic road map to heaven and explain how they could successfully complete the journey. The parish revival was a key component in the church's educational enterprise; for some people it was the primary point of contact with the church; for others it complemented and reinforced what they had already learned. Like the Protestant revival, it reached large numbers of people; aside from the schools, it was the most effective means of religious education that Catholics had.[40]

Catholics never developed the Sunday school as Protestants did. Catechism classes were important and were always mentioned as an item of concern, but the clergy and women religious were never as serious about the Sunday school as they were about the parochial school. The Sunday school was aimed at those children who did not attend the parish school; nationwide, this represented 60 percent or more of the school-age children at the turn of the century, though in some neighborhoods and cities it was not as high. In these catechism classes, most often taught by women religious teachers from the parish school, children were prepared for their first Communion and confirmation; the former was received in the third or fourth grade, the latter normally around age twelve. Once confirmed, the child graduated from catechism, and that was the end of formal religious instruction for this group of children.

Unlike most cities, San Francisco had a very organized Sunday-school program. At the heart of it were the Sisters of the Holy Family. Founded in San Francisco in 1872 by an Australian-born woman, Elizabeth Armer, this religious order of women was actively involved in catechetical work. They taught the immigrant Italian children in the North Beach section of the city and had classes in other parishes as well, often assisted by lay men and women. A 1915 report to the superintendent of schools stated that they were managing twenty-two Sunday schools and teaching close to eight thousand (7,763) children in the city of San Francisco; they were also teaching catechism in parishes in Oakland and San Jose.[41]

Shortly before World War I, a revival of the Confraternity of Christian Doctrine was beginning to take place. The Confraternity, originated in the sixteenth century, had a simple concept: an organized approach to religious instruction that promised spiritual benefits. Both Pope Pius X and the 1917 Code of Canon Law promoted the Confraternity, with the result that some larger dioceses, such as Los Angeles, began to develop a parish catechetical program to improve the teaching of religion to children who attended public schools. By the 1930s, the Confraternity of Christian Doctrine had become a nationwide movement, complete with its own national organization.

Another educative agency in the local church was the parish library. This became the Catholic counterpart to the reading room and lyceum, which were so common in large cities. Many parishes had such libraries, most often aimed at the young men and women of the parish. Isaac Hecker and the community of priests he founded, the Paulists, especially promoted the concept of a parish library and its offspring, the reading circle. By the 1890s it was a nationwide movement complete with its own organization and journal, the *Catholic Reading Circle Review*. At that time, about ten thousand people belonged to more than 250 reading circles across the country.[42] Mention should also be made of the omnipresent devotional society. Such societies deliberately sought to develop a Catholic ethos in their members by educating them in the finer points of spirituality; overwhelmingly female and largely adult, they reached only a small section of the parish; especially popular was the teenage sodality for girls, which sought to attract those young women who had graduated from elementary school but were not yet married. As mentioned earlier, an important men's society that developed in the late-nineteenth century was the Holy Name Society. Its origin lay in the distant past, and like so many confraternities, it was resurrected from obscurity during the nineteenth century. At first, Dominican priests promoted this society, whose explicit purpose was to encourage reverence for the name of Jesus. It also encouraged a militant and triumphant style of Catholicism by fostering public demonstrations of faith in which thousands of Catholic men paraded through city streets and gathered for huge rallies in baseball stadiums. By 1910, the Holy Name Society had been established in thousands of parishes and had as many as five hundred thousand members.[43]

Another major educational institution was the men's fraternal society. The fraternal society was an idea whose time had come in the second half of the nineteenth century. People joined such societies with increasing regularity, and they proliferated. Among the immigrants they took on a decided ethnic character and transmitted a particular cultural heritage. Founded initially as mutual-aid or insurance societies, they also had wider cultural and religious goals. Generally national organizations, they had local chapters or lodges based in individual parishes, or if not in a parish, they had one or more chapters serving parts of a city or an entire town. These fraternal societies were closely associated with the rising sense of nationality that was evident among various immigrant groups in the United States, and this gave religion a strong dose of ethnic nationalism. Among the Polish, the oldest and most noteworthy fraternal organization was the Polish Roman Catholic Union of America; founded in 1873 "to preserve Catholic and Polish tradition and culture among Polish immigrant groups," it reached a national membership of over 100,000 by the time of World War I. Every French-Canadian community had its own St. Jean Baptiste Society. Rooted in a deep attachment to the ethnic heritage of French Canada, this society, as noted earlier, was a major influence in preserving *la langue et la foi*. By 1890, New England had 210 such societies, with 30,840 members. Germans belonged to the Central Verein, which was founded in 1855. Like the other fraternals, it held national conventions, had its own national headquarters and officers, and published educational materials for its members; by 1916 it had about 125,000 members. The Ancient Order of Hibernians, founded in 1836 in New York City, was an important organization among the Irish; decidedly nationalistic and staunchly Catholic, it sought to pass on the culture of Irish Catholicism to future generations. It claimed 127,254 members by 1908.[44] The most famous and most successful fraternal organization was the Knights of Columbus.

Father Michael McGivney, a young priest in New Haven, Connecticut, founded the Knights of Columbus in 1882. Though a life-insurance program was central to its purpose, the Knights had much broader concerns. Like other fraternals, it developed an extensive educational program which aimed at religious as well as civic education. The Knights of Columbus also promoted a distinctly Catholic version of American nationalism, Columbianism, which looked to a new age characterized by a new Catholic maturity, "an end of Protestant hegemony, and full civil and social rights for persons of all religions."[45] It was both militantly Catholic and proudly American. Even though it did not limit its membership to those of Irish descent, the Irish occupied the important leadership positions and made up the majority of its members, who numbered 40,267 by 1899. The Knights of Columbus grew rapidly in the early years of the twentieth century, reaching a membership of over 300,000 by 1914. Eventually, parallel women's organizations developed, such as the Daughters of Isabella, an offshoot of the Knights of Columbus, and the Ladies Auxiliary of the Ancient Order of Hibernians. Like the men's societies, they sought to educate their members in the Catholic culture as well as provide a place where people could come together, enjoy one another's company, and share their concerns.

The summer school was another important educative agency. Resembling the much larger Chautauqua movement, of the late-nineteenth century, the Catholic summer school was held to foster intellectual and religious growth through lectures and special courses; people learned "the Catholic point of view in all the issues of the day in history, in literature, in philosophy, in political science, upon the economic questions agitating the world, upon the relations between science and religion." Summer schools first began to appear in the 1890s in Connecticut, New York, Wisconsin, Louisiana, and Maryland. A permanent site was soon established near Plattsburg, New York, on the shores of Lake Champlain. Named Cliff Haven, the school brought together Catholics from all parts of the country, with as many as ten thousand people annually attending its summer fare of lectures, courses, concerts, and dramatic recitals.[46] Catholic settlement houses were also quite common during this period, with 27 in operation by 1915; they offered education courses and taught catechism to hundreds of immigrant children. Orphanages were also very widespread; 296 such institutions were caring for 45,687 children by 1920. Taking the place of home and family, the orphanage sought to provide moral and religious training for its residents.[47]

The church's educational network went far beyond the parish school, reaching out to all types of people in its effort to develop a strong and enduring Catholic culture in the United States. As we have already seen, the *newspaper* and *book publishing* enterprises figured prominently here.

In the 1830s and after, newspapers began to multiply like rabbits. New technology, better postal service, partisan politics, increasing literacy, and a growing population stimulated this growth. As an "educator of the populace," the newspaper interpreted public affairs for its readers in a special way, reflecting a particular ethnic, religious, or political bias. People selected newspapers that reflected their own ethnic, religious, and political preferences, and Catholics did not have to look far for their kind of paper. Between 1830 and

1900 over seven hundred Catholic newspapers appeared in print; add to this parish, school, and society newspapers as well as magazines, and the number almost doubles. Since publishing religious and ethnic newspapers was a financial challenge, relatively few people were successful at it for any length of time. As a result, the survival rate of Catholic serials was quite low: out of the 1,278 serials published between 1830 and 1900, only 349 survived into the twentieth century.[48]

Every ethnic group had its own newspaper. English-speaking Catholics had the largest representation; Germans and French Canadians were a distant second, followed by the Polish, Czechs, and Lithuanians. All but a few of these papers had very small circulation—a few thousand subscribers at best. The *Pilot,* of Boston, with approximately 72,000 subscribers, and the *Catholic News,* of New York, with an estimated circulation of 100,000 in the late 1880s, were the two leading Catholic newspapers in the country. Both were English-language papers, and they catered to Irish- and American-born Catholics.[49]

The *Pilot* was "one of the most influential immigrant newspapers, the Irish Bible, of nineteenth century America."[50] Founded in 1829 it interpreted the world for the immigrants as well as reporting news from Ireland. It defended the Irish and their religion when they came under attack; it celebrated their victories with appropriate chauvinism and sought to assist people in the adaptation of the Irish to the American way of life. As owner and publisher, the Irish-born Patrick Donahoe was the moving force behind the paper during the middle decades of the century, when it became "the Irish Bible." In the 1870s, John Boyle O'Reilly became editor, and circulation increased. O'Reilly, a noted Irish writer, gave the paper a progressive, reform orientation and a decidedly Irish flavor. When he died, in 1890, another outstanding journalist, James Jeffrey Roche, became editor and continued the orientation of O'Reilly. When Roche retired, in 1904, Katherine Conway took over as editor. A novelist and poet, Conway had written for the paper for a number of years and was one of the outstanding writers of her time. With O'Reilly, Roche, and Conway guiding the paper, the *Pilot* maintained a high standard of quality and received "the coveted gold marks of distinction awarded by the American Newspaper Directory" in 1904. As the Directory noted, "The *Pilot* is the one religious journal accorded the gold marks, and while fundamentally a Roman Catholic publication, it is best known as the organ of the Irishman of America."[51] In 1908 the Donahoe family sold the paper to the archbishop of Boston, William O'Connell; no longer an immigrant newspaper, it now became the official paper of the diocese and has remained so to this day. Both Irish and Catholic, the *Pilot* helped to educate thousands of people into the Catholic immigrant culture.

Just as newspapers multiplied during this period, so, too, did book publishers. Catholics saw a need not only for their own newspapers, but also for their own books. Understanding this, immigrant Irishmen such as P. J. Kenedy and John Doyle of New York, John Murphy in Baltimore, and Patrick Donahoe in Boston set up shop and, before long, became important Catholic publishers. Other ethnic groups had their own publishing firms as well. The Herder Company in St. Louis catered to the Germans, as did Benziger Brothers, the American branch of a well-known Swiss firm; the Bohemian Benedictine Press published books for the Czechs, while a major publisher of Polish literature was Antoni Paryski of Toledo. As the Catholic population increased, so did the number of publishers, reaching a peak in the 1890s. New York City was the center of the industry, and during the 1890s sixty-eight firms published a total of 1,183 Catholic books. The major reason for this increase in publishers was the expanding educational network among Catholics; schools, colleges, reading circles, summer schools, parish libraries, revivals, and sodalities encouraged the reading of Catholic books, and enterprising publishers sought to capture a portion of the market. Relatively few publishers made it, however; like the newspaper industry, book publishing was a precarious business, and more failed than survived. Those that did—P. J. Kenedy & Sons, Benziger Brothers, and Herder—grew stronger by buying up their competitors' plates and stock and "gradually adding works not exclusively tailored for the Catholic market." Moreover, by the early-twentieth century, major non-Catholic firms such as Macmillan and Scribner's began to publish Catholic works.[52]

Catholic publishers printed such items as bibles, novels, school readers, prayer books, text books, devotional pamphlets, and catechisms. But it was the catechism that kept the Catholic firms financially solvent. P. J. Kenedy & Sons had a list of five hundred titles in 1904, but the money-maker for the firm was an expanded version of the Baltimore Catechism; ". . . at one time it was estimated that if anyone wanted to stack the Kenedy Catechism printed in a year the pile would reach 17½ times the height of the Woolworth Building."[53]

Family, church, newspapers, and books were important educative agencies. They helped to shape a culture and provided a means for one generation to educate the next. To underestimate their influence is to misunderstand the educative process which shapes the minds of people. One New Jersey schoolmaster emphasized this point in 1838. "As a nation," he said, "we are educated more by contact with each other, by business, by newspapers, magazines, and circulating libraries, by public meetings and conventions, by lyceums, by speeches in Congress, in the state legislatures, and at political gatherings, and in various other ways, than by direct instructions imparted in the schoolroom."[54] Such an informal configuration of education raised the level of general intelligence and established a distinctive American ethos. Like most subcultures, Catholics had their own network of educative agencies, and these helped to form a Catholic ethos. Notwithstanding the importance of such agencies, it was the school that became the principal educational institution in the course of the nineteenth century.

X

Schools

THE NINETEENTH CENTURY was a time when the schoolhouse became the sacred temple of the American nation. The school had replaced the family as the principal educational institution and, by mid-century, politicians and educators were working together for a common goal: state-supported education for all children. The public school was the key to the realization of this goal. Though a similar movement was underway in Canada and Western Europe, the United States became the acknowledged leader in the public school movement as educators and politicians pushed their campaign forward with the zeal of religious crusaders. By the late-nineteenth century, the public school had acquired a sacred aura and anyone opposed to this institution would likely be regarded not only as "an enemy of education, of liberty, of progress," but also guilty of "treason to our country."[1] It was within this context that the Catholic parochial school emerged. Like its counterpart, the public elementary school, it became the principal educational institution in the Catholic community, and Catholic educators promoted it with the same type of zeal found among public school crusaders. By the 1880s, the parochial school, rather than the men's college, was the most important school in the Catholic community.

The Catholic elementary school, like its public counterpart, developed over the course of time. It did not appear as a fully developed institution complete with eight separate grades housed in a building especially designed as a schoolhouse. On the contrary, it began as a shoestring operation in a damp church basement or log-cabin room where a single instructor taught the basic four R's to a group of children ranging from ages six to twelve. Moreover, schooling did not develop at the same rate and according to the same patterns throughout the nation. Rather, various regions exhibited their own distinctive patterns in this regard.

In New York City, most Catholic parishes during the 1830s had some type of school. Generally it was in the basement of the church, where children were "so closely pushed together that they hardly had room to move." By 1840 about five thousand children attended these schools.[2] The major problem for the schools was finances; this threatened to close some of them. For this reason, Catholics petitioned the city's Common Council for financial aid. Another principal reason for the petition was religion. The Public School Society operated the schools in New York, and this society of Protestant gentlemen promoted an evangelical Protestant piety in the city's schools. Many Catholics found this offensive. For almost two years, Catholics pushed their campaign for public funds. In the end their petition was denied. Defeated in their attempt to obtain public funds, Catholics began to concentrate on building their own schools. The key person in this was John Hughes, the Irish-born bishop of New York. A priest in Philadelphia prior to his promotion to the episcopacy in 1838, Hughes was an accomplished orator and achieved public prominence during the two-year campaign for public funds. Defeated in that battle, Hughes directed his energies to organizing Catholic schools; before he died in 1864, he had become the acknowledged champion of the Catholic school. Hughes's famous dictum—"to build the school-house first, and the church afterwards"—was picked up by many Catholic educators throughout the century and became a slogan on behalf of the parochial school.[3]

True to his word, Hughes began to build new schoolhouses; he recruited orders of religious women along with the Christian Brothers to teach in the schools; 75 percent of the parishes in the city had schools by 1865. These schools were instructing sixteen thousand students, or about one third of the Catholic school population.[4] But all the world was not New York.

Boston offered a striking contrast to New York. At mid-century, Irish Catholics were immigrating to this Yankee citadel in record numbers, with the result that, by the 1860s, close to half the city's population was Catholic. Like New York, the city's schools promoted a Protestant piety that was openly offensive to Catholics. In addition, anti-Catholic feelings ran high in this community. Catholics could not forget the burning of the Ursuline convent in Charlestown in 1834; anti-Catholic riots increased hostility; then, in 1859, the celebrated Eliot School case took place. At issue was the refusal of Thomas Wall, an Irish Catholic boy, to recite the Protestant version of the Ten Commandments; when, at the suggestion of the local priest, other boys followed his example, bedlam reigned in the school for days, and as many as three hundred students were dismissed for following Wall's example. Then, singling Wall out as the ringleader, his schoolteacher beat the boy's hands until they bled, and after twenty to thirty minutes of this treatment, Wall gave in and recited the Ten Commandments. The parents sued and a trial followed. The schoolteacher was acquitted, and Boston's schools remained Protestant, with the Protestant Bible and the Protestant version of the Lord's Prayer and the Ten Commandments being recited each school day. Within a few months, however, the Boston School Committee ruled that Catholic children could no longer be forced to recite anything contrary to their beliefs.[5]

Given the Protestant piety of the public schools and the deep-rooted anti-Catholic feelings of Yankee Boston, the city seemed ripe for a campaign for Catholic schools. But it did not happen. The people did not push for it, and the bishops, John Fitzpatrick (1846–66) and John Williams (1866–1907), were reluctant to exercise the necessary leadership. The best explanation for this is that, unlike New York's, Boston's bishops sought to build the church first and the school later. As a result, no more than 40 percent or so of the city's parishes had schools throughout the entire nineteenth century. Such figures, one historian observed, "suggest a kind of collective ambivalence in Boston's approach to parochial education. The building of Catholic schools was neither completely neglected nor totally implemented." A similar lack of commitment was evident throughout the rest of New England, where most dioceses could not even match Boston's 40 percent.[6] What schools were built in this region were the result of a local parish's initiative, and not a concerted campaign promoted by aggressive Catholic educators.

Cincinnati offered a striking contrast to Boston. As in New York, the force behind Catholic schools in Cincinnati was the bishop, John Purcell. Purcell arrived in Cincinnati in 1833 and remained as bishop until his death in 1883. During these years, he became the midwestern leader of the campaign for Catholic schools. In fact, along with Hughes, Purcell was one of the church's most effective leaders on behalf of Catholic schools. Whereas few Catholic schools existed in Cincinnati in 1833, by 1850 four fifths of the city's parishes had schools and were educating a total of two thousand children. Twenty years later, the number of children in Catholic schools rose to somewhere between twelve and fifteen thousand, or approximately one third of the city's total school population.[7] In promoting this growth, Purcell adopted a very conciliatory attitude toward the public schools and their Protestant supporters. Unlike Hughes, he was not hostile to the public schools; rather, he sought to achieve some compromise with them so that they would be more acceptable to Catholics. He first attempted to have schoolbooks amended so they would be less offensive to Catholics; he sought to allow Catholic children to read from their own version of the Bible, rather than the Protestant King James version; and he also sought public funds for Catholic schools. Even though he was not successful in any of these efforts, he did not attack the public school as if it were public enemy number one. After failing to achieve a compromise, he realized that it was time to build a Catholic school system.

By the 1850s, Purcell had emerged as the midwest champion of Catholic schools.

In less developed regions of the country, the evolution of schools was quite different from that of New York and Cincinnati. In Iowa and Nebraska, schooling at mid-century followed a pattern reminiscent of the earlier, republican period. Most often, an individual priest or schoolmaster organized a school in a small town. It would be a typical one-room school that opened and closed depending on the availability of a teacher. Vital to the church's missionary work in these regions, was the presence of female religious orders. They were viewed as essential to the educational apostolate of the region, and one of the first things a frontier bishop did was to recruit a religious order of women for his diocese. Though the sisters often became involved in a variety of activities, their main work was teaching. Their primary educational attention was given to the female academy; only secondarily were they involved in the more basic elementary parochial school. Thus, in the formative years of these rural regions, the girls' academy was the principal school; after they were settled and established, women religious would expand their work and undertake the operation of parochial schools. The coming of the Sisters of Providence to Washington offers a good example of this pattern of development.

The Sisters of Providence were a religious order of women founded in Montreal in 1843. Their chaplain was Augustin M. Blanchet, who later would become bishop of Walla Walla in the Oregon territory. One of the first things Blanchet did as bishop was to recruit the Sisters of Providence for his missionary diocese. Led by Mother Joseph of the Sacred Heart, a group of five sisters arrived in Vancouver, Washington, on December 8, 1856, after a forty-five day journey on land and water from Montreal via the Isthmus of Panamá. Within a year, they had opened Providence Academy, a catchall school that took in boarders, orphans, and day students. In 1858, Mother Joseph founded a hospital in Vancouver, the first of fifteen such hospitals she would establish in the West before her death in 1902. Mother Joseph was a remarkable person: carpenter, architect, fund raiser, and religious superior, she guided the expansion of the Sisters of Providence throughout the western states of Washington, Oregon, Idaho, and Montana, as well as British Columbia. Her achievements were deservedly memorialized when a statue of Mother Joseph was placed in Statuary Hall in the nation's Capitol, one of five women and the only nun so honored. Like women religious in other frontier regions, the Sisters of Providence took on a variety of tasks, with schooling and caring for the sick occupying the bulk of their time and energy. After they were established in Vancouver, they began to found schools in other towns. A major reason why they first established their academies was that these schools provided a necessary source of income for the religious community; securing their livelihood in this manner, they could then branch out and care for the sick, the poor, and the needy.[8]

Another aspect of schooling in such frontier regions was the blurring of the public/private school distinction. Definitions of public and private schools "were neither precise nor static during the nineteenth century; they were rather in the process of evolution."[9] For this reason, church-affiliated elementary schools were often designated as the local public schools. This was evident in rural Ohio, where entire towns were made up of German Catholic settlers. In the town of Glansdorf, for example, the district school, built and supported by public funds, was a Catholic school "staffed by Catholic teachers who taught Catechism and Bible History along with secular subjects." Similar arrangements occurred in Indiana and Arizona, where the Catholic school served as the local district school.[10] In some cities, Catholic schools received government funds along with the state schools. Parochial schools in Lowell, Massachusetts, received public funds in the 1830s and 1840s; the same was true in Milwaukee in the 1840s and Hartford and Middletown, Connecticut, in the 1860s along with towns in New Jersey.[11] In towns like Glansdorf, anti-Catholic bias or a local Protestant school culture clearly did not exert much influence on the organization of the Catholic school. As the boundary lines separating public and private schools became more defined, such Catholic public schools began to disappear.

The principal influence on the development of a separate Catholic school system was the emergence of the common school, or what is today called the public school. The concept of the common school, "an elementary school intended to serve all the children in an area," developed in the pre-Civil War period.[12] During this period, many reform movements were sweeping across the nation: antislavery, women's rights, temperance, and politics, to name a few. The common-school movement was part of this wave of reform, which began to peak in the 1830s and 1840s, with the result that by 1860 most Americans were ready to support the concept of the common school. Such reformers as Horace Mann of Massachusetts and Henry Barnard of Connecticut spearheaded this movement for a "strong state regulated common school system." Driving these reformers was an ideology that gave flesh to their ideas on education and guided them in their crusade. This ideology "centered on Republicanism, Protestantism, and Capitalism, three sources of social belief that were intertwined and mutually supporting."[13] Rooted in the Protestant culture of the United States, it promoted an American Protestant imperialism that recaptured the vision of John Winthrop's "city on a hill," to which all nations would look for guidance and inspiration. Once this movement took hold, its supporters promoted it with a crusader's zeal, and before long the schoolhouse became the established church of the American republic.

As spectacular as this movement was, it had a basic flaw. It was rooted in a white, Anglo-Saxon, Protestant ideology which was not very tolerant of those outside this cultural matrix. Thus, for Indians, blacks, Jews, Catholics, Mormons, and people of other religious heritages, the culture of the public school was alien and its benefits questionable. It was this basic conflict between the ideology of the common school and Roman Catholicism that led to the development of the Catholic school system.

In the 1830s, Catholic leaders were not anxious about organizing Catholic schools. Education was very much a priority, but the family was still viewed as the primary educator. This point of view was eloquently stated in the pastoral letter written by John England and issued by the American bishops after their council meeting in 1829. This emphasis on the family as the primary educative institution would remain dominant throughout the 1830s and 1840s. The major point of concern during the 1830s was the type of textbook used in the public schools; bishops wanted such books to be less offensive to Catholics. Without a doubt, most church leaders still believed that some sort of compromise with the common school was still possible and indeed desirable.

In the 1840 council of bishops, church leaders discussed "whether the public [school] system is to be favored or rejected," and ambivalence seemed to dominate the discussion. Most likely, the bishops "would have settled for a truly non-sectarian public school."[14] But such was not to be. During the 1840s, John Hughes led the campaign for Catholic schools in New York; in most other places, ambivalence about their need remained. The issue was discussed in the three national church councils of that decade, but it was clearly not a priority of the bishops. In the 1850s, however, a major shift took place.

By the 1850s, the public school had become a genuine part of American society. As a committee of Catholic theologians observed in 1852, "The public School System" was "now generally established in this country." This development forced the hands of Catholics, since this system was, in the opinion of many bishops, "both heretical and infidel."[15] They believed this because of the Protestant culture of the public school, with its Protestant hymns, prayers, and Bible reading. Previously they had sought some type of compromise with the public schools, but that no longer seemed possible or even desirable. The Catholic hierarchy was also more confident about Catholics' place in American society during the 1850s. This decade was a heady time. The church was riding the crest of an unprecedented wave of growth, having become by mid-century the largest denomination in the country. Such Protestants as the historian Philip Schaff noted that the Catholic church was beginning "to make its influence felt in the public life of the United States."[16] Notable individuals such as John Henry Newman, Orestes Brownson, and Levi S. Ives, an Episcopal bishop in North Carolina, converted to Catholicism, along with lesser known individuals. Catholic apologists happily recorded these conversions, viewing them as harbingers of future success. Catholic journalists also became more confident and aggressive, celebrating the glories of the church both at home and abroad. The revival of Catholicism in Europe and the self-assured attitude of Pope Pius IX reinforced the confidence of American church leaders; moreover, the Pope's positive support for the Catholic education of youth strengthened the campaign for schools, and the example of the Irish hierarchy, who were also opposing a Protestant system of education, increased their resolve.

The First Plenary Council of Baltimore, in 1852, revealed the attitude of the bishops on the school issue. Unlike previous ones, this council took a decided step forward in defining the concept of the parochial school and in urging its establishment in Catholic parishes. A committee of theologians defined parochial schools as

> institutions, in which none but Catholic children are admitted, and which are conducted by teachers having the approbation of the pastor, exercising their office under his direction and superintendence, and making the catechism the frequent subject of their instructions to those under their charge.[17]

In their opinion, such schools were "indispensable for the security of faith and morals among Catholic children." They also put together a report that was "the most detailed plea for a system of schooling tied to the parish that had been given up to this time." The committee went on to urge the immediate establishment "of free schools for the education of Catholic children in our cities, & other places where it is practicable to do so." In addition, if parents did not send their children to these schools, the committee recommended that they be "denied the sacraments."[18]

This report, compiled by a committee of theologians and bishops, was an important step in the evolution of the parochial-school concept. Its forthright, indeed harsh, tone contrasted sharply with the ambivalence of previous council statements. When the final decrees of the council were voted on, however, the harshness of the report and its aggressive support for the parochial school were considerably toned down. The bishops merely exhorted the clergy and laity "to see that schools are established in connection with the churches of their diocese."[19] This was obviously a step back from the recommendations of the committee, and it accurately reflected the lack of total commitment on the part of the bishops to parochial schools. Nevertheless, for the first time, Catholic educators had taken a decisive step toward the establishment of a parochial-school system.

During the 1850s and 1860s, the public-school movement gained greater momentum as the concept of state-supported education became more widely accepted. Archbishop Hughes of New York continued to promote the cause of Catholic schools. Martin J. Spalding, bishop of Louisville, joined Purcell of Cincinnati in leading the midwest campaign for schools, and when the midwestern bishops met at the Second Provincial Council of Cincinnati, in 1858, they came out strongly on behalf of parochial schools. In fact, they passed a decree that required every pastor to build a parochial school under pain of mortal sin; Spalding was instrumental in drawing up this stringent legislation.[20] Across the nation, Catholic pastors were now beginning to deny the sacraments to parents who refused to send their children to the Catholic school. But when the nation's bishops met in Baltimore in 1866 for the Second Plenary Council, they issued a rather mild statement on parochial schools. Similar to the one approved in 1852, it recommended that "in every diocese" a school be built "next to each and every church."[21] Given the fact that Martin J. Spalding was now the archbishop of Baltimore and the main force behind this council, such a mild statement in comparison with the one Spalding had gotten passed in Cincinnati eight years earlier suggests that the majority of the nation's bishops were still not ready to go all out for the parochial school.

It would be almost twenty years before the next national church council would meet; during this time, the school became a topic of nationwide debate. Fueling this was the 1869 decision of the Cincinnati Board of Education to exclude Bible reading, religious instruction, and hymn singing from the public schools. This decision was the result of action taken by "a temporary coalition of Jews, Catholics, free thinkers, and a few strong minded Protestants," who argued that because of the' religious pluralism of Cincinnati and the nation, schools must be devoid of all religion.[22] By their action they hoped to make the public schools more attractive to the large Catholic population of Cincinnati. The school board's decision sparked a nationwide debate and persuaded the Superior Court of Cincinnati to overrule the board's decision. The Supreme Court of Ohio, however, upheld the decision of the board as constitutional, thus adding another brick to the wall separating church and state. It was clear, however, that in 1870 the Cincinnati school board and the justices of the Ohio Supreme Court were in the minority. The vast majority of Americans were now championing the public school as the nation's sacred temple, and any attempt to remove the Bible from the school was seen as "a blow at the very foundations of republicanism."[23] The Protestant clergy took the lead in this campaign and made "the public school a major plank in the Evangelical Protestant missionary platform. Protestants heaped paeans of praise upon it as God's chosen instrument for religionizing and Americanizing the youth, and they roundly castigated those who opposed it—chiefly the Roman Catholics."[24]

Catholics could not understand the fuss. They claimed to be loyal Americans, but because they challenged the Protestant culture of the public schools they were labeled "un-American" and enemies of the republic. Because they attacked the public school, Catholics were perceived as assaulting the basic Protestant ideology that inspired not only the school, but also the nation. Thus, to attack the school was to attack God, nation, and government as well. Catholics could not understand the logic of such reasoning. Nevertheless, the accusations continued throughout the late-nineteenth and early-twentieth centuries.[25]

During the 1870s, the school debate intensified, when it entered the national political arena. The Republican platform in the campaign of 1876 came out in favor of a constitutional amendment that would prohibit the use of tax funds to support schools under the control of any religious organization. This idea remained part of the Republican political strategy throughout the decade. The more intense the school question became, the more Catholic journalists spoke out on behalf of Catholic schools. One of the leading journalists was James McMaster, editor of *Freeman's Journal,* a New York Catholic newspaper. McMaster spoke for many when he inveighed against the "Godless" public schools, and he was instrumental in getting the Vatican to intervene on the issue. The Vatican intervention took the form of an instruction sent to the American bishops in 1876 which spoke firmly against public schools while supporting the need for "the establishment of Catholic schools in every place"; it also discussed the sensitive issue of Catholic attendance at public schools, since most Catholic children did in fact attend these schools. Though it acknowledged that this could be permitted for a "sufficient cause," those parents who sent their children to public schools without such cause could, "if obstinate," be denied absolution in confession.[26] This was the opening that the hard-line school people wanted, and the practice of denying the sacraments to the parents of public-school children now became common. Though many bishops and clergy spoke out against this, it was a popular tactic to force parents to send their children to the Catholic school; it was practiced in the Chicago, Milwaukee, Boston, Rochester, Cincinnati, Dubuque, Louisville, Buffalo, Brooklyn, Pittsburgh, and Cleveland dioceses, to name but a few. For those bishops and pastors lukewarm about parochial schools, the 1876 instruction left the door open as well, since it did condone the practice of children's attending public schools as long as there was sufficient cause.

Another major spokesman for Catholic schools to emerge at this time was Bernard McQuaid, bishop of Rochester since 1868. McQuaid entered the arena of debate in 1871, when he gave a lecture in Rochester in support of what he called "Christian Free Schools"; a year later he gave a second lecture. These talks received such wide publicity that McQuaid was invited to speak in cities throughout the country. This national exposure enhanced his reputation, and before long he was being lionized as a champion of the Catholic school. McQuaid continually hammered home three basic points: the need for religion in education, the priority of parents over the state in education, and the right of Catholics to a fair share of public funds for education. What McQuaid wanted was state-supported Christian free schools, both Catholic and Protestant, where religion was an essential part of the curriculum. Such sectarian public schools were just what the Republican party and many other Americans opposed, but McQuaid's program found a receptive ear among many Catholics, as well as some Protestants. In promoting his plan, McQuaid lashed out against the secularism of the public schools; so forthright a stance won him wide support.[27]

McQuaid and McMaster represented one school of thought in the Catholic community during the 1870s; they vigorously promoted Catholic schools and did so by attacking what they believed to be the godless, secular character of the public schools. It was true, of course, that many public school systems were removing prayers, hymn singing, and even Bible readings from their schools, thus becoming more "secular." But this trend went against the wishes of many Americans, who still viewed the school as the nation's church. The other school of thought within the Catholic community still sought to seek a compromise with the nation's public schools. Local communities in New York, Connecticut, Pennsylvania, Illinois, and Georgia had worked out such arrangements, whereby Catholic children were educated in Catholic schools supported by state funds. These arrangements were generally the result of a local pastor's initiative and reflected the desire of many Catholics, mainly for financial reasons, to work through the public-school system, rather than oppose it. Like McQuaid, representatives of this position, such as Bishop Thomas L. Grace of St. Paul, Minnesota, and his auxiliary bishop, John Ireland, believed strongly in the need for religion in education, but they sought to achieve such Christian schools by working through the public-school system wherever possible.[28]

McMaster spoke out vehemently against such compromise when he heard about its enactment in Poughkeepsie, New York, in 1873. In this town, the Board of Education rented the Catholic school and took control of instruction during school hours, paid the teachers, and then let the owners have control of the school at other times. In practice this meant that Catholic teachers taught Catholic children secular subjects during regular school hours and then taught religion outside these hours, when the school was no longer under the control of the public-school board. McMaster stated that such an arrangement was "a bargain with the devil," and such schools "cannot in conscience be attended."[29] Despite such vehemence, McMaster could not persuade many to join his crusade. Thus, on the eve of the third national church council, most bishops and clergy, in contrast to the 1840s, were now committed to the need for Catholic schools, but how this could best be accomplished was still an issue of debate.

The Third Plenary Council of Baltimore met in November 1884 and promulgated a body of legislation that would guide the direction of the church for the next forty years and more. About one fourth of this legislation focused on education, the centerpiece of which was the decrees on the parochial school. In these decrees the bishops centered on four points: the establishment of parochial schools, the pastor's obligation in this matter, the people's obligation to support such schools, and finally the obligation of parents to send their children to Catholic schools. In the end, they voted to command the building of a parochial school within two years "near each church where it does not exist"; if pastors did not attend to this within this time period, they could be removed from their parish; if parish communities were negligent in the support of schools, they "should be reprehended by the Bishop and by the most efficacious and prudent means possible, be induced to contribute the necessary support"; and finally, all Catholic parents were "bound to send their children to the parochial schools."[30]

A debate took place on each of these four points. These debates revealed the extent and nature of division within the hierarchy. A few bishops wanted the decrees to encourage, rather than command, the building of Catholic schools, but the majority wanted the stronger statement. Much more sensitive was the issue of sanctions against parents who sent their children to public schools. The hard-liners wanted to deny the sacraments to such parents; after a lengthy discussion they lost out to a compromise position by the slim margin of five votes; the compromise position deleted any references to the denial of the sacraments to uncooperative parents; this was a victory for those who opposed this harsh tactic, but a close one indeed. The hard-liners won the debate on sanctions for uncooperative priests, however, and passed legislation that stated that such pastors should be removed; they also got their way in recommending spiritual penalties—interdiction of a parish, for example—if parishioners refused to support a parish school. When it came time for the Vatican to review and approve the council decrees, they wisely toned down these hard statements against pastors and parishioners.[31]

The bishops were also concerned about the quality of education in the schools and passed legislation stating that teachers had to pass examinations that tested their competency. Each diocese was to establish a school board of examiners to administer these exams; normal schools to train teachers were also mandated. Encouragement was given to the establishment of Catholic high schools, and the bishops urged wealthy Catholics to support "the founding and enlargement of Catholic colleges." Through such legislation, the Catholic hierarchy was clearly encouraging the development of a separate Catholic school system. But dissent remained. At one extreme was the position of the bishop of Little Rock, Arkansas, Edward Fitzgerald, who told his fellow bishops at the council, "We were ordained to teach catechism not to teach school. If we know that children are learning the catechism it is enough." At the other extreme was Bernard McQuaid, who, appropriating the slogan of John Hughes, said that he "would rather see the schoolhouse without the church than the church without the schoolhouse."[32]

The dissension evident at the Baltimore Council did not go away. McQuaid and others became more insistent on the need for Catholic schools and stepped up their attack on the "state school system thoroughly godless, in name and in law. . . ."[33] Other prelates still sought a compromise with the public schools. Most notable of these was John Ireland, appointed the archbishop of St. Paul in 1884. Ireland had always believed in such a compromise, and in an address before a National Educational Association convention held in St. Paul in 1890 he took the opportunity to publicize his point of view once again. In some ways his philosophy of education resembled that of McQuaid. Ireland favored religion in education, as well as state-supported schools permeated "with the religion of the majority of the children of the land"; in other words, state-supported sectarian schools.[34] But he also offered another solution, modeled on the arrangement in Poughkeepsie, New York, and this clearly indicated that Ireland was willing to work through the public-school system in order to establish a way for Americans to receive both religious and secular instruction in the public schools. McQuaid and others would not take that step. Ireland did because it was part of his overall philosophy of attempting to build a bridge between the American and the Roman Catholic cultures. His compromise plan was as much the result of his social and theological thinking as it was an educational policy. McQuaid's stance in this regard was quite different. Rather than build bridges and seek accommodation with the American system, he sought to erect walls to protect the children from the "wolves of the world," who were "destroying countless numbers of the unguarded ones"; and so "if the walls are not high enough," said McQuaid, "they must be raised, if they are not strong enough, they must be strengthened."[35] A clearer statement of the Catholic fortress mentality would be hard to find. Rather than condemn the state school, Ireland praised it, calling it "our pride and our glory." "The free school of America!" he said. "Withered be the hand raised in sign of its destruction!"[36] McQuaid choked on that statement, as did many others. But Ireland's talk was only the beginning. In 1891 he implemented the Poughkeepsie plan in his diocese in the towns of Faribault and Stillwater. This action, coming so soon after his speech, ignited a major controversy in the church.

This "school controversy," as it has come to be known, lasted for two years, but the bad feeling it generated within the hierarchy endured much longer. The basic issue of the controversy was whether or not the school decrees of the Third Baltimore Council would be the norm for the church, or some compromise solution like the one Ireland worked out in Faribault and Stillwater would become, if not the norm, at least an acceptable practice. Clearly Ireland's plan was not so earthshaking; such an arrangement had been in operation in Poughkeepsie since 1873, as well as in other communities. But Ireland had proposed it and he had many enemies within the hierarchy, bishops who believed that he was too liberal and too American in his thought. Thus, Ireland's compromise plan must be viewed against the backdrop of a broader cultural and theological debate within the church. It was more than just an educational debate; a political and theological question was at stake as well: Who would occupy the seat of power in the United States and have a prevailing influence with Vatican authorities—the liberals like Ireland or the conservatives like McQuaid? This larger issue engulfed the school question and turned it into a *cause célèbre*.

The school controversy generated a pamphlet debate between liberals and conservatives; it split the hierarchy into bitterly opposed factions; it was one reason why Rome sent an apostolic delegate to the United States; it prompted two inquiries from the Vatican and eventually became the personal concern of Pope Leo XIII; and finally, it has generated numerous books and dissertations. The outcome of the controversy was ambiguous. At one time, in April 1892, the Vatican wrote to Ireland and told him that his plan could be tolerated. This caused such a stir among the bishops that Rome was forced to reconsider its decision. The Pope then sent his delegate Francesco Satolli to the United States; Satolli made a statement in favor of Ireland's plan, thus confirming the 1892 letter. Nevertheless, the debate continued, and finally the Vatican took a second polling of the American hierarchy on the issue. The results were interesting: seventeen bishops favored Ireland's concept, six of them with reservations, while fifty-three were opposed to it either completely or partially.[37] Thus, it was clear where the majority of the bishops stood on the issue. But when the Pope wrote to Cardinal Gibbons in a letter designed to settle the issue once and for all, diplomatic ambiguity prevailed. In one part of his letter, Leo XIII praised his delegate, Francesco Satolli, and his statement approving the Ireland plan; yet, in another paragraph, he praised the decrees of Baltimore III. He concluded by stating that the decrees of Baltimore III concerning parochial schools "and whatever else has been prescribed by the Roman Pontiffs, whether directly or through the Sacred Congregations concerning the same matter are to be steadfastly observed." Included in "whatever else" of course would be the 1892 letter to Ireland stating that his plan could be tolerated as well as Satolli's statement favorable to Ireland. Ireland and his supporters believed they had won the battle; Michael Corrigan, the archbishop of New York and a leader of the opposition, accepted it with a "spirit of resignation," as did McQuaid. But it was a hollow victory.[38]

Although Rome approved Ireland's plan, it failed where it mattered most: in Faribault and Stillwater. The Stillwater arrangement collapsed by 1892, and Faribault followed in the fall of 1893. In Stillwater, public opposition on the part of Protestants was so strong and persistent that the plan was scuttled in June of 1892; in Faribault the Catholic public school remained in existence longer, but when difficulties arose in 1893 over staffing of the school, Ireland seemed unwilling to pursue the matter and the arrangement was terminated in September of that year. Even more telling was Ireland's decision never to establish this type of compromise arrangement in any other parish in his diocese. Furthermore, after 1894 the number of separate Catholic schools in his diocese steadily increased.[39] Thus, the end of this last-ditch effort at compromise with the public school had failed, and few of Ireland's episcopal colleagues were eager to attempt his plan in their own dioceses.

An obvious reason for the failure of the Faribault-Stillwater arrangement was that Ireland's solution was going against the tide of church/state developments in the area of education. Public schools were becoming less sectarian, and any attempt to try to establish state-supported church schools in the 1890s was not very feasible. The wall separating church and state was now high enough that such a compromise was no longer a viable solution to the Catholic-school issue. Indicative of this was that in 1898 New York State ruled that the arrangement in Poughkeepsie was illegal.

Over the course of the nineteenth century, the concept of a separate, parochial school system had gained increasing support. The concept of such a school had been around for some time, but it was not until the 1840s in such places as New York and Cincinnati that a school was viewed as normative for the parish community. In most places, however, the school was not a priority in the 1840s; immigration was the top concern. The legislation passed at the 1852 Baltimore Council was decisive in defining the concept of the parochial school and urging its adoption. Vigorous debate in the 1870s increased support, and buoyed by the Vatican's intervention, many clergy were confident enough to punish uncooperative parents through denial of the sacraments. By the 1884 Council, the parochial school had become the norm as far as the majority of bishops were concerned. But that is the key point: the *majority* favored it, not everyone.

Throughout the nineteenth century, there never was a total commitment to the parochial school either on the part of the bishops or on the part of the people. Some bishops sought compromise with the public-school system, and though never very widespread, that remained a viable option even into the twentieth century, when Catholic educators lobbied on behalf of released time for religious instruction for public-school children. Other bishops, such as John Williams of Boston and Edward Fitzpatrick of Little Rock, wanted to build the church first and the school later. Even those bishops who opposed any sort of compromise with the public schools could not follow the mandate of Baltimore III, which they so enthusiastically supported. The reason was money. In New York, for example, where Michael Corrigan was archbishop, only one half of the parishes in the diocese had schools in 1898, and they were able to educate only one third of the eligible Catholic children. Such a commitment, modest as it was, placed a tremendous financial burden on the archdiocese by creating a $7,000,000 debt.[40] Schools were very expensive to run, and not all Catholics—neither clergy nor laity—were prepared to make the financial commitment, regardless of what the bishops said. Thus, in 1900, despite the legislation of Baltimore III and the rhetoric of the schoolhouse before the church, no more than 37 percent of the nation's parish communities were able to support schools; in 1883, it was 38 percent; thus, sixteen years after the Baltimore Council, the percentage was virtually identical. By 1920, it had declined to 35 percent.[41] Financial reality tempered the school crusade, and when a new wave of immigrants from southern and Eastern Europe began to flow into the United States during the early-twentieth century, churches, not schools, once again became the priority.

Why did Catholics establish schools in the first place? This is a question that deserves an answer. In the first place, Catholic lay people put a primary value on the need for religious instruction. Parents wanted to pass on their religious culture to their children, and the principal way this was being done in the late-nineteenth century was through the schools. Family and church had not abdicated this responsibility, but after mid-century the school increasingly became the primary institution in the religious education of children. For most Protestants, a Sunday school filled this role. For others, the German Lutherans being the best example, separate parochial schools were necessary. So, too, with Catholics. Thus, the school became an essential part of the church's evangelization program. The shift from the primacy of informal religious education to formal religious instruction, from family to school, was critical to the development of a Catholic school system.

It should also be noted that the Catholic commitment to parochial schools got stronger just as the public-school commitment to religion weakened. The walls separating church and state in the area of education had steadily risen in the late-nineteenth century; this development canceled out any attempt at compromise between Catholics and a state-supported system of education. In addition, the boundary line separating public and private schools was more defined by 1900, so the two spheres no longer overlapped as they had twenty-five to fifty years previously.

A second major reason was the development of the common-school system. The widespread acceptance of the public school and the general belief at mid-century that learning demanded a religious foundation forced the hands of Catholics. Catholic educators rejected schools operated according to a Protestant ideology. Archbishop John Hughes made this the basis for his campaign in the 1840s, and others followed his lead. Anti-Catholic prejudice on the part of some educators also influenced Catholics. This took a variety of forms: forced reading of the Bible, convent and church burnings, the passing of laws that overtly discriminated against Catholic schools, and prejudice against hiring Catholic schoolteachers. Such practices, less violent but more subtle as the century progressed, strengthened the Catholic commitment to separate schools.

A third major reason for the establishment of Catholic schools was the commitment of Catholic immigrant groups to hand on the faith according to their own cultural traditions. In the case of the Irish, religion, rather than language, was the major motivation. For other foreign-language groups, both religion and language were major influences in the commitment to support separate schools. Within these communities the school became a key part of the local parish culture, and the commonplace crusade to preserve culture through religion strengthened its importance. Thus, German bishops and clergy became ardent champions of the parochial schools; French Canadians and Polish were also strong advocates and, along with second- and third-generation Germans and Irish, they helped to strengthen the Catholic commitment to schools in the early-twentieth century. Strengthening this determination was the antiforeign ideology of the public-school system. Schools were committed to Americanizing their students and were not very tolerant of language and cultural differences. A New York school-committee report in 1843 expressed this attitude very emphatically.

> In educating children in our schools, it is intended to give them habits and feelings adapted to our institutions and Government; and when a foreigner adopts our country as his home, it is expected that he should subscribe to our forms, and particularly to our system of education, which is intimately and inseparably connected with our forms of government.[42]

A necessary prerequisite for the establishment of Catholic schools was the availability of teachers. By the middle of the century, teaching had become the preserve of women, and Catholics were fortunate to have available a large pool of women religious—sisters—to staff the schools. Some of these women were American-born and belonged to religious orders founded in the United States specifically to work in the area of education. The Sisters of Charity of Emmitsburg, founded by Elizabeth Seton in 1809, were representative of this type. Close to 1,600 women belonged to this community in 1900, and they taught in schools throughout the country. Numerous religious orders were transplanted to the United States from various parts of Europe, and they, too, became involved in teaching; 91 of the 119 women's religious communities in the nineteenth century were European or Canadian in origin. The largest order was the School Sisters of Notre Dame. They first came to the United States in 1847 and worked mainly though not exclusively in German parishes; by 1900, this community comprised 2,752 women. Whereas in 1850 only about 1,344 sisters were at work in the United States, compared to approximately 1,109 priests, in 1900 their numbers had risen to 40,340, compared to 11,636 priests.[43] This phenomenal increase in the number of women religious made the growth of schools possible, since they were the people who staffed the schools. Their willingness to work for low wages lowered the cost of Catholic schooling considerably and made feasible an otherwise financially impossible undertaking.

These four factors explain why Catholics made a commitment to a separate school system in the nineteenth century. As already noted, however, this commitment was not total on the part of either bishops or clergy; neither was it total on the part of the people, since never more than one third of the nation's eligible children attended parochial schools during the age of the immigrant church. Like the clergy, some Catholics were more committed than others to the parochial school. Ethnic background had a lot to do with this, as well as geographical location and the size of the community to which people belonged.

The Irish offer a good example of how delicate it is to attempt to describe a particular immigrant group's commitment to the parochial school. Irishmen like John Hughes, Bernard McQuaid, and Michael Corrigan led the episcopal battle for Catholic schools; pastors like Father Thomas Scully of Cambridge, Massachusetts, were neighborhood crusaders, while women like Mary Frances Clark, founder of the Sisters of Charity of the Blessed Virgin Mary, committed their religious communities to Catholic schools. But Irishmen also led the opposition; John Ireland was a national crusader for compromise; New York's Edward McGlynn was one of many local pastors who spoke out in favor of the public schools, as did Irish journalists. In other words, the Irish, like other immigrant communities, were divided on the issue. Given this understanding, it is still possible to measure the degree of their commitment as a group. An indicator of this would be whether or not an Irish parish built a parochial school and, if so, how soon it was built after the formation of the parish. A study of eighty-seven Irish immigrant parishes concluded that about one quarter of them, 27 percent, founded a school within two years; for almost half of them, 46 percent, it took more than ten years to take this step. Though not conclusive, when compared with German parishes the contrast is quite striking. Among a group of 278 German parishes, two thirds of them had a school within two years and 86 percent of them within ten years. Even more striking was the fact that, in 1914, 95 percent of German parishes had schools.[44]

The Germans, of course, had an added incentive—language—and this definitely influenced their commitment to the parish school. The Irish, on the other hand, did not face this problem; consequently, large numbers of them sent their children to public schools, rather than support a separate Catholic school system. In Boston, for example, about three quarters of the Irish schoolchildren attended public schools in 1908; in New York a little more than half did, while in Minneapolis and Kansas City the percentage was even higher. A study of twenty-four selected cities in 1908 found that Irish-American children in public schools outnumbered those in parochial schools 67,229 to 59,521.[45] German Catholic children attended public schools as well, but never to the extent that the Irish did during the century of immigration.

The language issue, so evident with the Germans, also influenced the decision of other immigrant groups. Religion and language were so intertwined that to lose one meant the loss of the other. Faced with this dilemma, foreign-language groups opted in large numbers for the parochial school. This was especially evident among the French Canadians. Wherever they settled, a school was quickly established. "A parish without a church is preferable to a parish without a Catholic school," argued a French-Canadian journalist, "for the excellent reason that where the second is lacking the first often becomes useless."[46] In New England, French Canadians stood out as the most ardent supporters of the parochial school. In those areas where they were especially concentrated, Rhode Island and New Hampshire, the overall ratio of churches with schools was much higher than in other regions. By 1909, fifty-five thousand children were attending 133 French-Canadian parochial schools in New England; this was 41 percent of the region's parochial schools. In Woonsocket, Rhode Island, 75 percent of the French-Canadian children attended parochial schools; in Holyoke, Massachusetts, more than half attended parochial schools.[47]

Like other immigrant groups, the Polish had their Catholic-school advocates. One was Father Wenceslaus Kruszka, who believed that the school served as "the foundation of the Polish Catholic church." "Without the Polish school," he wrote, "the Polish church might remain Catholic but will eventually evolve into an Irish, English, or an American church. . . . without them the Polish church might sink in the Anglo-American sea."[48] Not all Poles were as enthusiastic about parochial schools as Kruszka; in fact, many criticized those schools because of their low educational standards, and regarded public schools as superior. This was a common complaint about Catholic schools and undoubtedly influenced some people to choose the public school over the parochial school. This seemed to be the situation in Buffalo, where by 1912, 6,071 Polish children were attending public schools and 5,729 were in parochial schools, a dramatic turnaround from earlier years, when parochial-school students outnumbered those in public schools four to one. A 1905 estimate put Polish parochial-school attendance nationwide at 70,000, or about 36 percent of the eligible elementary-school population; a study done a few years later put it around the 50 percent level. Another indication of their commitment to schools was the ratio of parishes with schools; in 1914, 71 percent of the seven hundred Polish parishes in the United States supported schools.[49]

Slovaks exhibited patterns of support similar to other groups. All Slovak educators attacked the public schools; secular leaders accused them of turning "children against their parents," while Catholic Slovaks labeled them "anti-religious."[50] As with the Polish, there seems to have been widespread support for the parochial school if one existed in a parish. In other words, where a parochial school was in operation, the vast majority of people sent their children to the Catholic school. In Pittsburgh the local Slovak fraternal even went so far as to expel people if they failed to send their children to the local Slovak parish school. If a Slovak Catholic school did not exist, many—

almost half, according to one study—sent their children to a nearby non-Slovak Catholic school.[51] But the problem was that not every parish community supported a parish school. By 1916, only 38 percent of the Slovak parishes had schools; this caused some clergy to repeat that familiar battle cry: build the school before the church. It seemed to work, as the situation improved so that by 1930 approximately 53 percent of the parishes were supporting schools.[52] Czech, Lithuanian, and Ukrainian Catholics supported Catholic schools at approximately the same level as the Slovaks, with between 28 and 36 percent of those national parishes having parochial schools in the early-twentieth century.[53]

The Italians did not support the parochial school to the same degree that other immigrant groups did. James Sanders's study of Catholic schools in Chicago demonstrated how weak this support was. In 1910 there were 73,000 first- and second-generation Italians in Chicago; ten Catholic parishes served this community, and only one of them had a school. As Sanders observed, "This was extraordinary in a diocese where most of the parishes had schools."[54] A U.S. Government report in 1908 found that less than 15 percent of the Italian children in twenty-four selected cities attended parochial schools; it reported that in New York 59,645 Italian children were in the public schools and only 8,301 in Catholic schools; in Philadelphia, site of another major Italian settlement, the ratio was better but the public-school enrollment was still twice as large as that of the parochial school. John Briggs, in his study of Italians in Utica and Rochester, New York, and Kansas City, Missouri, concluded, ". . . a figure of one-third is a reasonable upper limit on the proportion of Italian children who attended Italian parochial schools in the early twentieth century."[55] This would compare favorably with other immigrant groups, but the situation in these three cities appeared to be more the exception than the norm as regards Italian support for parochial schools. Their lack of support for parochial schools reflected their general alienation from official church religion. As unimpressive as the Italian situation was Mexican-American support for parochial schools was virtually nonexistent. Isolated in the Southwest, the Mexican-American church was short on personnel, and this hindered the development of parochial schools. In the nineteenth century, many public schools in New Mexico were in effect Catholic schools run by Italian Jesuits. This changed, however, as Protestant public-school advocates protested this arrangement. Later on, parochial schools were so scarce that a study in 1906 estimated that, of the 514 Spanish-speaking parishes in the United States, only 6 were listed as having parochial schools.[56] This was graphically illustrated in New Mexico, where twelve parochial schools were in operation in 1910 and all but one of these was most likely made up of English-speaking Catholics. The San Antonio diocese had thirty-six parish schools in 1910, and all but two of them served the non-Mexican community.[57]

In assessing the support of various immigrant groups for the parochial school, certain conclusions are evident. Of the foreign-language-speaking groups, the Germans and the French Canadians were the most ardent supporters of the parochial school; close behind were the Polish. Next came the Slovaks, Czechs, Lithuanians, and Ukrainians. The Italians and Mexicans were the least ardent supporters of the parochial school. As regards the Irish, they would rank behind the Germans, French Canadians, and Polish, most likely at the level of the Slovaks.

The reasons for this difference of commitment to parochial schools are as various as the groups themselves. German Catholics launched a campaign to preserve language and culture, as did the French Canadians; both viewed the school as critical to the survival of language and faith. Another important reason was the availability of women religious teachers for both groups from the very beginning of their immigration to the United States. Both Germans and French Canadians also tended to settle in specific areas, in large concentrations, with French Canadians settling in New England's mill towns and Germans in both the rural and urban Midwest. Such large concentrations made support of schools more feasible. Among the Eastern European groups, certain factors seemed to lessen support. A major reason was a lack of teachers; even though all groups had their own orders of women religious to teach in the schools, their numbers were never sufficient to keep up with the demand. This was dramatically illustrated in the diocese of Green Bay, Wisconsin, where the bishop, Sebastian Messmer, an ardent advocate of Catholic schools, was unable to provide schools for the Polish because he could not get Polish teachers, and Green Bay, he claimed, had more Polish parishes than any other diocese in the country.[58]

In addition, many Eastern European Catholic secularists or nationalists did not believe in the value of a Catholic education. Such opposition not only fostered debate over the value of a parochial school, but it also precluded any widespread campaign for schools, as was true with the Germans. Finally the quality of education in Eastern European parochial schools was quite suspect because of the poor educational background and preparation of the sisters who taught in these schools. A Slovak priest, Stefan Furdek, in an article on education, listed the advantages of a public-school education. These schools were free, he noted; they supplied the children with books and clothes and had nurses to care for the sick; they also had small classes taught by certified teachers who spoke good English. Then he observed that Slovak Catholic schools were expensive, had large classes, often eighty to a hundred in one room; their teachers had no diplomas and a poor command of English. Despite the obvious benefits of the public school, the priest claimed that the parochial schools were superior because they taught religion, and "the saving of souls," he said, "was more important than a good secular education."[59]

Many Eastern European Catholics did not agree, however, and for the very reasons Furdek mentioned, they chose the public school.

The lack of teachers certainly had a negative influence in Italian and Mexican communities. In addition, Italian and Mexican Catholics followed a religious tradition that was not as parish-oriented as other groups, and this also weakened the demand for parish schools. The Mexican pattern of settlement was also very important. They tended to settle in small rural towns or villages, and such low concentrations of people were not conducive to financing parish schools.

Geographical location and the size of the local Catholic community also influenced a group's decision to support a parochial school. New England was not a center of parochial-school support. A notable exception was those regions where French Canadians were heavily concentrated: Rhode Island and New Hampshire. Unlike in New York and Cincinnati, church leaders in Boston in the nineteenth century never pushed hard for parochial schools. The Irish were heavily concentrated in New England and they were not very ardent in their support of parochial schools. In contrast to New England, the midwestern states of Ohio, Illinois, Indiana, Missouri, and Wisconsin were very supportive of Catholic schools. This was no doubt due to the early leadership and commitment of Bishop John Purcell as well as the high concentration of Germans in these states. Though such regional differences did exist, the most significant difference was rural versus urban. Southern dioceses like New Orleans exhibited a good if not better church–school ratio than northern dioceses; the same could be said for West Coast dioceses in relation to those on the East Coast. But this was not true of rural areas when compared with urban areas. This was noticeable in Minnesota, New York, Pennsylvania, Iowa, and virtually every other state in the union. The cities had schools, while many small towns and villages did not. A study of 982 parishes pointed this out; 371 of these parishes were situated in places of fewer than twenty-five hundred people, and in this group of rural parishes only 29 percent had parish schools. Among the remaining parishes, only 11 percent were without schools. The pattern of Czech parochial schools reflected this. Of 120 rural parishes in 1914, only 38 had schools, while all 30 urban parishes had them.[60] Moreover, in rural parishes it took considerably longer to found a school than in urban parishes. The length of time it took a parish to build a school was directly related to the size of the area in which the parish was situated. In rural areas, fewer than twenty-five hundred people, it took on the average at least fourteen years before a parish founded a school; in small towns, between twenty-five hundred and ten thousand people, it took an average of eleven years. In cities with over fifty thousand people, however, an average of only five years passed before a parish built a school.[61] In addition, the bulk of the Catholic school-age population was in the cities, not in small towns or rural areas. The Philadelphia archdiocese offered a dramatic illustration of this. In 1900, 33,025 students attended fifty-seven schools in the city of Philadelphia, while 8,096 students were enrolled in forty-two schools outside the metropolis. These small-town and rural schools were one-room schools, while urban schools were specially designed buildings complete with six to eight grades with principals and staffs of teachers.[62]

Another important point to realize is that people's support for the parish school was very selective. A study of Catholic immigrants living in the Chicago Stock Yards district concluded that the vast majority of these families felt "an obligation to send their children to the parochial school for part of their training"; "this feeling," the report noted, "arises from a deep religious conviction that conquers even those who recognize the greater potential value of the public school."[63] What was taking place in Stock Yards neighborhood was a very common practice. Parents would send their children to the parochial school for basic religious instruction, and once they received their first Communion, then many would transfer their children to the public school. Some pastors even forced students to transfer to public schools after their first Communion in order to make room for younger children preparing for that sacrament.[64] While bemoaning the overcrowding of classes, a Philadelphia school report in 1900 observed, "The lower grades provide education for the vast majority of our children; a small percentage of those who begin the first year, ever enter the last." Then, citing figures "from one of our city schools," the report concluded that "more than seventy-five percent of the children in this school are in the classes of the first four years." Some dioceses, Chicago and Cleveland for example, did not allow children to receive first Communion unless they attended the parochial school for at least one year.[65] Some children attended the public school first and then transferred to the parochial school later on so they could receive first Communion, which generally took place in the third or fourth grade. Confirmation was generally received around age twelve, or at about the fourth- or fifth-grade level, around the turn of the century. For all effective purposes, this was the termination point of an immigrant child's education. School reports show this pattern very clearly, and educators complained about it, but they could not prevent the exodus of children after they received Confirmation. Immigrant families needed their help at home as well as the income they could bring in from work outside the home. Thus attendance at parochial schools was quite selective; underlying the religious value of the schools, parents sent their children to them so that they could receive one or both of the childhood sacraments. For many, first Communion marked the end of a Catholic education; for others, education terminated with Confirmation.[66]

An important aspect of the history of the Catholic school movement was the emergence of the Indian mission school. Many European priests initially came to the United States to work among the Indians. Like their seventeenth-

and eighteenth-century predecessors, they came fired with missionary zeal to Christianize and civilize the Indians. Most of them never saw an Indian and ended up working in the urban centers of the immigrant Catholic community. Some priests did become missionaries, and their heroic exploits in the face of enormous obstacles gained them an important niche in Catholic history. Samuel Mazzuchelli was one. An Italian-born Dominican priest, he labored among the Indians in northern Michigan and Wisconsin. Traveling by canoe or on snowshoes, he tried to keep in touch with the nomadic tribes that inhabited this part of the country. Frederic Baraga was born in Slovenia and educated at the University of Vienna. His one ambition in life was to be a missionary to the American Indians. Like his contemporary Mazzuchelli, he worked among the Indians in northern Michigan. His apostolic zeal and austere lifestyle became legendary; in 1853 he became a bishop and was appointed head of the church in the Michigan Upper Peninsula. Farther west, the Belgian Jesuit Peter DeSmet promoted missions among the Plains Indians in Montana; one of his colleagues was Nicholas Point. A gifted linguist, sensitive to the culture of the Indians, Point was also a decent artist and left a valuable legacy of sketches and paintings depicting Indian life in the Rocky Mountain region.[67]

Point, DeSmet, Baraga, and Mazzuchelli were but a few of the many priests who worked among the Indians in the pre-Civil War period. This was a time when the Indian population was being forcibly removed to lands west of the Mississippi, where eventually they were gathered together on reservations. All along, it was the hope of the American Government that the Indians would become acculturated to the American way of life. To carry out this policy of acculturation, the government relied on the work of Protestant and Catholic missionaries. For these missionaries, the school was the central agent in the Christianization and civilization of the Indian population.

In the words of a Jesuit priest, "To give instructions and to teach Catechism, are the principal occupations of the missionary."[68] Teaching was the missionary's primary work and the way by which he sought to convert the Indian to the God of Christianity and the culture of America. To augment the work of the priest and organize the task of teaching was the purpose of the Indian mission school. Though popular in the colonial period, ". . . schools became the most important focal point of nineteenth-century missionary activity."[69] There were several reasons for this. One was the influence of the common-school movement, which made the schoolhouse the principal agency of education. Another was the support of those men and women who sought to reform Indian affairs in the late-nineteenth century; for these reformers, schools were the principal way to bring about the Americanization of the Indian. A third reason was the financial support of the federal government, which made such a vast educational enterprise possible. Thus, by the last quarter of the nineteenth century, the school had become the focal point of the mission complex, and the men and women who ran the mission spent most of their time and energy building and maintaining the school.

In 1874, Catholic missionaries operated two boarding schools and five day schools. By 1910, the number of Indian mission schools had increased to fifty-five boarding schools and eight day schools, which enrolled a total of 4,924 students. An especially revealing statistic was that of the 137 Catholic Indian missions in the United States, 87 of them did not have any school at all; this proportion was about the same as that of schools to parishes in the immigrant community. In California, where very few Indian Catholics lived, hardly any schools existed; in New Mexico, where large numbers of Indian Catholics lived, only two schools were in operation. The most notable Indian missions were in the northern plains states. The largest of these were the Sioux reservations at Rosebud and at Pine Ridge, South Dakota. Jesuit priests, brothers, and Franciscan sisters staffed the mission schools there. White Earth, Minnesota, was the site of a well-known Indian mission run by Benedictine priests and sisters. At Harbor Springs, Michigan, an Indian mission school had been in operation since the early-nineteenth century; in 1910, Franciscan priests and School Sisters of Notre Dame ran a mission school there for 147 children. Even larger was the Franciscan Mission at Gila Crossing, Arizona, an area where Father Kino had once traveled; 1,367 Indian Catholics lived on this reservation, and its school, staffed by the Sisters of St. Joseph, had an enrollment of two hundred students.[70]

By the late-nineteenth century, the boarding school had clearly become the school of choice for Indian children. Various communities of religious women ran these Catholic boarding schools, and they followed a monastic routine, with prayer and work taking up the bulk of the day. The curriculum was quite similar to that of the parochial and public schools, with the added ingredient of agricultural and industrial training for the boys and domestic training for the girls. Never very large in enrollment (most having fewer than a hundred students), the boarding schools were very costly to operate. The lack of finances plagued them continually. Financial support from the federal government did help, but this was eventually outlawed and made the situation even more precarious. A Philadelphia heiress, Katherine Drexel, gave a substantial portion of her fortune to support these Indian schools; she even founded an order of religious women, the Sisters of the Blessed Sacrament, to work among the Indians and Negroes. A Bureau of Catholic Indian Missions, established in 1874, sought to rally moral and financial support for the missions. Indian missions, however, were not a priority in the Catholic community, and neither clergy nor laity ever gave them the moral and financial support they needed. Another major problem at the schools was the resistance of the Indians themselves. Children often ran away from the schools; parents even had to be coerced to send their children to the schools. Like their colonial ancestors, nineteenth-century Indians strongly resisted attempts to convert them to the ways of the white people.[71]

By 1910, the American Indian population was estimated at about 220,000; of these, 61,456, or 28 percent, were Catholic.[72] That was a sizable percentage and reflected the centuries-old commitment of Catholic missionaries to the Indian population. For many of these Indians, however, the importance of the church remained marginal; for them, Christianity was a veneer religion; their native religion remained their major system of belief. Others did embrace the Christian gospel, and the church became for them a point of stability and identification in the disintegrating world of Indian culture. As was true in colonial times, however, the attempt of both the missionaries and the government to Christianize and civilize the Indians had a destructive effect. Just at the time when the reservation system was undermining their outer world and their traditional way of life, the missionaries attacked their inner world of beliefs. Such attacks further weakened their culture and had destructive consequences. What limited positive influence the church had on the quality of Indian life was, in the final analysis, far outweighed by the destruction that resulted from the disintegration of American Indian life.

At the Indian reservation and in the immigrant neighborhood, the school day began with prayers or, in some instances, attendance at Mass; the course of study was like that in the public schools, and Catholic educators always mentioned this, implying that their schools were as good as, if not better than, the public schools. The last class every day was religious instruction. Religion was the obvious margin of difference in these schools, and its presence was continuously manifest throughout the day; pictures and statues were constant visual reminders; short prayers said throughout the day brought children back from thoughts of "taffy and molasses candy."[73] James Burns, C.S.C., a noted educator and historian, described how religion permeated the school:

> The selection of teachers with special reference to their moral and religious character; the admission of only such pupils as belong to the religious faith which the school endeavors to foster and propagate; the placing of religious pictures and objects of piety in conspicuous places on the school walls; the use of religious songs, as well as common oral prayers and devotion; the organization of religious societies—through these and kindred means the pupil is continually surrounded with an atmosphere of religion and piety in the schoolroom which supplements and reinforces the work of formal religious instruction.[74]

At the turn of the century, most elementary schools had only four or five grades; some had six, and very few had eight. A common complaint was overcrowding. Classes were quite large throughout the period, ranging from seventy to one hundred students, with the lower grades much larger than the upper levels. Viewing this as "a crying evil," educators sought to remedy such overcrowding, but it persisted well into the twentieth century.[75] Such overcrowded conditions naturally raised the question of the quality of education in Catholic schools. A common complaint was that they were inferior to public schools, and though these charges would be almost impossible to verify nationwide, the complaint was loud enough and persistent enough on the part of parents and educators that there had to be some degree of truth to it. A major reason for this was not just overcrowding, but the quality of teachers. Most women religious were poorly prepared for teaching.

There were many reasons for the poor preparation of elementary-school teachers. The most obvious one was the level of education. Most teachers entered the classroom with no more than an elementary level of education. Sisters generally entered religious life at an early age—after elementary school or in their mid-teens. After a year of spiritual formation, called the novitiate, they were sent off to teach. While teaching, they received on-the-job training from an older, experienced teacher; then, during the summer, they would attend classes run by the religious order in order to upgrade their education.

The Third Baltimore Council had encouraged the establishment of Catholic normal schools and also teacher certification requirements in the hope of raising the quality of education in Catholic schools. By the 1890s, most religious orders did have some sort of novitiate training school, and they supplemented these with summer institutes. But these schools were very elementary in what they tried to do. "The novices have regular classwork," wrote one superior to William Cardinal O'Connell of Boston. "I think the teachers start in by reviewing the Primary and Grammar school work. Those who have gone through the High School take advanced subjects." This was quite a sparse program, considering that it describes conditions in 1921.[76] As a result, ". . . young girls were often clothed with the religious habit, and sent out to teach in parish schools where upper scholars were fully their equal in knowledge if not in age."[77] Moreover, the expectations of the clergy were quite low. "The old idea," educator James Burns wrote, "that anyone could teach well a subject he had thoroughly mastered himself, still obtained very widely."[78] Catholic colleges were male institutions, and this precluded the attendance of women religious at such schools; living a secluded life in a convent reinforced their intellectual isolation. When a group of sisters did aspire to higher education, wishing to take summer courses at Catholic University, for example, their bishop told them, ". . . such eagerness . . . would diminish the religious spirit of an Institute whose first care was the instruction of the poor."[79]

Another reason for poor teacher preparation was that each religious order went its own way in this area. Because they were so competitive and jealous of one another, religious orders never banded together to establish a common normal school. Each order jealously guarded its own tradition and remained aloof from other teaching orders. Such isolation fostered narrow-minded attitudes, the perpetuation of antique teaching methods, and weak teacher preparation. Bishops did little to correct this situation. Their expectations were low and their attitude quite casual. Cardinal O'Connell of Boston was typical in this regard. He sponsored summer institutes for teachers, but they were short-term programs and not very well funded. When a woman religious superior outlined "an extremely weak educational program to him, his response was: 'That is good. Keep it up.' This private reaction was a sharp contrast to his public statements on quality education and reflects his unwillingness to commit church resources to its attainment."[80]

The preparation of teachers received a major shot in the arm with the opening of a teachers college at Catholic University in 1911. Founded by Father Thomas E. Shields, it offered summer courses to women religious desirous of educational advancement. Since they could not attend men's colleges, and few women's colleges existed, this was an opportunity for sisters to begin work, in a part-time manner, on a college degree. Such other schools as Creighton in Nebraska and DePaul in Chicago offered similar programs; this development was a major advance in the professional training of Catholic-school teachers. The principal impetus, however, came from the need for teacher certification. By 1920 this was becoming quite common in most states. "Certification of teachers," wrote a religious superior, "is the immediate and imperative need."[81] As a result, teacher preparation programs were stepped up. Teachers obtained their high school diplomas and the required extra hours in educational courses. Teachers with college degrees were still the exception at this time.

Another influence on the quality of education was the inability of foreign-speaking sisters to speak English. This was quite common and caused concern. A Chicago study in the mid 1920s found that among Polish sisters many could speak only broken English. These sisters lived in a culture in which the mother tongue was Polish; hardly ever did they speak English, and their convents included few if any books or newspapers in English.[82] The same was true of other immigrant communities of women religious. Many people did not view this as a serious liability, since they sent their children to school to learn the language and culture of the old country. Other parents put a priority on their children's learning English, and this was indeed difficult when the teacher herself often knew less than the students. In Polish schools this persisted into the twentieth century, when it was still common for children to look upon English as a second language. This changed dramatically after the 1920s, when Americanization programs pushed for the exclusive use of English in all schools.

Of all the problems facing Catholic educators, however, the most serious was finances. This had been a problem since the earliest days of the nineteenth century and remained so throughout the twentieth century. It was a principal reason why John Ireland sought some compromise with the public-school system in his diocese; it was the motivating factor for the Poughkeepsie plan in New York and for similar arrangements in other towns. Many schools were forced to close because of financial difficulties, and those that remained open were a financial drain, adding 30 to 50 percent to the total cost of operating the parish.[83] The major reason why parochial schools made it at all financially was because the sisters subsidized them through their low salaries. By the early-twentieth century, sisters generally received an annual salary of about two hundred dollars, or one third less than female public-school teachers and one half that received by teaching brothers. Many times, pastors failed to pay the full salary; one year, the Sisters of Charity of the Blessed Virgin Mary did not receive salaries in twenty-four of the fifty-nine schools in which they taught. In Buffalo, New York, most parishes did not pay the Sisters of Mercy any salaries at all during their first thirty years of teaching in the diocese.[84] Such free labor was not uncommon. But in order to operate the convent and support the order, the sisters needed money and so they were forced "to rely heavily on supplementary income sources to compensate" for inadequate salaries; chief among these was the teaching of music to children after school hours. A single music teacher could earn twice as much as a poorly paid teacher, and this helped to put food on the table and heat in the convent. Religious orders also established tuition academies for girls to subsidize their work in parish schools. Some orders received a commission on books and school supplies; often, they sponsored an end-of-the-year entertainment, and in this manner they "made up for the differential between school income and their household expenses."[85]

Compounding the problem was the status of sisters in the church. They were the Catholic serfs, having fewer rights and fewer options than priests, brothers, or lay people. Bishops possessed the ultimate authority and frequently sought to interfere in the internal affairs of the community. Some pastors treated them worse than hired help: refusing to honor contract agreements, providing poor living accommodations, and removing them from the schools if the pastors so desired. In the parish, the pastor was the local superintendent of education, and he did pretty much what he wanted in the school. Obviously, all bishops and pastors did not act in this manner, but those that did were so numerous that this aspect of American Catholic history would constitute a book in itself.[86] Women religious fought back against meddling bishops and tyrannical pastors, but their options were few. The experience of the School Sisters of St. Francis was very illuminating in this regard.

The School Sisters of St. Francis was founded by three German women religious who left Germany in 1873 to establish a religious order in the United States. A teaching order, they were concentrated mainly in rural parishes in the Midwest and quite typically received more requests for teachers than they could fill. In many instances, they worked in the parish "on a charity basis"; at other times they received a salary. But they frequently withdrew from some of their missions "when pastors failed to pay in accordance with their prior agreement."[87] But "the most common reason for leaving missions was pastors who, though untrained in educational work, insisted upon running the school, interfering with the work of sisters. Inadequate housing for the sisters was another frequent cause of withdrawals." The above-quoted historian of the community went on to observe:

> One is struck by the number of parish histories which recount that when the rectory was no longer satisfactory for the pastor, he had a new one built and gave the old one to the sisters for a convent. The Congregation had leverage, however, because pastors in rural missions generally had great difficulty in finding religious orders of women who would serve as teachers, musicians, domestics and church workers. The School Sisters of St. Francis had begun with rural missions and gained a reputation for doing whatever needed to be done. Consequently, the mere threat of withdrawal was often sufficient to correct any difficulties with rural pastors. When the congregation did withdraw, it was usually with an offer to return when the unsatisfactory conditions were corrected.[88]

Despite the problems encountered in religious life, young women joined religious orders in large numbers. Teaching was an attractive career in the late-nineteenth and early-twentieth centuries, and by this time, most women religious were involved in teaching. Catholics also held religious life in high esteem, so it was socially acceptable for a daughter to choose this vocation. The austerity of convent life did not deter youthful idealism, and for daughters of working-class families, religious life offered a career, be it teaching or nursing, that would have been difficult to attain outside the church. Without this reservoir of talent, Catholic schools would never have been as numerous or significant as they were.

A major development in the late-nineteenth century was the trend toward the organization of a Catholic school system. American society was experiencing a trend toward centralization in the formation of organizational bureaucracies. Coupled with this was a movement toward professionalization and specialization in the workplace. These developments fostered the systematization of public schools. Educators believed that the quality of education in public schools was poor and needed improvement. Teachers were not well trained, students' attendance was sporadic, and lack of coordination among schools was commonplace. Improvement, they believed, was obtainable through the systematization of schools. Thus, educational bureaucracies began to develop, with superintendents of schools, school boards, examiners, truant officers, and principals being the major figures. Once standards became important, educators stressed testing and compulsory attendance, along with the certification of teachers.[89]

The same cultural trends of centralization, professionalization, and specialization also influenced Catholic educators. In seeking to improve the quality of education, the Third Baltimore Council urged the establishment of school boards and the testing of teachers. Other dioceses took the cue and began appointing diocesan superintendents of schools to organize the Catholic educational enterprise. Larger urban dioceses such as New York, Philadelphia, and Cincinnati led the way in this regard. But progress was slow, and it was not until the early-twentieth century that the move toward organization gained wide support. School superintendents then began to issue annual reports, which reflected concerns common to public-school educators at the time. Overcrowding of classrooms, irregular attendance at school, disorder in the classrooms, poor record keeping, and faulty methods of teaching became major concerns as educators sought to establish a Catholic school system in which common standards would result in better quality.[90] It was in this atmosphere that teacher training developed as a major priority, and as in so many other areas, Catholic University took the lead in providing such training for the teaching sisters.

A major obstacle to the systematization of Catholic schools was the independence of each parochial school. The pastor was the supreme authority in both parish and school, and for all practical purposes he functioned as the local superintendent of schools. As pastor he built the school, hired the teachers, and paid the bills. Diocesan school superintendents could legislate progressive reform measures, but it was up to the local pastor to implement them if he so chose. Many would choose not to, and the superintendent was powerless to force them to do otherwise. Another obstacle to the systematization of Catholic schools was the diversity of immigrant groups in urban areas. Each group had its own schools and its own teaching sisters, and used its own set of textbooks. In effect, each immigrant group was a separate school system within the larger system. A typical working-class neighborhood would have numerous parochial schools, each serving a different immigrant community. The school configuration in Chicago's Stock Yards neighborhood was commonplace. Within walking distance of each other were three Polish schools, along with an Irish, a German, a Slovak, a Lithuanian, and a Czech school, eight schools in all, as well as a German Lutheran school. These parochial schools enrolled more than twice as many students as the three public schools in the area.[91] It would prove to be impossible to standardize such an ethnically diverse network of schools during the era of immigration. As a result, school systems focused on English-language schools, most of which were Irish. This could clearly be seen in New York, where in 1905 the Catholic school superintendent introduced the history of Ireland as "part of the course of study in the entire seventh and eighth grades."[92] It is hard to imagine such courses being taught in Polish schools. On the contrary, Polish sisters introduced students to the glories of Poland's past. In New York, at least, Catholic educators were as oblivious to the cultural heritage of their immigrant coreligionists as were their public-school counterparts.

An important part of the educational system was the high school. High schools first emerged in the middle of the nineteenth century, but they attracted very few students. In the first two decades of the twentieth century, the high school came into its own, enrolling more and more students. Catholics had to move in this direction if they were going to compete with what the public-school educators were offering. In 1899 the new superintendent of Catholic schools in Baltimore wrote that high schools were "the crying need in Baltimore, Washington, and other parochial centers."[93] Other educators repeated his concern, and the establishment of high schools soon became a top priority of Catholic educators.

Throughout the nineteenth century, both male and female students had been attending private academies where they could receive a secondary-school education. Numerous such academies were in operation by 1900, but they were principally college preparatory schools for men and finishing schools for women. By the late-nineteenth century, educators were calling for schools that would educate children graduating from parochial elementary schools; a high school, they said, would complete the parochial school system and enable Catholics to compete more effectively against its rival, the public school system. For most children, it would be the end of formal schooling; for others, it would be preparation for college. Catholics, however, were slow to organize high schools, with the first Catholic central high school being established in 1890 in Philadelphia through a generous gift of Thomas E. Cahill. The concept of a central high school serving an area of the city became the recommended norm, since few parishes could afford to organize their own high schools. By 1912, fifteen central Catholic high schools were in operation. But these schools reached only a fraction of the eligible children. In Philadelphia, for example, 60,000 students were enrolled in the parochial schools in 1912; the city's Roman Catholic High School had an enrollment of only 394.[94]

The tradition of the private academy as the place for secondary education retarded the growth of Catholic high schools. Thus in Chicago the private academy, not the central high school, remained the principal secondary school. Many of these academies were mixed institutions. Calling themselves colleges, they offered both high school and college education, with the high school classes enrolling the largest number of students. A study of men's colleges in 1916 underscored this point. In the eighty-four colleges surveyed, the college student population numbered 8,304; the high school population was 16,288. In other words, there were two high school students for every college student enrolled in Catholic colleges. Furthermore, only eleven of the eighty-four colleges had undergraduate enrollments over 200; more than one third had fewer than 50 undergraduates, and in these schools the high school population was around 100 to 150.[95] Before Catholic schools could come into their own, a clearer differentiation between collegiate and secondary education was needed.

Catholics had a view of college education that was quite different from the prevailing American pattern. Modeled on a European Jesuit system, the Catholic college was a seven-year institution combining both secondary and collegiate instruction. This meant that the two major Catholic schools in the early-twentieth century were the elementary school and the college; there were few high schools, because ". . . high school work was actually going on in the Catholic colleges."[96] Until the Catholic college could be better defined and made to correspond to the American system, high schools would be slow to develop. Such differentiation did take place under the pressure of accreditation, and with the change of a name, many Catholic colleges disappeared overnight and became what they actually were: high schools. This sorting out was pretty much completed by the 1920s, and only then did Catholic high schools and colleges develop according to the American pattern.

Another development in the early-twentieth century was the establishment of colleges for women. The first such college was the College of Notre Dame of Maryland; established in 1896 by the School Sisters of Notre Dame, it granted its first degrees in 1899. The College of Notre Dame had evolved from a female academy founded in 1863; this pattern of a women's college evolving from a female academy was quite common in the twentieth century. Some schools were initially founded as colleges. Trinity College was the first of this kind, receiving its first students in 1900. When they held their first commencement, four years later, the college enrollment numbered eighty-one students. By 1915, nineteen Catholic colleges for women were in operation; like their male counterparts, they survived on small enrollments, optimistically looking ahead to more prosperous days.[97]

Without a doubt, the development of the parochial school as a keystone of Catholic institutional life was a notable achievement during a century of immigration. In these schools, thousands of children acquired the basic learning skills needed in a developing modern society. Together with other educational agencies, the school had a major influence in shaping the Catholic ethos. It had become the centerpiece of a school system that, by 1920, was second only in size and scope to the public-school system. It was clearly one of the wonders of the immigrant Catholic world.

XI

Religion and Society

EVEN BEFORE MASSES OF IMMIGRANTS started coming to the United States, Roman Catholicism was experiencing a fundamental conflict in its relationship to American society. Some Catholics wanted a church that would be thoroughly American. Rooted in American soil, it would be independent of any foreign interference; its clergy would be in tune with the "American way of life"; church and state would be separate and religious toleration would be a virtue, not a vice; and English, not Latin, would be the language of church prayer. These Catholics were mostly American- or Irish-born people. Other Catholics, however, had a different view of the relation between Catholicism and American society. Composed mainly of French-born clerics and German-born priests and lay people, they wanted to transplant a European model of Roman Catholicism to the United States. For the French, it would be shaped *à la Française;* for the Germans, it would reflect the influence of the German Catholic heritage. For these Europeanists, the United States was a stage on which Catholicism would play out its role in the history of salvation. Little, if any, interaction would take place between religion and society, according to this point of view. For the Americanists, however, religion would adapt itself to the culture in which it was situated in order to be better in tune with the culture of the people. At the heart of the conflict were two basic issues: the definition of *American* and the definition of *church.* The Americanists defined American identity in clearly American terms; the Europeanists were much more cosmopolitan, defining it more broadly, so that it included ingredients from both sides of the Atlantic. As regards the church, the Americanists, exhibiting evidence of an Enlightenment influence, defined it in a positive, interventionist stance as regards society, whereas the Europeanists viewed the church as a perfect society whose mission was to conquer the world and ultimately bring all culture under its control. From this point of view, society was an adversary, not an ally.[1]

After 1820 or so, two developments took place that not only fueled the conflict but also shaped the eventual outcome. The first was large-scale immigration. As millions of foreign-born people came to the United States, the answer to the question of what it meant to be an American became more problematical. Discussions turned into heated arguments; racism and nationalism intensified the situation, and controversy continued throughout the nineteenth and early-twentieth centuries, until Americans finally decided to keep out as many foreigners as possible by passing immigration restriction laws in the 1920s. A second development was the consolidation of the Papacy. For Catholics, this meant that the church became increasingly more centered in Rome. By the end of the century, the Vatican had become the nerve center of the church, and the Pope, wrapped in the cloak of infallibility, was restored to a position of power reminiscent of medieval times. But unlike in medieval times, church and society were no longer united; in fact, they were at odds with one another. The Pope had become a prisoner in his own palace; anticlericalism and indifference to religion were sweeping through Italy and France; and modern science challenged ageless truths. For some, the Catholicism of the Old World was standing still while the modern world passed it by. People began to ask whether the church should stand still or join the modernist parade into the twentieth century.

During the era of the immigrant church, the issues of nationality and church periodically surfaced and stepped out onto the national stage, sparking lively controversy among Catholics. The stance that people took and the outcome of the controversies revealed how Catholics thought about the relation between religion and American society. In analyzing this debate, it is important to realize that the two issues of American identity and the definition of church could and did indeed overlap. They were closely related, but for the sake of clarity it is best to discuss them separately. The first issue to emerge was the debate over American identity.

By the middle of the nineteenth century, the number of Catholics in the United States had swelled to record numbers, and American Protestants were seriously concerned about a papist takeover. This concern spilled over into anti-Catholic demonstrations and riots; eventually a political party was formed—the Know-Nothings—whose platform was explicitly antiforeign and anti-Catholic. According to the nativist, anti-Catholic mind, Catholic immigrants could not be considered true Americans, because of their religion and their foreign birth. Catholics scoffed at such charges and defended themselves by proclaiming their loyalty to the American republic and the values that inspired it. Nevertheless, the problem remained, and it was indeed a real problem, not just one conjured up by anti-Catholic nativists. The problem was, How could an adult person, born and raised in Ireland or Germany, become an American without abandoning his or her ethnic heritage? Compounding the issue was the nativist fear that Catholics, in being loyal to the Pope in Rome, could not be completely loyal citizens of the United States. Against this background of nativist attack and Catholic defensiveness, the Yankee convert Orestes Brownson ignited a controversy by publishing a series of articles in his quarterly, *Brownson Quarterly Review*, in the summer and fall of 1854.

The essay that sparked the controversy was on the topic of "Native Americanism."[2] In this essay, Brownson wrote in such a paternal, condescending style that this alone would have caused problems with his Irish Catholic readers. The thrust of the essay was that native Americanism was a legitimate aspiration of the American-born. The Irish, strongly nationalistic themselves, should understand this and accept it, he said. Brownson repudiated the anti-Catholicism of the native Americanists, but endorsed their Americanist platform and was willing to limit the right to vote to American-born citizens. He told the Irish and all immigrants that they "must ultimately lose their own nationality and become assimilated in general character to the Anglo-American race."[3] Strongly assimilationist, Brownson wanted Irish and German Catholics to shed their nationalities and become American. In the process, however, he did not want them to lose their religion. As he later put it, "The Americanization of the Catholic body does and will go on of itself, as rapidly as is desirable, and all we have to do with it is, to take care that they do not imbibe the notion that to Americanize is necessarily to Protestantize. The transition from one nationality to another is always a dangerous process, and all the Americanization I insist on is, that our Catholic population shall feel and believe that a man may be a true American and a good Catholic."[4] Clearly and concisely, Brownson had stated the issue that would continue to haunt Catholic immigrants for the next one hundred years.

Brownson's essay on native Americanism stirred up a hornet's nest among Irish journalists. He harbored a strong prejudice against the Irish, and it came out between the lines of his essay. Irish journalists picked this up, and "In July and August 1854 he was censured in at least nine Catholic journals for insulting honest immigrants and kindling anti-Irish feeling."[5] They accused him of being anti-Irish and soft on anti-Catholic nativists. Brownson sought to defend himself and clarify his position in subsequent essays. But, as Arthur M. Schlesinger, Jr., noted, "He was caught between two fires. As he remarked, he was trying to defend against Americans his right to be a Catholic and against Catholics his right to be an American. The outcome was not happy."[6]

Though the Brownson-Irish controversy was only a brief flurry, it did point out the issues involved in the American identity debate. One point of view, articulated by Brownson and shared by American-born Catholics, was that immigrants should shed their foreign habits and loyalties and become American. For the immigrants, in this case the Irish, this was unthinkable; being Irish meant being Catholic, and to downplay their nationality would weaken religion as well. Thus the question was posed, Could immigrant Catholics become American Catholics?

Thirty years later, the question surfaced once again. This time it involved the Germans, and the controversy exploded into a prolonged and bitter debate that became international in scope. At the heart of the issue was the question of language. Like most immigrants, German Catholics closely identified their religion with their native culture, customs, and language. Under the slogan "Language Saves the Faith," they strongly resisted any attempts to weaken their attachment to German language and culture.

The focal point of this struggle was the local parish. German Catholics, led by their priests, resented the fact that in some dioceses—St. Louis, for example—their parishes did not enjoy the same rights and privileges as English-language parishes, which were virtually all Irish. Moreover, they saw such secondary status not only as an obstacle to preserving their language and culture, but also as a means of forced Americanization. To promote their campaign for equal rights, a group of eighty-two priests sent a petition to the Vatican in 1884 asking that German parishes and pastors be granted the same rights and independence as English-speaking parishes and pastors. This fueled the controversy over the German nationality issue and got some of the American bishops involved, along with church authorities in Rome. Then, in 1886, a German priest from Milwaukee, Peter Abbelen, went to Rome and presented a similar petition on behalf of the clergy in the German triangle region of Milwaukee, St. Louis, and Cincinnati. In asking for equal rights for Germans, he spoke out strongly against forced Americanization on the part of Irish clergy and bishops. Abbelen's petition added fuel to the fire, and Bishops John Ireland and John J. Keane led a counterattack against this German campaign for equal rights. Many bishops wrote to Rome protesting that the nationality question was hurting the church and giving credence to the charge that Catholics were indeed foreigners in the United States and not true and loyal Americans. They also feared that the Germans wanted to set up their own, national church, and this, too, could cause great harm to Catholics in the United States. The letter-writing campaign of the hierarchy made its point. The response of the Vatican to the Abbelen petition recognized the legitimacy and independence of separate parishes for diverse language groups —a practice that was already widespread in the United States—but refused to grant the Germans any further privileges and left the resolution of disputes over language in a parish to the decision of the local bishop.

Rome's decision did not end the debate, and controversy over the forced Americanization of German Catholics continued. Fueling the controversy was the organization of the German clergy in 1882 into a national organization, Deutsch-Amerikaner Priester-Verein, and the inauguration in that same year of an annual German Catholic national assembly, or *Katholikentag*. Modeled on similar conventions in Germany, it was a manifestation of German Catholic solidarity. Such gatherings of large numbers of clergy and laity helped to keep the nationality issue alive. In 1891 the controversy once again took on an international dimension.

The catalyst for the 1891 explosion was a German Catholic layman, Peter Paul Cahensly. He was interested in protecting the interest of German emigrants, and through his efforts the St. Raphaelsverein was established in Germany. The purpose of this society was to help the German Catholic emigrant "in every possible way before he sailed, during his voyage, and at the ports of debarkation."[7] An international organization, it had branches in several countries. An American branch was founded in 1883, and within a few years, a home for traveling emigrants, Leo House, was established in New York City. German Catholic clergy and laity had rallied behind the organization of Leo House, and their contributions made the home possible.

In 1890 the leaders of the various national branches of the St. Raphaelsverein held a meeting in Lucerne, Switzerland, at which they drafted a memorial to the Pope outlining ways and means to protect the faith of immigrants after they had arrived in the United States. Cahensly himself delivered the document to the Pope. Citing losses to the church in the United States of "more than ten million souls," the Lucerne Memorial made several recommendations for the care of immigrants in the United States. These included separate parishes for each nationality, administered by priests of "the same nationality to which the faithful belonged," catechetical instruction in the mother tongue, separate parochial schools for each nationality, equal rights for the clergy of each nationality, and representation within the hierarchy of each nationality.[8]

Once the Lucerne Memorial became public, the nationality debate exploded. Catholics and Protestants alike discussed the implications of the document. Even President Benjamin Harrison took an interest in the debate. Some saw it as foreign interference in American affairs—a German plot, they said, to gain influence in the United States. Archbishop John Ireland labeled it "Cahenslyism" and the name stuck, thus unjustly singling out Peter Paul Cahensly as the chief culprit of an imagined political conspiracy. On one side of the debate were Ireland, James Cardinal Gibbons of Baltimore, and a host of other bishops who wanted Catholic immigrants to become American; they favored the Americanization of the foreign-born and abhorred any step that would promote "a spirit of nationalism" among the diverse groups of immigrants in the church.[9] On the other side were the German clergy and people, who wanted recognition of their needs and equal rights in the church; their common enemy was the Irish, whom they feared "would Americanize everything." Before long, Pope Leo XIII responded to the Lucerne Memorial saying that its proposals were "neither opportune nor necessary."[10]

With the nationalist demands of the Lucerne Memorial defeated, the Americanizers felt vindicated. For German Catholics, life in the parish went on as before, but a certain defensiveness about their minority status persisted. Attention was soon diverted to other issues that were engaging Catholics in debate, a constellation of issues centering around a liberal-versus-conservative definition of the Church in relation to American society. Furthermore, the social process of Americanization was transforming the Germans as it had the Irish. As a result, German Catholics soft-pedaled their resistance to Americanism; pleas for equal rights and the slogan "Language Saves the Faith" were seldom heard among the Germans. But the nationality debate and the question of American identity did not disappear. New immigrants took up the cause and once again challenged the prevailing definition of what it meant to be both American and Catholic.

The new immigrants from southern and Eastern Europe faced the dilemma of how to become an American while still remaining Italian, Czech, Polish, or Slovak. This became even more difficult as the nation grew more aggressively American and nationalistic in the early decades of the twentieth century. World War I intensified the spirit of 100 percent Americanism to the point that all foreigners were suspect. Within the Catholic community, herculean efforts were made to demonstrate Catholic loyalty to the American republic. War-bond drives, fund-raising rallies, loyalty banquets, promotion of recruiting for the military, and episcopal statements of patriotism were the order of the day. Such an intense commitment to nationalism and patriotism was bound to clash with the nationalist feelings of the new immigrants. Though all groups were caught in this bind, the Polish were the ones who mounted the most aggressive and significant campaign against Americanization.

The first phase of this campaign involved the appointment of more Polish bishops. Like the Germans before them, the Poles very much resented the Irish domination of the church and wanted a proportionate representation in the hierarchy. The Wisconsin priest Wenceslaus Kruszka led the campaign to gain the appointment of Polish bishops for the United States. A strong-willed nationalist who was also a gifted writer, Kruszka eventually went to Rome to present his petition to the Pope. Rome was slow to act, but eventually a Polish priest, Paul Rhode, was consecrated auxiliary bishop of Chicago in 1908. Then, in 1913, another Polish priest, Edward Kozlowski, was appointed auxiliary bishop for Milwaukee, site of another large Polish community. But these two appointments did not silence the Polish demand for more power and independence in the church. World War I served to heighten the sense of Polish nationalism as the dream of an independent Poland appeared to be a not too distant reality. Such nationalist feelings ran head-on into the aggressive Americanization position taken by the Catholic hierarchy. Conflict was inevitable.[11]

The main setting for the clash was Chicago. In 1916, George Mundelein was installed as the new archbishop of Chicago. A third-generation German-American Catholic, Mundelein was a staunch supporter of 100 percent Americanism. For this reason, he was very reluctant to organize separate national parishes for differing foreign language groups; he also ordered that English become the principal medium of instruction in Catholic parochial schools. As he explained in a letter to Theodore Roosevelt, ". . . there is hardly any institution here in the country that does so much to bring about a sure, safe, and sane Americanization of immigrant people as do our parochial schools."[12] Such aggressive Americanization was new to Chicago and did not sit well with the Polish community. Moreover, Mundelein's authoritarian style (he was known as the Dutch Master) and his German background did not win him many friends among the Polish. Polish clergy quarreled frequently with Mundelein and soon banded together to protest policies he had initiated which, they believed, would undermine the strength and vitality of the Polish Catholic community in Chicago.[13] These were minor, local quarrels and were commonplace in the church. In the 1920s, however, a major controversy broke out that was reminiscent of the Cahensly episode thirty years earlier.

Frustrated by their losing battles with Mundelein and angered by their second-class status in the church, a group of Polish clergy from Chicago and across the nation sent a lengthy document to the Vatican protesting the Americanization policies of the bishops in the United States. The Polish Embassy at the Vatican supported the clergy in their effort. The clergy were convinced that the American bishops, Mundelein in particular, were "not only neglectful of Polish interests but intent upon destruction of their nationality." They pointed out the loss of faith among the Polish because the transition to an "Americanized church" was so difficult for the immigrants. Under no circumstances did they want the "Catholic church through its bishops to become the instrument of Americanization among the Polish immigrants." To prevent this, they asked for more Polish bishops, a curriculum of Polish studies in the seminary, and the continued establishment of separate Polish parishes.[14]

Once the American hierarchy heard about the letter, they prepared a lengthy reply to counter the charges. The response condemned the interference of the Polish Government, through its Vatican embassy, in American ecclesiastical affairs and warned what dire consequences such intervention could have in Protestant America. Then, in a section written largely by Mundelein, the response went on to rebut the particulars of the charges, stating that granting special concessions to one national group would have adverse effects throughout the entire Catholic community. In an eloquent passage, written by Archbishop Sebastian Messmer of Milwaukee, the bishops put forth a powerful defense of Americanization:

> It is of the utmost importance to our American nation that the nationalities gathered in the United States should gradually amalgamate and fuse into one homogeneous people and, without losing the best traits of their race, become imbued with the one harmonious national thought, sentiment and spirit, which is to be the very soul of the nation. This is the idea of Americanization. This idea has been so strongly developed during the late war that anything opposed to it would be considered as bordering on treason.[15]

The Vatican accepted the bishops' defense and no action was ever taken on the Polish petition. Polish bishops continued to remain a rare sight in the United States. Mundelein's star, however, was on the rise, and in 1924 he was appointed to the College of Cardinals, one of four bishops so honored at the time.

In all of these controversies, the main issue centered on immigrants becoming American. Brownson wanted the Irish to become American; Ireland cajoled the Germans; and Mundelein worked on the Polish. It was not a neat, clear-cut case of a person totally shedding his or her national loyalties, customs, and cultures and becoming 100 percent pure American. Ireland and the others were not so simplistic in their demands, since they recognized the value of cultural traditions. On the other hand, the immigrants were willing to accept a gradual Americanization; in other words, the inevitable change that would take place sometime in the distant future. But such amenability and conciliation got lost in the heat of debate.

Intensifying the controversy was the religious dimension. People were not arguing about such accidental issues as dress, social behavior, or proper speech, but about the sensitive issue of how to pray, how to worship, and how to educate their children; in other words, how to keep alive a cultural heritage that had been passed on in families for generations and was a vital link both with the past (their family) and the present (their God). Such commitment to family, culture, and God naturally strengthened the resistance of immigrants to anything that would threaten that bond.

Strengthening the tenacity of the Americanists was the fear of public opinion. Catholics generally saw themselves as outsiders in the United States, a minority group that was forced to suffer persecution because of their religion. But the hierarchy desperately wanted to become insiders and be accepted as part of mainstream America. To gain such acceptance, Catholics had to shed any taint of foreign loyalties, customs, and languages. Time and again this argument was used in Rome in defense of an Americanization policy. If the nationalists were to win the day, then Catholics would continue to remain outsiders and possibly even suffer because of such foreign separatism. Viewed in this manner, more than just the desires of one group were at stake: the very future of Catholics in the United States appeared to hang in the balance.

The Americanizers clearly wanted the immigrants to blend into American society. They should adopt American ways, learn the language, and become loyal citizens. Archbishop Ireland expressed it in the following manner:

> What I do mean by Americanization is the filling up of the heart with love for America and for her institutions. It is the harmonizing of ourselves with our surroundings, so that we will be as to the manner born, and not as strangers in a strange land, caring but slightly for it, and entitled to receive from it but meagre favors. It is the knowing of the language of the land and failing in nothing to prove our attachment to our laws, and our willingness to adopt, as dutiful citizens, all that is good and laudable in its social life and civilization.[16]

This was rather vague, and few immigrants would balk at such adaptation. What raised their ire were efforts to impose or force Americanization—e.g., forbidding the use of a foreign language in public and parochial schools or not establishing national foreign-language parishes. The immigrants never hesitated to display their loyalty to the United States, and their patriotism became legendary. But they still wanted to remain loyal to their own national heritage and strongly resisted any attempt to force them to abandon it. Such national loyalty did set them apart from the rest of society and gave to both church and nation a quality of diversity unmatched throughout the world.

Lurking behind the issue of nationality and American identity was the question of power. By the closing decades of the nineteenth century, the Irish occupied the seats of power in the church. In 1900, bishops of Irish birth or descent were presiding over such key dioceses as New York, Baltimore, Boston, Philadelphia, Detroit, St. Paul, and San Francisco. In fact, two thirds of all the bishops in the United States were of Irish birth or descent; even in the diocese of St. Louis, where the clergy of German descent outnumbered the Irish, all but one of the twelve St. Louis priests promoted to the episcopacy between 1854 and 1922 were Irish.[17] Other immigrant groups resented such Irish domination, and before long the Irish became the common enemy of non-Irish immigrant Catholics. To counter this Irish power, Germans and Poles petitioned for better representation in the hierarchy. The Germans did achieve a measure of such representation, so that by 1900 about 15 percent of the hierarchy were of German descent. In the course of the twentieth century, this percentage increased somewhat, while that of the Irish leveled off around the 50 percent range. No other group could come close to such representation in the hierarchy, however. Even the Polish, who mounted the strongest campaign for bishops, ultimately failed. The 1908 appointment of the Polish priest Paul Rhode as an auxiliary bishop was a token offer; during the next seventy years, only about fifteen priests of Polish descent became bishops in the United States; even fewer French Canadians and Italians made it to the episcopacy.[18] The immigrants wanted power and control but were not able to gain it. The Irish continued to occupy the episcopal seats of power, and before long people began describing the church in the United States as One, Holy, Irish, and Apostolic.[19]

Another dimension to the nationality debate was social class. Though this was never explicitly articulated by either side in the debate, it seems clear that it was an ingredient in the controversy. This was most true in the Polish episode. These immigrants were lower-class working people, and the Americanist bishops wanted them to conform to values that legitimately can be called those of middle-class respectability. By 1920, large numbers of Irish and Germans had moved into the middle classes and were gaining a measure of respectability in society. But the immigrant newcomers weakened the very image of respectability that the bishops were so desperately seeking to cultivate. Though the class issue did not enter the German controversy, it certainly can be applied to the Brownson-Irish flurry. This issue of class tended to harden the lines of division separating the protagonists in these controversies and made accommodation all the more difficult.

What is an American? This is a question that has fascinated people since the founding of the republic. It captured the attention of immigrant Catholics and sparked controversy and conflict. Just when the controversy appeared over, a new group of immigrants raised the issue again. Though the question is timeless, the answer is not. It has changed with each new generation of people and each new age of history. For Catholics, another timeless issue that over the centuries has ignited intense debate is the definition of the church.

Over time, the theological understanding of the church has shifted depending on what aspect of the church was understood as primary. In the early centuries, for example, the spiritual or incarnational nature of the church as the body of Christ was emphasized. From the late Middle Ages on, however, the institutional nature of the church was stressed. As centuries passed and Roman Catholicism experienced the stresses initiated by the Protestant Reformation, the institutional nature of the church became its determinative element. The more Protestants attacked the Papacy and the hierarchy, the more Roman Catholic theologians emphasized these very features of the church. The result was that the normative model of the church became the institution, ". . . that is to say, the view that defines the Church primarily in terms of its visible structures, especially the rights and powers of its officers." This institutional model of the church dominated the mental landscape of Roman Catholicism throughout the seventeenth and eighteenth centuries and reached its culmination in the late-nineteenth and early-twentieth centuries.[20]

Allied to this understanding of the church as institution was the classicist or neo-Scholastic view which dominated the Roman Catholic theological world. According to this perspective, the church was perceived as "a static, essentially unchanging reality, by divine decree and guidance immune to process. The Church moves through history, but is affected by it only at the most external levels."[21] Thus, as a perfect society, the church was not only superior to all other human societies, but it was also immune to any change. Any influence of culture upon the church was unthinkable.

This classicist perspective, dominant from 1850 to 1950, infused the institutional model of the church with a timeless reality and meaning. Founded by Jesus Christ, it acquired a divine quality, which elevated everyone and everything it touched. It was this meaning of the church—divine institution, visible and perfect society, immune to change—which was viewed as the one and only true meaning of the church in the late-nineteenth century. But all the world was not Roman Catholic. Other influences were at work, and they would eventually transform the institutional view of the church. The key to this change was the rise of historical consciousness.

Hegel's philosophy of change and Darwin's theory of evolution clearly and definitively pointed the direction toward the future by way of the past. After Hegel and Darwin, theologians began to think differently about religion; more and more, they saw the need for cultural adaptation on the part of religion. A more immanent understanding of God and history and the concept of a progressive realization of the kingdom of God also began to be stressed. For nineteenth-century American Protestants, there emerged a discernible modernist impulse which embraced these three ideas of adaptation, the immanence of God, and religious progressivism; by the early-twentieth century, it would divide Protestants into two bitterly opposed camps.[22] While American Catholics never experienced the bitter division that split the Protestant community, a modernist impulse did indeed emerge to challenge the prevailing understanding of the church as a timeless, unchanging institution.

For Roman Catholics, modernism is a term generally associated with a theological controversy that surfaced in the late-nineteenth and early-twentieth centuries. But the rise of historical-mindedness, or what can be called the modernist mentality, clearly predated this controversy. As regards European Catholicism, the evidence for this is extensive.[23] Even though the evidence is not so extensive for American Catholicism, a definite modernist impulse can be discerned in some leading American Catholic thinkers. Though they did not call themselves modernists, nor did they self-consciously think of themselves as such, they were thinking and acting according to a modern perspective that theologically viewed the church as historically conditioned—unlike the classicist or neo-Scholastic mentality, which viewed it as unchanging and immune to the influence of history.

John Carroll was an intellectual heir of the Enlightenment, and his thinking on the nature of the church leaned in the modern direction. As previously noted in the chapter on republican Catholicism, John Carroll wanted to adapt certain practices of the church to the American environment. These included the training of priests, an English liturgy, friendly relations and cooperation with Protestants, and a church independent of foreign interference. In this manner he envisioned a church in the United States distinct from Roman Catholic churches in other countries. Such a program of adaptation to the American cultural situation clearly pointed in the modernist direction. Though these types of adaptation were more external and would not alter the intrinsic meaning of the church, Carroll did go further. He advocated the separation of church and state and promoted the idea of religious liberty. This touched on the very meaning of the church. According to the institutional model, the church was the one perfect society, and the state or civil society was subject to the rule of the church. Carroll promoted a different point of view, and in doing so modified the institutional model of the church as the one perfect visible society. Though he never fully explained how church and state would be separated and the consequent relationship between the two, his advocacy of the general concept of separation according to the American model clearly put him at odds with the prevailing model of the church as the one perfect society. In addition, Carroll celebrated religious liberty, not as a pragmatic concession to a religiously pluralist society, but as a natural human right. This, too, challenged the prevailing Roman Catholic position that said error had no rights and false religious beliefs could not be tolerated. The logic of Carroll's position suggested that, in a religiously pluralist society, Roman Catholicism could not claim to be the one and only visible church.[24]

In advocating these positions on religious liberty and the separation of church and state, Carroll was implying that the understanding of the church should be adapted to the cultural context, in this case the United States. Such thinking reflected a historical consciousness, a modern mentality in other words, when it came to defining the meaning of the church. This does not mean that Carroll self-consciously was adopting a historical, modern perspective in place of the classicist point of view. Nor was Carroll alone. During the Republican era, other American Catholics advocated religious liberty and separation of church and state. Unlike in Europe, such thinking did not result in a new school of thought or a new theology, but it did set a precedent. The precedent was the need of the church to adapt itself to the American context, not just in externals, but even in its very definition.

Bishop John England's thoughts on the understanding of the church and its relationship to society were much more developed than those of Carroll. England was clearly one of the more gifted churchmen of the nineteenth century and left a large body of writings as testimony to his fertile intellect. Raised in Ireland, he came to the United States in 1820 imbued with progressive ideas on the relationship between church and state. A nineteenth-century liberal, he developed a theory of church and state relations that advocated a free church in a free society. He not only championed the separation of church and state, but he also spelled out the implications of this arrangement both for individual Catholics and for the institutional church. In addition, he supported religious liberty and "the right of every man to follow the dictates of his conscience in the belief of doctrines purely religious without being subject, on that account, to civil pains and disabilities."[25] England also defined the church in a more republican, less monarchical, manner than most of his Catholic contemporaries. His advocacy of local church councils and the trustee system were clear indications of this. By advocating a republican church government, religious liberty, and separation of church and state, England was seeking to adapt the church to the age in which he lived. In other words, his thinking pointed in the direction of the historically conditioned, modern perspective. Though he was not self-consciously aware of this shift, his thought reflected the modern impulse toward cultural, historical adaptation on the part of religion.

Equally important was his understanding of the church. For England, the church was "the congregation of the faithful, an undying, perpetual and still living body." Grounding his understanding in the Pauline image of the body of Christ, England placed his emphasis on the work of the Holy Spirit within the church, rather than on the church as the one perfect visible institution.[26] Like Carroll before him, he also viewed the church as a visible institution with a government and authority. Nevertheless, he did modify this considerably by introducing the concept of the church as the body of Christ, along with his ideas on church and state, religious liberty, and Catholic republicanism. In so doing he suggested more emphatically than Carroll an alternative to the prevailing model of the church as institution. England's liberal views did meet with strong opposition from some of his more traditional-minded episcopal colleagues. They recognized his thinking for what it was: a new, and to them unorthodox, concept of the church. Such opposition was widespread enough so that England's vision remained a solitary challenge to the prevailing concept of the church during the 1820s and 1830s.

The significance of England and Carroll is that both realized the need of the church to adapt itself to a new historical situation, namely the American republic. Moreover, by advocating the separation of church and state, religious liberty and, in the case of England, republicanism in church government and the biblical model of the church as the body of Christ, they were modifying the prevailing institutional model of the church as the one perfect society. The implications of these modifications would become clearer in the 1890s, when the modernist perspective would become more fully developed and more widely endorsed.

The next person who sought to recast the definition of the church was Orestes Brownson. This Yankee convert grounded his understanding of the church in the concept of communion with God, which was achieved in the Incarnation, through which the divine and the human were united. For Brownson, the church became the visible extension of the Word made flesh, the mystical body of Christ, and through the church humanity achieved communion with God. Brownson clearly was shaping his understanding of the church according to a model quite different from the prevailing, institutional one. "In an age when American Catholics were tending to see the Church chiefly in terms of her external structure, Brownson was referring to her as 'communion,' 'vital organism,' 'living body of Christ,' and 'person of Christ.' In this way, Brownson began to buck the current. . . ."[27] Because he focused on the concept of communion, Brownson viewed the church as "the congregation of the faithful," which "includes in one indissoluble whole, both clergy and laity. The clergy," he went on to say, "are not the church, but are functionaries in the Church."[28] By stressing the role of the laity in the church, Brownson was again going against the current of mainstream Catholic thinking, which emphasized the clerical, hierarchical nature of the church.

An American to the core, Brownson supported separation of church and state and regarded religious liberty as a human right. But he went further and advocated a progressive concept of religion and church which would establish harmony between religion and society, church and state. The laity would have a major responsibility in bringing about this harmonious, complementary relationship between religion and society. According to Brownson, the United States had a special destiny in the working out of this new relationship. For him, "manifest destiny" was not simply geographical expansion or political domination, but "the inauguration of a new kind of civilization, one based on Christian principles."[29] This was a special theme in American history, articulated centuries earlier by John Winthrop to his Puritan colleagues as they were about to set foot on New England soil. Since then, Americans never failed to sound the call of manifest destiny, but with Brownson it took on a new twist. Catholics, not Protestants, were the hope of America. Nation and church, religion and society were bound together in a common quest for a "higher order of civilization," and it was the destiny and responsibility of Catholics to lead the way. "The salvation of the country and its future glory depend on Catholics," Brownson wrote, "and therefore they must prove themselves superior in intelligence, independence, public spirit, all the civic virtues, to non-Catholics, or else they will do nothing to save and develop American civilization."[30]

The Paulist priest Isaac Hecker, a close friend of Brownson as well as an influential speaker and writer in the middle decades of the nineteenth century, also articulated a concept of the church quite different from the prevailing, institutional model. Influenced by Brownson, he adopted the concept of "life through Communion," by which the believer can be united with God. Hecker also focused on the spiritual nature of the church. But, for Hecker, it was the divine Spirit, the indwelling Spirit, that shaped his understanding of the church. For Brownson, the church was first of all the body of Christ, whereas for Hecker the church was primarily where the Spirit dwelled. This emphasis on the divine Spirit in the church led Hecker to stress the spiritual nature of the church more than its visible quality. Like Brownson, Hecker viewed the separation of church and state as a condition favorable to the growth of religion. In his opinion, church and state did not contradict or oppose one another; rather, they supported and complemented each other.[31]

Hecker was most eloquent when he wrote about the relationship between religion and society, or the church and what he called "the age." Hecker had a progressive notion of history; in other words, he believed that the divine Spirit becomes more manifest as history unfolds; i.e., God becomes more present in the world through the medium of the church with each passing age. Hecker's emphasis on the Spirit enabled him to conclude that the divine Spirit acts in the world through the church. For Hecker, the laity had a central role to play in the realization of God's kingdom on earth. Since the Spirit would dwell in the soul of every Christian, it was each person's duty to follow "the promptings of the Holy Spirit."[32] Such promptings would lead them to become actively engaged in the work of realizing God's kingdom on earth.

Hecker's notion of history was also very American. He believed that a new age was dawning and that the United States had a special destiny to usher in this new age for both church and world. The key to it was Roman Catholicism. According to Hecker, the destinies of the United States and American Catholicism were so bound together that Catholics alone would be able to guide the nation toward "its highest destinies."[33]

Brownson died in 1876 and Hecker in 1888. They were transitional figures, individuals living in one age whose thinking pointed to a future era. They both thought of the church as ahistorical, transcending time, and immune to change; in other words in a neo-Scholastic sense. Nevertheless, at the same time they both evidenced a historical consciousness that was unusual in the American Catholic community. A commitment to a historical, developmental view of reality was an essential ingredient in their thinking; for that reason, they were convinced that the church must adapt itself to a particular time and culture.[34]

The modern impulse in American Catholicism did not end with Hecker and Brownson. Through their essays and books, they persuaded another generation of Americans to continue the search for ways to adapt the church to the age. The major figures in this group were clergymen, including bishops, who in the 1880s and 1890s mounted what one proclaimed was "the new, the most glorious crusade. Church and age!"[35] This crusade ignited a bitter and prolonged controversy in the United States and eventually spilled over to Europe, where it threatened to challenge the old order of traditional Catholicism; then, in 1899, the "new crusade" to unite church and age (which was by then labeled Americanism) prompted a papal condemnation. The unquestioned leader of this group was John Ireland, archbishop of St. Paul. In numerous speeches, he outlined the ideology of this new crusade in which "the Church must herself be new, adapting herself in manner of life and in method of action to the conditions of the new order, thus proving herself, while ever ancient, to be ever new, as truth from heaven it is and ever must be."[36] Joining Ireland were John Keane, bishop of Richmond, Virginia, and later rector of Catholic University, and Denis O'Connell, rector of the North American College in Rome. Another prelate with a decidedly modernist impulse was John L. Spalding, Bishop of Peoria, Illinois, but he was not as actively involved in mounting the new crusade as the others. James Cardinal Gibbons, archbishop of Baltimore, was a strong supporter of Ireland and the others in their efforts to unite church and age.

Reading the speeches of John Ireland still remains a moving experience. They were powerful talks conveyed in a language and style designed to inspire his listeners. Ireland had a crusader's vision and sought to persuade others to join him in this new and glorious crusade to unite church and age. Like Hecker and Brownson, both of whom influenced his thinking, Ireland articulated an understanding of the church that differed from the prevailing one. Yet he differed from Hecker and Brownson in that his thinking focused "almost exclusively on the Church's relationship to the world, and on the Church's mission. His concern is not so much with what the church is, as with what the church does. . . ."[37] In describing what the church should do, Ireland articulated an understanding of the church in its relation to society that clearly reflected a modern, not a neo-scholastic, perspective. This is not to say that he abandoned the prevailing understanding of the church as a visible institution, transcendent and immune to change. Not at all. A typical transitional figure, living between two intellectual epochs, Archbishop Ireland embraced both neo-scholastic and modern points of view.

For Ireland, church and age were in harmony with each other; ". . . in both the self-same God" works, he said, so that "They pulsate alike." He also advocated an active laity, who "must think, work, organize, read, speak, act as circumstances demand." Quoting a line from Hecker, he stated, "Layman need not wait for priest, nor priest for bishop, nor bishop for Pope." "Laymen," he went on to say, "have in this age a special vocation."[38]

An enthusiastic Americanist, he saw "the Church and the Republic" to be "in thorough harmony." Like Hecker and Brownson, he supported the complete separation of church and state, basing his judgment on the belief that they had "separate and distinct spheres" of action. He also believed that just as America was the hope of the world, Catholics were the hope of America. Their mission was "to make America Catholic" and thereby solve "for the Church universal the all-absorbing problems with which religion is confronted in the present age."[39] This was Ireland's ultimate goal: to reform Roman Catholicism throughout the world; for Ireland, this meant Europe, and both the model and agent of reform would be American Catholicism. It was precisely this ambitious, international program that did in Ireland and his liberal colleagues.

Since Denis O'Connell did not leave a large corpus of speeches and essays, his ideas on the church are not as richly developed as Ireland's. Nevertheless, it is clear that he affirmed Ireland's vision, and when the opportunity presented itself, he did speak out on behalf of the gospel of "Americanism" that Ireland was preaching. For O'Connell, however, Americanism was more a political philosophy grounded in English common law and the American system of separation of church and state.[40] John Keane was an intellectual heir of Hecker, and thus his understanding of the church mirrored Hecker's. He stressed the importance of the Holy Spirit in defining the church, thus modifying the prevailing tendency to stress the visible, institutional character of the church. Like the others, he supported the separation of church and state and had a progressive notion of history in which the church, in adapting itself to the age, would take on a new shape as the new century dawned. For Keane, as for Hecker, the basis for this was the doctrine of divine providence, according to which God directs the progress of both church and world.[41]

John L. Spalding's corpus of essays and talks rivaled Ireland's. His intellectual interest ranged far and wide, and according to one historian, "The extent of his influence on Catholic thought was probably greater than that of any other American Catholic prelate."[42] He, too, exhibited a modernist impulse, believing firmly that "the Catholic church must fit herself to a constantly changing environment, to the character of every people, and to the wants of each age." For Spalding, this meant that such adaptation would take place in areas of church discipline as well as by "the development of the verbal forms of Christian truth."[43] He favored the American system of separation of church and state as a model for the rest of the world; he also believed that the divine Spirit was present in and active through the human soul. This was very similar to Hecker's position on the immanence of God through the Spirit dwelling in the individual.

Using a broad definition of modernism, three basic ideas emerge as central: the adaptation of religious ideas to modern culture, the idea that God is immanent in human cultural development and revealed through it, and the belief that human society is moving toward the realization of the kingdom of God.[44] Fundamental to this way of thinking was a historical consciousness which viewed religion in a developmental manner. In a nutshell, this was what modernist thought was about insofar as it referred to nineteenth-century religion. American Protestants clearly evidenced such tendencies, and so, too, did American Catholics. Cultural adaptation was a central theme to Brownson, Hecker, Ireland, and the others; an immanent God who acts in history was present most explicitly in Hecker and Keane's concept of the indwelling Spirit; Spalding's emphasis on the divine Spirit pointed in the same direction, and John Ireland implied as much throughout his writings; a progressive doctrine of providence through which the kingdom of God was being more fully realized in history was also central to their thinking, though for them as Catholics this development would take place in and through the Catholic church, which was the kingdom of God on earth. The major difference that set this group of Catholics apart from their liberal Protestant counterparts was that they focused their attention on the church and did not examine the more explosive issues of the Bible and revelation.

Though Ireland and his contemporaries in the 1880s and 1890s were consciously aware that what they were proposing was new for the Catholic Church, they did not view their "movement," as they called it, as theologically unorthodox or threatening the beliefs of Catholics. In other words, they did not fully recognize the extent of the implications their modernist impulse posed for Roman Catholicism. They were confronted with a paradox; as Ireland put it, "the Church never changes, and yet she changes."[45] They worked at reconciling this paradox by distinguishing between the absolute and the relative, essentials and accidents, but they did not have the tools—either the theological language or the historical-critical method—to deal fully with the paradox. For this reason they never completely developed the implications of their thought about the church and the age.

Ireland, Keane, and the others actively promoted their concept of the church. Many Catholics, both clergy and lay people, supported their viewpoint, and before long a school of thought, labeled "American Catholicity" by one of its critics, was making itself known.[46] Conflict was inevitable, and for the last fifteen years of the nineteenth century, liberals and conservatives engaged in a series of bitter controversies. The conservative position supported the institutional concept of the church, stressing the need for authority and order; according to this point of view, the church as a divine institution was immune to change. The liberals also accepted this view. What divided one group from the other was the conservative group's impulse to absolutize its concept of the church as visible institution; it admitted no modifications and very rigidly defined the church as the one perfect visible society. An even greater point of difference was the conservative attitude toward American society. Conservative Catholics were hostile toward Protestants, wary of government reform efforts, and alienated from the progressive thinking of the times. They were not at all enthusiastic about the opportunity of uniting church and age; for them, the church was incompatible with modern culture. Like their liberal counterparts, they were patriotic Americans and loyal citizens, but being Catholic had nothing to do with being American. Their crusade was not to unite church and age, but to strengthen the church so that it could withstand the attacks of the modern world.[47]

The leaders of the conservative wing were Michael A. Corrigan, archbishop of New York, and his long-time mentor and friend, Bernard J. McQuaid, bishop of Rochester; allied with them were most of the German hierarchy and clergy, together with the Jesuits. The conservative position was also the majority viewpoint among the rank-and-file clergy and laity. In labeling Corrigan, McQuaid, and the others as conservatives and Ireland and his colleagues as liberals, it is important to note that such simple labels of identification misrepresent the complexity of these people. At times, Ireland could behave as the most authoritarian, unenlightened pastor in Minnesota, whereas McQuaid could adopt progressive positions on clerical education and social justice. On some issues, John L. Spalding sided with Ireland, while at other times he supported Corrigan. Complicating the matter is the current state of research. A great deal of research on liberal churchmen has revealed the nature of their theology, but similar work needs to be done on the conservative clergy before a complete understanding of their thought on the meaning of the church in the modern age can be acquired. Nevertheless, it is fair to say that Corrigan, McQuaid, and their allies among the German hierarchy, together with the Jesuits, were indeed conservative in their thinking about the relationship of the church to the age. Even more clear was their opposition to Ireland, Keane, and the others, whom McQuaid accused of fomenting "a spirit of false liberalism that if not checked in time, will bring disaster on the Church."[48]

The split between liberals and conservatives began to develop in the 1880s. Division of opinion and conflicting points of view surfaced at the Third Baltimore Council, in 1884, but in the end a sense of unity prevailed. The unity was short-lived, however, and in the next fifteen years a continuous storm of controversy raged within the church. These controversies hardened party lines and served to set those whom contemporaries called liberals apart from those labeled conservatives.

The prolonged debate over parochial schools was the issue that shaped the opposing coalitions. The conservatives championed the parochial school and attacked any effort at compromise with the "Godless" public schools. The liberals sought some type of compromise with the public-school enterprise and gave more authority to the state in the realm of education than the conservatives would tolerate. Strengthening the conservative position was the support of German Catholics. Since the parochial school was a key component in the "Language Saves the Faith" campaign, they defended it with vigor. This allied them with Corrigan and McQuaid and broadened the scope of the conservative coalition. The school debate also brought the Jesuits into the conservative camp and solidified the coalition once and for all.

Another issue that bitterly divided liberals and conservatives was membership in secret societies. To a twentieth-century person, this sounds odd, but in the nineteenth century, fraternal societies were very popular and many of them had secret rituals of initiation. In Europe the classic example of this was the Masons, and they were notoriously anti-Catholic. This colored the attitude of church leaders toward secret societies in general. In the United States, the Ancient Order of Hibernians, an Irish benevolent society, was one example of such a society, as was the Knights of Columbus; the most popular labor organization in the United States in the 1880s, the Knights of Labor, also had a secret ritual of initiation. Conservative Catholics wanted to forbid their coreligionists to join these societies, while liberals were more tolerant about membership. Fearing that such societies would draw Catholic laymen away from the church, with the "lodge" becoming "a substitute for the church," conservative prelates such as McQuaid vehemently opposed them.[49] The liberals tried to avoid any blanket condemnation of secret societies because of the adverse effect such condemnation would have on the public's opinion of Catholics in the United States. Gibbons, Ireland, and Keane were able to persuade the Vatican not to condemn the Knights of Labor, but Corrigan and McQuaid got their way in 1894, when a decree came forth from Rome condemning such secret societies as the Knights of Pythias, the Odd Fellows, and the Sons of Temperance.[50]

Another area of intense debate was the attitude toward Protestants. Conservatives were generally suspicious of Protestants—and on occasion explicitly hostile—while liberals were more tolerant. For the conservative, such tolerance smacked of religious indifferentism, since Protestantism, as one of them put it, could not be "a species of the true Christian religion."[51] Fraternization with Protestants really made conservative blood boil, and when Bishop John Keane spoke at Harvard University in 1890, Bernard McQuaid was beside himself. Then, in 1893, Gibbons, Ireland, and Keane, along with other Catholic priests and laymen, took part in the international Parliament of Religions, held in Chicago. Such public collusion with Protestants, even praying with them, served to harden the lines of division between liberals and conservatives.

The controversy between conservatives and liberals was not only bitter, but it also generated public debate. Both the religious and the secular press commented on it at great length. What was at issue was not just fraternization with Protestants, membership in secret societies, or support for the parochial school. These were but singular manifestations of a larger issue, namely the attitude of the church toward the modern age. A Baptist minister captured the meaning of this controversy in a sermon he preached in Rochester in 1894:

> . . . there are two distinct and hostile parties in the Roman Catholic Church in America. One is led by Archbishop Ireland. It stands for Americanism and a larger independence. It is sympathetic with modern thought. It believes the Roman Catholic Church should take its place in all the great moral reforms. It is small, but progressive, vigorous, and brave.
>
> The other party is led by the overwhelming majority of the hierarchy. It is conservative, out of touch with American or modern ideas. It is the old medieval European Church, transplanted into the Nineteenth Century and this country of

freedom, interesting as an antiquity and curiosity, but fast losing its power and consequently, growing in bitterness.[52]

Catholic conservatives also perceived the central meaning of the controversy and viewed liberalism as a threat to the true faith. In the words of Father Thomas Preston, a chief aide to Archbishop Corrigan, "There is no more dangerous disposition, if it should ever become popular, than the belief that there is an American Catholicity which is in advance of past times, which differs materially from the faith once delivered to the Church and always preserved by her, which boasts of a freedom from restrictions which bind the ages of the past."[53] For Preston and others, more was at stake than just praying with Protestants or lecturing at Harvard.

Such division of opinion was not unusual in the United States in the late-nineteenth century. The 1880s and 1890s were tumultuous decades, distinguished by economic growth and labor conflict. Reform was in the air as progressives and populists, socialists and communists sought to build a better America. It was also a time of intellectual ferment and theological controversy. Seen in this context, a liberal-conservative debate among Catholics was right in step with the changing times. There was a difference, however. The Catholic controversy had a European dimension to it, which would make all the difference in the world. This shifted the debate from America to Europe, and eventually it involved church authorities in Rome. Moreover, the debate shifted to a more theological level and thus got at the heart of the liberal-conservative controversy. Once this happened, a domestic quarrel became an international affair.

Just about every issue that sparked debate among liberals and conservatives eventually found its way to the Vatican and forced church authorities to take a position one way or the other. Both parties lobbied in Rome to win support for their points of view. Hardly monolithic, the Vatican had prelates of equally conflicting points of view. Complicating the situation was a general liberal-conservative debate going on within European Catholicism at this time. Ireland and Keane carried their "new and glorious crusade" to Europe. Since they viewed liberal American Catholicism as the key for a renewal of the church in Europe, they traveled about the Continent speaking before sympathetic audiences, outlining their liberal Catholic platform. In France, Ireland became a folk hero among liberal Catholics, who looked upon the American republican form of government as a model for France. Complicating the issue in Italy was the question of the Pope's temporal power. Liberals, advocating a separation of church and state, did not see the wisdom of the Papacy's maintaining temporal or civil jurisdiction over a portion of Italy. But the Pope and his Italian supporters were not about to give up the Papacy's claim to temporal power.

The event that brought the issue to a crisis stage was the publication in

1897 of a French translation of a biography of Isaac Hecker written by a fellow Paulist, Walter Elliott. When Elliott's biography was first published, in 1891, complete with a glowing preface by John Ireland, it hardly created a ripple of controversy. As Bernard McQuaid said, the book "fell dead from the press."[54] But when some French liberal Catholics got hold of it and published it in France, it created an unparalleled controversy throughout Europe. Félix Klein, a French priest of the liberal persuasion, wrote a thirty-five-page Preface praising Hecker in glowing terms, comparing him favorably with such individuals as Augustine and John of the Cross, and proposed him as not only "a man of our times, but a man of the future."[55] The book was an instant bestseller and went through seven editions in a brief period of time. Liberal Catholic clergy in France liked Hecker and Ireland's understanding of the church and the age. They also favored the American system of democracy and separation of church and state; this clashed with the prevailing conservative position in France, which supported a monarchical form of government. A war of words ensued. A French priest, Charles Maignen, led the attack against the liberals and got church authorities in Rome to support his position.

Characterizing Hecker as "a victim of delusions and badly instructed in his religion and in his duties," Maignen sought to discredit Hecker and those called "the Ireland party," who were "the liberal and innovating party among American Catholics."[56] Complicating the issue even more was the outbreak of the Spanish American War in the spring of 1898. O'Connell and Ireland viewed the war as a golden opportunity to persuade Vatican authorities that the United States was a power to be reckoned with; this of course would enhance their campaign to Americanize (i.e., modernize) the church in Europe. European conservatives viewed the war differently. For them the war was a battle between the New World and the Old, and the United States was clearly a threat to the old order both politically and theologically. Thus what was once a domestic controversy became an international crisis.

All these issues—the threat of theological modernism, the temporal power of the Papacy, the French controversy between republicans and monarchists, and the Spanish-American War—came together to influence the European debate over Americanism. Given this atmosphere, it is not surprising that Pope Leo XIII sided with the conservatives and in 1899 issued a letter, *Testem Benevolentiae,* which condemned a constellation of ideas he labeled "Americanism." The Pope said that it was a French translation of "the book entitled *The Life of Isaac Thomas Hecker*" and the ideas contained therein "concerning the manner of leading a Christian life" that prompted him to issue the letter.[57] In this letter, Leo XIII condemned the concept that the Church ought to adapt its doctrine to the modern age; he also warned against the idea that the church in America could be "different from that which is in the rest of the world."[58] Then he specifically mentioned as suspicious ideas such notions as the rejection of external guidance in the spiritual life, the placing of natural virtues ahead of supernatural virtues, the suitability of active virtues for the present age, a feeling of disdain for religious life, and the desire for new ways and methods to seek converts.

The reaction in the United States was understandable. Liberals like Ireland claimed that such ideas were alien to them and never existed in the United States. Conservatives like McQuaid and Corrigan were pleased that the Pope had condemned such liberal ideas, which they believed were being promoted in the United States.

What did Leo XIII censure? He was condemning a cluster of ideas found in Klein's Preface to the French translation of the life of Isaac Hecker and reiterated in an exaggerated manner in the essays of Charles Maignen. This cluster of ideas is what Leo XIII called Americanism. Similar concepts could be found in the writings and speeches of Hecker, Ireland, Keane, Spalding, and O'Connell, to name the most noteworthy representatives of the liberal, or Americanist, mentality. All of these men espoused a liberal view when it came to defining the meaning of the church in the modern age. From this flowed certain ideas such as the espousal of active virtues, or an active, energetic laity, the dwelling of the divine Spirit in individuals, a more tolerant attitude toward Protestants, the need for the church to adapt itself to the age, and the superiority of the American version of Catholicism to that of the Old World. Though the Pope did not explicitly condemn Hecker, Ireland, or the others, the ideas he labeled as erroneous were ideas that these men had championed. Though they never fully developed them or contemplated the implications of their thinking, the liberals were promoting a cluster of ideas that were alien to the prevailing neo-Scholastic school of theology. Compounding the problem was a difference of perspective. The liberals manifested sensitivity to the idea of historical development in the area of religion, whereas in Rome the neo-Scholastics were of the classical frame of mind, which viewed religion as absolutely immune to change. Thus, the crisis over Americanism represented a clash not only between opposing cultures but also between conflicting worldviews. It was not the first time that the church in Rome and in America had experienced such a cultural conflict, nor would it be the last.

Testem Benevolentiae put an end to the "Americanism" question. John Ireland's "New and Glorious Crusade" to unite church and age was finished. But the encyclical did not close the door on the debate over the need for religion to adapt itself to modern culture. Other individuals in the United States had been pursuing this issue in a different manner, but they were not actively involved in the Americanist debate. Mostly priests teaching in seminaries, they were primarily interested in the relationship between the modern disciplines of philosophy, history, and biblical criticism and how new developments in these areas affected traditional Catholic teaching. *Testem Benevolentiae* did not halt their work, and for the first few years of the new century they continued to explore the implications of modernity for theology. But a changing of the guard in Rome and the election of a new Pope in 1903 did not bode well for the future of modern Catholic theology. As if to send a signal to the Catholic world, the new Pope, Giuseppe Sarto, took the name of Pius X, "in memory of the Popes of the same name who, in past centuries, had courageously fought against sects and rampant errors."[59]

What worried Pius X most was a movement in Catholic Europe that would eventually become known as modernism. In a very general sense, it was an attempt to reconcile traditional Catholic teachings with the new religious sciences; an effort at intellectual renewal, it sought to keep Roman Catholicism in step with the modern world. Viewed in this general sense, Americanism was clearly a part of the Catholic modernist movement. In a more specific sense, however, modernism was the self-conscious attempt of scholars to re-examine traditional Catholic teachings "on a number of fundamental points: the nature of revelation, of biblical inspiration and of religious knowledge, the personality of Christ and his true role in the origins of the Church and of its sacraments, the nature and function of the living tradition in the Catholic system and the limits of dogmatic evolution, the authority of the Church's *magisterium* and the real import of the concept of orthodoxy, the value of the classical apologetic."[60] These were explosive issues; modernist scholars knew this and realized the implications of their work but, for them, intellectual renewal demanded such a confrontation between tradition and modernity. This recognition of the threat that such thinking posed to Catholicism set them apart from earlier liberals such as Hecker and Ireland.[61]

Some of what was done in the name of modernism was legitimate and sound in principle though perhaps unconventional and seemingly dangerous, given "the baldness of their expression"; other manifestations of it "verged on the heretical" and in some cases eventually became "entirely devoid of Christian content."[62] Though France was the center of the modernist movement, it was underway in other parts of Europe as well; by the time of the new Pope's election, it had succeeded in destroying the tranquillity of the Roman Catholic world. American involvement in the movement was minimal.

Prior to 1900, the most noted episode regarding Catholic modernist thought in the United States was the condemnation of the work of the Holy Cross priest John A. Zahm, professor of physics and chemistry at the University of Notre Dame. The most able Catholic scientist of his day, Zahm had lectured widely throughout the United States on the topic of evolution; in 1896 he published these lectures in a book, *Evolution and Dogma*, wherein he vigorously advanced the idea of a theistic evolution that "admits the existence of a God, and the development, under the action of His providence, of the universe and all it contains."[63] In 1898 the Vatican censured Zahm and forced him to withdraw his book from circulation. At the time, Zahm's condemnation was entangled with the Americanist controversy, but it was a clear indication of Vatican thinking about the relationship between Catholic theology and the new sciences. Nevertheless, it did not stop Catholic scholars in the United States from pursuing their attempt at intellectual and theological renewal.

Several seminaries in the United States were centers of modernist thought, in particular St. Joseph's in New York, Catholic University in Washington, D.C., and Saint Mary's in Baltimore. Those involved were priests who taught at these and some few other seminaries. They wrote articles for scholarly journals, kept in touch with Catholic modernists in Europe through correspondence and by reviews of their work in various publications, and in general embraced the idea that traditional Catholic theology was in need of renewal. The first few years of the new century were heady times for these Catholic intellectuals, and the future appeared bright with hope.

The foremost center of such intellectual activity was St. Joseph's Seminary, in Yonkers, New York. The Sulpician Fathers had been in charge of St. Joseph's since 1896 and had succeeded in gathering together a distinguished faculty. Numbered in this group were James F. Driscoll, who from 1901 to 1909 was president of the seminary and a man considered by some to be "the best theological thinker in the United States at that time."[64] The French-born Francis E. Gigot, an accomplished Scripture scholar, was a noted member of the faculty; another Frenchman, Joseph Bruneau, S.S., taught dogmatic theology, and Francis P. Duffy and John F. Brady taught philosophy. Duffy and Brady promoted the idea of a scholarly journal, and with Driscoll's support they succeeded in publishing *The New York Review* in 1905. The *Review* was clearly the finest American Catholic theological journal published up to that time. As president of the seminary, Driscoll, who was also editor of the *Review*, encouraged intellectual inquiry by inviting notable Catholic and Protestant scholars to lecture at the seminary. He encouraged students to take courses at New York University and Columbia, and in general fostered an atmosphere that encouraged students to keep in touch with modern thought. But Pius X was Pope and he thought differently about the relationship between Catholicism and modern thought.

The ax fell in 1907, when the Pope issued his encyclical against modernism, *Pascendi Dominici Gregis.* In one fatal blow the Pope destroyed the budding renewal of Catholic theology. The encyclical spelled out in summary fashion the "errors of the modernists." But it went even further and prescribed concrete, practical remedies to combat modernism. These ranged from promoting—indeed canonizing—scholastic philosophy, to establishing a "council of vigilance" in each diocese to be on the lookout for modernist errors. Then, three years later, the Pope imposed an oath against modernism that all priests and candidates for the priesthood had to take. These actions ended the modernist crisis and cast a gloomy pall over Catholic intellectual life throughout the world. With some few, notable exceptions, Catholics accepted the decision of Pius X. But the church paid a heavy price.[65]

In the United States the effects of the condemnation of modernism soon became apparent. In 1908 *The New York Review* ceased publication. Seminaries were a special target, and soon seminary libraries closed their doors except for a few hours a week; suspicious books were removed from library shelves; secular newspapers and periodicals became forbidden reading for seminarians; intellectual curiosity was discouraged. Brain rot set in as a climate of fear gripped the academy. Some scholars took up new pursuits. Father Zahm, for example, turned to writing travel books, rather than scientific treatises. Driscoll was forced out of his position at St. Joseph's Seminary and became pastor of a New York parish. Francis Duffy also became a New York pastor and later a famous World War I chaplain. Witch-hunts to purge all vestiges of modernist thinking from Catholic seminaries began to occur. Even the slightest suspicion of modernism was enough to damage a person's reputation. The fear of heresy "settled over episcopal residences, chanceries, seminaries, and Catholic institutions of higher learning. Security, safety, conservatism became national imperatives. Free intellectual inquiry in ecclesiastical circles came to a virtual standstill. The nascent intellectual movement went underground or died. Contact with Protestant and secular thinkers was broken off. It was as though someone had pulled a switch and the lights had failed all across the American Catholic landscape."[66] A half century later, American Catholics wondered why the church had produced so few intellectuals; the answer lay scattered among the heap of rubble produced by the fallout of *Pascendi Dominici Gregis.*

The condemnation of modernism, coupled with the condemnation of Americanism, brought an end to the American Catholic romance with modernity. Conservatism had triumphed and the church now moved into a period of consolidation. Devotional Catholicism fostered an ethos that supported tradition and authority in the church. Its intimate link with the Papacy through indulgences, encyclicals, and religious congresses enveloped the Pope with a spiritual aura of authority and importance. *Pascendi Dominici Gregis* expanded this sphere of authority and put the Papacy in an unprecedented position of power. It now claimed power over the minds as well as the souls of Catholics. The popularity of devotional Catholicism facilitated this development and paved the way for the Romanization of the church in the United States. This Romanization bound the American church more closely to the Vatican and its way of thinking. The spirit of independence articulated by Carroll, England, Hecker, Ireland, and others disappeared. Novelty and pluralism were cast aside in favor of order and discipline. Rome had become not just the spiritual center of American Catholicism, but the intellectual center as .well. This put Catholics in a strange stance; they were both 100 percent American, loyal patriots to the core, and 100 percent Roman, loyal Catholics to the core. It was a unique blend of religion and nationalism which most other Americans failed to understand.

XII

Toward a Social Gospel

IN 1876 THE NATION celebrated its one hundredth birthday with a Centennial Exposition in Philadelphia. Spread across 236 acres of parkland were 180 buildings housing such technological wonders as the telephone, the typewriter, and the self-binding reaper. A nineteenth-century world's fair, the Exposition celebrated technological progress by highlighting "the glorious triumphs of skill and invention." A major attraction was the giant Corliss steam engine, which provided power for the exhibits in Machinery Hall. People strained their necks to get a good look at the twenty-five-hundred-horsepower engine that rose thirty-nine feet above the building floor. William Dean Howells, a noted essayist, called it a "giant," "an athlete of steel and iron"; in its presence, he wrote, "one thinks only of the glorious triumphs of skill and invention. . . . it is in these things of iron and steel that the national genius most freely speaks." Howells's paean to the machine age captured the meaning of the transformation that the United States was undergoing. For Howells and scores of other Americans the machine symbolized the industrial epoch that the nation was passing through.[1]

In 1820, people traveled by horse or boat, worked at home or in small shops, read by candlelight, and made their own clothes. By 1876, the railroad had replaced the horse, small shops had given way to large factories, the sewing machine had revolutionized the clothing industry, and Thomas Edison was getting ready to turn night into day with the electric light bulb. The next half century witnessed even more startling changes as "skill and invention" continued to triumph and turned the nation into the industrial giant of the world. The automobile and the skyscraper replaced the railroad and the Corliss engine as the symbols of a new age.

The Industrial Revolution had a profound impact on the lives of Americans. As the economy expanded, progress seemed natural, but the cycle of boom and bust demonstrated how fickle and fragile the economy really was. New titans of industry emerged, and names like Rockefeller and Carnegie were permanently etched into American history; alongside such great wealth was a sea of poverty that increased with each economic depression. In 1890 it was estimated that of the 12.5 million families in the United States, 11 million had an average income of less than $380 a year; and 1890 was a year of prosperity.[2] In the cities, housing became a serious problem as more and more people crowded into already congested neighborhoods. Rows of four- and five-story tenements lined city streets, and families were packed into them like sardines in a can. To make ends meet, women and children went to work for meager wages in less than desirable conditions. Workers began to protest such low wages, and soon strikes and labor violence became commonplace. To many people, the nation seemed out of joint and too high a price was being paid for the dream of prosperity and success. Each age brought forth its reformers. At mid-century some looked to the school as the key to stability and social harmony; others championed the cause of temperance as a cure to social problems. Later on, labor saw the hope of the future in organizing; others advocated better housing legislation or political reform as the hoped-for salvation. Americans wanted decent housing, less poverty, and a better life. The urge for such basic human desires launched a moral crusade, and by the turn of the century reform had become part of the American way of life. The nation entered the twentieth century riding a crest of reform enthusiasm; labeled progressivism, this reform movement captured the idealism of many people who dedicated their energies and talents to building a better world for all.

No segment of American society was left untouched by the spirit of reform, least of all the churches. Some Protestants championed such traditional reform measures as temperance, the Sunday school, and moral conversion. Others were more socially oriented and wanted to reform society itself, the economic system which, they believed, was the major cause of poverty and the unequal distribution of wealth. By the 1890s this trend became known as the social gospel. Applying the principle of the gospel to all aspects of human life—the public and social realms as well as the private and individual spheres —the social-gospel movement transformed American Protestantism. The impact of the industrial age and the spirit of reform also affected American Catholicism.

In analyzing the Catholic response to the industrial age it is clear that a definite change of attitude took place in the 1880s. In order to understand the significance of this shift it is necessary to look at the previous period, 1820–80, when industrialization and urbanization first made their impact on the United States.

As thousands and eventually millions of Catholic immigrants from Ireland and Germany settled in the United States, Catholicism became a working-class church. Made up mainly of lower-class immigrants, the church was centered in the cities and towns of the Northeast, the economic core of the nation, where industrialization had its most visible impact. Given their heavy concentration in the working class, Catholics were especially vulnerable to the fickleness of the economy and the hard times of depression. They lived close to the edge economically; the slightest turn for the worse would have serious consequences in any Catholic community. The 1830s was a case in point. Transfiguration parish was situated in New York City's Sixth Ward; an Irish parish made up mostly of working-class people, it enjoyed the people's financial support during the early 1830s. When economic depression hit in 1837, however, the climate quickly changed. People who had loaned money to the church now besieged the trustees for return of their funds; others, out of work for months and "in the utmost distress," had to sell their furniture to pay the rent; other parishioners were running out of food and sent messages "from their bed of sickness begging a small portion of their money to procure necessary food and care."[3] The finances of the parish deteriorated so badly that the church was scheduled to be sold at a public auction. When the economy collapsed again in the 1850s, Irish and German immigrants were hit hard once more. Some chose to return to the old country, rather than live in poverty in a strange city; the city's Alms House attracted large numbers of the poor, and the Irish led the way, constituting two thirds of its residents in 1858.[4] Nor was New York unique. In such large cities as Boston and Philadelphia and in small towns like Troy, New York, and Newburyport, Massachusetts, similar patterns prevailed. Given their heavy concentration in the lower rungs of the occupational ladder, Catholics were especially vulnerable to the problems and distress that accompanied the emergence of the new industrial economy. Confronted with this reality, the church, through its laity and clergy, mounted a crusade of charity.

The parish was the center around which neighborhood charitable societies were organized. The most important of these was the Society of St. Vincent de Paul. Founded in France and imported to the United States, it was first organized in America in St. Louis in 1845. Made up of laymen, its goal was "the exercise of charity in many ways, but chiefly, to visit poor families, to minister to their physical wants as far as means will admit and to give such counsel for their spiritual good as circumstances may require and to look after male orphans when they shall have left the asylum."[5] By mid-century, St. Vincent de Paul societies could be found in New York, Buffalo, Milwaukee, and New Orleans. With each passing decade, the number of local chapters increased, and by the 1880s it was the most important charitable agency in the church. Though a priest served as spiritual director, the society was the best expression of the nineteenth-century lay apostolate. Men from all walks of life joined the organization; they spent their time collecting money and visiting the homes of the poor and sick and providing them with food, clothing, and fuel. During the 1860s the society increasingly turned its attention to the care of destitute young boys, and before long child care became the principal work of the society. Another major parish organization was the mutual benefit society; it was especially popular among the Germans. Made up of laymen from the parish, its manifest purpose was to provide financial benefits to its members in times of sickness or disability. Such aid helped people cope with a loss of income during hard economic times. Prior to the 1880s, female charitable societies were not as numerous as those of men. In those years the crusade of charity on the parish level was a man's work. Some female charitable organizations did of course exist; generally they distributed clothing to the poor or sponsored annual fairs or bazaars for the benefit of the poor.

The most visible and impressive aspect of the Catholic response to the social problems of the age was the founding of hospitals and orphanages. The people most responsible for this were women religious. Recruited by bishops and priests as teachers and missionaries, women religious soon involved themselves in a variety of ministries in the local church. Care of the sick and of orphans was an area that attracted their attention from the very beginning. When the Sisters of Mercy came to Chicago, in the 1840s, they founded not only schools but also a hospital and two orphan asylums. Mercy Hospital opened its doors in 1851 and to this day remains a symbol of Catholic charity. The Sisters of Charity arrived in Milwaukee at about the same time and repeated a similar pattern by founding orphan asylums and a hospital.[6] Mother Joseph of the Sisters of Providence became a legend through her work in establishing fifteen hospitals in various cities throughout the Northwest. The dedicated service of women religious during the epidemics that periodically ravaged the nation won them public acclaim. In New York the Sisters of Charity were singled out for their work in the 1832 and 1849 cholera epidemics; when cholera struck again in 1866, hitting hardest in the immigrant neighborhoods, their services as nurses were once more requested. In San Francisco the Sisters of Mercy gained similar acclaim when cholera struck that city. By 1880, 119 Catholic hospitals were in operation, along with 267 orphan asylums.[7] That was remarkable progress in a half century and underscored the commitment of the church to the care of the sick and the orphaned. Such a commitment had been a long-standing tradition within Roman Catholicism, and it met an obvious need in an immigrant community caught up in the industrial age.

The most obvious reason for the Catholic crusade of charity was the need of the people. Poverty, sickness, and death were frequent visitors to working-class neighborhoods. Such misfortune and distress were hardly new to the United States, but in densely crowded nineteenth-century city neighborhoods their victims were very numerous, and this dramatically underscored the need for assistance. Moreover, poverty was no longer being accepted as a normal ingredient in the human community. The early-nineteenth century was a time when Americans were beginning to view poverty as a social problem, a disorder in society; with this change in attitude came a heightened sense of moral concern, which persuaded many people to work to alleviate human suffering. Numerous hospitals and public institutions to aid the orphans, the insane, the poor, and the delinquent were built during the pre-Civil War period. Through these institutions, Americans sought to correct disorders of society and in so doing bring order and harmony to the republic.[8] The proliferation of charitable institutions and the general moral concern for the plight of the poor, noble as it was, posed a problem for Catholics. The reason was obvious. The institutions and the social workers were Protestant in spirit and ethos, and this caused grave concern among Catholics. Nor was the concern illusionary. In many cities, Catholic clergy were refused admittance to public hospitals and asylums. Boston, long a citadel of anti-Catholic feeling, was a case in point. Catholic clergy were not welcome in the city's hospitals and orphanages. Even though they fought such discrimination in the courts, it was not until 1879 that priests were legally allowed to visit Catholics in such public institutions. In some cities such as Chicago and Milwaukee, where such institutionalized discrimination was absent, the needs of the community, rather than the fear of proselytization, was a major reason for establishing hospitals and asylums.[9]

The Catholic crusade for charity prior to 1880 was quite traditional. Aimed at the poor, the sick, and the homeless, its emphasis was on bettering the lot of the individual, with the guiding principle always being the salvation of souls. This was the highest law, and ". . . as for the rest, though you should be stripped of all your worldly possessions, all this is nothing if you arrive at length at the happy term of salvation." Social disorders, those "social evils which afflict mankind are the result of Adam's sin," wrote one priest, and "all reform, properly understood, begins with a return to religion and the Church."[10] Such thinking did not allow for social change and reform. According to Catholic thinking at this time, society was a static, stratified social system, and each level of this divinely designed order had its own responsibilities. John Hughes, the archbishop of New York, expressed this typically Catholic viewpoint to a Baltimore audience:

> To every class and condition [the church] assigned its own peculiar range of Christian obligations: to sovereigns and legislators, those of justice and mercy in the enactment and execution of laws. To the rich, moderation in enjoyment and liberality toward the poor. To the poor, patience under their trials and affection toward their wealthier brethren. Toward all, the common obligation of loving one another, not in word, but in deed.[11]

Since God had permitted poverty, the church had to protect the poor; as representatives of Christ, Catholics were reminded that "to extend a generous and charitable hand to a fellow creature in distress is one of the most exalting and noble acts of man." This was the motivating impulse behind the crusade for charity, and traditional though it was, Catholics distinguished themselves, laymen and women religious especially, in bringing comfort and solace to the poor, the sick, and the homeless.[12]

Such conservative social thought put Catholics out of step with any attempts at social reform during the pre-1880 period. The Protestant character of American reform movements made such a stance appear quite reasonable, given the hostile feelings between Catholics and Protestants at that time. Nevertheless, there was one reform cause to which Catholics gave their wholehearted support: temperance. Crusading for temperance was as Catholic as going to Sunday Mass. If there was poverty in society, it was because of intemperance. This was a popular American response to the social problems brought on by a flawed economy, and it fit right in with the Catholic mentality. The national president of the St. Vincent de Paul Society, Henry J. Anderson, put it very clearly: "Where there is health, temperance and industry, there cannot be poverty." It was as simple as that, and "Intemperance," Anderson went on to say, "is the great evil we have to overcome; it is a source of misery for at least three-quarters of the families we are called upon to visit and relieve."[13] Church councils urged support for the temperance movement; parish communities sponsored local temperance societies; all revival preachers had temperance sermons in their repertoires, and they administered the total-abstinence pledge to thousands of people. A national society, the Catholic Total Abstinence Union of America, was formed in 1872; its annual conventions were national rallies for temperance.

Begun in the 1830s, the temperance crusade continued into the early-twentieth century. It was the most enduring reform movement that Catholics sponsored in the nineteenth century. Of course, Catholics were not alone in their support for temperance; many Americans supported the temperance crusade as well; among Catholics it enjoyed support because it fit in not only with their conservative social thought, but also with their evangelical code of morality. Personal salvation was at the heart of the Catholic ethos, and an individual code of morality was central to this spirituality. Temperance blended in with this spirituality and became the touchstone of the Catholic moral code in the nineteenth century. It would not be an exaggeration to say that temperance was to late-nineteenth-century Catholicism what birth control was to mid-twentieth-century Catholicism: the *cause célèbre* of moral reform.

While many Americans were beating the drum of temperance, the economy was beginning to come apart. The most visible sign of this was the 1873 depression. One of the nation's worst depressions, it left one fifth of the nation's workers completely unemployed by 1877; another two fifths were able to find work for six or seven months a year, and only one fifth were working full-time. Wages were cut and working hours got longer. People lost their homes, ninety thousand in New York City alone; shantytowns sprung up, and parades of the unemployed dramatized the plight of the poor as people shouted, "Bread for the needy, clothing for the naked, and houses for the homeless." Then, in 1877, took place "the most violent and most significant labor upheaval in the nineteenth century—the Railway Strike of 1877."[14] To protest continuous wage cuts, workers with the Baltimore and Ohio Railroad went on strike in July; with tornado force the strike spread to New York, Pennsylvania, and west across the country. A nationwide protest against the injustices of the railroad industry and the miseries endured during the depression, the strike involved thousands of workers; it also involved hundreds of militiamen and federal troops. When the strike ended, in early August, less than three weeks after it began, the toll was heavy: $10,000,000 in property damage, hundreds of people dead, countless numbers injured. The violence of the strike shocked the nation, but its true significance was that ". . . it gave working men a class consciousness on a national scale."[15]

In the next quarter century, labor strikes became a way of life. In 1886 alone, 1,572 strikes took place, involving 610,000 workers; Homestead, Pennsylvania, was the site of a famous strike against the Carnegie Steel Corporation; the mining region of Coeur d'Alene, Idaho, was the scene of labor violence; Pullman, Illinois, where railroad cars were manufactured, was the scene of another violent strike, during the summer of 1894. The strikes at Homestead, Coeur d'Alene, Pullman, and hundreds of other, less notorious, places awakened the consciences of many Americans and made them more aware of and more sensitive to the social distress brought on by a flawed industrial capitalism.[16] In Congress, churches, parlors, and saloons, people debated the social consequences of the unequal distribution of wealth. The relations between labor and capital were getting worse, not better. Many Americans questioned the prevailing economic doctrine of laissez-faire, which allowed the economy to proceed naturally, with no governmental regulation or modification; for many, such a theory was not only seriously defective, but also terribly insensitive to human needs. Poverty and unemployment were the result of this misguided economic doctrine and not the result of personal sin or laziness. This was the cry of the reformers, and increasingly people accepted their reasoning and voted for a reform of the economic and social system.

It was in this atmosphere of increased labor activity and a mounting call for reform that Catholics began to evaluate their response to the new social order brought on by industrialization. For the majority, the answer seemed very clear: more charity; for others, the times demanded something more.

After 1880 the Catholic crusade for charity intensified. At the parish level, the St. Vincent de Paul Society continued to be the mainstay of the charity apostolate; by 1902 the number of parish branches of the society had increased to 428. Though this was a significant increase since the 1880s, it was evident that most parishes still did not support the St. Vincent de Paul Society. It was clearly an English-speaking organization, with heavy concentration in Irish parishes. Among Eastern-European-immigrant parishes, it was the mutual benefit organization and not the St. Vincent de Paul Society that sought to provide relief in times of economic distress. In conjunction with the St. Vincent de Paul Society, some parishes opened up employment bureaus; others provided day care for children of working mothers.[17]

Much more significant than the social apostolate of the parish was the work of citywide institutions and groups. The numbers of hospitals increased substantially, with 225 being founded between 1877 and 1906; in the next decade, another 102 were added. Women religious operated the vast majority of these hospitals; the Alexian Brothers, a unique religious order of male nurses, were also engaged in hospital work in Chicago, St. Louis, Oshkosh, Wisconsin, and Elizabeth, New Jersey. Orphan asylums also increased, and by 1910, 285 orphanages were caring for 51,938 children.[18] Women religious operated asylums for female orphans, but since the constitutions of many orders forbade them to work with boys, male religious orders of brothers ran the boys' orphanages. Industrial schools for boys to train them in the skills needed for an industrial economy were established in the 1870s and 1880s; the Christian Brothers operated such schools in New York and Philadelphia. Shelters for homeless men, where the poor could receive shelter, food, and clothing, were also established. A layman, William F. Downey, and his fellow workers in the St. Vincent de Paul Society of Washington, D.C., opened the first such shelter in 1895; several years later, Holy Name Mission situated in New York's Bowery neighborhood opened up, and in St. Louis a local pastor, Timothy Dempsey, founded Father Dempsey's Hotel for the homeless poor. The Little Sisters of the Poor opened homes for the aged poor, thirty-four of them between 1870 and 1900; the Sisters of the Good Shepherd established homes for delinquent women; the Sisters of Charity and other groups of women religious founded homes for abandoned infants and unwed mothers.[19] The charity crusade met obvious needs in an urban and industrial nation, and its scope was extraordinary. In Chicago one observer commented that it was "patent that the Roman Catholic church is unexcelled in charities."[20] The same could be said for many cities at the turn of the century. In New Orleans, for example, Catholics were supporting thirteen orphan asylums, an infant asylum, an industrial school for boys, a deaf-mute asylum, three homes for the aged poor, three hospitals, a home for newsboys, and a home for unwed mothers.[21] Such an intense commitment to works of charity had a long and noble tradition in the church and the demands made by the industrial age brought forth the best in this tradition.

A new dimension to the charity crusade after 1880 was the increased involvement of laywomen. With the emergence of a sizable middle class among Catholics of Irish and German descent, more women began to become involved in activities outside the home. The ideal and recommended type of involvement was charitable work. This was spelled out quite emphatically by a group of women who were forming a federation of women's societies in Louisiana; they resolved to "take up the work peculiar to women only, viz.: work of mercy and charity, on the lines of the St. Vincent de Paul Society, social work among the women such as establishing of girl's homes, protection of traveling girls and women, saving the wayward and fallen girls . . ."[22] Such a commitment led Catholic laywomen to organize citywide charitable organizations, and by the 1890s they were focusing their attention on the needs of the new immigrants. "They did for the new immigrants," wrote the historian of Catholic charities, "what the Vincent de Paul Society did for the older immigrants."[23] Their most notable endeavor was their involvement in the social settlement movement. The late-nineteenth century witnessed the emergence of settlement houses in the United States, the most famous being Jane Addams's Hull House in Chicago. To meet the needs of the new immigrants and to counteract the work of Addams and other Protestant humanitarians, Catholic women began to organize settlement houses in cities across the nation. In opening these homes, laywomen chose to live among the poor and provide education classes for children and adults, health-care programs, cooking classes, English-language classes, and recreation. In this way they sought to improve the "moral, physical, educational and social welfare of the people in the neighborhood." In cities such as Chicago and New York, settlement houses were established in Italian and Polish neighborhoods; in Los Angeles they served the Mexican population. By 1915, twenty-seven such settlements were in operation across the country.[24]

The crusade for charity that swept through the church in the late-nineteenth and early-twentieth centuries was rooted in traditional Catholic social doctrine. Conservative as regards social reform, its focus was individual, personal reform; in other words, it emphasized the corporal works of mercy. This differed very little from the earlier phase of the charity crusade; it meant more hospitals and more asylums; it added settlement houses and industrial schools to its list of charitable institutions and involved more women than previously. But many Catholics came to the conclusion during the 1880s that the times demanded more than charity and mercy; justice was also necessary. Though clearly a minority in the Catholic community, those who called for social justice did make an impact on the clergy and lay people, so that by the time of World War I, American Catholicism had acquired a social-gospel tradition.

The catalyst for this change was the labor movement. Before the Civil War, workers began to organize and push for better wages and a ten-hour workday. The 1860s and 1870s witnessed increased labor activity in the organization of trade unions. Since Catholics were predominantly a working-class people, they were naturally attracted to the labor movement. The Irish were especially involved. In Lynn, Massachusetts, Irish factory workers joined the shoemakers' union, the Knights of St. Crispin, in the late 1860s; in San Francisco they rallied behind their countryman Denis Kearney and the Working Men's Party in the late 1870s; a similar pattern developed in other manufacturing towns and cities.[25] But it was their involvement with the Knights of Labor in the 1880s that best illustrated the commitment of the Irish to the cause of labor and the problem this posed for clergy and bishops.

Founded in Philadelphia in 1869, the Knights of Labor reached its peak of popularity in the 1880s, when Terence V. Powderly, the son of Irish-born parents, was its grand master. One big union, it welcomed everyone into its ranks, "men and women of every craft, creed and color . . . every race worth saving."[26] It not only championed the cause of the worker, but it also preached a program of social reform. Catholics joined the Knights of Labor in large numbers; Powderly himself estimated that about two thirds of its members were Catholic and a very large percentage of these were Irish (the Knights numbered over seven hundred thousand in 1886).[27] In the Pennsylvania coalfields, large numbers of Irish workers joined the Knights of Labor. In the marble-quarry region of Rutland, Vermont, Irishmen joined the Knights of Labor local, and their pastor supported them. In De Soto, Missouri, large numbers of Irish railroad workers belonged to the Knights of Labor, and their pastor, Father Cornelius O'Leary, stood by them in 1886 when they went on strike.[28] Irish women also joined the Knights. Two of the more well known were Elizabeth Rogers and Leonora Barry. The Irish-born Rogers became active in the Chicago labor movement, and in 1882, "despite the burden of housework and a growing number of children," she became head of a local Knights of Labor chapter. Barry emerged to prominence in Amsterdam, New York, and became a noted organizer for the Knights of Labor.[29] It was obvious that wherever the Knights were organized, Irish men and women joined their ranks. Yet, such allegiance to the Knights of Labor on the part of Catholic men and women posed a serious problem for many Catholic clergy. At issue was the secrecy of the order and the quasireligious character of its initiation ritual.

Bishops and priests were suspicious of labor organizations from their very inception. Secrecy was a characteristic feature of labor organizations at the time, and this made them suspect in the eyes of the Catholic clergy; labor violence was also commonplace, and this, too, made the clergy wary of supporting labor. With the Knights of Labor, suspicion turned into open opposition. Though some clergymen were sympathetic to the Knights, the vast majority were not. Some priests even went so far as to deny the sacraments to people who belonged to the Knights; others refused them burial. Such strong opposition definitely slowed the growth of the union among Catholics and led one Knight to declare that "the greatest curse to our order seems to me to be the priest."[30] Powderly sought to defuse the opposition by having any hint of religious oath-swearing removed from the order's initiation ritual in 1881, but secrecy remained a feature of the union and so clerical opposition stood firm.

Reinforcing the Irish commitment to labor and reform was a deep strain of Irish nationalism. This became especially clear in the late 1870s and early 1880s, when the Irish in America rallied to the cause of the Land League in Ireland. The Land League, headed by Charles Stuart Parnell, sought to reform Irish society by transferring ownership of the land from a few thousand aristocratic families to the tenant farmers. The New York newspaper *Irish World* and its editor, Patrick Ford, championed the cause of the Land League and "consistently sought to link the land struggles in Ireland with social issues in the United States."[31] Terence Powderly also linked land reform in Ireland with reform in the United States and, according to Ford, represented "the joining of the Land League and American labor forces." In some Pennsylvania mining towns where clerical opposition precluded a local Knights of Labor chapter, ". . . the Land League functioned as kind of a surrogate" organization. Such Irish nationalism galvanized by the cause of the Land League clearly intensified Irish support of labor; and as the historian Eric Foner has convincingly argued, it gave rise to a strong strain of radicalism among Irish Americans.[32]

When the Land League collapsed in the early 1880s, the issue of land reform in the United States did not fade away. Henry George, a charismatic social reformer, linked the Irish love for land ownership with social reform. For George, the root cause of social disorder and distress was the ability of a few landowners to profit from rising land values. To correct this injustice and thus achieve a more equal distribution of wealth, George proposed a single tax. This single tax on the "unearned increment" of the land—that rise in land values caused by market demand, rather than by any improvement the owners made—would bring in sufficient money to ensure social progress. Utopian though it was, George's program attracted an enthusiastic response, and his book *Progress and Poverty* was widely read. One of George's strongest supporters was a New York priest, Edward McGlynn. Known as a priest of the people, McGlynn was a strong advocate of social reform. He supported the Land League and spoke at their rallies, articulating in an evangelical and appealing style a Catholic version of the social gospel. He was also a strong supporter of Henry George and his program for reform. When George unsuccessfully campaigned for mayor of New York in 1886, McGlynn actively supported him, along with Powderly and Ford. In a very poignant way, the George mayoralty campaign symbolized the fusion of labor, Irish nationalism, and social reform. These three forces had come together in the Irish Catholic community during the early 1880s and substantially changed the thinking of many people, with the result that by the 1880s the Irish as a group stood firmly behind the labor movement.

The change taking place among the Irish was notable in other segments of the Catholic community as well. By the mid-1880s, the Catholic press, including both newspapers and journals of opinion, was much more sympathetic to the cause of labor and social problems than it had been a decade earlier. It was also more critical of laissez-faire economics and the injustices it caused in society. Clearly the 1880s was a heady time for all Americans. The depression of the 1870s and the great strike of 1877 ushered in a climate of crisis and an urge for reform. Labor was riding a wave of popularity, and criticism of capitalism and laissez-faire economics had become more commonplace. Catholic lay men and women, the Irish especially, were heavily committed to this call for reform. Nevertheless, some Catholic bishops still remained opposed to labor and social reform. One strong opponent was Peter Kenrick, archbishop of St. Louis. He showed his opposition by reprimanding Father Cornelius O'Leary for his support of the Knights of Labor in De Soto, Missouri, and transferring him out of town to another parish. Archbishop Corrigan of New York was strongly opposed to the work of Edward McGlynn on behalf of the Land League and Henry George; after repeated attempts to curb the work of McGlynn, he suspended him in 1886 from his priestly ministry. This created a public uproar in New York. Such actions tended to confirm the suspicion of many Americans that the Catholic hierarchy was opposed to labor and social reform. Fortunately the majority of bishops were not so reactionary.[33] They began to follow the lead of the people by supporting labor unions and economic reform. The most dramatic and symbolic incident in this regard was the intervention in Rome of James Cardinal Gibbons on behalf of the Knights of Labor.

At the request of Archbishop Taschereau of Quebec, the Vatican had issued a ruling in 1884 that forbade Catholics to belong to the Knights of Labor. Most American bishops interpreted this as applying to Canada only and were reluctant to prohibit Catholics from joining the Knights of Labor, but Taschereau forced their hand by asking Rome to make the condemnation universal. At this juncture, Gibbons, who had previously counseled "a masterly inactivity and a vigilant eye" in the whole affair, decided to act. When in Rome in February 1887 to receive the red hat, the symbol of his recent elevation to the College of Cardinals, Gibbons presented Vatican officials with a lengthy statement defending the rights of workers to organize and urging that the Knights of Labor not be condemned. Written by Bishops John Ireland and John Keane and signed by Gibbons, the statement marked a major turning point in the church's position on labor and social reform.

The document recognized the "social evils, public injustices . . . heartless avarice" that plagued the nation, and the need, indeed the right, of workers to organize. It was foolish to think, stated Gibbons, that the "struggle of the great masses of the people against the mail-clad power which . . . often refuses them the simple rights of humanity and justice" and their desire for "organizing which is their only hope of success" can be deterred. Prudence forces the church to accept this fact of life. Then, in a manner quite typical of Gibbons and his episcopal collaborators, the document in a very shrewd political move went on to point out the consequences of a condemnation. As in Europe, the working class would become estranged from the church, souls would surely be lost, public opinion would turn against Catholics in the United States, the revenues of the church "would suffer immensely" (the effect of which would be felt in Rome), and the Holy See would be looked upon "as a harsh and unjust power." To prove his point, Gibbons cited the public outcry against the suspension of McGlynn; such deplorable consequences resulted "from the condemnation of only one priest, because he was considered to be the friend of the people, . . . what will not be the consequences to be feared from a condemnation which would fall directly upon the people themselves in the exercise of what they consider their legitimate right?"[34]

A year and a half later, the Vatican finally rendered a decision. It lifted the ban on the Knights of Labor and stated that the organization could be tolerated on the condition that the Knights revise their constitution in order to omit any references "which seem to savor of socialism and communism."[35] Hardly a resounding endorsement of labor, it was an approval of the Knights, nevertheless. More important, the American public perceived Gibbons's defense of the Knights and Rome's favorable decision as a victory for labor. Thenceforth, the leadership of the Catholic Church in the United States would officially be on the side of labor. This was a dramatic turnabout. For the first time, the bishops stood behind the people in their commitment to the cause of labor. This marked the first step in the formation of a Catholic social-gospel tradition.

The late 1880s witnessed the decline of the Knights of Labor and the emergence of the American Federation of Labor. Founded in 1886, the A.F. of L. was a federation of national craft unions. Unlike the Knights, it had no secret oaths or religious-like rituals. Though Samuel Gompers, a Jewish cigar maker, was the principal founder of the A.F. of L., the Irish soon rose to prominence in the union. They often occupied leadership positions at the local level, and at the national level they "occupied the presidencies of more than 50 of the 110 unions in the American Federation of Labor" by the first decade of the twentieth century.[36] The new immigrants from Eastern Europe also supported the labor movement by joining unions. The Polish who worked in the meat-packing industry in Chicago's Stockyards district joined the meatcutters' union along with Irish, Lithuanians, and Germans; Irish women led the struggle to form a women's union in the Stockyards, and once the union was formed, "Slavic women, especially the Poles, joined in large numbers." In the coalfields of Pennsylvania, Polish, Lithuanian, Slovak, and Ukrainian immigrants were in the forefront of labor protests and became members of the United Mine Workers of America. Mexican miners and farmworkers joined labor unions in the Southwest.[37] Such widespread participation of Catholics in the labor movement at both leadership and rank-and-file levels made it expedient for bishops and clergy to support labor unions. To do otherwise would have been institutional suicide, as Cardinal Gibbons wisely pointed out in his memorial to Rome. Thus, by the turn of the century, ". . . the acceptance of organized labor was complete" within the Catholic church. The press, with few dissenting voices, defended the cause of labor during the Homestead strike of 1892 and the Pullman strike of 1894. Along with the customary condemnation of violence was a strong endorsement of the workers' rights to organize and to strike, together with an advocacy of settlement by arbitration. Catholic journalists were also more critical of the abuses of industrial capitalism and laissez-faire economics.[38] The commitment of the Catholic laity to the labor movement, together with Gibbons's strong defense of the Knights of Labor, were among the major reasons for this change in thinking. Another major influence was the publication in 1891 of the papal encyclical *Rerum Novarum*.

Compared to his predecessor, Pius IX, Pope Leo XIII was a progressive church leader. *Rerum Novarum* was an excellent example of such progressivism. Drawing upon a European tradition of social Catholicism, *Rerum Novarum* sought to analyze the conditions of labor in the modern world and offer a program of reform based on the concept of social justice. The Pope condemned socialism, the perceived archenemy of the church and the main target of the encyclical, but he also spoke out against the excesses of capitalism and individualism. In addition, he upheld the right to private property, the right of workers to organize, and the need for the intervention of the state to protect the rights of the people. Such an endorsement of the labor movement and the concept of social justice by the Papacy would ultimately have "a truly epoch-making effect in driving home the idea that Catholics must have a social conscience and above all that they must actively concern themselves with the conditions of workers."[39]

The initial American reaction to the encyclical was quite favorable. Labor unions now appealed to papal authority for support of their cause; Protestant social-gospel advocates welcomed the publication of the encyclical; Catholic church leaders were also enthusiastic. Bishop John L. Spalding observed that the encyclical drove home the point that "the mission of the church is not only to save souls, but also to save society." In the diocese of Rochester, New York, Bishop McQuaid had the encyclical read from the church pulpits on successive Sundays; in other dioceses, the Catholic press publicized its message.[40] In 1893, a national Catholic congress of laity and clergy met in Chicago. This was the second of two such national congresses organized by the laity. The first was held in Baltimore in 1889. Unlike at Baltimore, both men and women participated in the Chicago congress, and for three days they discussed the Pope's encyclical and the social question in general. The bulk of the resolutions adopted by the participants were related to social issues; progressive in tone, they were both prolabor and procapital; the St. Vincent de Paul Society and the cause of temperance were also singled out as potent remedies to social problems.[41]

On a national level, it is difficult to find any further recognition of the Pope's social encyclical. Initially it was welcomed with enthusiasm, but within a few years it was put on the shelf to gather dust. There were several reasons why the encyclical failed to ignite a Catholic crusade for social justice. First of all, social justice was not a burning issue for the church's episcopal leaders in the 1890s. They were concerned with internal disputes—Cahenslyism, the school debate, Americanism, to name a few—and the social question was not a priority. Furthermore, these internal disputes had badly divided the hierarchy into factions, and such division precluded any united effort on behalf of social justice. The 1890s and the early-twentieth century was also a time when conservatism was on the rise in the church, and this school of thought was generally suspicious of social reform. The 1890s was also the heyday of the anti-Catholic organization the American Protective Association, and church leaders were busy defusing their attacks. In addition, the ideology of social conservatism, which emphasized charity, rather than justice, was still the dominant force in shaping Catholic social thought. Devotional Catholicism, the bedrock of Catholic piety, was also a factor; it nurtured a private, personal religion, not a religion with social consequences. Thus, for most Catholics the crusade for charity was judged to be a more than adequate response to the social question. A crusade for justice would have to wait for another time.

Another key reason why Catholics failed to use the encyclical as a catalyst for a crusade for justice was that intellectually they had no tools, no methodology, by which they could adapt its abstract universal principles to the American scene. Catholics were devoid of any intellectual system at this time that would have allowed them to do this. The response of Gibbons and other church leaders to labor unions and reform was rooted in expediency and not in intellectual principles. The historian Mel Piehl has argued this point very convincingly:

> The problem for Protestantism was how to reach a lower class with whom it had little in common; for Catholicism, it was to keep abreast of the pressing demands from a working-class membership eager for its ministrations. American Catholicism's encounter with industrialization, therefore, was more institutional and practical than intellectual or moral, more an unconscious necessity than a conscious choice. Its leaders were not a minority of articulate prophets challenging accepted beliefs, but numerous clergy and laypersons who seldom understood or proclaimed their activities as a distinctly religious response to industrialization. Many Catholics, therefore, had a long experience in coping with social problems before they began to reflect on them.[42]

The principal way in which bishops and priests appropriated the encyclical was as another arrow in their quiver to use in the battle against socialism. Like most papal encyclicals, *Rerum Novarum* was open to a variety of interpretations: it had an anticapitalist, prolabor perspective as well as an antisocialist, proprivate-property perspective. American bishops and priests focused on the latter and ignored the Pope's criticism of capitalism and his call for social reform. This was not surprising, given the antisocialist tradition of Catholicism. Church leaders had continually battled the evils of socialism.[43] Pius IX had condemned it; Leo XIII had issued an encyclical against socialism in 1878, and this served to heighten Catholic opposition. Their negative attitude toward socialism had made American Catholic bishops very suspicious of labor unions and helps to explain their initial distrust of the Knights of Labor. It also made them wary of any reform movement, such as Henry George's single-tax program, that threatened the sanctity of private ownership of land.[44] The antisocialist emphasis of *Rerum Novarum* appeared to justify their concern, and for the next quarter century, church leaders, progressives as well as conservatives, waged a continuous crusade against socialism.

The formation of the Socialist political party in 1901 brought unity to the socialist movement, but this served to intensify the opposition and to escalate the rhetoric. Bishops issued pastoral letters condemning socialism because, as the socially liberal prelate James E. Quigley wrote, it "denies the existence of God, the immortality of the soul, eternal punishment, the right of private ownership, the rightful existence of our present social system, and the independence of the Church as a society complete in itself and founded by God." Archbishop Sebastian Messmer of Milwaukee, where socialists were especially strong, warned Catholics that "A man cannot be a Catholic and a Socialist."[45] German Catholics were especially sensitive to the issue, since socialism was very popular among the Germans. The German Central Verein was an important national organization which had not been terribly interested in the social question, but the rise of socialism brought fear to the hearts of German Catholics. This "Fear of socialism was perhaps the most important single factor in turning the attention of the German-American Catholics to the social question" and making the Central Verein one of the most socially conscious Catholic organizations in the early-twentieth century.[46]

The sacredness of private property in the modern Catholic tradition was a key reason for the church's opposition to socialism. Adding fuel to the fire was the strident anticlerical and antichurch position of many socialist leaders. For socialists like Eugene Debs and Victor Berger, the Catholic Church was "the implacable foe of socialism," because it had a vested interest in capitalism. Other attacks on the church were more virulent and served to heighten the fear of socialism among Catholics.[47] Nevertheless, not all Catholics were opposed to socialism. Father Thomas J. Hagerty from Las Vegas, New Mexico, joined the socialist cause and became a very popular lecturer; in fact, one contemporary stated that he was "without a doubt the brainiest and certainly one of the most eloquent speakers in the Labor and Socialist movement in the world." Another popular lecturer and advocate of socialism was Father Thomas McGrady of Bellevue, Kentucky. Hagerty and McGrady were the exceptions, however.[48] Eventually both men left the ministry and the church. More telling than the conversion of Hagerty and McGrady to socialism was Catholic support for socialist political candidates. Milwaukee was the best example of this. For a number of years in the twentieth century, the Socialist party ran the city of Milwaukee; they were able to do this because Irish, Polish, and German Catholics voted for the Socialist ticket despite the protestations of bishops and clergy.[49]

A significant development in the 1890s was the increased involvement of clergy in the labor movement. This marked the beginning of the labor-priest tradition. The popularity of the Knights of Labor among Catholics had forced the clergy to reexamine their generally hostile attitude toward labor unions; the subsequent coming of age of the labor movement and the heavy participation of Catholics kept the issue alive. Gibbons's defense of labor, together with the Pope's endorsement in *Rerum Novarum*, also influenced the thinking of the clergy. More and more became sympathetic to unions and the struggles of workers against the large monopolies of coal, oil, and steel. Others went beyond just being sympathetic, however, and adopted an aggressive advocacy role on behalf of labor. Such individuals would later become known as labor priests. The prototypes of the labor priests were most visible during the time of a strike.

During the coal strike of 1902, ". . . practically all of the priests" in the Pennsylvania mining region "were solidly behind the strike." Some of the priests had worked in the mines themselves and personally understood the workers' grievances. Especially prominent was John J. Curran of Wilkes-Barre. Known as "the miners friend," he worked closely with John Mitchell, head of the United Mine Workers of America, and even went to the White House to intercede with President Theodore Roosevelt in order to bring about a settlement of the strike.[50]

Work in Chicago's Stock Yards came to a halt in 1904 when the meatcutters' union went on strike. As in the coal mines of Pennsylvania, most of the strikers were immigrant Catholics. Priests in the stockyard neighborhoods supported the strikers; some went further and tried unsuccessfully to arbitrate a settlement.[51] Father Thomas H. Malone of Denver, Colorado, was a strong advocate of trade unionism and wielded significant influence among Irish workers. In the great steel strike of 1919, the clergy were again active. One of the more well known was the Slovak priest Adelbert Kazincy, pastor of St. Michael's Church in Braddock, Pennsylvania. Together with other priests and ministers, Kazincy supported the strikers. Hundreds of steelworkers attended his morning Masses and evening talks. His sermons boosted the workers' morale and won Kazincy a legendary reputation.[52] Some few bishops were also becoming involved. Bishop James E. Quigley of Buffalo actively supported the labor movement and successfully arbitrated a local dock strike in 1899 after all other efforts had failed. Bishop John L. Spalding of Peoria served on the presidential commission appointed to arbitrate a settlement of the 1902 coal strike.[53]

Unquestionably one of the more charismatic labor priests at the turn of the century was Peter C. Yorke of San Franciso. Born in Ireland, Yorke entered the seminary at Maynooth to prepare for the priesthood. Like many of his contemporaries, he applied for a diocese in the United States and was accepted by the archbishop of San Francisco. Soon after his arrival in San Francisco, in 1888, he began to make his mark. He was appointed editor of the local Catholic newspaper and gained notoriety for his spirited defense of Catholicism against the anti-Catholic attacks leveled by the local American Protective Association. Then, in the summer of 1901, a major strike closed the port of San Francisco, which had long been a union stronghold. The city's major employers decided in the spring of 1901 to band together and crush the labor movement. A confrontation was inevitable, and it took place in July 1901 with a lockout of union workers. A strike ensued and the usual pattern of events took place: strikebreakers were recruited to replace the union workers, violence erupted, the police intervened, and violence escalated. By early September, business in the city had come to a standstill; twenty thousand people were out of work and two hundred ships lay idle in the harbor. Local leaders sought a settlement, and after much negotiation the strike ended in early October. A major actor throughout the strike was Father Yorke.[54]

Yorke joined the cause of the workers early on and provided them with leadership throughout the long weeks of the strike. He helped to plan strike strategy and composed much of the written material published on behalf of labor during the strike. He gave public lectures and donated the admission fee to the strike fund. A morale booster and fund raiser, he also played a major role in bringing about a settlement of the strike. Yorke's most effective intervention, however, was on the lecture platform. He was a gifted orator and used his skills to the utmost during the strike. His popularity was such that people packed the halls to hear him speak. In supporting the strikers, Yorke appealed to the encyclical *Rerum Novarum.* This became his labor bible, and he never ceased to refer to it in his personal campaign on behalf of labor. What is especially important is that Yorke emphasized the natural-human-rights tradition that Leo XIII had incorporated into his defense of the workers. This was an important step. Supporting labor was no longer the pragmatic, expedient thing to do; according to *Rerum Novarum,* such support was rooted in the natural-law tradition, and the organization of labor unions was a natural human right, not a pragmatic concession to troubled times. This was the intellectual principle that progressive Catholics needed in order to build a social-gospel tradition. Yorke was one of the first to apply it to the labor movement.[55]

In later years, Yorke continued to champion the cause of labor in San Francisco. He took their side when they went on strike; he founded a newspaper, the *Leader*, which was explicitly prolabor. A man of many talents, he was an educator, orator, Irish Nationalist, and labor priest. But it was his work on behalf of labor for which he was most remembered. At his death in 1925 a San Francisco labor newspaper memorialized him with the epitaph "Father of the organized labor movement of San Francisco."[56]

Like McGlynn of New York, Malone of Colorado, and many other priests actively involved in the cause of labor and social reform, Yorke was an ardent Irish Nationalist. For these people, labor struggles and economic oppression in the United States were linked to the struggles of the old country; by making this connection, their appeal to Irish workers became more intensely nationalistic, and this helped to galvanize opposition against their oppressors. Furthermore, the appeal of men like McGlynn and Yorke was most popular among the working class Irish, a distinct group within the larger Irish-Catholic community. These were the lower class, the shanty Irish, as they were derisively referred to by their middle-class, lace-curtain-Irish detractors. San Francisco offered a good example of this class division within the Catholic community. Yorke and the union men who went on strike in 1901 represented working-class Irish Nationalists; they had developed their own culture, which was very ethnocentric and set apart from the more middle-class Irish. The archbishop of San Francisco, Patrick Riordan, and the mayor, James D. Phelan, both Irish Catholics, represented the upper-class Irish Catholic community, the economically and socially successful. They supported the employers in the strike of 1901, and their antiunion sympathies clearly set them apart from the working class. Irish by descent, they were American in aspiration, concerned with fitting into American society. They shunned the radicalism and ethnocentrism of the working class. A similar division was present in New York City during the 1880s and 1890s; Father McGlynn was a folk hero among the Irish working class and the nationalists who supported the Land League and the single-tax campaign of Henry George. The archbishop, Michael A. Corrigan, was not at all sympathetic to the Knights of Labor and found support for his views among the Irish-dominated Tammany Hall Democrats, whose political fortunes were threatened by George and McGlynn. As both New York and San Francisco suggest, the Irish-Catholic community was a house divided. To ignore this is to fall prey to the facile generalization that Irish Catholics were conservative on social issues; that is a half-truth. The middle- and upper-class Irish best fit this description, whereas the working class—the miners, teamsters, meatcutters, laborers—evidenced a strong impulse for reform. A similar division can be seen among the clergy; most bishops were moderates or conservatives as regards social issues; among the parish clergy, however, the tradition of the labor priest was emerging. Such distinctions must be made in order to understand more accurately the history of social Catholicism in the United States. This said, it is also important to realize that labor priests were few and far between in the early-twentieth century. The vast majority were concerned more with charity than with justice, with parochial schools, rather than labor unions. As for the workers themselves, the vast majority did not belong to a union and were not as class conscious as the more nationalistic segment of the Irish community.

In the early years of the twentieth century, by 1910 or so, a definite shift had occurred in the Catholic community. The labor movement still attracted large numbers of Catholic men and women, and most priests and bishops remained sympathetic to their cause. But Catholics were moving beyond labor and beginning to support other types of social reform. Like many Americans, Catholics were caught up in a spirit of reform that was capturing the popular imagination. Labeled progressivism, it was a reform movement made up principally of the new middle class emerging at the turn of the century; educated men and women, they believed in progress and the ability of people to fashion a better world. Centered in the cities, it focused on such urban issues as poverty and housing, along with political and educational reform. Most often, people found their agency of change in the voluntary organization, an institution that had become very popular as the nation moved toward more organization and centralization in virtually every area of American life.

The influence of progressivism on the Catholic crusade for charity was very visible. For some time, people in the St. Vincent de Paul Society realized the need for better coordination and organization of relief efforts. William Mulry, a New York layman, was especially active in this regard and worked closely with the Charity Organization Society in New York. Along with other Vincentians, he pushed for some type of national organization that would guide Catholic charity work. The desire for organization was also present among large numbers of laywomen active in the charity apostolate. At the local level, some bishops were beginning to organize their numerous charity programs around a central office so that the charity crusade would become better coordinated and more efficient. These local efforts at organization finally blossomed into a national organization, the National Conference of Catholic Charities. Father William Kerby, a professor of sociology at Catholic University, was a major force in the organization and subsequent development of the Catholic charity movement. Kerby advocated a more professional, more scientific approach to charity; in the classroom and on the lecture circuit he educated a new generation of Catholic charity workers.[57] In addition to organization, the charity crusade also began to shift its focus beyond individual relief work to the more basic issue of the causes underlying poverty and the social distress associated with it. Called "preventive charity," its rationale was that poverty has "its origins in economic, social or industrial conditions which are inherently wrong but against which the poor are power-less to protect themselves." Therefore, as one charity worker said, "There is a very sacred duty resting upon us to throw our power into the unequal conflict on the side of the weak and oppressed against the power of the unscrupulous strong who habitually exploit for their own gain the needs of their less fortu-nate neighbor."[58] This was a far cry from the traditional view, which under-stood poverty not only as part of the divine plan, but also as a personal fault. This environmental or social view of poverty was characteristic of the pro-gressive movement, as was the desire for organization and professionaliza-tion. The crusade for charity had clearly taken a new turn in the twentieth century and set forth a new agenda for the next half century.

Another indication of the Catholic shift toward progressive reform was the organization of the American Federation of Catholic Societies in 1901. For some years, Catholic laymen and laywomen had sought to organize them-selves on a national level in order to have a more substantial influence on church and nation. The Catholic Congress in Baltimore in 1889 and another one four years later in Chicago were the direct result of such thinking. The hierarchy, however, with Cardinal Gibbons being the chief protagonist, suc-cessfully put an end to the lay-congress idea. But the desire for organization remained, and in 1901 a group of national Catholic organizations formed the American Federation of Catholic Societies. An enthusiastic supporter of the Federation was James A. McFaul, bishop of Trenton, New Jersey; together with Sebastian Messmer, the archbishop of Milwaukee after 1903, McFaul provided the Federation with the necessary episcopal patronage and support. Composed of middle-class men, and after 1912 of women as well, the organi-zation was a clear-cut example of Catholic progressivism. Its stated objectives were "the cementing of the bonds of fraternal union among the Catholic laity and Catholic societies of the United States; the fostering of Catholic interests and works of religion, piety, education and charity; the study of conditions in our social life; the dissemination of the truth and the encouragement of the spread of Catholic literature and of the circulation of the Catholic Press."[59] Its goal was to build a Christian America, one built on Catholic principles. To achieve this, they promoted the moral reformation of society, focusing on such evils as intemperance, violation of the Sabbath, and divorce. In many respects, the Federation had the same dream as many evangelical Protestants who were engaged in their own crusade to build a Christian America. After 1910 the Federation adopted a program of social reform that focused on the labor issue. The person most responsible for this shift was Peter E. Dietz.[60]

Son of German-born parents, Dietz was a priest of the diocese of Cleve-land, Ohio. Since his days in the seminary, he had had an interest in the social question, and after his ordination in 1904 he began to become actively in-volved in the labor movement. At first he joined forces with the Central

Verein, the leading German Catholic organization at the time. Unfortunately he had a basic disagreement with Frederick P. Kenkel, the new progressive leader of the Central Verein. Kenkel's vision of social reform required "a fundamental restructuring of society and a concomitant reordering of attitudes and values so that human life could again be lived in something like the organic, integrated community that had obtained in the Middle Ages."[61] Dietz's vision focused on the role of labor unions in solving social problems. Less utopian than Kenkel, Dietz wanted action-oriented programs. Pushed out of the Central Verein, he brought his talents and agenda to the American Federation of Catholic Societies and succeeded in turning the vision of this group toward active support for labor unions. Prior to Dietz, the Federation had evidenced mild support for labor more as a consequence of its strong antisocialist stance than as a prolabor commitment. With Dietz now guiding the Federation's Committee on Social Reform, the organization became a strong advocate of labor unions. Through lectures, pamphlets, and books, it sought to educate Catholics on the social question; it also put the support of the Federation, about three million members strong in 1912, behind legislation favoring labor and related reform issues. This emphasis on education and legislation was characteristic of progressive reformers. Dietz also strengthened the ties between the Federation and the heavily Catholic American Federation of Labor. To this end, he organized the Militia of Christ for Social Service in 1910; composed of Catholic union men, it sought to build a bridge between the church and labor unions.[62]

During this era of reform enthusiasm, there emerged a person who more effectively than anyone else blended together the spirit of progressivism and Catholic social thought. This was John Ryan. The oldest of eleven children, Ryan was born in 1869 to Irish immigrant parents who lived in the small farming community of Vermillion, Minnesota. John Ryan grew up in an environment where populism and reform were topics of table talk. A subscription to Patrick Ford's *Irish World*, published in New York, not only kept the Ryan family in touch with life back home in Ireland, but it also heightened their sense of Irish nationalism and their taste for social reform. As Ryan later acknowledged, "One could not read the *Irish World* week after week without acquiring an interest and a love of economic justice, as well as political justice."[63] This interest in economic justice was the main sail of Ryan's life.

After ordination to the priesthood in 1898, Ryan went to Catholic University for further studies in moral theology. His doctoral dissertation, "A Living Wage," was published in 1906 and included a laudatory preface by the well-known economist Richard Ely. Like Ely, Ryan argued that moral principles should shape economic policies; in his book he argued that "wages should be sufficiently high to enable the laborer to live in a manner consistent with the dignity of a human being."[64] The book, an excellent synthesis of morality and economics, was well received. The success of his book and Ryan's commitment to "social doctrine in action" propelled him into the reform movement. His work as a professor of moral theology at St. Paul's Seminary in St. Paul, Minnesota, kept him busy much of the year, but he found time to write numerous articles for Catholic publications on the issue of social reform; he also became a popular speaker on the lecture circuit. He allied himself with such other Catholic reformers as Dietz and Kerby and supported the reform thrust of the American Federation of Catholic Societies and the National Conference of Catholic Charities. A typical progressive, he mingled freely with reform groups not associated with the church and became a recognized advocate of minimum-wage legislation. He helped to write the new minimum-wage law in Minnesota and testified on behalf of similar laws in numerous states. Such activity "enhanced Ryan's reputation among re-formers. His phrase, living wage, had shown up in quotation marks in the platform of the Progressive Party in 1912. In the fight for state legislation, no name was more common than his. He was on the committee of the National Consumers' League that drew up the model bill on which many state laws were based."[65] In addition to all this involvement, Ryan found time to write another major book, *Distributive Justice: The Right and Wrong of Our Present Distribution of Wealth.* Published in 1916, it represented his major synthesis of ethics and economics. With the publication of this book, ". . . the basic frame of Father Ryan's program for social justice was set" and the best of his serious scholarly work was completed.[66]

The genius of Ryan was his ability to merge Catholic social thought with the American current of reform. The basis for this merger was the natural-law tradition. With Pope Leo XIII, the natural law had become the founda-tion of Catholic social ethics in a new and fresh manner. Ryan took this aspect of papal social thought, best articulated in *Rerum Novarum,* and sought to apply it to the American economic and industrial environment. This link with the natural-law tradition explains Ryan's insistence on natural human rights and the dignity of the individual person. Such insistence placed him in the mainstream of American reform thought, though, all the time, he insisted—and rightly so—that he was following the thrust of *Rerum Novarum,* the Magna Charta of Catholic social thought. From the basic prin-ciple of the natural law flowed Ryan's emphasis on a living wage, the impor-tance of labor unions, and the need of the state to intervene and effect change in the social order. These were both progressive and Leonine principles. Ryan brought them together in a meaningful and convincing manner and gave to American Catholics the foundations of a social gospel. Prior to him, Catholic reformers had operated more from the principle of expediency, what the times demanded, than from principles articulated in a coherent social ethics. Ryan changed that by formulating a system of social ethics that was both very Catholic and very American. Thenceforth, the natural-law tradition would become the keystone of American Catholic social thought.[67]

The outbreak of World War I gave the Catholic hierarchy an opportunity to demonstrate its patriotic Americanism, and the bishops did so with vigor. They supported President Woodrow Wilson in his crusade "to make the world safe for democracy"; they sponsored Liberty Bond rallies; they sought to boost the morale of the people at home and the spirit of the troops abroad. To bring unity to the Catholic response, the bishops established the National Catholic War Council in 1917; throughout the war, the council coordinated Catholic participation in the war effort both at home and abroad. Once the war ended, people began to look toward the reconstruction of American society, and numerous groups, religious as well as secular, put forth plans for postwar reconstruction. The Catholic bishops wanted to present their own program of social reconstruction, and they set up a committee to draft a document. Father John O'Grady, secretary of the Committee on Reconstruction, had the responsibility to produce such a plan. He turned to John Ryan, who at the time was writing his own program of reconstruction; Ryan had hoped to present it in a speech in Louisville, Kentucky, but "realized that it was much too long for an address on such an occasion." O'Grady saw the unfinished talk on Ryan's desk and, after reading it, begged and pleaded with Ryan to expand it. Ryan reluctantly agreed. "Inasmuch as he seemed to be in a hurry to get to production," wrote Ryan, "I refrained from rewriting it and merely dictated with a few verbal corrections the contents of the pencil draft to the operator of a typewriting machine and added a final carefully written paragraph."[68] In February 1919 it appeared as the "Bishops' Program of Social Reconstruction." Without a doubt it was "the most forward-looking social document ever to have come from an official Catholic agency in the United States."[69]

Thoroughly progressive and explicitly Catholic, the Bishops' Program sought to adapt the "principles of charity and justice . . . to the social and industrial conditions and needs" of the times.[70] In a rambling style it advocated minimum-wage legislation; a minimum working age; public housing; laws enforcing the right of labor to organize; insurance against old age, sickness, and unemployment; regulation of public utility rates; control of monopolies; and a partnership between labor and management through cooperative enterprises and worker ownership of the stock of corporations.

The public reaction to the doctrine was very favorable. Its release, on Lincoln's birthday, was but one calculated step in an elaborate publicity campaign orchestrated by the press agent of the National Catholic War Council. The campaign paid off, and its publication generated unusual interest among Catholics and Protestants alike. For many years, Americans had looked upon the Catholic Church as conservative on social issues. Thus, the bishops' statement took many people by surprise. People were amazed that the Catholic hierarchy could be so socially progressive. The progressive secular press ex-pressed "incredulous delight" with the document; liberal Protestants re-sponded favorably, as did labor leaders. Upton Sinclair called it nothing less than a "Catholic miracle."[71] Not everyone, however, was as impressed. Some bishops feared its socialistic tendencies and its endorsement of the positive role of the state on behalf of social legislation. The reaction of big business was particularly hostile, but Ryan and Bishop Peter J. Muldoon of Rockford, Illinois, defended the document as both Catholic and American. Muldoon was especially instrumental in the publication and defense of the document. He was chairman of the committee that administered the National Catholic War Council and was the bishop most responsible for the publication of the Bishops' Program. Socially progressive, he represented a new generation of bishops who had come of age during the progressive period and were very much in support of social reform.

Catholics had come a long way since the days of John Hughes. The concept of justice was now central to their program of reform; in addition to a deeply engrained tradition of personal religion, a new dimension of public religion, or what can be called a social gospel, became part of the Catholic tradition. Catholics were now known not just for what they opposed—socialism—but also for what they advocated: social reform. Three major events stood out in this transition. The first was Gibbons's defense of the Knights of Labor; another was Pope Leo XIII's encyclical *Rerum Novarum;* and the final one was, of course, The Bishops' Program of Social Reconstruction. These were the high points of a transformation that took place over the course of some thirty years and more. During this period, the labor movement had come of age; a progressive reform movement had captured the imagination of Ameri-cans; Catholic workers joined unions in large numbers and rose to leadership positions; labor priests began to emerge, and charity workers sought to pre-vent poverty and social distress as well as lessen their harsh effects. Viewed from this long-range perspective, the bishops' statement was not "a miracle" at all; it represented the culmination of three decades of increased Catholic involvement on behalf of reform. Modest to be sure, but real nonetheless. Beginning with the people and the labor movement, expanding with the in-creased participation of the clergy, it finally reached the hierarchy in the wake of World War I. The absence of much episcopal support for reform prior to the postwar period should not obscure the reality of an impulse for reform at other levels in the Catholic community. Both people and priests provided the initial thrust for reform, and only after this gained headway during the progressive period did the hierarchy unite to support such reform.

Unfortunately the Bishops' Program came at a very inopportune time. The nation was heading into a decade when, in Ryan's words, ". . . social think-ing and social action were chilled and stifled in an atmosphere of pseudo prosperity and thinly disguised materialism."[72] During the 1920s, the vitality of the progressive movement died out; the bishops, like most Americans, lost interest in plans for social reconstruction. Conservatism, rather than progressivism, characterized the spirit of the times, and social reform became a victim of the age. Nevertheless, American Catholicism had taken an important step forward in the development of a social-gospel tradition. Further development of this impulse would have to wait until another time.

The End of an Era,
1920-60

XIII

Changes in Church and Nation

CHICAGOANS WHO VENTURED OUT for a lunchtime stroll on Michigan Avenue on Thursday, June 17, 1926, received quite a shock. The sidewalks were packed with people, and lining the avenue were thousands more onlookers waiting to greet one of the most unusual motorcades ever seen in the Windy City. Nothing like this had ever happened in Chicago—or in any American city for that matter. It was a motorcade of nine cardinals of the Roman Catholic Church. Coming from France, Germany, Ireland, Spain, Austria, Hungary, and Italy, these church dignitaries had traveled to Chicago from New York on a special train painted cardinal red for the occasion. Seated in open-top cars and dressed in their brightly colored robes and strange-looking hats, they rode solemnly along a three-mile stretch of Michigan Avenue. The Chicago *Tribune* reported that "not fewer than 120,000 onlookers, and perhaps as many as 150,000" cheered the prelates as they made their way to the city's Catholic cathedral. It took "an hour and twenty-two minutes" before the motorcade finally reached the church, where hundreds of people, along with the cardinal archbishop of Chicago, George Mundelein, waited to welcome them.[1]

The Catholic prelates had come to Chicago for the International Eucharistic Congress, a massive pilgrimage of faith to honor Christ in the Blessed Sacrament. Since this was the first time an International Eucharistic Congress was being held in the United States, it generated a great deal of excitement in Chicago and throughout Catholic America. Catholics from all parts of the country traveled to Chicago to take part in it. For five days they put on an unparalleled display of devotion and faith; an open-air Mass at Soldier Field attracted an estimated 150,000 people; even more people participated in evening candlelight services held at the lakefront stadium. The main event of the congress was the procession of the Eucharist on the last day. It was held on the spacious grounds of the Catholic seminary situated beyond the city, where an estimated "400,000 to 500,000 men, women, and children, knelt in prayer and lifted their voices in praise while the magnificent pageantry of their Mother Church was unfolded before them."[2] This was Catholic triumphalism, Catholic big, at its best.

The Catholic spectacle in Chicago was a fitting symbol of the church as it entered into the second quarter of the twentieth century. Catholics were filled with confidence about their place in American society and their future in the nation. The number of Catholics was continuing to grow, reaching an estimated twenty million by the 1920s. The brick-and-mortar phase of Catholicism picked up momentum after World War I, and new churches, schools, hospitals, and convents took their places in the cities' skylines. Philadelphia offered a classic example of brick-and-mortar Catholicism. In 1918 a new archbishop, Dennis Dougherty, was appointed to Philadelphia; three years later he was elevated to the cardinalate. In his first ten years in Philadelphia, Dougherty compiled an impressive record as a brick-and-mortar prelate:

> he established ninety-two new parishes; eighty-nine new parish schools; forty-eight new churches; three new diocesan high schools; a new college for women; fourteen new academies; and the $5,000,000 preparatory diocesan seminary, totally paid for the day of its completion. So frequently was he photographed laying a cornerstone during his administration that he laughingly referred to himself as "God's bricklayer."[3]

The pace did not change in the next two decades as "God's bricklayer" presided over the construction of more churches and schools.

The confidence and boosterism evident in Chicago and Philadelphia in the 1920s continued throughout the depression and into the post-World War II era. The Catholic spectacle became commonplace as huge religious rallies filled baseball stadiums with thousands of supporters. In 1934, Maryland Catholics commemorated the three-hundredth anniversary of the founding of Maryland with a mammoth parade. One hundred thousand Catholics, led by the Georgetown University band and three hundred Jesuits in cassock and biretta, marched into Baltimore stadium, where Mass was celebrated amid drum rolls, bugles, and the roar of a ten-cannon salute. Boston was the site of the national gathering of the Holy Name Society in 1947; fifty thousand men rallied in Braves Field for a demonstration of Catholic faith; two days later, they paraded for eight and one half hours through the streets of Boston. Such Catholic spectacles symbolized the confidence and pride people had in being Catholic in America.[4]

Brick-and-mortar Catholicism continued to be the norm throughout the

1920–60 period. Dougherty was not God's only bricklayer. Builder priests could be found throughout the nation, especially in such rapidly growing areas as California. About half a million people lived in Los Angeles in 1920, but their numbers skyrocketed to two and a half million by 1960, and about 15 percent of them were Catholic. The need for churches, schools, and other church-related buildings was obvious. By 1960 the city of Los Angeles had 101 parishes and 80 parochial schools, a sizable increase from the 29 parishes and 18 schools of 1920. The South was also experiencing a population boom. Louisiana offered a dramatic illustration of Catholic growth. Catholicism had been visibly present in Louisiana since the eighteenth century, and each generation witnessed the building of new parish churches, but the increase in building that took place in the twentieth century was unparalleled. From 1720 to 1960, 390 parishes had been organized in Louisiana, two thirds of them founded in the first sixty years of the twentieth century. It was this type of rapid growth in Louisiana and California as well as in other areas of the country that forced many bishops and clergy to become bricklayers for God.[5]

When Catholics built, they loved to build big. It was a matter of pride to have a magnificent church and a large complex of parish buildings housing school, faculty, and clergy. "Noble and dignified buildings," wrote a California pastor, "are a sign of a noble and dignified people"; for his parish he wanted "a church building better than the best."[6] Catholics believed that they were the best God had to offer in the twentieth century. Such optimism and confidence permeated the entire culture of Catholicism. Visibly present in church buildings and religious spectacles, it also shaped the Catholic mind during these decades.

Catholics had emerged from the experience of World War I confident and optimistic about the future. The anti-Catholic paranoia of the Ku Klux Klan during the 1920s and the bitter taste of anti-Catholic hostility occasioned by the 1928 presidential campaign of the Irishman Al Smith, took the wind out of their sails for a while, yet Catholics moved on, deterred but not defeated. They also became publicly more aggressive with each successive decade. Priests and lay people became involved in highly publicized convert crusades to win America to Christ. Bishops and priests viewed themselves as the moral conscience of the nation and publicly condemned birth control, divorce, and morally suspect movies. Philadelphia's Cardinal Dougherty even went so far as to urge Catholics to boycott all movies. Church leaders also waged a continuous campaign on behalf of public aid to parochial schools. Catholic intellectuals believed that Catholicism was more than just a religion, it was "an important cultural reality." As a group of educators put it, "The Catholic College will not be content with presenting Catholicism as a creed, a code, or a cult. Catholicism must be seen as a culture."[7] Binding this culture together was a system of philosophy known as Thomism, a school of thought rooted in the writings of the medieval philosopher Thomas Aquinas and recently revived in Catholic intellectual circles. Thomism provided a sense of security in a world of change and furnished the intellectual cement that could bind religion and culture together. The medieval and Thomistic ideal of the unity of religion and life, the natural and divine, became the model for integrating Catholicism and American culture in the twentieth century. Filled with self-confidence and enthusiasm about the future, Catholic activists sought to bring about a synthesis between Catholicism and American culture. It was the gospel of Americanism all over again, but this time it was not aimed at the adaptation of religion to culture, but at the conversion of culture to religion; another way of putting it is that the culture of Catholicism would permeate American culture and thus change a culture which, in the minds of Catholics, was in a state of decay.

World War II did not shake the confidence of Catholic intellectuals and activists. A new generation of men and women emerged to usher in a period of revival and religious enthusiasm. Inspired by the writings of European Catholics such as Jacques Maritain, Catholics, more than ever before, sought to build a new society in which religion and life were integrated. Christian humanism became the ideal. Grounded in the incarnation of Jesus and inspired by hope, it fired the imagination of a new generation of Catholics who had come of age in the post-World War II period. They sought to bring about a synthesis between religion and life, faith and culture, and they rushed into the marketplace eager to convert others to their point of view. The culture of Catholicism was to permeate everything: literature, politics, philosophy, indeed even athletics.

Catholics not only sought to write the Catholic novel or define a Catholic philosophy, but they also celebrated Catholic all-Americans in basketball. That the dream of unity was not yet realized did not matter, since working toward its realization provided sufficient excitement for Catholic enthusiasts. Religious spectacles, a booming population, a plethora of new churches and schools, record numbers of religious vocations—these were all visible signs to the plain people of the triumph of Catholicism in the United States. The superiority of Thomism and its systematic synthesis of religion and life provided the intellectual and the activist with equally persuasive proof of Catholicism's superiority. Catholicism was not just the hope of America, it would also be the salvation of Western civilization. Such self-confidence, or what the writer Flannery O'Connor called "Catholic smugness," defined the spirit of Catholicism in the pre-1960 period.[8]

Another major development at this time was the organization of the church at the national level. Between 1829 and 1866, national church councils met rather frequently; these councils gave some degree of unity to the church by formulating a body of legislation to regulate church life. The last national meeting, the Third Baltimore Council in 1884, was the culmination of this conciliar movement; it passed a body of legislation that surpassed all previous councils in terms of detail and inclusiveness. The legislation of Baltimore III remained the Magna Charta of American Catholic church life for the next several decades. After 1884, the only attempt to achieve unity of purpose and action at a national level was through the annual meeting of American archbishops. This never worked, however, and so the church remained strikingly devoid of unity at the national level. Internal disputes over such issues as the school question, Americanism, and the rights of immigrant groups in the church made unity especially difficult to achieve. The organization of the National Catholic War Council in 1917 was a major step toward national organization. The success of the Council in coordinating Catholic involvement in the war effort persuaded church leaders that the organization should continue to function after the war. In a letter to his episcopal colleagues, Cardinal Gibbons strongly recommended such a national organization because ". . . the Catholic Church in America, partly through defective organization, is not exerting the influence which it ought to exert in proportion to our numbers and the individual prominence of many of our people." Though it was, in Gibbons's opinion, well organized at the local, diocesan level,

> the Church in America as a whole has been suffering from the lack of a unified force that might be directed to the furthering of those general policies which are vital to all.[9]

To remedy this, the bishops agreed to meet each year to discuss issues of national concern and to establish a National Catholic Welfare Council as a successor to the War Council. With headquarters in the nation's capital, the National Catholic Welfare Council (later named Conference) became the primary agency to coordinate and promote Catholic interests and activities at a national level. Though some bishops opposed the council, because they feared it would limit their autonomy and authority, it succeeded in providing the church with the type of national organization it needed. Such organization did give the bishops a national consciousness and taught them to think about issues that transcended local diocesan concerns. The Bishops' Program of Social Reconstruction in 1919 was a concrete example of such grand thinking. In later years, they issued numerous statements on a variety of issues of both national and international importance. Through these national pastoral letters, often prepared by the staff at the National Catholic Welfare Conference, and their annual meetings in Washington, D.C., the bishops acquired a sense of corporate confidence not present in the nineteenth century. Such confidence blended in well with the booster spirit so evident at the local level. The hierarchy's move toward organization and action at a national level also enabled the Catholic people to identify with a church that was now more visibly national and thus seemingly more important and powerful. The NCWC, the more common name of the Conference, also sought to educate people to think in more national, less parochial, terms. Such an enlarged vision of church life seemed only natural, given the boosterism and confidence that permeated Catholic life the first half of the twentieth century.

The tendency toward greater organization was also evident at the local, diocesan level. Throughout much of the nineteenth century, parish schools were independent of one another. Each pastor was the local neighborhood superintendent of schools, and each religious order followed its own guidelines and chose its own textbooks for teaching. Nationality and language differences added another ingredient of diversity. By the early-twentieth century, Catholic schools began to be organized in much the same manner as the public schools. Superintendents were appointed, uniformity in education became a desired goal, and better organization and record keeping were also encouraged. By the 1920s, the Catholic educational system was beginning to be organized on both the local and the national levels. Such organization gave the Catholic educational enterprise a powerful position in the public arena. Education was no longer a parochial concern, but a national priority. The Catholic charity apostolate underwent a similar pattern of organization in the first half of the century. Disparate and disconnected charitable societies were organized into a diocesan system of charity; diocesan directors of Catholic charities were appointed, and a national organization was founded to coordinate activities at the national level. As with education, the whole was greater than any one of the parts; diocesan bureaus were a more powerful force than parish societies and the national organization became an effective lobbying group at the national level.

The organization of church finances was another key development in the twentieth century. Priests were often promoted to the hierarchy because of their success as fund-raisers and money managers. Each bishop was the head banker of the diocese; some even acted like bankers, with their offices resembling counting rooms; a few actually set up their own banks. The failure of one such church bank in Cincinnati in 1878 caused grief and hardship to large numbers of people who had deposited over $13,000,000 in the bank since 1847. When the bank collapsed, it owed close to $4,000,000 to its depositors. Though the Cincinnati incident was unique, the emphasis on finances was so widespread that it was regarded as a serious evil in the church.[10] Nevertheless, the pressing need for more churches, schools, hospitals, and orphanages undermined any attempt at serious reform. Like education and charity, the financial enterprise in the nineteenth century was noted for its lack of organization. Each pastor was financially quite independent of the bishop. He raised his own funds, personally directed the construction of the parish complex of buildings, and paid off his own debt. Only a small percentage of parish funds was turned over to the bishop to support diocesan programs. But all that changed in the twentieth century. Bishops began to adopt modern business practices to organize church finances more efficiently. Cardi-

CHANGES IN CHURCH AND NATION   355

nal Mundelein of Chicago set up a central banking system, established elaborate regulations to be followed before a church could be built, placed limits on the debt a parish could incur, and issued bonds, one as large as 5.5 million dollars, to raise money for the diocese. In effect he set up a central banking system in the archdiocese of Chicago. By doing so he acquired greater control over pastors, and parishes became considerably less autonomous. In 1939, the new archbishop of New York, Francis J. Spellman, found a $28,000,000 debt awaiting him. He quickly acted to reduce interest payments on the debt, and within a few years had streamlined church finances to a remarkable degree. Financial wizardry had taken over, and the church in New York became famous for its business acumen. Elaborate guidelines regulated parish finances, building committees supervised the construction of parish buildings, a central bank was set up to lend money to parishes at favorable interest rates, group health-insurance plans were established, and a central purchasing organization was set up so that anything from pencils to bricks could be purchased at reduced prices. Mundelein and Spellman were not unique. They were just the best known of a new breed of episcopal businessmen who brought organization and efficiency to the institutional church in the early-twentieth century.[11]

As the Third Plenary Council of Baltimore had pointed out, bishops were supposed to be in control. That was the prevailing theology of the church. But in reality they had to fight fiercely to gain such authority during the nineteenth century. Clerical independence, rather than episcopal control, was clearly the prevailing pattern at that time. But the situation changed dramatically during the course of the twentieth century. The organization and centralization of church life did what theology could never achieve. It gave the bishop control over the church. If the nineteenth century was a time that witnessed the demise of the laity, the first half of the twentieth century saw the weakening of the clergy's independence and the expansion of episcopal authority and control over both priests and people. Archbishop Joseph P. Hurley, head of the church in Florida during the 1940s and 1950s, articulated this new attitude very clearly. In a letter to a prominent and independent-minded pastor, William Barry of St. Patrick's parish in Miami Beach, Hurley informed the Irish-born priest, "You will have to understand, once and for all, that I am running this diocese, and that in matters of grave moment I shall set the policy."[12] Like Mundelein in Chicago, Dougherty in Philadelphia, and O'Connell in Boston, Hurley was the self-proclaimed boss of the church. Such boss rule was not so commonplace or real in the nineteenth century, but by the twentieth century it had become the accepted norm. One obvious result of this development was that people became fascinated with bishops. They became the object of much attention in the media, and bishop-watching became a popular pastime. Such colorful personalities as Cardinals Dougherty of Philadelphia, Glennon of St. Louis, Mundelein of Chicago,

Spellman of New York, and Cushing of Boston were local Catholic heroes. They commanded public attention and personified the spirit of confidence and boosterism so evident at other levels of the community. In the popular mind, the bishop not only represented the church, he was the church. As a result, a top-heavy episcopal (or monarchical) understanding of the church became quite popular. Popes and theologians had always said that this was supposed to be true; but only in the twentieth century, with increased centralization and the public glorification of bishops, did this theology become real.

A major change that had a substantial impact on the future of American Catholicism was the decision of Congress in 1924 to limit the number of immigrants admitted to the United States. After opposing the principle of immigration restriction for some time, Catholic leaders had finally come around to support the concept. But when the Johnson-Reed Immigration Act of 1924 permitted admittance into the country according to a quota system based on race and ethnicity, Catholics strongly objected. They viewed such a discriminatory quota system as an attack on Catholics, which it was, since it discriminated against the new immigrants from southern and Eastern Europe, who were overwhelmingly Catholic. The protest of Catholics and other Americans soon passed, however, and the law went into effect in 1929. Under the new quota system, just under 154,000 people could enter the United States each year. This legislation had a dramatic effect on the development of twentieth-century Catholicism. For one thing, it slowed the growth of Catholicism considerably, with the result that from the mid-1920s to the mid-1950s it experienced an increase in population of approximately 42 percent, or slightly higher than the growth of Protestantism during the same period. This was a dramatic turnaround from the nineteenth century, when in a thirty-year period, 1830–60, the number of Catholics increased by almost 900 percent. Another major consequence was that newly arrived European immigrants no longer defined the agenda of the church. The social consequences of this were particularly significant. It meant that within the next generation, by about the mid-1950s, Catholicism would become a church of the middle class.[13]

In the 1920s, class lines were clearly evident in the Catholic community. Some few people comprised the rungs of the upper class, Irish and Germans made up the large bulk of the middle class, and the more recently arrived immigrants from Eastern and southern Europe, along with the French Canadians and the Mexicans, were overwhelmingly lower-class. Though the size of the middle class had increased since the mid-nineteenth century, Catholicism was still preponderantly a church of the working class. A study of the factory town of Holyoke, Massachusetts, in 1947 found that two thirds of the Catholic workers were involved in jobs that were described as lower-class. Predictably, three out of six Irish parishes were middle-class while the other three were lower-class. The Polish and French-Canadian parishes, however, were all described as lower-class. In the steel-producing center of Steelton, Pennsylvania, Italian and Slovak workers evidenced a modest degree of occupational mobility prior to World War II. Nevertheless, they remained heavily concentrated in unskilled and semiskilled occupations. Similar patterns prevailed in Cleveland and Boston, where both first- and second-generation immigrant Catholics remained preponderantly blue-collar; though the sons had fared better than their fathers, they were still working in lower-class occupations. A national survey conducted in the mid-1940s confirmed the pattern found in places like Holyoke and Boston. Two thirds of the Catholics surveyed belonged to the lower class, 25 percent to the middle class, and 9 percent to the upper class. The occupational distribution of Baptists and Mormons was remarkably similar to that of Catholics.[14]

After World War II, the United States experienced an economic boom that benefited most Americans. Immigrant Catholics and their descendants certainly profited. By the early 1960s, Catholics had made a decisive move into the middle class; as one study reported, "While both religious groups have enjoyed the benefits of the last quarter century of prosperity, it appears that Catholics have been able to use this period of time to achieve rough social and economic parity with Protestants, at least among those who are under forty."[15] Though Catholics were still underrepresented in the upper classes, this would change in the 1960s and 1970s.

A second major change that affected all Americans in the twentieth century was the emergence of the modern suburb. In 1920 a significant milestone was reached when, for the first time in American history, a majority of Americans lived in cities. It revealed what many people had known for some time: the city, not the farm, had become the vital center of the nation. Fifty years later, another milestone would be reached when the 1970 census would reveal that, for the first time, more Americans lived in suburbs than in cities. Even though streetcar suburbs predated the twentieth century, the 1920s ushered in a period of sustained centrifugal movement from the city to those regions around it, namely the suburbs. The mass production of the automobile hastened the pace of suburbanization; motorized buses could outdistance streetcars more quickly and economically; highways and better roads made suburbia more accessible; and federal home-loan policies made it easier for people to purchase homes in the suburbs. Prior to 1950, downtown U.S.A. still possessed a magnetic appeal. As a retail, financial, and entertainment center, the city attracted many people. But things changed rapidly after World War II. The modern shopping center, born in the 1920s, skyrocketed to popularity in the 1950s. Housing construction increased as the government expanded its generous home-loan policies to World War II veterans; more highways and more automobiles made the suburban trend possible, and commuting became a way of life for the majority of American workers.

As Americans began to move to the suburbs in the post-1920 period, the church followed. New parishes were organized and the clergy mobilized the people for the building of new churches and schools. When Cardinal Dougherty of Philadelphia went to lay the cornerstone of a new church, the odds were that he would travel to the suburbs, not the city. Of the twenty-eight parishes he founded in his first three years as archbishop, twenty-one were in the suburbs; 1925 was a particularly busy year for "God's bricklayer": nineteen new parish schools were opened that year, and fourteen of them were situated in the suburbs around Philadelphia.[16] The suburban population around Chicago was also booming, and the result was that half of the parishes founded during the episcopacy of Cardinal Mundelein (1916–39) were outside Chicago, "most of them in bedroom communities." It is worth noting that Mundelein's predecessor, Archbishop Quigley, established 113 parishes in twelve years, 75 percent of them in the city of Chicago. Such a rapid transition from city to suburb illustrated the sudden shift in population that took place throughout the nation in the post-World War I period. With good reason, Quigley has been remembered as "the bishop of the immigrants" and Mundelein as "the bishop of the suburbs."[17] The same pattern prevailed in Boston, St. Louis, and New Orleans as people picked up and moved to the suburbs. The emergence of modern suburbia and the suburban parish posed a new challenge for the churches in the 1920–60 era. People lived differently along the "crabgrass frontier"; the single-family dwelling and the automobile emphasized the privacy of life, as opposed to the public dimension nurtured in the immigrant neighborhood; in suburban America, individual suburbs became identified with a particular class of people, since income defined where people would live; homogeneity was a characteristic of suburban culture, as opposed to the diversity of urban life. These and other differences meant that the church would have to shift its focus from an immigrant constituency to an American-born, suburban constituency, which after World War II was becoming increasingly middle-class.

As Catholics moved from city to suburb, from the blue-collar working class to the white-collar middle class, two other major social changes were underway that would eventually present a mighty challenge to the church. The first was the migration north of thousands of black Americans. In 1900, most black Americans lived south of the Mason-Dixon line, and only 20 percent of them lived in urban places. In the next half century a dramatic population shift took place, so that by 1960 about half of black America lived in the North, and three out of four lived in the cities. The transition of Harlem in New York City dramatized how quickly and thoroughly an urban neighborhood could change.

In the 1890s Harlem was described as a genteel community of the upper-middle class, Manhattan's "first suburb." In the early-twentieth century the area changed when real estate developers overbuilt and an excess of residential buildings flooded the market. Spurred on by black realtors, many blacks began to settle in Harlem, so that by 1920 it had become "the Mecca of the colored people of New York City."[18] After World War I, the black migration North intensified as wave after wave of people moved to Chicago, Detroit, Philadelphia, and New York. This was the decade when black Americans turned from "farm life to city life." New York reflected this shift, and from 1920 to 1930 the city's black population increased 115 percent, from 152,467 to 327,706. In Harlem the black population rose to 164,566 by 1930. As the blacks moved into Harlem the whites moved out, 118,792 of them during the 1920s alone; as a result, Harlem became the nation's major black ghetto.[19] Chicago experienced a similar transformation during and after World War I. The city's black population expanded from 44,103 in 1910 to 233,903 by 1930. As in New York, one section of the city became the center of the black population; in Chicago the black metropolis was situated on the city's South Side. The black migration North transformed such other cities as Newark and Detroit. Large numbers of blacks migrated to Los Angeles in the 1940s and 1950s, with the result that 334,916 blacks lived in the city by 1960, whereas in 1940 only 63,774 blacks called Los Angeles their home.[20]

As black Americans moved to the urban North, they were moving into the heartland of Catholic America: the urban Northeast. This posed a serious challenge to the church, religious as well as economic. Throughout the era of the immigrant church, 1820–1920, relatively few blacks were attracted to Catholicism. A 1928 Catholic census placed the black population at 203,986, or less than 2 percent of the total black population. All indications suggested that during the nineteenth century the relative percentage of black Catholics was no higher than the 1928 level. About half of the 1928 black Catholic population was in Louisiana, a southern stronghold of Catholicism. The next-largest concentration was in New York City, where about 25,000 lived; then came Baltimore and Washington, D.C., with a combined total of about 22,000. The remainder were scattered across the country.[21]

Many reasons help to explain why so few blacks were attracted to Catholicism during the era of the immigrant church. During the nineteenth century blacks lived in the South, where the Catholic Church was very underdeveloped in terms of institutional and human resources. Protestant churches had evangelized the black slave population during the revival of the second Great Awakening (1800–35). Then, after the Civil War blacks began to organize their own churches, and the independent black church became an important center in the community. Catholic clergy were never really involved in this phase of evangelization. Of course, some few bishops, priests, and women religious did seek to evangelize southern blacks but their success was limited. Catholic clergymen looked upon black Americans much as they viewed the Indians; in other words, they had little or no religion and needed to be evangelized in a manner similar to the Indians. When church leaders talked about the evangelization of the blacks, it was almost always in conjunction with talk about the evangelization of the Indians with whom the focus was on the youth, not the adults. The two were viewed similarly, and the chosen remedy for both was the school. Church leaders acknowledged, however, that ". . . far more in proportion is being done for the support of mission work among the Indians than among the Negroes."[22] This general lack of interest continued until the 1920s.

Racial discrimination was another obvious influence. It was the main reason for the lack of black clergy. Throughout the entire nineteenth century, only two blacks were ordained, and as late as 1930 only three black priests were at work in the American Catholic Church.[23] The absence of a black clergy certainly hindered the work of the church among black Americans. This meant that responsibility for the black Catholic apostolate remained with white clergymen. The one group most closely identified with this work in the twentieth century were the Josephites, an order of priests established in 1893 to work among the "colored missions." As regards women religious, there were three communities of black sisters in the United States in the early-twentieth century: the Oblates of Providence, centered in Baltimore with 122 members; the Sisters of the Holy Family, in New Orleans with 153 members; and a very small community in New York, the Handmaids of the Most Pure Heart of Mary, with 11 members. The Sisters of the Blessed Sacrament was the major order of white women religious who had members working in black Catholic communities.[24]

Racial discrimination also drew a color line through the local parish church. As one historian put it, Jim Crow had come to church. This meant segregated seating arrangements and Communion services at which blacks received the Eucharist only after all the whites had been served.[25] The immigrant church was clearly a white people's church, and few blacks found a home there; those that did were clearly third-class citizens. This attitude, built up over a hundred-year period, did not disappear overnight. As long as the blacks lived down South, few people cared, since, like the Indians, they were far removed from where most Catholics lived. As long as people did not feel threatened, racist attitudes remained dormant. But once blacks moved North, into the heartland of Catholic America, Catholics were forced to reexamine their attitudes toward black Americans. Church leaders also had to ponder what to do with churches left empty by the flight of the immigrants and their children.

The other significant change during the 1920–60 period was a large increase in the Hispanic population, principally Mexican and Puerto Rican. By 1900, somewhere in the vicinity of half a million people of Mexican descent lived in the United States. Immigration was casual and moderate in the early years of the century as people moved back and forth across the border. When revolution broke out in Mexico in 1910, many people migrated to the United States. In the 1920s, immigration soared, and close to half a million people came to the United States. During the depression and World War II, immigration slacked off, but it boomed again in the 1950s. By 1960 the number of people of Mexican descent in the United States had reached an estimated 3,842,100 people, the vast majority of whom lived in five states of the Southwest: Arizona, California, Colorado, New Mexico, and Texas.[26] In the early years of the century, Mexican immigrants were attracted primarily to rural agricultural work, but by the 1950s they were becoming more and more urbanized. The pattern of settlement was also shifting at the time to California, Los Angeles in particular, which in 1960 was the city with the largest Mexican-American population in the Southwest region. Outside the Southwest, the major Mexican-American settlement was in Illinois, particularly the industrial center of Chicago, where the 1950 census counted 24,000 Mexicans, a figure that was undoubtedly much lower than the real number of Mexicans living in the city at the time. Economically, Mexican-American families fared very poorly. Their family income as late as 1959 was only 65 percent of that of Anglo families in the Southwest region. Though some progress had been made during the 1950s, Mexican Americans, after sixty years and more of residency in the United States, were still "substantially below the income standing of the general population."[27]

The Puerto Ricans were the other major Hispanic group to migrate to the United States during the twentieth century. Migration was steady but moderate prior to World War II; by the late 1940s it had increased substantially. By that time, ". . . all the elements of a large-scale migration were in place: unrestricted travel, unemployment at home, a community awaiting the newcomers on the mainland, and cheap, fast transportation." The result was that the Puerto Rican population in the United States increased to 887,662 by 1960; the most popular place of residence was New York City, where 612,574 Puerto Ricans lived in 1960—69 percent of the total U.S. population.[28] Like most Hispanics, the Puerto Ricans did poorly economically. They were "the poorest segment of the New York City population" in 1960, with a median family income "considerably lower than that of the blacks."[29] Mexicans and Puerto Ricans were clearly the new lower class in the Catholic community. Mexicans had been in that position since the nineteenth century, and even as late as 1960 they still clung to the lower ranks of the occupational scale, joined by the Puerto Ricans and a small number of black Catholics. Along with their lower-class status, Mexicans and Puerto Ricans introduced the element of color into the church. Neither black nor white, but a multiracial group, both Mexicans and Puerto Ricans came to a society and a church where color played a decisive role in identifying who a person is and where he or she belongs. In other words, racial discrimination would have a major influence in shaping the attitude of people and priests toward Hispanic Catholics.

Looking back over the 1920–60 era, two major trends stand out. One was a spirit of confidence and optimism, Catholic boosterism if you wish, which permeated the entire white Catholic Anglo community. These were the descendants of the immigrants, second and third generation and beyond, who proudly celebrated their religion and their Americanism. By the 1950s, they were becoming more and more like the rest of the American population. They reached the pinnacle in 1960, when one of their own, John F. Kennedy, was elected President of the United States. The other trend was the emergence of a large Hispanic community, a people whose tradition was very Catholic, and the migration North into the heartland of Catholic America of large numbers of black Americans, a people whose tradition was not Catholic at all. Colored and poor, black and Hispanic, these newcomers settled in old Catholic neighborhoods and presented a mighty challenge to a church that was white, middle-class, and proudly American. For much of the period, these two worlds, like ships passing in the night, did not take much notice of one another. When they finally did, the reality of the new social situation tempered the enthusiastic spirit of Catholic boosterism and forced church leaders to formulate a new agenda that would include black and brown poor Catholics as well as suburban middle-class white Catholics.

The changes in both church and society had a substantial impact on the parish community. The end of large-scale immigration, the black migration North, the Hispanic movement North from Mexico and the Caribbean, and the development of suburbia altered the landscape of the nation. For the church, a new social situation demanded a new agenda. In the 1820s, the church had faced a similar challenge and had responded in a remarkable manner. The 1920s was quite different, however, and the changes it ushered in posed a serious challenge. Hispanic immigrants were different from European Catholics, and the blacks were traditionally Protestant; the descendants of the old immigrants were becoming more American, and to some this inevitably meant less Catholic; and the sense of community nurtured in the old immigrant neighborhood got lost somewhere along the way to suburbia. The new social environment challenged the immigrant church to change; how it met this challenge constitutes the most important chapter of American Catholic history in the first half of the twentieth century.

Even though the immigration laws of the 1920s greatly reduced the number of new immigrants, the Catholic community still retained a distinctive immigrant quality. The Boston archdiocese had forty-two foreign-language parishes in 1907; in the next thirty-five years, thirty-five new foreign-language parishes were founded, most prior to 1930. In Chicago, 55 percent of the Catholic population in 1936 still belonged to national parishes and the clergy remained divided along nationality lines. The immigrant character had changed, however, as the number of foreign-born people decreased and those born in the United States increased. Among Italians and Polish, for example,

71 percent of the foreign-stock population in 1950 belonged to the second generation, i.e., individuals born in the United States whose parents were born in a foreign country. A study of the Catholic community in the early 1960s found that 60 percent of the people surveyed were either first- or second-generation.[30] Even though second-generation immigrants were born and raised in the United States, they were still very much the product of immigrant households and cultures. Surrounded by the sounds of the immigrant language at home and in the streets, bombarded by the community's insistence on preserving the culture, they carried with them a strong dose of the family's national heritage. The immigrant quality of Catholic life, maintained and nurtured by both first and second generations, was most visible among the immigrants from Eastern and southern Europe, as well as the French Canadians.

A study of Holyoke, Massachusetts, in the 1940s highlighted the ethnic character of the city. As the author put it, "When you speak of Catholics in Paper City [Holyoke] it is important to know whether you mean Irish Catholics, French Catholics or Polish Catholics."[31] Parishes were still divided along nationality lines; ethnic rivalry was present and pastors worked hard to keep their national culture alive; fraternal societies had a definite ethnic flavor, with the Knights of Columbus being Irish and St. Jean Baptiste being French. In New Britain, Connecticut, a group of second-generation Polish Catholics became tired of the autocratic policies of their pastor and formed a new parish. Founded in 1927, Holy Cross represented the epitome of the second-generation Polish parish. Nevertheless, it remained very Polish into the 1940s. Parishioners spoke Polish at home; sermons were in Polish, and only in 1942 was a Mass in English introduced, the other five Masses remaining in Polish. The parish school featured Polish language and culture; the people regularly celebrated Polish customs, and when it came time to marry, 75 percent of these second-generation Polish men and women chose Polish partners.[32] St. Philip Benizi, founded in 1904, was a vibrant center of Italian Catholic life in Chicago. Despite the loss of parishioners to suburbia, St. Philip's remained a center of Italian life for more than four decades. It supported numerous parish societies; it hosted the popular Italian festivals; and its pastor was a great booster of Italian language and culture. In St. Louis, the neighborhood known as the Hill was another local center of Italian life and culture, and the major institution on the Hill was St. Ambrose Church. The same was true in San Francisco, where SS. Peter and Paul remained an important center of the Italian colony throughout the first half of the century.

The other side of parish life was the decisive move toward Americanization. The nation was engaged in an Americanism crusade during the 1920s. Church leaders joined in and promoted the Americanization of immigrant Catholics. A key agent in this was the parish. In the nineteenth century, most bishops and pastors viewed the parish as the guardian of the immigrant's culture and religion. This commitment to the national parish began to wane by the 1920s as bishops, most of whom were Irish, gave wholehearted support to the concept of Americanization. At the national level, the National Catholic Welfare Conference orchestrated an impressive "Campaign for Civic Instruction," and many dioceses adopted this educational program to aid immigrants. The major center in this program was the parish. Parishes sponsored classes that taught the immigrants how to read and write; American citizenship training was also encouraged; pastors urged their parishioners to become American citizens by filing their papers for naturalization, and often doctors and lawyers of the parish would tutor the immigrants and then "go down and sponsor them for their papers."[33] Immigrants generally offered little resistance to such parish-sponsored Americanization programs. Like their nineteenth-century counterparts, they wanted to learn English and succeed in America. Moreover, relatively few immigrants contemplated returning permanently to the old country after World War I, and this made citizenship and language classes particularly appealing.

Americanization was a sensitive issue and had to be treated gingerly. When a bishop became insensitive to national pride and tried to force the people to Americanize, conflict inevitably erupted. Forced Americanization generally meant the banishment of foreign languages from parochial schools or the refusal to build national parishes for particular groups. Cardinal Mundelein of Chicago antagonized the Polish community by issuing an "English only" edict for parochial schools, refusing to establish new Polish parishes, and assigning Polish priests to mixed territorial parishes. Bishop William Hickey of Providence, Rhode Island, became the archenemy of many French Canadians because of his strong assimilationists views. "It is not the blood in one's veins that makes the Catholic," he told the people, "but it is belief in a doctrine and submission."[34] This point of view clashed with the fiercely proud French Canadians and resulted in a five-year battle between the Irish bishop and militant French Canadians who viewed assimilation as apostasy.

Time, however, was on the side of the Americanizers. With each new generation, the ties to the cultures and languages of the Old World weakened. Immigrants passed their cultural heritage on to their children, and the national parish was an important agency in this process. During the era of the second generation, between the two world wars, the national parish remained strong, but it began to encourage Americanization as well as loyalty to a particular national culture. After World War II a noticeable shift toward Americanization and assimilation set in. Bilingualism gradually gave way to English only; American-born and American-trained clergy replaced priests born and raised in the Old World; intermarriage between ethnic groups increased; large numbers of people moved out of the city to the suburbs, where they lived and worshiped in culturally mixed neighborhoods and parishes; travel, television, and participation in various aspects of American mass culture encouraged Americanization and cultural uniformity. People now identified themselves as Americans of Polish or Italian descent, not Polish Americans or Italian Americans. In some old immigrant neighborhoods, the parish remained a citadel of national loyalty and a museum of cultural pride into the 1950s. Eventually the bulldozers that ushered in urban renewal and new highways turned many of these churches into heaps of rubble. For white ethnic Catholics, however, the bulldozer was not the major threat. It was their new black neighbors.

City neighborhoods were always in a state of flux, with people moving in and out. Throughout the nineteenth century this often meant that as one ethnic group moved out, another group moved in to replace it. Italians settled where the Irish once lived, and Poles took over German neighborhoods. Because the parish church remained, it was able to serve the needs of successive groups of people in a city neighborhood. When an Irish parish turned Italian, as often happened, or a German parish acquired large numbers of Polish members due to the absence of a nearby Polish church, the transition was often quite difficult for clergy and people alike, but in the end the parish survived, poised for another possible change in the future. New York City's Transfiguration parish was not untypical. Founded as an Irish parish in 1836, it later became an Italian parish and then, in the twentieth century, it became the Catholic church in Chinatown. Over the course of a century such change was common. But when blacks moved into the neighborhood, people and clergy were ill prepared to deal with the presence of the newcomers.

The Catholic policy toward blacks as they moved into the northern cities was to segregate them in their own separate parishes. This had been the policy since the mid-nineteenth century, and like the national-parish concept, both people and clergy viewed this arrangement as appropriate at that time. But racism hardened the line separating black and white Catholics. What was once viewed as pastorally appropriate now became racially desirable. This was true in the North as well as the South. If blacks were permitted to attend services in a white parish, they were clearly considered outsiders, and as was the policy in Chicago, they could not become full members of the white parish. Black Catholics, led by Daniel Rudd of Cincinnati, organized five national congresses in the 1880s and 1890s at which they protested such segregation and discrimination in church and school. But nothing changed. Separate churches and schools for blacks remained the norm.

In some southern parishes, blacks and whites did worship together, but segregation separated them at the altar and in the pew. When northern cities began to acquire sizable black populations, one church in each city was designated as exclusively for blacks. This was where they were supposed to worship and receive the sacraments. To care for the spiritual needs of the black Catholic community in a given city, the bishop would assign a religious order of priests. This pattern of assigning a religious order to care for a specific group of people, be they Italian, Indian, or black was quite common in the church. In this manner, a bishop was able to cope with a particularly difficult pastoral situation, but it also meant that other priests felt no responsibility for the people being cared for by religious-order priests. In the case of European immigrants or reservation Indians, this posed little or no problem, but in the case of the blacks it only served to cut them off from the neighboring white Catholic community and allowed the diocesan clergy to abdicate their responsibility for them. One church, however, could never adequately serve the needs of increasing numbers of people scattered throughout the city. Some blacks did attend the local neighborhood church, but the racial biases of most clergy and people discouraged black Catholics from joining white parishes.[35] As the numbers of blacks moving North increased, the problem became more serious. Whites would flee the neighborhood, parish populations would decline along with parish revenues, and pastors would despair. What happened in Harlem after World War I clearly illustrated the problem and the challenge posed to the church in the city.

In the nineteenth century, St. Benedict the Moor, founded in 1883, was the one church for blacks in New York City. People came from all over the city to attend Mass and receive the sacraments at St. Benedict's. Situated in Greenwich Village at first, St. Benedict's moved uptown to a new location at West 53rd Street in 1898; the old Greenwich Village church was then converted into an Italian parish, Our Lady of Pompeii. But Harlem, not the West Side, was becoming the chosen residence for migrating blacks. The church was well represented in Harlem, but the parishes catered to a white, very Irish, population. In 1912 the pastor of St. Mark's church, unable to cope with the changes in the neighborhood, resigned. The archbishop turned the parish over to a religious order of priests, the Holy Ghost Fathers, and for all practical purposes St. Mark's became the exclusively black parish in Harlem. The pastor at nearby St. Charles parish clearly understood it in this manner; on Sunday mornings he would stand on the church steps directing black Catholics to go to their own church, "pointing his cane in the direction of St. Mark's." By 1928 the old Irish pastor at St. Charles was gone, replaced by the pastor of St. Benedict the Moor, a man who had worked with black Catholics for more than forty years. A few blocks away, All Saints parish tried to ignore the presence of the black newcomers and hold on to the old traditions. The parish schools remained exclusively white throughout the 1920s. Then, in the 1930s, the inevitable happened. The girls' academy and the boys' high school closed and the elementary school became integrated. St. Thomas the Apostle was another prosperous Irish parish in Harlem and had $300,000 in its savings account in the 1920s. Throughout the transitional years of the late 1920s and early 1930s, the parish maintained a business-as-usual policy, but the construction of a new subway in the neighborhood and the increased number of black newcomers persuaded many people to leave the area. By 1935 the parish was not able to pay its bills. The response of Harlem's German parish, St. Joseph's, was very typical of strong national parishes in black communities. It resisted all attempts at adaptation and remained very German. Only in 1948, through the intervention of Archbishop Spellman and against the bitter protest of the German pastor, did the parish begin to adapt to the needs of black newcomers. The German pastor was transferred and the German order of women religious left, replaced by priests and sisters involved in the black Catholic apostolate.[36]

What happened in Harlem took place in many northern cities. Lacking any clear policy and forceful leadership, the clergy responded as they desired. Some despaired and fled; others resisted and clung to the past; and a few sought to minister to the needs of the black newcomers. As a result, the number of black Catholics in Harlem did not increase very much during the 1920s and 1930s. Fortunately, the churches did not close. They remained open, ready to welcome a new breed of priests who would respond positively and creatively to the needs of the newcomers.

In Harlem the new breed first surfaced in the late 1930s at St. Charles parish. The recognized leader was William McCann, who became the pastor of St. Charles in 1933 and remained there until his death in 1949. The energetic McCann was part of a new type of priest emerging across urban America who saw hope and promise in the black community. Viewing themselves as urban missionaries, they sought to win converts among the blacks. Instruction classes for potential converts became standard practice at St. Charles parish, and throughout the 1930s and 1940s, McCann, along with his assistants, baptized an estimated two hundred converts a year. Other parishes in Harlem followed McCann's example, and priests from other cities even came to St. Charles to view at first hand the work of McCann and his colleagues. In 1943 McCann boasted, "Ten years ago the Catholic church was not known in Harlem but was sneeringly referred to as 'the white man's Church.' Today it needs no advertisement and is known as a potent instrument of good in our Negro community. . . ." During that decade he claimed that five thousand people "received the light of Faith and Baptism, and we have created a record unequaled in the country."[37]

Just about every northern city had a charismatic figure like McCann. In Philadelphia it was Edward Cunnie, the newly appointed pastor of St. Elizabeth's parish in 1937. He turned St. Elizabeth's, a parish that successively served the Germans and the Irish, into the showcase of Philadelphia's black Catholic community. By 1955 the parish had three thousand members, 90 percent of whom were Cunnie's converts, and the parish school had an enrollment of nine hundred.[38] In St. Louis, the Jesuit priest William Markoe led the fight for racial justice. Pastor of the city's black parish from 1927 to 1941, William Markoe, along with his brother John, battled with the cardinal archbishop of St. Louis, John Glennon, over the issue of racial justice and equal rights in the church. Though convert-making remained a central priority in St. Louis, the Markoe brothers, along with other clergy, realized the need for more than just catechism classes. Black Catholic lay people in St. Louis also raised their voices for "equal rights" in the church.

In St. Louis the color line ran right through the heart of the Catholic community, segregating churches, grade schools, high schools, and colleges. A small black Catholic high school, St. Joseph's, "could not even engage in competitive sports within the city's Catholic High School League." Cardinal Glennon believed that "eliminating the color line altogether was impractical for the present at least in a city such as St. Louis which is by sentiment and by tradition a Southern city."[39] Black Catholics desiring to eliminate the color bar protested vigorously. By the 1940s some priests also began to become more militant and demanded racial justice in a segregated church. The first breakthrough came in 1944, when St. Louis University admitted its first black students. A year later, the process of integration was set in place in a local parish school. The militancy of black Catholics and some few white priests did not change things very much, however. Then, in 1946, Glennon died, and his successor, Joseph E. Ritter, wasted little time in tackling the issue of integration. In 1947 he issued an edict that demanded the integration of parochial schools. He threatened those who opposed his policy with excommunication. By the stroke of the pen, Ritter accomplished what lay people and parish priests acting together could not. The power of the bishop could not have been more clearly demonstrated. Though Ritter met with strong opposition, his decision, supported by church authorities in Rome, prevailed. Ritter exemplified a new type of bishop, who, unlike Glennon and Mundelein, did not believe the time was "inopportune" for integration. Bishops Francis J. Spellman in New York, Vincent S. Waters in North Carolina, Patrick A. O'Boyle in Washington, D.C., and Robert E. Lucey in San Antonio were other advocates of racial justice who demanded integration in their dioceses.

The militancy of clergy and laity and the concern for integration and equal rights represented a new direction in Catholic thought and action in the twentieth century. Among lay people, the Federation of Colored Catholics, organized in 1924 by Howard University Professor Thomas W. Turner, sought to promote equal rights in the church on a national scale. The Federation was an outgrowth of a small committee of twenty-five people who had first gathered in Turner's home in 1917 to discuss the place of blacks in the Catholic Church. The Federation held annual conventions during the 1920s and 1930s and sought "to bring about a closer union and better feeling among all Catholic Negroes, to advance the cause of Catholic education throughout the Negro population, to seek to raise the general church status of the Negro and to stimulate colored Catholics to a larger participation in racial and civic affairs."[40] Like the Afro-American congresses in the 1880s and 1890s, the annual convention of the Federation attracted Catholic attention nationwide and provided a forum for discussion. Clergy working in black parishes also organized in the 1930s. In Newark, Mobile, Richmond, and Raleigh, local and regional organizations were established. A Midwest Clergy Conference on Negro Welfare was set up in 1938. Support groups for priests involved in the black Catholic apostolate, these organizations encouraged integration and equal rights and sought "to make our priests and nuns color conscious by every available form of publicity."[41]

Another, less militant organization was taking shape in New York. Under the guidance of John LaFarge, a Jesuit priest who had worked in the Negro missions in Maryland, a select group of about twenty black Catholics met in 1924 to study and discuss the ways of improving the condition of blacks, especially within the church. In 1934 the group, now called the Laymen's Union, sought to promote a biracial approach to racial justice. An Interracial Council was formed in New York, and by 1936 it began to expand to other cities. By 1959, thirty-five Catholic interracial councils were functioning in cities throughout the North and the South. LaFarge was the key person in the organization and became nationally known and respected for his promotion of racial justice. Stressing education and a biracial or interracial approach, the Catholic Interracial Council sought to instruct Catholics on the need for racial equality in the church. LaFarge's educational and biracial approach gained wide support, and by the 1940s the Catholic Interracial Council had become the most important church organization engaged in the promotion of racial justice. At the local level, interracial councils succeeded in persuading numerous Catholics to join the cause of racial justice and civil rights.[42]

The civil rights movement gained considerable momentum when, in 1954, the Supreme Court ordered the integration of the nation's public schools with all deliberate speed. The Montgomery bus boycott in 1955 propelled a young Baptist minister, Martin Luther King, Jr., onto the national stage and marked the beginning of a nationwide crusade for civil rights. This crusade, publicized on national television, reached into every home in the nation and forced people to take a stand on the issue of equal rights for all Americans regardless of their race. The civil rights crusade also persuaded many people that more direct action was needed before racial justice could be achieved. During the 1950s, large-scale urban-renewal programs got underway, and they forced the removal of people by destroying their homes in the hope of building better housing or more profitable urban institutions. Inspired by the crusade for civil rights and challenged by the human destruction inherent in urban renewal, some Catholic clergy shifted their attention from integration and equal rights in the church to social justice in the city. A prominent example of this transition took place in Chicago.

Since the days of Cardinal Mundelein, Chicago had been a center for social action. Clergy and lay people were involved in numerous organizations concerned with issues of social justice. On the issue of race, Chicago resembled

New York, St. Louis, and Philadelphia. It had a Catholic Interracial Council, and its chaplain, Daniel Cantwell, became a recognized leader in the campaign to improve race relations in the city. Convert-making was another very active apostolate in the black community. In the 1940s and 1950s, two priests in particular, Joseph Richards and Martin Farrell, led the drive to win converts in the black community. In this manner they were able to revitalize inner-city parishes abandoned by white parishioners. But broader issues of social and racial justice forced Catholics to expand their horizons. In Chicago, the catalyst for this change was Saul Alinsky and his priest protégé, John Egan.

Alinsky was a nationally known community organizer who sought to organize "powerless urban neighborhoods into active self-help communities." Egan was head of the Cana Conference, a family-life organization. When they met, in 1954, ". . . the young priest was interested in finding flesh and blood ways to bring to life for Chicago's younger Catholic families the Church's social teachings about work, poverty, education, family and community life. At that time Alinsky was looking for a way to involve the churches in his plan to reorganize America's city dwellers in mass-based organizations. It was a match made in heaven."[43] Egan and Alinsky worked together promoting community organization in Chicago, with the result that by the early 1960s three major neighborhood organizations were in operation; the backbone of these organizations was the Catholic Church. By the use of political power gained through community organization, clergy and people sought to place the power of the church in the forefront of the struggle for social justice. Priests became activists and opposed poorly conceived urban-renewal programs and worked to provide better housing for the city's poor. In the 1950s and early 1960s this was a radical step.

There is no question that the church, through its clergy and people, had come a long way since the 1930s. The transition from convert-making and interracial educational programs to community organization and direct action on behalf of issues of social justice broadened the horizons of the black Catholic apostolate considerably. It also put the urban church in a good position to respond to the social problems of the 1960s. The black apostolate was no longer the preserve of one parish and a single religious order of priests. It had become the concern of many priests and numerous parishes. Because of the church's increased commitment during these years, the number of black Catholics increased significantly. By 1959 they numbered 595,155, almost three times the number in 1928. Most of the increase was through conversions, which by 1959 were at the annual level of about 12,000. This represented a little more than 3 percent of the total black population, a proportion about twice as large as in 1928.[44] During the 1950s the number of black priests also increased, and by 1961 they numbered 120, with most of the increase having taken place during the 1950s. Unlike in the 1940s, seminaries across the country now accepted blacks as candidates for the priesthood. As regards women religious, blacks were no longer forced into exclusively black religious orders but were welcomed in most orders.[45] The church had met the challenge of the black migration in a positive and creative manner. While most people fled, church and clergy remained in the changing neighborhoods and began a new apostolate that would expand during the 1960s.

It is important to remember, however, that racism still remained a serious problem in the Catholic community in the late 1950s. The majority of clergy and lay people lived in the suburbs, far from the problems and challenges of the inner city, and many of these people harbored deep racist feelings. Nor were all city priests and lay people well disposed to their black neighbors. In Chicago, a city notorious for its racism, some pastors were still trying to keep blacks out of their churches and neighborhoods, and high schools, hospitals, and orphanages were still segregated in the late 1950s. In heavily Catholic neighborhoods, people even resorted to violence to keep out blacks. In the South, segregation died hard. Despite the strong integrationist stand of the archbishop of New Orleans, Joseph F. Rummel, many clergy and laity in Louisiana remained firm in their southern tradition of segregation. The Catholic church had clearly experienced an awakening on the issue of race, but in 1960 it still had a way to go before it could claim to be a racially integrated institution.

The immigration of Mexicans presented a special problem for the church. Though Catholic, their style of religion was quite different from mainline Catholicism in the United States. As one immigrant put it, "I am a Catholic and pray in my house, but I hardly ever go to church."[46] For American Catholics, such a statement was a self-contradiction, since a person could not be a Catholic and "hardly ever go to church." But Mexican Catholics were not church-centered, they were family-centered; for this reason, domestic family rituals and the public celebration of a saint's feast day were much more important than regular attendance at Sunday Mass. Nevertheless, the church did have a special importance in their lives. The basic sacraments, those fundamental rights of passage, baptism, marriage, and burial "were always of special significance to the Mexican American. Even if he never attended a Mass, he felt these sacraments to be as essential as life itself."[47] Anglo clergy and people never understood this. As one priest put it, "The Mexicans coming into our States come here almost entirely ignorant of their duties to God and church."[48] This stereotype of Mexican immigrants as a people "ignorant of their duties to God and church" was a standard image among American Catholics. Given this "ignorance" of things religious, the clergy viewed working with the newcomers as part of the missionary apostolate. Like the Indians and the blacks, the Mexicans, even though Catholic by birth and tradition, were in need of conversion to the true religion of church-going, dues-paying American Catholics. In other words, they needed to become "Mass and sacraments" Catholics. The clergy's inability to understand and appreciate the religious world of the Mexican immigrants created a cultural chasm between the two groups. It should be noted that in this regard the Catholic clergy were no different from the rest of Americans at the time. Indeed, they were more concerned and less nativistic as regards the Mexicans than were most Americans. Compounding the problem was that scarcely any Mexican clergy followed the immigrants in their migration North. The church in Mexico had suffered greatly from the Mexican revolution in the early-twentieth century; anticlerical feelings were widespread and the clergy were in short supply, with only 230 registered in Mexico in 1935. This shortage of clergy would prove to be a severe liability.[49]

Of course the American church posed many problems for the newcomers as well. Mass-and-sacraments Catholicism was foreign to them, and the popular religious festivals of the old country were missing in the United States. As a result, the church did not evoke in the immigrants the same satisfying emotions that their Mexican religious experience did. The language barrier was another formidable obstacle, and so was discrimination. In some churches they had to sit in special pews in the back of the church; and other churches had signs, "Mexicans Prohibited." Another common practice was to have one Mass on Sunday for Mexicans, and if they attended any other Mass, they would be asked to leave. Even at the special early morning Mass they would have to wait outside church until all the Anglos had entered, and only then could they enter and take their place in the back of the church.[50] Such blatant discrimination alienated many Mexicans.

Although the Southwest had been home to Mexican-American Catholics for centuries and numerous Mexican-American parishes existed in the area, the twentieth-century migration North from Mexico was on such a large scale that it presented new problems and challenges for the church in the Southwest. Catholicism in the region was still in its missionary phase; clergy were scarce, financial resources were meager, and many people lived in isolated communities scattered across the vast areas of the rural Southwest. Thus, when the immigrants began to cross the border in large numbers, the church in the Southwest was ill prepared to minister to them. Nevertheless, bishops and priests did respond, and the 1920s ushered in a period of increased apostolic commitment to the Mexican immigrant community.

The Mexican population in Los Angeles increased dramatically during the 1920s, and by 1930, the city had a population of 97,116 Mexicans, making Los Angeles the largest community of Mexicans in the United States. This was a threefold increase in ten years. The response of the church to this influx was impressive, and by 1930 a large number of churches were in operation in Mexican neighborhoods. A major reason for this response was the fear of Protestant proselytization.[51]

During the nineteenth century, Mexicans in Los Angeles had been progressively isolated and segregated from the rest of the Catholic community. Set apart in their own neighborhoods, they went to their own separate parishes. In 1920 the principal Mexican church was Our Lady Queen of Angels. A religious order, the Claretian Fathers, ran the parish, and Spanish-speaking priests worked there. In addition, a small mission chapel was affiliated with the Anglo cathedral; among the remaining twenty-seven parishes, there was only one priest with a Spanish surname. In the next ten years a dramatic increase took place, and by 1930 the number of Catholic parishes in the city had grown to sixty-nine. Though foreign-born Irishmen staffed the vast majority of these parishes, thirteen churches in the city had Spanish-surname clergy and were clearly engaged in some type of ministry to the Mexican newcomers.[52] Because of the lack of Mexican clergy, religious-order priests from Spain had to be recruited to minister to the newcomers. Even though they spoke Spanish, culturally they were oceans removed from the Mexican immigrants and had difficulty, according to one priest, "understanding the psychology, manner, religious feeling, and educational problems of the Mexicans."[53] They were also criticized for being too aristocratic and aloof.

In Los Angeles, as in most of southern California, the separate national parish became the norm in the Mexican community. As was the pattern among blacks and Indians, certain religious orders, in Los Angeles the Claretians and Franciscans in particular, were given responsibility for the group. As a result, the rest of the parish clergy waived any responsibility for the Mexicans. This served only to reinforce the isolation and segregation of the newcomers from the rest of the Catholic community.

The neighborhood settlement house was another key institution in the church's ministry among the Mexicans. The first one in Los Angeles was founded in 1901; by 1930, four more were in operation, with a membership of well over twenty-three hundred people.[54] Though recreation was a vital part of these community centers, they also fostered religious instruction through an active catechetical program. Mexican lay men and women worked in this program visiting homes and conducting catechism classes for children. Women religious from Mexico were also involved in this catechetical work. Organized locally and eventually nationally into the Confraternity of Christian Doctrine, catechetics became a major feature of the apostolate to the Mexican community during the twentieth century. In this manner there was hope that their "religious ignorance" would be corrected and the children of the newcomers would be educated in the rituals and dogma of mainline, devotional Catholicism. The hope was that "in making better Catholics we shall make them better citizens."[55] In other words, church leaders viewed religious conversion as intimately linked with conversion to the American way of life. In keeping with the spirit of the 1920s, the church in Los Angeles inaugurated an extensive Americanization program. The bishop of Los Angeles, John Cantwell, was a big supporter of this movement and received help from the Knights of Columbus, who published a civics catechism in Spanish. Cantwell's successor, Francis McIntyre, continued this emphasis on Americanization; during his episcopacy, the parish school became the principal agency in the Americanization of the Mexican population.[56]

Mexicans were also moving into northern cities, and once again the separate national parish, operated by a religious order of priests, became the standard response of the church. Chicago had a growing Mexican population in the 1920s; many of these newcomers settled in the steel-mill community of South Chicago, where a small wooden church, Our Lady of Guadalupe, was opened for services in 1925. Cardinal Mundelein put the Claretian Fathers in charge of the parish, and they soon became closely identified with the Spanish-speaking apostolate in Chicago. A second Mexican parish opened on the city's near West Side. Once a German parish, then Italian for a brief time, St. Francis of Assisi parish began celebrating a Mass for Mexicans in 1925. The Claretians also operated this parish as well as several missions, or catechetical centers as they were called, in Mexican neighborhoods. They were assisted in this catechetical work by the Cordi-Marian sisters from Mexico. Americanization programs were also a priority in Chicago, where a Spanish-born priest urged his parishioners "to learn the language and adopt the customs of the United States."[57] Though some Mexicans did disperse to northern cities like Chicago or rural areas like Kansas, the vast majority remained in the rural Southwest in such border states as Texas and New Mexico.

Since colonial times, large numbers of Mexicans had lived in the Southwest region. The new immigrants of the twentieth century increased the Mexican, Spanish-speaking presence significantly and thus intensified the Mexican nature of the Southwest. The newcomers, however, were clearly different from those Mexican Americans whose families had lived in the Southwest for generations. Because of this, the old Spanish and Mexican-American families harbored a certain measure of prejudice against the newcomers. But the discrimination they encountered from the Anglos was much more harsh. Robert E. Lucey, bishop of Amarillo, Texas, in the 1930s, summed it up quite succinctly in a letter written in 1941. Speaking of the Mexicans, he said, "They are a people apart, ostracized and held in social and economic subjection. . . . If a Mexican is murdered, the officials do little or nothing about it. The Mexicans in Texas, even if born here, are classed with the Negroes." Such discrimination forced them into economic culs-de-sac—farm labor especially —where they received low wages and "barely managed to exist in poverty, disease and squalor."[58] Segregated economically, they were also segregated geographically and lived either in isolated towns and villages scattered about the Southwest or in crowded *barrios* in the city. The segregation and discrimination evident in the Southwest had also infiltrated into the American Catholic community.

In Texas, as was true in New Mexico, the institutional church was still very poor and underdeveloped. Unlike Boston or Chicago, Texas was mission country, and Catholics in the Northeast thought about it in much the same way as they did the missions of China or India. Thousands of Catholic families in the Northeast received the Catholic magazine *Extension;* there they learned of the poverty of the church in the Southwest. Inspired by illustrated reports written by missionary priests in Texas and New Mexico, Catholics contributed thousands of dollars to support the church in the Southwest. *Extension* magazine was a monthly publication of the Catholic Church Extension Society. Founded in 1905, the society was the brainchild of a Michigan priest, Francis C. Kelley. For decades, Extension raised funds to build chapels, schools, and other institutions in the Southwest. By 1930 it had contributed close to a million dollars to the church in Texas, and in the next twenty years the Lone Star State received another 1.5 million dollars from the Extension Society.[59] Other Catholic mission-aid societies in the United States also raised money to aid the church in the Southwest, much as foreign mission societies did to aid the church in the Northeast during the nineteenth century. One such group was the American Board of Catholic Missions. Founded by the bishops, it contributed 1.5 million dollars to the church in Texas from 1925 to 1951. Of course the Catholic population of Texas was heavily Mexican, with about two of every three Catholics being Mexican. Nevertheless, English-speaking parishes received $980,866 and the Spanish-speaking $390,000, or about one quarter of the total funds distributed by the Board.[60] Such a distinction clearly indicated that the apostolate to the Mexicans came in a distant second to that of the Anglos.

The lack of financial resources was one problem that organizations like the Extension Society were able to remedy to some degree. Less easily remedied was the isolated nature of church life in the rural areas. Many small towns and villages dotted the region, and priests visited these isolated settlements at occasional and distant intervals. A single parish would cover an immense territory. Sacred Heart parish, for example, was in the center of the state of Texas, in San Angelo; it covered a territory 195 miles long and 175 miles wide, an area almost seven times the size of Connecticut. When the Franciscans took over the parish, in 1925, the bishop told them that they had "a vast field like a diocese for the Mexican missions"; in the town of San Angelo itself there were "75 Catholic American families well disposed and doing all they can for their Church and parish." Beyond the town were several chapels or missions which priests visited on a regular basis, but no priest lived at these missions.[61] Insofar as the Catholic church was concerned, Texas in the 1920s was much like Maryland in the 1720s, except it was bigger.

Compounding the problem of isolated patterns of settlement was the lack of clergy. In comparison with other dioceses in the Northeast, the Southwest was clearly in need of priests. Desperate for clergy, bishops would accept just about any able-bodied priest who passed through, with the result that the clergy in the Southwest were, in the words of one Texas bishop, "quite mediocre."[62] As regards the pastoral care of the Mexicans, bishops were eager to recruit a religious order and give them total responsibility for the Spanish-speaking apostolate in the diocese. In this way, the bishop would not have to worry about recruiting Spanish-speaking priests, since the religious order would have to supply its own personnel for its parishes. As a result, the Claretians, the Oblates, and the Holy Cross Fathers became involved in the Spanish-speaking apostolate in Texas.

The Claretians were in charge of Immaculate Heart of Mary parish in San Antonio, and every indication suggests that it was a very active parish in the 1920s. It had numerous devotional societies, just like its Anglo counterpart; it solemnly celebrated several religious feasts including the feast of Our Lady of Guadalupe; it also sponsored a local branch of the Knights of Columbus; and in 1926, like many parishes, it was in the midst of fund-raising activities "for the benefit of the new school." As was customary, priests assigned to the parish were responsible for the pastoral care of several mission settlements.[63] The Franciscans were in charge of the parish of San José in the rural village of Los Ojos, New Mexico. There were also several missions, or chapels as they were called, in the sparsely populated area surrounding Los Ojos. Though a poor community, San José had its own school, which opened in 1923 in a solidly built brick structure. After the demolition of the old church, the men of the parish built a new brick church. In Los Ojos, as in other isolated settlements in the Mexican Southwest, the church occupied an important place in the people's lives.[64]

San José in Los Ojos and Immaculate Heart of Mary in San Antonio resembled many parishes in the Southwest. As religious and educational centers, they were engaged in a multitude of activities. They came alive on special feast days and burst with activity when it came time to raise money for a new school or church. As centers of pastoral concern, they cared for the sick, comforted the dying, and buried the dead. As educational centers, they helped to hand down the faith to a new generation of people. Indeed, paternalism and discrimination permeated the church in the Southwest. No one can deny that. Nonetheless, the parish remained a vital center for religion and succeeded in passing on the faith to a generation of people whose voices eventually would rise up in protest against paternalism and discrimination. As with the challenge presented by the black migration north, the church responded to Mexican immigration in a positive though flawed manner. One concrete result of this was that by 1960 Catholicism still remained the religion of more than 90 percent of the Mexican immigrants and their descendants.

In the black community, convert making was clearly the most creative and active response of the parish church in the 1930s and 1940s. In the Mexican community, the most creative apostolic work was catechetics. Catechetics and convert making had the same goal: instructing people in the Catholic faith. With the blacks, this also meant receiving them formally into the church. By the 1920s and 1930s, the catechetical movement had captured the imaginations of numerous Catholics. For many, the area most ripe for the harvest was the Southwest. Because of the shortage of clergy in this area, the presence of lay catechists proved to be especially advantageous. Traveling through the region, lay and religious volunteers taught children in school-rooms, pool halls, shacks, "or just a space in the open air."[65] They followed migrant workers and taught catechism in the camps. In the cities, catechetical centers often became launching pads for new parishes. A new order of women religious, the Victory Noll Sisters, was founded in 1922 by John Sigstein, a Chicago priest intensely interested in catechetics. For a number of years, these women catechists worked principally among Hispanics in New Mexico, California, Texas, and northwestern Indiana. In communities too poor and too small to support parish schools, catechists, in typical missionary fashion, concentrated their efforts on the young children, seeking to educate them in the dogma and ritual of devotional Catholicism. In larger and more estab-lished communities, lay catechists became the nucleus of social-action-minded parishioners, who began to discuss issues of social justice as well as religious instruction.[66]

As was true in the black Catholic apostolate, a shift toward issues of social justice began to take place in the 1940s and 1950s. A major catalyst in this transition was the Bishops' Committee for the Spanish-Speaking. Raymond A. McGowan, a priest working out of the Social Action Department of the National Catholic Welfare Conference, and Robert E. Lucey, the archbishop of San Antonio, hit on the idea of having a regional organization for the Spanish-speaking communities of the Southwest. After some initial meetings, the Bishops' Committee was organized in 1945, with Lucey as its executive chairman; for the next twenty-five years, Lucey was the key person in di-recting the activities of the committee. A social-action bishop, Lucey led a crusade against social injustices in Texas, and in the Mexican community the principal weapon in his fight for justice was the Bishops' Committee. It spon-sored catechism and child-care programs; it established health clinics and community centers; it also became involved in public housing and unioniza-tion efforts. In the 1950s, Lucey turned the committee into a "virtual farm workers' organization, using it to expose the migrants' plight and broaden the church's involvement in confronting this injustice."[67] Lucey was particularly active in opposing the government bracero program. Established in 1942 as a temporary work program, the bracero program legally provided for the re-cruitment of Mexican laborers for work in the United States. In effect, the United States Government became a supplier of cheap labor and in this man-ner subsidized the agricultural industry. The program not only kept wages for farm workers at a very low level, but it was riddled with corruption. It finally ended in 1964, after years of debate about the injustices it fostered in the Mexican farm workers' community. The persistent stance of the Bishops' Committee against the bracero program, along with its other work on behalf of social justice, helped to raise the public consciousness. This was the committee's "principal long range accomplishment." In this way, "It contributed to the political coming of age of the Mexican American in Texas and the Southwest at large by keeping before the public eye the prejudice and discrimination suffered by the Spanish-speaking."[68]

As a result of the Committee's success in raising public awareness of the problems of the migrant farm workers, dioceses in California and Florida inaugurated a traveling mission band to work with the migrants during the 1940s and 1950s. In California, priests involved in this ministry eventually became concerned with social-justice issues and encouraged farm workers to organize unions. Though such activity angered growers, a trend was set; by the 1960s, the Catholic clergy in California would become deeply involved in the cause of the farm workers.[69]

By the 1950s another chapter in the Hispanic phase of American Catholic history began to unfold. The heavy influx of Puerto Ricans to the United States, New York City in particular, presented new problems and new challenges for the church. New York City had a few separate parishes for the Spanish-speaking in the early-twentieth century, but Cardinal Spellman did away with the practice and told pastors to accept the newcomers and integrate them into the existing parish community. Since priests were in short supply in Puerto Rico, there was an immediate need to train the New York clergy in the language and culture of the newcomers. To achieve this, New York launched an ambitious pastoral program in 1953. Each year, priests and seminarians were sent off to language school in Puerto Rico. Then, in the summer of 1957, "a brilliant young Dalmatian priest," Ivan Illich, inaugurated a special program at the Catholic University of Puerto Rico for mainland church personnel working with Puerto Ricans. This program profoundly influenced a generation of ministers, both male and female, and the priests trained in Puerto Rico "became the pastoralist vanguard of the archdiocese."[70]

The plan to integrate Puerto Ricans into existing parishes had enormous implications. Not only would priests and religious have to be retrained, but "all diocesan programs, offices, and agencies would have to begin to address themselves to a bilingual, bicultural reality."[71] The church in New York responded to these new demands with a vast network of pastoral programs geared to the Puerto Ricans. What developed in New York eventually became the model for other eastern dioceses where Puerto Ricans were settling. As expected, discrimination against the Puerto Ricans on the part of many Catholics, both clergy and lay, short-circuited efforts at integration at the parish level. Puerto Rican Masses were held in church basements and school auditoriums while whites worshiped in the main church. Many older clergy, without the benefit of the Puerto Rican training program, resisted the efforts of the new breed of bilingual priests and clung to the traditions of the past. The gap between mainline devotional Catholicism and the religious world of the newcomers was a major stumbling block. As with the Mexicans, the standard of Mass-and-sacraments Catholicism was the expected norm for all Catholics. But, by the 1950s, Catholic social scientists were beginning to emerge. In New York the name of the Jesuit sociologist Joseph Fitzpatrick stood out above all others. Sensitive to the culture and religion of the Puerto Ricans, he unlocked their rich cultural and religious heritage and, through his writings and talks, educated a generation of priests and lay people in the issue of cultural and religious adaptation.

Despite obvious shortcomings, the trend was set, and a new ministry to the Spanish-speaking became a permanent part of New York Catholicism. Because of this, the church in New York was prepared to meet the challenges of the 1960s, when Catholicism in Manhattan and the Bronx became a church of the Spanish-speaking.

The new direction toward social justice, so evident in the Mexican community in the 1950s, was a decisive turn for the church in the post-World War II period. The major impulse for this shift was not the parish, but the Bishop's Committee, which in turn gave birth to special social-action ministries at the local level. The local parish remained focused on pastoral concerns and was unable to deal effectively with the larger social issues that emerged in the barrios and farm fields where Mexican-Americans lived and worked. For this reason, specialized social-action ministries soon became standard. Just as a new type of urban minister emerged in the black community, so, too, a new breed of social-action priests surfaced in Spanish-speaking communities. By the 1960s, this spirit would filter down to the parishes, and only then would parish communities become centers for social action.

In the 1950s, traditional pastoral concern still remained the chief focus of Spanish-speaking parishes. In the Southwest, more and more Mexicans were integrated into parishes with Anglos. Schools became the primary agents of Americanization, and schoolchildren and their parents were taught to be what were then called "practical Catholics."[72] At home, Mexican religious customs remained a living tradition; the celebration of special Mexican feast days also kept alive the people's self-identity. Like the rest of Catholic America, Mexican-Americans grew up in a world defined by their religion. Reflecting back on his childhood, one Mexican-American writer described his feelings about that period:

> I remember my early Catholic schooling and recall an experience of religion very different from anything I have known since. Never since have I felt so much at home in the Church, so easy at mass. My grammar school years especially were the

years when the great church doors opened to enclose me, filling my day as I was certain the Church filled all time. Living in a community of shared faith, I enjoyed much more than mere social reinforcement of religious belief. Experienced continuously in public and private, Catholicism shaped my whole day. It framed my experience of eating and sleeping and washing; it named the season and the hour.[73]

As the author, Richard Rodriguez, put it, ". . . the Church filled my life."[74] Adulthood would bring new challenges and elicit different feelings. Nonetheless, for young Rodriguez and his family, together with scores of Mexican Americans like him, Catholicism remained a vital part of life.

The heavy concentration of Mexicans in the rural Southwest, where vast distances and rural isolation posed special problems for the church, underscored the unique nature of rural life. People have always had a love affair with the country, and church leaders never ceased to praise the virtue of the country over the city. God made the country, while the city was a human invention. That was a refrain heard numerous times throughout the nineteenth century. In the early-twentieth century, just when the national population was becoming more urban than rural for the first time in its history, the country church movement got underway. Even though only an estimated 6 percent of the Catholic population lived in rural areas, the church inaugurated an ambitious rural-life program during the 1920s. The person most responsible for this was Edwin V. O'Hara, a priest in Oregon. In a 1920 paper on Catholic rural life presented at the National Catholic Educational Association convention, O'Hara sounded the warning. In his opinion, the quality of religion in rural areas was declining and something had to be done. Bishop Peter J. Muldoon of the National Catholic Welfare Conference shared O'Hara's concern and set up a Rural Life Bureau as part of the Social Action Department of the Conference. O'Hara became its first director. Working out of a parish in Eugene, Oregon, O'Hara promoted the cause of rural life. In 1923, together with other rural pastors, he formed a National Catholic Rural Life Conference.[75]

This trend toward a national organization was typical of everything Catholic in the twentieth century; education, social action, catechetics, Indian missions, and the Spanish-speaking apostolate, to name but a few, were organized nationally, and most often the national organizations were affiliated with the National Catholic Welfare Conference in a committee type of arrangement. This had the obvious effect of turning the Conference into a super church agency at the national level. Much like its Protestant counterpart, the Federal Council of Churches, the offices of the Conference in Washington, D.C., became the national headquarters of American Catholicism.

While the National Catholic Welfare Conference concerned itself with the national arena, rural pastors became involved in their apostolate of work, prayer, and lots of fertilizer. The major thrust of the rural ministry was the summer vacation school, at which children gathered together for a brief but intense program of religious instruction. In the 1930s, over three thousand summer programs were in operation, reaching over a quarter of a million children.[76] This focus on catechetics and the child was quite standard at the time regardless of the environment or the group. When the depression of the 1930s heightened interest in the economic problems of the farmer, some rural pastors began to expand their horizons and look at such questions as wages, economic conditions, and housing. An energetic pastor in Granger, Iowa, Luigi G. Ligutti, took advantage of New Deal legislation and succeeded in obtaining funds to build homes for Granger's unemployed miners and their families, both Protestant and Catholic. Throughout the 1930s, Ligutti spoke out continually on the plight of the rural worker and gained a national reputation as an advocate of rural life. By 1941 he had become head of the National Catholic Rural Life Conference. Through numerous talks across the country, he sparked interest in the needs of the rural parish. His message was clear: farming must develop together with the overall development of a region; the center of rural life is the family; and the purchasing power of the poor must increase. Such bishops of rural dioceses as Aloysius J. Muench of Fargo, North Dakota, gave strong support to the rural life movement; colleges such as St. John's University in Collegeville, Minnesota, sponsored rural-life summer schools for priests and lay people during the 1940s and 1950s.[77] Virtually unknown in the urban East, the rural-life movement occupied an important place in the lives of Catholic communities west of the Mississippi.

The move to suburbia was a major residential shift that challenged the church. As people flocked to tree-lined suburbs and septic-tank developments, the church followed. The response of the church was quite simple. The parish of the immigrant neighborhood was transplanted to the American suburb. The model suburban parish included church and elementary school, and by the 1950s some even were building their own high schools. Of course the suburbs were white and they also tended to be very mixed in nationalities, though some few did acquire a decisive ethnic quality. Like much of Catholicism at the time, the suburban parish became very child-centered, with the school being the central point of parish life.

By the 1950s, a good deal was being written about the quality of life in suburbia. The man in the gray flannel suit, the organization man, and the child-bound, car-caged housewife were popular stereotypes that denigrated suburban culture. In suburbia the old immigrant organizations had disappeared, the closeness of city neighborhoods was gone, and the moral integrity of family life seemed threatened. The fast-paced, highly mobile, seemingly secular suburban society did not appear to be a healthy environment for church religion. When compared to the city, however, suburbia seemed to be a pleasant place. The problems of race and poverty were downtown, out of sight and out of mind. That is just where the vast majority of Catholics in the 1950s wanted them: out of sight and out of mind. In suburbia, life's problems tended to be more personal and family-oriented, and they remained hidden in the privacy of the home or the confessional.

One major trend in suburbia was the concern for parish finances. The move to suburbia, begun in the 1920s and developing rapidly after World War II, placed huge debts on new suburban parishes. Central financing was one way to cope with these problems, but parishes still had to struggle to raise funds to pay off the cost of new churches, schools, rectories, and convents. The problem of finances was obviously not new to the twentieth century, but it is clear that from the 1920s through the 1950s, parish indebtedness became a major concern. Bingo signs became commonplace, and fund-raising events defined the church year in much the same way as Easter and Christmas. The Sunday envelope system was introduced around 1920; it soon became the main source of ordinary parish income, replacing the practice of pew rents and door collections. But it was never enough. An endless round of fund-raising events took place: card parties, dinners, raffles, picnics, entertainments, and fashion shows. They culminated in the largest event of all, the parish festival, or bazaar. These were great events throughout the nineteenth century; in those days parishes raffled off a horse and buggy, and numerous games of chance raised money for the parish. But financial concern did not define nineteenth-century parish life to the degree that it did in the twentieth century. The increasing emphasis on the parish school, which in most cases made up about 40 percent of the parish budget, and the need to support Catholic high schools was the primary reason for this financial fixation.[18] The Catholic "big" syndrome, with its penchant for large, costly churches, also drove up the debts of new suburban parishes. The Sunday envelope system or passing the basket at Mass was never sufficient to meet the rising cost of the twentieth-century parish. Thus, from their earliest days, Catholics were educated to support the church and did so with remarkable generosity.

Financial concerns eventually took over the pulpit, and the Sunday sermon frequently turned into an appeal for funds. A study of one parish indicated that 25 percent of the Sunday sermons during the course of a year were financial appeals. Coupled with this was the bishop's letter. With the rise in central financing and the centralization of various church ministries, bishops had to raise a lot of money for diocesan projects, and they did this by appealing to the people. In the New Orleans diocese, about half of the letters from the bishop were appeals for funds for diocesan and national needs; this meant that, at least once a month, people in the parish were asked to contribute to the bishop's treasury. When this was added to the pastor's appeal for money, it meant that in a given parish it would be quite normal to have half of the Sunday sermons during the course of a year given over to appeals for funds.[19]

Concern for finances has been a constant presence in church life regardless of time or place. But the challenges presented by the changing social environment of twentieth-century America added new and more vital issues to the church's agenda. The racial issue, the presence of black and brown Americans in the shadow of the church steeple, was clearly the most critical issue the church had to face since the days of immigration. Catholics responded slowly and with great difficulty to the racial issue. Nevertheless, progress had been made by the 1950s, and the course of the future was set. When the racial issue became a central concern of the entire nation in the 1960s, the church, through its priests and lay people, was prepared to become involved in a constructive fashion.

All the world was not in a state of flux during the 1920–60 period. There were some anchors in a sea of change which people could hold on to. For Catholics, one central constant in their lives was their religion.

XIV

Religion, Education, and Reform

THE THIRTY YEARS after World War I was the time when devotional Catholicism hit its peak. As was true in the nineteenth century, the Papacy vigorously promoted this type of religion through encyclical letters, indulgences, and the establishment of new religious feasts. Bishops and priests followed the lead of the popes, and lay people responded with uncommon enthusiasm. One of the clearest examples of the growing popularity of devotional Catholicism was in the area of Marian piety.

The recitation of the rosary, the spring ritual of May crownings of Marian statues, and the celebration of Marian feast days still occupied a central place in the religious life of Catholics. The Mexican newcomers brought a strong Marian tradition with them; every city where they settled had a church named after Our Lady of Guadalupe in honor of the sixteenth-century Marian apparition near Mexico City. The celebration of the feast of Our Lady of Guadalupe, on December 12, was always a festive event in the community. When migrant workers came to the United States, they often began and ended their journey with a visit to the shrine of La Virgen de San Juan de los Lagos in San Juan, Texas, near the Rio Grande. During the twentieth century, other expressions of Marian devotion also became popular. One of the most popular of all was the novena. In the decades following World War I, the novena became the most popular devotion in the Catholic community. There were various types of Marian novenas, but clearly one of the most popular was the novena in honor of Our Sorrowful Mother, better known as the Sorrowful Mother novena. Inaugurated by a Servite priest, James R. Keane, at Our Lady of Sorrows Church in Chicago in 1937, it met with immediate and surprising success. Within a year, seventy thousand people were attending thirty-eight novena services at Our Lady of Sorrows every week. The novena spread to other cities across the country and to foreign countries as well. The novena prayer book was eventually translated into thirty-five languages, and a braille edition was also published. On its tenth anniversary, it was reported that the cumulative attendance at the novena in the United States was over thirty-five million.[1]

The Sorrowful Mother novena had become a mass movement promoted by a religious magazine, a radio program, and a national publicity campaign. Novena services soon began to attract large, enthusiastic crowds. Part of the novena's appeal was its Marian quality; Mary was clearly enjoying a renaissance of popularity in the early-twentieth century. The Marian apparition at Fátima, Portugal, in 1917 and the papal promotion of new Marian feast days, climaxing with the 1950 papal definition of Mary's Assumption into Heaven, encouraged popular Marian devotion. Spiritual writers became preoccupied with writing about Mary, and in the ten-year period 1948–57, ten thousand Marian titles were published; never before or since has so much been written about Mary. The Sorrowful Mother novena capitalized on this Marian renaissance and added the special dimension of focusing "on the sorrowful moments in Mary's life"; in this manner the person not only gave honor to Mary, "but also achieved consolation for his own troubles and guilt."[2] The service itself also had a special appeal. Conducted in English, it enabled the people to participate actively; sentimental tunes appealed to many people, the most notorious being the novena theme song, "Good Night Sweet Jesus." The petitions of people which focused largely on spiritual appeals—e.g., for the deceased, the sick, and good health—were also read aloud at these services. Another major reason for the novena's widespread popularity was the social situation of the people in the United States. The effects of the depression were still being felt throughout the nation in the late 1930s. In a time of crisis and hardship, working-class Catholics could relate quite readily to Our Lady of Sorrows. It gave them emotional relief and allowed them to pray for jobs and financial success. When World War II broke out, personal anxiety and sorrow continued to be a common experience for many people. Not surprisingly, the record shows that the novena began a steady decline after the early 1940s.

The Sorrowful Mother novena, like much of Marian piety, reinforced the Catholic ethos. Its intense focus on sorrow nurtured a sense of sin and guilt; the public performance of the novena underscored the central importance of ritual; and the emphasis on good health and miraculous cures kept alive a reverence and respect for the miraculous.

Another very popular aspect of Marian piety in the twentieth century was devotion to Our Lady of Fátima. Inspired by the Marian apparition in Fátima in 1917, the cult of Fátima received a papal endorsement in 1942. The message of Fátima was one of prayer and repentance, with a specific request of Mary reportedly being prayers for the conversion of Russia. In the Cold War atmosphere of the late 1940s and 1950s, devotion to Our Lady of Fátima took on a very strong anti-Communist quality. American Catholics, fearful of Communist expansion, the nuclear arms race, and subversion of America itself, found comfort and solace in devotion to Our Lady of Fátima. Catholics had long been ardent opponents of international communism, and Fátima was a heavenly sign of approval for such opposition. When much of the United States got caught up in the Communist scare of the McCarthy era of the 1950s, many Catholics, nurtured on a piety that had a decided anti-Communist quality, became ardent supporters of the anti-Communist crusade.[3]

In keeping with the twentieth-century emphasis on the apostolate of the young, the sodality movement experienced a renaissance in the 1920s and 1930s. The main force behind this was the Jesuit priest Daniel Lord. The sodality promoted devotion to Mary, and in the twentieth century frequent Communion also became an important theme. Lord targeted the sodality at high school students, who were rapidly increasing in number at this time. He promoted the sodality and its special brand of devotional Catholicism in a variety of ways: through a magazine, pamphlets, theater, summer schools of Catholic Action, and national conventions. The sales of his religious pamphlets—small booklets that cost ten cents—exceeded twenty-five million copies.[4]

Devotion to Jesus and the Eucharist was another aspect of Catholic piety that experienced a resurgence in the twentieth century. In the nineteenth century, the focus had been on adoration of the Eucharistic Christ through benediction and Eucharistic processions. This continued during the twentieth century and became very commonplace in parish devotional life. Added to the concept of adoration was the frequent reception of Communion. Pope Pius X first promoted the "Communion movement," by urging frequent Communion, in 1905. The reception of Communion at Mass soon became more and more frequent; it even became common for Communion to be distributed before and after Mass, and eventually Communion was distributed entirely apart from the Mass. The transformation that took place in one parish, St. Ignatius in Portland, Oregon, indicated how swift and extensive the change was. In 1919, 330 Communions were recorded for the year; by 1923 the number had jumped to 14,400, and during these four years the number of parishioners had remained the same.[5] Linked to frequent Communion was frequent confession, and the nineteenth-century tradition of long lines at Saturday confessions remained standard during these years.

Parish missions continued to be very popular, but in the early-twentieth century another pastoral technique, the retreat, developed. Aimed at lay men and eventually lay women, it was an intense period of prayer and devotional rituals that generally took place over the course of a weekend. Rooted in the spiritual exercises of St. Ignatius, the retreat movement became popular in the post-World War I period. By the end of 1930, over fifty-five retreat houses were operating in the United States, and they had conducted 3,274 retreats for men that year. The Jesuits were the main promoters of the movement, but other religious orders also conducted retreats for men. Retreats for high school students were popular and had much the same effect as a parish mission because of the heavy emphasis on sin, judgment, heaven, and hell. A women's retreat movement began to take shape in the 1930s, and women religious had a central role in this. Predictably the retreat movement was organized nationally and sponsored the usual annual conventions.[6]

Mainline devotional Catholicism was the normative religion nurtured in both the black Catholic community and the Mexican community. Among the Mexicans, the tradition of family-oriented, folk religion remained very strong; in the Mexican parish the pattern was to add special devotions popular with the people—such as devotion to Our Lady of Guadalupe—to the regular calendar of mainline devotional Catholicism. In every community, the Catholic ethos remained very much the same as in the nineteenth century. Shrines or pilgrimage sites increased during the 1920s. Fascination with healing remained very strong, and the growing popularity of such international shrines as Lourdes, in France, strengthened this. Added to the sense of the miraculous was a strong dose of sin and guilt. Marian piety, especially after Fátima, stressed this; the retreat movement and the sodality movement did so as well. Ritual increasingly occupied a more central role in the community as Catholics went public with parades and other outdoor religious events; the ritualized nature of the novena, which included the repetition of a set formula of prayers over a prescribed period of time, not only reinforced the sense of ritual, but it also gave it a very magical quality. During these years, the growing popularity of the popes culminated in the pontificate of Pope Pius XII. A popular cult of the Papacy developed, and this facilitated its promotion of devotional Catholicism. The Bishop and priest still remained very powerful in the spiritual life of the faithful, but the communications revolution of radio and television brought the Papacy closer to home. The deaths and elections of popes became front-page news and table talk. Such popularity reinforced the Pope's position as monarch in the church.

As was true in the nineteenth century, organized religion still remained more popular with women than men. Sociological studies of Catholic life confirmed this trend and suggested that, at the parish level, women made up a two-to-one majority at religious exercises.[7] The men's retreat movement was a notable exception, as was the popular Holy Name Society. The popularity of Marian piety strengthened the female nature of the people's religion. Not surprisingly, large numbers of women continued to be attracted to religious life. Even though the life of the convent was a more difficult path to follow, women religious continued to outnumber priests; in 1960 there were 164,922 women religious to 52,689 priests.

As in the nineteenth century, not all Catholics brought up in the "novena-rosary tradition" liked it. Flannery O'Connor, the noted writer, described it as "vapid Catholicism" and confided to a friend, ". . . you have to save yourself from it some day or dry up."[8] In her own inimitable style she said what she thought about novenas:

> Having grown up with them, I think of novenas the same way I think of the hideous Catholic churches you all too frequently find yourself in, that is, after a time I cease to see them even though I'm in them. The virtue of novenas is that they keep you at it for nine consecutive days and the human attention being what it is, this is a long time. I hate to say most of these prayers written by saints-in-an-emotional-state. You feel you are wearing somebody else's finery and I can never describe my heart as "burning" to the Lord (who knows better) without snickering.[9]

By the 1950s, devotional Catholicism was clearly on the decline, and critics were quite common though usually not as eloquent as Flannery O'Connor. Never more than a small part of the community, nonetheless they represented the vanguard of a movement that was slowly but doggedly changing the nature of Catholic piety. The main source of criticism came from supporters of the liturgical movement.

The liturgical movement originated in the nineteenth century in French Benedictine monasteries. After World War I it gained wide support and initiated a movement of renewal in the church. The drive for reform in the liturgy or the public prayer life of the church was but one of several reform movements going on in Catholic Europe at that time. Others touched on biblical studies, theology, and church history. Due to the antimodernist climate, such reform movements proceeded cautiously and quietly. The reform of the liturgy, however, was quite public. Even the Pope, Pius X, urged reform in certain aspects of the liturgy. He favored the frequent reception of Communion, and this was seen as increasing a person's participation in the Mass; Pius X also encouraged the solemn chanting of parts of the Mass. In this manner he helped to encourage "the active participation of the faithful in the sacred mysteries in the public and solemn prayer of the Church."[10] With the Benedictines pointing the way and with the support of many clergy and bishops in Germany, the liturgical movement expanded throughout Europe. By the 1920s it arrived in the United States as part of the cultural baggage of priests who had studied in Europe and saw at first hand the effects of the liturgical movement. Chief among these priests was Virgil Michel, a Benedictine monk at St. John's University in Collegeville, Minnesota. Together with Martin Hellriegel, a St. Louis pastor, and Gerald Ellard, a Jesuit seminarian, Michel founded a periodical in 1926, *Orate Fratres,* later known as *Worship.*

Orate Fratres became the bible of the American liturgical movement. Michel also founded a publishing enterprise, Liturgical Press, whose books and pamphlets promoted liturgical renewal. Until his death in 1938, he was the major force behind the movement. St. John's continued to be a major center for the promotion of liturgical renewal, and Michel's successor, Godfrey Diekmann, O.S.B., eventually became a nationally recognized authority on the liturgy.

At the pastoral level, Hellriegel was the recognized authority on liturgy in the parish. Every year, hundreds of priests would visit his parish to observe how pastor and people celebrated the liturgy. After ordination to the priesthood and study in Europe, Ellard devoted his time to the scholarly study of the liturgy; his 1933 book *Christian Life and Worship* was used in many colleges throughout the pre-Vatican II period. In 1940, the first of many national liturgical conventions was held; people returned from these annual conventions energized and fortified for their struggle against the much more pervasive "novena-rosary" Catholicism.[11]

The goal of the liturgical movement was to create a better understanding of the Mass through a more active participation on the part of the people. It encouraged singing at Mass, at first by chanting parts of the Mass in Latin and then, by the 1950s, singing popular hymns in English. It urged people to follow the Mass in an English-language hand missal; and it promoted the dialogue Mass, in which the people would respond in Latin to the prayers of the priest celebrant. By the 1950s, supporters of the liturgical movement even wanted to have the entire Mass said in English, rather than the traditional Latin. At the time this was a very radical proposal.

The basis for liturgical renewal was a new theology of the church. Originating in Europe, it made its way to the United States in the 1930s and 1940s. It was a more biblical, less institutional, type of theology, which emphasized the spiritual nature of Catholicism. Its focus was Jesus Christ, not the saints; its chief prayer was the Mass, not the novena; it encouraged a social spirit, rather than individualism; it sought to foster community, rather than isolation; it stressed the public quality of religion, not the private. Such a radical shift was not always warmly received, and arguments between advocates of the new liturgy, derisively called "litniks," and adherents of the old-style religion, were common. The new theology received papal approval when, in 1943, Pope Pius XII published an encyclical on the mystical body wherein he defined the church in the more biblical and spiritual manner as the mystical body of Christ. Then, four years later, he published another encyclical, *Mediator Dei*, which became the Magna Charta of the liturgical movement. In the 1950s, Pope Pius XII inaugurated programs for liturgical renewal such as a new, liturgically inspired ritual for Holy Week; by then it was clear that the "litniks" were gaining strength in their efforts to reform devotional Catholicism. Nevertheless, it would take some time before the majority of the people would feel comfortable with changes in the liturgy.

Unlike in Germany, the bishops in the United States did not provide a leadership role in liturgical renewal. Most bishops and priests were raised in the "novena-rosary" tradition and never questioned its value. They looked with suspicion, if not hostility, at liturgical innovation. Since liturgical reform touched a very sensitive nerve—the nature of a person's relationship with God—most people felt threatened by any suggested changes in this relationship. Even though all indications pointed to a decline in the popularity of devotional Catholicism by the 1950s, the vast majority of Catholics still clung to the old-style religion. As a result, they were poorly prepared for the sweeping changes in the liturgy that took place in the 1960s as a result of the Second Vatican Council.[12]

During the twentieth century, the Catholic educational network expanded to a considerable degree. As American society became more modern and metropolitan, the educational experience of people became broader and more complex. With the extension of education to all segments of society, an incredible array of educational agencies developed. Along with this came a desire to export American culture and civilization to the rest of the world. These tendencies received a decided push from the progressive reform period and the educational ideas of people such as John Dewey. By World War I, the course was charted, and a communication revolution and the development of mass media served to expand "the range and complexity" of the educational experience.[13] These powerful cultural trends greatly influenced the configuration of education in the Catholic community.

During the decades following World War I, the Catholic configuration changed in a subtle but substantial manner. The church remained an important educational institution, but the range and complexity of its educational enterprise increased to an incredible degree. A brief glance at the 1960 edition of the *Catholic Almanac* strikingly illustrates this. There were 223 different "associations, movements and societies" that had an explicit educational purpose; they ranged from a professional sociological organization to a Catholic poetry society; from the Blue Army of Our Lady of Fatima, which urged prayers for the conversion of Russia, to the League of Tarcisians of the Sacred Heart, which organized children "as Apostles of the Sacred Heart in their homes." In addition, there were Catholic camps, religious correspondence courses, and book clubs.[14] By the 1950s, Catholics clearly believed that all segments of American society needed the benefits of a Catholic influence. The expansive trend of the modern educational experience certainly influenced this, but a strong feeling of confidence, or "Catholic smugness," had a lot to do with it as well. Both intellectuals and factory workers believed that Catholicism was just what society needed.

A paean of praise to religion and football, written by the Prefect of Religion at the University of Notre Dame, John F. O'Hara, C.S.C., when Notre

Dame beat Nebraska for the national championship in 1924, is a perfect example of this smugness:

> . . . the world is beginning to realize the source of Notre Dame's brand of sportsmanship. The teamwork of a Notre Dame eleven is not inspired by the philosophy of Nietzsche, it has none of the earmarks of Schopenhauer or Kant; it is neither bloodless pessimism, nor festering selfishness; it is neither cynical nor brutal; it is a red-blooded play of men full of life, full of hope, full of charity, of men who learn at the foot of the altar what it means to love one another, of men who believe that clean play can be offered as a prayer in honor of the Queen of Heaven, Notre Dame football is a new crusade: it kills prejudice and it stimulates faith.[15]

Though bitten by theological hyperbole, O'Hara, who would one day become the cardinal archbishop of Philadelphia, evidenced a passionate belief in the influence of Catholicism. Such belief, coupled with the American shift to educational expansion and complexity, launched a period of tremendous growth in the Catholic educational enterprise.

A separate book would be needed to examine the twentieth-century church as an educational agency. Nevertheless, some general trends can be noted. Up until the 1960s, the *Baltimore Catechism* remained the staple of the Catholic Sunday school and of children's religious instruction in general. Because of strong and persistent criticism of its pedagogical flaws and arcane theology, a new and revised version appeared in 1941. But the question-and-answer format remained central and the memorization of scholastic terminology was still necessary. However, in the mid-twentieth century, there was more to religious instruction that just the *Baltimore Catechism*. A vigorous catechetical movement had gained a full head of steam by the 1930s; summer-vacation schools, discussion clubs, and a number of other programs became very popular. Included in the catechetical movement was a concern for convert-making. In the rural areas of America where neither priest nor Catholic church existed, Paulist priests brought Catholicism to the people by means of a "trailer chapel." Made of steel and pulled by a Ford car, the St. Lucy trailer was "equipped with a rather complicated electrical system, a public address system and phonograph, a complete sound movie projector and screen, as well as a Catholic encyclopedia, a supply of selected pamphlets, and several Bibles, both Douay and King James Versions." The missionary claimed, "The loudspeakers had been heard at a distance of three miles, and questions had been sent in by people who were listening to the service at a distance of over a mile."[16] In 1939, a new religious order, the Glenmary Missioners, was founded "for the care and conversion of souls in neglected 'no priest land.' " Inspired by the success of such noted convert-makers as Fulton J. Sheen and John A. O'Brien, priests zealously sought to convert people to Catholicism. In 1960, the number of converts peaked at 146,212.

The fraternal societies of the nineteenth century remained in existence throughout the period, but they lost their strong Old World quality with each new generation. The Knights of Columbus emerged as the premier organization for men. Though run by Irishmen, it had a decided American spirit to it. This enabled the Knights of Columbus to cut across nationality differences and appeal to a variety of nationalities.

With more children in school and more leisure time available, societies for young people increased dramatically. Nineteenth-century parish organizations were clearly adult-oriented, but by the twentieth century, youth-oriented societies multiplied. Chief among these was the Catholic Youth Organization, referred to as the CYO. Founded in 1930 by a Chicago priest, Bernard J. Sheil, it spread across the country. Based in the parish but organized on a city, regional, and national level, it promoted all types of programs for young men, but it was clearly most successful in its athletic programs. Dramatic clubs also remained popular, but competition from movies and television weakened their attraction. Summer institutes organized by Catholic colleges began to replace the popular Catholic Chautauqua at Cliff Haven, New York.

At the national level, the National Catholic Welfare Conference became a very important educational agency through its promotion of social action, Americanization, youth movements, lay organizations, journalism, and political lobbying. The professionalization of the charity apostolate led to the emergence of the Catholic social worker, who, as a home visitor, became an important instructor in the domestic and family virtues.

Though the pulpit remained an important part of Catholic worship, preaching did not seem to improve very much in the twentieth century. "Priests were competent and pedestrian preachers, but they lacked great eloquence and artistic merit," noted one study.[17] A Protestant observer made a similar assessment:

> The sermon is of minor importance in the Catholic Sunday morning service or Mass. It is usually no more than eight to ten minutes in length. It is prefaced by the priest's reading of a selection from the Scriptures. Usually the reading is rapid and sometimes intoned almost as if it were liturgy. The Scripture reading is seldom used as a basis for development of the sermon. The sermons are usually straight, rational expositions of doctrine with much less general use than the Protestant pastors employ of devices to interest and persuade, (such as illustrations, narrative, dramatic figures of speech, personal witness). The role of the priest in the service is primarily that of performance of the ritual, not of instruction.[18]

The rise of the mass media was of course a major development and had a powerful impact on all churches. Like Protestants, Catholics took to the airways and became heavily involved in religious broadcasting. "The Catholic Hour" was inaugurated in 1930 and transmitted across the country by twenty-two radio stations of the National Broadcasting Company; by 1940, the number of stations had increased to seventy-one, and in 1959 one hundred fifty stations carried the program to an estimated four million people. Religious broadcasting at the local level also developed. In 1948 a person in Boston could tune in to the following programs: "A Novena to Our Lady of Perpetual Help," "Our Lady of Fatima Devotions," "Mother of Sorrows Novena," "Meditations on the Life of Christ," "The Sacred Heart Program," "The Hour of St. Francis," "The Ave Maria Hour," "The Rosary Hour," and weekly segments of "The Greatest Story Ever Told," to name but a few.[19]

The star of Catholic radio and television was Fulton J. Sheen. Born in rural Illinois, he was ordained a priest in 1919; after graduate studies in philosophy, he taught at the Catholic University in Washington, D.C. His talents as a preacher and lecturer soon became known, and in 1930 he was selected to speak on the national program "The Catholic Hour." A spellbinding speaker, Sheen was a most successful radio preacher. His listening audience numbered more than seven million people, and he received about six thousand letters a day from people all over the country. In 1951 he turned to television; by this time he was a bishop. Even though his evening program, "Life Is Worth Living," was scheduled opposite Milton Berle's comedy show, it still reached an estimated audience of thirty million people and remained on the air until 1957. That year, Sheen received an Emmy Award in recognition of his television accomplishments. In the opinion of Billy Graham, Sheen was "one of the greatest preachers of our century"; he was a true Catholic hero, and his success made Catholics proud and indeed smug.[20]

Twentieth-century Catholics also shared the American desire to export their culture and religion to other countries. Throughout the nineteenth century, Catholics were very parochial, but the horizon of the clergy and the people expanded in the twentieth century. This sparked a foreign-mission campaign. In 1911 a new religious order was founded, The Catholic Foreign Mission Society, generally known as Maryknoll. Founded by two priests, James A. Walsh and Thomas Price, it was the first American order established for overseas mission work. Other religious orders also became involved in foreign missions, with Asian countries having a special attraction for many. The Jesuit, Maryknoll, and La Salette orders had the largest numbers of priests and brothers, while Maryknoll and the Missionary Sisters of the Immaculate Conception had the most women religious missionaries. By 1958 3,496 priests and brothers were working on the foreign missions along with 2,532 women religious. In addition, 96 lay missionaries were also working overseas. This was a new development as well as a sign of the increasing involvement of the laity in the work of the church.[21]

Newspapers took on a new life in the twentieth century. Though fewer in number, their circulation was much larger. A significant development was the newspaper chain. *Our Sunday Visitor,* founded in Fort Wayne in 1912, began to publish editions for other dioceses in 1937; the same pattern developed with the *Catholic Register* in Denver. By the early 1960s, *Our Sunday Visitor* and the *Catholic Register* had a combined national circulation of over 1.5 million. An active Catholic Press Association promoted Catholic journalism; in 1959 it reported "a record total of 24,273,972 subscribers to 580 Catholic publications in the United States."[22] Of these, 111 were diocesan newspapers. Unlike the nineteenth century, when some Catholic newspapers were owned and operated by lay people, newspapers in the twentieth century were controlled by the local bishops. A notable exception is the weekly magazine *Commonweal*. Founded in 1924 as a weekly review of literature, the arts, and politics, it is owned and operated by laymen. Other independent, lay-operated publications did emerge in later years, but none matched the success and achievements of *Commonweal*. Book publishing was another important aspect of the Catholic subculture. Catholic book clubs became popular, and Catholic literary awards were also common.

The extensive and complex network of Catholic educational programs promoted a very specific culture, an ethos that in the twentieth century was becoming increasingly more American while it remained traditionally very Catholic.

The family was another major part of the modern configuration of education. The family underwent some subtle changes in the first half of the twentieth century. The size of the household decreased, the divorce rate continued to rise, and beginning in the 1940s, more married women went to work outside the home. During the 1920s and after, increased attention was directed to the family. As a result, a host of new organizations emerged, both secular and church-related, to strengthen and assist family life. Some of these came about as the result of increased specialization in such disciplines as counseling and sociology; others emerged from a concern over a perceived moral crisis in family life. After World War II, America celebrated home and family life as a haven in a world threatened by atomic bombs and Communist infiltration. Religion also experienced a revival, and with this renewed interest came more family-oriented organizations.

Catholics were caught up in the concern for family life, and like many other Americans, they became alarmed about "the moral crisis" of the family. By the 1930s this concern approached "hysteric proportions." One bishop feared that the increase in divorce would unleash a "moral gangrene" that would destroy the nation. In 1949 the American hierarchy issued a pastoral letter on family life which described the family crisis as a "present danger more fearsome than the atomic bomb."[23]

The Catholic position, articulated principally by sociologists and clergymen, was that rapid social change posed a threat to family life. Therefore, sound principles of family life were required, in other words a clear articulation of the Catholic principles of family life. The procreation and education of children were stressed as the primary goals of marriage, and the ultimate goal of the child was not worldly success, but eternal salvation. Beset by the "disintegration" of family life, the home was to become, in the words of a noted Catholic sociologist, "a little world set apart from the turmoil and strife of the outside world." There the family, nurtured by devotional Catholicism, would be safe from the "moral gangrene" of American society. In 1930 a papal encyclical, *Casti Connubii,* highlighted these concerns and gave church leaders the desired Catholic proclamation on marriage.[24]

Numerous organizations were created to strengthen family life. At the national level, a Family Life Bureau was set up at the National Catholic Welfare Conference in 1931, but it never penetrated parish and family life to a significant degree. A more successful program was the Cana Conference, which originated from a married couples' retreat held in New York City in 1943. Stressing personal responsibility and the need for education and attitudinal change, Cana's focus was on the person, not the environment. In other words, "Reform began with the formation of the individual and only then could spread to the larger society."[25] Because of its upbeat nature, Cana became very popular, and by 1950 75 percent of the dioceses in the United States had Cana conferences. The nerve center of the movement was Chicago, where it prospered under the energetic leadership of a young priest, John Egan.

For many Catholics, Cana was not enough. The answer to the family crisis was to be found not in the home or with the married couple, but in society. As historian Jeffrey Burns noted, ". . . if better family life was to be attained, the environment had to be changed."[26] The group that advocated this position became known as the Christian Family Movement.

The Christian Family Movement, more commonly known as CFM, grew out of a unique Catholic Action movement that captured the imagination of many young people in the 1930s and 1940s. Developed by a Belgian priest, Joseph Cardijn, it was an apostolic technique that stressed the reform of society through the formula of "observe, judge, and act." Its primary orientation was toward action and the reform of society, rather than the education and formation of the individual. Catholic Action groups, following the Cardijn model, began to emerge in various cities throughout the country, with Chicago being an especially active area. An adult version of Catholic Action, the concept of CFM emerged during the mid 1940s from Catholic Action groups meeting in Chicago, South Bend, and other cities. In 1949 an organizational meeting of these kindred spirits was held and Chicago was chosen as the site for the national headquarters. A Chicago lawyer and his wife, Pat and Patty Crowley, were selected as the leaders of the group. The following year, the name Christian Family Movement was chosen as the title of the adult Catholic Action movement. CFM became very popular, and by 1958, its membership numbered thirty thousand couples in the United States and in several foreign countries. Because of their energetic leadership, the

Crowleys, often referred to as Mr. and Mrs. CFM, became the leading couple in the movement.[27]

The Christian Family Movement was radically new in several ways. Its focus on the relationship between the social order and the family was quite unusual in family-life organizations. Its social-action orientation reflected the growing involvement of lay Catholics in issues related to social justice, issues that were not strictly Catholic but touched all people regardless of their race or religion. This social-action focus intensified during the 1950s, and by 1960 the goal of CFM had become the formation of "members of Christian families through spiritual development and action on temporal problems to assume their place in the lay apostolate so that they can completely bear witness to Christ in the particular field of endeavor or circumstance in which they find themselves."[28] Based in metropolitan areas and drawing from the new Catholic middle class, CFM was militantly lay-oriented. Priests had an advisory role, but lay people controlled the group. In addition, CFM promoted the new concept of the church as the mystical body of Christ. This emphasis on the communal nature of Catholicism undercut the individualism of traditional devotional Catholicism and made members of CFM and other social-action Catholics more conscious of their responsibility to other people in both church and society.

CFM provides a good indication of the changes that were taking place in Catholicism during the 1940s and 1950s. A minority movement, to be sure, nevertheless it pointed in a new direction, toward a new future. The concern for social justice and for issues that were not strictly Catholic was a definite shift from the parochialism of the past. A new understanding of the church as the mystical body of Christ introduced a more social and communal quality to the religion of the people. The emergence of lay leadership after so many years of clerical control during the twentieth century was also new. A new generation of Catholics was emerging, many of whom were college-educated professionals, and they were beginning to seek leadership roles in the Catholic community. The Catholic Action movement, because of its distant stance from the institutional church, was a good training ground for such leadership. Though CFM drew its members from parish communities, it transcended particular parish loyalties and remained fiercely independent of the local pastor. This did create problems, but many priests in the 1950s welcomed the emergence of lay leadership in the Catholic community.

The success of CFM suggested that the parish was no longer the one vital center of Catholic life. Because Catholic Action movements focused on special groups of people (married couples, college students, and businessmen or workers), they were not oriented toward the parish. The twentieth-century trend of modernization fostered this development of special-interest apostolates with national organizations. This, too, shifted the focus from parish and neighborhood. Though the parish still remained a vital center of Catholic life in the 1950s, new trends were on the horizon which would challenge this in the years ahead. A study of Catholic parish life in New Orleans in the late 1940s already suggested as much. As the author of the study, the sociologist Joseph Fichter, S.J., pointed out, "The facts showed that these Catholics associated more closely on the basis of similar educational, occupational, and especially racial characteristics than on the basis of their shared Catholicism. In general we had to conclude that the parish was a kind of service station where the people had their religious and spiritual needs satisfied."[29] This was a decisive shift from the immigrant era, when the parish had a powerful influence in the formation of the immigrants' sense of identity in the New World. As Catholics became more American and farther removed from the immigrant experience, the parish was clearly beginning to take on a new function.

The centerpiece of the Catholic educational network was still the school. The nineteenth century had set the patterns for the development and growth of the parochial school. The ideal remained a school in every parish and Catholic children in Catholic schools. Bishops tried to enforce this and were able to use the new 1917 Code of Church Law, which forbade Catholic children to attend schools open to non-Catholics. Fortunately for the United States, the law allowed the local bishop to determine if attendance at such schools could be allowed, and most American bishops did not enforce the 1917 Roman regulation.[30] Despite the laws of the Third Baltimore Council and the Code of Canon Law, the hoped-for ideal was never realized. The number of schools increased dramatically during the twentieth century, but so did the number of elementary-school children. By 1959 only 59 percent of the nation's Catholic parishes had schools. That was a sizable increase over the 1920 level of 35 percent but still far from the ideal of the Third Baltimore Council. What this meant was that about one half of Catholic elementary-school children attended public schools.

The twentieth-century emphasis on organization and specialization strengthened the move toward the systematization of Catholic schools. The number of diocesan superintendents increased, and at the national level the National Catholic Educational Association, founded in 1904, served as the main coordinating agency for educational enterprises. The education department of the NCWC also promoted the cause of Catholic education at the national level. The trend toward organization did mean that schooling was becoming more and more centralized at the local diocesan school office. Nevertheless, pastors still protected their authority as the local school bosses, and this tended to retard efforts toward greater standardization and centralization. Much more influential in shaping Catholic schools was the move toward accreditation and testing, which helped to make Catholic schools very much like their public counterparts.

As in the nineteenth century, the elementary school continued to be a key promoter of devotional Catholicism and the Catholic ethos. It also had a major influence on the increased Americanization of the children of immigrants. Both Catholic and public educators were pushing for the elimination of the use of foreign languages in teaching. The more recent immigrants, such as the Poles, resisted, but in the end they, too, succumbed to the desire of the Americanizers. Religion class remained the one area where Polish was the language of instruction, but as more and more children came to school not knowing Polish, religion was soon explained in English. In the end, the study of Polish became an extracurricular activity. This was a long process that began in the 1920s, when already some children knew little or no Polish, and culminated in the 1950s, when most children and adults knew little or no Polish. With the Mexican newcomers the same pattern was present. The parochial school not only educated them in the mainline religion of devotional Catholicism, but also was a powerful agent for Americanization.

After World War I, the trend toward the certification of teachers became widespread and forced women religious to upgrade themselves professionally. Of course, public-school teachers in the early twentieth century were not highly educated either. A 1918 report noted that one sixth of all public-school teachers did not even have a tenth-grade education.[31] As high school education became more common, more women entered religious life with at least a high school education; this was an improvement over earlier years, when many had little more than an elementary education. Catholic colleges did offer teacher training programs, and some women religious attempted to obtain college degrees on a part-time basis. But this was very difficult and it took a minimum of ten years and usually longer to complete work for the degree. Given the heavy teaching schedule of women religious, the large classes, the obligation to teach catechism after school hours to public-school children, their religious obligations, which occupied several hours a day, "Professional study despite all rhetoric to the contrary, could possibly not have had high priority in their daily schedules."[32]

Another major reason for the lack of training was the rapid increase in school enrollments and the subsequent demand for more teachers. Since pastors were still reluctant to hire lay teachers because of the cost, they asked for more women-religious teachers. Pressured by both pastors and bishops, superiors of women's religious orders continued to postpone any serious educational training program for teaching sisters. In the 1950s, however, a movement finally got underway to promote the professional preparation of women-religious schoolteachers. This began to turn things around, and more women religious attended college-level courses and some even received their degrees prior to stepping into the classroom. But it took some time before the program could achieve its desired results. The Sisters of the Holy Cross was one order that vigorously promoted the professional education of its members, but 40 percent of the Holy Cross Sisters teaching in elementary schools as late as 1964 still did not have college degrees. In other religious communities the percentage was higher.[33]

The emergence of the high school was a major development in twentieth-century American society. Never as extensive as the elementary parochial school, nonetheless the Catholic high school became a central part of the educational enterprise. The nineteenth-century Catholic pattern of mixing high school and college students in one institution gradually became obsolete, and the American system of four years of high school and four years of college became standard. Given the high cost of education, few parishes sponsored high schools. For this reason, the central high school serving a citywide population became the more common pattern. By 1959 there were 2,428 Catholic high schools educating 810,763 students; the corresponding elementary-school population for that year was 4,083,860, or five times as large.[34]

Throughout the period, separate high schools for men and women was the pattern. Women religious taught in the female academies and high schools, and men taught in the schools for boys. Religious brothers became especially involved in high school teaching. The Christian Brothers were the largest such order and had a total membership of 1,906 in 1959. The Jesuits also became very involved in boys' high school education and concentrated on the education of students from middle- and upper-class families. As the high school program expanded to include sports, clubs, entertainment, and religious sodalities, it became a surrogate parish for many youth. This, of course, weakened the influence of the parish on high school youth.

The Catholic college shared in the twentieth-century expansion of American higher education. The increase was not so much in the number of new colleges founded, but in the size of the college student population. In 1916, the number of students enrolled in Catholic colleges was 8,304; by 1950, the number of full-time students had reached 112,765, two thirds of them being male. Despite the large number of male students, the number of colleges for men had actually declined, whereas the number of colleges for women had increased significantly. In 1915 there were 19 Catholic colleges for women, but by 1950 the number had jumped to 116, or 66 percent of the total number (175) of Catholic colleges in the United States. These figures can be deceiving, however. Many women's colleges had enrollments of fewer than one hundred students and could hardly qualify as genuine schools of higher education. Other institutions, however, were first-rate. Clearly one of the best was the College of St. Catherine in St. Paul, Minnesota. During the presidency of Sister Antonia McHugh in the 1920s and 1930s, St. Catherine's became a noted women's college. Run by the Congregation of St. Joseph, its faculty of women religious were highly educated, having earned doctoral degrees from such universities as Minnesota, Chicago, Columbia, Michigan, and the Catholic University of America. Some had studied at Oxford and other universities in England and France. In recognition of its excellence, the college received a chapter of the exclusive National Honor Society, Phi Beta Kappa, in 1937. As late as 1960, only one other Catholic college, Catholic University, had earned this distinction.[35]

A significant development during the twentieth century was the Jesuit take-over of Catholic higher education for men. The Jesuits had founded numer-ous colleges during the nineteenth century, and as the number of Jesuits increased they were able to expand these schools and turn them into solid undergraduate institutions. In time their dominant presence in Catholic higher education solidified, and by 1950 the Jesuits were operating twenty-five colleges, or 42 percent of the total number of men's colleges (fifty-nine) in the United States.[36] What this meant was that the Jesuits were educating about half the male Catholic college population at the time. Such Jesuit col-leges as Georgetown, Holy Cross, Fordham, and St. Louis gained well-de-served reputations during these years as fine undergraduate schools that ex-celled in liberal-arts education.

Prior to World War II, with the notable exception of Catholic University, colleges were overwhelmingly centered on undergraduate education. After the war, with the increase in enrollment and the expansion of graduate stud-ies, Catholic colleges began to develop graduate programs. One of the most dramatic examples of this shift took place at the University of Notre Dame, a school operated by priests of the Congregation of Holy Cross. Notre Dame's reputation had been made on the football field, not in the classroom. A new president in 1946, John J. Cavanaugh, C.S.C., wanted to change this by upgrading the quality of education offered at Notre Dame. Under Cava-naugh, research in advanced studies became a high priority. To achieve this goal he recruited faculty from Europe. Refugee scholars, "these professors and their colleagues enlarged Notre Dame's participation in the wider Ameri-can academic community . . . and also brought a new cultural heterogene-ity to the campus, helped make research and publication an integral part of university life, and contributed greatly to the expansion of the graduate school."[37] Cavanaugh's successor in 1952 was a thirty-five-year-old Holy Cross priest, Theodore M. Hesburgh. As one observer put it, "What Hes-burgh inherited was a university ready for take-off."[38] Under Hesburgh's lead-ership, Notre Dame did take off, and in 1960 the Ford Foundation singled it out as one of the six rapidly improving universities in the United States and awarded Notre Dame a six-million-dollar grant. Robert Hutchins, former chancellor of the University of Chicago, commented in 1962 that "the Notre Dame efflorescence has been one of the most spectacular developments in higher education in the last twenty-five years. I suspect that Notre Dame has done more than any other institution possibly because there was more to do."[39]

The Notre Dame transformation was only part of the story of the 1950s. More fundamental and more engaging was a nationwide debate among Catholic intellectuals on the quality of Catholic education in general and the impoverishment of Catholic intellectual life in particular. The spark that ignited the debate was a 1955 essay by the historian John Tracy Ellis on "The American Catholic and the Intellectual Life." Reprinted extensively, it prompted Catholics to ponder why there were no "Catholic Salks, Oppenheimers, Einsteins." The debate highlighted the absence of Catholic intellectual leadership and pointed out the anomaly that "although American Catholics have the largest and most expensive educational system of any national group in the world, a genuine Catholic intellectual life is still dependent upon translations of European works and books of British origin."[40] Such novelists as Flannery O'Connor and J. F. Powers, sociologists such as Thomas O'Dea and theologians such as Gustave Weigel, S.J., pointed out the liabilities of devotional Catholicism and the culture it created. At issue was the larger question of what it meant to be Catholic in the modern world. "Out of the great debate on Catholicism and the intellectual life" came questions that had no easy answer. An influential Catholic writer, Daniel Callahan, put it very succinctly:

> It was one thing to decide, as many Catholic colleges did, that honors programs for the brighter students would be a fruitful venture. It was quite another to decide how free the Catholic ought to be to inquire into the teachings of the Church, how independent he ought to be as a citizen of the Church's social teachings, how much freedom he had to differ with his parish priest, his bishop or the pope. But these were exactly the kinds of problems which were to come out of the great debate on Catholics and the intellectual life. . . .[41]

The debate about Catholicism and the intellectual life was but another sign that for Catholics the times were changing. Another area of change was the Catholic reform movement. The Bishops' Program of Social Reconstruction in 1919 was a landmark statement for social reform, but in the 1920s Catholics turned away from reform. When economic depression strangled the nation in the 1930s, Americans became preoccupied with reform. Breadlines, soup kitchens, business failures, and high unemployment dramatized the plight of the people. The election of Franklin Delano Roosevelt in 1932 and his New Deal for the American people fostered a climate for reform. The labor movement attracted numerous supporters in the automobile, steel, and meat-packing industries. The founding of the Congress of Industrial Organizations (CIO) in 1935 marked a major step forward for labor, and by the end of the thirties it had organized millions of workers who never before had had the opportunity to join a union. During these years, reform was in the air, and a new social contract, grounded in the socially progressive legislation of the New Deal, gained wide support. Like the rest of America, Catholics became involved in numerous projects and movements on behalf of social reform. The one distinguishing feature of this movement was its diversity.

Though they had a common concern for social justice, Catholic reformers in the 1930s supported programs that ranged from the radical left to the radical right.

John Ryan was a prominent Catholic reformer. From his position as head of the Social Action Department of the NCWC, he kept the torch of social Catholicism burning during the 1920s. Through essays, lectures, and personal involvement in a variety of issues, he sought to awaken the Catholic conscience to the demands of a social gospel. His cause received a big boost in 1931, when Pope Pius XI published a social encyclical, *Quadragesimo Anno.* Issued on the fortieth anniversary of *Rerum Novarum,* it affirmed the church's support for labor and endorsed the "law of social justice" as the great equalizer of society's riches. In 1931 a sense of urgency and concern was in the air because of the stock market crash and the ensuing economic downturn. Given this environment, Catholics were inclined to receive the encyclical of Pope Pius XI with much more enthusiasm than they had its 1891 predecessor, *Rerum Novarum.* This helped Ryan's work considerably. The election of Roosevelt in 1932 and the enactment of New Deal programs was another major boost to his work. Citing the encyclicals, he reiterated the need for the state to establish economic justice through legislation, and he applauded the work of Roosevelt in this regard. During the 1930s, Ryan became a cheerleader for Roosevelt and the New Deal. In turn, the Roosevelt administration sought his advice on numerous occasions and he became a valuable ally as "the New Deal's Ambassador to Catholics."[42] Ryan's main work until his death in 1945 was to interpret the American reform tradition to Catholics and persuade them of the need for a social gospel.

Ryan's assistant at the Social Action Department, Raymond A. McGowan, also had a significant influence on the Catholic reform movement. But because he worked in the shadow of Ryan, McGowan has never received the attention that his achievements merited. Nevertheless, it was his vision and organizing abilities that made the Social Action Department an effective agency in promoting social reform at the local level. He helped to organize the Catholic Conference on Industrial Problems, the Bishops' Committee for the Spanish-Speaking, and the Catholic Association for International Peace. He also was a driving force in promoting national social-action congresses and labor schools for priests and lay people. Sensing the temper of the times, he became a strong advocate of the need for the laity to work with the clergy in the area of social action. Ryan himself acknowledged that McGowan "has done by far the greater share of the work, both in planning and execution, and originated the majority of the decisions" of the Social Action Department. "Moreover," Ryan acknowledged, "he has furnished most of the new ideas for the department."[43]

Another priest who worked at a national level and achieved remarkable success was Francis J. Haas. Like McGowan, he studied at Catholic University under John Ryan. Unlike Ryan, his mentor, who was "primarily a thinker and teacher, a man apart," Haas was "a man of action, a doer, and influential government official."[44] During the 1930s and 1940s, he held numerous important government positions, and as a labor mediator his record was remarkable. He was "one of the New Deal's most successful labor mediators and in hundreds of disputes throughout the 1930s and '40s he was instrumental in restoring industrial peace and protecting workers' right to an adequate wage, reasonable hours, unrestricted unionization, and steady employment."[45] Another priest prominent at the national level was John O'Grady. An Irish-born priest, he served as secretary of the National Conference of Catholic Charities from 1920 until 1961; like Ryan, he also taught at Catholic University. O'Grady's chief influence was as a lobbyist in Congress on behalf of social welfare legislation. He was an especially strong advocate of social security and federally funded housing for low-income families. As a speaker and writer and through his work as secretary of the National Conference of Catholic Charities, he also helped to shape Catholic opinion on social welfare legislation and programs.[46]

Ryan the thinker, McGowan the organizer, Haas the mediator, and O'Grady the lobbyist were part of the labor-priest tradition that had emerged from the Catholic community during the late-nineteenth and early-twentieth centuries. As priests, they preached a social gospel; as activists, they were involved in public affairs and public service. Teachers and administrators, these men operated at the national level and sought to educate Catholics about the social dimension of Christianity, while at the same time they sought to instruct other Americans about Catholic social thought. Politically and economically liberal, they were ardent supporters of the New Deal; traditionally Catholic, they grounded their liberalism in the social encyclicals of the popes. Their work represented one type of Catholic reform activity during the 1930s and 1940s: the New Deal Catholic liberal who looked to the state and traditional politics as the one hope for social reform.

Much more popular and famous than any of these liberal clergymen was the radio priest, Charles E. Coughlin. Coughlin rose to national prominence in the early 1930s as a radio preacher. At first pleasant talks on religious subjects, his radio sermons became exclusively political. With the depression as a backdrop, he preached a message of "want in the midst of plenty." Anticapitalist as well as anti-Communist, he was heard by millions of people and his name became a household word. He received more mail than the President and at one time needed over one hundred secretaries to handle it. High school football games stopped so that players and fans could listen to his Sunday-afternoon sermon. People walking down the street remember "hearing out of every window the voice of Father Coughlin blaring from the radio. You could walk for blocks, they recalled, and never miss a word."[47]

At first Coughlin was a supporter of Roosevelt and the New Deal as the answer to the nation's economic problems, but by the 1936 election he had become an outspoken opponent of Roosevelt and joined with other critics of the New Deal to form a third political party, the Union party. From his parish in Royal Oak, Michigan, a Detroit suburb, Coughlin kept up his radio preaching throughout the late 1930s and augmented this with a newspaper, *Social Justice*. His attacks against communism appealed to many people who feared Communist infiltration and subversion. But he had added a new theme —anti-Semitism—and his verbal attacks on Jews were soon turned into physical attacks by his followers, who were now organized into neighborhood clubs called the Christian Front. His bigoted attacks on Jews led to his downfall; in 1942 he was forced to abandon public life and return to his parish. His voice was silent. He died in 1979, a fallen, but not forgotten, hero.

Coughlin was one of those rare individuals who, for a variety of reasons, were able to attract national followings. He was a populist preacher, like a Henry George or a Huey Long, who offered a simple solution to a complex problem. Viewing reality in black and white, Coughlin interpreted life as a cosmic struggle between good and evil. The choice was always between Christ and his enemy. "Thus," as David O'Brien noted, "whether the issue was the revaluation of gold, the New Deal, the C.I.O., or the Spanish Civil War, the choice was always 'Civilization or Communism: Christ or Chaos.' "[48] Such a message, packaged in emotional, biblical, and nationalistic language, appealed to many people. In his early years of radio preaching, Coughlin was in tune with the Catholic community, ". . . helping its members to relate their economic and social problems to their faith. In that period he made constructive contributions, opening the minds of his listeners to the possibility of an active and dynamic government seeking to realize the ideals of justice and equality." Historian David O'Brien went on to conclude, ". . . even more than Ryan, he succeeded in communicating to his listeners the basic immorality of the old orders of concentration of wealth, low wages, and social insecurity."[49] Without a doubt, Coughlin inspired many Catholics to embrace the social gospel in the early 1930s. But after Roosevelt's victory in 1936 Coughlin went downhill. His public career descended into bigotry and hysteria. Sympathetic to Hitler and the Nazis, he lost popularity; by 1940 he was a pathetic figure and, for most Catholics, an embarrassment.

All the world was not Royal Oak, Michigan, or Washington, D.C. In cities across the nation, Catholic clergy and laity were turned on to the crusade for social justice during the decade of the depression. The major catalyst in this was the Social Action Department of the NCWC. Through the organizing efforts of Raymond A. McGowan, Catholic conferences on industrial problems had been held throughout the 1920s and 1930s. Their purpose was "to discuss and promote the study and understanding of industrial problems." The conferences were really a "traveling school of social thought" that sought to educate Catholic clergy and laity on questions related to industry and labor.[50] Using the model of these conferences, McGowan organized a National Catholic Social Action Conference in Milwaukee in 1938 and another one the following year in Cleveland. The Milwaukee conference attracted thirty-five bishops, seven hundred and fifty priests, and several thousand lay people. In addition to these congresses, McGowan promoted Schools for Social Action for clergy. In 1937, the first of many such institutes was held in Milwaukee, Toledo, San Francisco, and Los Angeles; they attracted three hundred priests from twenty-four dioceses. Labor schools for the laity also became very popular and were underway in many cities across the nation; by 1945, about one hundred of these schools were in operation, with the Jesuits operating about one fourth of them.[51]

The primary thrust of all this activity was educational. The congresses, summer institutes, and labor schools sought to educate a generation of people in the principles of social Catholicism as expounded in the papal encyclicals and then apply these principles to the American industrial and economic environment. There was no question that these educational programs had a decisive impact on numerous clergy and laity. Though they numbered only in the thousands, nevertheless an increasing number of Catholics were becoming conscious of their social responsibility. Pro labor and pro social justice, they began to be heard throughout Catholic America. An increasing number of bishops also became advocates for the workers and defended the CIO when it came under attack because of suspected Communist sympathies.

The main preoccupation of these Catholic reformers was the labor question. For Catholics at this time, social justice was limited to economic and industrial issues. Preoccupied with the labor question and the rights of workers, most Catholic social activists were blind to the issue of race. Only in the 1950s did the Catholic concept of social justice expand to include racial justice.

Though the thrust of NCWC-sponsored activities was primarily educational, they did provide the stimulus for action. McGowan's philosophy was to educate the leaders so that, once informed, they could then influence change from their positions of leadership. His trickle-down strategy worked, insofar as many future labor leaders did attend these conferences and schools. But other social activists favored more action-oriented programs, through which change could be effected more rapidly. One such group was the Association of Catholic Trade Unionists, commonly referred to as ACTU. Founded in New York in 1937 by a group of Catholic laymen, it quickly spread to other cities, fifteen in all by 1940. The labor-school concept was the primary thrust of ACTU along with a newspaper. But it also became very involved in promoting union organization. ACTU supporters joined picket lines, participated in labor rallies by giving speeches, and distributed leaflets urging Catholics to support striking workers. From 1939 to 1949, "ACTU provided support for over three hundred strikes." Activists, as they called themselves, helped to mediate labor disputes and defended the CIO against the attacks of Charles Coughlin. The Catholic wing of the CIO, ACTU "became an effective propaganda and pressure group within several major industrial unions, notably the auto, steel, transport, and electrical workers."[52] During the 1940s, ACTU became increasingly concerned about the Communist influence in the CIO, and as its focus narrowed, so did its influence.

One of the most militant chapters of ACTU was situated in Pittsburgh. Heart of the steel industry, Pittsburgh was a logical place for union activity, and during the 1930s no one promoted this more than Charles Owen Rice. Ordained a priest in 1936, Rice had spent a good part of his youth in Ireland, where he learned about "the Irish struggle for justice." An heir of the Irish radical tradition that first surfaced with the Land League and Edward McGlynn, Rice became a legend in Pittsburgh because of his dynamic work on behalf of labor and the working class. He claimed to be a radical, "a Catholic radical" he said, and he believed "that the present social and economic system is a mess and should be changed from top to bottom." But Rice's prescriptions for change were not very radical. His basic remedy was a labor union, and in this regard he was typically American and Catholic. In 1936, along with other Pittsburgh labor priests, Rice founded the Catholic Radical Alliance, an organization that "spent most of its time aiding the labor movement." Two years later, he organized a chapter of ACTU in Pittsburgh. Rice also founded a house of hospitality that became a refuge for the poor, the homeless, and the unemployed. Like most Catholic activists at the time, Rice focused heavily on educational programs—speaking, writing, and conducting labor schools—in order to educate the people of Pittsburgh about the rights of the worker. But he was also an activist. He helped workers to organize, spoke at their rallies, and joined them on the picket lines. He defended the CIO and was so identified with its cause that he became known as "Chaplain of the C.I.O."[53] He also became involved with community action groups and tried to obtain better public housing for the city's workers. Because of his interest in public housing, he was appointed to several government positions.

Rice represented one type of labor priest in the 1930s, the young activist who was "committed to change, and willing to agitate in the streets for the worker and the labor movement."[54] Numerous priests and bishops were similarly involved; some resembled Rice in their militancy on behalf of labor; others inclined more to the role of mediator and educator, like Haas or Ryan; others, like McGowan, were behind-the-scenes organizers who sought to convert clergy and laity to the cause of labor and social justice. By the late 1930s, the labor-priest tradition had clearly come into its own, with hundreds of representatives and many styles of action. But it is important to realize that of the more than thirty-three thousand priests in the United States at that time, the vast majority were more interested in novenas than labor unions. Nevertheless, the emerging tradition of the labor priest and the increased Catholic commitment to a social gospel would have a decisive influence on the future of Catholicism.

As nation and church moved into the 1940s and 1950s, the concerns of the depression decade faded. The influence of communism became a major concern, and Rice and his ACTU counterparts spent much of the 1940s seeking to rid unions of suspected Communist influence. Corruption in the unions became another concern, and clergy and laity sought to purge unions of criminal influence. The work of labor mediation still engaged many priests, and when right-to-work laws became popular, Catholic social actionists spoke out against them. The struggles of the 1930s and 1940s had won unprecedented popularity and respectability for labor unions, and by the 1950s they were an accepted part of American life. But a new social issue appeared on the horizon—racial justice—and when the civil rights movement took off in the mid-1950s, Catholic Action took on a new focus.

It was clear that by the 1950s the marriage between Catholicism and the American liberal reform movement was consummated. The idea that Catholicism and liberalism were compatible was no longer in question. Catholic support for the labor movement during the 1930s and 1940s was a major reason for this development. Even though Catholic social thought "exerted little influence on labor's development," the intense and widespread support of Catholics for labor brought a significant segment of the Catholic community into the mainstream of the American reform movement and helped labor at a time when it desperately needed help.[55] Such participation in the reform movement of the Roosevelt era not only demonstrated to other Americans that Catholicism was compatible with the American liberal tradition, but it also made Catholicism a more American religion. The Americanization of the Catholic reform movement was one more sign that Catholics were becoming part of the American mainstream.

Through participation in the labor movement, Catholic reformers also became less parochial in their vision and less smug about their religion. This was a decidedly different attitude from that of the Catholic majority, in which parochialism and smugness were still very much in evidence. The expanded vision of liberal Catholics prepared them to meet the challenges of the post-Vatican II era.

There was another, potentially more significant, dimension to the Catholic reform movement during this era. This was the involvement of the laity in reform efforts other than the labor movement. Of its nature, the labor movement was decidedly one-dimensional, quite pragmatic, and very political. Though it would involve numerous lay people, men especially, bishops and priests were in the forefront and for the most part in control. ACTU was a notable exception. The tradition of the labor priest and the controlling leadership of the Social Action Department of the NCWC help to explain this clerical dominance. Yet, in the 1930s and 1940s, a decisive development occurred when increasing numbers of lay people became involved in social action. Throughout the nineteenth and early-twentieth centuries, lay men and women had been active in the crusade for charity. As home visitors, settlement-house workers, and social workers, scores of people became involved in the traditional charity crusade. But something new emerged in the decade of the depression. Lay Catholics became more action-oriented and turned their attention to the public arena, where they sought to effect needed changes. This new breed of Catholic activist was independent and wanted to be as free as possible from clerical control. Seeking to develop lay responsibility in the church, they wanted to work with the clergy, rather than be controlled by them.

During the 1930s and 1940s, several developments both in society and the church came together to create a very receptive atmosphere for the emergence of a new style of social action. The poverty and want of the depression pricked the consciences of many people; the struggle of labor to gain recognition fired the imagination of others; the emergence of the black in the cities of the Northeast and the blatant racial discrimination that followed awakened many to the cause of racial injustice. The popularity of communism at home and abroad, together with the fear of fascism and the subsequent outbreak of World War II persuaded many people that materialism and secularism were gaining control of the world's destiny. Symptomatic of the time was the American hierarchy's November 1941 pastoral letter "Crisis of Christianity." It claimed, "Christianity faces today its most serious crisis since the Church came out of the catacombs." The two great evils "bent on world dominance" were nazism and communism.[56] All these developments created a sense of urgency, even alarm, and many young people grasped the torch of reform and rushed out to improve society and make the world a better place in which to live. For some people the answer was communism, for others it was Roman Catholicism.

Certain developments were also going on within the Catholic community which fostered the emergence of a new breed of Catholic. A new understanding of the church as the mystical body of Christ stressed the corporate responsibility of the members of the body to one another. This heightened the sense of social responsibility and broke down a strong strain of individualism nurtured by the immigrant Catholic ethos. The liturgical movement, slowly gaining momentum during these years, reinforced this new understanding of the church. In the United States, the liturgical movement had a strong dose of social awareness mainly because of the pioneering work of Virgil Michel. Michel stressed the concept of human solidarity and the need for action on behalf of others. He believed that this flowed naturally from a correct understanding of the sacraments and the church. For him the liturgy was "the indispensable basis of Christian social regeneration."[57] Also popular at this time was Catholic Action. Promoted by Pope Pius XI, Catholic Action encouraged lay people to become active apostles in society and in that manner advance the kingdom of God on earth. The official church version of Catholic Action also stressed that the laity should act under the direction of the hierarchy.

The final development that prepared the way for the emergence of lay activists was the Catholic Revival. This "was a resurgence of Catholic thought and belief brought about by a brilliant crowd of novelists, poets, dramatists, historians, philosophers, biographers, and theologians. . . ."[58] The revival provided the intellectual stimulus and spiritual motivation that Catholic activists needed. It surfaced in the United States when Maisie Ward and Frank Sheed opened their publishing house in New York in 1933. By publishing the works of such noted European Catholic authors as G. K. Chesterton, Jacques Maritain and Paul Claudel, Sheed & Ward provided Catholics with the necessary tools to fashion a vision of Christian humanism that would be in tune with the modern world. A young Brooklyn schoolteacher, Ann Harrigan, recalled the impact that Sheed & Ward and their stable of authors had on her when she walked into their bookstore in New York City for the first time:

> A sort of elation accelerated the heartbeat as one entered the shop: Frank or Maisie might be there while you browsed among the books . . . or even one of those fascinating authors. And what books! The crème de la crème! For it was the time of a great flowering of Catholic literature. Sheed & Ward was attracting a stable of British and continental writers who were not only competitive or even top-notch in their various fields but who seemed to enjoy, to flaunt even, a no-nonsense, take-it-or-leave-it attitude about their faith—not the namby-pamby pap that passed for Catholic literature.[59]

These were exciting days for young Catholic men and women who were discovering for the first time the richness of the Catholic tradition. Each new book, each new contact, was an eye-opener; one day Maritain, the next day a social encyclical; one week the liturgical movement, the next week racial justice. It was a special moment in history, when the American Catholic imagination was set aflame in a unique manner.

One of the first reform movements to attract the new emerging generation of Catholic activists was the Catholic Worker. The Catholic Worker was born on May Day 1933 in New York's Union Square when a woman and three young men began selling a newspaper, *The Catholic Worker,* to a crowd of fifty thousand Socialists and Communists for a penny a copy. The newspaper was the brainchild of Dorothy Day, a leftist journalist and recent convert to Catholicism, and Peter Maurin, a French Catholic peasant and thinker. After the newspaper came the movement, which tried to implement the ideals defended in the newspaper. The purpose of the Catholic Worker was to make the Catholic church "the dominant social dynamic force." Maurin wrote numerous essays for the paper; one in particular succinctly expressed the purpose of the Catholic Worker:

What the Catholic Worker Believes

The Catholic Worker believes
in the gentle personalism
of traditional Catholicism.
The Catholic Worker believes
in the personal obligation
of looking after
the needs of our brother.
The Catholic Worker believes
in the daily practice
of the Works of Mercy.
The Catholic Worker believes
in Houses of Hospitality
for the immediate relief
of those who are in need.
The Catholic Worker believes
in the establishment
of Farming Communes
where each one works
according to his ability
and gets
according to his need.
The Catholic Worker believes
in creating a new society
within the shell of the old
with the philosophy of the new,
which is not a new philosophy
but a very old philosophy
a philosophy so old
that it looks like new.[60]

Translated into programs, this meant that in addition to the newspaper, the Catholic Worker opened houses of hospitality, halfway houses where the poor, homeless, and unemployed could find hot food, warm conversation, and a place to sleep.

The house of hospitality was the heart of the movement, and its commitment to serve the poor had a special attraction to young people and intellectuals. Living in voluntary poverty, they learned the meaning of the corporal works of mercy. The houses also became centers for regular discussions about everything from the steel strike to new developments in Catholic theology. The labor struggles of the 1930s were a special concern of the Catholic Worker; the newspaper reported strike activities, and hospitality houses fed the unemployed. Another phase of the movement was the rural commune or farm. A return to the farm was one of Maurin's solutions to the crisis of modern industrial society. As a social experiment the farms were a failure, but they did help to attract families to the movement and were able to serve as rural retreat centers, halfway houses, and suppliers of produce for the urban houses.[61]

The Catholic Worker was a radical movement. To define its radicalism, however, is like trying to bottle a morning fog. Day and Maurin were not systematic thinkers. They enunciated principles, lived according to them, and expected others to do the same. The Catholic Worker put no hope in the modern state; it put faith in the community of the sacred; the spiritual was more central to life tnan the material; peace was better than war; love in action was superior to love in dreams; the ideal of Christian perfection far surpassed the minimalism of the natural-law tradition; personalism out-ranked pragmatism; and in the end, the primacy of love would redeem history. Simple principles, they became profoundly radical when people followed them. The Catholic Worker wanted to change the hearts of people and in that way effect a radical reconstruction of society. Unlike Catholic liberals, the Catholic Worker recoiled from politics and argued for a spiritual solution to society's problems.

In the 1930s the Catholic Worker became a national movement, attracting followers across the country. By 1942 thirty-two houses of hospitality were in operation; there were also about twelve farms scattered throughout the East and the Midwest. The mixture of radicalism and Catholicism had an obvious appeal to people who had grown tired of the old immigrant church and sought something new and challenging. As one follower put it, ". . . it was as far Left as you could go within the Church."[62] What was also special about the Worker was that lay people ran the show; clergy joined the movement only as advisers or fellow travelers. In the 1930s this was indeed unusual among Catholics as well as Protestants.

People discovered a new type of church at the Catholic Worker. In Chicago, Ed Marciniak, the son of a Polish immigrant, joined the movement and, in his words, "discovered a church I had never heard about, never knew existed." His recollection captures the enthusiasm and excitement of the times:

> All of a sudden there was this new world for me, a world of great intellectual vitality. There were many of us, and we read avidly, every learned Catholic maga-zine we could locate. We raised every question, we challenged every conceivable position, we subjected the Church to so much scrutiny because we loved her so much. Sometimes our sessions would go from Sunday afternoon right through to early Monday morning—one week, Maritain; the next, perhaps, the steel strike.[63]

The heart and center of the Catholic Worker was Dorothy Day. She was indeed a special person. Michael Harrington described her as "a presence." "When she comes into a room," he wrote, "even a stranger who had never heard of her would realize that someone significant had just entered."[64] She kept the movement going and held it together through the 1930s and 1940s. Her radical-pacifist stand forced many men to leave the movement during the Second World War, and as a result many houses closed; by the end of the war only ten houses of hospitality were left. Through it all, Day remained radically committed to peace, and in the 1950s the Catholic Worker became the vital center of an emerging Catholic peace movement. Politically radical, she was devoutly Catholic. This puzzled many people, but for Day and her fellow travelers it made eminent sense.

Because of Day's unique charisma and the movement's appeal, numerous men and women joined the Catholic Worker. Once in touch with its spirit, they were transformed into Catholic activists. Most stayed for a brief period of time and then moved on to other apostolic work. Many "became prominent Catholic writers, social activists, and religious leaders, and through them, as well as by its own activities, the Worker played a critical role in American Catholic intellectual life." One Catholic activist, John Cort, a member of the Catholic Worker and one of the founders of ACTU, described Day "as a great woman and the mother of us all." He went on to say, ". . . the Catholic Worker has taught us magnificent lessons about these same works of mercy, about love and the importance of poverty, about the primacy of the spiritual and the importance of faith." Michael Harrington joined the Worker after he graduated from college and there discovered "the terrible reality of involuntary poverty and the magnificent ideal of voluntary poverty." After he left the Worker, he went on to write *The Other America,* a book that sparked a nationwide discussion and a presidential war on poverty. In a moment of exaggeration he claimed, "The Catholic Worker had inspired almost every one of the Catholic social movements"; not every one, but many indeed. "In any case," he said, "there were very few people who agreed with [Day] on everything but hundreds of thousands were profoundly influenced by her life."[65]

During the 1930s, another woman appeared in New York and opened a storefront operation in Harlem to promote interracial justice. The woman was Catherine de Hueck. Born into an aristocratic family in Russia, she experienced the depths of poverty during World War I and the Russian revolution. With her husband she emigrated to Canada, where after separating from him she began a new career as a lecturer. Then she discovered racial discrimination and founded an organization in Toronto—Friendship House—to promote interracial justice. At the invitation of some New York priests, she came to Harlem in 1938 and established another Friendship House. The concept caught on and eventually there were Friendship Houses in Chicago

(1942), Washington, D.C. (1949), Portland, Oregon (1951), and Shreveport, Louisiana (1954); in addition there were farms in Wisconsin, Virginia, and New York, which served as educational and spiritual centers for the movement. At one time, as many as two hundred people were on the staffs of these houses and farms; ". . . hundreds would work as volunteers, and thousands would visit or participate in its various programs." The people who joined Friendship House "were for the most part young, well educated, idealistic, outraged at injustice, and determined to change the world."[66] It held a special attraction for women, and they were able to assume leadership roles in the movement.

Friendship House engaged in three areas of work: direct assistance to the needy by providing food and clothing and helping people find housing; educational efforts to change the thinking of people through lectures, workshops, pamphlets, and a monthly newspaper; and social action to effect change at local, state, and national levels by conducting surveys and nonviolent demonstrations against discrimination.

The Baroness, as De Hueck was known, was an exceptional speaker and had an ability to inspire people to follow her in her work on behalf of social justice. What was especially attractive to young Catholics was the challenge to become lay leaders. As one admirer, Ann Harrigan, put it, "Her genius was in being a lay person, and offering this kind of leadership to us who wanted to work for change as lay people."[67] Harrigan, who left a job as a New York high school teacher to join the movement, recalled those days in 1938 when many young Catholics were intoxicated with social action. "I found it exciting," she said, "to observe the church now beginning to emerge from its post-Tridentine trauma, restating ever more clearly in the papal encyclicals the unity and dignity of all peoples. This growing sense of freedom was intoxicating. I discovered that I could think for myself, that what I did with my life was ultimately my own decision."[68] Priests played an important role in supporting the movement, and Bishops Bernard J. Sheil of Chicago and Patrick A. O'Boyle of Washington, D.C., were strong backers of Friendship House. But, like the Catholic Worker, lay people ran Friendship House and made it work. The spirit behind it was both uniquely Catholic and commonly Christian. The mystical-body concept of the church as a caring and sharing community of people was the cornerstone of its ethos; the Protestant social-gospel dictum, the brotherhood of man under the fatherhood of God, was another part of its manifesto, as was the demand for interracial justice.

Friendship House had an important influence in awakening the consciences of many Catholics to the issue of racial justice. Along with the Catholic Interracial Council, it was an oasis of racial justice which forced people to confront the reality of racial discrimination in both church and nation. Unquestionably, one reason for its success was the awakening that was taking place in America as regards the issue of racial justice and civil rights. Another obvious reason was its appeal to lay people as a movement in which they could realize a vocation as lay apostles. Profoundly Catholic and militantly lay, these were the characteristics of the new breed of Catholics emerging in the 1930s and 1940s.

Another important lay movement for reform was the Grail. Founded by a Dutch Jesuit in 1921, the Grail spread throughout Europe and was finally imported to the United States in 1940. It was a movement that aimed at training women lay apostles who would go forth to convert the world. In the words of their founder, Jacques van Ginneken, S.J., they were

> to counterbalance in the world all masculine hardness, all the angles of masculine character, all cruelty, all the results of alcoholism and prostitution and capitalism, which are ultra masculine, and to Christianize that with a womanly charity.[69]

The first center was in a Chicago suburb; in 1944 they moved to a farm in Loveland, Ohio. From there the movement spread, and by the 1950s Grail centers were operating in half a dozen cities; Grail-trained women were also working as lay missionaries in foreign countries.

The Grail movement entered the United States just at the time that the liturgical movement, the rural-life movement, and Catholic Action were gaining headway. All these movements influenced the shaping of its program. As a result, Grail in America became centered at the farm at Loveland, known as Grailville; hard work, a monastic routine centered in the liturgy, with elaborate celebrations of feast days, deep asceticism, and an eagerness to convert the world from secularism to Christian humanism became the chief features of Grail. Young, city-bred Catholic women came to Grailville for a few days, a few weeks, or several months to learn the Grail way of life. In the city centers a group of women would live together, working at their own jobs or training new lay apostles. By the 1950s, Grail had become quite popular; Janet Kalven, a leader in the movement, recalled:

> every summer, carloads came from the cities to Grailville for weeklong or summerlong courses, some staying on for the full year. Grailville burst at its seams, all the barns becoming sleeping places, the dining rooms spilling over to the porch and lawns. As strange as the lay apostolate, the liturgical movement, social action were to most Catholics, the momentum was gaining on all fronts, a quiet revolution, for new life in the church.[70]

Like the Catholic Worker and Friendship House, the Grail was run by lay people, in this case women, and the clergy played a supporting role. Its apostolic activities were similar to the Catholic Worker and Friendship House: service to the poor, as well as educational programs. Not surprisingly, a concern for interracial justice was a top priority. Each center also developed a strong liturgical life, around which a variety of activities took place. Like Friendship House, the Grail reached relatively few people in the United

States; an estimated fourteen thousand had participated in Grail programs by 1962. But as Kalven suggested, it was preparing these women for the church of the future. When the time came, Grail-trained women would emerge as advocates of a new Catholicism.

A final reform movement worth noting was Catholic Action. Promoted by the Papacy, it urged the involvement of lay people in the apostolate of the church under the supervision of the hierarchy. But in the United States, Catholic Action acquired a new twist and eventually emerged into autonomous, independent lay movements. In the late 1930s, Catholic Action for the laity was a popular issue, and such labor priests as Raymond A. McGowan promoted it enthusiastically. But a priest from Oklahoma, Donald Kanaly, who had studied in Louvain, Belgium, introduced a new dimension to the prevailing notion of Catholic Action in the United States. In Belgium, Kanaly had come in contact with a priest, Joseph Cardijn; his new technique, whereby people would systematically observe and discuss their environment, judge the situation in the light of the gospel, and then act, was called the inquiry method. Cardijn's method focused on small groups of people, defined by occupation, age, and sex, who would meet weekly and end their gathering in a decision for action. The thrust was clearly on action, not education. This was a major difference from the study-club method, which was the chosen model for Catholic Action at the time. Kanaly made his important speech in Chicago in 1938 at a clergy summer school for social action. In Chicago it was like throwing a match into a puddle of gasoline. Before long a new chapter in the history of the American lay apostolate unfolded.[71]

During the era of Cardinal Mundelein (1916–39), Chicago had become a center of reform. A key person in this development was a young Chicago priest whom Mundelein later had promoted to the rank of bishop, Bernard J. Sheil. Sheil became a legend in his own time and a local Catholic hero in the 1930s. He was a tough, activist priest who believed in the social gospel and used his prestige to work for social justice. He was the founder of the Catholic Youth Organization in 1930; he worked with the community organizer Saul Alinsky in organizing the Catholic immigrant neighborhood around the Chicago Stock Yards; he was an ardent supporter of labor and intervened dramatically at a labor rally in 1939 at the Chicago Coliseum, where thirty thousand meat-packers had gathered. Sheil needed fifty police bodyguards to protect him from the hooligans hired to keep him from speaking. Alinsky, an admirer of Sheil, wrote, ". . . the little bishop made history that night."[72] Sheil was outspoken on the issue of racial discrimination and defended the CIO against Coughlin and other critics. He it was who invited Friendship House to Chicago. He also got the Grail to come to the United States. But Sheil was not alone. A young priest, Reynold Hillenbrand, had been appointed head of the Chicago seminary in 1936. Hillenbrand was a typical liberal priest of the 1930s. He understood the church as the mystical body, he promoted active participation in the liturgy, and he was a strong advocate of social justice. As rector of the seminary, he influenced numerous priests and made them into advocates for the social gospel. Less flamboyant than Sheil and a virtual unknown outside Chicago circles, Hillenbrand nonetheless made a decisive impact on the future of social action in the United States.

Once Hillenbrand heard Kanaly's talk, he became a convert to the Cardijn method and began to promote it. The arrival in the United States of another priest, Louis Putz, C.S.C., brought Hillenbrand just the person he needed to launch a national movement. Putz had used the Cardijn method in France, where he had worked as a parish priest. In 1940, after the war broke out, he returned to the United States and the University of Notre Dame, where he began to promote the Cardijn concept of Catholic Action among the students. At Notre Dame his group's first action was to persuade the university administration to admit black students! Surprisingly, they succeeded, but only after a student petition convinced the administration that integration would be accepted.[73]

With Chicago as the nerve center and Hillenbrand and Putz the promoters, the new style of Catholic Action spread across the country. The two major groups were called the Young Christian Students (YCS) and Young Christian Workers (YCW). YCW groups existed in about thirty-five cities by 1947, and the YCS existed at a number of colleges and high schools. Their thrust was action, not education. They sought to change their environment at work or school through a specific action program. At Notre Dame the work of the YCS resulted not only in the integration of the university, but in the establishment of a college press and courses on marriage. In factories it meant promoting unions as well as encouraging a strong spiritual life. The key was to develop lay responsibility. Priests such as Putz and Hillenbrand encouraged this and sought to keep the movement as far removed as possible from the hierarchy and official church bureaucracy. This was a very different thrust from the official version of Catholic Action, in which lay people acted under the control of the hierarchy. YCS and YCW eventually became autonomous lay movements, run by the laity with priests as advisers. The major result of the movement was the organization of the Christian Family Movement, which was founded in Chicago by men and women who came out of the social-action ferment nurtured by YCW and YCS. In an unusual turn of events, the Christian Family Movement, an American organization, was eventually exported to other parts of the world. Significantly, it was a concept that had a very strong American quality to it, namely independence; in this case, the independence of the laity within the church.

The Catholic Worker, Friendship House, Grail, and the new style of Catholic Action represented a new type of apostolate in the church.[74] In one respect they were a response to the new metropolitan America. Rather than being rooted in the neighborhood parish, they were organized around a special interest; in a mobile and suburban society this made sense. Rather than being run by the clergy, they tapped the resources of educated, independent-minded Catholics. This also fit in well with a middle-class constituency. These movements were also the result of a strong reform impulse in twentieth-century Catholicism. They represented a new direction in the church. No longer would priests alone be the stars of Catholic reform. A new age, the age of the laity, was emerging, and it was just in time.

By the end of the 1950s, Catholicism in the United States had clearly come of age. More accepted by the Protestant majority, Catholics entered the 1950s confident about their place in American society. Being Catholic was indeed compatible with being American. The religious revival of the 1950s demonstrated how conducive the United States was to religion, and this only served to boost the confidence of Catholics about their place in the nation. Reasons for Catholic pride were everywhere: the successful television preacher Fulton J. Sheen, record numbers of converts, record numbers of priests and nuns, and numerous new churches; a new Pope in 1958 charmed the world and filled Catholics with pride. The possibility of a Catholic in the White House also contributed to a sense of Catholic boosterism. But beneath the surface were strong undercurrents of reform, which challenged the smug confidence of mainstream Catholicism. The liturgical movement and a new theology of church challenged the relevance of devotional Catholicism in the twentieth century. A rising concern for social and racial justice pointed out the flaws and limitations of a parochial Catholicism. An emerging laity, determined to become active apostles in church and society, were challenging the hegemony of the clergy. Catholic intellectuals began to question fundamental aspects of their religion and wanted to know what it meant to be Catholic in a postimmigrant, modern America.

These undercurrents of reform pointed out what most Catholics did not want to hear: the church of the immigrants, with its own unique style of devotional Catholicism, was no longer making it in the twentieth century. A new age and a new people demanded a new Catholicism. More and more frequently came the call for reform and renewal. The new Pope seemed to sense the need better than most, and in January 1959 John XXIII called a council to bring the church up to date. It would not be long before the strong undercurrents of reform would surface and change the nature of mainstream Catholicism both in the United States and throughout the world.

The Catholic Reformation, 1960-84

XV

A New Catholicism

ON JANUARY 20, 1961, John F. Kennedy took the presidential oath of office and stepped to the microphones to deliver his inaugural address. He spoke of a new frontier, of sacrifice on behalf of the country, and of America's strength in the world. Millions of people watched the event on television and, many years later, could still recall the stirring appeal of the youthful President. Throughout his presidential campaign, Kennedy had stirred up the idealism of many young people who saw Kennedy as "our remedy." His youth, intelligence, and wit appealed to many people, and his vision of the future captivated others. For Kennedy, the Roman Catholic, his greatest liability was his religion. He confronted the religion issue head-on and, at a meeting of Protestant ministers in Houston, told them and thousands more watching on television, "I do not accept the right of any ecclesiastical official to tell me what to do in the sphere of my public responsibility as an elected official."[1] Kennedy was telling the voters that he would take orders from the people, not the Pope; that in the United States, church and state were separate. Even though Kennedy's declaration of independence won him wide support, religion still remained an issue in the campaign. His victory in November was by the slimmest of margins; undoubtedly, anti-Catholic prejudice cost him votes. At the same time, many people voted for Kennedy *because* he was Catholic. As the first Catholic elected to the presidency, Kennedy put to rest the idea that a Catholic could not be elected President. In later years, other Catholics campaigned for the presidency and religion was no longer an issue.

Kennedy did more than prove that a Catholic could be President. The Kennedy style, "his poise, sophistication, the modernity worn as casually as his London-tailored clothes, suggested more than any proclamation could that Catholics at long last were comfortably integrated into American society." For Catholics, Kennedy became a symbol of success; wealthy and well educated, he had achieved the dream of every American: the presidency of the United States. His popularity enabled Catholics to stand a little taller, because one of their own "became an authentic folk hero during his lifetime and after his tragic death was quickly assigned to the company of American legends."[2] Of course, the legend was bigger than life and the hero had his flaws. But in those early years of the 1960s Americans wanted a hero, and so they created the Kennedy myth. It was sealed in blood on the streets of Dallas in November 1963, when a sniper's bullet killed Kennedy and brought an end to the days of Camelot.

About a decade later, in 1973, Richard M. Nixon took the presidential oath of office and stepped to the microphone to promise great things for the nation. But the United States had changed in the time since Dallas. Cynicism had replaced idealism, and disillusionment prevailed, rather than hope. In the interval between 1963 and 1973 the course of American history was decisively altered. A war in Vietnam took the lives of thousands of young Americans and left countless others maimed for life. A massive peace movement, unheard of in American history, galvanized support against the war, while presidents and generals urged Americans to support the cause of "freedom and democracy" in Southeast Asia. Vietnam divided the nation into bitterly opposed factions. Fathers argued with their sons, politicians fought with one another, and for the first time in the twentieth century, Americans began to doubt their invincibility as a world power.

Another major issue was race. The civil rights movement had gained momentum during the Kennedy years and achieved a decisive victory when President Lyndon B. Johnson signed into law the Civil Rights Act of 1964 in the presence of Martin Luther King, Jr., and other activists who had fought a bitter, ten-year struggle to achieve racial justice. The issue of race did not go away, however. Race riots broke out in cities across the nation. Then, in 1968, King was assassinated and riots broke out again in 168 cities and towns. A national advisory commission was appointed to investigate the violence and concluded—to the surprise of few—that the nation was "rapidly moving toward two increasingly separate Americas, . . . a white society principally located in suburbs, and in smaller central cities, and in peripheral parts of large central cities; and a Negro society largely concentrated within large central cities."[3] The riots had gutted large parts of major cities. In Detroit, Los Angeles, and Chicago, burned-out urban wastelands remained stark symbols of the poverty and discrimination imbedded into American society. Frustrated by ever-rising expectations, many black Americans became more militant in their demands for justice and equality. Racial integration, so long the goal of both blacks and whites, became discredited, and black separatism became a slogan as well as a lifestyle.

In addition to the issues of war and race, people became concerned about the rights of women. This concern gave life to a women's movement that, by 1973, was gathering wide support. The pollution and destruction of the environment was another concern that captured the attention of many. But nothing gripped the nation in 1973 like Watergate, the name given to a Republican "dirty tricks" campaign to steal the 1972 presidential election, and the attempted cover-up that followed. At issue was the abuse of power. Credibility was a popular theme in those years, and people looked for it in their leaders. When President Nixon tried to lie his way out of Watergate, he lost the respect of the people; it was not long before he resigned the presidency, rather than face the embarrassment of impeachment.

For many, Watergate was the last straw. The prolonged war had created bitter conflicts and divisions between young and old; the issue of race divided neighborhoods; the politics of confrontation, rather than conciliation, seemed to threaten the future of democracy. The mood of the people had clearly changed from the days of Camelot and the Kennedy presidency. By the early 1970s, the hopes of a new frontier were relocated to fantasyland; the American promise of unlimited opportunity proved false. Conflict, rather than consensus, was the prevailing spirit.

Nevertheless, within every crisis lies the promise of growth and the seeds for reconstruction. It was no different in the America of the 1960s. The issues of war, race, feminism, the environment, and political honesty involved "the fundamental question of justice," which, as historian Sydney E. Ahlstrom pointed out, "is the first virtue of any society."[4] A crusade for justice had come to life during the 1960s with the result that America entered the 1970s concerned about social justice and reform to a degree unparalleled in the twentieth century. Though the prevailing mood was suspicion of reform, the issues would not go away, and increasing numbers of people began to become sensitized to the cause of justice. By the end of the 1970s, the issues of the '60s were taken for granted, and this alone showed how far the nation had progressed. Women's rights, concern for the environment, racial justice, political accountability, and a desire for peace in a nuclear age had become part of the American mainstream. The 1960s had unleashed a contagion of justice which substantially changed the nature of American society. To overlook this is to miss the other half of the story that took shape between Dallas and Watergate.

The social and cultural changes that reshaped the nation also affected religion. Religion lives and breathes in a specific time and place, in a particular culture; for this reason, it is shaped "by the ideas, attitudes, values, and forms that prevail in the society in which that religion lives." Thus the social changes that turned America inside out had an immense effect on religion and church life. One dramatic illustration of this was a 1970 poll that revealed that 75 percent of the people interviewed believed religion was losing its influence; in 1957, a similar poll could find only 14 percent of the people sharing that belief.[5] The Vietnam debate that divided Americans split the churches, as did the racial issue. The disintegration of urban life sparked a concern for a new type of urban ministry. City pastors became more political and more involved in community organizations. Women pushed for equal rights in the church and sought to become ordained ministers in increasing numbers. For many young people, the traditional churches suffered from a severe credibility gap in the face of war, poverty, and racism. As a result, they were "turned off" and joined new religious cults and sects to get "turned on." Mainline Protestant churches suffered a significant decline in membership, and seminaries began to close. Protestant theologians started to question the relevance of religion in a modern age; some went so far as to proclaim a "death of God" theology. "In summary," wrote Sydney E. Ahlstrom, "one may safely say that America's moral and religious tradition was tested and found wanting in the '60s."[6]

Only against this backdrop of social and religious turbulence is it possible to understand and measure the meaning and significance of the changes that transformed Catholicism in the United States. Catholics not only had to cope with changes in American society, they also had to contend with changes initiated by the Second Vatican Council. The events from Dallas to Watergate rocked the nation and the churches; add to these the revolution sparked by Vatican II, and the result is a powerful one-two punch that sent American Catholics reeling.

Shortly after his election to the papacy, John XXIII announced that he wanted "to offer to the Catholic Church and to the world the gift of a new Ecumenical Council." Called the Second Vatican Council, it would be the first church council in almost a century. Its goal was, in the word of John XXIII, *aggiornamento;* that is, to bring the church up to date. A pastoral Pope, John wanted Catholicism to be in tune with the times and its dogmas presented in a language reflective of modern thought. Preferring the "medicine of mercy rather than severity," the Pope also made an eloquent plea for Christian unity. When the council opened, in the fall of 1962, Protestants were in attendance as invited observers. Though a simple gesture, it was loaded with profound significance, since it symbolized the break with past tradition. That was the genius of John XXIII. He cut through tradition like a hot knife passing through butter, simply but decisively. Gone was the tiara, seclusion in the Vatican palace, aloofness, the trappings of imperial splendor, and harshness toward people of other religions. In their place stood warmth, concern, openness, simplicity—an urbane, modern style not unlike that of John F. Kennedy. The momentous impact of these two men persuaded many people to speak of the two Johns as if they had a common destiny. The death of both in 1963 sealed this connection.

Though Pope John died before the Council finished its business, his successor, Paul VI, took up where he left off and brought the Council to a conclusion in the fall of 1965.

The Second Vatican Council ushered in a new era for Roman Catholics. The age of Tridentine Catholicism had come to an end, and a new Catholicism came to life. Rooted in the past but living in the present, this new spirit of Catholicism sought to revitalize both church and world. The Council produced sixteen documents; taken together, they charted the future course of Catholicism. Some were quite ordinary and lacking in vision; others represented a brilliant synthesis of Catholic thought. At the time, the most revolutionary document was on the liturgy. It spelled out an agenda for reform that radically changed the way Catholics prayed. Equally important was the new understanding of the church as the people of God. Gone was the juridical, institutional image of the church, and in its place was a more biblical understanding first captured in the concept of the mystical body of Christ and developed further by the notion of the church as the people of God. Joined with this was the idea of the servant church, by which the church put itself at the service of the human family. Ecumenism was another major thrust of the council; it urged efforts at union, rather than separation. Another important statement of the Council was the declaration of religious freedom. A key architect of the document was the American Jesuit John Courtney Murray, who for years had studied the issue of religious freedom in civil society. Together with Murray, a number of American bishops, most notably Cardinal Spellman of New York, spearheaded the passage of this document, which was not only the most controversial of all, but perhaps the most significant as well.

The Second Vatican Council was not as revolutionary as it seemed at first glance. It did not appear out of nowhere, but emerged from a general reform movement that had been sweeping through Roman Catholicism. This movement had begun to crest in the 1950s, and one of its more prominent representatives was the archbishop of Milan, Giovanni B. Montini, who later became Pope Paul VI. The link between the Council and earlier reform movements was most visible in the area of liturgy, the definition of the church, and the declaration of religious freedom. All these issues were discussed with great vigor during the 1940s and 1950s, and once the winds of renewal blew through the church, they became a central concern of the Council fathers.

Underlying all the issues debated at the Council was the general theme of *aggiornamento*. What this meant was that for the first time Catholic church leaders came to grips with the issues of modernity in a constructive manner. American Catholics such as John Carroll, John England, Isaac Hecker, and

John Ireland had grappled with such issues in imperfect and incomplete ways. By the 1960s, however, Catholics were better prepared and better equipped to deal with the fundamental issue of change in theology. The classicist or neo-Scholastic worldview, which focused on the static, unchanging nature of theology, was giving way to the modern, historical perspective, which emphasized development in theology. Change in theology and church life was one of the key issues of the Council. As the writer Garry Wills put it, the Council "let out the dirty little secret. It forced upon Catholics, in the most startling symbolic way, the fact that the church changes."[7] This simple revelation turned Catholicism on its head, and it has caused serious division in the church.

Another underlying issue of great significance was the emergence of dissent in the church. This first happened in a dramatic way. At the very first session of the Council, some bishops protested the proposed agenda and the people selected for major committee positions. The next day, the papers carried the headlines BISHOPS REVOLT. This marked the beginning of an open Council and an open church, in which debate and dissent became accepted. This was unheard of in a church accustomed to authoritarianism and papal absolutism. As a result of the Council, however, Catholics acquired the authority to dissent.

Living in the midst of fundamental social and cultural changes and prodded by Vatican II to bring itself up to date, American Catholicism was about to pass through the most turbulent period of its short history. It was a time of both disillusionment and hope, of conflict and harmony, of crisis and growth. Though the significance of the changes still remained uncertain, one thing was clear. A new Catholicism was coming to life in the United States.

By the 1960s, Catholics in the United States were becoming more like the rest of the American population. A 1974 Carnegie report on higher education revealed that Catholics were now attending colleges at a rate higher than Protestants; they were entering graduate schools in record numbers and were just as likely as other Americans "to plan careers as scholars."[8] As regards their economic situation, they were becoming more middle-class; in other words, more like the rest of the American population in terms of income. Though Jews scored higher educationally and economically, Catholics and Protestants were remarkably similar in both areas. Among Catholics it was also clear that certain ethnic groups were more responsible than others for this improved performance. The Irish in particular were especially successful educationally and economically. Regarding their political attitudes, Catholics described themselves as more liberal and less conservative than the rest of white America. When compared with Protestants "on a variety of controversial social questions," Catholics proved to be as liberal as Protestants. A case in point was the Vietnam War when, as early as 1967, 24 percent of the Catholic population opposed the war, while only 16.5 percent of the Protestants adopted such a position. It was thus evident that the descendants of Catholic immigrants had become fully American by the 1960s. Educationally and economically, they no longer stood apart as inferior or below par. Not only was this a most significant achievement, but it is an important consideration in understanding the nature of contemporary American Catholicism.[9]

Another important point to consider is the large influx of new Catholic immigrants into the United States. Not only do Mexican Americans continue to migrate to the United States; but record numbers of Cubans, Haitians, and Puerto Ricans also immigrated during the 1960s and 1970s. In recent years, a large number of Vietnam refugees and other Asian people, many of whom are Catholic, also chose the United States as their new home. These new immigrants, for the most part economically and educationally inferior to other Catholics, present a mighty challenge to the church. This is especially true in the case of the Spanish-speaking, who are the fastest-growing minority in the United States, presently making up about 25 percent of the American Catholic population. In Florida, Texas, and New Mexico, they constitute about two thirds of the Catholic population. Along with their increased presence is a militancy reminiscent of the Germans and the Polish.

The 1960s was a period of ethnic awakening among Hispanics, blacks and many white ethnic groups. They all began to argue for more recognition in just about every phase of American life. Influenced by the civil rights movement, these groups also pushed their cause in the nation's churches. Hispanic Catholics became especially militant and demanded equal rights in the church, better representation in the hierarchy, and in general more recognition in the Catholic Church in the United States. Such militancy did result in the appointment of Mexican Americans to the hierarchy, the first coming in 1970, when Patricio Flores, the son of migrant farm workers, became the first Mexican-American bishop in the history of the United States. Hispanics also began to have more of a say in church affairs. They are making their mark on American Catholicism not simply because of their numbers, but also because of the leadership of Mexican-American Bishops Flores, the archbishop of San Antonio, and Robert Sanchez, the archbishop of Santa Fe, New Mexico, as well as the work of such priests as Virgil Elizondo, head of the Mexican American Cultural Center in San Antonio. Organized nationally and possessing forceful leaders, Hispanic Catholics will make a major impact on the future of Catholicism in the United States in much the same way the Irish did in the nineteenth century.

When the first Vatican Council ended, in 1870, most Catholics in the United States hardly noticed, and most Americans hardly cared. That was not the case when the Second Vatican Council ended, in 1965. In 1870, Catholics were still outsiders in the United States; in 1965, that was no longer true. In 1870, Catholics were overwhelmingly Irish and German; in 1965, they represented numerous nationalities from around the world. In 1870, Catholics were struggling with the question of what it meant to be an American; comfortably American in 1965, they now struggled with a more fundamental question: what it meant to be Catholic. Just when they had solved one half of the riddle—what it meant to be American—the other half came unraveled. For the first time in modern history, Catholics no longer agreed on an answer to the question of what it meant to be Catholic. Vatican II was largely responsible for forcing Catholics to rethink the meaning of Catholicism in the modern world. In all likelihood, the church would have undergone a period of reform and renewal even if the Council had never taken place. The undercurrents for reform were so strong and widespread in the 1950s that they eventually would have surfaced and changed the nature of the Catholic mainstream. What the Council did was to unlock the gates and let the currents of reform burst forth with much greater force than would have been otherwise true. A church council not only sanctioned reform, it accelerated it. What this meant was that Catholics tried to solve the riddle of religion and modernity overnight. It proved to be quite difficult. The Protestant theologian Langdon Gilkey explained why:

> Protestantism has in one way or another, both successfully and unsuccessfully, sought for 200 years or more to deal with, absorb, and reinterpret the culture of modernity—a modernity that has developed more and more radically over those two centuries. Thus Protestantism has had the good fortune to be able to see the structure and the effects of this interaction of Christianity and modernity slowly unfold before it, first on one level and then on the other. Catholicism, on the other hand, has really for the first time tried to absorb the effects of this whole vast modern development from the Enlightenment to the present in the short period between 1963 and 1973! Thus *all* the spiritual, social, and technological forces that had structured and transformed the modern history of the West have suddenly, and without much preparation, impinged forcefully on her life, and they have had to be comprehended, reinterpreted, and dealt with by Catholicism in one frantic decade.[10]

The process of implementing the changes unleashed by Vatican II began even before the Council ended. Many bishops returned from Rome renewed in spirit and enthused about the prospects of renewal; they made pastoral visits throughout their dioceses urging priests and people to catch the spirit of Vatican II and embrace the changes taking place. In Baltimore, Archbishop Lawrence J. Shehan implemented a two-year plan whereby he or one of his assistants would visit every region and then every parish of the diocese to promote the new spirit of Catholicism. Other bishops set up similar programs. Some dioceses went even farther and convened a church synod, which, modeled on Vatican II, sought to establish new guidelines for the church and its people. Detroit, under the leadership of Archbishop John F. Dearden, undertook one of the more ambitious programs, in 1966. After two years of preparation in which thousands of people participated, clergy and lay people met in Detroit's Cobo Hall in February 1969 to discuss the final synod documents, which were officially promulgated a month later. The Detroit synod became a model for other dioceses.

Something different was happening in the American church. Many bishops were taking up the cause of renewal in an untypically aggressive manner. For many, participation in Vatican II was a conversion experience, and once they returned home to their dioceses they spearheaded programs for renewal. Bishops like Dearden and Shehan were now the progressives, the reformers, and this was unusual. In the 1940s and 1950s, reform came from below, from priests and laity. After Vatican II, reform began to come from the top as well. This put the bishops out in front and exposed them to criticism as well as praise. This new style of episcopal leadership was only one of many changes ushered in by the Council. More fundamental was the change in devotional life.

The most visible changes took place in the Catholic Mass. In the 1980s, people now take for granted changes which in the 1960s were considered earthshaking; as a result, life before Vatican II and the painful process of change are often forgotten. In 1960, Mass was said in Latin, the priest faced the wall and prayed the prayers of the Mass silently and alone; occasionally the tinkle of a bell or the sound of the organ would break the spell of silence; the sanctuary, where the altar stood, was the holy of holies, and only clergy and authorized lay people would dare to enter; people knelt in reverent silence, separated from the altar by an imposing guardrail; they prayed the rosary, recited prayers, or followed the Mass in an English-language hand missal; no one except the priest was supposed to talk in church. This was the way Catholics had always worshiped, and in 1960 no one dreamed that it would ever be any different. But it was. The first issue the Council discussed was liturgy; the result was a document that charted the course for a decade of liturgical change. Gradually, piece by piece, the rules for celebrating Mass changed. By the end of the 1960s, most changes were in place and a new Catholic Mass had replaced the old-style, Latin Mass.

The suddenness and finality of the liturgical changes jolted many. A jingle printed in a Darlington, Wisconsin, parish bulletin captured the feelings of many people:

Latin's gone, peace is too; singin' and shoutin' from every pew. Altar's turned around, priest is too; commentators yellin': "page 22." Communion rail's gone, stand up straight! Kneelin' suddenly went outta date . . . rosary's out, psalms are in; hardly ever heard a word against sin. Listen to the lector, hear how he reads; please stop rattlin' them rosary beads . . . I hope all changes are just about done; that they don't drop Bingo, before I've won.[11]

More bitter was the reaction of a Detroit Catholic:

> It's ridiculous. We don't feel holy when we go to church, anymore. It's too loud to say the rosary and they tell us it don't do no good to use the missals we paid good money for. So what the hell do we do? You ain't gonna catch the wife and I singing those songs from TV and radio. Not in church. Why, it's sacrilegious. Like shaking hands with the person next to you, and holding the communion host in your hands. Hell, when we were kids they told us our fingers would fall off if we touched the host; and that we were committing a sin if we tried to chew it. Now everything is different. But we don't feel comfortable. And somehow it just don't seem right, if you know what I mean.[12]

The changes in the Mass had touched the very soul of Catholic devotional life, and many people openly rebelled. Poorly prepared for such changes, they did not understand why the Council, and later the Pope, would urge such changes. Some clergy also rebelled and even went so far as to establish an organization for traditional-minded Catholics who wanted the Latin Mass. But these were rearguard actions. The vast majority of Catholics went along with the changes and in time began to understand why it all had taken place. The key theme was "active participation." This was the basic principle enunciated by the Council document on the liturgy, and all else flowed from it. Thenceforth, people were to become active participants in the Mass and the sacraments. This eventually took on a variety of forms, so that by the 1980s many parishes had liturgy committees to plan Sunday Mass, directors of liturgical music, lay ministers of the Eucharist who assisted the priest, and lay readers of the Scriptures. The congregation eventually became accustomed to singing hymns at Mass, exchanging greetings of peace with each other, and standing instead of kneeling. The priest became the celebrant of the liturgy and took on a more public role at Mass, facing the people and praying with them, not just for them. Church sanctuaries were reconstructed and old altars discarded, communion rails were removed and in their place came freestanding altars and open sanctuaries. The many statues and pictures so characteristic of the era of devotional Catholicism disappeared as simplicity replaced the cluttered look in churches. Another key development was that different types of liturgies or Masses were designed for different groups of people and different occasions. Ranging from a simple, quiet Mass to an elaborate celebration, the Catholic liturgy began to evidence a degree of diversity and adaptability unknown in the recent past.

Of course not all priests and people took to the new liturgy with enthusiasm. As a result, Sunday Mass in many churches is not much different from before; the language is English, the structure of the celebration is different, but the spirit is clearly pre-Vatican II. In these parishes the active participation of the people is discouraged. Many people obviously feel at home in such parishes and support them by their presence. There are undoubtedly as many pre-Vatican-II-style parishes as there are liturgically advanced parishes. The vast majority of Catholic parishes appear to be somewhere in between; in these parishes the new Catholic liturgy is still in the development stage.

In addition to the Mass, other aspects of Catholic devotional life have also changed. The old-style parish mission has disappeared; novenas are considerably less popular; and fewer Catholics pray the rosary. At the same time, new devotional rituals have appeared. Prayer services centered around readings from the Bible are now standard; home liturgies at which a priest celebrates Mass for small groups of people are commonplace. Among Spanish-speaking Catholics especially, but among others as well, the *cursillo*, an intense weekend of prayer, has become popular. Marriage encounter, a weekend of prayer for married couples, has also attracted a large following. In black Catholic parishes, evangelical-style revivals reminiscent of the old parish mission, have become a popular form of evangelization. Several programs aimed at the spiritual renewal of entire parishes were developed during the 1970s. One of the most popular was called RENEW. Developed by a team of priests, women religious, and lay people in the archdiocese of Newark, it is a three-year program designed to help parishes in the task of spiritual renewal. Launched in Newark in 1978, it spread like wildfire, and within five years over four thousand parishes across the country were participating in the RENEW program; it has also been exported to Canada, Australia, and New Zealand.[13]

Clearly one of the most remarkable developments in religious renewal is the charismatic movement. In the 1950s and 1960s, a Pentecostal style of religion, which emphasized the baptism of the Holy Spirit and such gifts as speaking in tongues and healing, began to surface in mainline Protestant denominations. It was not long before Catholics came under the influence of Pentecostalism. Another major influence on the Catholic charismatic movement was the *cursillo*. In the 1960s, the cursillo had become quite popular; many of the first leaders of the charismatic movement were influenced by the intense emotional experience of a cursillo retreat. This led one historian to conclude, ". . . the seeds of the charismatic movement in the Catholic Church were planted and nurtured in the Cursillo Movement."[14]

Duquesne University in Pittsburgh was the site of the first stirrings of a Catholic Pentecostal movement. Two faculty members, William Storey and Ralph Keifer, were keenly interested in the renewal taking place in Catholicism; they both had made a cursillo and had participated in Protestant Pentecostal prayer meetings. In February 1967 they organized a weekend retreat for students, and over the course of the weekend, as one student recalled, ". . . the Holy Spirit came upon them to reveal the Lord to them in a new way and to introduce a new dimension of Christian living." The rest is history. In the spring of 1967 the movement spread to the campuses of Michigan State and Notre Dame, and it was not long before "people were speaking of a

'Pentecostal Movement' in the Catholic Church." For the first couple of years, growth was slow. Many Catholics were very suspicious of the demonstrative style of Pentecostal prayer and the intense emotionalism evident at some Pentecostal prayer meetings. Others regarded it as just another strange expression of religion so prevalent at the time. Nonetheless, the Catholic hierarchy gave the movement their cautious approval in 1969, and the leaders of the Catholic Pentecostal movement made the most of this endorsement. By 1973, an estimated 50,000 Catholics in the United States and Canada were seriously involved in the Pentecostal movement. Throughout the 1970s the movement continued to grow and attract national attention. By 1984 there were about 5,700 prayer groups in the United States; each week about 250,000 people attended a charismatic prayer meeting; another 250,000 were also actively involved in the movement. The estimated number of Catholics who have passed through the movement since 1967 ranges anywhere from eight to ten million.[15]

The Catholic charismatic movement is organized nationally, with its headquarters in South Bend, Indiana; it has its own magazine and publishing house; and it sponsors annual conventions, most of which are held at the University of Notre Dame. The crowds are so large at these conventions that they have to use the Notre Dame basketball arena and football stadium for their liturgies. Bishops, priests, and women religious belong to the movement, but it is preponderantly a lay Catholic movement with men in the decision-making positions. In addition to the prayer group, which is the core of the movement, there are also covenant communities in which groups of people "discern life in Christ together" by making decisions in common as a community; members also share their financial resources by contributing part of their income to the covenant community. A more intense commitment to charismatic piety, such covenant communities existed in about a hundred locations in 1984; about 10 percent of their membership came from denominations other than Catholic. Another feature of the movement is its focus on healing. By the late 1970s, healing services conducted by Catholic charismatic leaders were drawing large crowds of people, and many healings were reported.[16]

Not surprisingly, the emergence of a Pentecostal style of religion disturbed a great many Catholics. Emphasis on the personal experience of religion and the tendency to express this in a very emotional and demonstrative way made many Catholics suspicious of the movement. Others criticized it because women were assigned a more traditional, secondary role in the movement; still others spoke out against abuses of authority and efforts to manipulate the lives of young people. Activists did not like it because charismatic piety was too personal and not oriented enough toward action on behalf of social justice. The tendency of charismatics to interpret the Bible in a fundamentalist manner has come under criticism, as has the tendency to consider charismatic piety superior to all other types of prayer. Despite prolonged criticism and widespread misunderstanding, the charismatic movement continues to prosper. Though its growth has slowed in recent years, it has gained a permanent place in contemporary Catholicism. Its stress on the value of personal prayer and giving witness to a person's faith has been widely accepted. Without a doubt, it has been one of the most powerful movements for religious renewal that has swept across Catholic America in the twentieth century. It was a phenomenon the Second Vatican Council never envisioned and never considered. Rather, it emerged out of the broader spiritual renewal taking place in American society during the 1960s and 1970s, when millions of Americans turned to new forms of religious expression in order to fill a need in their lives.

There was no question that in the decade following the Second Vatican Council many people were quite disturbed about the changes in Catholic devotional practices. Imposed from the top by the Council and the clergy with little preparation, they confused people. At a time when American society was undergoing dramatic changes and social upheaval, many turned to the churches and religion for an anchor in a sea of change and confusion. For Catholics, the anchor appeared to have disappeared; disappointed and disillusioned, many stopped going to church. A 1974 survey reported that only about 50 percent of the people questioned attended church regularly, whereas the 1963 level had been 71 percent. During the same period, the rate of those not going to church at all had doubled.[17]

By the late 1970s, a measure of calm had settled into the area of Catholic devotionalism. Church attendance had increased, and people better understood the new style of liturgy. Young people raised in the new tradition took it for granted. Grumblings remained, but they were less strident and widespread. Catholic charismatics were more accepted and more integrated into parish life. The "novena-rosary" style of devotional Catholicism was gone. In its place was a new Catholic piety whose distinguishing trademarks were its strong biblical flavor and its radically pluralistic nature. Thenceforth, there would be no one, Catholic way to pray, but a variety of ways for Catholics to pray.

In recent years, Catholics have not only discovered new ways to pray, but they have also learned new attitudes about Protestants. In no area was the impact of the Council more visible and dramatic. Suspicion disappeared overnight. Catholic and Protestant clergy began to talk to one another more frequently and more cordially. Local dialogues took place among clergy of various churches, and soon interdenominational worship services became commonplace. Religiously mixed marriages became more frequent and less scorned. Official church committees between Catholics and Lutherans, as well as between Catholics and Baptists, began to explore the theological bonds that united these churches in a common Christian faith. By the 1980s, people took such happenings for granted and forgot how dramatic the move toward ecumenism had been in the 1960s. Easily the most talked about aspect of the Council in its early days, ecumenism remained front-page news for a few years. After the novelty wore off, the formidable reality of separation between denominations remained. Nonetheless, a whole new attitude has reshaped relations between Catholics and Protestants and brought an end to the long cold war of hostility and suspicion.

Another change that transformed the religious world of Catholics was a new understanding of sin. The traditional concept of sin was grounded in a system of laws, some of which were rooted in Scripture or the natural law, while others were promulgated by the church. The new Catholic morality argued for a more personal, less legalistic, approach to sin. The virtue of love became primary, together with the individual conscience. The implications of this shift, publicized in both scholarly and popular works, was tremendous. Perhaps most dramatic was the decline in confession. A 1974 study found that only 17 percent of the Catholics surveyed went to confession monthly, compared to 37 percent in 1963.[18] Soon form followed function, and reconciliation rooms, where priest and penitent could interact face to face, replaced the dark confessional box. Penitential services became popular, and on some occasions a public general absolution replaced private confessions.

The most publicized impact of the new morality was, predictably, in the area of sex, specifically the issue of birth control. For years, church authorities had placed a taboo on sex. As late as the 1950s, seminarians in some places were not allowed to view high school biology films describing the reproductive cycle; marriage courses for college students were rare; preachers and confessors were admonished to deal gingerly with the issue of sex; only reluctantly were boys and girls allowed in the same classrooms; and sex education was unheard of. Given this environment, the Catholic clergy were poorly prepared to cope with the sexual revolution of the 1960s. The more permissive society became, the more adamant church leaders were in their desire to uphold traditional Catholic teaching. The most explosive issue was birth control.

At Vatican II, bishops wanted to discuss the traditional teaching of the church prohibiting the use of any artificial means of birth control. Rather than debate it openly, Pope John set up a papal commission to investigate the matter. Composed of clergy and laity, it spent more than two years studying the church's teaching on birth control. Complicating the issue was the development of the birth-control pill and its success in controlling conception. This was clearly one reason why, in the 1960s, American women, Catholics included, were much more inclined to practice birth control. Also entering into the discussion was the new phenomenon of dissent in the church. The bishops demonstrated this in a remarkable manner at the Council, demonstrating that loyalty to the church did not mean blind obedience. The Council sanctioned the right to dissent, and Catholics were quick to learn this. A dramatic illustration of this took place in 1967 when the trustees of Catholic University refused to renew the contract of Charles E. Curran, a priest who taught moral theology and whose teaching on birth control was suspect in the opinion of several bishops on the board. This sudden action, taken against the will of the theology faculty that had voted to promote Curran, set off a storm of protest that closed the university down when students and faculty boycotted classes. In the end, Curran's contract was renewed. In the 1960s, such protest and dissent were becoming more common both in society and in the church. Thus, when Pope Paul VI finally issued an encyclical on marriage, in the summer of 1968, in which he upheld the traditional ban of the church against all artificial means of birth control, Catholics were primed for dissent.

In 1967, a year prior to the publication of the encyclical, *Humanae Vitae,* the report of the papal birth-control commission had been leaked to the press along with a dissenting, minority report. Published in the *National Catholic Reporter,* the report concluded that the decision to regulate the size of the family should be left to the individual couple. This raised the expectations of Catholics, and they looked for a change in church teaching. When the Pope issued the encyclical and went against the commission's conclusion, all hope for change vanished.

Of course, many Catholic women had made up their minds prior to *Humanae Vitae.* Whereas in 1955 only about 30 percent of Catholic women used some artificial means of birth control, by 1965 the rate had increased to 51 percent; it would continue to rise, so that by 1970 it reached a level of 68 percent. Obviously the encyclical had done little to change the minds of women; in fact, close to 90 percent of the American Catholic laity rejected the encyclical's teaching on birth control.[19]

Much more publicized than the dissent of the laity was the dissent of the clergy. Throughout the world, bishops tried to soft-pedal the implications of the Pope's decision. In the United States, priests and theologians began a storm of protest; at the eye of the storm was Charles E. Curran, the theologian some bishops had tried to discredit a year earlier. Theologians and clergy held news conferences, signed petitions, and publicly dissented from the papal teaching. In Washington, D.C., the dissent became especially bitter when the archbishop, Patrick A. O'Boyle, disciplined fifty-one priests who refused in conscience to accept the encyclical's teaching. Cut off from exercising their ministry until they recanted, many of the fifty-one—twenty-five at least— eventually left the priesthood.[20]

For Catholics, birth control was the issue of the decade that separated Dallas from Watergate. Andrew Greeley, a noted priest-sociologist-journalist-novelist and one of the more perceptive observers of contemporary American Catholicism, concluded that *Humanae Vitae* canceled out the positive results of Vatican II and sent the church into a sudden and dramatic decline: priests refused to endorse the teaching in the confessional; Sunday church attendance dropped off sharply; church collections diminished; resignations from the priesthood increased, while those who remained diminished their efforts to recruit young men for the vocation and family support for religious vocations eroded. Acceptance of papal authority declined dramatically.[21]

The furor over the encyclical was a symbol of fundamental changes in both religion and society that were reshaping contemporary Roman Catholicism. It was but one of many elements that contributed to the transformation of Catholicism in the post-Vatican II era. As Greeley pointed out, more than sex was at issue. At stake was the question of authority in the church and how it would be exercised; religious freedom and the primacy of the individual conscience were also at issue. The Council had broadened the concept of authority in the church to counteract the narrow papalism of the nineteenth century. Vatican II also proclaimed the right of the individual conscience to "immunity from coercion in matters religious." The encyclical and the harsh reprisal against dissenting clergy undercut this and created a severe credibility gap for the church. Catholics were not only disappointed, but disillusioned. For these reasons, *Humanae Vitae* was a shattering blow to "the euphoria that had flourished after Vatican II."

Another area that has undergone substantial revision is the church's attitude toward divorce. Simply put, a pastoral revolution has taken place. Clergy and bishops are recognizing the reality of divorce among Catholics and have sought to minister to divorced Catholics in a more effective and compassionate manner. In addition, church authorities have become more willing to grant divorce with the right to remarry (i.e., marriage annulments). Statistics demonstrate this quite dramatically. In 1967, the church in the United States granted seven hundred annulments; in 1978, twenty-five thousand annulments were issued.[22] Many dioceses have also set up pastoral programs for separated and divorced Catholics, and national conventions began to become regular events in the early 1970s. A Paulist priest, James Young, and a Franciscan sister, Paula Ripple, were most responsible for developing and promoting this ministry to separated and divorced Catholics.

As revolutionary as the new Catholic morality was the change in the concept of ministry. Clearly, one of the most publicized issues in the 1960s was the large number of priests who left the active ministry. A worldwide phenomenon, it created quite a stir in the Catholic community. In the United States, an estimated 3,413 men resigned from the priesthood between 1966 and 1969. Such an exodus was unprecedented, and the news media gave it extensive coverage. Closely tied to the clerical exodus was the issue of married clergy. For several centuries the Roman Catholic tradition allowed for married priests, but eventually the priesthood was limited to celibates; in Eastern Catholic churches, married priests have always been accepted, though in the United States the hierarchy succeeded after decades of struggle to outlaw Eastern-rite married clergy. Though the issue of a married clergy for the Roman rite was discussed at Vatican II, the Council document on the priesthood upheld the celibate model for priests in the Roman Catholic rite while it praised the tradition of married clergy in Eastern Catholic churches. The distinction underlined the point that celibacy "is not," in the words of the Council fathers, "demanded by the very nature of the priesthood." The question of a married clergy would not go away, and at the 1971 synod of bishops in Rome it was a major topic of debate. By this time, many bishops were urging the Pope and their episcopal colleagues to allow for a married clergy. Surveys taken in the United States indicated that a large majority of the laity—62 percent—did indeed favor a married clergy. Nevertheless the law was not changed, and celibacy remains a requirement for ordination to the priesthood in the Roman Catholic church.[23]

The crisis in the priesthood stemmed from a significant shift in the understanding and meaning of ministry. Prior to the mid-1960s, ministry in the Catholic church was identified with the ordained priesthood. But a new theology of church and priesthood began to change this. A broader concept of ministry developed which included priest, laity, and nonordained religious. No longer did the priest have a monopoly on ministry. This shift in understanding tended to create a crisis of identity for priests. The broader concept of ministry, with its increasing emphasis on the plurality of ministries in the church, substantially narrowed the definition of ordained priesthood; as a consequence, it became increasingly limited to the celebration of Mass and the sacraments. The question of celibacy served to intensify the identity crisis. One concrete result of this was a growing shortage of priests. Throughout the 1970s, priests continued to resign, and by 1978 it was estimated that in the United States about ten thousand priests had left the active ministry since 1966. During these years, the number of those preparing to become priests had declined dramatically. In 1964, the number of seminarians preparing for the priesthood in the United States stood at 47,500, but by 1984 the number had dropped to about 12,000. Reflecting this decrease, 241 seminaries closed their doors during this twenty-year period. Because of the decrease in the number of new recruits and the resignation of large numbers of younger priests, the clergy as a group were aging rapidly, and with age were tending to become more conservative. Equally significant is that more parishes, especially in small, isolated communities, are without resident priests for the first time; those parishes that do have priests have fewer than before. As the number of priests has declined, the number of Catholics has increased. This compounds the problem of the shortage of clergy. As serious as the problem is in the United States, it is worse in other countries.[24]

The departure of large numbers of women religious has intensified the problem of personnel shortage. Throughout the 1950s and early 1960s, the number of women leaving religious life was steadily increasing; in the three-year period 1963–66, an estimated 4,332 left. Yet recruits kept coming, so the total number of women religious in the United States increased and peaked in 1966 at 181,421. Then a steady decline set in. Recruits stopped coming, more sisters left, and by 1980 the total population of women religious in the United States was 126,517. Like that of the priests, the median age of women religious has increased significantly. The same pattern of fewer recruits, smaller numbers, and an aging population was also present in communities of religious brothers throughout the 1960s and 1970s.[25]

Why was there such a massive exodus from religious life? Certainly the social and cultural changes of the 1960s had some influence, as did the new spirit of independence unleashed by Vatican II. Sociologists have probed the question in some detail and come up with fairly consistent answers. The reasons why priests left the active ministry are quite clear. "They left," concluded a 1970 study commissioned by the bishops, "because they found difficulties with the structure of the Church and the work they were doing as priests and because they wanted to get married." As regards women religious, the desire for greater self-fulfillment, rather than marriage, was the primary personal reason. Others offered reasons related to religious life itself; some women no longer saw a value in it, while others believed that their religious order was not following the lead of the Second Vatican Council and thus was not changing fast enough.[26]

Fortunately, as the number of clergy and religious declined, laity became more involved in ministry. During the 1950s, greater participation in the church and the world on the part of lay people was being encouraged. Vatican II continued this thrust, so that by the 1970s lay people were becoming much more involved in the ministry of the church. As one person put it, "The degree to which nonordained people are serving in functions that were once reserved for priests is absolutely mind boggling."[27] Many dioceses have inaugurated training programs for lay ministers; lay people have gone back to school to get prepared for work in the church. In recent years, laymen, most of whom are married and have secular jobs, have been ordained as deacons and are authorized to preside at baptisms and weddings as well as distribute Communion and preach; by 1982 their number had increased to 4,725. Religious education has become an especially popular field for lay ministers; others are in charge of parish music programs, youth programs, or social-justice activities; some do more traditional pastoral work such as counseling or visiting the sick and the elderly; and a few have even been put in charge of priestless parishes. By the 1970s, full-time, paid lay ministers had become quite accepted in Catholic parish life. In addition, many women religious have left the traditional work of teaching and entered a variety of new ministries. It is not uncommon to see sisters directing public social-service agencies or working as prison chaplains, as lobbyists on Capitol Hill, or as community organizers.

An important development in the area of lay ministry is the extensive participation of women; in fact, they outnumber men to a significant degree. This is not surprising, given the traditionally heavy involvement of women in organized religion. Nonetheless, the women's movement of the 1960s and 1970s reinforced the trend by urging women to become more involved in all aspects of public life. Many began to use their professional skills in the local church and became lay ministers. The women's movement also emphasized the rights of women in all institutions of society, including the church. As a result, Catholic women, sisters especially, have become more vocal in challenging the institutional church in those areas where the rights of women are ignored. This awakening has led to the development of a feminist theological school of thought, the leading representatives of which are Rosemary Radford Ruether and Elisabeth Schüssler Fiorenza. In the 1970s, a movement on behalf of the ordination of women to the priesthood also got underway.[28]

The expansion of the concept of ministry to include nonordained people as well as ordained clergy was not without its problems. One major complaint has been the low salaries paid to full-time lay ministers. Another bone of contention is the lack of authority and decision-making power that lay ministers have in a clerically controlled church. Another problem is that, as of the mid 1980s, the new theology of ministry was still in the process of development.

Lacking a clear focus, confusion, rather than clarity, remains a dominant feature of ministry in contemporary Catholic life. The most explosive issue has been the need to reexamine the nature of priesthood. "Catholics are witnessing ministerial leadership ably exercised by nonclerics," wrote the journalist Robert McClory; "the next question is inevitable: Why can't these leaders (be they women, married or whatever) be legitimately ordained and authorized to preside over the community liturgy?" As one seminary rector put it, that is "the ultimate question and it's coming. It threatens the hell out of priests and believe me, it's gonna blow the roof off the church some day!"[29] The issue of women priests has become especially divisive, as many theologians vigorously argue for the ordination of women, while the hierarchy, taking their cue from the Pope, remain strongly opposed to it.

As the nature of ministry was undergoing redefinition, seminaries experienced dramatic changes. Not only are they fewer in number, but seminaries are operated quite differently from before. Men interested in the priesthood enter the seminary at a later age, most often after graduation from college; seminarians are less cut off from the rest of society than was previously true and also have become more pastorally involved. For women entering religious life, the years of preparation in the convent have also changed. They enter as candidates at a much older age, are better prepared educationally, and are not as separated from the rest of society as before. The dress of women religious has also changed, as the traditional habit has either been modernized or discarded in favor of contemporary dress.

As might be expected, new structures and organizations have emerged in the church since the 1960s. At the national level, the NCWC was reorganized into the National Conference of Catholic Bishops and its administrative agency, the United States Catholic Conference. Priests became organized for the first time on both local and national levels. The Association of Chicago Priests, founded in 1966, was one of the first; other dioceses organized priests' senates or councils. Then, in 1968, with Chicago priests leading the way, the National Federation of Priests' Councils was founded to give the rank-and-file clergy a more powerful voice in church affairs. National organizations for women religious became prominent, with the most notable being the Leadership Conference of Women Religious and the National Assembly of Women Religious. Hispanic Catholics held national pastoral meetings in 1972 and 1977. The closest parallel to a national church council was the Call to Action conference held in Detroit in October 1976; two years of regional hearings preceded the national meeting, at which 1,340 delegates debated a variety of resolutions focusing on the issue of justice in society.

To involve lay people in the decision-making process of the church, some dioceses have organized pastoral councils to assist the bishop in determining the priorities of the local church and its future direction. Much more common is the parish council. Reminiscent of nineteenth-century lay trustees, council members are elected to office and assist the clergy in managing parish affairs. A 1982 study found that about three of four parishes have such councils, but their effectiveness varies greatly.[30] Vatican II encouraged these developments by emphasizing the role of the laity in the church and the concept of collegiality, or shared authority. Nevertheless, democracy has yet to penetrate the government of the Catholic church to any significant degree. Though there tends to be more consultation, the clergy still control the church. But the priest is no longer the one and only parish leader. Lay ministers have emerged as recognized parish leaders. As a result, a classic dilemma, so common in the nineteenth century, once again confronts lay people and priests. Who will control parish affairs, the clergy acting alone or priests and people acting together? How this issue is resolved will determine the future vitality of parish life in the United States.

The social and religious changes that swept across America had a twofold impact on the Catholic educational network. First, as Catholics became socially and culturally more American, they began to rethink the meaning of Catholicism in American society. Then, as a result of the changes initiated by Vatican II, they began to rethink the meaning of Catholicism in the modern world. From this questioning emerged a crisis of identity. On a personal level, it clearly had a profound impact: for some it meant personal and spiritual renewal; for others it resulted in dropping out of the church. On an organizational level the crisis was quite visible. Ernan McMullin, president of the American Catholic Philosophical Association in 1967, put it most succinctly in his presidential address when he asked the question, "Who Are We?"[31] Catholic sociologists asked the same question, as did members of other professional societies. The end result was that in redefining their role in American society, many Catholic organizations, fraternal as well as professional, either passed out of existence or acquired a new self-understanding that was deliberately more American and less exclusively Catholic.

Along with the decrease in Catholic organizations was a notable decline in the popularity of Catholic newspapers. Though the number of newspapers actually increased, circulation figures plummeted. Many Catholic book-publishing firms also closed their doors, while others redefined their objectives in the light of Vatican II. One of the more significant developments was the founding, in 1964, of the *National Catholic Reporter,* a newspaper, independently owned and operated by lay people, that has been seeking to keep liberal-minded Catholics up to date on developments in the church. The crisis of identity also deflated the smugness and confidence of Catholics. The 1940s and 1950s crusade to win converts disappeared, and interest in foreign missions declined.

Like just about everything else in Roman Catholicism, the area of catechetics has undergone substantial change. The Baltimore Catechism has disappeared from use. In its place are many other catechisms, designed and written in the spirit of Vatican II. The style of teaching religion has also changed; less concerned about the rote learning of theological dogmas, educators emphasized personal understanding and appropriation of the gospel message. Adult religious education programs have become especially popular in recent years. Nevertheless, the new catechetics has brought new problems. The clarity and precision of the Baltimore Catechism era has given way to less precise, popular expressions of theological truths. As a result, many Catholics have questioned the orthodoxy of some new catechetical texts. This has resulted in either the revision of some texts or, in a few cases, the actual withdrawal of official church approval from suspected texts. Another major problem is the preparation of lay religious educators. While not new, by any means, the changes in theology, together with a shortage of clergy and religious, have necessitated the use of more lay teachers in religious education. Yet most laity are not theologically prepared for the task or, if they are, the salaries of full-time religious educators remain too low to keep them working in the area for any length of time.

One of the obvious reasons for the increased commitment to catechetics is the decline of the parochial school. After a hundred years of sustained growth, attendance at Catholic elementary schools began to decline in the 1960s. An obvious reason was the declining birth rate, which affected the growth of all schools. More peculiarly Catholic was the 1960s debate on the value of a parochial-school education. Many people questioned the value of educating children in separate, denominational schools. Another obvious reason was financial. As large numbers of women religious either left religious life altogether or abandoned teaching for other ministries, the need to hire more lay teachers and thus pay higher salaries became paramount. As a result, school budgets increased, and before long they became unbearable. Thus, schools were forced to close. Lay people had already begun to take up teaching positions in elementary and secondary schools in steadily increasing numbers in the 1950s, but the virtual disappearance of women religious from the classroom in the late 1960s and 1970s accelerated the trend. The change in the diocese of Bridgeport, Connecticut, told the story: in 1970, of the teachers in Catholic elementary and high schools, 85 percent were members of religious orders; by 1984, 85 percent were lay people. On a national level it was not much better: 41 percent of the faculty in Catholic schools were lay teachers in 1969; by 1984, the level had risen to 77 percent. Such a sudden shift in personnel was financially too much for many parishes to handle. The result was that, between 1964 and 1984, 40 percent of the nation's Catholic high schools and 27 percent of its elementary schools closed their doors.[32] In order to survive, the Catholic school system had to trim down. Inner-city schools were particularly hard hit; many were forced either to close or to consolidate. Those that remained open began to educate large numbers of children from other religious backgrounds. Nationally, children from other denominations made up about 10 percent of the Catholic elementary-school enrollment in 1984, but in inner-city schools the level was much higher. In Chicago, for example, half of the black students in the city's Catholic schools were not Catholic. In some southern cities the same pattern prevailed.[33] The Catholic character of such schools was negligible, and this has sparked a debate over whether or not these schools should continue to operate under church auspices.

Surveys taken in the 1970s indicated that the majority of Catholics favored parochial schools. In 1977, Andrew Greeley noted, ". . . at least three quarters of the Catholics in the United States have endorsed the principle of Catholic schools, and there is simply no evidence that the level of endorsement is falling." Few people would quarrel with Greeley's assessment. In fact, recent trends suggest that Catholic schools may be enjoying a renaissance after a prolonged period of decline. But, as has always been true, economic realities threaten their future, particularly in inner-city schools, "which have been providing outstanding educational services for the poor and minorities."[34]

Economic realities have also persuaded many Catholic parents to send their children to publicly supported universities and colleges. The falling birth rate has also had an impact on college enrollment. As a result, many smaller Catholic colleges have been forced to close, while others have survived only by merging with nearby Catholic institutions. The increased attendance of Catholics at secular universities (the best estimates conclude that about two of every three Catholic college students attend non-Catholic institutions) has given a big boost to the Newman Movement. First begun at the University of Wisconsin in 1883, the Newman Movement attempts "to supply pastoral care and religious education in non-Catholic colleges and universities." In the 1960s, it began to attract increasing numbers of priests and religious, who moved to secular campuses with the zeal of missionaries.[35]

Even though Catholics have become better educated and more involved in the intellectual and cultural life of the nation, Catholic colleges and universities still remain mediocre institutions of learning. Schools like Notre Dame, Georgetown, Holy Cross, and Boston College continue to excel in undergraduate education. But as research institutions, Catholic schools are at best a little above average. A 1982 assessment of universities offering research doctorate programs in the United States not only confirmed this, but it indicated which Catholic universities American educators perceived to be the best. Across the board, the University of Notre Dame was ranked the highest. Nonetheless, its highest-ranked programs, philosophy and chemical engineering, were considered to be slightly better than average. Other universities that fared well were Catholic University and Loyola University of Chicago. When compared with similar reports in the 1960s, Catholic universities appeared to be holding their own, with places like Notre Dame and Loyola evidencing some improvement. The only area where a Catholic university has broken into the charmed circle of the top twenty is in endowment funds. Notre Dame, with a 1984 endowment of 250 million dollars, was ranked nineteenth in the nation, far above its closest Catholic rival, Loyola University of Chicago, which ranked fifty-first with an endowment of 107 million dollars.[36]

The changes initiated by Vatican II affected Catholic colleges in a variety of ways. Several universities established lay boards of trustees, which has tended to shift control of these schools from the clergy to the lay-dominated boards. More significant has been the issue of academic freedom.

Vatican II encouraged intellectual freedom, and American educators were quick to endorse it. Nonetheless, all did not go smoothly. Intense debate and bitter confrontations took place in the late 1960s over this issue. Catholic University, the bishops' university, was a major catalyst in sparking the debate. In 1963 the university administration banned four distinguished priest-scholars—Godfrey Diekmann, O.S.B., Hans Küng, John Courtney Murray, S.J., and Gustave Weigel, S.J.—from speaking on campus. Such suppression was common in the 1950s, but Vatican II had already breathed a new spirit into the church. The publicity associated with the ban was widespread and led one observer to write that it marked "a turning point in the history of freedom in the Catholic church in America."[37] Undaunted, the administration of Catholic University struck again in 1967, when they sought to dismiss the moral theologian Charles E. Curran from the faculty; this time they failed. Even more publicized and more prolonged was the dismissal of thirty-three faculty members from St. John's University in New York in 1965; twenty-two of them were suspended immediately and without a hearing. A basic issue at St. John's was the faculty's right to organize a union as well as the larger question of academic freedom. For its action, the American Association of University Professors censured St. John's University. Other universities got caught in the changing times and attempted to use 1950s tactics to solve 1960s issues of academic freedom. In 1966 the historian Philip Gleason observed that academic freedom "was the most crucial problem facing Catholic higher education."[38] To explore the issue, a group of Catholic educators led by Theodore M. Hesburgh, C.S.C., met in the summer of 1967 at Land O'Lakes, Wisconsin. They drafted a statement which asserted "that institutional autonomy and academic freedom are essential conditions of life and growth and indeed of survival for Catholic universities as for all universities." The Land O'Lakes document became a key statement on behalf of academic freedom and the value of the Catholic university.[39]

Since the 1960s, academic freedom has, for the most part, vanished as a major issue in American Catholic universities. Conservative-minded church authorities in Rome, unfamiliar with the nature of higher education in the United States, have from time to time sought to emphasize the right of the hierarchy to monitor intellectual life at Catholic universities, especially in the area of theology. Thus far no major confrontations have occurred, mainly because most American university presidents and bishops are strongly committed to uphold the principle of intellectual freedom articulated at Vatican II.

Closely related to this issue was the question of Catholic identity, or What is the uniquely Catholic character of the Catholic university? Part of the broader question of what it means to be a Catholic in the United States, it has generated considerable discussion in the past twenty years. In the 1980s, Catholic educators are still trying to build the perfect Catholic university, but a workable definition has proved to be quite elusive. Throughout the 1960s and 1970s, Notre Dame followed the direction of service to the church, and in an impressive manner used its academic resources to aid the cause of church renewal in the United States. No Catholic university was able to match Notre Dame's performance in this regard. The key catalyst for this was its president, Theodore M. Hesburgh, C.S.C., whose public-service record in the 1950s, 1960s, and 1970s was unparalleled. Recently, Notre Dame has sought to reaffirm its Catholic character in a new manner, and in doing so has once again raised the question, "What is specifically Catholic about Catholic colleges and universities?" The suspicion is that an answer satisfactory to all will be as elusive in the 1980s as it was in the 1960s. Nonetheless, the very fact that the question is still being raised is a positive sign for the future of Catholic higher education.

Since Vatican II, a new atmosphere prevails in the Catholic academy. Freedom of inquiry is clearly the most significant advance. Suppression of theological dissent was a feature of pre-Vatican II Catholicism, but this is no longer true. Indeed, church authorities still remain zealous monitors of theological orthodoxy, and suppression of theologians suspected of unorthodox positions still takes place. But in the United States during the 1960s and 1970s such suppressive tactics were less likely to be used. The Council had sanctioned the right to dissent, and the majority of Catholic intellectuals welcomed this. In this new atmosphere, American Catholic theologians began to make important strides. For years, theology in the United States was derived from the work of European theologians. Though this still remains true, American theologians have begun to be recognized for the quality and originality of their own work. Scripture scholars like John L. McKenzie, Raymond E. Brown, S.S., and Joseph A. Fitzmyer, S.J., have acquired international reputations. The writings of moral theologians or ethicists, like Richard A. McCormick, S.J., and Charles E. Curran, are highly regarded, as is the work of such theologians as Avery Dulles, S.J., and David Tracy. Not surprisingly, all these individuals are priests, that segment of the community to which theological study has been traditionally limited. A new development in recent years has been the emergence of lay men and women in the theological academy. The major feature of the new Catholic theology is its diversity, or pluralism; this is the most important theological development since the 1960s. No longer is there one Catholic way to do theology; rather, plurality of method and style has taken over. Coupled with freedom of inquiry, it constitutes the major trademark of American Catholic theology in the post-Vatican II era.

Other issues of reform were sweeping through the Catholic church during this period. One was a renewed commitment to social justice. Social justice became a major national concern during the 1960s as poverty, racial violence, and war singed the consciences of a generation of Americans. At Vatican II, the bishops made social justice a top priority. In the United States, church leaders had traditionally evidenced strong support for the labor movement; this remained true throughout the 1960s and 1970s, but added to the agenda was a more intense commitment to racial justice and an honest concern for peace.

On the labor front, the major issue of the 1960s and 1970s was the farm workers' movement. Mexican Americans had long labored as migrant farm workers, but they were never effectively organized. Cesar Chavez changed that. The son of migrant farm workers, Chavez was discovered by a Catholic priest, Donald McDonnell, in the barrio Sal Si Puedes of San Jose, California. McDonnell was part of the traveling band of San Francisco priests who were ministering to farm workers in the 1940s and 1950s. After meeting Chavez, McDonnell began to talk to him about labor organizing. Chavez recalled their late-night conversations: "He told me about social justice and the Church's stand on farm labor and reading from the encyclicals of Pope Leo XIII, in which he upheld labor unions. I would do anything to get the Father to tell me more about labor history. I began going to the *Bracero* camps with him to help with the Mass, to the city jail with him to talk to the prisoners, anything to be with him. . . ."[40] In the early 1950s, McDonnell also aided a community organizer, Fred Ross, in finding his way around Sal Si Puedes. Eventually Chavez and Ross joined forces and began organizing Mexican-American communities. Then, in 1962, Chavez set out on his own to establish the National Farm Workers Association. Born in an age of protest and civil disobedience, the farm workers' movement, popularly known as *la causa,* captured public attention. Chavez became a prominent public figure as he pushed vigorously but nonviolently for justice for the farm workers. Since he is a religious person, Christian principles were a decisive influence on the thought and work of Chavez; he invoked the symbol of Our Lady of Guadalupe in his cause, and the celebration of Mass became part of the movement's ritual.

The organizing efforts of Chavez and the farm workers angered many people, mainly the growers. In California, Catholic clergy and lay people were bitterly divided over *la causa.* Nonetheless, after years of protest, picketing, and boycotting stores that sold nonunion-picked grapes and lettuce, Chavez and the farm workers gained a major victory. It came in 1970 when the United Farm Workers signed the first of several labor contracts with major California growers. A central figure in these negotiations was George Higgins, a priest associated with the United States Catholic Conference. A labor priest in the tradition of John A. Ryan and Raymond A. McGowan, Higgins was a member of the Bishops' Ad Hoc Committee on Farm Labor, a group set up by the hierarchy to attempt to mediate the dispute between Chavez and the growers. The Bishops' Committee succeeded, and Higgins's skills as a mediator as well as his long support of *la causa* led Chavez to state, "I doubt that anyone has done as much for us as Monsignor Higgins has."[41]

The involvement of bishops in the farm workers' movement was part of a new trend. In 1975 the bishops of Appalachia put together an eloquent statement on behalf of social justice in this forgotten pocket of poverty, "where in a wilderness of idolatrous destruction," they wrote, "the great voice of God still cries out for life." Another notable instance of bishops becoming involved in the struggle of workers was the conflict between labor and the textile company of J. P. Stevens. In 1980, a group of southern bishops endorsed a union boycott of the company; their action helped to resolve the dispute between the company and the union. Members of clergy and lay people were heavily involved in these and similar issues, but the public stance of an increasing number of bishops on behalf of social justice was something new in American Catholicism.

Nothing shocked the nation like the civil rights crusade and the racial violence that erupted during the 1960s. Because of the advances made in the 1950s, Catholics were better prepared to join forces with the movement; because of their concentration in the cities, they had little choice. The '60s was a decade of sit-ins and protest marches. Certainly one of the most significant marches took place in Alabama in March 1965, when thousands of people walked from Selma to Montgomery to demonstrate for the right of blacks to vote. Clergy of all religions took part in this demonstration; over four hundred Catholic priests plus numerous nuns, brothers, and lay people walked together with blacks and whites, Protestants and Jews, publicly demonstrating on behalf of civil rights for blacks. To be out on the front line publicly demonstrating for social justice was something new for Catholic priests and religious. Eventually a priest or nun standing on the picket line or participating in a protest march became quite a common sight. Such activity angered many traditional-minded Catholics, who wanted their priests out of the streets and back in the sanctuary. In 1966, King took his civil rights crusade to Chicago. A Mecca of Catholic reform, Chicago's clergy and laity worked with King and his aides to dramatize the plight of blacks in the Windy City. But when demonstrators marched through heavily Catholic neighborhoods, they got pelted with bottles and racist epithets. The following year, the Milwaukee priest James Groppi made national news when he led open-housing marches throughout Milwaukee.

Though the media focused on the activities of priests and nuns, the laity were also heavily involved. What was different, however, was that as they became more integrated into American society, they relied less on church organizations as outlets for their social concern. Catholic laity were finally beginning to take their places in society as socially involved Christians. For this reason, special-interest groups such as YCS, YCW, and CFM became less popular. As the civil rights movement engulfed an entire nation, Catholic interracial councils also began to disappear. The Friendship House movement redefined its vision, as did Grail; they became less exclusively focused on Catholic concerns and more oriented to justice issues affecting all of society. Black Catholics became militant once again. In 1970, the National Office of Black Catholics was opened; priests, nuns, and laity set up national organizations and pushed for equal rights in the church. For the first time in over a century, black priests were appointed to the hierarchy.

The civil rights crusade had dramatized the pitiful condition of black urban America. When urban-renewal programs and new highway construction gutted large parts of the nation's cities, whites fled to the suburbs, and blacks and other newcomers got left behind. This population shift radically transformed city churches. What happened in Harlem after World War I happened all across the nation in the 1960s. White parishes lost parishioners, school populations declined, and huge churches stood as cavernous reminders of a past age. The transformation of Most Blessed Sacrament parish in West Philadelphia was typical. A population change swept through West Philadelphia as Irish Catholics moved out and black Protestants moved in. As late as 1964, the parish school had about 3,200 students, and only 12 were black. Within a decade a radical change took place and, by 1976, the school had only 532 students; 378 were black, and of these 164 were not Catholic.[42] Nor was such change limited to the Northeast; in the South as well, urban parishes changed from white to black during the 1960s and 1970s. At the same time, suburban parishes were booming as more Catholics set down their roots in the white belt that circled the nation's cities. The relative prosperity of Catholic suburbia and the economic decline of many urban parishes provided the impetus for cooperative sharing programs between parishes. Suburban parishes gave financial support to poor inner-city parishes; children and families of differing races and parishes visited one another in the hope of building better understanding between the races. Though most of these programs were short-lived, they offered a partial solution to the financial poverty of many city parishes and the racial separation among Catholic parishes.

A major trend of the civil rights movement was the goal of integration. Church leaders had fought for this, and in the 1960s they pushed even harder. In the South this resulted in the closing of separate black parishes. The integration of parishes generally meant the closing of the black parish and the integration of the white parish. Though this did not go smoothly for anyone, blacks were especially offended, because they had to witness the closing of their churches, many of which were quite old and of venerable memory. Many blacks were so angry that they left the Catholic church.[43]

Race was not the only issue troubling urban America in the decade between Dallas and Watergate. Poverty, inadequate housing, and job discrimination were other issues that attracted national attention. A presidential War on Poverty and federal public housing projects were launched with great enthusiasm. Catholic clergy became involved in urban affairs, and before long urban ministry became the desired apostolate of many priests; many dioceses established offices for urban affairs. Young social-action priests joined forces with the old guard of the 1950s, and in 1967 they formed a new organization, the Catholic Committee on Urban Ministry (CCUM), which sought to promote the cause of social justice. Within a decade, CCUM had become a national network of over five thousand men and women who were working in some phase of social ministry. The godfather of CCUM and the 1970s dean of urban ministry was John Egan of Chicago. A Washington, D.C., priest, Geno Baroni, also became noted for his work on behalf of social justice, and before long acquired a national reputation. He was appointed assistant Secretary of Housing and Urban Development in the Carter administration. Both Baroni and Egan were instrumental in establishing the Campaign for Human Development, a national program funded by the bishops to eliminate poverty. Founded in 1970, the Campaign for Human Development distributed over 75 million dollars to fifteen hundred self-help projects during its first ten years of operation. Alinsky-inspired community organizations also became more widespread. One of the most successful was Communities Organized for Public Service (COPS), founded in San Antonio in 1973. A grass-roots political organization in the Mexican-American community, it was based in thirty parish communities and enjoyed the active support of the archbishop, Patricio Flores.

City parishes took on a new look in the 1960s and 1970s. Breaking out of narrow parochial concerns, they began to redefine their mission. As one priest put it, they were "groping for relevance." Many became community institutions committed to serving the needs of all people regardless of race or religion. In New York City, the showcase of this new-style parish was St. Gregory the Great, on the city's West Side. Its pastor, Henry J. Browne, had become an important community leader during the 1960s. A colorful public speaker possessing a sharp wit and political savvy, Browne was in the tradition of the radical Irish. As the first president of the local neighborhood community organization, he led the fight to modify the neighborhood urban renewal program so that more low- and middle-income housing units were provided. During this ten-year struggle, St. Gregory's took on a new image. "The church," wrote Browne, "had become identified with the effort to increase the opportunities for poor people— especially many Puerto Ricans—to find roots in their community, to survive the renewal process, to have new housing they could afford, and thus to live in a neighborhood where they wanted very much to remain."[44] Liturgical celebrations were linked to neighborhood concerns and the church hall became a community meeting place. The spirit of Vatican II permeated the parish, and clergy and lay people worked together designing programs for spiritual renewal. But as was true everywhere, not everyone liked the change. Old-time parishioners protested, and one wrote Browne the following note:

> I would also like to point out at this time that I feel St. Gregory is now a Political Organization and a meeting place for the liberals, hippies, anti-establishment, etc. characters, and since the many incidents of the past year . . . it is with regret that now after more than thirty years, I am no longer a parishioner of St. Gregory, but will follow the people you, yourself, say you have lost to the North and to the South of St. Gregory.[45]

This anonymous protest underscored the point that not everyone was pleased with the turn to relevance in the urban parish. In time it became clear that as regards social justice the clergy were becoming more progressive than the laity. This caused serious conflict. In no area would this difference become more pronounced than on the question of peace.

American Catholics traditionally were superpatriots. When the United States went to war in 1917 and again in 1941, Catholics never questioned the legitimacy of these decisions. One major exception was the Catholic Worker movement. During the 1930s, Dorothy Day adopted a pacifist stand and strongly opposed American involvement in World War II. About two hundred Catholics did register as conscientious objectors and refused to take up arms. Some did alternative service, others went to jail, and some served out the war in public-service camps. Once the war ended, the issue of peace faded into the background. Beginning in the late fifties, a revival of the American peace movement occurred as people began to reexamine the nature of war in light of the development of nuclear weapons. Some Catholics also became more concerned about the threat of nuclear war. In 1963, Pope John XXIII issued an encyclical, *Pacem in Terris,* in which he questioned the legitimacy of the Catholic just-war tradition in a nuclear age. At Vatican II, bishops discussed the issues of war and peace. Despite the lobbying efforts of Catholic pacifists, the Council fathers upheld the doctrine of the just war and refused to condemn nuclear weapons; one small step forward was taken when they came out in support of conscientious objection. In her study of the Catholic peace movement, historian Patricia McNeal concluded, "At best the council fathers opened the way for a new ethic of peace based on their affirmation of the dignity of man, the Gospels, and nonviolence."[46] It was the Vietnam War, however, that proved to be the major catalyst in mobilizing the American Catholic peace movement.

The war not only sparked widespread debate, it also gave life to a national peace movement. Moreover, for the first time in their history, Catholics were in the forefront of the movement. When the Vietnam debate eventually forced President Johnson to refuse to run for reelection, the two peace candidates who sought his job, Robert F. Kennedy and Eugene McCarthy, were both active Catholics. Their candidacies symbolized how far Catholics had progressed on the issue of peace.

A central figure in the development of the Catholic peace movement was the Trappist monk Thomas Merton. A convert to Catholicism in 1938, he entered a Kentucky monastery three years later; by the time he died, in 1968, he had become the most influential monk of the twentieth century. Through his books, essays, correspondence, and retreats he influenced enormous numbers of people from quite different religious traditions. In the 1950s he was a Catholic folk hero, and his autobiography, *The Seven Storey Mountain,* was a national best-seller. In the 1960s he turned to the mysticism of the East and opened the door to a new realm of thought. A contemplative activist, he urged people to become socially involved and to reject the destructive materialism of the nuclear age in favor of the divine reality intimately present in the human person. He wrote over sixty books and more than three hundred essays while keeping up a voluminous correspondence. Through his writings in the 1960s, Merton continually prodded Catholics to take a stand against war in the nuclear age; he also encouraged nonviolence as a chosen tactic for resistance. Merton's support gave the Catholic peace movement a degree of respectability and enabled it to gain a wider audience than would have been otherwise possible.

The other major figures in the Catholic peace movement were the Berrigan brothers, Daniel and Philip. In the mid-1960s the peace movement centered on opposition to the draft. Draft-card burnings became the public symbol of resistance, while privately clergy and laity counseled young Catholic men on their legal right to register for the draft as conscientious objectors. Resistance to the draft intensified, and more Catholics than ever before declared themselves to be conscientious objectors. Then, in May 1968, the Catholic peace movement took a radical turn when the Berrigan brothers, along with seven other Catholic resisters, seized the records of the Catonsville, Maryland, draft board and burned them outside the building with homemade napalm—the substance used in bombing raids over Vietnam. Daniel, a Jesuit priest, and Philip, a priest of the Josephite order, had been socially involved for some time. Once the war in Vietnam escalated, they became active in the peace movement and gradually increased their involvement and the intensity of their protest. The action of the Catonsville 9, as they called themselves, and their subsequent arrest propelled the Berrigan brothers onto center stage. Dan, a poet and writer, sought to mobilize public opinion through numerous speeches and writings. Phil, the organizer, focused on recruiting more followers and initiating more disruptive draft-board actions. The result was that after Catonsville, numerous draft boards were raided, records destroyed, and Catholic activists arrested. Their trials turned into courtroom theater as defendants spoke out against the war and upheld the right of nonviolent resistance. A Catholic resistance movement was underway. Though nonviolent in nature, the movement was pursued by the Federal Bureau of Investigation as if it were public enemy no. 1, and many were placed behind bars. To avoid arrest, Daniel Berrigan went underground for some time, but he was caught and jailed for his acts of resistance.

The Catholic peace movement was something new in American history. Though the number of activists was small, their influence ranged far and wide among Catholics, Protestants, and Jews. Priests, nuns, brothers, and lay people made up the Catholic peace movement in the 1960s. With few exceptions, the bishops were notably absent. As a group they remained publicly silent until the early 1970s, when opposition to the war had already become quite widespread throughout the nation. Their one major contribution was a 1968 pastoral letter which supported the right of Catholics to conscientious objection.

Once the Vietnam War ended, in 1973, the peace movement took a back seat, but not for long. As the nuclear arms race escalated, more people became frightened of the potential for total destruction inherent in nuclear missiles. The Berrigan brothers and other Catholic activists began a campaign against nuclear weapons. Then, in 1980, the hierarchy began to consider seriously the consequences of war in a nuclear age. After three years of discussion and a process of consultation that was remarkable for the Catholic hierarchy, they issued a pastoral letter in 1983, The Challenge of Peace: God's Promise and Our Response, which stunned people by its bold advocacy of peace. One respected scholar and diplomat, George F. Kennan, described it "as the most profound and searching inquiry yet conducted by any responsible collective body into the relations of nuclear weaponry, and indeed of modern war in general, to moral philosophy, to politics and to the conscience of the national state." An editorial in the National Catholic Reporter stated, "Despite the document's shortcomings, it could well be the most important religious statement of our times. This is not because of any single insight or particular line of reasoning contained in the pastoral, rather because at long last moral analysis can no longer be ignored as an essential element in any discussion of nuclear strategies."[47]

The American hierarchy had come a long way since Vatican II, when they patriotically resisted any serious examination of war in a nuclear age. By 1983 they had moved to the forefront of the peace movement. Liberal Catholics cheered their boldness. Conservative Catholics chided them because they were meddling in politics and foreign affairs. The action of the bishops in 1983 revealed just how far the social-justice revolution had transformed Catholicism in the post-Vatican II era. For the first time, large numbers of bishops, priests, and laity were involved in a crusade for social justice. The unusual became common, as bishops publicly spoke out on war and peace, the rights of workers, the shame of poverty, and the need for racial justice.

The civil rights movement, Vietnam, American involvement in the social and political upheavals of Central America, and the threat of nuclear destruction had a cumulative impact on church and nation. By 1980, social justice had become a central concern in American Catholicism. Theologians and activists defined such concern as an essential part of the church's mission in the world. Inner-city parishes were transformed into community centers for social justice; men and women, both clerical and lay, took up full-time jobs as social-action ministers; bishops became advocates of peace and critics of American foreign policy. Such activity was unheard of in the 1950s. No longer a fortress church, set off from the rest of society, Catholics were now part of the American mainstream. In its search for relevance, the church found its answer in the gospel mandate of social justice. Many Catholics, in fact the vast majority, found this offensive. They wanted their bishops and priests to stop meddling in worldly affairs and leave the cause of justice to other people better versed in politics and business. Most suburban parish communities evidenced little concern for social-justice issues and left this field to more progressive-minded clergy and laity. Nonetheless, in the mid-1980s, the torch of reform burns brightly. The rekindling of this spirit to an unparalleled degree is one of the most significant transformations of American Catholicism in the past quarter century.

A new Catholicism has come to life during the past two decades, and one of its most striking features is pluralism. There is no longer one way to do theology, to worship at Mass, to confess sin, or to pray. There are various ways of being Catholic, and people are choosing the style that best suits them. Though this is something new for modern Catholicism, it is not new in the history of the church. For centuries there were always differing schools of theology, differing liturgical traditions, and differing ways of being Catholic. This inclination to diversity emerged at the very beginning, when the apostle Paul left Peter in Jerusalem to forge a new Christianity among the Gentiles. Since the sixteenth-century Reformation, that ancient tradition of diversity had been lost, as a rage for order and uniformity engulfed Catholicism. Nevertheless, ethnic diversity did give to Catholicism in the United States a unique measure of cultural pluralism not present in other countries. A common faith, a common theology, and clerical control held it together. Then, just as the immigrants were becoming united in a common bond as Americans, the cement that held them together as Catholics crumbled.

With the emergence of a new Catholicism, the immigrant Catholic ethos has changed. A new model of church and authority is replacing the old, monarchical, clerical concept of church and authority. A new Catholic morality is replacing the traditional moral code with its exaggerated emphasis on sin and guilt. Ritual still remains very much a part of the new Catholicism, but new rituals are taking the place of old ones. The sense of the transcendent, the miraculous, also remains prominent, especially among evangelical, charismatic Catholics. Though the future shape of this new Catholicism remains uncertain, one thing is clear: the traditions of the past will not always work.

American Catholics are living in a period of transition. One model of church is passing away and another is coming to life. Since the new has not yet replaced the old, conflict and division are very real problems. This became clear in the fall of 1979, when the new Pope, John Paul II, visited the United States. Everywhere he went during his week-long tour—Boston, New York, Philadelphia, Des Moines, Chicago, and Washington, D.C.—enthusiastic crowds welcomed him. A charismatic individual, he had become a genuine hero whom people wanted to see and touch. But, intellectually and spiritually, he was out of touch with many Catholics. He spoke to them like a headmaster to his schoolchildren, and each visit seemed to bring forth only another set of denunciations. At the United Nations he spoke out against war, materialism, and the arms race. Many Catholics applauded that. But, at other stops along the way, the list of denunciations grew. He spoke out against divorce, birth control, abortion, the ordination of women, married clergy, and homosexuality. As one journalist put it, "It was a formidable listing of prohibitions; and the most formidable thing about it was its finality."[48] No modifications were allowed and little pastoral sensitivity permitted. John Paul II was calling Catholics back to the old church and trying to restore uniformity and control. But it would no longer work. He could utter the command, but the Papacy had lost the ability to enforce it.

The pontificate of John Paul II, which began in 1978, coincided with a conservative swing in religion. Among Catholics, the most notable evidence for this was the official investigation of theologians suspected of unorthodox teaching, the attempted suppression of books, a renaissance of sexophobia with its accompanying denunciation of artificial birth control, the suspension of priests and nuns who held public office, and a reassertion of male supremacy and clerical control. Such actions have hardened the lines of division in the church. Traditional Catholics welcomed them, while progressive Catholics denounced them. But the ways of the past will no longer work. A new spirit is alive in American Catholicism, and the twenty-first century belongs to it. The challenge of the future still remains the timeless question that people have wrestled with for two hundred years: how to be both Catholic and American. How the new generation of Catholics solves this riddle will determine the shape that American Catholicism will take in the years ahead.

Notes

NOTES TO CHAPTER I

1. Edwin Scott Gaustad, *A Religious History of America* (New York: Harper & Row, 1966), p. 7.

2. Samuel Eliot Morison, *The European Discovery of America: The Southern Voyages A.D. 1492–1616* (New York: Oxford University Press, 1974), p. 41.

3. Samuel Eliot Morison, *Admiral of the Ocean Sea: A Life of Christopher Columbus* (Boston: Little, Brown, 1946), p. 222.

4. Robert Ricard, *The Spiritual Conquest of Mexico*, trans. Lesley Byrd Simpson (Berkeley: University of California Press, 1966), p. 15.

5. A. G. Dickens, *The Counter Reformation* (London: Thames & Hudson, 1968), p. 25.

6. J. H. Elliott, *Imperial Spain* (New York: St. Martin's Press, 1964), p. 53.

7. William Weber Johnson, *Cortés* (Boston: Little, Brown, 1975), p. 59.

8. Finbar Kenneally, O.F.M., *Writings of Fermín Francisco de Lasuén* (2 vols.; Washington, D.C.: Academy of American Franciscan History, 1965), II, p. 202.

9. *Documents from Early Peru: The Pizarros and the Almagros 1531–1578* in The Harkness Collection in the Library of Congress (Washington, D.C.: U.S. Government Printing Office, 1936), no. 41, p. 171.

10. Stephen Neill, *A History of Christian Missions* (Baltimore: Penguin Books, 1964), pp. 170–71.

11. Ibid.

12. Lewis Hanke, *The Spanish Struggle for Justice in the Conquest of America* (Philadelphia: University of Pennsylvania Press, 1949), p. 1.

13. Fray Francisco Atanasio Domínguez, *The Missions of New Mexico*, trans. Eleanor B. Adams and Fray Angelico Chavez (Albuquerque: University of New Mexico Press, 1956), p. 180.

14. Herbert E. Bolton, *Wider Horizons of American History* (Notre Dame, Ind.: University of Notre Dame Press, 1967), p. 118.

15. Michael V. Gannon, *The Cross in the Sand* (Gainesville: University of Florida Press, 1965), p. 75.

16. Frederick Webb Hodge, George P. Hammond, and Agapito Rey (eds.), *Fray Alonso de Benavides' Revised Memorial of 1634* (Albuquerque: The University of New Mexico Press, 1945), p. 80.

17. Ibid.

18. Domínguez, *The Missions of New Mexico,* p. 295.

19. John L. Kessell, *Mission of Sorrows: Jesuit Guevavi and the Pimas 1691–1767* (Tucson: University of Arizona Press, 1970), p. 21.

20. Carlos E. Castaneda, *The Mission Era: The Passing of the Mission 1762–1782,* Vol. IV: *Our Catholic Heritage in Texas 1519–1936* (7 vols.; Austin: Von Boeckmann-Jones, 1936–58), p. 4.

21. Sherburne F. Cook, *The Conflict Between the California Indian and White Civilization* (Berkeley: University of California Press, 1976), p. 6.

22. Yves F. Zoltvany (ed.), *The French Tradition in America* (Columbia, S.C.: University of South Carolina Press, 1969), pp. 34–35, 43.

23. Jean Delumeau, *Catholicism Between Luther and Voltaire: A New View of the Counter-Reformation* (London: Burns & Oates, 1977), p. 35.

24. Zoltvany, *The French Tradition in America,* p. 5.

25. Cornelius J. Jaenen, *Friend and Foe* (New York: Columbia University Press, 1976), p. 190.

26. Ibid., p. 16.

27. Ibid., p. 159.

28. Morison, *The European Discovery,* p. 594.

29. Delumeau, *Catholicism Between Luther and Voltaire,* p. 46.

30. Reuben Gold Thwaites (ed.), *The Jesuit Relations and Allied Documents* (73 vols.; Cleveland: The Burrows Brothers, 1896–1901), LXI, p. 131.

31. Albert Léon Guérard, *France: A Modern History* (Ann Arbor: University of Michigan Press, 1959), p. 198.

NOTES TO CHAPTER II

1. James P. Ronda, "We Are as Well as We Are: An Indian Critique of Seventeenth-Century Christian Missions," *William and Mary Quarterly,* 34 (1977), 67.

2. Kessell, *Mission of Sorrows,* pp. 40–41.

3. Edna Kenton (ed.), *The Jesuit Relations and Allied Documents* (New York: A. Boni and C. Boni, 1925), p. 118.

4. *Benavides' Revised Memorial of 1634,* p. 58.

5. Kenton (ed.), *The Jesuit Relations,* pp. xv ff.

6. Quoted in Robert Conkling, "Legitimacy and Conversion in Social Change: The Case of French Missionaries and the Northeastern Algonkian," *Ethnohistory,* Vol. 21, no. 1 (Winter 1974), 8.

7. Kessell, *Mission of Sorrows,* p. 92.

8. Ibid.

9. Quoted in Conkling, "Legitimacy and Conversion in Social Change," p. 14.

10. The issue of forced conversions in the California missions is a disputed issue; see Cook, *The Conflict Between the California Indian and White Civilization,* p. 76, where the author states, ". . . all pretense of voluntary conversion was discarded . . ." in the later period of the California missions and forced conversion became the norm; a persuasive critique of Cook's thesis is contained in Francis F. Guest, O.F.M., "An Examination of the Theses of S. F. Cook on the Forced Conversion of Indians in the California Missions," *Southern California Quarterly,* Vol. 61, no. 1 (Spring 1979), 1–77.

11. Kessell, *Mission of Sorrows,* p. 92.

12. Quoted in Bolton, *Wider Horizons of American History,* p. 131.

13. Thwaites, *The Jesuit Relations*, LXVI, pp. 150–51.
14. Zephyrin Engelhardt, O.F.M., *The Missions and Missionaries of California* (4 vols.; San Francisco: James H. Bally, 1908–15), II, p. 251.
15. Kessell, *Mission of Sorrows*, p. 130.
16. Elsie Clews Parsons, *Pueblo Indian Religion* (2 vols.; Chicago: The University of Chicago Press, 1939), II, p. 1132.
17. Thwaites, *The Jesuit Relations*, LXIII, p. 31.
18. Engelhardt, *The Missions and Missionaries*, II, p. 253.
19. Thomas J. Steele, S.J., *Santos and Saints* (Albuquerque: Ancient City Press, 1974), p. 139.
20. Marta Weigle, *Brothers of Light, Brothers of Blood: The Penitentes of the Southwest* (Albuquerque: University of New Mexico Press, 1976), p. 28.
21. Thwaites, *The Jesuit Relations*, LXIII, p. 193.
22. *Benavides' Revised Memorial of 1634*, pp. 84–85.
23. Fay Jackson Smith, John L. Kessell, and Francis J. Fox, S.J., *Father Kino in Arizona* (Phoenix: Arizona Historical Foundation, 1966), p. 64; and Herbert Eugene Bolton, *Rim of Christendom* (New York: Macmillan, 1936), pp. 272–73.
24. Thwaites, *The Jesuit Relations*, LXIII, pp. 67–69.
25. Bolton, *Wider Horizons of American History*, p. 137.
26. Edward H. Spicer, *Cycles of Conquest* (Tucson: University of Arizona Press, 1962), p. 291.
27. Kessell, *Mission of Sorrows*, p. 94.
28. Spicer, *Cycles of Conquest*, p. 307.
29. Eleanor B. Adams (ed.), *Bishop Tamaron's Visitation of New Mexico, 1760* (Albuquerque: Historical Society of New Mexico, 1954), p. 67.
30. Ibid., p. 48.
31. Ibid., p. 49.
32. Quoted in Martha Voght, "Shamans and Padres: The Religion of the Southern California Mission Indians," *Pacific Historical Review* 36 (1967), n. 5, p. 364.
33. Quoted in James Axtell, "The European Failure to Convert the Indians: An Autopsy," in William Cowan (ed.), *Papers of the Sixth Algonquian Conference 1974*, (Ottawa: National Museums of Canada, 1975), p. 278.
34. Jaenen, *Friend and Foe*, p. 54.
35. Ibid., p. 52.
36. Fray Silvestre Vélez de Escalante, "Letter to the Missionaries of New Mexico," in Eleanor B. Adams, (ed.), *New Mexico Historical Review*, Vol. 40, no. 4 (October 1965), 323.
37. Adams, *Bishop Tamaron's Visitation*, p. 49.
38. Ibid., p. 102.
39. Jaenen, *Friend and Foe*, p. 53.
40. Ibid., p. 145.
41. Cook, *The Conflict Between the California Indian and White Civilization*, p. 25.
42. Jaenen, *Friend and Foe*, p. 109.
43. Ibid., p. 24.
44. Ibid., p. 103.
45. Ibid., pp. 102–3.
46. Spicer, *Cycles of Conquest*, p. 306.
47. *Benavides' Revised Memorial of 1634*, p. 51.
48. Ibid., p. 43.
49. Ruth M. Underhill, *Red Man's Religion* (Chicago: University of Chicago Press, 1965), p. 3.
50. Gerónimo Boscana, *Chinigchinich*, ed. Phil Townsend Hanna, trans. Alfred Robinson (Santa Ana, Calif.: Fine Arts Press, 1933), p. 17.
51. Ibid., pp. 29–30.

52. Ibid., pp. 34–38.

53. See Alfonso Ortiz, *The Tewa World* (Chicago: University of Chicago Press, 1969), on Pueblo Indian religious ideology.

54. Edward P. Dozier, *The Pueblo Indians of North America* (New York: Holt, Rinehart & Winston, 1970), p. 184; this book is indispensable for a basic understanding of the Pueblo Indian culture.

55. W. Vernon Kinietz, *The Indians of the Western Great Lakes, 1615–1760* (Ann Arbor: University of Michigan Press, 1940), p. 29.

56. Ronda, "We Are as Well as We Are," p. 72.

57. Quoted in Axtell, "The European Failure . . . ," p. 286.

58. Jaenen, *Friend and Foe,* p. 72.

59. Kenneally, *Writings of . . . Lasuén,* II, p. 211.

60. Boscana, *Chinigchinich,* p. 61.

61. Voght, "Shamans and Padres," p. 369.

62. Domínguez, *The Missions of New Mexico,* p. 254.

63. Ibid., pp. 255–57.

64. Quoted in Charles H. Lange, *Cochiti: A New Mexico Pueblo, Past and Present* (Austin: University of Texas Press, 1959), pp. 20–21.

65. George C. Barker, "Some Functions of Catholic Processions in Pueblo and Yaqui Culture Change," *American Anthropologist,* Vol. 60, no. 3 (June 1958), p. 453.

66. Spicer, *Cycles of Conquest,* p. 507.

NOTES TO CHAPTER III

1. J. C. H. Aveling, *The Handle and the Axe* (London: Blond & Briggs, 1976), p. 31.

2. John D. Krugler, "Puritan and Papist: Politics and Religion in Massachusetts and Maryland Before the Restoration of Charles II" (unpublished Ph.D. dissertation, University of Illinois, 1971), p. 10.

3. Ibid., p. 15.

4. Russell R. Menard, "Economy and Society in Early Colonial Maryland" (unpublished Ph.D. dissertation, University of Iowa, 1975), p. 4.

5. Krugler, "Puritan and Papist," p. 252.

6. Robert Wintour, *To Live like Princes,* ed. John Krugler (Baltimore: Enoch Pratt Free Library, 1976), p. 12.

7. John D. Krugler, "Lord Baltimore, Roman Catholics, and Toleration: Religious Policy in Maryland During the Early Catholic Years," *Catholic Historical Review,* Vol. 65, no. 1 (January 1979), 60.

8. Clayton Colman Hall (ed.), *Narratives of Early Maryland 1633–1684* (New York: Scribner's, 1910), p. 16.

9. Ibid., p. 41.

10. Ibid., p. 40.

11. Lois Green Carr and David William Jordan, *Maryland's Revolution of Government, 1689–92* (Ithaca, N.Y.: Cornell University Press, 1974).

12. William Hand Browne et al. (eds.), *Archives of Maryland . . .* (Baltimore: Maryland Historical Society, 1883–), I, p. 246, hereafter cited as *Md. Archives.*

13. Wesley Frank Craven, *The Southern Colonies in the Seventeenth Century, 1607–1689* (Baton Rouge, La.: Louisiana State University Press, 1949), p. 235.

14. Hall, *Narratives of Early Maryland,* p. 118.

15. Ibid., p. 136.

16. Krugler, "Lord Baltimore, Roman Catholics, and Toleration," p. 67.

17. Michael James Graham, "Lord Baltimore's Pious Enterprise: Toleration and Community

in Colonial Maryland 1634–1724" (unpublished Ph.D. dissertation, University of Michigan, 1983), p. 91.

18. Henry F. Thompson, "Maryland at the End of the Seventeenth Century," *Maryland Historical Magazine,* Vol. 2, no. 2 (June 1907), 167.

19. Ibid.; Thomas Hughes, S.J., *History of the Society of Jesus in North America, Colonial and Federal* (4 vols.; New York: Longmans, Green, 1908–17), Text, II, p. 77.

20. Gilbert Chinard (ed.), *A Huguenot Exile in Virginia* (New York: The Press of the Pioneers, 1934), pp. 156–61.

21. See Lorena S. Walsh, "Charles County, Maryland, 1658–1705: A Study of the Chesapeake Social and Political Structure" (unpublished Ph.D. dissertation, Michigan State University, 1977), p. 298.

22. Richard Beale Davis (ed.), *William Fitzhugh and His Chesapeake World, 1676–1701* (Chapel Hill: University of North Carolina Press, 1963), p. 203.

23. Graham, "Lord Baltimore's Pious Enterprise," pp. 97, 104, 123–25.

24. Ibid., pp. 104–6; John Bossy, *The English Catholic Community 1570–1850* (New York: Oxford University Press, 1976), pp. 158–62, 170 ff.

25. *Md. Archives,* XXVI, pp. 340–41.

26. "Petition of Sundry Roman Catholics Against the Imposition upon Them of a Double Tax as a Discrimination Against Their Religion," *Maryland Historical Magazine,* Vol. 5 (1910), 51–52.

27. Ibid., p. 57; Timothy W. Bosworth, "Anti-Catholicism as a Political Tool in Mid-Eighteenth Century Maryland," *Catholic Historical Review,* Vol. 61, no. 4 (Oct. 1975), 539–63.

28. Russell R. Menard, P. M. G. Harris, and Lois Green Carr, "Opportunity and Inequality: The Distribution of Wealth on the Lower Western Shore of Maryland, 1638–1705," *Maryland Historical Magazine,* Vol. 69, no. 2 (Summer 1974), 182; Menard, "Economy and Society . . . ," p. 448.

29. Aubrey C. Land (ed.), *Letters from America by William Eddis* (Cambridge, Mass.: Harvard University Press, 1969), p. xvi.

30. Graham, "Lord Baltimore's Pious Enterprise," pp. 373–84.

31. Thomas Spalding, "The Premier See: A History of the Archdiocese of Baltimore," Ch. III, pp. 29–30. I want to thank Thomas Spalding for allowing me to read his unpublished history of the Archdiocese of Baltimore. I am especially indebted to him for the information pertaining to some of the Catholic families in colonial Maryland.

32. Hughes, *History of the Society of Jesus,* Documents, I, pp. 337 and 352; "Letter of Rev. Henry Neale, Philadelphia, 1741," *American Catholic Historical Researches,* Vol. 6, no. 4 (Oct. 1889), 182–83; Martin I. J. Griffin, "Rev. Robert Harding," *American Catholic Historical Researches,* Vol. 7, no. 2 (April 1890), 82–92.

33. Edward I. Devitt, S.J., "Letters of Father Joseph Mosley, S.J., and Some Extracts from His Diary, 1757–1786," *Records of the American Catholic Historical Society of Philadelphia,* Vol. 17 (1906), 202.

34. Hughes, *History of the Society of Jesus,* Text, II, p. 556.

35. Devitt, "Letters of Father Joseph Mosley," pp. 186 and 208.

36. Thomas O'Brien Hanley, S.J. (ed.), *The John Carroll Papers* (3 vols.; Notre Dame, Ind.: University of Notre Dame Press, 1976), I, p. 160.

37. Sister Marion Norman, "John Gother and the English Way of Spirituality," *Recusant History,* Vol. 11, no. 6 (October 1962), 313.

38. John Gother, *Instructions for Particular States and Conditions of Life,* ed. Rev. M. Comerford (Dublin: M. H. Gill, 1888), p. 337.

39. Georgetown University Archives, Sermons of Peter Atwood, S.J.

40. Edwin H. Burton, *The Life and Times of Bishop Challoner, 1691–1781* (2 vols.; New York: Longmans, Green, 1909), I, p. 131.

41. John Gother, *Instructions and Devotions for Hearing Mass* (London: T. Meighan, 1740), pp. 4–5.

42. Hanley, *The John Carroll Papers*, I, p. 32.

43. Devitt, "Letters of Father Joseph Mosley," pp. 297–98.

44. Charles Arbro Barker, *The Background of the Revolution in Maryland* (New Haven: Yale University Press, 1940), p. 351.

45. Aubrey C. Land, *The Dulanys of Maryland* (Baltimore: Maryland Historical Society, 1955), p. 303.

NOTES TO CHAPTER IV

1. Hanley, *The John Carroll Papers*, I, p. 53.

2. Joseph P. Chinnici, "American Catholics and Religious Pluralism 1775–1820," *Journal of Ecumenical Studies* 16 (Fall 1977), 727–28.

3. See Joseph A. Agonito, "Ecumenical Stirrings: Catholic-Protestant Relations During the Episcopacy of John Carroll," *Church History*, 45 (September 1976), 358–73.

4. *The John Carroll Papers*, I, p. 53.

5. Annabelle M. Melville, *John Carroll of Baltimore* (New York: Scribner's, 1955), p. 44.

6. *The John Carroll Papers*, I, p. 78.

7. Ibid., I, p. 71.

8. Ibid., I, p. 68.

9. Hughes, *History of the Society of Jesus*, Documents, Vol. I, Part II, p. 619.

10. Melville, *John Carroll of Baltimore*, p. 69.

11. *The John Carroll Papers*, I, pp. 80–81.

12. Ibid., I, p. 156.

13. Ibid., pp. 156–57.

14. Ibid., p. 171.

15. Ibid., p. 168.

16. Ibid., p. 309.

17. Ibid., p. 146.

18. Ibid., p. 256.

19. Ibid., p. 275.

20. Ibid., II, p. 46.

21. Ibid., I, p. 192.

22. Ibid., p. 354, and II, p. 105.

23. Chinnici, "American Catholics and Religious Pluralism," 729.

24. Ibid., 736, and also Agonito, "Ecumenical Stirrings," 268–70.

25. Quoted in Chinnici, "American Catholics and Religious Pluralism," 734.

26. *The John Carroll Papers*, I, p. 168.

27. Thomas Spalding, "History of the Archdiocese of Baltimore," unpublished manuscript, Ch. 4, p. 32; see also Patrick Carey, "The Laity's Understanding of the Trustee System, 1785–1855," *Catholic Historical Review* 64 (July 1978), 367.

28. *The John Carroll Papers*, I, pp. 219 and 149.

29. Carey, "The Laity's Understanding of the Trustee System," p. 358.

30. Ibid., p. 373.

31. *The John Carroll Papers*, I, pp. 517 and 524.

32. Ibid., II, pp. 29 and 121.

33. Ibid., I, p. 548.

34. Ibid., II, p. 95.

35. Ibid., I, p. 548, and also II, p. 129.

36. Ibid., III, p. 207, and I, p. 309.

37. Ibid., III, p. 109.

38. Ibid., p. 133, and I, p. 148.

39. Carey, "The Laity's Understanding of the Trustee System," pp. 365–66.

40. *The John Carroll Papers*, II, p. 224.

41. Bishop Leonard Neale to Rev. James Lucas, April 19, 1816, quoted in Patrick Carey, "Two Episcopal Views of Lay-Clerical Conflicts, 1785–1860," *Records of American Catholic Historical Society of Philadelphia*, 87, nos. 1–4 (Mar.–Dec. 1976), 91.

42. *The John Carroll Papers*, II, p. 120.

43. Ibid., I, p. 524.

44. Joseph William Ruane, *The Beginnings of the Society of St. Sulpice in the United States 1791–1829* (Washington, D.C.: The Catholic University of America, 1935), p. 92.

45. See Sr. Mary Ramona Mattingly, *The Catholic Church on the Kentucky Frontier 1795–1812* (Washington, D.C.: The Catholic University of America, 1936), and also Robert Trisco, *The Holy See and the Nascent Church in the Middle Western United States 1826–1850* (Rome: Gregorian University Press, 1962), pp. 97–98.

46. Mattingly, *The Catholic Church on the Kentucky Frontier*, pp. 139–40.

47. Thomas W. Spalding, *Martin John Spalding: American Churchman* (Washington, D.C.: Catholic University of America Press, 1973), p. 20.

48. Trisco, *The Holy See and the Nascent Church . . . .*, p. 109.

49. *The John Carroll Papers*, II, p. 248.

50. Gerald P. Fogarty, S.J., Joseph T. Durkin, S.J., and R. Emmett Curran, S.J., *The Maryland Jesuits 1634–1833* (Baltimore: n.p., 1976), pp. 49–50.

51. See Joseph I. Dirvin, C.M., *Mrs. Seton, Foundress of the American Sisters of Charity* (New York: Farrar, Straus & Cudahy, 1962), pp. 268 ff.

52. Mary Ewens, O.P., *The Role of the Nun in Nineteenth Century America* (New York: Arno Press, 1978), p. 50; see also Barbara Misner, "Highly Respectable and Accomplished Ladies: Early American Women Religious 1790–1850," Working Paper Series, no. 3, Spring 1978, Charles and Margaret Hall Cushwa Center for the Study of American Catholicism, University of Notre Dame, pp. 41–42.

53. Quoted in Ewens, *The Role of the Nun*, p. 72.

54. Joseph P. Chinnici, "Organization of the Spiritual Life: American Catholic Devotional Works 1791–1866," *Theological Studies* 40 (June 1979), 237; also Joseph P. Chinnici, "Politics and Theology: From Enlightenment Catholicism to the Condemnation of Americanism," Working Paper Series, no. 9, Spring 1981, Charles and Margaret Hall Cushwa Center for the Study of American Catholicism, University of Notre Dame.

55. Chinnici, "Organization of the Spiritual Life," p. 255.

NOTES TO CHAPTER V

1. Philip Taylor, *The Distant Magnet: European Emigration to the U.S.A.* (New York: Harper & Row, 1971).

2. John Higham, *Send These to Me: Jews and Other Immigrants in Urban America* (New York: Atheneum, 1975), p. 16.

3. See Patrick J. Blessing, "Irish," in *Harvard Encyclopedia of American Ethnic Groups*, ed. Stephan Thernstrom (Cambridge: Harvard University Press, 1980), pp. 524–45.

4. Quoted in Patrick J. Blessing, "West Among Strangers: Irish Migration to California 1850–1880" (unpublished dissertation, University of California at Los Angeles, 1977), p. 132.

5. Ibid., p. 53.

6. Ibid., p. 68.

7. See Kathleen Neils Conzen, "Germans," in *Harvard Encyclopedia of American Ethnic Groups*, pp. 405–25.

8. Quoted in Joseph M. White, "Religion and Community: Cincinnati Germans 1814–1870" (unpublished Ph.D. dissertation, University of Notre Dame, 1980), p. 20.

9. Conzen, "Germans," p. 411.

10. Josef J. Barton, *Peasants and Strangers: Italians, Rumanians and Slovaks in an American City 1890–1950* (Cambridge: Harvard University Press, 1975), p. 47.

11. Quoted in John W. Briggs, *An Italian Passage: Immigrants to Three American Cities 1890–1930* (New Haven: Yale University Press, 1978), p. 10.

12. Quoted in Virginia Yans-McLaughlin, *Family and Community: Italian Immigrants in Buffalo 1880–1930* (Ithaca: Cornell University Press, 1977), p. 97.

13. Ibid., p. 96.

14. Quoted in Victor R. Greene, "Pre-World War I Emigration to the United States: Motives and Statistics," *The Polish Review*, Vol. VI (Summer 1961), 52–53.

15. Caroline Golab, *Immigrant Destinations* (Philadelphia: Temple University Press, 1977), p. 81.

16. Ibid., p. 84.

17. Ibid., p. 90.

18. Ibid., p. 75.

19. Greene, "Pre-World War I Emigration . . . ," p. 47.

20. *Religious Bodies, 1916: Part I, Summary and General Tables* (Washington, D.C.: U.S. Government Printing Office, 1919), pp. 81–82.

21. Ibid.

22. M. Mark Stolarik, "Slovaks," *Harvard Encyclopedia of American Ethnic Groups*, p. 928.

23. Karen Johnson Freeze, "Czechs," in *Harvard Encyclopedia of American Ethnic Groups*, pp. 261–72.

24. Bohdan P. Procko, "Soter Ortynsky: First Ruthenian Bishop in the United States, 1907–1916," *The Catholic Historical Review*, Vol. LVIII (January 1973), 529.

25. Arunas Alisauskas, "Lithuanians," *Harvard Encyclopedia of American Ethnic Groups*, p. 669.

26. Golab, *Immigrant Destinations*, p. 74.

27. Taylor, *The Distant Magnet*, p. 145.

28. Greene, "Pre-World War I Emigration . . . ," p. 66.

29. Kathleen Neils Conzen, *Immigrant Milwaukee 1836–1860: Accommodation and Community in a Frontier City* (Cambridge: Harvard University Press, 1976), p. 34.

30. Joseph Cada, *Czech-American Catholics 1850–1920* (Lisle, Ill.: Center for Slav Culture, 1964), p. 53.

31. Blessing, "West Among Strangers," p. 197; Stephan Thernstrom, *The Other Bostonians* (Cambridge: Harvard University Press, 1973), p. 187.

32. Clyde Griffen and Sally Griffen, *Natives and Newcomers: The Ordering of Opportunity in Mid-Nineteenth Century Poughkeepsie* (Cambridge: Harvard University Press, 1978), p. 232; and Carol Groneman, "She Earns as a Child—She Pays as a Man: Women Workers in a Mid-Nineteenth Century New York City Community," in Richard L. Ehrlich (ed.), *Immigrants in Industrial America 1850–1920* (Charlottesville, Va.: University Press of Virginia, 1977), p. 35.

33. Griffen and Griffen, *Natives and Newcomers*, p. 225.

34. Douglas V. Shaw, *The Making of an Immigrant City: Ethnic and Cultural Conflict in Jersey City, New Jersey, 1850–1877* (New York: Arno Press, 1976), p. 40; and Griffen and Griffen, *Natives and Newcomers*, p. 233.

35. Quoted in *Natives and Newcomers*, pp. 249–50.

36. Stephan Thernstrom, *Poverty and Progress: Social Mobility in a Nineteenth Century City* (Cambridge: Harvard University Press, 1964), p. 156.

37. Griffen and Griffen, *Natives and Newcomers*, p. 48.

38. Quoted in Jo Ellen Vinyard, *The Irish on the Urban Frontier: Nineteenth Century Detroit, 1850–1880* (New York: Arno Press, 1976), p. 90.

39. Dennis Clark, *The Irish in Philadelphia: Ten Generations of Urban Experience* (Philadel-

phia: Temple University Press, 1973), pp. 56–57; and R. A. Burchell, *The San Francisco Irish* (Berkeley: University of California Press, 1980), p. 41.

40. Conzen, *Immigrant Milwaukee*, p. 77; see also Clark, *The Irish in Philadelphia;* Vinyard, *The Irish on the Urban Frontier;* and Burchell, *The San Francisco Irish.*

41. George Potter, *To the Golden Door* (Boston: Little, Brown, 1960), p. 183.

42. See Clark, *The Irish in Philadelphia;* Vinyard, *The Irish on the Urban Frontier;* and Burchell, *The San Francisco Irish.*

43. Thernstrom, *The Other Bostonians,* p. 132.

44. Ibid., p. 136.

45. Margaret E. Conners, "Their Own Kind: Family and Community Life in Albany, New York, 1850–1920" (unpublished manuscript), p. 27; see also David M. Doyle, *Irish Americans, Native Rights and National Empires* (New York: Arno Press, 1976). For a good description of Catholic middle-class culture, see John Talbot Smith, *The Catholic Church in New York* (2 vols.; New York: Hall & Locke, 1908), II, pp. 446–59.

46. See Charles Fanning and Ellen Skerrett, "James T. Farrell and Washington Park: The Novel as Social History," *Chicago History,* Vol. 8, no. 2 (Summer 1979), 80–91.

47. Conners, "Their Own Kind," p. 34; and also Blessing, "Irish," *Harvard Encyclopedia of American Ethnic Groups.*

48. For Chicago, see James W. Sanders, *The Education of an Urban Minority: Catholics in Chicago 1833–1965* (New York: Oxford University Press, 1977), p. 131; for Albany, see Conners, "Their Own Kind," p. 89.

49. Daniel O'Neill, "St. Paul's Priests 1850–1930: Recruitment, Ethnicity, and Americanization," in David J. Alvarez (ed.), *An American Church* (Moraga, Calif.: Saint Mary's College of California, 1979), p. 38; see also O'Neill's dissertation "St. Paul's Priests 1851–1900: Recruitment, Formation, and Mobility" (unpublished Ph.D. dissertation, University of Minnesota, 1979); Richard A. Schoenherr, "Ethnicity and Status Attainment: The Case of the Roman Catholic Clergy" (unpublished paper).

50. See John Corry, *Golden Clan! The Murrays, the McDonnells, and the Irish American Aristocracy* (Boston: Houghton Mifflin, 1977); and Stephen Birmingham, *Real Lace* (New York: Harper & Row, 1973).

51. See Griffen and Griffen, *Natives and Newcomers,* pp. 72–78.

52. Kathleen Neils Conzen, "Foundations of a Rural German-Catholic Culture: Farm and Family in St. Martin, Minn. 1857–1915," Charles and Margaret Hall Cushwa Center for the Study of American Catholicism, University of Notre Dame, Working Paper Series, Vol. 1, no. 2 (Spring 1977), p. 23.

53. Conzen, *Immigrant Milwaukee,* p. 71.

54. Ibid., pp. 69–74; Jay P. Dolan, *The Immigrant Church: New York's Irish and German Catholics 1815–1865* (Baltimore: Johns Hopkins University Press, 1975), p. 75.

55. See Conzen, *Immigrant Milwaukee,* p. 73; and Vinyard, *The Irish on the Urban Frontier,* p. 316.

56. Bruce Laurie, Theodore Hershberg, and George Alter, "Immigrants and Industry: The Philadelphia Experience, 1850–1880," in Ehrlich (ed.), *Immigrants in Industrial America,* p. 146.

57. Conzen, *Immigrant Milwaukee,* p. 93; and Groneman, "She Earns as a Child—She Pays as a Man," p. 46.

58. Griffen and Griffen, *Natives and Newcomers,* pp. 232–34.

59. See ibid., p. 79; Conzen, *Immigrant Milwaukee,* p. 77; Conners, "Their Own Kind," pp. 104–5; and Laurence Glasco, "Ethnicity and Occupation in the Mid-Nineteenth Century: Irish, Germans, and Native-born Whites in Buffalo, New York," in Ehrlich (ed.), *Immigrants in Industrial America,* pp. 166–67.

60. Griffen and Griffen, *Natives and Newcomers,* p. 259.

61. See Conners, "Their Own Kind," pp. 227–28.

62. Doyle, *Irish Americans*, p. 67.

63. Barton, *Peasants and Strangers*, p. 146.

64. Briggs, *An Italian Passage*, pp. 11–14; and Thomas Kessner, *The Golden Door: Italian and Jewish Immigrant Mobility in New York City 1880–1915* (New York: Oxford University Press, 1977), pp. 32–36.

65. Thernstrom, *The Other Bostonians*, pp. 131 and 136.

66. Kessner, *The Golden Door*, p. 52; Yans-McLaughlin, *Family and Community*, p. 45; Humbert S. Nelli, *The Italians in Chicago 1880–1930: A Study in Ethnic Mobility* (New York: Oxford University Press, 1970), pp. 72 ff.; Dino Cinel, *From Italy to San Francisco: The Immigrant Experience* (Stanford: Stanford University Press, 1982), pp. 134–38.

67. Kessner, *The Golden Door*, p. 39.

68. Golab, *Immigrant Destinations*, p. 60.

69. Cinel, *From Italy to San Francisco*, pp. 138–39, 154, and 156.

70. Ibid., pp. 211–17.

71. Yans-McLaughlin, *Family and Community*, p. 173; and Kessner, *The Golden Door*, p. 75.

72. Yans-McLaughlin, *Family and Community*, pp. 53 and 180 ff.

73. Ibid., pp. 203–4.

74. Golab, *Immigrant Destinations*, p. 52.

75. Nelli, *The Italians in Chicago*, p. 77; and Kessner, *The Golden Door*, p. 75.

76. Quoted in Yans-McLaughlin, *Family and Community*, p. 157.

77. Raymond S. Dondero, "The Italian Settlement in San Francisco" (M.A. thesis, University of California, Berkeley, 1953), p. 52.

78. Barton, *Peasants and Strangers*, p. 102; see also Nelli, *The Italians in Chicago*, and Yans-McLaughlin, *Family and Community*.

79. Kessner, *The Golden Door*, pp. 169–70; see also the studies by Nelli, *The Italians in Chicago*, Cinel, *From Italy to San Francisco*, pp. 134–61, and Barton, *Peasants and Strangers*.

80. Cinel, *From Italy to San Francisco*, pp. 146–47.

81. Golab, *Immigrant Destinations*, p. 36.

82. Ibid., pp. 102–3; and William J. Galush, "Forming Polonia: A Study of Four Polish-American Communities, 1890–1940" (unpublished Ph.D. dissertation, University of Minnesota, 1975), p. 115.

83. Golab, *Immigrant Destinations*, pp. 149 and 151–52.

84. Quoted in Caroline Golab, "The Impact of the Industrial Experience on the Immigrant Family: The Huddled Masses Reconsidered," in Ehrlich (ed.), *Immigrants in Industrial America*, p. 3.

85. Quoted in Victor Greene, *For God and Country: The Rise of Polish and Lithuanian Ethnic Consciousness in America 1860–1910* (Madison: State Historical Society of Wisconsin, 1975), p. 57.

86. Frank Anthony Renkiewicz, "The Polish Settlement of St. Joseph County, Indiana, 1855–1935" (unpublished Ph.D. dissertation, University of Notre Dame, 1967), p. 127; and Greene, *For God and Country*, pp. 40–41.

87. Galush, "Forming Polonia," pp. 115–21.

88. William MacDonald, "The French Canadians in New England," *The Quarterly Journal of Economics*, Vol. 12 (1898), 264–65.

89. Peter Haebler, "Habitants in Holyoke: The Development of the French-Canadian Community in a Massachusetts City 1865–1910" (unpublished Ph.D. dissertation, University of New Hampshire, 1976), p. 71; Tamara K. Hareven, "Family and Work Patterns of Immigrant Laborers in a Planned Industrial Town," in Ehrlich (ed.), *Immigrants in Industrial America*, p. 52; Iris Saunders Podea, "Quebec to 'Little Canada': The Coming of the French Canadian to New England in the Nineteenth Century," *New England Quarterly* 23 (1950), 69.

90. Leon E. Truesdell, *The Canadian Born in the United States: An Analysis of the Statistics of*

the Canadian Element in the Population of the United States 1850 to 1930 (New Haven: Yale University Press, 1943), p. 204.

91. Hareven, "Family and Work Patterns . . . ," p. 56; and Podea, "Quebec to 'Little Canada,' " pp. 369–73.

92. MacDonald, "The French Canadians . . . ," p. 269.

93. Carlos E. Cortes, "Mexicans," *Harvard Encyclopedia of American Ethnic Groups,* p. 707.

94. Albert Camarillo, *Chicanos in a Changing Society: From Mexican Pueblos to American Barrios in Santa Barbara and Southern California 1848–1930* (Cambridge: Harvard University Press, 1979), pp. 132–33.

95. Ibid., pp. 221–22; and Mario Barrera, *Class in the Southwest: A Theory of Racial Inequality* (Notre Dame, Ind.: University of Notre Dame Press, 1979), p. 98.

96. Freeze, "Czechs," *Harvard Encyclopedia of American Ethnic Groups,* pp. 264–65.

NOTES TO CHAPTER VI

1. Quoted in Jay P. Dolan, *Catholic Revivalism: The American Experience 1830–1900* (Notre Dame, Ind.: University of Notre Dame Press, 1978), p. 4.

2. Quoted in Leo R. Ryan, *Old St. Peter's: The Mother Church of Catholic New York 1785–1935* (New York: United States Catholic Historical Society, 1935), p. 42.

3. Robert H. Lord, John E. Sexton, and Edward T. Harrington, *History of the Archdiocese of Boston* (3 vols.; New York: Sheed & Ward, 1944), I, pp. 375–91.

4. Mattingly, *The Catholic Church on the Kentucky Frontier,* pp. 55–59.

5. Edwin Scott Gaustad, *Historical Atlas of Religion in America* (New York: Harper & Row, 1962), pp. 43 and 52; Gerald Shaugnessy, *Has the Immigrant Kept the Faith?* (New York: Macmillan, 1925), pp. 71–72; see Dolan, *Catholic Revivalism,* pp. 28–29.

6. Dolan, *The Immigrant Church . . . ,* p. 22.

7. Martin J. Spalding, *Life, Times, and Character of the Right Reverend Benedict Joseph Flaget* (Louisville: Webb & Levering, 1852), pp. 334–36; and Trisco, *The Holy See and the Nascent Church . . . ,* pp. 73–74.

8. Timothy L. Smith, "Religion and Ethnicity in America," *American Historical Review,* Vol. 83, no. 5 (Dec. 1978), 1169.

9. See Jay P. Dolan, "Philadelphia and the German Catholic Community," in Randall M. Miller and Thomas D. Marzik (eds.), *Immigrants and Religion in Urban America* (Philadelphia: Temple University Press, 1977), pp. 69–70; and Dolan, *The Immigrant Church . . . ,* p. 71.

10. Hanley, *The John Carroll Papers,* I, 411.

11. Quoted in Dolan, "Philadelphia and the German Catholic Community," p. 71.

12. Dolan, *The Immigrant Church . . . ,* p. 69.

13. White, "Religion and Community," pp. 208–10.

14. For Cincinnati, see White, "Religion and Community," pp. 210–16; for Chicago, *Gedenkblätter zum Goldenes Jubiläum der St. Michael's Gemeinde Chicago 1852–1902* (Chicago, 1902).

15. Quoted in Dolan, *The Immigrant Church . . . ,* p. 54.

16. Oscar Handlin, *Boston's Immigrants* (New York: Atheneum, 1970), p. 128.

17. Vinyard, *The Irish on the Urban Frontier,* p. 103; and James H. O'Donnell, *History of the Diocese of Hartford* (Boston: D. H. Hurd, 1900), pp. 324–34.

18. Lord et al., *History of the Archdiocese of Boston,* II, p. 39.

19. Quoted in O'Donnell, *History of the Diocese of Hartford,* p. 182.

20. Quoted in Peter Clarke, *A Free Church in a Free Society* (Rome: Pontifical Gregorian University, 1980), p. 182.

21. The Right Reverend Ignatius Aloysius Reynolds (ed.), *The Works of the Right Rev. John England* (5 vols.; Baltimore: J. Murphy, 1849), V, p. 104.

22. Ibid., p. 101.

23. See minute book of board of trustees of St. Mary's Church, Philadelphia, from 1782 to

1829, published in *Records of the American Catholic Historical Society of Philadelphia*, Vol. 4 (1893), pp. 242–459; Vol. 42 (September 1931), pp. 197–232; Vol. 43 (1932), pp. 246–79 and 320–59; and Vol. 49 (1938), pp. 171–87, 249–61, and 334–69; and Stephen C. Worsley, "Catholicism in Antebellum North Carolina," *The North Carolina Historical Review*, Vol. 60, no. 4 (October 1983), 412–16.

24. Martin J. Becker, *A History of Catholic Life in the Diocese of Albany 1609–1864* (New York: United States Catholic Historical Society, 1975), p. 205.

25. Francis E. Tourscher, O.S.A., *The Hogan Schism and Trustee Troubles in St. Mary's Church Philadelphia 1820–1829* (Philadelphia: Peter Reilly, 1930), pp. 83–84; and James F. Connelly (ed.), *The History of the Archdiocese of Philadelphia* (Philadelphia: The Archdiocese of Philadelphia, 1976), p. 96.

26. Carey, "The Laity's Understanding of the Trustee System," p. 357.

27. Jay P. Dolan and Jeffrey Burns, "Parish History Study" (unpublished, 1982); this study examined the published histories of 980 parishes in the United States. Various data were collected, cross-tabulated and summarized for the purpose of analysis. The printouts of the data, together with an essay summarizing the results, are available at the Charles and Margaret Hall Cushwa Center for the Study of American Catholicism, University of Notre Dame.

28. White, "Religion and Community," p. 201; see also David Gerber, "Modernity in the Service of Tradition: Catholic Lay Trustees at Buffalo's St. Louis Church and the Transformation of European Communal Traditions 1829–1855," *Journal of Social History*, Vol. 15, no. 4 (Summer 1982), 655–84.

29. Quoted in Silvano Tomasi, *Piety and Power* (New York: Center for Migration Studies, 1975), p. 83.

30. Dolan and Burns, "Parish History Study"; and Conzen, *Immigrant Milwaukee*, pp. 158–67.

31. Quoted in *The Church of St. Joseph of Yorkville* (New York: n.p., 1932), n.p.

32. See S. J. Connolly, *Priests and People in Pre-Famine Ireland 1780–1845* (New York: St. Martin's Press, 1982), pp. 55–56, and 269–70 for clergy-laity relations; and Burchell, *The San Francisco Irish*, pp. 94–115, and Vinyard, *The Irish on the Urban Frontier*, pp. 283–308, for Irish associational life.

33. O'Neill, "St. Paul's Priests 1851–1900," pp. 18 and 129; James Hitchcock, "Secular Clergy in Nineteenth Century America: A Diocesan Profile," *Records of American Catholic Historical Society of Philadelphia*, Vol. 88 (March 1977) 38.

34. Nelson J. Callahan (ed.) *The Diary of Richard L. Burtsell Priest of New York* (New York: Arno Press, 1978), pp. 413–22.

35. Quoted in Dolan, *The Immigrant Church*, p. 65.

36. Philip J. Murnion, *The Catholic Priest and the Changing Structure of Pastoral Ministry, New York 1920–1970* (New York: Arno Press, 1978), p. 89.

37. Dolan and Burns, "Parish History Study."

38. Harry C. Koenig (ed.), *A History of the Parishes of the Archdiocese of Chicago* (2 vols.; Chicago: Archdiocese of Chicago, 1980), I, pp. 302–4; Ellen Skerrett, "The Irish and Polish Parish: Chicago 1880–1920," paper delivered at 1979 annual meeting of American Catholic Historical Association.

39. Peter Guilday, *History of the Councils of Baltimore, 1791–1884* (New York: Macmillan, 1932), p. 88.

40. See *Acta et Decreta Sacrorum Conciliorum Recentiorum. Collectio Lacensis* (Freiburg: Herder, 1875), III, col. 298, no. VII (Third Provincial Council of New York); col. 454, no. 201 (Second Plenary Council of Baltimore); and *Decreta Concilii Plenarii Baltimorensis Tertii* (Baltimore: J. Murphy, 1884), pp. 163–65.

41. See Connolly, *Priests and People in Pre-Famine Ireland*, pp. 55–56 and 269–70; as Con-

nolly suggests, lay deference was not complete by any means, but it soon became the norm in nineteenth-century Ireland.

42. White, "Religion and Community," pp. 212 ff.

43. Clement Steltenpohl, *Stray Leaves from the History of St. Paul's Congregation of Cincinnati, Ohio* (Cincinnati: n.p., 1900), pp. 14–26 and 89 ff.; also Dolan and Burns, "Parish History Study."

44. See Leonard Covello, *The Social Background of the Italo-American School Child: A Study of the Southern Italian Family Mores and Their Effect on the School Situation in Italy and America* (Leiden, 1967), pp. 103–45.

45. Quoted in Dolan, *The Immigrant Church,* p. 23; see also Tomasi, *Piety and Power.*

46. Quoted in Tomasi, *Piety and Power,* p. 119.

47. Donald E. Byrne, Jr., "Maria Assunta: An Italian Religious Festival in Berwick, Pennsylvania" (unpublished paper).

48. Quoted in Rudolph J. Vecoli, "The Italians," in *They Chose Minnesota,* ed. June Drenning Holmquist (St. Paul: Minnesota Historical Society Press, 1981), p. 459; see also John Briggs, "Church Building in America: Divergent and Convergent Interests of Priests and Lay People in Italian-American Communities" (unpublished paper).

49. Lord et al., *History of the Archdiocese of Boston,* III, pp. 224–28 and 735–36; George E. Pozzetta, "The Mulberry District of New York City: The Years Before World War One," in *Little Italies in North America,* ed. Robert F. Harney and J. Vincenza Scarpaci (Toronto: Multicultural History Society of Ontario, 1981), pp. 7–40.

50. Charles Shanabruch, *Chicago's Catholics* (Notre Dame, Ind.: University of Notre Dame Press, 1981), pp. 51–52 and 125–26; also Deanna Paoli Gumina, *The Italians of San Francisco 1850–1930 (Gli Italiani di San Francisco 1850–1930)* (New York: Center for Migration Studies, 1978).

51. Covello, *The Social Background of the Italo-American School Child,* p. 133.

52. Paul Horgan, *Lamy of Santa Fe: His Life and Times* (New York: Farrar, Straus & Giroux, 1975), p. 127.

53. John L. Kessell, *The Missions of New Mexico Since 1776* (Albuquerque: University of New Mexico Press, 1980), p. 14.

54. Horgan, *Lamy of Santa Fe,* p. 127; and James H. Defouri, *Historical Sketch of the Catholic Church in New Mexico* (San Francisco: McCormick Brothers, 1887), pp. 67 and 122.

55. Robert E. Lucey, "The Catholic Church in Texas," in Louis J. Putz (ed.), *The Catholic Church U.S.A.* (Chicago: Fides Publishers Association, 1956), p. 228.

56. Kessell, *The Missions of New Mexico Since 1776,* p. 19.

57. Josef J. Barton, "Land, Labor and Community in Nueces: Czech Farmers and Mexican Laborers in South Texas, 1880–1930," Working Paper Series 5, no. 1 (Spring 1979), Charles and Margaret Hall Cushwa Center for the Study of American Catholicism, University of Notre Dame, p. 15.

58. Ibid., p. 16; and Weigle, *Brothers of Light, Brothers of Blood.*

59. Richard S. Sorrell, "The Sentinelle Affair (1924–1929) and Militant *Survivance:* The Franco-American Experience in Woonsocket, Rhode Island" (unpublished Ph.D. dissertation, State University of New York at Buffalo, 1975), p. 14.

60. Richard S. Sorrell, "The *Survivance* of French Canadians in New England 1865–1930: History, Geography and Demography as Destiny," *Ethnic and Racial Studies,* Vol. 4, no. 1 (January 1981), 98.

61. Mason Wade, "The French Parish and Survivance in Nineteenth-Century New England," *Catholic Historical Review,* Vol. 36, no. 2 (July 1950), 163; see also Horace Miner, *St. Denis: A French Canadian Parish* (Chicago: University of Chicago Press, 1939).

62. Quoted in Elliott Robert Barkan, "French Canadians," in *Harvard Encyclopedia of American Ethnic Groups,* p. 392.

63. See Miner, *St. Denis*, pp. 54–55; and Cornelius J. Jaenen, *The Role of the Church in New France* (Toronto: McGraw-Hill Ryerson, 1976), pp. 90–91.

64. See Haebler, "Habitants in Holyoke," pp. 104–6; Dolores Ann Liptak, "European Immigrants and the Catholic Church in Connecticut, 1870–1920" (unpublished Ph.D. dissertation, University of Connecticut, 1978), pp. 255–56; and Patrick J. Conley and Matthew J. Smith, *Catholicism in Rhode Island: The Formative Era* (Providence: Diocese of Providence, 1976), p. 141.

65. Conley and Smith, *Catholicism in Rhode Island*, p. 136; and Michael Guignard, "Maine's Corporation Sole Controversy," *Maine Historical Society Newsletter*, Vol. 12 (Winter 1972), 112.

66. Sorrell, "The *survivance* of French Canadians in New England," p. 102; Guignard, "Maine's Corporation Sole Controversy"; Robert Rumilly, *Histoire des Franco-Américains* (Montreal: n.p., 1958), pp. 102–14, 146–58, and 177–86.

67. *Handbook for Parishioners of the Archdiocese of Milwaukee*, pp. 23–24, quoted in Anthony J. Kuzniewski, "The Catholic Church in the Life of the Polish-Americans," in Frank Mocha (ed.), *Poles in America* (Stevens Point, Wis.: Worzalla Publishing, 1978), p. 413.

68. William I. Thomas and Florian Znaniecki, *The Polish Peasant in Europe and America* (2 vols.; New York: A.A. Knopf, 1927), I, p. 276, and II, p. 1523.

69. Quoted in Mary Cygan, "Ethnic Parish as Compromise: Spheres of Authority in a Polish American Parish, 1911–1930," Charles and Margaret Hall Cushwa Center for the Study of American Catholicism, University of Notre Dame, Working Paper Series 13, no. 1 (Spring 1983), p. 15.

70. Paul R. Magocsi, *The Ukrainian Experience in the United States: A Symposium* (Cambridge: Harvard Ukrainian Research Institute, 1979), p. 107.

71. Thomas and Znaniecki, *The Polish Peasant* . . . , II, p. 1523.

72. Quoted in Galush, "Forming Polonia," p. 92.

73. Ibid., p. 58.

74. William Galush, "The Polish National Church: A Survey of the Origins, Development and Mission," *Records of the American Catholic Historical Society of Philadelphia*, Vol. 83 (Sept.–Dec. 1972), 133.

75. John Joseph Parot, *Polish Catholics in Chicago 1850–1920* (Dekalb, Ill.: Northern Illinois University Press, 1981), pp. 55, 72, et passim.

76. Galush, "The Polish National Church," pp. 131–45.

77. Quoted in Arunas Alisauskas, "Changing Patterns of Religious Behavior, Organization and Belief in Immigrant Subcultures: The Lithuanian Settlement at Lawrence, Massachusetts, 1890–1930" (unpublished paper).

78. Mark Stolarik, "Building Slovak Communities in North America," in Keith P. Dyrud, Michael Novak, and Rudolph J. Vecoli (eds.), *The Other Catholics* (New York: Arno Press, 1978), p. 87.

79. William Wolkovich-Valkavicius, *Lithuanian Pioneer Priest of New England* (Brooklyn, N.Y.: Franciscan Press, 1980), p. 128.

80. Cada, *Czech-American Catholics*, pp. 26, 35–36.

81. Wolkovich-Valkavicius, *Lithuanian Pioneer Priest* . . . , p. 81.

82. Renkiewicz, "The Polish Settlement of St. Joseph County, Indiana," pp. 39–44.

83. Magocsi, *The Ukrainian Experience* . . . , p. 106.

84. Keith S. Russin, "Father Alexis G. Toth and the Wilkes-Barre Litigations," *St. Vladimir's Theological Quarterly*, Vol. 16, no. 3 (1972), 132–33.

85. See Gerald P. Fogarty, S.J., "The American Hierarchy and Oriental Rite Catholics, 1890–1907," *Records of the American Catholic Historical Society of Philadelphia*, Vol. 85 (Mar.–June 1974), pp. 17–28.

86. Magocsi, *The Ukrainian Experience* . . . , p. 123; Paul Robert Magocsi, "Ukrainians," *Harvard Encyclopedia of American Ethnic Groups*, pp. 999–1001; Keith P. Dyrud, "The Estab-

lishment of the Greek Catholic Rite in America as a Competitor to Orthodoxy," in *The Other Catholics*, pp. 191–92.

87. Magocsi, *The Ukrainian Experience* . . . , pp. 84 and 125.

88. Dyrud, "The Establishment of the Greek Catholic Rite . . . ," p. 216.

89. Bernard Bailyn, David Brion Davis, David Herbert Donald, John L. Thomas, Robert H. Wiebe, and Gordon S. Wood, *The Great Republic* (2 vols., Lexington, Mass.: Little, Brown, 1977), I, p. 402.

90. See Dolan, *The Immigrant Church*, pp. 50–51, and Carey, "The Laity's Understanding of the Trustee System," p. 359.

91. See Sylvia Granatir Alexander, "The Immigrant Church and Community: The Formation of Pittsburgh's Slovak Religious Institutions 1880–1914" (unpublished Ph.D. dissertation, University of Minnesota, 1980), pp. 388–94.

92. Carey, "The Laity's Understanding of the Trustee System," p. 359.

93. Dolan, *The Immigrant Church*, p. 52; and Gerber, "Modernity in the Service of Tradition," pp. 667–68.

94. Alexander, "The Immigrant Church and Community," pp. 650 and 395–402.

95. *Vehementer Nos* (encyclical of Pope Pius X, 1906), in Claudia Carlen, I.H.M. (ed.), *The Papal Encyclicals, 1903–1939*, (Raleigh, N.C.: McGrath Publishing, 1981), p. 48.

NOTES TO CHAPTER VII

1. Quoted in *Annual Report of Association for Improving the Conditions of the Poor, 1867*, p. 42.

2. See David Ward, *Cities and Immigrants* (New York: Oxford University Press, 1971); and Sam Bass Warner, *The Urban Wilderness* (New York: Harper & Row, 1972).

3. Glen E. Holt and Dominic A. Pacyga, *Chicago: A Historical Guide to the Neighborhoods: The Loop and South Side* (Chicago: Chicago Historical Society, 1979), pp. 113–19. Al Smith's autobiography, *Up to Now* (New York: Viking Press, 1929), pp. 25–49, gives an excellent account of life in a city neighborhood in the late-nineteenth century.

4. See Dolan, *The Immigrant Church*, pp. 29 ff. and 52–53.

5. Joseph Parot, "Steelmills, Stockyards, Sweatshops and Slums: The Social Fabric of the Polish Catholic Working Class in Chicago, 1870–1900" (unpublished paper), p. 14; Thomas Lee Philpott, *The Slum and the Ghetto: Neighborhood Deterioration and Middle Class Reform* (New York: Oxford University Press, 1978), pp. 29–32.

6. Mario T. García, *Desert Immigrants: The Mexicans of El Paso 1880–1920* (New Haven: Yale University Press, 1981), pp. 127–54 and 214–19.

7. Dolan, *The Immigrant Church*, p. 37.

8. Tamara K. Hareven and Randolph Langenbach, *Amoskeag: Life and Work in an American Factory-City* (New York: Pantheon Books, 1978), p. 265.

9. Dolan, *The Immigrant Church*, p. 20.

10. Sam Bass Warner, *Streetcar Suburbs: The Process of Growth in Boston, 1870–1900* (Cambridge: Harvard University Press, 1962), pp. 79–83; Dennis Clark, "A Pattern of Urban Growth: Residential Development and Church Location in Philadelphia," *Records of the American Catholic Historical Society of Philadelphia*, Vol. 82, no. 3 (Sept. 1971), 163–70; Fanning and Skerrett, "James T. Farrell and Washington Park," p. 85.

11. Howard P. Chudacoff, *The Evolution of American Urban Society* (Englewood Cliffs, N.J.: Prentice-Hall, 1975), p. 129; Tamara K. Hareven, *Family Time and Industrial Time: The Relationship Between the Family and Work in a New England Industrial Community* (New York: Cambridge University Press, 1982), p. 21; Philpott, *The Slum and the Ghetto*, p. 138.

12. Edward Kantowicz, "Church and Neighborhood," *Ethnicity*, Vol. 7, no. 4 (Dec. 1980), 351–55; for similar neighborhoods in Philadelphia, see Golab, *Immigrant Destinations*, pp. 122–33.

13. Hareven, *Family Time and Industrial Time,* p. 21.

14. Chudacoff, *The Evolution of American Urban Society,* p. 130.

15. Philpott, *The Slum and the Ghetto,* pp. 131–35.

16. Ray Allen Billington, *The Protestant Crusade* (New York: Macmillan, 1938), p. 89; this is the classic study of anti-Catholicism before the Civil War.

17. Patrick Blessing, "Culture, Religion and the Activities of the Committee of Vigilance, San Francisco 1856," Working Paper, Series 8, no. 3 (1980), Charles and Margaret Hall Cushwa Center for the Study of American Catholicism, University of Notre Dame, p. 4.

18. See Donald L. Kinzer, *An Episode in Anti-Catholicism: The American Protective Association* (Seattle: University of Washington Press, 1964); and John Higham, *Strangers in the Land* (New Brunswick, N.J.: Rutgers University Press, 1955).

19. See Ralph Janis, "Ethnic Mixture and the Persistence of Cultural Pluralism in the Church Communities of Detroit, 1880–1940," *Mid-America* 61 (April–July 1979), 99–115.

20. Thernstrom, *The Other Bostonians,* pp. 221–25.

21. Chudacoff, *The Evolution of American Urban Society,* p. 92; and Dolan, *The Immigrant Church,* p. 42.

22. Sam Bass Warner, Jr., *The Private City: Philadelphia in Three Periods of Its Growth* (Philadelphia: University of Pennsylvania Press, 1968), p. 61.

23. Dolan and Burns, "Parish History Study."

24. Smith, *The Catholic Church in New York,* II, p. 470.

25. Koenig, *A History of the Parishes of the Archdiocese of Chicago,* p. 374; Thomas M. Mulkerins, S.J., *Holy Family Parish* (Chicago: Universal Press, 1923), pp. 189, 195–96.

26. Bonaventure Hammer, O.S.F., *Gedenk-Büchlein der St. Johannes Baptista Gemeinde in Cincinnati, Ohio* (Cincinnati: Braunwart & Brockhoff, 1895), pp. 77–90.

27. Alfred J. Ede, "The Lay Crusade for a Christian America: A Study of the American Federation of Catholic Societies 1900–1919" (unpublished Ph.D. dissertation, Graduate Theological Union, 1979), p. 58.

28. Philip J. Murnion, *The Catholic Priest and the Changing Structure of Pastoral Ministry, New York 1920–1970* (New York: Arno Press, 1978), pp. 127, 121, 152; see issues of *American Ecclesiastical Review* in the 1920s for such articles; see also Smith, *Up to Now,* pp. 40–49.

29. Hugh McLeod, "Insecure, unknowledgeable, frightened: The New York City Immigrant and Religion, c. 1900" (unpublished paper), pp. 6–7.

30. Ibid., pp. 5 and 27; Dolan, *Catholic Revivalism,* p. 133; Alisauskas, "Changing Patterns of Religious Behavior. . . ."

31. See Robert Orsi, "The Madonna of 115th Street: Faith and Community in Italian Harlem 1880–1950" (unpublished Ph.D. dissertation, Yale University, 1982), pp. 21–34.

32. Father John Grassi, "The Catholic Religion in the United States in 1818," in Philip Gleason (ed.), *Documentary Reports on Early American Catholicism* (New York: Arno Press, 1978), p. 237.

33. Ambrose Marechal, "Report to Propaganda October 16, 1818," in Gleason (ed.), *Documentary Reports on Early American Catholicism,* pp. 204–5.

34. Stephen T. Badin, "Origin and Progress of the Mission of Kentucky," in Gleason (ed.), *Documentary Reports on Early American Catholicism,* p. 834.

35. See Hanley, *John Carroll Papers,* II, pp. 10–11, for Carroll's Lenten Pastoral (1792); pp. 336–37 for his Advent Sermon (1801); and III, pp. 375–466, for others.

36. See Thomas Wangler, "Toward a Religious History of American Catholicism: The Boston Experience 1900–50" (unpublished paper).

37. Grassi, "The Catholic Religion in the United States in 1818," pp. 238–39.

38. Quoted in O'Donnell, *History of the Diocese of Hartford,* p. 182.

39. Joseph Chinnici, "Politics and Theology: From Enlightenment Catholicism to the Condemnation of Americanism," Working Paper, Series 9, no. 3 (Spring 1981), Charles and Marga-

ret Hall Cushwa Center for the Study of American Catholicism, University of Notre Dame, pp. 21 and 27.

40. See *Dictionnaire de Spiritualité* (Paris: G. Beauchesne, 1957), III, pp. 747–95.

41. Ann Taves, "Relocating the Sacred: Roman Catholic Devotions in Mid-Nineteenth Century America" (unpublished Ph.D. dissertation, University of Chicago, 1983), pp. 10–13.

42. "Catholic Literature and the Catholic Public," *Catholic World* 12 (Dec. 1870), 405, cited in Taves, "Relocating the Sacred," p. 17.

43. Taves, "Relocating the Sacred," pp. 45–46.

44. Dolan, *Catholic Revivalism*, p. 178.

45. Ellen H. Walworth, *Life Sketches of Father Walworth* (Albany: J. B. Lyon, 1907), p. 207.

46. Dolan and Burns, "Parish History Study."

47. See Eugene P. Willging and Herta Hatzfeld, *Catholic Serials of the Nineteenth Century in the United States, Part 15: A Statistical Analysis* (Washington, D.C.: Catholic University of America Press, 1968), pp. 117–18.

48. Ibid., Series 2, Part 10, no. 1, pp. 19–20 *(Pilot);* Series 2, Part 14, no. 1, pp. 42–44 *(Catholic News);* Series 2, Part 11, no. 1, p. 75 *(Messenger of the Sacred Heart);* Series 2, Part 4, no. 1, p. 25 *(Ave Maria).*

49. Paul R. Messbarger, *Fiction with a Parochial Purpose* (Boston: Boston University Press, 1971), pp. 56, 70, and 134 ff.

50. Eileen Mary Brewer, "Piety and Religious Education in the Catholic Girls Convent School, 1860–1920" (unpublished paper).

51. Antonia White, *Frost in May* (New York: Viking Press, 1933), pp. 45–46, cited in Brewer, "Piety and Religious Education . . . ,"

52. Christa Ressmeyer Klein, "The Jesuits and Catholic Boyhood in Nineteenth-Century New York: A Study of St. John's College and the College of St. Francis Xavier 1846–1912 (unpublished Ph.D. dissertation, University of Pennsylvania, 1976), pp. 249 and 316–18.

53. Charles W. Churchill, *The Italians of Newark: A Community Study* (New York, 1975), pp. 99–100; Orsi, "The Madonna of 115th Street"; Rudolph J. Vecoli, "Prelates and Peasants: Italian Immigrants and the Catholic Church," *Journal of Social History* II (Spring 1969), 217–68.

54. Marianne L. Stoller and Thomas J. Steele, S.J. (eds.), *Diary of the Jesuit Residence of Our Lady of Guadalupe Parish, Conejos, Colorado,* trans. by José B. Fernández (Colorado Springs: Colorado College, 1982), p. 94.

55. Steele, *Santos and Saints,* pp. 69–70.

56. Elsa G. Herzfeld, *Family Monographs* (New York: J. Kempster Printing, 1905), pp. 45–46 and 15.

57. Roger Aubert, *The Church in a Secularised Society,* Vol. V of *The Christian Centuries* (New York: Paulist Press, 1978), p. 117.

NOTES TO CHAPTER VIII

1. Martin E. Marty, *The Modern Schism* (New York: Harper & Row, 1969).

2. See Chapter 4 for a discussion of the spirit of independence in the republican period. Evidence for the immigrant-church period is extensive but diverse; see, e.g., Mary Ewens, O.P., *The Role of the Nun in Nineteenth Century America;* and Archives of University of Notre Dame, Edward Sorin, Chronicles of Notre Dame du Lac, Vol. I, p. 25.

3. *Vehementer Nos,* pp. 47–48.

4. Dolan, *The Immigrant Church,* p. 161; Joseph Wuest, *Annales Congregationis SS. Redemptoris Provinciae Americanae* (Boston: Angel Guardian Press, 1923), V, Part 2, pp. 55, 163–64, 173, 191 and 352–53. Roger Aubert, *Le Pontificat de Pie IX* (Paris: Bloud & Gay, 1963), pp. 292–95.

5. *The Mission Book* (Baltimore: Kelly & Piet, 1862), p. 329.

6. Quoted in Parot, *Polish Catholics in Chicago,* p. 124.

7. Messbarger, *Fiction with a Parochial Purpose*, p. 134.

8. Cygan, "Ethnic Parish as Compromise," pp. 5–6.

9. See *The Mission Book*, pp. 253–88.

10. *The Ursuline Manual* (New York: Edward Dunigan, 1840), pp. 519–20.

11. Eugene A. Walsh, *The Priesthood in the Writings of the French School: Bérulle, De Condren, Olier* (Washington, D.C.: Catholic University of America Press, 1949), p. 115.

12. Quoted in Hareven and Langenbach, *Amoskeag*, p. 257.

13. Dolan, *The Immigrant Church*, p. 62; and Edward Roberts Moore, *Roman Collar* (New York: Macmillan, 1950), pp. 8–9.

14. See *The Ursuline Manual*, pp. 139 ff.; and *The Mission Book*, pp. 247 ff.

15. Dolan, *The Immigrant Church*, pp. 62–63.

16. Dolan, *Catholic Revivalism*, pp. 139–40.

17. Ibid., p. 109.

18. Klein, "The Jesuits and Catholic Boyhood . . . ," p. 310; and *The Mission Book*, p. 323; see pp. 321–29 of *The Mission Book* for a typical discussion on the need for purity.

19. See Robert D. Cross, *The Emergence of Liberal Catholicism in America* (Cambridge: Harvard University Press, 1958), pp. 1–21.

20. *The Mission Book*, p. 322.

21. Moore, *Roman Collar*, p. 41; and Cross, *The Emergence of Liberal Catholicism . . . ,* pp. 51–70.

22. See George Deshon, *Guide for Catholic Young Women* (New York: Sadlier, 1863), pp. 297–99; and Lelia Hardin Bugg, *The People of Our Parish* (Boston: Marlier, Callanan, 1900), pp. 45–59.

23. Quoted in Murnion, *The Catholic Priest and the Changing Structure of Pastoral Ministry*, p. 128.

24. *The Mission Book*, p. 267; and Dolan, *The Immigrant Church*, p. 63.

25. *The Mission Book*, p. 323.

26. Ibid., p. 237.

27. Messbarger, *Fiction with a Parochial Purpose*, p. 140.

28. Dolan, *Catholic Revivalism*, pp. 108–9.

29. Patrick O'Farrell, "Lay Spirituality and Historical Conditioning," *The Australasian Catholic Record*, Vol. 55, no. 1 (January 1978), 39.

30. Quoted in Klein, "The Jesuits and Catholic Boyhood . . . ," p. 318.

31. Messbarger, *Fiction with a Parochial Purpose*, p. 93.

32. Klein, "The Jesuits and Catholic Boyhood . . . ," p. 321.

33. Daniel A. Lord, S.J., *Played by Ear: The Autobiography of Father Daniel A. Lord, S.J.* (Garden City, N.Y.: Doubleday, 1959), p. 27; and Orsi, "The Madonna of 115th Street," p. 257.

34. Peter W. Bardaglio, "Italian Immigrants in the Catholic Church in Providence 1890–1930," *Rhode Island History*, Vol. 34, no. 2 (May 1975), 52.

35. McLeod, "Insecure, unknowledgeable, frightened," Table 2; the corresponding Protestant level of female churchgoers was 60 percent.

36. See Dolan, *Catholic Revivalism*, pp. 136–37.

37. Data on gender are based on Dolan and Burns, "Parish History Study"; for marital status, see Conners, "Their Own Kind," pp. 122 and 126.

38. Herzfeld, *Family Monographs*, pp. 18–22; Connolly, *Priests and People in Pre-Famine Ireland*, pp. 148–74; and Dolan, *The Immigrant Church*, pp. 60–62.

39. See Carol Jensen, "Cleofas Jaramillo's View of Marriage: An Example of the Interplay of Folk Religion and Institutional Religion in Territorial New Mexico" (unpublished M.A. thesis, Religious Studies, Indiana University, 1981); Carla Bianco, *The Two Rosetos* (Bloomington, Ind.: Indiana University Press, 1974), pp. 102–3.

40. See, for example, "Devotion to St. Ann," *Ave Maria*, Vol. 35, no. 6 (August 6, 1892), 157–

59; and "Saved by the Scapular," *Ave Maria*, Vol. 35, no. 4 (July 23, 1892), 102–3; these are but two of numerous such stories; Dolan, *Catholic Revivalism*, pp. 177–78

41. Ralph L. Woods and Henry F. Woods, *Pilgrim Places in North America: A Guide to Catholic Shrines* (New York: Longmans, Greene, 1939), pp. 88–89, 108–10, et passim, for a list of Catholic shrines; see also Orsi, "The Madonna of 115th Street."

42. The religious magazine *Ave Maria* published many such miracle stories.

43. Isaac Hecker, *The Church and the Age* (New York: Office of the Catholic World, 1887), p. 7.

44. Ibid., p. 33.

45. Ibid., pp. 25 and 170.

46. Archives of the Paulist Fathers, Mission Chronicles II, p. 13 (November 1863 mission in St. Louis, Mo.); George Deshon, *Guide for Young Catholic Women*, p. 143; and Bernard O'Reilly, *Mirror of True Womanhood* (New York: P. F. Collier, 1905), p. 260.

47. See Joseph P. Chinnici, "Theology, Politics, and Spirituality: Images of Christ in the Americanist Controversy" (paper presented at spring meeting of American Catholic Historical Association, St. Louis, 1982).

48. Quoted in Dolan, *Catholic Revivalism*, p. 88.

49. Murnion, *The Catholic Priest and the Changing Structure of Pastoral Ministry*, p. 133; see also Vecoli, "Prelates and Peasants: Italian Immigrants and the Catholic Church."

50. Thomas J. Steele, S.J., "The Spanish Passion Play in New Mexico and Colorado," *New Mexico Historical Review* 53 (1978), 239–59; and Weigle, *Brothers of Light, Brothers of Blood*.

51. Smith, "Religion and Ethnicity in America," p. 1169.

52. McLeod, "Insecure, unknowledgeable, frightened," pp. 8–9.

NOTES TO CHAPTER IX

1. Bernard Bailyn, *Education in the Forming of American Society: Needs and Opportunities for Study* (Chapel Hill, N.C.: University of North Carolina Press, 1960), p. 14.

2. The work of Lawrence A. Cremin, especially his book *American Education: The National Experience 1783–1876* (New York: Harper & Row, 1980), has influenced my thinking about the historical study of education.

3. *Fifth Annual Report of the Reverend Superintendent of Catholic Schools in the Archdiocese of New York* (New York: New York Catholic School Board, 1909), p. 18.

4. Quoted in Joseph H. Lackner, S.M., "Bishop Ignatius F. Horstmann and the Americanization of the Roman Catholic Church in the United States" (unpublished Ph.D. dissertation, St. Louis University, 1977), p. 238.

5. Carl N. Degler, *At Odds: Women and the Family in America from the Revolution to the Present* (New York: Oxford University Press, 1980), p. 26.

6. Ibid., pp. 63–73; and Cremin, *American Education*, pp. 372–78.

7. Hanley, *The John Carroll Papers*, I, pp. 334, 355, 435, and 493; II, pp. 250 and 353; III, pp. 81–82 and 132; also Lord et al., *History of the Archdiocese of Boston*, I, p. 540.

8. Lord et al., *History of the Archdiocese of Boston*, I, pp. 540–41.

9. Hanley, *The John Carroll Papers*, I, pp. 43, 45, and 48.

10. S. M. Hester Valentine, S.S.N.D., *The North American Foundations: Letters of Mother M. Theresa Gerhardinger* (Winona, Minn.: School Sisters of Notre Dame, 1977), p. 64.

11. Ibid.

12. Quoted in Dolan, *Catholic Revivalism*, p. 5.

13. Quoted in Dolan, *The Immigrant Church*, p. 142.

14. Dolan, *Catholic Revivalism*, pp. 15–19.

15. Eugene P. Willging and Herta Hatzfeld, *Catholic Serials of the Nineteenth Century in the United States, First Series: Part II* (Washington, D.C.: Catholic University of America Press, 1968), p. 223; and *Second Series: Part XV*, pp. 118–19. See also Peter Guilday, *The Life and*

Times of John England: First Bishop of Charleston, 1786–1842 (New York: American Press, 1927), I, pp. 453–73.

16. Willging and Hatzfeld, *Catholic Serials . . . , Second Series: Part XV,* p. 107.

17. See Lord et al., *History of the Archdiocese of Boston,* I, p. 540; and Hanley, *The John Carroll Papers,* I, pp. 334, 355, and 502; II, pp. 135 and 250.

18. Dolan, *The Immigrant Church,* pp. 114–15; *U.S. Catholic Almanac* (Baltimore: James Myres, 1833), pp. 118–20; Taves, "Relocating the Sacred," pp. 278–82.

19. Quoted in George Paré, *The Catholic Church in Detroit 1701–1888* (Detroit: Gabriel Richard Press, 1951), pp. 317–18.

20. Frank B. Woodford and Albert Hyma, *Gabriel Richard* (Detroit: Wayne State University Press, 1958), pp. 68–71.

21. Earl L. Bradsher, *Mathew Carey* (New York: Columbia University Press, 1912), p. vi.

22. Hanley, *The John Carroll Papers,* I, p. 275.

23. Philip Gleason, "From an Indefinite Homogeneity: The Beginnings of Catholic Higher Education in the United States" (unpublished paper), pp. 3–8; Edward J. Power, *A History of Catholic Higher Education in the United States* (Milwaukee: Bruce Publishing, 1958), p. 333.

24. Hanley, *The John Carroll Papers,* II, p. 6; and also Philip Gleason, "The Main Sheet Anchor: John Carroll and Catholic Higher Education," *Review of Politics,* Vol. 38 (October 1976), 584–85.

25. Gleason, "From an Indefinite Homogeneity," p. 13.

26. Ibid., pp. 2 and 19.

27. Ibid., pp. 18–19.

28. Frederick Rudolph, *The American College and University: A History* (New York: Vintage Books, 1965), p. 310.

29. Quoted in Mother M. Benedict Murphy, R.S.H.M., "Pioneer Roman Catholic Girls Academies: Their Growth, Character, and Contribution to American Education: A Study of Roman Catholic Education for Girls from Colonial Times to the First Plenary Council of 1852" (unpublished Ph.D. dissertation, Columbia University, 1958), p. 120.

30. Ibid., pp. 267 and 271.

31. Ibid., pp. 157 ff.; also *U.S. Catholic Almanac* (Baltimore: Sadlier, 1833) for advertisements describing the curricula of these academies.

32. Barbara Misner, "Highly Respectable and Accomplished Ladies: Early American Women Religious, 1790–1860," Working Paper Series, Cushwa Center for the Study of American Catholicism, University of Notre Dame, Series 8, no. 1, Fall 1980.

33. Quoted in Thomas J. Donaghy, F.S.C., *Philadelphia's Finest: A History of Education in the Catholic Archdiocese 1692–1970* (Philadelphia: American Catholic Historical Society, 1972), p. 49.

34. O'Reilly, *Mirror of True Womanhood,* p. 6.

35. Walter Elliott, *Mission Sermons* (Washington, D.C.: Apostolic Mission House, 1926), p. 134; Bugg, *The People of Our Parish,* pp. 97–98; Dolan, *Catholic Revivalism,* p. 102.

36. O'Reilly, *Mirror of True Womanhood,* p. 261.

37. Degler, *At Odds,* p. 136; see also Jeremy Brecher, Jerry Lombardi, and Jan Stackhouse, *Brass Valley: The Story of Working People's Lives and Struggles in an American Industrial Region* (Philadelphia: Temple University Press, 1982), for the family life of immigrants.

38. Orsi, "The Madonna of 115th Street," p. 141.

39. Vecoli, "Prelates and Peasants," p. 233.

40. See Dolan, *Catholic Revivalism.*

41. D. J. Kavanagh, S.J., *The Holy Family Sisters of San Francisco: A Sketch of Their First Fifty Years 1872–1922* (San Francisco: Gilmartin, 1922), p. 116 et passim.

42. John T. Driscoll, "Summer Schools, Catholic," in *The Catholic Encyclopedia* (New York: Encyclopedia Press, 1912), XIV, p. 334; Messbarger, *Fiction with a Parochial Purpose,* pp. 57–58.

43. Clement M. Thuente, "Holy Name, Society of the," *The Catholic Encyclopedia* (New York: Encyclopedia Press, 1910), VII, pp. 420–21.

44. Walter Zachariasiewicz, "Organizational Structure of Polonia," in Mocha (ed.) *Poles in America*, p. 637; E. Hamon, S.J., *Les Canadiens-Français de la Nouvelle Angleterre* (Quebec: N. S. Hardy, 1891), p. 51; Philip Gleason, *The Conservative Reformers: German-American Catholics and the Social Order* (Notre Dame, Ind.: University of Notre Dame Press, 1968), p. 122.

45. Christopher J. Kauffman, *Faith and Fraternalism: The History of the Knights of Columbus, 1882–1982* (New York: Harper & Row, 1982), p. 90.

46. *Catholic Mirror*, August 26, 1899, p. 8; Driscoll, "Summer Schools, Catholic," XIV, 334–35; see also James A. White, *The Founding of Cliff Haven* (New York: United States Catholic Historical Association, 1950).

47. Aaron I. Abell, *American Catholicism and Social Action* (Notre Dame, Ind.: University of Notre Dame Press, 1963), pp. 163–65; Robert Biggs, "What We Are Doing in Settlement Work," *St. Vincent de Paul Quarterly*, XIX (Nov. 1914), 237–45; *U.S. Catholic Directory* (New York: P. J. Kenedy, 1920).

48. Willging and Hatzfeld, *Catholic Serials . . . Second Series: Part XV: A Statistical Analysis*, pp. 68–69, 118–19.

49. Ibid., pp. 120, 153–54.

50. Francis Robert Walsh, "The Boston *Pilot:* A Newspaper for the Irish Immigrant 1829–1908" (unpublished Ph.D. dissertation, Boston University, 1968), p. v.

51. Ibid., p. 254.

52. Bernard Pacyniak, "An Historical Outline of the Polish Press in America," in Mocha (ed.), *Poles in America*, pp. 515–18; Patricia Feiten, "A Survey of Catholic Americana and Catholic Book Publishing in the United States 1896–1900 (M.A. thesis, Library Science, Catholic University, 1958), pp. 128–29 et passim; Messbarger, *Fiction with a Parochial Purpose*, p. 56.

53. Robert C. Healey, *A Catholic Book Chronicle: The Story of P. J. Kenedy and Sons, 1826–1951* (New York: Kenedy, 1951), pp. 43–44.

54. Quoted in Cremin, *American Education*, p. 370.

NOTES TO CHAPTER X

1. Quoted in Robert Michaelsen, *Piety in the Public School* (New York: Macmillan, 1970), p. 119.

2. *Freeman's Journal*, July 2, 1842; Dolan, *The Immigrant Church*, p. 102.

3. Vincent P. Lannie, *Public Money and Parochial Education: Bishop Hughes, Governor Seward and the New York School Controversy* (Cleveland: Press of Case Western Reserve, 1968), p. 255.

4. Dolan, *The Immigrant Church*, p. 106.

5. James W. Sanders, "19th Century Boston Catholics and the School Question," Charles and Margaret Hall Cushwa Center, University of Notre Dame, Working Paper Series, no. 2, Fall 1977, pp. 28–29; and Lord et al., *History of the Archdiocese of Boston*, II, pp. 587–601.

6. Sanders, "19th Century Boston Catholics . . . ," pp. 7–8; See Timothy H. Morrissey, "Archbishop John Ireland and the Faribault-Stillwater School Plan of the 1890s: A Reappraisal" (unpublished Ph.D. dissertation, University of Notre Dame, 1975), Appendix.

7. Francis Michael Perko, "A Time to Favor Zion: A Case Study of Religion as a Force in American Educational Development 1830–1870" (unpublished Ph.D. dissertation, Stanford University, 1981), pp. 90 and 156–57.

8. Dorothy Lentz, S.P., *The Way It Was in Providence Schools* (Montreal: Sisters of Providence, 1978), p. 35 et passim.

9. Cremin, *American Education*, p. 165.

10. Perko, "A Time to Favor Zion," p. 89; and Ewens, *The Role of the Nun in Nineteenth Century America*, pp. 101–2 and 261–62.

11. Carl F. Kaestle, *Pillars of the Republic* (New York: Hill & Wang, 1983), pp. 166–67.

12. Ibid., p. xi.

13. Ibid., pp. 103 and 76.

14. Bernard J. Meiring, *Educational Aspects of the Legislation of the Councils of Baltimore 1829–1884* (New York: Arno Press, 1978), pp. 94 and 97.

15. Quoted in ibid., pp. 143 and 141.

16. Philip Schaff, *America: A Sketch of the Political, Social and Religious Character,* ed. Perry Miller (Cambridge, Mass.: Harvard University Press, 1961), p. 183.

17. Meiring, *Educational Aspects . . . ,* p. 137.

18. Ibid., pp. 137 and 144.

19. Ibid., p. 144.

20. Thomas W. Spalding, *Martin John Spalding: American Churchman* (Washington, D.C.: Catholic University of America Press, 1973), pp. 126–27.

21. Meiring, *Educational Aspects . . . ,* p. 185.

22. Michaelsen, *Piety in the Public School,* p. 90.

23. Quoted in ibid., p. 118.

24. Ibid., pp. 121–22.

25. See Kaestle, *Pillars of the Republic,* p. 101.

26. Neil G. McCluskey. S.J., *Catholic Education in America* (New York: Bureau of Publications, Teachers College, Columbia University, 1964), pp. 123 and 125–26.

27. See Norlene M. Kunkel, C.S.F.N., "Bishop Bernard J. McQuaid and Catholic Education" (unpublished Ph.D. dissertation, University of Notre Dame, 1974), pp. 110–27.

28. Morrissey, "Archbishop John Ireland . . . ," pp. 98–105.

29. Quoted in Kunkel, "Bishop Bernard J. McQuaid . . . ," p. 200.

30. Meiring, *Educational Aspects . . . ,* p. 301.

31. Francis Cassidy, "Catholic Education in the Third Plenary Council of Baltimore," *Catholic Historical Review,* Vol. 34 (January 1949), 415–16.

32. See Meiring, *Educational Aspects . . . ,* pp. 314 and 234 for Fitzgerald quote; Kunkel, "Bishop Bernard J. McQuaid . . . ," p. 154.

33. B. J. McQuaid, *Christian Free Schools* (Rochester, N.Y.: n.p., 1892), p. 147.

34. John Ireland, *The Church and Modern Society* (New York: D. H. McBride, 1903), I, p. 229.

35. For Ireland's thought, see Morrissey, "Archbishop John Ireland . . . ," pp. 113 and 136; for McQuaid's, see Kunkel, "Bishop Bernard J. McQuaid . . . ," p. 160.

36. Ireland, *The Church and Modern Society,* I, p. 220.

37. Robert James Wister, *The Establishment of the Apostolic Delegation in the United States of America: The Satolli Mission, 1892–1896* (Rome: Gregorian University, 1981), pp. 100–1.

38. See David F. Reilly, *The School Controversy 1891–1893* (Washington, D.C. 1943), p. 229; and John Tracy Ellis, *The Life of James Cardinal Gibbons* (Milwaukee: Bruce Publishing, 1952), I, p. 702.

39. See Morrissey, "Archbishop John Ireland . . . ," pp. 264–71, for Stillwater, and pp. 304–10 for Faribault.

40. Robert Emmett Curran, S.J., *Michael Augustine Corrigan and the Shaping of Conservative Catholicism in America 1878–1902* (New York: Arno Press, 1978), p. 507.

41. See *U.S. Catholic Directory* for 1883, 1900, and 1920, where each church is understood as representing a parish community.

42. Quoted in William Bourne, *History of the Public School Society of the City of New York* (New York: W. Wood, 1870), p. 529.

43. Mary Ewens, O.P., "The Impact of Sisters on the Nineteenth-Century American Church" (unpublished paper, April 1979), Tables I and II; Mary Ewens, O.P., "The Leadership of Nuns in Immigrant Catholicism," in Rosemary Radford Ruether and Rosemary Skinner Keller (eds.),

Women and Religion in America. Vol. I, *The Nineteenth Century* (San Francisco: Harper & Row, 1981), p. 103.

44. Colman J. Barry, O.S.B., *The Catholic Church and German Americans* (Milwaukee: Bruce Publishing, 1953), p. 272. Dolan and Burns, "Parish History Study."

45. Howard R. Weisz, *Irish Americans and Italian-American Educational Views and Activities 1870–1900: A Comparison* (New York: Arno Press, 1976), pp. 95–96.

46. Quoted in Elliott R. Barkan, "French Canadians," in *Harvard Encyclopedia of American Ethnic Groups*, p. 396.

47. Ibid.; Sorrell, "The Sentinelle Affair . . . ," pp. 118–19; Haebler, "Habitants in Holyoke," pp. 224–25.

48. Quoted in Ellen Marie Kuznicki, C.SS.F., "An Ethnic School in American Education: A Study of the Origin, Development, and Merits of the Educational System of the Felician Sisters in the Polish-American Catholic Schools of Western New York" (unpublished Ph.D. dissertation, Kansas State University, 1973), p. 248.

49. Ibid., pp. 96–97 and 120; see Josephine Marie Peplinski, S.S.J.-T.O.S.F., *A Fitting Response: The History of the Sisters of St. Joseph of the Third Order of St. Francis* (South Bend: The Order, 1982), I, p. 79; James A. Burns, C.S.C., *The Growth and Development of the Catholic School System in the United States* (New York: Benziger Brothers, 1912), p. 320; Kuzniewski, "The Catholic Church in the Life of the Polish Americans," pp. 346 and 457.

50. Marian Mark Stolarik, "Immigration and Urbanization: The Slovak Experience" (unpublished Ph.D. dissertation, University of Minnesota, 1974), p. 163.

51. Ibid., p. 165; and Alexander, "The Immigrant Church and Community," p. 597.

52. Stolarik, "Immigration and Urbanization: The Slovak Experience," pp. 160–68.

53. See Burns, *The Growth and Development of the Catholic School System . . .* , pp. 330–36, for data on parish-school percentages, where he puts Czechs at 43 percent, Lithuanians at 29 percent, and Ukrainians at 36 percent; for Czechs, see also Cada, *Czech-American Catholics*, pp. 53–56, and Freeze, "Czechs," *Harvard Encyclopedia of American Ethnic Groups*, 266–67.

54. James W. Sanders, *The Education of an Urban Minority: Catholics in Chicago 1833–1965* (New York: Oxford University Press, 1977), p. 69.

55. Weisz, *Irish Americans and Italian-American Educational Views*, p. 401, and Briggs, *An Italian Passage*, p. 202; Burns put the Italian parish-school percentage at 22 (see *The Growth and Development of the Catholic School System*, pp. 307–10).

56. Burns, *The Growth and Development of the Catholic School System*, p. 329; see Frederick G. Bohme, *A History of the Italians in New Mexico* (New York: Arno Press, 1975).

57. See *The Official Catholic Directory 1910* (New York: P. J. Kenedy, 1910), pp. 210–16 and 603–8.

58. Peplinski, *A Fitting Response*, p. 78.

59. Stolarik, "Immigration and Urbanization: The Slovak Experience," pp. 164–65.

60. See *U.S. Catholic Directory 1890* for geographical distribution of schools; Dolan and Burns, "Parish History Study"; Cada, *Czech-American Catholics*, pp. 53 and 56.

61. Dolan and Burns, "Parish History Study."

62. *Sixth Annual Report of the Superintendent of Parochial Schools of the Archdiocese of Philadelphia for the Year Ending June 30, 1900* (Philadelphia: n.p., 1900), pp. 129–32; see also *Second Annual Report of the Superintendent of the Parochial Schools of the Archdiocese of Cincinnati 1908–1909* (Cincinnati: Diocesan School Board, 1910) for differences between urban and rural schools; also Sister Jo Ann Euper, O.S.F., *First Century of Service: The School Sisters of St. Francis* (Milwaukee: n.p., 1976), p. 25, for description of rural schools.

63. Louise Montgomery, *The American Girl in the Stockyards District* (Chicago: University of Chicago Press, 1913), pp. 5–6.

64. Kuznicki, "An Ethnic School . . . ," pp. 115–16.

65. *Sixth Annual Report . . . of Philadelphia . . . ,* p. 7; Sanders, *The Education of an Urban Minority,* p. 35; Lackner, "Bishop Ignatius F. Horstmann," p. 240.

66. See Kuznicki, "An Ethnic School . . . ," pp. 115–18; Weisz, *Irish Americans and Italian-American Educational Views,* p. 94; Galush, "Forming Polonia," p. 182; also Philadelphia, Cincinnati, and New York annual school reports.

67. See Nicholas Point, S.J., *Wilderness Kingdom: Indian Life in the Rocky Mountains, 1840–1847* (trans. Joseph P. Donnelly, S.J.; New York: Holt, Rinehart & Winston, 1967); Samuel Mazzuchelli, O.P., *The Memoirs of Father Samuel Mazzuchelli, O.P.* (trans. Sisters Maria M. Armeto, O.P., and Mary J. Finnegan, O.P.; Chicago: Priory Press, 1967); P. J. DeSmet, *Western Missions and Missionaries: A Series of Letters* (New York: J. B. Kirker, late E. Dunigand and Brother, 1859); Joseph Gregori, *The Apostle of the Chippewas: The Life Story of the Most Rev. Frederick Baraga, the First Bishop of Marquette* (Lemont, Ill.: Franciscan Fathers, 1932).

68. Quoted in Howard L. Harrod, *Mission Among the Blackfeet* (Norman, Okla.: University of Oklahoma Press, 1971), p. 59.

69. Henry Warner Bowden, *American Indians and Christian Missions* (Chicago: University of Chicago Press, 1981), p. 167.

70. See *Report of the Director of the Bureau of Catholic Indian Missions for 1910* (Washington: n.p., 1911); these annual reports are valuable sources of information; Francis Paul Prucha, *The Churches and the Indian Schools 1888–1912* (Lincoln, Neb.: University of Nebraska Press, 1979), p. 3.

71. For Indian resistance and finances, see Harrod, *Mission Among the Blackfeet,* pp. 86–90, 94–95, and Dominic B. Gerlach, "St. Joseph's Indian Normal School 1888–1896," *Indiana Magazine of History,* Vol. 69, no. 1 (March 1973), 30–33 et passim; Gerlach also describes curriculum and daily schedule; see annual reports of Bureau of Catholic Indian Missions for financial woes of schools.

72. *Report of the Director of the Bureau of Catholic-Indian Missions for 1910,* p. 16, and Alvin M. Josephy, Jr., *The Indian Heritage of America* (New York: A. A. Knopf, 1968), p. 51.

73. Valentine, *The North American Foundations: Letters of Mother M. Theresa Gerhardinger,* p. 75; for curriculum see Kuznicki, "An Ethnic School . . . ," p. 448; Mulkerins, *Holy Family Parish,* p. 434; and John O'Kane Murray, *A Popular History of the Catholic Church in the United States* (New York: Sadlier, 1876), p. 430.

74. James A. Burns, C.S.C., *The Principles, Origin and Establishment of the Catholic School System in the United States* (New York: Benziger Brothers, 1912), p. 27.

75. *Sixth Annual Report . . . of Philadelphia,* p. 7; John E. O'Breza, "Philadelphia Parochial School System from 1830–1920: Growth and Bureaucratization" (unpublished Ph.D. dissertation, Temple University, 1979), pp. 39–40; Ellen Marie Kuznicki, C.SS.F., "The Polish American Parochial Schools," in Mocha (ed.), *Poles in America,* p. 447; Mary J. Oates, "Learning to Teach: The Professional Preparation of Massachusetts Parochial School Faculty, 1870–1940," Charles and Margaret Hall Cushwa Center, University of Notre Dame, Working Paper Series 10, no. 2 (Fall 1981), pp. 32–33.

76. Oates, "Learning to Teach," p. 19; Burns, *The Growth and Development . . . ,* pp. 210–16.

77. Burns, *The Growth and Development,* p. 212.

78. Ibid.

79. Oates, "Learning to Teach," p. 8.

80. Ibid.

81. Quoted in M. Jane Coogan, B.V.M., *The Price of Our Heritage* (Dubuque: Mount Carmel Press, 1978), II, p. 426; see also Sister Maria Concepta, C.S.C., *The Making of a Sister-Teacher* (Notre Dame: University of Notre Dame Press, 1965).

82. Sanders, *The Education of an Urban Minority,* p. 61; Kuznicki, "An Ethnic School . . . ," p. 94.

83. Briggs, *An Italian Passage*, pp. 191 ff., for a discussion of parish school finances; Michael J. McNally, "A Peculiar Institution: Roman Catholic Parish Life in the South Atlantic Region 1850–1980" (unpublished manuscript), p. 70, states, ". . . it was not unusual for the school to take from one-third to one-half of the parish budget from 1850 to 1960."

84. See Mary J. Oates, "Organized Voluntarism: The Catholic Sisters in Massachusetts, 1870–1940," in Janet Wilson James (ed.), *Women in American Religion* (Philadelphia: University of Pennsylvania Press, 1980), pp. 154–60; David B. Tyack, *The One Best System* (Cambridge: Harvard University Press, 1974), p. 62; Coogan, *The Price of Our Heritage*, II, p. 358; Mary J. Oates, "Management and Control in Communities of Religious Women in America: 1840–1940" (unpublished paper), p. 17; Mary J. Oates, "Circles of Usefulness: Occupational Choices and Work Organization in Catholic Sisterhoods 1850–1940," paper presented at Organization of American Historians Annual Meeting, April 1983, p. 13 and Table III.

85. Oates, "Circles of Usefulness," p. 13 and Table III; Coogan, *The Price of Our Heritage*, II, p. 359.

86. Ewens, *The Role of the Nun in Nineteenth Century America*, pp. 284–87, for a general discussion of this; Oates, "Circles of Usefulness," pp. 1–12, discusses Cardinal O'Connell's relationship with the sisters in the Boston Archdiocese; Florence Wolff, S.L., *From Generation to Generation* (Louisville: F. Wolff, 1982) discusses the terrible grief Bishop William G. McCloskey caused the Sisters of Loretto in Kentucky.

87. Euper, *First Century of Service*, p. 25.

88. Ibid., pp. 25–26.

89. See Tyack, *The One Best System*, for a discussion of these developments.

90. See O'Breza, "Philadelphia Parochial School System . . . ," and Thomas J. Donaghy, F.S.C., *Philadelphia's Finest: A History of Education in the Catholic Archdiocese 1692–1970*.

91. Montgomery, *The American Girl in the Stockyards District*, pp. 8–10.

92. *Report of the Reverend Superintendents of the New York Archdiocesan Schools, February 1905–July 1906* (New York: New York Catholic School Board, 1906), p. 7.

93. *Catholic Mirror*, Aug. 26, 1899.

94. Sanders, *The Education of an Urban Minority*, p. 166; O'Breza, "Philadelphia Parochial School System . . . ," p. 165; see also "Report of the Committee on High Schools," *Catholic Educational Association Bulletin*, Vol. 8 (Nov. 1911), 45–73, and "The Condition of Catholic Secondary Education in the United States," *Catholic Educational Association Bulletin*, Vol. 12 (Nov. 1915), 377–440, for extensive reports on Catholic high schools. These bulletins, like the annual diocesan school reports, are a valuable source of information.

95. "Report on the Attendance at Catholic Colleges and Universities in the United States," *Catholic Educational Association Bulletin*, Vol. 12 (August 1916), 1–17; also Philip Gleason, "Confronting the 20th Century: the Reorganization of Catholic Higher Education: 1900–1925" (unpublished paper), p. 5.

96. Gleason, "Confronting the 20th Century," p. 8.

97. Power, *A History of Catholic Higher Education* . . . , pp. 192–94.

NOTES TO CHAPTER XI

1. See Chinnici, "American Catholics and Religious Pluralism."

2. See "Native Americanism," *Brownson Quarterly Review*, Third Series, II (July 1854), 328–54; this entire discussion on American identity draws substantially from the essay by Philip Gleason, "American Identity and Americanization," in *Harvard Encyclopedia of American Ethnic Groups*, pp. 31–58.

3. "Native Americanism," pp. 336–37.

4. "Conversations of Our Club," *Brownson Quarterly Review*, III (April 1858), 190; also Philip Gleason, "Coming to Terms with American Catholic History," *Societas*, Vol. 3, no. 4 (Autumn 1973), 284–90.

5. Arthur M. Schlesinger, Jr., *Orestes A. Brownson: A Pilgrim's Progress* (Boston: Little, Brown, 1939), p. 215.

6. Ibid., pp. 215–16; for more on this, see Isaac McDaniel, O.S.B., "Orestes A. Brownson on Irish Immigrants and American Nativism," *The American Benedictine Review*, Vol. 32, no. 2 (June 1981), 122–39.

7. Barry, *The Catholic Church and German Americans*, p. 30; this book is the standard history of the German episode.

8. Ibid., pp. 312–13.

9. Ibid., p. 163, for this quote of James Cardinal Gibbons.

10. Ibid., p. 155; and Tomasi, *Piety and Power*, p. 89.

11. See Anthony J. Kuzniewski, *Faith and Fatherland: The Polish Church War in Wisconsin, 1896–1918* (Notre Dame, Ind.: University of Notre Dame Press, 1980).

12. Quoted in Edward R. Kantowicz, *Corporation Sole: Cardinal Mundelein and Chicago Catholicism* (Notre Dame, Ind.: University of Notre Dame Press, 1983), p. 25.

13. See John Joseph Parot, *Polish Catholics in Chicago*, for an account of these quarrels.

14. Shanabruch, *Chicago's Catholics*, pp. 217 ff., for a discussion of this episode.

15. Ibid., pp. 222–23; and Gerald P. Fogarty, *The Vatican and the American Hierarchy from 1870 to 1965* (Stuttgart: Anton Hiersemann, 1982), pp. 211–13.

16. Quoted in Gleason, "Coming to Terms with American Catholic History," pp. 291–92.

17. James Hitchcock, "Secular Clergy in Nineteenth Century America: A Diocesan Profile," *Records of the American Catholic Historical Society of Philadelphia*, Vol. 88 (Mar.–Dec. 1977), 58.

18. For Polish, see Kuzniewski, "The Catholic Church in the Life of the Polish Americans," p. 408; for Irish, see Richard A. Schoenherr, "Ethnicity and Status Attainment: The Case of the Roman Catholic Clergy" (unpublished paper).

19. Quoted in Kuzniewski, "The Catholic Church in the Life of the Polish Americans," p. 408.

20. Avery Dulles, S.J., *Models of the Church* (Garden City, N.Y.: Doubleday, 1974), pp. 31 and 46–47.

21. Richard McBrien, *Catholicism* (Minneapolis: Winston Press, 1980), II, p. 609; a good discussion of this is William L. Portier, "Isaac Hecker and Testem Benevolentiae: A Study in Theological Pluralism," in John Farina (ed.), *Hecker Studies: Essays on the Thought of Isaac Hecker* (New York: Paulist Press, 1983), pp. 11–48; also Bernard J. F. Lonergan, S.J., "The Transition from a Classicist World-View to Historical Mindedness," in William F. J. Ryan, S.J., and Bernard J. Tyrell, S.J. (eds.), *A Second Collection* (Philadelphia: Westminster Press, 1975), pp. 1–10.

22. See William R. Hutchison, *The Modernist Impulse in American Protestantism* (Cambridge: Harvard University Press, 1976).

23. See Mark Schoof, O.P., *A Survey of Catholic Theology 1800–1970* (New York: Paulist Newman Press, 1970); also Thomas F. O'Meara, *Romantic Idealism and Roman Catholicism: Schelling and the Theologians* (Notre Dame, Ind.: University of Notre Dame, 1982).

24. See Chinnici, "American Catholics and Religious Pluralism"; and Chapter 4 above.

25. *United States Catholic Miscellany*, Jan. 27, 1827, quoted in Patrick Carey, *An Immigrant Bishop: John England's Adaptation of Irish Catholicism to American Republicanism* (Yonkers, N.Y.: United States Catholic Historical Society, 1982), p. 88.

26. Ibid., pp. 133–34.

27. Dennis J. Dease, "The Theological Influence of Orestes Brownson and Isaac Hecker on John Ireland's Americanist Ecclesiology" (unpublished Ph.D. dissertation, Catholic University of America, 1978), p. 56.

28. Ibid., pp. 88–89.

29. Ibid., pp. 260 and 160–69.

30. Quoted in ibid., p. 265.

31. Ibid., pp. 56–61 et passim.

32. Hecker, *The Church and the Age*, p. 136.

33. Quoted in Dease, "The Theological Influence . . . ," p. 283.

34. See Portier, "Isaac Hecker and Testem Benevolentiae"; in his later years, Brownson became very pessimistic about the possibility of achieving a harmony between church and society.

35. Ireland, *The Church and Modern Society*, I, p. 115.

36. Ibid., p. 107.

37. Dease, "The Theological Influence . . . ," p. 63.

38. Ireland, *The Church and Modern Society*, I, pp. 115, 99, and 90.

39. Ibid., pp. 28 and 73; Dease, "The Theological Influence . . . ," p. 215.

40. Gerald P. Fogarty, S.J., *The Vatican and the Americanist Crisis: Denis J. O'Connell, American Agent in Rome 1885–1903* (Rome: Università Gregoriana, 1974); and Margaret Mary Reher, "The Church and the Kingdom of God in America: The Ecclesiology of the Americanists" (unpublished Ph.D. dissertation, Fordham University, 1972), pp. 139–71.

41. Reher, "The Church and the Kingdom . . . ," pp. 78–79.

42. David P. Killen, "Americanism Revisited: John Spalding and *Testem Benevolentiae*," *Harvard Theological Review*, Vol. 66 (1973), 413.

43. Quoted in ibid., p. 435, fn. 63, and p. 452.

44. See Hutchison, *The Modernist Impulse* . . . , pp. 2–3.

45. Dease, "The Theological Influence . . . ," p. 220.

46. Thomas S. Preston, "American Catholicity," *American Catholic Quarterly Review*, Vol. 16, no. 62 (April 1891), 397.

47. See Robert D. Cross, *The Emergence of Liberal Catholicism in America* (Cambridge, Mass.: Harvard University Press, 1958), for an analysis of the liberal-conservative position; also Curran, *Michael Augustine Corrigan and the Shaping of Conservative Catholicism in America.*

48. Quoted in Frederick J. Zwierlein, *The Life and Letters of Bishop McQuaid* (Rochester: Art Print Shop, 1927), III, p. 224.

49. Robert F. McNamara, "Bernard J. McQuaid's Sermon on Theological 'Americanism,'" *Records of the American Catholic Historical Society of Philadelphia*, Vol. 90 (Mar.–Dec. 1979), 29.

50. Zwierlein, *The Life and Letters of Bishop McQuaid*, II, pp. 378–474, for a detailed account of the issue of secret societies.

51. Preston, "American Catholicity," p. 398.

52. Quoted in Zwierlein, *The Life and Letters of Bishop McQuaid*, III, p. 234.

53. Preston, "American Catholicity," p. 408.

54. McNamara, "Bernard J. McQuaid's Sermon . . . ," p. 27.

55. W. Elliott, *Le Père Hecker* (Paris: V. Lecoffre, 1897), p. xxiv.

56. Charles Maignen, *Father Hecker, Is He a Saint?* (London: Burns & Oates, 1898), pp. xvii and 181.

57. Thomas T. McAvoy, *The Great Crisis in American Catholic History 1895–1900* (Chicago: H. Regnery, 1957), p. 380; this is a thorough study of the Americanist episode and includes the letter in an appendix.

58. Ibid., p. 390.

59. Roger Aubert et al., *The Church in the Industrial Age*, Vol. 9 of Hubert Jedin and John Dolan (eds.), *History of the Church* (New York: Seabury, 1981), p. 384.

60. Roger Aubert et al., *The Church in a Secularised Society*, Vol. 5 of Louis J. Rogier et al. (ed.), *The Christian Centuries* (New York: Paulist Press, 1978), p. 191.

61. See Scott Appleby, "American Catholic Modernism: Dunwoodie and *The New York Review*," Charles and Margaret Hall Cushwa Center, University of Notre Dame, Working Paper Series 14, no. 3, Fall 1983.

62. Aubert, *The Church in a Secularised Society,* p. 187.

63. J. A. Zahm, *Evolution and Dogma* (Chicago: D. H. McBride, 1896), p. 279.

64. Michael J. DeVito, *The New York Review 1905–1908* (New York: United States Catholic Historical Society, 1977), p. 16.

65. See Aubert, *The Church in a Secularised Society,* pp. 186–203.

66. Michael V. Gannon, "Before and After Modernism: The Intellectual Isolation of the American Priest," in John Tracy Ellis (ed.), *The Catholic Priest in the United States: Historical Investigations* (Collegeville, Minn.: St. John's University Press, 1971), p. 341.

NOTES TO CHAPTER XII

1. Quoted in Henry Nash Smith (ed.), *Popular Culture and Industrialism 1865–1890* (New York: New York University Press, 1967), pp. 70–71.

2. Sigmund Diamond (ed.), *The Nation Transformed* (New York: G. Braziller, 1963), p. 18.

3. Dolan, *The Immigrant Church,* p. 49.

4. Ibid., pp. 32–33.

5. Quoted in ibid., p. 127.

6. See Timothy Walch, "Catholic Social Institutions and Urban Development: The View from Nineteenth Century Chicago and Milwaukee," *Catholic Historical Review,* Vol. 64, no. 1 (Jan. 1978), 16–32.

7. See *U.S. Catholic Directory 1881;* John O'Grady, *Catholic Charities in the United States* (Washington, D.C.: National Conference of Catholic Charities, 1930), pp. 186–87; Dolan, *The Immigrant Church,* p. 131.

8. See David J. Rothman, *The Discovery of the Asylum* (Boston: Little, Brown, 1971).

9. See Walch, "Catholic Social Institutions . . ."; Lord et al., *History of the Archdiocese of Boston,* III, pp. 69–74.

10. Quoted in Dolan, *The Immigrant Church,* pp. 122 and 124.

11. Quoted in ibid., p. 124.

12. Quoted in ibid.; see also James E. Roohan, *American Catholics and the Social Question 1865–1900* (New York: Arno Press, 1976), pp. 73–118.

13. Quoted in Aaron I. Abell, *American Catholicism and Social Action* (Notre Dame, Ind.: University of Notre Dame Press, 1960), p. 29.

14. Joseph G. Rayback, *A History of American Labor* (New York: Free Press, 1966), pp. 129, 130, and 133.

15. Ibid., p. 136.

16. Hugh Davis Graham and Ted Robert Gurr (eds.), *Violence in America* (New York: Bantam Books, 1969), p. 281.

17. Abell, *American Catholicism and Social Action,* p. 123; Daniel T. McColgan, *A Century of Charity* (Milwaukee: Bruce, 1951), II, pp. 532–33.

18. O'Grady, *Catholic Charities . . . ,* pp. 195–96; Christopher J. Kauffman, *The Ministry of Healing,* Vol. Two; *The History of the Alexian Brothers from 1789 to the Present* (New York: Seabury Press, 1978); *U.S. Catholic Directory 1911.*

19. Abell, *American Catholicism and Social Action,* pp. 125 and 160–61; O'Grady, *Catholic Charities . . . ,* pp. 216 ff.

20. Quoted in Shanabruch, *Chicago's Catholics,* p. 130.

21. *U.S. Catholic Directory 1901,* pp. 90–93.

22. Quoted in Ede, "The Lay Crusade for a Christian America," p. 241.

23. O'Grady, *Catholic Charities . . . ,* p. 324.

24. Shanabruch, *Chicago's Catholics,* p. 132; Biggs, "What We Are Doing in Settlement Work," 237–45, for list of settlements.

25. Burchell, *San Francisco Irish,* pp. 148–54; Alan Dawley, *Class and Community: The Industrial Revolution in Lynn* (Cambridge: Harvard University Press, 1976), pp. 143 ff.

26. Quoted in Thomas R. Brooks, *Toil and Trouble* (New York: Delacorte Press, 1964), p. 59.

27. Henry J. Browne, *The Catholic Church and the Knights of Labor* (Washington, D.C.: Catholic University of America Press, 1949), p. 190.

28. Leon Fink, *Workingmen's Democracy: The Knights of Labor and American Politics* (Urbana, Ill.: University of Illinois Press, 1983), pp. 76–79; Browne, *The Catholic Church and the Knights of Labor*, pp. 158–59.

29. Susan Levine, "Labor's True Woman: Domesticity and Equal Rights in the Knights of Labor," *Journal of American History*, Vol. 70, no. 2 (Sept. 1983), 331–39; Hasia R. Diner, *Erin's Daughters in America* (Baltimore: Johns Hopkins University Press, 1983), pp. 100–2.

30. Quoted in Eric Foner, "Class, Ethnicity, and Radicalism in the Gilded Age: The Land League and Irish-America," *Marxist Perspectives*, Vol. 1, no. 2 (Summer 1978), 26.

31. Ibid., p. 15.

32. Ibid., pp. 25–26.

33. Abell, *American Catholicism and Social Action;* Roohan, *American Catholics and the Social Question;* and Browne, *The Catholic Church and the Knights of Labor,* treat this issue; Cardinal Gibbons stated that seventy of seventy-five American bishops supported the Knights of Labor; see memorial on Knights of Labor in Browne, *The Catholic Church and the Knights of Labor,* p. 377.

34. Browne, *The Catholic Church and the Knights of Labor,* pp. 368, 375, and 376.

35. Ibid., p. 324.

36. David Montgomery, "The Irish and the American Labor Movement," in David Noel Doyle and Owen Dudley Edwards (eds.), *America and Ireland 1776–1976* (Westport, Conn.: Greenwood Press, 1980), p. 206.

37. Dominic A. Pacyga, "Villages of Packinghouses and Steel Mills: The Polish Worker on Chicago's South Side 1880 to 1921" (unpublished Ph.D. dissertation, University of Illinois at Chicago Circle, 1981), p. 238; Victor R. Greene, *The Slavic Community on Strike* (Notre Dame, Ind.: University of Notre Dame Press, 1968); and Matt S. Meier and Feliciano Rivera, *The Chicanos* (New York: Hill & Wang, 1972).

38. Roohan, *American Catholics and the Social Question,* pp. 431 ff.; Abell, *American Catholicism and Social Action,* pp. 54 ff.; Shanabruch, *Chicago's Catholics,* pp. 139–54.

39. Alec R. Vidler, *A Century of Social Catholicism* (London, 1964), p. 127; see also Aubert et al., *The Church in a Secularised Society,* pp. 150–51.

40. Quoted in Abell, *American Catholicism and Social Action,* p. 77; see Shanabruch, *Chicago's Catholics,* pp. 141–45.

41. Abell, *American Catholicism and Social Action,* pp. 103–5 and 109–19.

42. Mel Piehl, *Breaking Bread: The Catholic Worker and the Origin of Catholic Radicalism* (Philadelphia: Temple University Press, 1982), p. 34.

43. Aaron I. Abell, "The Reception of Leo XIII's Labor Encyclical in America, 1891–1919," *Review of Politics,* Vol. 7, no. 4 (Oct. 1945), p. 481; and also Joseph M. McShane, S.J., "The Bishops' Program of Social Reconstruction of 1919: A Study in American Catholic Progressivism" (unpublished Ph.D. dissertation, University of Chicago, 1981), p. 51.

44. Abell, *American Catholicism and Social Action,* pp. 137 ff.; and Ede, "The Lay Crusade for a Christian America," pp. 272 ff.

45. Quoted in Robert E. Doherty, "Thomas J. Hagerty, The Church, and Socialism," *Labor History,* Vol. 3, no. 1 (Winter 1962), pp. 45–46.

46. Philip Gleason, *The Conservative Reformers* (Notre Dame, Ind.: University of Notre Dame Press, 1968), pp. 125–26 and 74–76.

47. Quoted in Doherty, "Thomas J. Hagerty . . . ," p. 47.

48. Ibid., p. 48; and Abell, *American Catholics and Social Action,* pp. 143–45.

49. Fink, *Workingmen's Democracy,* pp. 204–11.

50. Paul Stroh, "The Catholic Clergy and American Labor Disputes 1900–37" (unpublished Ph.D. dissertation, Catholic University of America, 1939), pp. 37–54.

51. Shanabruch, *Chicago's Catholics*, pp. 150–51.

52. Stroh, "The Catholic Clergy and American Labor Disputes," pp. 106–9.

53. Ibid., pp. 37–54; and Shanabruch, *Chicago's Catholics*, p. 146.

54. Bernard C. Cronin, *Father Yorke and the Labor Movement in San Francisco 1900–1910* (Washington, D.C.: Catholic University of America Press, 1943), pp. 59 and 65; also Joseph S. Brusher, S.J., *Consecrated Thunderbolt: Father Yorke of San Francisco* (Hawthorne, N.J.: Wagner, 1973), pp. 57–69.

55. Cronin, *Father Yorke*, pp. 55–56 et passim.

56. Ibid., p. 221, and also Brusher, *Consecrated Thunderbolt*, p. 59 et passim, for Yorke's subsequent career.

57. See Donald P. Gavin, *The National Conference of Catholic Charities 1910–1960* (Milwaukee: Catholic Life Publications, 1962); O'Grady, *Catholic Charities . . . ,* pp. 425 ff.

58. Robert Biggs, "The Trained Worker," *Proceedings of the National Conference of Catholic Charities, 1912*, p. 104; my thanks to Dan McLellan for this reference.

59. Ede, "The Lay Crusade for a Christian America," p. 76.

60. Ibid., pp. 290–91 and 372.

61. Gleason, *The Conservative Reformers*, p. 102.

62. Ede, "The Lay Crusade for a Christian America," pp. 294–95; and Mary Harrita Fox, *Peter E. Dietz, Labor Priest* (Notre Dame, Ind.: University of Notre Dame Press, 1953), pp. 95–96.

63. John A. Ryan, *Social Doctrine in Action* (New York: Harper & Brothers, 1941), p. 8.

64. John A. Ryan, *A Living Wage: Its Ethical and Economic Aspects* (New York: Macmillan, 1906), p. viii.

65. Francis L. Broderick, *Right Reverend New Dealer John A. Ryan* (New York: Macmillan, 1963), p. 85.

66. Ibid., p. 92; see also Charles E. Curran, *American Catholic Social Ethics* (Notre Dame, Ind.: University of Notre Dame Press, 1982), pp. 26–91.

67. For an excellent discussion of Ryan and American reform thought, see McShane, "The Bishops' Program of Social Reconstruction," pp. 65–134.

68. Ryan, *Social Doctrine in Action*, p. 145; and McShane, "The Bishops' Program of Social Reconstruction," p. 294.

69. Broderick, *Right Reverend New Dealer John A. Ryan*, p. 105.

70. "The Bishops' Program of Social Reconstruction," in Aaron I. Abell (ed.), *American Catholic Thought on Social Questions* (New York: Bobbs-Merrill, 1968), p. 327.

71. See McShane, "The Bishops' Program of Social Reconstruction," pp. 336–408, for a discussion of the promotion and reception of the statement.

72. Ryan, *Social Doctrine in Action*, p. 149.

NOTES TO CHAPTER XIII

1. *The Eucharistic Congress as Reported in the Chicago Tribune* (Chicago: Chicago Tribune, 1926), p. 10.

2. Ibid., p. 28.

3. Connelly (ed.), *The History of the Archdiocese of Philadelphia*, p. 380.

4. James Hennesey, S.J., *American Catholics* (New York: Oxford University Press, 1981), p. 258; Thomas Wangler, "Toward a Religious History of American Catholicism—The Boston Experience, 1900–50" (unpublished paper), p. 36.

5. See *U.S. Catholic Directory* for 1920 and for 1960; Louisiana data were compiled by Charles Nolan, archivist for the archdiocese of New Orleans.

6. Jeffrey Burns, "The Catholic Parish in the Pacific States" (unpublished manuscript), p. 6.

7. Quoted in Philip Gleason, "In Search of Unity: American Catholic Thought, 1920–1960," *Catholic Historical Review*, Vol. 65, no. 2 (April 1979), 198; see also William M. Halsey, *The Survival of American Innocence* (Notre Dame, Ind.: University of Notre Dame Press, 1980), p. 14.

8. Sally Fitzgerald (ed.), *Letters of Flannery O'Connor* (New York: Farrar, Straus & Giroux, 1979), p. 131; Halsey's study *The Survival of American Innocence* examines one aspect of this Catholic confidence.

9. Quoted in Elizabeth McKeown, "War and Welfare: A Study of American Catholic Leadership" (unpublished Ph.D. dissertation, University of Chicago, 1972), p. 227.

10. See M. Edmund Hussey, "The 1878 Financial Failure of Archbishop Purcell," *The Cincinnati Historical Society Bulletin*, Vol. 36, no. 1 (Spring 1978); the report of Bishop George Conroy of Ireland, who visited the United States in 1878 as an official Vatican investigator, was very critical of the financial fixation of many bishops and described it as one of the more serious problems in the church, "Relazio sullo stato della Chiesa Cattolica negli Stati Uniti d'America," in *The Acta of the General and Particular Congregations of the Sacred Congregation "de Propaganda Fide,"* 1883, p. 2, v. 252, f. 1132r–1138v. My thanks to Robert Wister for providing me with a copy of this report.

11. For Mundelein, see Kantowicz, *Corporation Sole;* for Spellman, see Robert I. Gannon, S.J., *The Cardinal Spellman Story* (Garden City, N.Y.: Doubleday, 1962), and James Gollin, *Worldly Goods* (New York: Random House, 1971).

12. Quoted in Michael J. T. McNally, "Cross in the Sun: The Growth and Development of Catholicism in South Florida 1868–1968" (unpublished Ph.D. dissertation, University of Notre Dame, 1982) p. 134.

13. Richard M. Linkh, *American Catholicism and European Immigrants* (New York: Center for Migration Studies, 1975), pp. 167–81; Thomas J. Archdeacon, *Becoming American: An Ethnic History* (New York: Free Press, 1983), pp. 173–74; Will Herberg, *Protestant-Catholic-Jew* (Garden City, N.Y.: Anchor Books, 1955), p. 160; Dolan, *Catholic Revivalism*, p. 26.

14. Kenneth Wilson Underwood, *Protestant and Catholic* (Boston: Beacon Press, 1957), pp. 192–93, 400–2; John Bodnar, *Immigration and Industrialization* (Pittsburgh: University of Pittsburgh Press, 1977), pp. 132–38; Barton, *Peasants and Strangers*, pp. 91–116; Thernstrom, *The Other Bostonians*, pp. 145–59; Herbert Wallace Schneider, *Religion in 20th Century America* (Cambridge, Mass.: Harvard University Press, 1952), pp. 261–65.

15. Andrew M. Greeley and Peter H. Rossi, *The Education of Catholic Americans* (Chicago: Aldine Publishing, 1966), p. 29; also Thernstrom, *The Other Bostonians*, p. 51.

16. Connelly (ed.), *The History of the Archdiocese of Philadelphia*, pp. 362 and 372.

17. Kantowicz, *Corporation Sole*, pp. 41 and 81.

18. Gilbert Osofsky, *Harlem: The Making of a Ghetto* (New York: Harper & Row, 1963), pp. 71 and 123.

19. Ibid., pp. 128 and 130.

20. Population data on blacks is in Bayrd Still, *Urban America: A History with Documents* (Boston: Little, Brown, 1974), pp. 406–7.

21. John T. Gillard, S.S.J., *The Catholic Church and the American Negro* (Baltimore: St. Joseph's Society Press, 1929), pp. 47–66.

22. Archives of the archdiocese of San Francisco, Minutes of the Annual Meeting of the Archbishops of the United States, 1904.

23. Gillard, *The Catholic Church and the American Negro*, p. 86.

24. Ibid., pp. 163–65.

25. See Dolores Egger Labbé, *Jim Crow Comes to Church* (New York: Arno Press, 1978).

26. See Thernstrom (ed.), *Harvard Encyclopedia of American Ethnic Groups*, p. 702; Leo Grebler, Joan W. Moore, and Ralph C. Guzman, *The Mexican-American People* (New York: Free Press, 1970), pp. 605–6.

27. Grebler et al., *The Mexican-American People*, p. 193; Louise Año Nuevo Kerr, "Mexican Chicago: Chicano Assimilation Aborted, 1939–1952," in Melvin G. Holli and Peter d'A. Jones (eds.), *The Ethnic Frontier* (Grand Rapids, Mich.: Wm. B. Eerdmans, 1977), p. 312.

28. Thernstrom (ed.), *Harvard Encyclopedia of American Ethnic Groups*, p. 860.

29. Joseph P. Fitzpatrick, *Puerto Rican Americans* (Englewood Cliffs, N.J.: Prentice-Hall, 1971), p. 59.

30. Lord et al., *History of the Archdiocese of Boston*, III, 725 ff.; Kantowicz, *Corporation Sole*, p. 82; Archdeacon, *Becoming American*, pp. 185–86; Harold J. Abramson, *Ethnic Diversity in Catholic America* (New York: Wiley, 1973), pp. 26–27.

31. Underwood, *Protestant and Catholic*, p. 207.

32. Stanislas Blejwas, "A Polish Community in Transition: The Evolution of Holy Cross Parish New Britain, Connecticut," *Polish American Studies*, Vol. 35, nos. 1–2 (Spring–Autumn 1978), 23 ff.

33. Stephen Shaw, "A History of the Catholic Parish in the Midwest" (unpublished manuscript), p. 78; Linkh, *American Catholicism . . .*, p. 148.

34. Quoted in Richard S. Sorrell, "The Sentinelle Affair . . . ," p. 67.

35. See Gillard, *The Catholic Church and the American Negro*, pp. 67–78, and Labbé, *Jim Crow Comes to Church*.

36. Philip Murphy, "The Greenwich Village Mission" (unpublished seminar paper), Columbia University, 1968, relates the Harlem story.

37. Quoted in Gannon, *The Cardinal Spellman Story*, p. 269.

38. William A. Osborne, *The Segregated Covenant* (New York: Herder & Herder, 1967), pp. 169–70.

39. Donald J. Kemper, "Catholic Integration in St. Louis 1935–1947," *Missouri Historical Review*, Vol. 73, no. 1 (October 1978), 5.

40. Marilyn W. Nickels, "The Federated Colored Catholics: A Study of Three Variant Perspectives on Racial Justice as Represented by John La Farge, William Markoe, and Thomas Turner" (unpublished Ph.D. dissertation, Catholic University of America, 1975), p. 303.

41. Quoted in Osborne, *The Segregated Covenant*, p. 36; Kemper, "Catholic Integration in St. Louis," pp. 8–9.

42. See William A. Osborne, "The Race Problem in the Catholic Church in the United States" (unpublished Ph.D. dissertation, Columbia University, 1953), pp. 164–74.

43. P. David Finks, *The Radical Vision of Saul Alinsky* (New York: Paulist Press, 1984), pp. vii and 160.

44. Felician A. Foy, O.F.M. (ed.), *The 1960 National Catholic Almanac* (Paterson, N.J.: St. Anthony's Guild, 1960), pp. 473–74; Richard A. Lamanna and Jay J. Coakley, "The Catholic Church and the Negro," in Philip Gleason (ed.), *Contemporary Catholicism in the United States* (Notre Dame, Ind.: University of Notre Dame Press, 1969), p. 171.

45. Rev. Rollins E. Lambert, "The Negro and the Catholic Church," in Thomas T. McAvoy, C.S.C. (ed.), *Roman Catholicism and the American Way of Life* (Notre Dame, Ind.: University of Notre Dame Press, 1960), p. 163.

46. Quoted in Manuel Gamio, *The Life Story of the Mexican Immigrant* (New York: Dover Publications, 1971), p. 116.

47. Richard Griswold del Castillo, *The Los Angeles Barrio 1850–1890* (Berkeley: University of California Press, 1979), p. 169.

48. William Schaeferes, "The Parish Priest and Mexican Settlements," *The Ecclesiastical Review*, 7th Series, Vol. 63, no. 4 (Oct. 1920), p. 392.

49. David H. Garcia, "The Chicano and the Catholic Church—a Struggle of Faith" (unpublished paper), p. 6.

50. See Antonio M. Stevens Arroyo (ed.), *Prophets Denied Honor* (Maryknoll, N.Y.: Orbis

Books, 1980), pp. 161–62; Antonio R. Soto, "The Church in California and the Chicano: A Sociological Analysis," *Grito Del Sol*, 1979, p. 56.

51. Ricardo Romo, *East Los Angeles* (Austin: University of Texas Press, 1983), p. 80; Samuel Ortegon, *The Religious Status of the Mexican Population of Los Angeles* (San Francisco: Rand E Research Associates, 1972); reprint of 1932 thesis at University of Southern California), p. 50.

52. Ortegon, *The Religious Status . . . ,* pp. 10–13, 45–48; *U.S. Catholic Directory* for 1920 and 1930.

53. Quoted in Burns, "The Catholic Parish in the Pacific States," p. 55.

54. O'Grady, *Catholic Charities . . . ,* pp. 293–94; see also Linna E. Bressette, *Mexicans in the United States* (Washington, D.C.: National Catholic Welfare Conference, 1929), a report sponsored by the NCWC and a valuable overview of the Mexican population and church work among them.

55. *First Annual Report of the Bureau of Catholic Charities,* 1919, p. 11, quoted in Patrick H. McNamara, "Catholicism, Assimilation and the Chicano Movement: Los Angeles as a Case Study," in Rudolph O. de la Garza and Z. Anthony Kruszewski (eds.), *Chicanos and Native Americans* (Englewood Cliffs, N.J.: Prentice-Hall, 1973), p. 125.

56. Grebler et al., *The Mexican-American People,* pp. 459–60.

57. Quoted in Shanabruch, *Chicago's Catholics,* p. 211; see also Harry C. Koenig, *A History of the Parishes of the Archdiocese of Chicago* (Chicago: Archdiocese of Chicago, 1980), I, pp. 282–87, 691–95.

58. Quoted in Saul E. Bronder, *Social Justice and Church Authority* (Philadelphia: Temple University Press, 1982), pp. 63–64.

59. Carlos E. Castaneda, *The Church in Texas Since Independence 1836–1950,* Vol. VII of *Our Catholic Heritage in Texas* (Austin: Von Boeckmann-Jones, 1958), pp. 181–96.

60. Ibid., p. 204.

61. *Commemorating the Golden Jubilee Anniversary of Sacred Heart Church 1906–1956* (n.p., n.d.), pp. 32 ff.

62. Bronder, *Social Justice,* p. 63.

63. See *Church of the Immaculate Heart of Mary: A Prospectus Containing the Activities Religious Educational and Social of the Parish,* 1926.

64. See Robert J. Torrez, *El Primer Siglo: A Centennial History of San José Parish, Los Ojos, New Mexico, 1883–1983.* (Los Ojos: San José Parish Council, 1983).

65. Margaret Campbell, "Organization of Religious and Social Groups Among Our Mexicans," *Proceedings of National Catechetical Congress, 1939,* p. 359.

66. Elizabeth Ann Clifford, O.L.V.M., *The Story of Victory Noll* (Huntington, Ind.: Our Lady of Victory Missionary Sisters, 1981), p. 73; Bronder, *Social Justice,* pp. 87–99.

67. Bronder, *Social Justice,* p. 76.

68. Ibid., p. 83.

69. Grebler et al., *The Mexican-American People,* pp. 462–64; McNally, "Cross in the Sun," pp. 180–87.

70. Robert L. Stern, "Evolution of Hispanic Ministry in the New York Archdiocese," in *Hispanics in New York: Religious, Cultural, and Social Experiences* (New York: Office of Pastoral Research, 1982), II, pp. 297 and 310.

71. Ibid., p. 306.

72. See Foy, *National Catholic Almanac, 1960,* pp. 665–68, for detailed report on Spanish-speaking Catholics.

73. Richard Rodriguez, *Hunger of Memory* (New York: D. R. Godine, 1982), p. 80.

74. Ibid., p. 100.

75. J. G. Shaw, *Edwin Vincent O'Hara* (New York: Farrar, Straus & Cudahy, 1957), pp. 63–71.

76. Vincent A. Yzermans, *The People I Love: A Biography of Luigi G. Ligutti* (Collegeville,

Minn.: Liturgical Press, 1976), p. 59, for the slogan "work, prayer, and fertilizer"; Madeleine M. Schmidt, C.H.M., *Seasons of Growth: History of the Diocese of Davenport 1881–1981* (Davenport: The Diocese, 1981), p. 205.

77. See Yzermans, *The People I Love.*

78. See Joseph Casino, "The Catholic Parish in the Northeast" (unpublished manuscript), for data on parish schools and parish budgets.

79. Joseph H. Fichter, S.J., *Dynamics of a City Church* (Chicago: University of Chicago Press, 1951), pp. 198 ff.

NOTES TO CHAPTER XIV

1. John M. Huels, O.S.M., *The Popular Appeal of the Sorrowful Mother Novena* (Rome: Edizioni Marianum, 1976), p. 191.

2. Ibid., p. 194. See also John M. Huels, O.S.M., *The Friday Night Novena* (Berwyn, Ill.: Servite Press, 1977).

3. Steven Avella, "Let Us Pray for the Conversion of Russia: The Fatimazation of American Marian Piety 1945–54" (unpublished seminar paper), University of Notre Dame, 1982.

4. William Barnaby Faherty, S.J., *Dream by the River* (St. Louis: Piraeus, 1973), p. 177.

5. Burns, "The Catholic Parish in the Pacific States," p. 18.

6. Joseph Chinnici, O.F.M., "The Retreat Movement in the United States: Changing Structures of a Spiritual Vision, 1909–82" (unpublished paper).

7. See Fichter, *Dynamics of a City Church,* pp. 190 and 254; François Houtart, *Aspects Sociologiques du Catholicisme Americain* (Paris: Editions Ouvrières, 1957), pp. 300 ff.; George A. Kelly, *Catholics and the Practice of the Faith* (Washington, D.C.: Catholic University of America Press, 1946), p. 140, Table 25.

8. Fitzgerald, *Letters of Flannery O'Connor,* p. 139.

9. Ibid., p. 145.

10. Gabriel Adrianyi et al., *The Church in the Modern Age,* Vol. X of Hubert Jedin, Konrad Repgen, and John Dolan (eds.), *History of the Church* (New York: Seabury, 1981), p. 300.

11. See Paul B. Marx, O.S.B., *Virgil Michel and the Liturgical Movement* (Collegeville, Minn.: Liturgical Press, 1957); Noel H. Barrett, "The Contribution of Martin B. Hellriegel to the American Catholic Liturgical Movement" (unpublished Ph.D. dissertation, St. Louis University, 1976); John Leo Klein, S.J., "The Role of Gerald Ellard in the Development of the Contemporary American Catholic Liturgical Movement" (unpublished Ph.D. dissertation, Fordham University, 1971).

12. A brief summary of twentieth-century development in Catholic piety can be found in Adrianyi et al., *The Church in the Modern Age,* pp. 299–320.

13. See Lawrence A. Cremin, *Traditions of American Education* (New York: Basic Books, 1977), pp. 91–128.

14. Foy (ed.), *The National Catholic Almanac, 1960,* pp. 566–78.

15. Thomas T. McAvoy, C.S.C., *Father O'Hara of Notre Dame* (Notre Dame, Ind.: University of Notre Dame Press, 1967), p. 107.

16. Rev. Francis Broome, C.S.P., "The St. Lucy Catholic Trailer Chapel of Tennessee," in *Proceedings of the National Catechetical Congress of the Confraternity of Christian Doctrine,* 1939, p. 332.

17. Fichter, *Dynamics of a City Church,* p. 210.

18. Underwood, *Protestant and Catholic,* p. 80.

19. See Foy (ed.), *The National Catholic Almanac, 1960,* pp. 633–34; Wangler, "Toward a Religious History of American Catholicism," p. 38.

20. See *Democrat and Chronicle* (Rochester, N.Y.), Dec. 10, 1979, p. 1.

21. Foy (ed.), *The National Catholic Almanac, 1960,* pp. 476–78.

22. Adrianyi et al., *The Church in the Modern Age*, p. 664; Foy, (ed.), *The National Catholic Almanac, 1960*, p. 605.

23. Jeffrey M. Burns, "American Catholics and the Family Crisis, 1930–62; The Ideological and Organizational Response" (unpublished Ph.D. dissertation, University of Notre Dame, 1982), pp. 2–3.

24. Ibid., pp. 22 and 36.

25. Ibid., p. 228.

26. Ibid., p. 279.

27. Ibid., pp. 279–334.

28. Ibid., pp. 290–91.

29. Joseph H. Fichter, *Dynamics of a City Church* (New York: Arno Press, 1978), Preface to Arno Press reprint.

30. See Neil G. McCluskey, *Catholic Education Faces Its Future* (Garden City, N.Y.: Doubleday, 1968), p. 99.

31. Kuznicki, "The Polish American Parochial Schools," p. 446.

32. Oates, "Learning to Teach . . . ," p. 21; also Mary J. Oates, "The Professional Preparation of Parochial School Teachers 1870–1940," *Historical Journal of Massachusetts*, Vol. XII (January 1984), 64.

33. Sister Maria Concepta, C.S.C., *The Making of a Sister-Teacher* (Notre Dame, Ind.: University of Notre Dame Press, 1965), p. 229.

34. Foy (ed.), *The National Catholic Almanac, 1960*, p. 496.

35. James F. Whelan, S.J., *Catholic Colleges of the United States of America at the Middle of the Twentieth Century* (New Orleans: Loyola University, 1952), pp. 6–17; Sister Karen Kennelly, "The Dynamic Sister Antonia and the College of St. Catherine," *Ramsey County History*, Vol. 14, no. 1 (Fall–Winter 1978), 13 ff.

36. Whelan, *Catholic Colleges . . .*, pp. 6–17.

37. Thomas J. Schlereth, *The University of Notre Dame: A Portrait of Its History and Campus* (Notre Dame, Ind.: University of Notre Dame Press, 1976), p. 198.

38. *Time*, Feb. 9, 1962, p. 50.

39. Ibid., p. 48.

40. Thomas F. O'Dea, *American Catholic Dilemma* (New York: Sheed & Ward, 1958), p. 9.

41. Daniel Callahan, *The Mind of the Catholic Layman* (New York: Scribner's, 1963), pp. 99–100.

42. Broderick, *Right Reverend New Dealer . . .*, p. 242.

43. Ryan, *Social Doctrine in Action*, p. 154.

44. Thomas E. Blantz, C.S.C., *A Priest in Public Service: Francis J. Haas and the New Deal* (Notre Dame, Ind.: University of Notre Dame Press, 1982), p. 3.

45. Ibid., p. 290.

46. See Thomas W. Tifft, "Toward a More Humane Social Policy: The Work and Influence of Monsignor John O'Grady" (unpublished Ph.D. dissertation, Catholic University of America, 1979).

47. Quoted in Alan Brinkley, *Voices of Protest: Huey Long, Father Coughlin, and the Great Depression* (New York, 1982), p. 83; also David J. O'Brien, *American Catholics and Social Reform* (New York: Oxford University Press, 1968), pp. 150–81.

48. O'Brien, *American Catholics and Social Reform*, p. 173.

49. Ibid., pp. 179–80.

50. Abell, *American Catholicism and Social Action*, pp. 214–15.

51. Ibid., pp. 260 and 275; Ryan, *Social Doctrine in Action*, p. 156.

52. Mel Piehl, *Breaking Bread: The Catholic Worker and the Origin of Catholic Radicalism in America* (Philadelphia, 1982), p. 161.

53. Neil Betten, *Catholic Activism and the Industrial Worker* (Gainesville, Fla.: University Presses of Florida, 1976), pp. 77–78.

54. Ibid., p. 83.

55. O'Brien, *American Catholics and Social Reform*, p. 119.

56. Hugh J. Nolan (ed.), *Pastoral Letters of the American Hierarchy 1792–1970* (Huntington, Ind.: Our Sunday Visitor, 1971), p. 372.

57. Quoted in Marx, *Virgil Michel* . . . . , p. 210.

58. Dolores Elise Brien, "The Catholic Revival Revisited," *Commonweal*, Vol. 106, no. 23 (Dec. 21, 1979), 714.

59. Ann Harrigan Makletzoff, "Friendship House" (unpublished manuscript), p. 17.

60. Quoted in Piehl, *Breaking Bread*, p. 63.

61. Ibid., p. 131.

62. Michael Harrington, *Fragments of the Century* (New York: Saturday Review Press, 1972), p. 18; William D. Miller, *A Harsh and Dreadful Love* (New York, 1973), p. 174.

63. Quoted in Piehl, *Breaking Bread*, p. 150.

64. Harrington, *Fragments of the Century*, p. 19.

65. Ibid., p. 21; Piehl, *Breaking Bread*, pp. 145, 165, and 173.

66. Elizabeth L. Sharum, "A Strange Fire Burning: A History of the Friendship House Movement" (unpublished Ph.D. dissertation, Texas Tech University, 1977), pp. 125 and 614.

67. Makletzoff, "Friendship House," p. 54.

68. Ibid., p. 37.

69. Quoted in Alden V. Brown, "Women in the Lay Apostolate: The Grail Movement in the United States 1940–1962," Working Paper Series 15, no. 1 (Spring 1984), Charles and Margaret Hall Cushwa Center for the Study of American Catholicism, University of Notre Dame, p. 6.

70. Janet Kalven, et al., "The Grail in America, 1940–82" (unpublished manuscript), p. 4; my thanks to Pat Weber for sharing this brief essay with me.

71. Dennis M. Robb, "Specialized Catholic Action in the United States, 1936–49: Ideology, Leadership, and Organization" (unpublished Ph.D. dissertation, University of Minnesota, 1972), p. 73.

72. Saul Alinsky, "The Fights of Bishop Sheil," *The Catholic Digest*, Vol. 15, no. 10 (August 1951), p. 76.

73. An Oral History of American Catholics (Thomas More Association, Chicago, 1974) interview with Louis Putz; see also Robb, "Specialized Catholic Action . . . ," pp. 104 ff.

74. An excellent introduction to this new apostolate is the essays in Leo R. Ward, C.S.C., *The American Apostolate* (Westminster, Md.: Newman Press, 1952).

NOTES TO CHAPTER XV

1. Quoted in John Cogley, *Catholic America* (New York: Dial Press, 1973), p. 97.

2. Ibid., p. 98.

3. Quoted in Chudacoff, *The Evolution of American Urban Society*, p. 276.

4. Sydney E. Ahlstrom, "The Traumatic Years: American Religion and Culture in the '60s and '70s," *Theology Today*, Vol. 36, no. 4 (Jan. 1980), 511–12.

5. Langdon Gilkey, *Catholicism Confronts Modernity* (New York: Seabury Press, 1975), p. 32; Winthrop S. Hudson, *Religion in America* (3rd ed.; New York: Scribner's, 1981), p. 415.

6. Sydney E. Ahlstrom, *A Religious History of the American People* (New Haven: Yale University Press, 1972), p. 1085.

7. Garry Wills, *Bare Ruined Choirs* (Garden City, N.Y.: Doubleday, 1971), p. 21.

8. Stephen Steinberg, *The Academic Melting Pot* (New York: McGraw-Hill, 1974), pp. 101 and 105.

9. Archdeacon, *Becoming American*, p. 222.

10. Gilkey, *Catholicism Confronts Modernity*, pp. 34–35.

11. Quoted in Shaw, "A History of the Catholic Parish in the Midwest," p. 100.

12. Quoted in Paul Wrobel, *Our Way* (Notre Dame, Ind.: University of Notre Dame Press, 1979), pp. 92–93.

13. *National Catholic Reporter,* June 3, 1983, pp. 1 and 24.

14. James T. Connelly, C.S.C., "Legitimate Reasons for Existence: The Beginning of the Charismatic Movement in the American Catholic Church, 1967–1971," Charles and Margaret Hall Cushwa Center for the Study of American Catholicism, Working Paper Series 11, no. 3, Spring 1982, p. 20.

15. Kevin and Dorothy Ranaghan, *Catholic Pentecostals* (Paramus, N.J.: Paulist Press, 1969), p. 28; Edward D. O'Connor, C.S.C., *The Pentecostal Movement* (Notre Dame, Ind.: Ave Maria Press, 1971), p. 16; interview, William Beatty, July 5, 1984.

16. *National Catholic Reporter,* Mar. 7, 1980, pp. 1 and 4; Beatty interview.

17. Andrew M. Greeley, *The American Catholic* (New York: Basic Books, 1977), p. 127.

18. Ibid., p. 132.

19. See George A. Kelly, *The Battle for the American Church* (Garden City, N.Y.: Doubleday, 1979), p. 188; Greeley, *The American Catholic,* pp. 142–50.

20. See Kelly, *The Battle for the American Church,* p. 170.

21. Andrew M. Greeley, "Going Their Own Way," New York *Times Sunday Magazine,* Oct. 10, 1982, p. 36.

22. South Bend *Tribune,* July 15, 1979, p. 18.

23. *The Catholic Priest in the United States: Sociological Investigations* (Washington, D.C.: United States Catholic Conference, 1972), p. 279; Greeley, *The American Catholic,* p. 161; Peter Hebblethwaite, *The Runaway Church* (New York: Seabury Press, 1975), pp. 62–64.

24. *National Catholic Reporter,* May 5, 1978, p. 4; New York *Times,* Feb. 26, 1984, p. 18E.

25. Sister Marie Augustine Neal, S.N.D., "Implications of the Sisters' Survey for Structural Renewal," *Annual Assembly Proceedings, Conference of Major Superiors of Women,* n.p., 1967, pp. 10–11.

26. *The Catholic Priest in the United States,* p. 307; see Helen Rose Fuchs Ebaugh, *Out of the Cloister* (Austin, Texas: University of Texas Press, 1977), pp. 101–18.

27. Quoted in Chicago *Tribune,* Feb. 22, 1982, p. 10; see also *National Catholic Reporter,* May 12, 1978, p. 1.

28. *Women and Ministry: A Survey of the Experience of Roman Catholic Women in the United States* (Washington, D.C.: Leadership Conference of Women Religious of the U.S.A., 1980), pp. 9–17.

29. *National Catholic Reporter,* Oct. 22, 1982, p. 11.

30. *Parish Life in the United States: Final Report to the Bishops of the United States by The Parish Project* (Washington, D.C.: The Project, 1983), p. 29.

31. See Philip Gleason, "The Crisis of Americanization," in Philip Gleason (ed.), *Contemporary Catholicism in the United States* (Notre Dame, Ind.: University of Notre Dame Press, 1969), p. 17.

32. New York *Times,* Feb. 25, 1984, p. 46; also *National Catholic Reporter,* Aug. 13, 1982, p. 11.

33. New York *Times,* Apr. 22, 1984; Chicago *Sun-Times,* Jan. 30, 1981.

34. Greeley, *The American Catholic,* p. 169; New York *Times,* Apr. 22, 1984; Chicago *Tribune,* Oct. 21, 1983.

35. See John Whitney Evans, *The Newman Movement* (Notre Dame, Ind.: University of Notre Dame Press, 1980).

36. Lyle V. Jones, Gardner Lindzey, and Porter E. Coggeshall (eds.), *An Assessment of Research Doctorate Programs in the U.S.* (5 vols.; Washington, D.C.: National Academy Press, 1982); *National Catholic Reporter,* Sept. 23, 1983, p. 1; theology programs were not included in this evaluation.

37. Quoted in John Tracy Ellis, *American Catholicism* (2nd ed.; Chicago: University of Chicago Press, 1969), p. 212.

38. Quoted in ibid., p. 214.

39. Neil G. McCluskey, *Catholic Education Faces Its Future* (Garden City, N.Y.: Doubleday, 1968), pp. 251–55, 296.

40. Ronald B. Taylor, *Chavez and the Farm Workers* (Boston: Beacon Press, 1975), p. 81.

41. Quoted in Gerald M. Costello, *Without Fear or Favor: George Higgins on the Record* (Mystic, Conn.: Twenty-Third Publications, 1984), p. 89.

42. Joseph Casino, "The Catholic Parish in the Northeast" (unpublished manuscript), pp. 199–200.

43. Michael J. McNally, "Roman Catholic Parish Life in the South Atlantic Region" (unpublished manuscript), pp. 134–35.

44. Henry J. Browne, "Groping for Relevance in an Urban Parish: St. Gregory the Great, New York City, 1968–70" (unpublished paper), p. 5.

45. Ibid., p. 27.

46. Patricia F. McNeal, *The American Catholic Peace Movement 1928–1972* (New York: Arno Press, 1978), p. 205.

47. New York *Times,* May 1, 1983, Section EY, p. 23; *National Catholic Reporter,* May 13, 1983, p. 1.

48. John Whale (ed.), *The Man Who Leads the Church* (San Francisco: Harper & Row, 1980), p. 211.

Index

Abbelen, Peter, 297
Abnaki Indians, 38, 64
Alamo, 28, 29
Alemany, Joseph S., 177
Alexander, Sylvia Granatir, 193
Alexian Brothers, 328
Algonkians, 34
Alinsky, Saul, 370, 415
Allouez, Claude, 39–40
America
  discovery by Columbus, 15
  Spanish exploration of, 20–21
  See also English colonies; New France;
    Spanish colonies
American Board of Catholic Missions, 375
American Catholicism
  Americanist movement in, 236–37
    vs. Europeanists, 294–95
  and Americanization policy, 295–303,
    363–65
  attitude to divorce, 436
  birth control issue in, 434, 435–36
  boosterism in, 239, 351–52, 362, 417
  brick-and-mortar, 350–51
  broader concept of ministry in, 436–39
  charismatic movement in, 431–33
  class lines in, 356–59
  clergy of. See Bishops; Priests; Women
    religious
  in colonial period. See Maryland colony;
    Missions
  conservative wing of, 311–12

devotional
  authority in, 221–25, 231
  cult of papacy in, 387
  divergent attitudes from, 235–37
  evangelical nature of, 227
  feminine imagery of, 231–32
  God of, 235
  hostility to secular society in, 228
  Marian piety in, 384–86
  miraculous in, 233–35, 387
  obedience and docility as ideals of, 225
  popularity of, 237–40
  religious festivals of, 217, 234
  religious symbols of, 218
  ritual in, 229–31, 386, 387
  Romanization of, 319–20
  salvation as goal of, 231
  shift toward, 211–20
  sin in, 225–29
educative institutions of. See Colleges and
    universities; Education; Parochial
    schools; Schools
  in 1820, 160
evangelization in. See Missions
identity crisis in, 440–41
and immigration restriction, 356
immigrants in. See Immigrant Catholics
intellectual life in, 401
liberal-conservative split in, 312–16
liturgical movement in, 388–90, 408
local organization in. See Parish(es)
modernist impulse in, 304–11

papal condemnation of, 318–20
national organizations of, 352–54, 380, 440
new Catholicism, 453–54
in 1960s, 426–28
peace movement of, 450–52
population growth in, 160–61, 351
racial discrimination in, 360, 365–66
racial justice in, 367–71, 413, 447–48
in republican era
    ecumenical spirit of, 102–3
    educative institutions of, 242–53
    English liturgy of, 109–10, 113–14
    independence from foreign influence,
        105–7
    lay participation in, 110–11, 114–16
    plain style of, 208–11
    political freedom and, 101–2
    population distribution of, 111
    republican blueprint for, 111, 116, 304–
        5
    role of John Carroll, 103–5, 304–6
    separation of church and state in, 108–9,
        305
    shift to European model, 112–14, 117–
        23
    shortage of priests, 107–8
    schism in, 184, 186–89
and social reform. See Social reform
urbanization of, 161
and Vatican II reform, 428–31, 433–34
"American Catholicity," 311
American Federation of Catholic Societies,
    341
American Federation of Labor, 333
Americanist movement, 236–37
Americanization of Catholic immigrants,
    295–303, 363–65, 398
American Revolution, Catholic patriots in,
    96–97
Ancient Order of Hibernians, 257, 258, 313
Anderson, Henry J., 326
Annulment, 436
Apaches, 28–29
Aquinas, Thomas, 238, 351–52
Architecture, church, 208–9, 215
Arizona, Spanish missions in, 27–28
Armer, Elizabeth, 256
Association of Catholic Trade Unionists
    (ACTU), 405–6, 407
Atwood, Peter, 91, 92
Authority, culture of, 221–25, 231
Ave Maria, 215

Badin, Stephen, 116, 119, 120, 209
Baltimore, Lords. See Calvert, Cecil; Calvert,
    Charles; Calvert, George
Baltimore, Plenary Council of, 172, 180, 190,
    213, 222–23, 268, 271–72, 274, 312,
    352–53
Baltimore Catechism, 391, 441
Baraga, Frederic, 284
Bardstown (Kentucky), 119, 160, 161
Baroni, Geno, 448–49
Barry, Leonora, 330
Barton, Josef, 131
Barzynski, Vincent, 223
Benavides, Alonso de, 26, 44, 51, 60, 63
Benziger Brothers, 260
Berrigan, Daniel, 451, 452
Berrigan, Philip, 451, 452
Beschter, John William, 102
Birth control issue, 434, 435–36
Bishops
    and Americanization policy, 297, 298
    authority of, 117, 180–81, 191, 222–23,
        355
    and church finances, 354–55
    first American, 104–5
    Irish, 143–44, 180, 302–3
    and labor movement, 445–46
    in nineteenth century, 244–45
    and parochial school development, 268–69,
        275
    and peace movement, 451–52
    Program of Social Reconstruction, 344–46,
        353, 401
    progressive leadership by, 428–29
    public glorification of, 355–56
    selection of, 112–13, 118
Black Catholics
    clergy, 360, 447
    equal rights for, 367–71, 413, 447–48
    evangelization of, 359–60, 367, 370
    parishes of, 366–67, 369
    revivals of, 431
    segregation of, 360, 365–66, 368
Blacks, northern migration of, 358–59
Blanchet, Augustin M., 265
Bolton, Herbert E., 25
Book publishing, 212, 214, 247–48, 259–60,
    409, 441
Boscana, Gerónimo, 61, 65
Bossy, John, 83
Boston (Mass.)
    anti-Catholicism in, 263–64
    Irish Americans in, 142, 199
    parish organization in, 160
    parochial schools in, 264, 282
Brady, John F., 318
Brébeuf, Jean de, 36, 37, 44
Brick-and-mortar Catholicism, 350–51
Bridgeport (Chicago), 197, 200
Broadcasting, religious, 392–93, 403–4
Brooke, Robert, 86

Brooke family, 80
Browne, Henry J., 449
Brownson, Orestes, 296–97, 306–7
Building and loan associations, 141, 152
Bultos, 50
Burtsell, Richard L., 170

Cahensly, Peter Paul, 298
California
    Catholic growth in, 351
    Indian religion in, 61, 65
    Mexican Americans in, 372–74
    Spanish missions in, 29–30, 49–50, 53–54
    Spanish settlements in, 22
Callahan, Daniel, 401
Calvert, Cecil, 72, 74
Calvert, Charles, 75, 78–79
Calvert, George, 71–72
Calvert, Leonard, 74, 75
Cana Conference, 395
Canada. *See* New France
Cantwell, Daniel, 370
Cantwell, John, 373–74
Cardijn, Joseph, 415, 416
Carey, Mathew, 243, 248
Carey, Patrick, 193
Carroll, Charles, 80, 85
Carroll, Charles of Carrollton, 96–97, 103, 117
Carroll, John, 94, 95, 101, 108, 109, 209, 244, 249
    background of, 103
    conservative shift of, 113, 117, 123–24
    elected first American bishop, 104–5, 111
    founding of seminary by, 107
    and issues of authority, 115–16
    and organization of clergy, 104
    program of adaptation, 304–5
    as revolutionary diplomat, 103–4
    selection of clergy by, 112–13, 118
Cartier, Jacques, 31, 35
Catechetical movement, 376–77, 391
Catechism
    Baltimore, 391, 441
    classes, 246, 255–56, 373
    Kenedy, 260
    nineteenth century, 247
    in spirit of Vatican II, 441
Catholic Action movement, 396, 408–9, 415–16
Catholic Christian Instructed, The (Challoner), 247
Catholic Committee on Urban Ministry (CCUM), 448
Catholic Enlightenment, 108–11, 190
"Catholic Hour, The," 392–93
Catholicism

antisocialist tradition of, 336–37
centered in Rome, 295
devotional. *See* American Catholicism, devotional
diverse cultures of, 127–28
English, 70–71, 73
French, 33–34
institutional model of, 303–4
and modernism, 221–22, 317
and Second Vatican Council, 424–26, 428
Spanish, 18–20
spiritual revival in, 219–20
Tridentine, 231
See also American Catholicism
Catholic News, 214–15, 259
Catholic Radical Alliance, 406
Catholic Reading Circle Review, 256
Catholic Revival, 409
Catholic Worker, The, 409
Catholic Worker movement, 409–12, 450
Catholic Youth Organization, 392
Cavanaugh, John J., 400
Central Verein, 257, 336
Chabrat, Guy I., 119, 120
Challoner, Richard, 92, 122
Champlain, Samuel de, 31–32
Charismatic movement, 431–33
Charity, crusade of, 323–26, 327–29, 335, 340–41
Charles I, 71, 72, 73
Charleston (S.C.), pew-rental system in, 192, 193
Chavez, Cesar, 445, 446
Cheverus, Jean, 165, 243–44
Chicago (Ill.)
    black Catholics in, 369–70
    International Eucharistic Congress in, 349–50
    Irish Americans in, 197, 199–200, 201, 205
    Mexican Americans in, 374
    Polish Catholics in, 181, 183, 198, 200, 300–1
    social reform in, 415–16
Chihuahuita (El Paso), 198
Chinnici, Joseph, 122
Christian Brothers, 328
Christian Family Movement (CFM), 395–96, 416
Chudacoff, Howard, 200, 201
Church(es)
    architecture, 208–9, 215
    attendance, 207
    construction of, 350–51
    See also Parish(es)
Church and state, separation of, 108, 109, 305, 306, 307, 308, 310
Cincinnati (Ohio)

German Catholics in, 163–64, 173, 206
  parochial schools in, 264–65
  public schools in, 269
Civil rights movement, 447, 448
Claretians, 374, 376
Clergy. *See* Bishops; Priests; Women
  religious
Cliff Haven school, 258
Code of Canon Law, 223
College of Notre Dame, 293
College and universities
  academic freedom issue in, 443–44
  Catholic identity of, 444–45
  decline in enrollment, 442–43
  expansion and improvement of, 400
  founding of, 249–50
  ranking of, 443
  women's, 293, 399–400
Colonial period. *See* English colonies;
  Maryland colony; Missions; New
  France; Spanish colonies
Columbus, Christopher, religious mission of,
  15–16, 17
Common-school movement, 266–67
Communion movement, 386
Communities Organized for Public Service
  (COPS), 449
Concanen, Richard Luke, 113
Confession, 226, 227, 229, 386, 434
Confraternities, 50, 176, 213, 256, 373
Conway, Katherine, 259
Conzen, Kathleen Neils, 130, 145
Corrigan, Michael A., 274, 275, 311, 312,
  313, 316, 339
Cortes, Carlos, 154
Cortés, Hernán, 17, 20
Coughlin, Charles E., 403–4
Craven, William, 77
Cunnie, Edward, 367
Cures, miraculous, 234, 387
Curran, Charles E., 435, 444
Curran, John J., 337
Czechs, 135, 138, 155, 185–86, 282
Czyzewski, Valentine, 186

Darnall family, 79–80
Daughters of Isabella, 258
David, John B., 119, 120, 121, 122, 245
Day, Dorothy, 409, 411, 412, 450
Dearden, John F., 428
Degler, Carl, 243
De Hueck, Catherine, 412–13
Dempsey, Timothy, 328
Deshon, George, 236
DeSmet, Peter, 284
Devotional Catholicism. *See* American
  Catholicism, devotional

Devotional society, 256
Díaz del Castillo, Bernal, 20
Diekmann, Godfrey, 389
Dietz, Peter E., 341–42
Digges, Mary, 86
Divorce, 436
Domínguez, Francisco Atanasio, 27
Donahoe, Patrick, 259
Dorchester (Boston), 199
Dorney, Maurice J., 171
Dougherty, Dennis, 350, 351, 358
Driscoll, James F., 318, 319
Druillettes, Gabriel, 46
Du Bourg, William, 120, 121, 249
Duffy, Francis P., 318
Dulany, Daniel, 96–97

Eastern European community
  devotional Catholicism of, 217
  lay-trustee system in, 193–94
  parish organization in, 185–89
  parochial schools of, 279–80, 281–82
  peoples of, 135
  work patterns in, 155
  See also Polish Catholics
Ecumenism, 425, 433–34
Education
  church activities in, 244–46, 255–58, 390,
    391–92
  family role in, 242–44, 252–55, 394
  of immigrant Catholics, 253–61
  newspapers and books in, 246–48, 258–59,
    393–94
  primary institutions for, 241–42
  religious broadcasting in, 392–93
  in republican period, 242–52
  See also Colleges and universities;
    Parochial schools; Schools
Egan, John, 370, 448
Ellard, Gerald, 388, 389
Elliott, Walter, 315
El Paso (Texas), Mexican Americans in, 198
Encomienda, 24–25
England, 32, 38
  era of overseas expansion, 69–70
  Protestant Reformation in, 70–71
  takeover of New France, 40–41
England, John, 166, 192, 246, 267, 305
English Catholicism
  and Maryland colonization, 73
  prayer books of, 91
  and Protestant Reformation, 70–71
  toleration of, 71, 73
English colonies
  Catholic immigration to, 87
  See also Maryland colony

Ethnic groups. *See* Immigrant Catholics; specific groups
Eucharist, 224–25
Extension Society, 375

Family
 educative role of, 242–44, 252–55, 394
 principles of family life, 394–96
Faribault-Stillwater school compromise plan, 273–75
Farrell, Martin, 370
Fátima, cult of, 385–86
Federation of Colored Catholics, 368
Fenwick, Benedict, 165
Fenwick, Edward, 249
Finn, Francis, 232
Fitzgerald, Edward, 272
Fitzpatrick, Joseph, 379
Flaget, Benedict, 116, 119, 120, 249
Flores, Patricio, 427, 449
Florida, Spanish settlement in, 21, 25–26
Foreign-mission campaign, 393
Franklin, Benjamin, 103, 104, 105
Fraternal societies, 257–58, 312–13, 391–92
French Canadians
 family work patterns of, 153
 lay-trustee system of, 178–79
 neighborhoods of, 200
 parochial schools of, 279, 281
 reasons for emigration, 133–34
 resistance to centralized control, 179–80
 social mobility of, 154
 struggle for survival, 178
French Catholicism, 33–34
French colonies. *See* New France
Friendship House, 412–14
Furdek, Stefan, 281

Gallicanism, 34
Garden of the Soul, The, 92, 247
Gaston, William, 249–50
George, Henry, 331
Georgetown University, 107, 249, 250
German Catholics
 and forced Americanization issue, 297–99
 importance of parish to, 168–69
 lay participation by, 173
 occupational hierarchy of, 144–47
 parochial schools of, 278–79, 281, 312
 phases of emigration, 129–31
 property ownership by, 147
 settlement pattern of, 137–78
 social mobility of, 147–48
 and social reform, 336
Gibbons, James, 332–33, 334, 341, 353
Gilkey, Langdon, 428
Glenmary Missioners, 391

Glennon, John, 368
God, of devotional Catholicism, 235
Golab, Caroline, 136, 151
Gother, John, 91, 93, 122
Graessel, Laurence, 112
Graham, Michael, 80
Grail movement, 414–15
Grassi, John, 208, 209–10
Greeley, Andrew, 435–36, 442
Griffen, Clyde, 147
Griffen, Sally, 147
Guilt, and culture of sin, 228–29

Haas, Francis J., 402–3
Hagerty, Thomas J., 336–37
Hanke, Lewis, 25
Harlem (New York), 358–59, 366–67
Harrigan, Ann, 409, 413
Harrington, Michael, 412
Hecker, Isaac, 235–36, 256, 307–8, 315
Hellriegel, Martin, 388, 389
Henni, John Martin, 130
Herder Company, 260
Hesburgh, Theodore M., 400, 444
Hickey, William, 364
Higgins, George, 446
High schools, 292–93, 399
Hillenbrand, Reynold, 415–16
Hodur, Francis, 184
Holy Family parish, Chicago, 205–6
Holy Name Society, 233, 257
Horstmann, Ignatius F., 242
Hospitals, 324–25, 328
Howells, William Dean, 321
Hughes, John, 263, 267, 268, 276, 325
Humanae Vitae, 435–36
Hurley, Joseph P., 355
Hurons, 36–37, 62–63

Illich, Ivan, 378
Immigrant Catholics
 Americanization of, 295–303, 363–65, 398
 and anti-Catholicism, 201–3
 and anti-foreign sentiment, 202
 cultural diversity of, 136
 devotional Catholicism of, 238–40
 and economic depression, 323
 educative institutions of, 253–61
 ethnic conflicts among, 201, 203
 family in religious life of, 253–55
 folk religious practices of, 234, 237
 fraternal societies of, 257–58
 geographical distribution of, 136–39
 in labor movement, 329–31, 333–34
 lay participation by, 162–94
 major groups of, 128–36
 neighborhoods of, 195–201, 238

successive migrations in, 365, 448
newspapers of, 259
in 1960s and 1970s, 427
parish in life of, 204–8
parochial-school support by, 276–77, 278–82, 283
saints of, 230
second generation, 362–63
settlement patterns of, 136–39
social and economic hierarchy of, 139–57
transatlantic crossing by, 136
See also specific groups
Immigration restriction, 356
Indians
conversions, 64–67, 78
culture of, 23
displayed as curios, 35
diversity among, 22–23
and encomienda system, 24–25
in 1492, 22
in fur trade, 31
mission schools for, 284–86
northeastern tribes, 34–35
polygamy of, 63–64
relations with French, 35–36
religion of, 23, 60–63, 65–66
resistance to missionaries, 64
Spanish view of, 23–24
See also Jesuit missions; Missions; specific tribes
International Eucharistic Congress, Chicago, 349–50
Ireland, John, 187, 297, 298, 302, 311, 313, 314, 332
compromise school plan of, 273–75
program of adaptation, 308–10
Irish Americans
and American identity issue, 296–97
in church hierarchy, 143–44, 180, 302–3
female work force of, 140, 143, 146
folk beliefs of, 234
fraternal societies of, 257–58
in labor movement, 329–31, 333, 339–40
and Land League, 331
lay participation by, 164–65, 169
neighborhoods of, 197–200
newspapers of, 259
occupational hierarchy of, 139–40, 146
and parochial schools, 278
in politics, 143
property ownership by, 140–41
reasons for emigration, 128–29
settlement pattern of, 137
social structure of, 141–43, 144
Iroquois, 34–35, 37–38
Italian Americans, 136
anticlericalism of, 173–74

family in religious life of, 254–55
friction with Irish Catholicism, 237
lay participation by, 174–76
occupational hierarchy of, 148–50
and parochial schools, 280, 282
property ownership by, 150
reasons for emigration, 131–32
religious festivals of, 217, 237
return migration by, 132
settlement patterns of, 138
social mobility of, 150–51

James I, 71
Jesuit missions
in Catholic folklore, 41–42
evangelical tradition and, 52
hardships of, 44–45
Huron and Iroquois, 36–38
in Maine, 38–39
in Maryland colony, 77–79
circuit riders, 82, 89–90
decline of, 123
farms, 80–81, 87–88, 90, 123
native language proficiency in, 56–57
in Northwest, 39–40
opposition to Frenchification, 59
in republican era, 120–21
in Southwest, 27–28
See also Missions
Jesuits
colleges of, 400
expulsion from North America, 41
papal suppression of, 95–96
Jogues, Isaac, 37
John Paul II, Pope, 453–54
John XXIII, Pope, 424–25, 450
Joseph, Mother, 265, 324
Juaneños, religion of, 61, 65

Kalven, Janet, 414, 415
Kanaly, Donald, 415
Kazincy, Adelbert, 337–38
Keane, James R., 384
Keane, John, 309, 310, 313, 314, 332
Kearney, Denis, 330
Keifer, Ralph, 431
Kenedy, P. J. & Sons, 260
Kenkel, Frederick P., 342
Kennedy, John F., 421–22
Kenrick, Peter, 332
Kentucky
foreign-born clergy in, 118–20
parish organization in, 160
urbanization of Catholics in, 161
Kerby, William, 340
Kino, Eusebio, 27–28, 51
Klein, Félix, 315

Knights of Columbus, 257–58, 313, 392
Knights of Labor, 313, 330–31, 332–33
Know-Nothings, 202, 295
Kozlowski, Edward, 299
Kruszka, Wenceslaus, 279, 299
Kulturkampf, 130

Labor movement
  American Federation of Labor, 333
  Association of Catholic Trade Unionists
      (ACTU), 405–6, 407
  bishops and, 446–47
  Church acceptance of, 334–35
  farm workers in, 445–46
  Irish Americans in, 329–31, 333, 339–40
  Knights of Labor, 330–31, 332–33
  priests in, 337–39, 340, 406, 446
  and progressive reform, 342
  strikes in, 327
LaFarge, John, 369
Laity
  ministry of, 438–39
  ownership of church property, 172, 183–
      84, 185, 188
  in parish council, 440
  parish organization by, 163–64, 174–76
  in republican era, 114–16
  retreats by, 386–87
  in social action programs, 396, 407–17,
      447
  teachers, 441, 442
  trustee system of parish government, 110–
      11, 115, 116, 160, 164, 165–68, 170,
      171–72, 173, 175–76, 178–79
    representation in, 192–94
    shift to clerical model, 189–92
  women, 232–33, 328–29, 439
  See also Immigrant Catholics
Lalemant, Gabriel, 37
Lamy, Jean B., 176, 177
Land League, 331
"Language Saves the Faith" campaign, 297,
    299, 312
Las Casas, Bartolomé de, 24–25
Lasuén, Fermín F., 24, 64
Laws and authority, 223–24
Laymen's Union, 369
LeJeune, Paul, 45, 56–57
Leo House, 298
Leo XII, Pope, 245
Leo XIII, Pope, 274, 299, 315–16, 334, 343
Lewis, John, 104
Ligutti, Luigi G., 381
Lithuanians, 135, 136, 138, 155, 185, 186
Liturgy
  changes of Vatican II in, 429–31
  in mission program, 49

reform movement, 388–90, 408
  in republican period, 109–10, 113–14
Los Angeles (Calif.), Mexican Americans in,
    372–74
Louisiana, Catholic growth in, 351
Louisville (Ky.), 161
Lucerne Memorial, 298–99
Lucey, Robert E., 374, 377

McCann, William, 367
McDonnell, Donald, 445–46
McFaul, James A., 341
McGlynn, Edward, 278, 331, 332, 339
McGowan, Raymond A., 377, 402, 404–5
McGrady, Thomas, 337
McMaster, James, 270
McQuaid, Bernard, 270–71, 272, 273, 311,
    312, 313, 315, 316, 334
Magic, Christianity and, 17–18
Maignen, Charles, 315, 316
Malone, Thomas H., 337
Manchester (N.H.), French Canadians in,
    199, 200
Manual of Godly Prayers, 91
Marciniak, Ed, 411
Marechal, Ambrose, 209
Marian piety, 384–86
Markoe, John and William, 367–68
Marquette, Jacques, 39, 43
Marriage
  encounter, 431
  ethnically mixed, 203
  of priests, 436–37
  religiously mixed, 228, 433
Maryknoll, 393
Maryland colony
  Catholic community in
    gentry of, 79–80, 82, 86
    institutional development of, 80–81
    parish structure in, 88–89, 90
    and patriot cause, 96–97
    personal piety of, 91–93
    private worship by, 84–85, 89
    religious instruction in, 93–94
    religious observance in, 81–84, 94–95
    status of women in, 83, 94
    sustained growth and vigor of, 86–87,
        90–91. *See also* Jesuit missions, in
        Maryland colony
  economic and social change in, 85–86
  founding of, 69, 71–75, 350
  Jesuits *vs.* Calvert in, 78–79
  political unrest in, 75
  post-1689 anti-Catholic legislation in, 84–
      85
  religious toleration in, 74, 76–77
Mass

active participation in, 389
authority of clergy in, 224–25
Latin, 113
ritual of, 229, 230
in Spirit, 92–93
and Vatican II reforms, 429–31
Maurin, Peter, 409–10, 411
Mazzuchelli, Samuel, 284
Mediator Dei, 389
Merton, Thomas, 450–51
Messbarger, Paul, 230
Messenger of the Sacred Heart, 215
Messmer, Sebastian, 281, 301, 336, 341
Mexican Americans
    in Americanization program, 373–74
    and bracero program, 377–78
    catechism classes for, 373, 376–77
    confraternities of, 176, 373
    devotional Catholicism of, 217–18, 386
    discrimination against, 374
    and European clergy, 177
    family-centered religion of, 371–72
    in farm workers movement, 445–46
    integration into parish, 379–80
    land dispossession of, 154
    Marian piety of, 384
    militancy of, 427
    national parish for, 372–73, 374
    neighborhoods, 198
    parish organization for, 177–78
    and parochial schools, 280, 282
    pastoral care of, 375
    private chapels of, 176–77
    size of community, 134, 360–61
    in unskilled occupations, 154–55
Michel, Virgil, 388–89, 408
Militia of Christ for Social Service, 342
Milwaukee (Wisc.), German immigrants in,
    145
Minneapolis (Minn.)
    Eastern-rite schism in, 187–88
    Polish Catholics in, 182
Miraculous, openness to, 233–35, 387
Mission-aid societies, 375
Mission Book, The, 226
Missions
    Christian formation in, 44–45, 48–52
    coercive tactics of, 46–47
    confraternities in, 50
    contribution of, 67–68
    cultural conversion in, 43–44, 52–53
    daily life in, 47
    destructive effects of, 286
    economic aspects of, 53–54
    and evangelical tradition, 51–52
    foreign, 393
    Indian interpreters in, 47–48

martyrdom of missionaries, 37
obstacles to conversion in, 55–60, 63–66,
    77–78
parish, 212–13, 226–27, 245–46, 255, 386,
    431
parish model for, 50–51
pattern of conversions in, 64–65
political organization of, 54–55
of pre-Civil War period, 283–84
schools, 284–86
segregation in mission towns, 45–46
Spanish
    in California, 29–30, 53–54
    dissolution of, 30
    in Florida, 25–26
    sacred images of, 49–50
    in Southwest, 26–29
    See also Jesuit missions
Modernism
    and American Catholicism, 304–11
    challenge to authority in, 221–22
    and European Catholicism, 317
    papal condemnation of, 318–19
    and Second Vatican Council, 425–26
Molyneux, Robert, 247
Montesinos, Antonio de, 24
Mosley, Joseph, 87–88, 89, 90, 95, 96
Mount St. Mary's College, 249
Muldoon, Peter J., 345, 380
Mundelein, George, 300, 301, 349, 355, 358,
    364, 374
Murray, John Courtney, 425
Murray, Thomas E., 144
Mutual benefit societies, 174, 175, 179, 181–
    82, 185

National Catholic Reporter, 441
National Catholic Rural Life Conference,
    381
National Catholic Social Action Conference,
    405
National Catholic War Council, 344, 353
National Catholic Welfare Conference
    (NCWC), 353–54, 380, 392, 395, 402,
    404–5
Native Americans. *See* Indians; Missions
Neale, Leonard, 112, 116
Neale family, 80
Nerinckx, Charles, 119, 121, 122
New Deal, 401, 402, 403–4
New France
    British takeover of, 40–41
    colonization of, 31–32
    Indians of, 34–35
    missions in. *See* Jesuit missions; Missions
    relations with Indians, 35–36
    western expansion of, 39

Newman Movement, 443
New Mexico
    Mexican Americans in, 374–77
    Spanish settlement in, 21–22, 26–27, 30
Newspapers, 214–15, 246–47, 258–59, 393–94, 441
New York City
    black migration to, 358–59
    black parish in, 366–67
    economic depression in, 323, 327
    impact of immigration in, 161
    Irish Americans in, 197–98
    middle-class parish in, 199
    neighborhood flux in, 365
    new-style parish in, 449
    parish organization in, 159–60, 170
    parochial schools in, 263, 267
    Puerto Ricans in, 361, 378–79
New York Review, The. 318, 319
Notre Dame University, 400, 416, 443, 444
Novena, 230, 384–85, 387, 388, 431

O'Boyle, Patrick A., 435
O'Brien, David, 404
O'Connell, Denis, 309, 310
O'Connell, William, 259
O'Connor, Flannery, 352, 388
Odin, John M., 177
Odone, Nicola Carlo, 175
O'Grady, John, 344, 403
O'Hara, Edwin V., 380
O'Hara, John F., 390–91
O'Leary, Cornelius, 330, 332
Oñate, Juan de, 21
Orate Fratres, 388–89
O'Reilly, John Boyle, 259
Orphanages, 258, 324, 328
Other America, The (Harrington), 412
Our Sunday Visitor, 393–94

Pacem in Terris, 450
Panik, Gaspar, 185
Papacy
    birth-control teaching of, 435–36
    condemnation of modernism, 318–19
    cult of, 387
    and just-war doctrine, 450
    and liturgical renewal, 389
    papal infallibility, 180, 190, 221–22, 236, 295
    program for social justice, 334–36
    temporal power of, 314
Parish(es)
    black, 366–67, 369, 448
    changing role of, 397
    in colonial Maryland, 88–89, 90
    as community institution, 449

congregational, 114–16
    vs. hierarchical model, 172–73, 189–94
council, 440
in economic depression, 323
episcopal control of, 179–81, 355
finances, 354–55, 382
immigrant, 197, 204–8
lay ownership issue in, 172, 183–84, 185, 188
lay-trustee government, 110–11, 115, 116, 160, 164, 165–68, 170, 171–72, 173, 175–76, 178–79
    representation by, 192–94
    shift to clerical model, 189–92
laywomen in, 232–33
library, 256
membership levels, 207
membership regulations, 223–25
middle-class, 199–200
mission, 212–13, 226–27, 245–46, 255, 386, 431
organization of, 159–60
    lay initiative in, 163–65, 174–76
    mutual benefit society in, 174, 181–83, 185
    in national parishes, 162–63, 197
    priest in, 165, 170–71, 175, 177–78, 186
    territorially, 162
processions, 208, 217
racial segregation in, 360, 365–66
schools. See Parochial schools
societies, 204–6, 213–14, 233, 256–58, 391–92
of Southwest, 375–76
spiritual renewal programs in, 431
suburban, 357–58, 381–82, 448
Parochial schools
    as agent of Americanization, 398
    construction of, 350–51
    decline of, 441–42
    finances of, 288–90
    in frontier regions, 265–66
    high schools, 292–93, 399
    integration of, 366, 368
    in nineteenth century, 242, 251–52
    obligation to support, 270, 272, 283, 397
    organization of, 262–69
        reasons for, 276–77
    overcrowding in, 286–87
    public funding issue in, 270–71
    -public schools compromise, 271, 273–75, 312
    quality of education in, 272
    religious instruction in, 215, 216
    support for, 275–83
    systematization of, 290–91, 354, 397
    teachers. See Teachers

Pascendi Dominici Gregis, 318
Paulists, 235–36, 256, 391
Paul VI, Pope, 425, 435
Peace movement, 450–52
Penitentes, 50, 237
Pennsylvania
  colonial Catholics in, 87, 89
  German Catholics in, 130
  Polish Catholics in, 151
  See also Philadelphia (Pa.)
Pentecostal movement, Catholic, 431–33
Pew-rental system, 192, 193
Philadelphia (Pa.)
  black Catholics in, 367
  church and school construction in, 350
  colonial Catholics in, 87
  Irish parish in, 167
  middle-class parish in, 199
  parochial schools in, 282–83
Piehl, Mel, 335
Piety
  baroque tradition of, 122–23
  concept of adoration in, 386
  Jesus as model of virtue in, 210
  Marian, 384–86
  personal, interior, 92–93, 122
  plain style of, 209–11
  pluralistic, 433
Pilot, 214, 259
Pima Indians, 28
Pius IX, Pope, 268
Pius X, Pope, 222, 317, 318–19, 388
Pius XI, Pope, 402
Pius XII, Pope, 389
Plessis, Joseph-Octave, 247
Point, Nicholas, 284
Polish Catholics
  campaign against Americanization, 299–301, 364
  importance of parish to, 181
  lay participation by, 183–85
  mobility of, 152–53
  occupational hierarchy of, 151–52
  parish organization by, 181–83
  parochial schools and, 279, 281, 288, 398
  reasons for emigration, 132–33
Polish Roman Catholic Union of America, 257
Portier, Michael, 249
Poughkeepsie (N.Y.)
  German immigrants in, 147
  parochial-public school compromise plan in, 271, 273–75
Powderly, Terence V., 330–31
Prayer books
  of colonial period, 91–92, 247
  in devotional Catholicism, 212, 226

  use in family, 243–44
Preaching, 245, 392
Preston, Thomas, 314
Priests
  authority of, 189–94, 223, 224–25
    in parochial school, 291
  in black parishes, 367, 369
  builder, 350–51
  and celibacy issue, 436–37
  conflicts with lay trustees, 166–67
  decline in numbers, 437
  Eastern-rite, 187–89
  foreign-born, 118–21, 170, 177
  Irish, 143–44, 180
  in labor movement, 337–39, 340, 406, 446
  organizations, 440
  in parish organization, 165, 170–71, 175, 177–78, 186
  preaching of, 245, 392
  resignations by, 436, 438
  shortage of, 107–8, 249
  social-action, 379, 402–3, 415–16
  tenure of, 171
Processions, 208, 217
Protestantism
  and culture of modernity, 428
  ecumenism in, 433–34
  as public-school ideology, 266–67, 269, 276
  Reformation, in England, 70–71
  social-gospel movement in, 322
Protestants
  anti-Catholicism of, 201–3, 295
  Catholic prejudice against, 228, 238
  and fraternization issue, 313
Public schools
  emergence of, 252, 262, 266
  and compromise plans, 271, 273–75, 312
  Protestantism in, 263, 266–67, 269, 276
Publishing. *See* Book publishing; Newspapers
Pueblo Indians, 46
  and missions, 26
  pattern of conversion, 66–67
  religion of, 49, 60, 61–62, 65
Puerto Ricans
  integration into parish, 378–79
  migration of, 361
Purcell, John, 264–65, 282
Putz, Louis, 416

Quigley, James E., 336, 338, 358

Reading circle, 256
Relics, 234
Religion
  in sixteenth century, 17–18
  and social change, 423–24, 428
RENEW program, 431

Rerum Novarum. 334–36, 338, 343
Retreat movement, 386–87
Revivals. *See* Parish(es), mission
Rhode, Paul, 302
Rice, Charles Owen, 406
Richard, Gabriel, 247–48
Richards, Joseph, 370
Ritter, Joseph E., 368
Ritual, culture of, 229–31
Roche, James Jeffrey, 259
Rodriguez, Richard, 379–80
Rogers, Elizabeth, 330
Ronda, James P., 63
Rudd, Daniel, 365
Rudolph, Frederick, 250
Rummel, Joseph F., 371
Rural areas
    convert-making in, 391
    rural-life movement in, 380–81
    women religious in, 265–66
Ruthenians. *See* Ukrainians
Ryan, John, 342–44, 402

Sacred Heart parish (New York), 206–7
St. Augustine (Florida), 21, 25, 26
St. Benedict the Moor parish (New York), 366
St. Catherine's College, 399–400
St. Gregory the Great parish (New York), 449
St. Ignace mission, 39
St. Jean Baptiste Society, 257
St. John's University, 444
St. John the Baptist parish (Cincinnati), 206
St. Joseph's College, 249, 250
St. Joseph's Seminary, 318, 319
St. Louis University, 249
St. Mary's Seminary, 107, 118
St. Paul (Minn.), Italian parish in, 174–75
St. Raphaelsverein, 298
Saints, devotion to, 230, 231
St. Stanislaus (Stanislaswowo), Chicago, 181, 183, 198, 200
St. Vincent de Paul societies, 323–24, 327–28
Santos, 50
Schaff, Philip, 267
Schlesinger, Arthur M., Jr., 296
Schools
    convent, 215–16
    female academies, 250–51
    Indian mission, 284–86
    industrial, 328
    private academies, 292
    summer, 258, 381
    Sunday, 246, 255–56
    See also Parochial schools; Public schools
School Sisters of St. Francis, 289–90

Secret societies, 312–13
Seminaries, 107, 249–50, 318, 319, 439
Separation of church and state, 108, 109, 305, 306, 307, 308, 310
Serra, Junípero, 29
Seton, Elizabeth, 121, 250, 277
Settlement houses, 258, 329, 373
Sheed & Ward, 409
Sheen, Fulton J., 393
Shehan, Lawrence J., 428
Sheil, Bernard J., 415
Short Abridgement of Christian Doctrine, A, 247
Shrines, 234–35, 387
Sigstein, John, 377
Sin, 225–29, 434
Sisters. *See* Women religious
Sisters of Charity, 277, 324
Sisters of Mercy, 324
Sisters of Providence, 265–66
Sisters of the Holy Cross, 398–99
Sisters of the Holy Family, 256
Sixth Ward (New York), 197–98
Slovaks, 135, 155, 185, 193–94, 279–80, 281
Smith, Timothy, 161
Socialism, crusade against, 336–37
Social reform
    Bishops' Program for, 344–46, 353, 401
    Catholic Action movement, 396, 408–9, 415–16
    Catholic Worker movement, 409–12
    charities, 323–26, 327–29, 335, 340–41, 354
    community parish in, 449
    Friendship House, 412–14
    Grail movement, 414–15
    lay activism in, 396, 407–9, 416–17, 447
    in 1930s, 401–6
    progressivism in, 340–44
    Rerum Novarum and, 334–36
    temperance crusade and, 326
    See also Labor movement
Societies, 204–6, 213–14, 233, 256–58, 312–13, 391–92
Sodalities, 213, 256, 386
Sorrowful Mother novena, 384–85
Spalding, John L., 309, 310, 312, 338
Spalding, Martin J., 268, 269
Spanish Catholicism
    authority of Crown in, 18
    fanatical orthodoxy of, 19–20
Spanish colonies
    in California, 22, 29–30
    in Florida, 21, 25–26
    Indians and, 23–30
    in New Mexico, 21–22, 26–27
    See also Missions, Spanish

Spanish conquest
  desire for wealth in, 20
  religious mission in, 15–18
Spanish Inquisition, 19–20
Spellman, Francis J., 355, 378, 425
Spicer, Edward, 53
Spring Hill College, 249
Starkenburg (Mo.), 234–35
Storey, William, 431
Suburbanization, 357–58, 381–82
Summer school, 258, 381
Sunday school, 246, 255–56

Tamarón, Bishop, 55, 56
Taves, Ann, 212
Taylor, Philip, 127
Teachers
  availability of, 277
  foreign-speaking, 288
  lay, 441, 442
  preparation of, 287–88, 398–99
  salaries, 289–90
Temperance movement, 326
Testem Benevolentiae, 315–16
Texas
  Mexican Americans in, 374–77
  mission-aid funds in, 375
  Spanish missions in, 28–29
Thernstrom, Stephan, 140, 142, 148
Thomism, 351–52
Toth, Alexis, 187–88
Tridentine Catholicism, 231
Trustee system. See Laity, trustee system
Truth Teller, 246
Turner, Thomas W., 368

Ukrainians, 135, 155
  schism from Latin-rite Catholicism, 186–89
United States Catholic Miscellany, 246
Universities. See Colleges and universities
Ursuline Manual, 226

Vatican
  First Council, 180, 190, 221–22
  and forced Americanization policy, 297
  Second Council, 424–26, 428
Victory Noll Sisters, 377
Vietnam War, 424, 426–27
  and Catholic peace movement, 450–52

Walworth, Clarence, 213
Warner, Sam Bass, 204
Washington Park (Chicago), 199–200
Washington State, parochial schools in, 265–66
White, Andrew, 77, 78
Winthrop, John, 16
Women
  birth-control dissent by, 435
  colleges, 399–400
  in colonial Maryland, 83, 94
  education of, 250–51
  immigrant work force, 140, 143, 146–47, 149–50, 151–52, 153, 155
  in lay ministry, 439
  as moral guardian and educator, 243, 244, 251, 252–53, 255
  ordination of, 439
  role in devotional Catholicism, 232–33
Women religious
  black sisters, 360, 371
  care of sick and orphans, 324, 328
  catechists, 377
  convent preparation of, 439–40
  decline in numbers, 437–38
  in female academies, 251
  growth of, 387–88
  in Maryland colony, 86
  missionaries, 393
  in nontraditional ministries, 438–39
  organizations, 440
  in parochial schools, 227
    founding of, 265–66
    salaries of, 289–90
    teacher training for, 287–88, 398–99
  in republican period, 121
  shelters of, 328
  status in the church, 289, 290
World War I, Catholic response in, 344

Ximénez, Cardinal, 19

Yans-McLaughlin, Virginia, 150
Yorke, Peter C., 338–39
Young Christian Students (YCS), 416
Young Christian Workers (YCW), 416

Zahn, John A., 317–18, 319
Zebris, Joseph, 186